The Richard Hannay Collection

Volume I

The Thirty-Nine Steps
Greenmantle
Mr Standfast

By

John Buchan

British Library Cataloguing-in-Publication Data
A catalogue record for this book is available from the
British Library

John Buchan

John Buchan, first Baron Tweedsmuir of Elsfield, was born in Perth, Scotland in 1875. In his youth, his father immersed him in the history, legends and myths of Scotland, and he was an avid reader, stating some years later that John Bunyan's *The Pilgrim's Progress* was a "constant companion" to him. Buchan's education was uneven, but at the age of seventeen he obtained a scholarship to study classics at Glasgow University, where he began to write poetry. His first work, *The Essays and Apothegms of Francis Lord Bacon*, was published in 1894, and a year later he enrolled at Oxford University to study law.

In 1900, Buchan moved to London, and two years later accepted a civil service post in South Africa. In the years leading up to World War I, he worked at a publishers, and also wrote *Prester John* (1910) – which later became a school reader, translated into many languages – as well as a number of biographies. In 1915, Buchan become a war correspondent for *The Times*, and published his most well-known book, the thriller *The Thirty-Nine Steps*. After the war he became a director of the news agency Reuters.

Over the course of his life, Buchan would eventually publish some one hundred books, forty or so of which were novels, mostly wartime thrillers. In the latter part of his life he worked in politics, serving as Conservative MP for the Scottish universities and Lord High Commissioner of the Church of Scotland (1933-34). In 1935, Buchan moved to Canada, where he became the thirty-fifth Governor General of Canada. He died in 1940, aged 64.

Contents

The Thirty-Nine Steps

Greenmantle

Mr Standfast

PART I

PART II

THE THIRTY-NINE STEPS

By

JOHN BUCHAN

TO
THOMAS ARTHUR NELSON
(LOTHIAN AND BORDER HORSE)

My Dear Tommy,

You and I have long cherished an affection for that elemental type of tale which Americans call the 'dime novel' and which we know as the 'shocker'—the romance where the incidents defy the probabilities, and march just inside the borders of the possible. During an illness last winter I exhausted my store of those aids to cheerfulness, and was driven to write one for myself. This little volume is the result, and I should like to put your name on it in memory of our long friendship, in the days when the wildest fictions are so much less improbable than the facts.

J.B.

CHAPTER ONE

The Man Who Died

I returned from the City about three o'clock on that May afternoon pretty well disgusted with life. I had been three months in the Old Country, and was fed up with it. If anyone had told me a year ago that I would have been feeling like that I should have laughed at him; but there was the fact. The weather made me liverish, the talk of the ordinary Englishman made me sick, I couldn't get enough exercise, and the amusements of London seemed as flat as soda-water that has been standing in the sun. 'Richard Hannay,' I kept telling myself, 'you have got into the wrong ditch, my friend, and you had better climb out.'

It made me bite my lips to think of the plans I had been building up those last years in Bulawayo. I had got my pile—not one of the big ones, but good enough for me; and I had figured out all kinds of ways of enjoying myself. My father had brought me out from Scotland at the age of six, and I had never been home since; so England was a sort of Arabian Nights to me, and I counted on stopping there for the rest of my days.

But from the first I was disappointed with it. In about a week I was tired of seeing sights, and in less than a month I had had enough of restaurants and theatres and race-meetings. I had no real pal to go about with, which probably explains things. Plenty of people invited me to their houses, but they didn't seem much interested in me. They would fling me a question or two about South Africa, and then get on their own affairs. A lot of Imperialist ladies asked me to tea to meet schoolmasters from New Zealand and editors from Vancouver, and that was the dismalest business of all. Here was I, thirty-seven years old, sound in wind and limb, with enough money to have a good time, yawning my head off all day. I had just about settled to clear out and get back to the veld, for I was the best bored man in the United Kingdom.

That afternoon I had been worrying my brokers about investments to give my mind something to work on, and on my way home I turned into my club—rather a pot-house, which took in Colonial members. I had a long drink, and read the evening papers. They were full of the row in the Near East, and there was an article about Karolides, the Greek Premier. I rather fancied the chap. From all accounts he seemed the one big man in the show; and he played a straight game too, which was more than could be said for most of them. I gathered that they hated him pretty blackly in Berlin and Vienna, but that we were going to stick by him, and one paper said that he was the only barrier between Europe and Armageddon. I remember wondering if I could get a job in those parts. It struck me that Albania was the sort of place that might keep a man from yawning.

About six o'clock I went home, dressed, dined at the Cafe Royal, and turned into a music-hall. It was a silly show, all capering women and monkey-faced men, and I did not stay long. The night was fine and clear as I walked back to the flat I had hired near Portland Place. The crowd surged past me on the pavements, busy and chattering, and I envied the people for having something to do. These shop-girls and clerks and dandies and policemen had some interest in life that kept them going. I gave half-a-crown to a beggar because I saw him yawn; he was a fellow-sufferer. At Oxford Circus I looked up into the spring sky and I made a vow. I would give the Old Country another day to fit me into something; if nothing happened, I would take the next boat for the Cape.

My flat was the first floor in a new block behind Langham Place. There was a common staircase, with a porter and a liftman at the entrance, but there was no restaurant or anything of that sort, and each flat was quite shut off from the others. I hate servants on the premises, so I had a fellow to look after me who came in by the day. He arrived before eight o'clock every morning and used to depart at seven, for I never dined at home.

I was just fitting my key into the door when I noticed a man at my elbow. I had not seen him approach, and the sudden appearance made me start. He was a slim man, with a short brown beard and small, gimlety blue eyes. I recognized him as the occupant of a flat on the top floor, with whom I had passed the time of day on the stairs.

'Can I speak to you?' he said. 'May I come in for a minute?' He was steadying his voice with an effort, and his hand was pawing my arm.

I got my door open and motioned him in. No sooner was he over the threshold than he made a dash for my back room, where I used to smoke and write my letters. Then he bolted back.

'Is the door locked?' he asked feverishly, and he fastened the chain with his own hand.

'I'm very sorry,' he said humbly. 'It's a mighty liberty, but you looked the kind of man who would understand. I've had you in my mind all this week when things got troublesome. Say, will you do me a good turn?'

'I'll listen to you,' I said. 'That's all I'll promise.' I was getting worried by the antics of this nervous little chap.

There was a tray of drinks on a table beside him, from which he filled himself a stiff whisky-and-soda. He drank it off in three gulps, and cracked the glass as he set it down.

'Pardon,' he said, 'I'm a bit rattled tonight. You see, I happen at this moment to be dead.'

I sat down in an armchair and lit my pipe.

'What does it feel like?' I asked. I was pretty certain that I had to deal with a madman.

A smile flickered over his drawn face. 'I'm not mad—yet. Say, Sir, I've been watching you, and I reckon you're a cool customer. I reckon, too, you're an honest man, and not afraid of playing a bold hand. I'm going to confide in you. I need help worse than any man ever needed it, and I want to know if I can count you in.'

'Get on with your yarn,' I said, 'and I'll tell you.'

He seemed to brace himself for a great effort, and then started on the queerest rigmarole. I didn't get hold of it at first, and I had to stop and ask him questions. But here is the gist of it:

He was an American, from Kentucky, and after college, being pretty well off, he had started out to see the world. He wrote a bit, and acted as war correspondent for a Chicago paper, and spent a year or two in South-Eastern Europe. I gathered that he was a fine linguist, and had got to know pretty well the society in those parts. He spoke familiarly of many names that I remembered to have seen in the newspapers.

He had played about with politics, he told me, at first for the interest of them, and then because he couldn't help himself. I read him as a sharp, restless fellow, who always wanted to get down to the roots of things. He got a little further down than he wanted.

I am giving you what he told me as well as I could make it out. Away behind all the Governments and the armies there was a big subterranean movement going on, engineered by very dangerous people. He had come on it by accident; it fascinated him; he went further, and then he got caught. I gathered that most of the people in it were the sort of educated anarchists that make revolutions, but that beside them there were financiers who were playing for money. A clever man can make big profits on a falling market, and it suited the book of both classes to set Europe by the ears.

He told me some queer things that explained a lot that had puzzled me—things that happened in the Balkan War, how one state suddenly came out on top, why alliances were made and broken, why certain men disappeared, and where the sinews of war came from. The aim of the whole conspiracy was to get Russia and Germany at loggerheads.

When I asked why, he said that the anarchist lot thought it would give them their chance. Everything would be in the melting-pot, and they looked to see a new world emerge. The capitalists would rake in the shekels, and make fortunes by buying up wreckage. Capital, he said, had no conscience and no fatherland. Besides, the Jew was behind it, and the Jew hated Russia worse than hell.

'Do you wonder?' he cried. 'For three hundred years they have been persecuted, and this is the return match for the pogroms. The Jew is everywhere, but you have to go far down the backstairs to find him. Take any big Teutonic business concern. If you have dealings with it the first man you meet is Prince von und Zu Something, an elegant young man who talks Eton-and-Harrow English. But he cuts no ice. If your business is big, you get behind him and find a prognathous Westphalian with a retreating brow and the manners of a hog. He is the German business man that gives your English papers the shakes. But if you're on the biggest kind of job and are bound to get to the real boss, ten to one you are brought up against a little white-faced Jew in a bath-chair with an eye like a rattlesnake. Yes, Sir, he is the man who is ruling the world just now, and he has his knife in the Empire of the Tzar, because his aunt was outraged and his father flogged in some one-horse location on the Volga.'

I could not help saying that his Jew-anarchists seemed to have got left behind a little.

'Yes and no,' he said. 'They won up to a point, but they struck a bigger thing than money, a thing that couldn't be bought, the old elemental fighting instincts of man. If you're going to be killed you invent some kind of flag and country to fight for, and if you survive you get to love the thing. Those foolish devils of soldiers have found something they care for, and that has upset the pretty plan laid in Berlin and Vienna. But my friends haven't played their last card by a long sight. They've gotten the ace up their sleeves, and unless I can keep alive for a month they are going to play it and win.'

'But I thought you were dead,' I put in.

'MORS JANUA VITAE,' he smiled. (I recognized the quotation: it was about all the Latin I knew.) 'I'm coming to that, but I've got to put you wise about a lot of things first. If you read your newspaper, I guess you know the name of Constantine Karolides?'

I sat up at that, for I had been reading about him that very afternoon.

'He is the man that has wrecked all their games. He is the one big brain in the whole show, and he happens also to be an honest man. Therefore he has been marked down these twelve months past. I found that out—not that it was difficult, for any fool could guess as much. But I found out the way they were going to get him, and that knowledge was deadly. That's why I have had to decease.'

He had another drink, and I mixed it for him myself, for I was getting interested in the beggar.

'They can't get him in his own land, for he has a bodyguard of Epirotes that would skin their grandmothers. But on the 15th day of June he is coming to this city. The British Foreign Office has taken to having International tea-parties, and the biggest of them is due on that date. Now Karolides is reckoned the principal guest, and if my friends have their way he will never return to his admiring countrymen.'

'That's simple enough, anyhow,' I said. 'You can warn him and keep him at home.'

'And play their game?' he asked sharply. 'If he does not come they win, for he's the only man that can straighten out the tangle. And if his Government are warned he won't come, for he does not know how big the stakes will be on June the 15th.'

'What about the British Government?' I said. 'They're not going to let their guests be murdered. Tip them the wink, and they'll take extra precautions.'

'No good. They might stuff your city with plain-clothes detectives and double the police and Constantine would still be a doomed man. My friends are not playing this game for candy. They want a big occasion for the taking off, with the eyes of all Europe on it. He'll be murdered by an Austrian, and there'll be plenty of evidence to show the connivance of the big folk in Vienna and Berlin. It will all be an infernal lie, of course, but the case will look black enough to the world. I'm not talking hot air, my friend. I happen to know every detail of the hellish contrivance, and I can tell you it will be the most finished piece of blackguardism since the Borgias. But it's not going to come off if there's a certain man who knows the wheels of the business alive right here in

London on the 15th day of June. And that man is going to be your servant, Franklin P. Scudder.'

I was getting to like the little chap. His jaw had shut like a rat-trap, and there was the fire of battle in his gimlety eyes. If he was spinning me a yarn he could act up to it.

'Where did you find out this story?' I asked.

'I got the first hint in an inn on the Achensee in Tyrol. That set me inquiring, and I collected my other clues in a fur-shop in the Galician quarter of Buda, in a Strangers' Club in Vienna, and in a little bookshop off the Racknitzstrasse in Leipsic. I completed my evidence ten days ago in Paris. I can't tell you the details now, for it's something of a history. When I was quite sure in my own mind I judged it my business to disappear, and I reached this city by a mighty queer circuit. I left Paris a dandified young French-American, and I sailed from Hamburg a Jew diamond merchant. In Norway I was an English student of Ibsen collecting materials for lectures, but when I left Bergen I was a cinema-man with special ski films. And I came here from Leith with a lot of pulp-wood propositions in my pocket to put before the London newspapers. Till yesterday I thought I had muddied my trail some, and was feeling pretty happy. Then ...'

The recollection seemed to upset him, and he gulped down some more whisky.

'Then I saw a man standing in the street outside this block. I used to stay close in my room all day, and only slip out after dark for an hour or two. I watched him for a bit from my window, and I thought I recognized him ... He came in and spoke to the porter ... When I came back from my walk last night I found a card in my letter-box. It bore the name of the man I want least to meet on God's earth.'

I think that the look in my companion's eyes, the sheer naked scare on his face, completed my conviction of his honesty. My own voice sharpened a bit as I asked him what he did next.

'I realized that I was bottled as sure as a pickled herring, and that there was only one way out. I had to die. If my pursuers knew I was dead they would go to sleep again.'

'How did you manage it?'

'I told the man that valets me that I was feeling pretty bad, and I got myself up to look like death. That wasn't difficult, for I'm no slouch at disguises. Then I got a corpse—you can always get a body in London if you know where to go for it. I fetched it back in a trunk on the top of a four-wheeler, and I had to be assisted upstairs to my room. You see I had to pile up some evidence for the inquest. I went to bed and got my man to mix me a sleeping-draught, and then told him to clear out. He wanted to fetch a doctor, but I swore some and said I couldn't abide leeches. When I was left alone I started in to fake up that corpse. He was my size, and I judged had perished from too much alcohol, so I put some spirits handy about the place. The jaw was the weak point in the likeness, so I blew it away with a revolver. I daresay there will be somebody tomorrow to swear to having heard a shot, but there are no neighbours on my floor, and I guessed I could risk it. So I left the body in bed dressed up in my pyjamas, with a revolver lying on the bed-clothes and a considerable mess around. Then I got into a suit of clothes I had kept waiting for emergencies. I didn't dare to shave for fear of leaving tracks, and besides, it wasn't any kind of use my trying to get into the streets. I had had you in my mind all day, and there seemed nothing to do but to make an appeal to you. I watched from my window till I saw you come home, and then slipped down the stair to meet you ... There, Sir, I guess you know about as much as me of this business.'

He sat blinking like an owl, fluttering with nerves and yet desperately determined. By this time I was pretty well convinced that he was going straight with me. It was the wildest sort of narrative, but I had heard in my time many steep tales which had turned out to be true, and I had made a practice of judging the man rather than the story. If he had wanted to get a location in my flat, and then cut my throat, he would have pitched a milder yarn.

'Hand me your key,' I said, 'and I'll take a look at the corpse. Excuse my caution, but I'm bound to verify a bit if I can.'

He shook his head mournfully. 'I reckoned you'd ask for that, but I haven't got it. It's on my chain on the dressing-table. I had to leave it behind, for I couldn't leave any clues to breed suspicions. The gentry who are after me are pretty bright-eyed citizens. You'll have to take me on trust for the night, and tomorrow you'll get proof of the corpse business right enough.'

I thought for an instant or two. 'Right. I'll trust you for the night. I'll lock you into this room and keep the key. Just one word, Mr Scudder. I believe you're straight, but if so be you are not I should warn you that I'm a handy man with a gun.'

'Sure,' he said, jumping up with some briskness. 'I haven't the privilege of your name, Sir, but let me tell you that you're a white man. I'll thank you to lend me a razor.'

I took him into my bedroom and turned him loose. In half an hour's time a figure came out that I scarcely recognized. Only his gimlety, hungry eyes were the same. He was shaved clean, his hair was parted in the middle, and he had cut his eyebrows. Further, he carried himself as if he had been drilled, and was the very model, even to the brown complexion, of some British officer who had had a long spell in India. He had a monocle, too, which he stuck in his eye, and every trace of the American had gone out of his speech.

'My hat! Mr Scudder—' I stammered.

'Not Mr Scudder,' he corrected; 'Captain Theophilus Digby, of the 40th Gurkhas, presently home on leave. I'll thank you to remember that, Sir.'

I made him up a bed in my smoking-room and sought my own couch, more cheerful than I had been for the past month. Things did happen occasionally, even in this God-forgotten metropolis.

I woke next morning to hear my man, Paddock, making the deuce of a row at the smoking-room door. Paddock was a fellow I had done a good turn to out on the Selakwe, and I had inspanned him as my servant as soon as I got to England. He had about as much gift of the gab as a hippopotamus, and was not a great hand at valeting, but I knew I could count on his loyalty.

'Stop that row, Paddock,' I said. 'There's a friend of mine, Captain—Captain' (I couldn't remember the name) 'dossing down in there. Get breakfast for two and then come and speak to me.'

I told Paddock a fine story about how my friend was a great swell, with his nerves pretty bad from overwork, who wanted absolute rest and stillness. Nobody had got to know he was here, or he would be besieged by communications from the India Office and the Prime Minister and his cure would be ruined. I am bound to say Scudder played up splendidly when he came to breakfast. He fixed Paddock with his eyeglass, just like a British officer, asked him about the Boer War, and slung out at me a lot of stuff about imaginary pals. Paddock couldn't learn to call me 'Sir', but he 'sirred' Scudder as if his life depended on it.

I left him with the newspaper and a box of cigars, and went down to the City till luncheon. When I got back the lift-man had an important face.

'Nawsty business 'ere this morning, Sir. Gent in No. 15 been and shot 'isself. They've just took 'im to the mortiary. The police are up there now.'

I ascended to No. 15, and found a couple of bobbies and an inspector busy making an examination. I asked a few idiotic questions, and they soon kicked me out. Then I found the man that had valeted Scudder, and pumped him, but I could see he suspected nothing. He was a whining fellow with a churchyard face, and half-a-crown went far to console him.

I attended the inquest next day. A partner of some publishing firm gave evidence that the deceased had brought him wood-pulp propositions, and had been, he believed, an agent of an American business. The jury found it a case of suicide while of unsound mind, and the few effects were handed over to the American Consul to deal with. I gave Scudder a full account of the affair, and it interested him greatly. He said he wished he could have attended the inquest, for he reckoned it would be about as spicy as to read one's own obituary notice.

The first two days he stayed with me in that back room he was very peaceful. He read and smoked a bit, and made a heap of jottings in a note-book, and every night we had a game of chess, at which he beat me hollow. I think he was nursing his nerves back to health, for he had had a pretty trying time. But on the third day I could see he was beginning to get restless. He fixed up a list of the days till June 15th, and ticked each off with a red pencil, making remarks in shorthand against them. I would find him sunk in a brown study, with his sharp eyes abstracted, and after those spells of meditation he was apt to be very despondent.

Then I could see that he began to get edgy again. He listened for little noises, and was always asking me if Paddock could be trusted. Once or twice he got very peevish, and apologized for it. I didn't blame him. I made every allowance, for he had taken on a fairly stiff job.

It was not the safety of his own skin that troubled him, but the success of the scheme he had planned. That little man was clean grit all through, without a soft spot in him. One night he was very solemn.

'Say, Hannay,' he said, 'I judge I should let you a bit deeper into this business. I should hate to go out without leaving somebody else to put up a fight.' And he began to tell me in detail what I had only heard from him vaguely.

I did not give him very close attention. The fact is, I was more interested in his own adventures than in his high politics. I reckoned that Karolides and his affairs were not my business, leaving all that to him. So a lot that he said slipped clean out of my memory. I remember that he was very clear that the danger to Karolides would not begin till he had got to London, and would come from the very highest quarters, where there would be no thought of suspicion. He mentioned the name of a woman—Julia Czechenyi—as having something to do with the danger. She would be the decoy, I gathered, to get Karolides out of the care of his guards. He talked, too, about a Black Stone and a man that lisped in his speech, and he described very particularly somebody that he never referred to without a shudder—an old man with a young voice who could hood his eyes like a hawk.

He spoke a good deal about death, too. He was mortally anxious about winning through with his job, but he didn't care a rush for his life.

'I reckon it's like going to sleep when you are pretty well tired out, and waking to find a summer day with the scent of hay coming in at the window. I used to thank God for such mornings way back in the Blue-Grass country, and I guess I'll thank Him when I wake up on the other side of Jordan.'

Next day he was much more cheerful, and read the life of Stonewall Jackson much of the time. I went out to dinner with a mining engineer I had got to see on business, and came back about half-past ten in time for our game of chess before turning in.

I had a cigar in my mouth, I remember, as I pushed open the smoking-room door. The lights were not lit, which struck me as odd. I wondered if Scudder had turned in already.

I snapped the switch, but there was nobody there. Then I saw something in the far corner which made me drop my cigar and fall into a cold sweat.

My guest was lying sprawled on his back. There was a long knife through his heart which skewered him to the floor.

CHAPTER TWO

The Milkman Sets Out on his Travels

I sat down in an armchair and felt very sick. That lasted for maybe five minutes, and was succeeded by a fit of the horrors. The poor staring white face on the floor was more than I could bear, and I managed to get a table-cloth and cover it. Then I staggered to a cupboard, found the brandy and swallowed several mouthfuls. I had seen men die violently before; indeed I had killed a few myself in the Matabele War; but this cold-blooded indoor business was different. Still I managed to pull myself together. I looked at my watch, and saw that it was half-past ten.

An idea seized me, and I went over the flat with a small-tooth comb. There was nobody there, nor any trace of anybody, but I shuttered and bolted all the windows and put the chain on the door. By this time my wits were coming back to me, and I could think again. It took me about an hour to figure the thing out, and I did not hurry, for, unless the murderer came back, I had till about six o'clock in the morning for my cogitations.

I was in the soup—that was pretty clear. Any shadow of a doubt I might have had about the truth of Scudder's tale was now gone. The proof of it was lying under the table-cloth. The men who knew that he knew what he knew had found him, and had taken the best way to make certain of his silence. Yes; but he had been in my rooms four days, and his enemies must have reckoned that he had confided in me. So I would be the next to go. It might be that very night, or next day, or the day after, but my number was up all right.

Then suddenly I thought of another probability. Supposing I went out now and called in the police, or went to bed and let Paddock find the body and call them in the morning. What kind of a story was I to tell about Scudder? I had lied to Paddock about him, and the whole thing looked desperately fishy. If I made a clean breast of it and told the police everything he had told me, they would simply laugh at me. The odds were a thousand to one that I would be charged with the murder, and the circumstantial evidence was strong enough to hang me. Few people knew me in England; I had no real pal who could come forward and swear to my character. Perhaps that was what those secret enemies were playing for. They were clever enough for anything, and an English prison was as good a way of getting rid of me till after June 15th as a knife in my chest.

Besides, if I told the whole story, and by any miracle was believed, I would be playing their game. Karolides would stay at home, which was what they wanted. Somehow or other the sight of Scudder's dead face had made me a passionate believer in his scheme. He was gone, but he had taken me into his confidence, and I was pretty well bound to carry on his work.

You may think this ridiculous for a man in danger of his life, but that was the way I looked at it. I am an ordinary sort of fellow, not braver than other people, but I hate to see a good man downed, and that long knife would not be the end of Scudder if I could play the game in his place.

It took me an hour or two to think this out, and by that time I had come to a decision. I must vanish somehow, and keep vanished till the end of the second week in June. Then I must somehow find a way to get in touch with the Government people and tell them what Scudder had told me. I wished to Heaven he had told me more, and that I had listened more carefully to the little he had told me. I knew nothing but the barest facts. There was a big risk that, even if I weathered the other dangers, I would not be believed in the end. I must take my chance of that, and hope that something might happen which would confirm my tale in the eyes of the Government.

My first job was to keep going for the next three weeks. It was now the 24th day of May, and that meant twenty days of hiding before I could venture to approach the powers that be. I reckoned that two sets of people would be looking for me—Scudder's enemies to put me out of existence, and the police, who would want me for Scudder's murder. It was going to be a giddy hunt, and it was queer how the prospect comforted me. I had been slack so long that almost any chance of activity was welcome. When I had to sit alone with that corpse and wait on Fortune I was no better than a crushed worm, but if my neck's safety was to hang on my own wits I was prepared to be cheerful about it.

My next thought was whether Scudder had any papers about him to give me a better clue to the business. I drew back the table-cloth and searched his pockets, for I had no longer any shrinking from the body. The face was wonderfully calm for a man who had been struck down in a moment. There was nothing in the breast-pocket, and only a few loose coins and a cigar-holder in the waistcoat. The trousers held a little penknife and some silver, and the side pocket of his jacket contained an old crocodile-skin cigar-case. There was no sign of the little black book in which I had seen him making notes. That had no doubt been taken by his murderer.

But as I looked up from my task I saw that some drawers had been pulled out in the writing-table. Scudder would never have left them in that state, for he was the tidiest of mortals. Someone must have been searching for something—perhaps for the pocket-book.

I went round the flat and found that everything had been ransacked—the inside of books, drawers, cupboards, boxes, even the pockets of the clothes in my wardrobe, and the sideboard in the dining-room. There was no trace of the book. Most likely the enemy had found it, but they had not found it on Scudder's body.

Then I got out an atlas and looked at a big map of the British Isles. My notion was to get off to some wild district, where my veldcraft would be of some use to me, for I would be like a trapped rat in a city. I considered that Scotland would be best, for my people were Scotch and I could pass anywhere as an ordinary Scotsman. I had half an idea at first to be a German tourist, for my father had had German partners, and I had been brought up to speak the tongue pretty fluently, not to mention having put in three years prospecting for copper in German Damaraland. But I calculated that it would be less conspicuous to be a Scot, and less in a line with what the police might know of my past. I fixed on Galloway as the best place to go. It was the nearest wild part of Scotland, so far as I could figure it out, and from the look of the map was not over thick with population.

A search in Bradshaw informed me that a train left St Pancras at 7.10, which would land me at any Galloway station in the late afternoon. That was well enough, but a more important matter was how I was to make my way to St Pancras, for I was pretty certain that Scudder's friends would be watching outside. This puzzled me for a bit; then I had an inspiration, on which I went to bed and slept for two troubled hours.

I got up at four and opened my bedroom shutters. The faint light of a fine summer morning was flooding the skies, and the sparrows had begun to chatter. I had a great revulsion of feeling, and felt a God-forgotten fool. My inclination was to let things slide, and trust to the

British police taking a reasonable view of my case. But as I reviewed the situation I could find no arguments to bring against my decision of the previous night, so with a wry mouth I resolved to go on with my plan. I was not feeling in any particular funk; only disinclined to go looking for trouble, if you understand me.

I hunted out a well-used tweed suit, a pair of strong nailed boots, and a flannel shirt with a collar. Into my pockets I stuffed a spare shirt, a cloth cap, some handkerchiefs, and a tooth-brush. I had drawn a good sum in gold from the bank two days before, in case Scudder should want money, and I took fifty pounds of it in sovereigns in a belt which I had brought back from Rhodesia. That was about all I wanted. Then I had a bath, and cut my moustache, which was long and drooping, into a short stubbly fringe.

Now came the next step. Paddock used to arrive punctually at 7.30 and let himself in with a latch-key. But about twenty minutes to seven, as I knew from bitter experience, the milkman turned up with a great clatter of cans, and deposited my share outside my door. I had seen that milkman sometimes when I had gone out for an early ride. He was a young man about my own height, with an ill-nourished moustache, and he wore a white overall. On him I staked all my chances.

I went into the darkened smoking-room where the rays of morning light were beginning to creep through the shutters. There I breakfasted off a whisky-and-soda and some biscuits from the cupboard. By this time it was getting on for six o'clock. I put a pipe in My Pocket and filled my pouch from the tobacco jar on the table by the fireplace.

As I poked into the tobacco my fingers touched something hard, and I drew out Scudder's little black pocket-book ...

That seemed to me a good omen. I lifted the cloth from the body and was amazed at the peace and dignity of the dead face. 'Goodbye, old chap,' I said; 'I am going to do my best for you. Wish me well, wherever you are.'

Then I hung about in the hall waiting for the milkman. That was the worst part of the business, for I was fairly choking to get out of doors. Six-thirty passed, then six-forty, but still he did not come. The fool had chosen this day of all days to be late.

At one minute after the quarter to seven I heard the rattle of the cans outside. I opened the front door, and there was my man, singling out my cans from a bunch he carried and whistling through his teeth. He jumped a bit at the sight of me.

'Come in here a moment,' I said. 'I want a word with you.' And I led him into the dining-room.

'I reckon you're a bit of a sportsman,' I said, 'and I want you to do me a service. Lend me your cap and overall for ten minutes, and here's a sovereign for you.'

His eyes opened at the sight of the gold, and he grinned broadly. 'Wot's the gyme?'he asked.

'A bet,' I said. 'I haven't time to explain, but to win it I've got to be a milkman for the next ten minutes. All you've got to do is to stay here till I come back. You'll be a bit late, but nobody will complain, and you'll have that quid for yourself.'

'Right-o!' he said cheerily. 'I ain't the man to spoil a bit of sport. 'Ere's the rig, guv'nor.'

I stuck on his flat blue hat and his white overall, picked up the cans, banged my door, and went whistling downstairs. The porter at the foot told me to shut my jaw, which sounded as if my make-up was adequate.

At first I thought there was nobody in the street. Then I caught sight of a policeman a hundred yards down, and a loafer shuffling past on the other side. Some impulse made me raise my eyes to the house opposite, and there at a first-floor window was a face. As the loafer passed he looked up, and I fancied a signal was exchanged.

I crossed the street, whistling gaily and imitating the jaunty swing of the milkman. Then I took the first side street, and went up a left-hand turning which led past a bit of vacant ground. There was no one in the little street, so I dropped the milk-cans inside the hoarding and sent the cap and overall after them. I had only just put on my cloth cap when a postman came round the corner. I gave him good morning and he answered me unsuspiciously. At the moment the clock of a neighbouring church struck the hour of seven.

There was not a second to spare. As soon as I got to Euston Road I took to my heels and ran. The clock at Euston Station showed five minutes past the hour. At St Pancras I had no time to take a ticket, let alone that I had not settled upon my destination. A porter told me the platform, and as I entered it I saw the train already in motion. Two station officials blocked the way, but I dodged them and clambered into the last carriage.

Three minutes later, as we were roaring through the northern tunnels, an irate guard interviewed me. He wrote out for me a ticket to Newton-Stewart, a name which had suddenly come back to my memory, and he conducted me from the first-class compartment where I had ensconced myself to a third-class smoker, occupied by a sailor and a stout woman with a child. He went off grumbling, and as I mopped my brow I observed to my companions in my broadest Scots that it was a sore job catching trains. I had already entered upon my part.

'The impidence o' that gyaird!' said the lady bitterly. 'He needit a Scotch tongue to pit him in his place. He was complainin' o' this wean no haein' a ticket and her no fower till August twalmonth, and he was objectin' to this gentleman spittin'.'

The sailor morosely agreed, and I started my new life in an atmosphere of protest against authority. I reminded myself that a week ago I had been finding the world dull.

CHAPTER THREE

The Adventure of the Literary Innkeeper

I had a solemn time travelling north that day. It was fine May weather, with the hawthorn flowering on every hedge, and I asked myself why, when I was still a free man, I had stayed on in London and not got the good of this heavenly country. I didn't dare face the restaurant car, but I got a luncheon-basket at Leeds and shared it with the fat woman. Also I got the morning's papers, with news about starters for the Derby and the beginning of the cricket season, and some paragraphs about how Balkan affairs were settling down and a British squadron was going to Kiel.

When I had done with them I got out Scudder's little black pocket-book and studied it. It was pretty well filled with jottings, chiefly figures, though now and then a name was printed in. For example, I found the words 'Hofgaard', 'Luneville', and 'Avocado' pretty often, and especially the word 'Pavia'.

Now I was certain that Scudder never did anything without a reason, and I was pretty sure that there was a cypher in all this. That is a subject which has always interested me, and I did a bit at it myself once as intelligence officer at Delagoa Bay during the Boer War. I have a head for things like chess and puzzles, and I used to reckon myself pretty good at finding out cyphers. This one looked like the numerical kind where sets of figures correspond to the letters of the alphabet, but any fairly shrewd man can find the clue to that sort after an hour or two's work, and I didn't think Scudder would have been content with anything so easy. So I fastened on the printed words, for you can make a pretty good numerical cypher if you have a key word which gives you the sequence of the letters.

I tried for hours, but none of the words answered. Then I fell asleep and woke at Dumfries just in time to bundle out and get into the slow Galloway train. There was a man on the platform whose looks I didn't like, but he never glanced at me, and when I caught sight of myself in the mirror of an automatic machine I didn't wonder. With my brown face, my old tweeds, and my slouch, I was the very model of one of the hill farmers who were crowding into the third-class carriages.

I travelled with half a dozen in an atmosphere of shag and clay pipes. They had come from the weekly market, and their mouths were full of prices. I heard accounts of how the lambing had gone up the Cairn and the Deuch and a dozen other mysterious waters. Above half the men had lunched heavily and were highly flavoured with whisky, but they took no notice of me. We rumbled slowly into a land of little wooded glens and then to a great wide moorland place, gleaming with lochs, with high blue hills showing northwards.

About five o'clock the carriage had emptied, and I was left alone as I had hoped. I got out at the next station, a little place whose name I scarcely noted, set right in the heart of a bog. It reminded me of one of those forgotten little stations in the Karroo. An old station-master was digging in his garden, and with his spade over his shoulder sauntered to the train, took charge of a parcel, and went back to his potatoes. A child of ten received my ticket, and I emerged on a white road that straggled over the brown moor.

It was a gorgeous spring evening, with every hill showing as clear as a cut amethyst. The air had the queer, rooty smell of bogs, but it was as fresh as mid-ocean, and it had the strangest effect on my spirits. I actually felt light-hearted. I might have been a boy out for a spring holiday tramp, instead of a man of thirty-seven very much wanted by the police. I felt just as I used to feel when I was starting for a big trek on a frosty morning on the high veld. If you believe me, I swung along that road whistling. There was no plan of campaign in my head, only just to go on and on in this blessed, honest-smelling hill country, for every mile put me in better humour with myself.

In a roadside planting I cut a walking-stick of hazel, and presently struck off the highway up a bypath which followed the glen of a brawling stream. I reckoned that I was still far ahead of any pursuit, and for that night might please myself. It was some hours since I had tasted food, and I was getting very hungry when I came to a herd's cottage set in a nook beside a waterfall. A brown-faced woman was standing by the door, and greeted me with the kindly shyness of moorland places. When I asked for a night's lodging she said I was welcome to the 'bed in the loft', and very soon she set before me a hearty meal of ham and eggs, scones, and thick sweet milk.

At the darkening her man came in from the hills, a lean giant, who in one step covered as much ground as three paces of ordinary mortals. They asked me no questions, for they had the perfect breeding of all dwellers in the wilds, but I could see they set me down as a kind of dealer, and I took some trouble to confirm their view. I spoke a lot about cattle, of which my host knew little, and I picked up from him a good deal about the local Galloway markets, which I tucked away in my memory for future use. At ten I was nodding in my chair, and the 'bed in the loft' received a weary man who never opened his eyes till five o'clock set the little homestead a-going once more.

They refused any payment, and by six I had breakfasted and was striding southwards again. My notion was to return to the railway line a station or two farther on than the place where I had alighted yesterday and to double back. I reckoned that that was the safest way, for the police would naturally assume that I was always making farther from London in the direction of some western port. I thought I had still a good bit of a start, for, as I reasoned, it would take some hours to fix the blame on me, and several more to identify the fellow who got on board the train at St Pancras.

It was the same jolly, clear spring weather, and I simply could not contrive to feel careworn. Indeed I was in better spirits than I had been for months. Over a long ridge of moorland I took my road, skirting the side of a high hill which the herd had called Cairnsmore of Fleet. Nesting curlews and plovers were crying everywhere, and the links of green pasture by the streams were dotted with young lambs. All the slackness of the past months was slipping from my bones, and I stepped out like a four-year-old. By-and-by I came to a swell of moorland which dipped to the vale of a little river, and a mile away in the heather I saw the smoke of a train.

The station, when I reached it, proved to be ideal for my purpose. The moor surged up around it and left room only for the single line, the slender siding, a waiting-room, an office, the station-master's cottage, and a tiny yard of gooseberries and sweet-william. There seemed no road to it from anywhere, and to increase the desolation the waves of a tarn lapped on their grey granite beach half a mile away. I waited in the deep heather till I saw the smoke of an east-going train on the horizon. Then I approached the tiny booking-office and took a ticket for Dumfries.

The only occupants of the carriage were an old shepherd and his dog—a wall-eyed brute that I mistrusted. The man was asleep, and on the cushions beside him was that morning's SCOTSMAN. Eagerly I seized on it, for I fancied it would tell me something.

There were two columns about the Portland Place Murder, as it was called. My man Paddock had given the alarm and had the milkman arrested. Poor devil, it looked as if the latter had earned his sovereign hardly; but for me he had been cheap at the price, for he seemed to have occupied the police for the better part of the day. In the latest news I found a further instalment of the story. The milkman had been released, I read, and the true criminal, about whose identity the police were reticent, was believed to have got away from London by one of the northern lines. There was a short note about me as the owner of the flat. I guessed the police had stuck that in, as a clumsy contrivance to persuade me that I was unsuspected.

There was nothing else in the paper, nothing about foreign politics or Karolides, or the things that had interested Scudder. I laid it down, and found that we were approaching the station at which I had got out yesterday. The potato-digging station-master had been gingered up into some activity, for the west-going train was waiting to let us pass, and from it had descended three men who were asking him questions. I supposed that they were the local police, who had been stirred up by Scotland Yard, and had traced me as far as this one-horse siding. Sitting well back in the shadow I watched them carefully. One of them had a book, and took down notes. The old potato-digger seemed to have turned peevish, but the child who had collected my ticket was talking volubly. All the party looked out across the moor where the white road departed. I hoped they were going to take up my tracks there.

As we moved away from that station my companion woke up. He fixed me with a wandering glance, kicked his dog viciously, and inquired where he was. Clearly he was very drunk.

'That's what comes o' bein' a teetotaller,' he observed in bitter regret.

I expressed my surprise that in him I should have met a blue-ribbon stalwart.

'Ay, but I'm a strong teetotaller,' he said pugnaciously. 'I took the pledge last Martinmas, and I havena touched a drop o' whisky sinsyne. Not even at Hogmanay, though I was sair temptit.'

He swung his heels up on the seat, and burrowed a frowsy head into the cushions.

'And that's a' I get,' he moaned. 'A heid better than hell fire, and twae een lookin' different ways for the Sabbath.'

'What did it?' I asked.

'A drink they ca' brandy. Bein' a teetotaller I keepit off the whisky, but I was nip-nippin' a' day at this brandy, and I doubt I'll no be weel for a fortnicht.' His voice died away into a splutter, and sleep once more laid its heavy hand on him.

My plan had been to get out at some station down the line, but the train suddenly gave me a better chance, for it came to a standstill at the end of a culvert which spanned a brawling porter-coloured river. I looked out and saw that every carriage window was closed and no human figure appeared in the landscape. So I opened the door, and dropped quickly into the tangle of hazels which edged the line.

it would have been all right but for that infernal dog. Under the impression that I was decamping with its master's belongings, it started to bark, and all but got me by the trousers. This woke up the herd, who stood bawling at the carriage door in the belief that I had committed suicide. I crawled through the thicket, reached the edge of the stream, and in cover of the bushes put a hundred yards or so behind me. Then from my shelter I peered back, and saw the guard and several passengers gathered round the open carriage door and staring in my direction. I could not have made a more public departure if I had left with a bugler and a brass band.

Happily the drunken herd provided a diversion. He and his dog, which was attached by a rope to his waist, suddenly cascaded out of the carriage, landed on their heads on the track, and rolled some way down the bank towards the water. In the rescue which followed the dog bit somebody, for I could hear the sound of hard swearing. Presently they had forgotten me, and when after a quarter of a mile's crawl I ventured to look back, the train had started again and was vanishing in the cutting.

I was in a wide semicircle of moorland, with the brown river as radius, and the high hills forming the northern circumference. There was not a sign or sound of a human being, only the plashing water and the interminable crying of curlews. Yet, oddly enough, for the first time I felt the terror of the hunted on me. It was not the police that I thought of, but the other folk, who knew that I knew Scudder's secret and dared not let me live. I was certain that they would pursue me with a keenness and vigilance unknown to the British law, and that once their grip closed on me I should find no mercy.

I looked back, but there was nothing in the landscape. The sun glinted on the metals of the line and the wet stones in the stream, and you could not have found a more peaceful sight in the world. Nevertheless I started to run. Crouching low in the runnels of the bog, I ran till the sweat blinded my eyes. The mood did not leave me till I had reached the rim of mountain and flung myself panting on a ridge high above the young waters of the brown river.

From my vantage-ground I could scan the whole moor right away to the railway line and to the south of it where green fields took the place of heather. I have eyes like a hawk, but I could see nothing moving in the whole countryside. Then I looked east beyond the ridge and saw a new kind of landscape—shallow green valleys with plentiful fir plantations and the faint lines of dust which spoke of highroads. Last of all I looked into the blue May sky, and there I saw that which set my pulses racing ...

Low down in the south a monoplane was climbing into the heavens. I was as certain as if I had been told that that aeroplane was looking for me, and that it did not belong to the police. For an hour or two I watched it from a pit of heather. It flew low along the hill-tops, and then in narrow circles over the valley up which I had come' Then it seemed to change its mind, rose to a great height, and flew away back to the south.

I did not like this espionage from the air, and I began to think less well of the countryside I had chosen for a refuge. These heather hills were no sort of cover if my enemies were in the sky, and I must find a different kind of sanctuary. I looked with more satisfaction to the green country beyond the ridge, for there I should find woods and stone houses.

About six in the evening I came out of the moorland to a white ribbon of road which wound up the narrow vale of a lowland stream. As I followed it, fields gave place to bent, the glen became a plateau, and presently I had reached a kind of pass where a solitary house smoked in the twilight. The road swung over a bridge, and leaning on the parapet was a young man.

He was smoking a long clay pipe and studying the water with spectacled eyes. In his left hand was a small book with a finger marking the place. Slowly he repeated—

As when a Gryphon through the wilderness
With winged step, o'er hill and moory dale
Pursues the Arimaspian.

He jumped round as my step rung on the keystone, and I saw a pleasant sunburnt boyish face.

'Good evening to you,' he said gravely. 'It's a fine night for the road.'

The smell of peat smoke and of some savoury roast floated to me from the house.

'Is that place an inn?' I asked.

'At your service,' he said politely. 'I am the landlord, Sir, and I hope you will stay the night, for to tell you the truth I have had no company for a week.'

I pulled myself up on the parapet of the bridge and filled my pipe. I began to detect an ally.

'You're young to be an innkeeper,' I said.

'My father died a year ago and left me the business. I live there with my grandmother. It's a slow job for a young man, and it wasn't my choice of profession.'

'Which was?'

He actually blushed. 'I want to write books,' he said.

'And what better chance could you ask?' I cried. 'Man, I've often thought that an innkeeper would make the best story-teller in the world.'

'Not now,' he said eagerly. 'Maybe in the old days when you had pilgrims and ballad-makers and highwaymen and mail-coaches on the road. But not now. Nothing comes here but motor-cars full of fat women, who stop for lunch, and a fisherman or two in the spring, and the shooting tenants in August. There is not much material to be got out of that. I want to see life, to travel the world, and write things like Kipling and Conrad. But the most I've done yet is to get some verses printed in CHAMBERS'S JOURNAL.' I looked at the inn standing golden in the sunset against the brown hills.

'I've knocked a bit about the world, and I wouldn't despise such a hermitage. D'you think that adventure is found only in the tropics or among gentry in red shirts? Maybe you're rubbing shoulders with it at this moment.'

'That's what Kipling says,' he said, his eyes brightening, and he quoted some verse about 'Romance bringing up the 9.15'.

'Here's a true tale for you then,' I cried, 'and a month from now you can make a novel out of it.'

Sitting on the bridge in the soft May gloaming I pitched him a lovely yarn. It was true in essentials, too, though I altered the minor details. I made out that I was a mining magnate from Kimberley, who had had a lot of trouble with I.D.B. and had shown up a gang. They had pursued me across the ocean, and had killed my best friend, and were now on my tracks.

I told the story well, though I say it who shouldn't. I pictured a flight across the Kalahari to German Africa, the crackling, parching days, the wonderful blue-velvet nights. I described an attack on my life on the voyage home, and I made a really horrid affair of the Portland Place murder. 'You're looking for adventure,' I cried; 'well, you've found it here. The devils are after me, and the police are after them. It's a race that I mean to win.'

'By God!' he whispered, drawing his breath in sharply, 'it is all pure Rider Haggard and Conan Doyle.'

'You believe me,' I said gratefully.

'Of course I do,' and he held out his hand. 'I believe everything out of the common. The only thing to distrust is the normal.'

He was very young, but he was the man for my money.

'I think they're off my track for the moment, but I must lie close for a couple of days. Can you take me in?'

He caught my elbow in his eagerness and drew me towards the house. 'You can lie as snug here as if you were in a moss-hole. I'll see that nobody blabs, either. And you'll give me some more material about your adventures?'

As I entered the inn porch I heard from far off the beat of an engine. There silhouetted against the dusky West was my friend, the monoplane.

He gave me a room at the back of the house, with a fine outlook over the plateau, and he made me free of his own study, which was stacked with cheap editions of his favourite authors. I never saw the grandmother, so I guessed she was bedridden. An old woman called Margit brought me my meals, and the innkeeper was around me at all hours. I wanted some time to myself, so I invented a job for him. He had a motor-bicycle, and I sent him off next morning for the daily paper, which usually arrived with the post in the late afternoon. I told him to keep his eyes skinned, and make note of any strange figures he saw, keeping a special sharp look-out for motors and aeroplanes. Then I sat down in real earnest to Scudder's note-book.

He came back at midday with the SCOTSMAN. There was nothing in it, except some further evidence of Paddock and the milkman, and a repetition of yesterday's statement that the murderer had gone North. But there was a long article, reprinted from THE TIMES, about Karolides and the state of affairs in the Balkans, though there was no mention of any visit to England. I got rid of the innkeeper for the afternoon, for I was getting very warm in my search for the cypher.

As I told you, it was a numerical cypher, and by an elaborate system of experiments I had pretty well discovered what were the nulls and stops. The trouble was the key word, and when I thought of the odd million words he might have used I felt pretty hopeless. But about three o'clock I had a sudden inspiration.

The name Julia Czechenyi flashed across my memory. Scudder had said it was the key to the Karolides business, and it occurred to me to try it on his cypher.

It worked. The five letters of 'Julia' gave me the position of the vowels. A was J, the tenth letter of the alphabet, and so represented by X in the cypher. E was XXI, and so on. 'Czechenyi' gave me the numerals for the principal consonants. I scribbled that scheme on a bit of paper and sat down to read Scudder's pages.

In half an hour I was reading with a whitish face and fingers that drummed on the table.

I glanced out of the window and saw a big touring-car coming up the glen towards the inn. It drew up at the door, and there was the sound of people alighting. There seemed to be two of them, men in aquascutums and tweed caps.

Ten minutes later the innkeeper slipped into the room, his eyes bright with excitement.

'There's two chaps below looking for you,' he whispered. 'They're in the dining-room having whiskies-and-sodas. They asked about you and said they had hoped to meet you here. Oh! and they described you jolly well, down to your boots and shirt. I told them you had been here last night and had gone off on a motor bicycle this morning, and one of the chaps swore like a navvy.'

I made him tell me what they looked like. One was a dark-eyed thin fellow with bushy eyebrows, the other was always smiling and lisped in his talk. Neither was any kind of foreigner; on this my young friend was positive.

I took a bit of paper and wrote these words in German as if they were part of a letter—

... 'Black Stone. Scudder had got on to this, but he could not act for a fortnight. I doubt if I can do any good now, especially as Karolides is uncertain about his plans. But if Mr T. advises I will do the best I ...'

I manufactured it rather neatly, so that it looked like a loose page of a private letter.

'Take this down and say it was found in my bedroom, and ask them to return it to me if they overtake me.'

Three minutes later I heard the car begin to move, and peeping from behind the curtain caught sight of the two figures. One was slim, the other was sleek; that was the most I could make of my reconnaissance.

The innkeeper appeared in great excitement. 'Your paper woke them up,' he said gleefully. 'The dark fellow went as white as death and cursed like blazes, and the fat one whistled and looked ugly. They paid for their drinks with half-a-sovereign and wouldn't wait for change.'

'Now I'll tell you what I want you to do,' I said. 'Get on your bicycle and go off to Newton-Stewart to the Chief Constable. Describe the two men, and say you suspect them of having had something to do with the London murder. You can invent reasons. The two will come back, never fear. Not tonight, for they'll follow me forty miles along the road, but first thing tomorrow morning. Tell the police to be here bright and early.'

He set off like a docile child, while I worked at Scudder's notes. When he came back we dined together, and in common decency I had to let him pump me. I gave him a lot of stuff about lion hunts and the Matabele War, thinking all the while what tame businesses these were compared to this I was now engaged in! When he went to bed I sat up and finished Scudder. I smoked in a chair till daylight, for I could not sleep.

About eight next morning I witnessed the arrival of two constables and a sergeant. They put their car in a coach-house under the innkeeper's instructions, and entered the house. Twenty minutes later I saw from my window a second car come across the plateau from the opposite direction. It did not come up to the inn, but stopped two hundred yards off in the shelter of a patch of wood. I noticed that its occupants carefully reversed it before leaving it. A minute or two later I heard their steps on the gravel outside the window.

My plan had been to lie hid in my bedroom, and see what happened. I had a notion that, if I could bring the police and my other more dangerous pursuers together, something might work out of it to my advantage. But now I had a better idea. I scribbled a line of thanks to my host, opened the window, and dropped quietly into a gooseberry bush. Unobserved I crossed the dyke, crawled down the side of a tributary burn, and won the highroad on the far side of the patch of trees. There stood the car, very spick and span in the morning sunlight, but with the dust on her which told of a long journey. I started her, jumped into the chauffeur's seat, and stole gently out on to the plateau.

Almost at once the road dipped so that I lost sight of the inn, but the wind seemed to bring me the sound of angry voices.

CHAPTER FOUR

The Adventure of the Radical Candidate

You may picture me driving that 40 h.p. car for all she was worth over the crisp moor roads on that shining May morning; glancing back at first over my shoulder, and looking anxiously to the next turning; then driving with a vague eye, just wide enough awake to keep on the highway. For I was thinking desperately of what I had found in Scudder's pocket-book.

The little man had told me a pack of lies. All his yarns about the Balkans and the Jew-Anarchists and the Foreign Office Conference were eyewash, and so was Karolides. And yet not quite, as you shall hear. I had staked everything on my belief in his story, and had been let down; here was his book telling me a different tale, and instead of being once-bitten-twice-shy, I believed it absolutely.

Why, I don't know. It rang desperately true, and the first yarn, if you understand me, had been in a queer way true also in spirit. The fifteenth day of June was going to be a day of destiny, a bigger destiny than the killing of a Dago. It was so big that I didn't blame Scudder for keeping me out of the game and wanting to play a lone hand. That, I was pretty clear, was his intention. He had told me something which sounded big enough, but the real thing was so immortally big that he, the man who had found it out, wanted it all for himself. I didn't blame him. It was risks after all that he was chiefly greedy about.

The whole story was in the notes—with gaps, you understand, which he would have filled up from his memory. He stuck down his authorities, too, and had an odd trick of giving them all a numerical value and then striking a balance, which stood for the reliability of each stage in the yarn. The four names he had printed were authorities, and there was a man, Ducrosne, who got five out of a possible five; and another fellow, Ammersfoort, who got three. The bare bones of the tale were all that was in the book—these, and one queer phrase which occurred half a dozen times inside brackets. '(Thirty-nine steps)' was the phrase; and at its last time of use it ran—'(Thirty-nine steps, I counted them—high tide 10.17 p.m.)'. I could make nothing of that.

The first thing I learned was that it was no question of preventing a war. That was coming, as sure as Christmas: had been arranged, said Scudder, ever since February 1912. Karolides was going to be the occasion. He was booked all right, and was to hand in his checks on June 14th, two weeks and four days from that May morning. I gathered from Scudder's notes that nothing on earth could prevent that. His talk of Epirote guards that would skin their own grandmothers was all billy-o.

The second thing was that this war was going to come as a mighty surprise to Britain. Karolides' death would set the Balkans by the ears, and then Vienna would chip in with an ultimatum. Russia wouldn't like that, and there would be high words. But Berlin would play the peacemaker, and pour oil on the waters, till suddenly she would find a good cause for a quarrel, pick it up, and in five hours let fly at us. That was the idea, and a pretty good one too. Honey and fair speeches, and then a stroke in the dark. While we were talking about the goodwill and good intentions of Germany our coast would be silently ringed with mines, and submarines would be waiting for every battleship.

But all this depended upon the third thing, which was due to happen on June 15th. I would never have grasped this if I hadn't once happened to meet a French staff officer, coming back from West Africa, who had told me a lot of things. One was that, in spite of all the nonsense talked in Parliament, there was a real working alliance between France and Britain, and that the two General Staffs met every now and then, and made plans for joint action in case of war. Well, in June a very great swell was coming over from Paris, and he was going to get nothing less than a statement of the disposition of the British Home Fleet on mobilization. At least I gathered it was something like that; anyhow, it was something uncommonly important.

But on the 15th day of June there were to be others in London—others, at whom I could only guess. Scudder was content to call them collectively the 'Black Stone'. They represented not our Allies, but our deadly foes; and the information, destined for France, was to be diverted to their pockets. And it was to be used, remember—used a week or two later, with great guns and swift torpedoes, suddenly in the darkness of a summer night.

This was the story I had been deciphering in a back room of a country inn, overlooking a cabbage garden. This was the story that hummed in my brain as I swung in the big touring-car from glen to glen.

My first impulse had been to write a letter to the Prime Minister, but a little reflection convinced me that that would be useless. Who would believe my tale? I must show a sign, some token in proof, and Heaven knew what that could be. Above all, I must keep going myself, ready to act when things got riper, and that was going to be no light job with the police of the British Isles in full cry after me and the watchers of the Black Stone running silently and swiftly on my trail.

I had no very clear purpose in my journey, but I steered east by the sun, for I remembered from the map that if I went north I would come into a region of coalpits and industrial towns. Presently I was down from the moorlands and traversing the broad haugh of a river. For miles I ran alongside a park wall, and in a break of the trees I saw a great castle. I swung through little old thatched villages, and over peaceful lowland streams, and past gardens blazing with hawthorn and yellow laburnum. The land was so deep in peace that I could scarcely believe that somewhere behind me were those who sought my life; ay, and that in a month's time, unless I had the almightiest of luck, these round country faces would be pinched and staring, and men would be lying dead in English fields.

About mid-day I entered a long straggling village, and had a mind to stop and eat. Half-way down was the Post Office, and on the steps of it stood the postmistress and a policeman hard at work conning a telegram. When they saw me they wakened up, and the policeman advanced with raised hand, and cried on me to stop.

I nearly was fool enough to obey. Then it flashed upon me that the wire had to do with me; that my friends at the inn had come to an understanding, and were united in desiring to see more of me, and that it had been easy enough for them to wire the description of me and the car to thirty villages through which I might pass. I released the brakes just in time. As it was, the policeman made a claw at the hood, and only dropped off when he got my left in his eye.

I saw that main roads were no place for me, and turned into the byways. It wasn't an easy job without a map, for there was the risk of getting on to a farm road and ending in a duck-pond or a stable-yard, and I couldn't afford that kind of delay. I began to see what an ass I had been to steal the car. The big green brute would be the safest kind of clue to me over the breadth of Scotland. If I left it and took to my feet, it would be discovered in an hour or two and I would get no start in the race.

The immediate thing to do was to get to the loneliest roads. These I soon found when I struck up a tributary of the big river, and got into a glen with steep hills all about me, and a corkscrew road at the end which climbed over a pass. Here I met nobody, but it was taking me too far north, so I slewed east along a bad track and finally struck a big double-line railway. Away below me I saw another broadish valley, and it occurred to me that if I crossed it I might find some remote inn to pass the night. The evening was now drawing in, and I was furiously hungry, for I had eaten nothing since breakfast except a couple of buns I had bought from a baker's cart. Just then I heard a noise in the sky, and lo and behold there was that infernal aeroplane, flying low, about a dozen miles to the south and rapidly coming towards me.

I had the sense to remember that on a bare moor I was at the aeroplane's mercy, and that my only chance was to get to the leafy cover of the valley. Down the hill I went like blue lightning, screwing my head round, whenever I dared, to watch that damned flying machine. Soon I was on a road between hedges, and dipping to the deep-cut glen of a stream. Then came a bit of thick wood where I slackened speed.

Suddenly on my left I heard the hoot of another car, and realized to my horror that I was almost up on a couple of gate-posts through which a private road debouched on the highway. My horn gave an agonized roar, but it was too late. I clapped on my brakes, but my impetus was too great, and there before me a car was sliding athwart my course. In a second there would have been the deuce of a wreck. I did the only thing possible, and ran slap into the hedge on the right, trusting to find something soft beyond.

But there I was mistaken. My car slithered through the hedge like butter, and then gave a sickening plunge forward. I saw what was coming, leapt on the seat and would have jumped out. But a branch of hawthorn got me in the chest, lifted me up and held me, while a ton or two of expensive metal slipped below me, bucked and pitched, and then dropped with an almighty smash fifty feet to the bed of the stream.

Slowly that thorn let me go. I subsided first on the hedge, and then very gently on a bower of nettles. As I scrambled to my feet a hand took me by the arm, and a sympathetic and badly scared voice asked me if I were hurt.

I found myself looking at a tall young man in goggles and a leather ulster, who kept on blessing his soul and whinnying apologies. For myself, once I got my wind back, I was rather glad than otherwise. This was one way of getting rid of the car.

'My blame, Sir,' I answered him. 'It's lucky that I did not add homicide to my follies. That's the end of my Scotch motor tour, but it might have been the end of my life.'

He plucked out a watch and studied it. 'You're the right sort of fellow,' he said. 'I can spare a quarter of an hour, and my house is two minutes off. I'll see you clothed and fed and snug in bed. Where's your kit, by the way? Is it in the burn along with the car?'

'It's in my pocket,' I said, brandishing a toothbrush. 'I'm a Colonial and travel light.'

'A Colonial,' he cried. 'By Gad, you're the very man I've been praying for. Are you by any blessed chance a Free Trader?'

'I am,' said I, without the foggiest notion of what he meant.

He patted my shoulder and hurried me into his car. Three minutes later we drew up before a comfortable-looking shooting box set among pine-trees, and he ushered me indoors. He took me first to a bedroom and flung half a dozen of his suits before me, for my own had been pretty well reduced to rags. I selected a loose blue serge, which differed most conspicuously from my former garments, and borrowed a linen collar. Then he haled me to the dining-room, where the remnants of a meal stood on the table, and announced that I had just five minutes to feed. 'You can take a snack in your pocket, and we'll have supper when we get back. I've got to be at the Masonic Hall at eight o'clock, or my agent will comb my hair.'

I had a cup of coffee and some cold ham, while he yarned away on the hearth-rug.

'You find me in the deuce of a mess, Mr—by-the-by, you haven't told me your name. Twisdon? Any relation of old Tommy Twisdon of the Sixtieth? No? Well, you see I'm Liberal Candidate for this part of the world, and I had a meeting on tonight at Brattleburn—that's my chief town, and an infernal Tory stronghold. I had got the Colonial ex-Premier fellow, Crumpleton, coming to speak for me tonight, and had the thing tremendously billed and the whole place ground-baited. This afternoon I had a wire from the ruffian saying he had got influenza at Blackpool, and here am I left to do the whole thing myself. I had meant to speak for ten minutes and must now go on for forty, and, though I've been racking my brains for three hours to think of something, I simply cannot last the course. Now you've got to be a good chap and help me. You're a Free Trader and can tell our people what a wash-out Protection is in the Colonies. All you fellows have the gift of the gab—I wish to Heaven I had it. I'll be for evermore in your debt.'

I had very few notions about Free Trade one way or the other, but I saw no other chance to get what I wanted. My young gentleman was far too absorbed in his own difficulties to think how odd it was to ask a stranger who had just missed death by an ace and had lost a 1,000-guinea car to address a meeting for him on the spur of the moment. But my necessities did not allow me to contemplate oddnesses or to pick and choose my supports.

'All right,' I said. 'I'm not much good as a speaker, but I'll tell them a bit about Australia.'

At my words the cares of the ages slipped from his shoulders, and he was rapturous in his thanks. He lent me a big driving coat—and never troubled to ask why I had started on a motor tour without possessing an ulster—and, as we slipped down the dusty roads, poured into my ears the simple facts of his history. He was an orphan, and his uncle had brought him up—I've forgotten the uncle's name, but he was in the Cabinet, and you can read his speeches in the papers. He had gone round the world after leaving Cambridge, and then, being short of a job, his uncle had advised politics. I gathered that he had no preference in parties. 'Good chaps in both,' he said cheerfully, 'and plenty of blighters, too. I'm Liberal, because my family have always been Whigs.' But if he was lukewarm politically he had strong views on other things. He found out I knew a bit about horses, and jawed away about the Derby entries; and he was full of plans for improving his shooting. Altogether, a very clean, decent, callow young man.

As we passed through a little town two policemen signalled us to stop, and flashed their lanterns on us.

'Beg pardon, Sir Harry,' said one. 'We've got instructions to look out for a car, and the description's no unlike yours.'

'Right-o,' said my host, while I thanked Providence for the devious ways I had been brought to safety. After that he spoke no more, for his mind began to labour heavily with his coming speech. His lips kept muttering, his eye wandered, and I began to prepare myself for a second catastrophe. I tried to think of something to say myself, but my mind was dry as a stone. The next thing I knew we had drawn up outside a door in a street, and were being welcomed by some noisy gentlemen with rosettes. The hall had about five hundred in it, women mostly, a lot of bald heads, and a dozen or two young men. The chairman, a weaselly minister with a reddish nose, lamented Crumpleton's absence, soliloquized on his influenza, and gave me a certificate as a 'trusted leader of Australian thought'. There were two policemen at the door, and I hoped they took note of that testimonial. Then Sir Harry started.

I never heard anything like it. He didn't begin to know how to talk. He had about a bushel of notes from which he read, and when he let go of them he fell into one prolonged stutter. Every now and then he remembered a phrase he had learned by heart, straightened his back, and gave it off like Henry Irving, and the next moment he was bent double and crooning over his papers. It was the most appalling rot, too. He talked about the 'German menace', and said it was all a Tory invention to cheat the poor of their rights and keep back the great flood of social reform, but that 'organized labour' realized this and laughed the Tories to scorn. He was all for reducing our Navy as a proof of our good faith, and then sending Germany an ultimatum telling her to do the same or we would knock her into a cocked hat. He said that, but for the Tories, Germany and Britain would be fellow-workers in peace and reform. I thought of the little black book in my pocket! A giddy lot Scudder's friends cared for peace and reform.

Yet in a queer way I liked the speech. You could see the niceness of the chap shining out behind the muck with which he had been spoon-fed. Also it took a load off my mind. I mightn't be much of an orator, but I was a thousand per cent better than Sir Harry.

I didn't get on so badly when it came to my turn. I simply told them all I could remember about Australia, praying there should be no Australian there—all about its labour party and emigration and universal service. I doubt if I remembered to mention Free Trade, but I said there were no Tories in Australia, only Labour and Liberals. That fetched a cheer, and I woke them up a bit when I started in to tell them the kind of glorious business I thought could be made out of the Empire if we really put our backs into it.

Altogether I fancy I was rather a success. The minister didn't like me, though, and when he proposed a vote of thanks, spoke of Sir Harry's speech as 'statesmanlike' and mine as having 'the eloquence of an emigration agent'.

When we were in the car again my host was in wild spirits at having got his job over. 'A ripping speech, Twisdon,' he said. 'Now, you're coming home with me. I'm all alone, and if you'll stop a day or two I'll show you some very decent fishing.'

We had a hot supper—and I wanted it pretty badly—and then drank grog in a big cheery smoking-room with a crackling wood fire. I thought the time had come for me to put my cards on the table. I saw by this man's eye that he was the kind you can trust.

'Listen, Sir Harry,' I said. 'I've something pretty important to say to you. You're a good fellow, and I'm going to be frank. Where on earth did you get that poisonous rubbish you talked tonight?'

His face fell. 'Was it as bad as that?' he asked ruefully. 'It did sound rather thin. I got most of it out of the PROGRESSIVE MAGAZINE and pamphlets that agent chap of mine keeps sending me. But you surely don't think Germany would ever go to war with us?'

'Ask that question in six weeks and it won't need an answer,' I said. 'If you'll give me your attention for half an hour I am going to tell you a story.'

I can see yet that bright room with the deers' heads and the old prints on the walls, Sir Harry standing restlessly on the stone curb of the hearth, and myself lying back in an armchair, speaking. I seemed to be another person, standing aside and listening to my own voice, and judging carefully the reliability of my tale. It was the first time I had ever told anyone the exact truth, so far as I understood it, and it did me no end of good, for it straightened out the thing in my own mind. I blinked no detail. He heard all about Scudder, and the milkman, and the note-book, and my doings in Galloway. Presently he got very excited and walked up and down the hearth-rug.

'So you see,' I concluded, 'you have got here in your house the man that is wanted for the Portland Place murder. Your duty is to send your car for the police and give me up. I don't think I'll get very far. There'll be an accident, and I'll have a knife in my ribs an hour or so after arrest. Nevertheless, it's your duty, as a law-abiding citizen. Perhaps in a month's time you'll be sorry, but you have no cause to think of that.'

He was looking at me with bright steady eyes. 'What was your job in Rhodesia, Mr Hannay?' he asked.

'Mining engineer,' I said. 'I've made my pile cleanly and I've had a good time in the making of it.'

'Not a profession that weakens the nerves, is it?'

I laughed. 'Oh, as to that, my nerves are good enough.' I took down a hunting-knife from a stand on the wall, and did the old Mashona trick of tossing it and catching it in my lips. That wants a pretty steady heart.

He watched me with a smile. 'I don't want proof. I may be an ass on the platform, but I can size up a man. You're no murderer and you're no fool, and I believe you are speaking the truth. I'm going to back you up. Now, what can I do?'

'First, I want you to write a letter to your uncle. I've got to get in touch with the Government people sometime before the 15th of June.'

He pulled his moustache. 'That won't help you. This is Foreign Office business, and my uncle would have nothing to do with it. Besides, you'd never convince him. No, I'll go one better. I'll write to the Permanent Secretary at the Foreign Office. He's my godfather, and one of the best going. What do you want?'

He sat down at a table and wrote to my dictation. The gist of it was that if a man called Twisdon (I thought I had better stick to that name) turned up before June 15th he was to entreat him kindly. He said Twisdon would prove his bona fides by passing the word 'Black Stone' and whistling 'Annie Laurie'.

'Good,' said Sir Harry. 'That's the proper style. By the way, you'll find my godfather—his name's Sir Walter Bullivant—down at his country cottage for Whitsuntide. It's close to Artinswell on the Kenner. That's done. Now, what's the next thing?'

'You're about my height. Lend me the oldest tweed suit you've got. Anything will do, so long as the colour is the opposite of the clothes I destroyed this afternoon. Then show me a map of the neighbourhood and explain to me the lie of the land. Lastly, if the police come seeking me, just show them the car in the glen. If the other lot turn up, tell them I caught the south express after your meeting.'

He did, or promised to do, all these things. I shaved off the remnants of my moustache, and got inside an ancient suit of what I believe is called heather mixture. The map gave me some notion of my whereabouts, and told me the two things I wanted to know—where the main railway to the south could be joined and what were the wildest districts near at hand. At two o'clock he wakened me from my slumbers in the smoking-room armchair, and led me blinking into the dark starry night. An old bicycle was found in a tool-shed and handed over to me.

'First turn to the right up by the long fir-wood,' he enjoined. 'By daybreak you'll be well into the hills. Then I should pitch the machine into a bog and take to the moors on foot. You can put in a week among the shepherds, and be as safe as if you were in New Guinea.'

I pedalled diligently up steep roads of hill gravel till the skies grew pale with morning. As the mists cleared before the sun, I found myself in a wide green world with glens falling on every side and a far-away blue horizon. Here, at any rate, I could get early news of my enemies.

CHAPTER FIVE

The Adventure of the Spectacled Roadman

I sat down on the very crest of the pass and took stock of my position.

Behind me was the road climbing through a long cleft in the hills, which was the upper glen of some notable river. In front was a flat space of maybe a mile, all pitted with bog-holes and rough with tussocks, and then beyond it the road fell steeply down another glen to a plain whose blue dimness melted into the distance. To left and right were round-shouldered green hills as smooth as pancakes, but to the south—that is, the left hand—there was a glimpse of high heathery mountains, which I remembered from the map as the big knot of hill which I had chosen for my sanctuary. I was on the central boss of a huge upland country, and could see everything moving for miles. In the meadows below the road half a mile back a cottage smoked, but it was the only sign of human life. Otherwise there was only the calling of plovers and the tinkling of little streams.

It was now about seven o'clock, and as I waited I heard once again that ominous beat in the air. Then I realized that my vantage-ground might be in reality a trap. There was no cover for a tomtit in those bald green places.

I sat quite still and hopeless while the beat grew louder. Then I saw an aeroplane coming up from the east. It was flying high, but as I looked it dropped several hundred feet and began to circle round the knot of hill in narrowing circles, just as a hawk wheels before it pounces. Now it was flying very low, and now the observer on board caught sight of me. I could see one of the two occupants examining me through glasses.

Suddenly it began to rise in swift whorls, and the next I knew it was speeding eastward again till it became a speck in the blue morning.

That made me do some savage thinking. My enemies had located me, and the next thing would be a cordon round me. I didn't know what force they could command, but I was certain it would be sufficient. The aeroplane had seen my bicycle, and would conclude that I would try to escape by the road. In that case there might be a chance on the moors to the right or left. I wheeled the machine a hundred yards from the highway, and plunged it into a moss-hole, where it sank among pond-weed and water-buttercups. Then I climbed to a knoll which gave me a view of the two valleys. Nothing was stirring on the long white ribbon that threaded them.

I have said there was not cover in the whole place to hide a rat. As the day advanced it was flooded with soft fresh light till it had the fragrant sunniness of the South African veld. At other times I would have liked the place, but now it seemed to suffocate me. The free moorlands were prison walls, and the keen hill air was the breath of a dungeon.

I tossed a coin—heads right, tails left—and it fell heads, so I turned to the north. In a little I came to the brow of the ridge which was the containing wall of the pass. I saw the highroad for maybe ten miles, and far down it something that was moving, and that I took to be a motor-car. Beyond the ridge I looked on a rolling green moor, which fell away into wooded glens.

Now my life on the veld has given me the eyes of a kite, and I can see things for which most men need a telescope ... Away down the slope, a couple of miles away, several men were advancing, like a row of beaters at a shoot ...

I dropped out of sight behind the sky-line. That way was shut to me, and I must try the bigger hills to the south beyond the highway. The car I had noticed was getting nearer, but it was still a long way off with some very steep gradients before it. I ran hard, crouching low except in the hollows, and as I ran I kept scanning the brow of the hill before me. Was it imagination, or did I see figures—one, two, perhaps more—moving in a glen beyond the stream?

If you are hemmed in on all sides in a patch of land there is only one chance of escape. You must stay in the patch, and let your enemies search it and not find you.

That was good sense, but how on earth was I to escape notice in that table-cloth of a place? I would have buried myself to the neck in mud or lain below water or climbed the tallest tree. But there was not a stick of wood, the bog-holes were little puddles, the stream was a slender trickle. There was nothing but short heather, and bare hill bent, and the white highway.

Then in a tiny bight of road, beside a heap of stones, I found the roadman.

He had just arrived, and was wearily flinging down his hammer. He looked at me with a fishy eye and yawned.

'Confoond the day I ever left the herdin'!' he said, as if to the world at large. 'There I was my ain maister. Now I'm a slave to the Goavernment, tethered to the roadside, wi' sair een, and a back like a suckle.'

He took up the hammer, struck a stone, dropped the implement with an oath, and put both hands to his ears. 'Mercy on me! My heid's burstin'!' he cried.

He was a wild figure, about my own size but much bent, with a week's beard on his chin, and a pair of big horn spectacles.

'I canna dae't,' he cried again. 'The Surveyor maun just report me. I'm for my bed.'

I asked him what was the trouble, though indeed that was clear enough.

'The trouble is that I'm no sober. Last nicht my dochter Merran was waddit, and they danced till fower in the byre. Me and some ither chiels sat down to the drinkin', and here I am. Peety that I ever lookit on the wine when it was red!'

I agreed with him about bed. 'It's easy speakin',' he moaned. 'But I got a postcard yestreen sayin' that the new Road Surveyor would be round the day. He'll come and he'll no find me, or else he'll find me fou, and either way I'm a done man. I'll awa' back to my bed and say I'm no weel, but I doot that'll no help me, for they ken my kind o' no-weel-ness.'

Then I had an inspiration. 'Does the new Surveyor know you?' I asked.

'No him. He's just been a week at the job. He rins about in a wee motor-cawr, and wad speir the inside oot o' a whelk.'

'Where's your house?' I asked, and was directed by a wavering finger to the cottage by the stream.

'Well, back to your bed,' I said, 'and sleep in peace. I'll take on your job for a bit and see the Surveyor.'

He stared at me blankly; then, as the notion dawned on his fuddled brain, his face broke into the vacant drunkard's smile.

'You're the billy,' he cried. 'It'll be easy eneuch managed. I've finished that bing o' stanes, so you needna chap ony mair this forenoon. Just take the barry, and wheel eneuch metal frae yon quarry doon the road to mak anither bing the morn. My name's Alexander Turnbull, and I've been seeven year at the trade, and twenty afore that herdin' on Leithen Water. My freens ca' me Ecky, and whiles Specky, for I wear glesses, being waik i' the sicht. Just you speak the Surveyor fair, and ca' him Sir, and he'll be fell pleased. I'll be back or mid-day.'

I borrowed his spectacles and filthy old hat; stripped off coat, waistcoat, and collar, and gave him them to carry home; borrowed, too, the foul stump of a clay pipe as an extra property. He indicated my simple tasks, and without more ado set off at an amble bedwards. Bed may have been his chief object, but I think there was also something left in the foot of a bottle. I prayed that he might be safe under cover before my friends arrived on the scene.

Then I set to work to dress for the part. I opened the collar of my shirt—it was a vulgar blue-and-white check such as ploughmen wear—and revealed a neck as brown as any tinker's. I rolled up my sleeves, and there was a forearm which might have been a blacksmith's, sunburnt and rough with old scars. I got my boots and trouser-legs all white from the dust of the road, and hitched up my trousers, tying them with string below the knee. Then I set to work on my face. With a handful of dust I made a water-mark round my neck, the place where Mr Turnbull's Sunday ablutions might be expected to stop. I rubbed a good deal of dirt also into the sunburn of my cheeks. A roadman's eyes would no doubt be a little inflamed, so I contrived to get some dust in both of mine, and by dint of vigorous rubbing produced a bleary effect.

The sandwiches Sir Harry had given me had gone off with my coat, but the roadman's lunch, tied up in a red handkerchief, was at my disposal. I ate with great relish several of the thick slabs of scone and cheese and drank a little of the cold tea. In the handkerchief was a local paper tied with string and addressed to Mr Turnbull—obviously meant to solace his mid-day leisure. I did up the bundle again, and put the paper conspicuously beside it.

My boots did not satisfy me, but by dint of kicking among the stones I reduced them to the granite-like surface which marks a roadman's foot-gear. Then I bit and scraped my finger-nails till the edges were all cracked and uneven. The men I was matched against would miss no detail. I broke one of the bootlaces and retied it in a clumsy knot, and loosed the other so that my thick grey socks bulged over the uppers. Still no sign of anything on the road. The motor I had observed half an hour ago must have gone home.

My toilet complete, I took up the barrow and began my journeys to and from the quarry a hundred yards off.

I remember an old scout in Rhodesia, who had done many queer things in his day, once telling me that the secret of playing a part was to think yourself into it. You could never keep it up, he said, unless you could manage to convince yourself that you were it. So I shut off all other thoughts and switched them on to the road-mending. I thought of the little white cottage as my home, I recalled the years I had spent herding on Leithen Water, I made my mind dwell lovingly on sleep in a box-bed and a bottle of cheap whisky. Still nothing appeared on that long white road.

Now and then a sheep wandered off the heather to stare at me. A heron flopped down to a pool in the stream and started to fish, taking no more notice of me than if I had been a milestone. On I went, trundling my loads of stone, with the heavy step of the professional. Soon I grew warm, and the dust on my face changed into solid and abiding grit. I was already counting the hours till evening should put a limit to Mr Turnbull's monotonous toil. Suddenly a crisp voice spoke from the road, and looking up I saw a little Ford two-seater, and a round-faced young man in a bowler hat.

'Are you Alexander Turnbull?' he asked. 'I am the new County Road Surveyor. You live at Blackhopefoot, and have charge of the section from Laidlawbyres to the Riggs? Good! A fair bit of road, Turnbull, and not badly engineered. A little soft about a mile off, and the edges want cleaning. See you look after that. Good morning. You'll know me the next time you see me.'

Clearly my get-up was good enough for the dreaded Surveyor. I went on with my work, and as the morning grew towards noon I was cheered by a little traffic. A baker's van breasted the hill, and sold me a bag of ginger biscuits which I stowed in my trouser-pockets against emergencies. Then a herd passed with sheep, and disturbed me somewhat by asking loudly, 'What had become o' Specky?'

'In bed wi' the colic,' I replied, and the herd passed on ... just about mid-day a big car stole down the hill, glided past and drew up a hundred yards beyond. Its three occupants descended as if to stretch their legs, and sauntered towards me.

Two of the men I had seen before from the window of the Galloway inn—one lean, sharp, and dark, the other comfortable and smiling. The third had the look of a countryman—a vet, perhaps, or a small farmer. He was dressed in ill-cut knickerbockers, and the eye in his head was as bright and wary as a hen's.

'Morning,' said the last. 'That's a fine easy job o' yours.'

I had not looked up on their approach, and now, when accosted, I slowly and painfully straightened my back, after the manner of roadmen; spat vigorously, after the manner of the low Scot; and regarded them steadily before replying. I confronted three pairs of eyes that missed nothing.

'There's waur jobs and there's better,' I said sententiously. 'I wad rather hae yours, sittin' a' day on your hinderlands on thae cushions. It's you and your muckle cawrs that wreck my roads! If we a' had oor richts, ye sud be made to mend what ye break.'

The bright-eyed man was looking at the newspaper lying beside Turnbull's bundle.

'I see you get your papers in good time,' he said.

I glanced at it casually. 'Aye, in gude time. Seein' that that paper cam' out last Setterday I'm just Sax days late.'

He picked it up, glanced at the superscription, and laid it down again. One of the others had been looking at my boots, and a word in German called the speaker's attention to them.

'You've a fine taste in boots,' he said. 'These were never made by a country shoemaker.'

'They were not,' I said readily. 'They were made in London. I got them frae the gentleman that was here last year for the shootin'. What was his name now?' And I scratched a forgetful head. Again the sleek one spoke in German. 'Let us get on,' he said. 'This fellow is all right.'

They asked one last question.

'Did you see anyone pass early this morning? He might be on a bicycle or he might be on foot.'

I very nearly fell into the trap and told a story of a bicyclist hurrying past in the grey dawn. But I had the sense to see my danger. I pretended to consider very deeply.

'I wasna up very early,' I said. 'Ye see, my dochter was merrit last nicht, and we keepit it up late. I opened the house door about seeven and there was naebody on the road then. Since I cam' up here there has just been the baker and the Ruchill herd, besides you gentlemen.'

One of them gave me a cigar, which I smelt gingerly and stuck in Turnbull's bundle. They got into their car and were out of sight in three minutes.

My heart leaped with an enormous relief, but I went on wheeling my stones. It was as well, for ten minutes later the car returned, one of the occupants waving a hand to me. Those gentry left nothing to chance.

I finished Turnbull's bread and cheese, and pretty soon I had finished the stones. The next step was what puzzled me. I could not keep up this roadmaking business for long. A merciful Providence had kept Mr Turnbull indoors, but if he appeared on the scene there would be trouble. I had a notion that the cordon was still tight round the glen, and that if I walked in any direction I should meet with questioners. But get out I must. No man's nerve could stand more than a day of being spied on.

I stayed at my post till five o'clock. By that time I had resolved to go down to Turnbull's cottage at nightfall and take my chance of getting over the hills in the darkness. But suddenly a new car came up the road, and slowed down a yard or two from me. A fresh wind had risen, and the occupant wanted to light a cigarette. It was a touring car, with the tonneau full of an assortment of baggage. One man sat in it, and by an amazing chance I knew him. His name was Marmaduke Jopley, and he was an offence to creation. He was a sort of blood stockbroker, who did his business by toadying eldest sons and rich young peers and foolish old ladies. 'Marmie' was a familiar figure, I understood, at balls and polo-weeks and country houses. He was an adroit scandal-monger, and would crawl a mile on his belly to anything that had a title or a million. I had a business introduction to his firm when I came to London, and he was good enough to ask me to dinner at his club. There he showed off at a great rate, and pattered about his duchesses till the snobbery of the creature turned me sick. I asked a man afterwards why nobody kicked him, and was told that Englishmen reverenced the weaker sex.

Anyhow there he was now, nattily dressed, in a fine new car, obviously on his way to visit some of his smart friends. A sudden daftness took me, and in a second I had jumped into the tonneau and had him by the shoulder.

'Hullo, Jopley,' I sang out. 'Well met, my lad!' He got a horrid fright. His chin dropped as he stared at me. 'Who the devil are YOU?' he gasped.

'My name's Hannay,' I said. 'From Rhodesia, you remember.'

'Good God, the murderer!' he choked.

'Just so. And there'll be a second murder, my dear, if you don't do as I tell you. Give me that coat of yours. That cap, too.'

He did as bid, for he was blind with terror. Over my dirty trousers and vulgar shirt I put on his smart driving-coat, which buttoned high at the top and thereby hid the deficiencies of my collar. I stuck the cap on my head, and added his gloves to my get-up. The dusty roadman in a minute was transformed into one of the neatest motorists in Scotland. On Mr Jopley's head I clapped Turnbull's unspeakable hat, and told him to keep it there.

Then with some difficulty I turned the car. My plan was to go back the road he had come, for the watchers, having seen it before, would probably let it pass unremarked, and Marmie's figure was in no way like mine.

'Now, my child,' I said, 'sit quite still and be a good boy. I mean you no harm. I'm only borrowing your car for an hour or two. But if you play me any tricks, and above all if you open your mouth, as sure as there's a God above me I'll wring your neck. SAVEZ?'

I enjoyed that evening's ride. We ran eight miles down the valley, through a village or two, and I could not help noticing several strange-looking folk lounging by the roadside. These were the watchers who would have had much to say to me if I had come in other garb or company. As it was, they looked incuriously on. One touched his cap in salute, and I responded graciously.

As the dark fell I turned up a side glen which, as I remember from the map, led into an unfrequented corner of the hills. Soon the villages were left behind, then the farms, and then even the wayside cottage. Presently we came to a lonely moor where the night was blackening the sunset gleam in the bog pools. Here we stopped, and I obligingly reversed the car and restored to Mr Jopley his belongings.

'A thousand thanks,' I said. 'There's more use in you than I thought. Now be off and find the police.'

As I sat on the hillside, watching the tail-light dwindle, I reflected on the various kinds of crime I had now sampled. Contrary to general belief, I was not a murderer, but I had become an unholy liar, a shameless impostor, and a highwayman with a marked taste for expensive motor-cars.

CHAPTER SIX

The Adventure of the Bald Archaeologist

I spent the night on a shelf of the hillside, in the lee of a boulder where the heather grew long and soft. It was a cold business, for I had neither coat nor waistcoat. These were in Mr Turnbull's keeping, as was Scudder's little book, my watch and—worst of all—my pipe and tobacco pouch. Only my money accompanied me in my belt, and about half a pound of ginger biscuits in my trousers pocket.

I supped off half those biscuits, and by worming myself deep into the heather got some kind of warmth. My spirits had risen, and I was beginning to enjoy this crazy game of hide-and-seek. So far I had been miraculously lucky. The milkman, the literary innkeeper, Sir Harry, the roadman, and the idiotic Marmie, were all pieces of undeserved good fortune. Somehow the first success gave me a feeling that I was going to pull the thing through.

My chief trouble was that I was desperately hungry. When a Jew shoots himself in the City and there is an inquest, the newspapers usually report that the deceased was 'well-nourished'. I remember thinking that they would not call me well-nourished if I broke my neck in a bog-hole. I lay and tortured myself—for the ginger biscuits merely emphasized the aching void—with the memory of all the good food I had thought so little of in

London. There were Paddock's crisp sausages and fragrant shavings of bacon, and shapely poached eggs—how often I had turned up my nose at them! There were the cutlets they did at the club, and a particular ham that stood on the cold table, for which my soul lusted. My thoughts hovered over all varieties of mortal edible, and finally settled on a porterhouse steak and a quart of bitter with a welsh rabbit to follow. In longing hopelessly for these dainties I fell asleep.

I woke very cold and stiff about an hour after dawn. It took me a little while to remember where I was, for I had been very weary and had slept heavily. I saw first the pale blue sky through a net of heather, then a big shoulder of hill, and then my own boots placed neatly in a blaeberry bush. I raised myself on my arms and looked down into the valley, and that one look set me lacing up my boots in mad haste.

For there were men below, not more than a quarter of a mile off, spaced out on the hillside like a fan, and beating the heather. Marmie had not been slow in looking for his revenge.

I crawled out of my shelf into the cover of a boulder, and from it gained a shallow trench which slanted up the mountain face. This led me presently into the narrow gully of a burn, by way of which I scrambled to the top of the ridge. From there I looked back, and saw that I was still undiscovered. My pursuers were patiently quartering the hillside and moving upwards.

Keeping behind the skyline I ran for maybe half a mile, till I judged I was above the uppermost end of the glen. Then I showed myself, and was instantly noted by one of the flankers, who passed the word to the others. I heard cries coming up from below, and saw that the line of search had changed its direction. I pretended to retreat over the skyline, but instead went back the way I had come, and in twenty minutes was behind the ridge overlooking my sleeping place. From that viewpoint I had the satisfaction of seeing the pursuit streaming up the hill at the top of the glen on a hopelessly false scent.

I had before me a choice of routes, and I chose a ridge which made an angle with the one I was on, and so would soon put a deep glen between me and my enemies. The exercise had warmed my blood, and I was beginning to enjoy myself amazingly. As I went I breakfasted on the dusty remnants of the ginger biscuits.

I knew very little about the country, and I hadn't a notion what I was going to do. I trusted to the strength of my legs, but I was well aware that those behind me would be familiar with the lie of the land, and that my ignorance would be a heavy handicap. I saw in front of me a sea of hills, rising very high towards the south, but northwards breaking down into broad ridges which separated wide and shallow dales. The ridge I had chosen seemed to sink after a mile or two to a moor which lay like a pocket in the uplands. That seemed as good a direction to take as any other.

My stratagem had given me a fair start—call it twenty minutes—and I had the width of a glen behind me before I saw the first heads of the pursuers. The police had evidently called in local talent to their aid, and the men I could see had the appearance of herds or gamekeepers. They hallooed at the sight of me, and I waved my hand. Two dived into the glen and began to climb my ridge, while the others kept their own side of the hill. I felt as if I were taking part in a schoolboy game of hare and hounds.

But very soon it began to seem less of a game. Those fellows behind were hefty men on their native heath. Looking back I saw that only three were following direct, and I guessed that the others had fetched a circuit to cut me off. My lack of local knowledge might very well be my undoing, and I resolved to get out of this tangle of glens to the pocket of moor I had seen from the tops. I must so increase my distance as to get clear away from them, and I believed I could do this if I could find the right ground for it. If there had been cover I would have tried a bit of stalking, but on these bare slopes you could see a fly a mile off. My hope must be in the length of my legs and the soundness of my wind, but I needed easier ground for that, for I was not bred a mountaineer. How I longed for a good Afrikander pony!

I put on a great spurt and got off my ridge and down into the moor before any figures appeared on the skyline behind me. I crossed a burn, and came out on a highroad which made a pass between two glens. All in front of me was a big field of heather sloping up to a crest which was crowned with an odd feather of trees. In the dyke by the roadside was a gate, from which a grass-grown track led over the first wave of the moor.

I jumped the dyke and followed it, and after a few hundred yards—as soon as it was out of sight of the highway—the grass stopped and it became a very respectable road, which was evidently kept with some care. Clearly it ran to a house, and I began to think of doing the same. Hitherto my luck had held, and it might be that my best chance would be found in this remote dwelling. Anyhow there were trees there, and that meant cover.

I did not follow the road, but the burnside which flanked it on the right, where the bracken grew deep and the high banks made a tolerable screen. It was well I did so, for no sooner had I gained the hollow than, looking back, I saw the pursuit topping the ridge from which I had descended.

After that I did not look back; I had no time. I ran up the burnside, crawling over the open places, and for a large part wading in the shallow stream. I found a deserted cottage with a row of phantom peat-stacks and an overgrown garden. Then I was among young hay, and very soon had come to the edge of a plantation of wind-blown firs. From there I saw the chimneys of the house smoking a few hundred yards to my left. I forsook the burnside, crossed another dyke, and almost before I knew was on a rough lawn. A glance back told me that I was well out of sight of the pursuit, which had not yet passed the first lift of the moor.

The lawn was a very rough place, cut with a scythe instead of a mower, and planted with beds of scrubby rhododendrons. A brace of black-game, which are not usually garden birds, rose at my approach. The house before me was the ordinary moorland farm, with a more pretentious whitewashed wing added. Attached to this wing was a glass veranda, and through the glass I saw the face of an elderly gentleman meekly watching me.

I stalked over the border of coarse hill gravel and entered the open veranda door. Within was a pleasant room, glass on one side, and on the other a mass of books. More books showed in an inner room. On the floor, instead of tables, stood cases such as you see in a museum, filled with coins and queer stone implements.

There was a knee-hole desk in the middle, and seated at it, with some papers and open volumes before him, was the benevolent old gentleman. His face was round and shiny, like Mr Pickwick's, big glasses were stuck on the end of his nose, and the top of his head was as bright and bare as a glass bottle. He never moved when I entered, but raised his placid eyebrows and waited on me to speak.

It was not an easy job, with about five minutes to spare, to tell a stranger who I was and what I wanted, and to win his aid. I did not attempt it. There was something about the eye of the man before me, something so keen and knowledgeable, that I could not find a word. I simply stared at him and stuttered.

'You seem in a hurry, my friend,'he said slowly.

I nodded towards the window. It gave a prospect across the moor through a gap in the plantation, and revealed certain figures half a mile off straggling through the heather.

'Ah, I see,' he said, and took up a pair of field-glasses through which he patiently scrutinized the figures.

'A fugitive from justice, eh? Well, we'll go into the matter at our leisure. Meantime I object to my privacy being broken in upon by the clumsy rural policeman. Go into my study, and you will see two doors facing you. Take the one on the left and close it behind you. You will be perfectly safe.'

And this extraordinary man took up his pen again.

I did as I was bid, and found myself in a little dark chamber which smelt of chemicals, and was lit only by a tiny window high up in the wall. The door had swung behind me with a click like the door of a safe. Once again I had found an unexpected sanctuary.

All the same I was not comfortable. There was something about the old gentleman which puzzled and rather terrified me. He had been too easy and ready, almost as if he had expected me. And his eyes had been horribly intelligent.

No sound came to me in that dark place. For all I knew the police might be searching the house, and if they did they would want to know what was behind this door. I tried to possess my soul in patience, and to forget how hungry I was.

Then I took a more cheerful view. The old gentleman could scarcely refuse me a meal, and I fell to reconstructing my breakfast. Bacon and eggs would content me, but I wanted the better part of a flitch of bacon and half a hundred eggs. And then, while my mouth was watering in anticipation, there was a click and the door stood open.

I emerged into the sunlight to find the master of the house sitting in a deep armchair in the room he called his study, and regarding me with curious eyes.

'Have they gone?' I asked.

'They have gone. I convinced them that you had crossed the hill. I do not choose that the police should come between me and one whom I am delighted to honour. This is a lucky morning for you, Mr Richard Hannay.'

As he spoke his eyelids seemed to tremble and to fall a little over his keen grey eyes. In a flash the phrase of Scudder's came back to me, when he had described the man he most dreaded in the world. He had said that he 'could hood his eyes like a hawk'. Then I saw that I had walked straight into the enemy's headquarters.

My first impulse was to throttle the old ruffian and make for the open air. He seemed to anticipate my intention, for he smiled gently, and nodded to the door behind me.

I turned, and saw two men-servants who had me covered with pistols.

He knew my name, but he had never seen me before. And as the reflection darted across my mind I saw a slender chance.

'I don't know what you mean,' I said roughly. 'And who are you calling Richard Hannay? My name's Ainslie.'

'So?' he said, still smiling. 'But of course you have others. We won't quarrel about a name.'

I was pulling myself together now, and I reflected that my garb, lacking coat and waistcoat and collar, would at any rate not betray me. I put on my surliest face and shrugged my shoulders.

'I suppose you're going to give me up after all, and I call it a damned dirty trick. My God, I wish I had never seen that cursed motor-car! Here's the money and be damned to you,' and I flung four sovereigns on the table.

He opened his eyes a little. 'Oh no, I shall not give you up. My friends and I will have a little private settlement with you, that is all. You know a little too much, Mr Hannay. You are a clever actor, but not quite clever enough.'

He spoke with assurance, but I could see the dawning of a doubt in his mind.

'Oh, for God's sake stop jawing,' I cried. 'Everything's against me. I haven't had a bit of luck since I came on shore at Leith. What's the harm in a poor devil with an empty stomach picking up some money he finds in a bust-up motor-car? That's all I done, and for that I've been chivvied for two days by those blasted bobbies over those blasted hills. I tell you I'm fair sick of it. You can do what you like, old boy! Ned Ainslie's got no fight left in him.'

I could see that the doubt was gaining.

'Will you oblige me with the story of your recent doings?'he asked. 'I can't, guv'nor,' I said in a real beggar's whine. 'I've not had a bite to eat for two days. Give me a mouthful of food, and then you'll hear God's truth.'

I must have showed my hunger in my face, for he signalled to one of the men in the doorway. A bit of cold pie was brought and a glass of beer, and I wolfed them down like a pig—or rather, like Ned Ainslie, for I was keeping up my character. In the middle of my meal he spoke suddenly to me in German, but I turned on him a face as blank as a stone wall.

Then I told him my story—how I had come off an Archangel ship at Leith a week ago, and was making my way overland to my brother at Wigtown. I had run short of cash—I hinted vaguely at a spree—and I was pretty well on my uppers when I had come on a hole in a hedge, and, looking through, had seen a big motor-car lying in the burn. I had poked about to see what had happened, and had found three sovereigns lying on the seat and one on the floor. There was nobody there or any sign of an owner, so I had pocketed the cash. But somehow the law had got after me. When I had tried to change a sovereign in a baker's shop, the woman had cried on the police, and a little later, when I was washing my face in a burn, I had been nearly gripped, and had only got away by leaving my coat and waistcoat behind me.

'They can have the money back,' I cried, 'for a fat lot of good it's done me. Those perishers are all down on a poor man. Now, if it had been you, guv'nor, that had found the quids, nobody would have troubled you.'

'You're a good liar, Hannay,' he said.

I flew into a rage. 'Stop fooling, damn you! I tell you my name's Ainslie, and I never heard of anyone called Hannay in my born days. I'd sooner have the police than you with your Hannays and your monkey-faced pistol tricks ... No, guv'nor, I beg pardon, I don't mean that. I'm much obliged to you for the grub, and I'll thank you to let me go now the coast's clear.'

It was obvious that he was badly puzzled. You see he had never seen me, and my appearance must have altered considerably from my photographs, if he had got one of them. I was pretty smart and well dressed in London, and now I was a regular tramp.

'I do not propose to let you go. If you are what you say you are, you will soon have a chance of clearing yourself. If you are what I believe you are, I do not think you will see the light much longer.'

He rang a bell, and a third servant appeared from the veranda.

'I want the Lanchester in five minutes,' he said. 'There will be three to luncheon.'

Then he looked steadily at me, and that was the hardest ordeal of all.

There was something weird and devilish in those eyes, cold, malignant, unearthly, and most hellishly clever. They fascinated me like the bright eyes of a snake.

I had a strong impulse to throw myself on his mercy and offer to join his side, and if you consider the way I felt about the whole thing you will see that that impulse must have been purely physical, the weakness of a brain mesmerized and mastered by a stronger spirit. But I managed to stick it out and even to grin.

'You'll know me next time, guv'nor,' I said.

'Karl,' he spoke in German to one of the men in the doorway, 'you will put this fellow in the storeroom till I return, and you will be answerable to me for his keeping.'

I was marched out of the room with a pistol at each ear.

The storeroom was a damp chamber in what had been the old farmhouse. There was no carpet on the uneven floor, and nothing to sit down on but a school form. It was black as pitch, for the windows were heavily shuttered. I made out by groping that the walls were lined with boxes and barrels and sacks of some heavy stuff. The whole place smelt of mould and disuse. My gaolers turned the key in the door, and I could hear them shifting their feet as they stood on guard outside.

I sat down in that chilly darkness in a very miserable frame of mind. The old boy had gone off in a motor to collect the two ruffians who had interviewed me yesterday. Now, they had seen me as the roadman, and they would remember me, for I was in the same rig. What was a roadman doing twenty miles from his beat, pursued by the police? A question or two would put them on the track. Probably they had seen Mr Turnbull, probably Marmie too; most likely they could link me up with Sir Harry, and then the whole thing would be crystal clear. What chance had I in this moorland house with three desperadoes and their armed servants?

I began to think wistfully of the police, now plodding over the hills after my wraith. They at any rate were fellow-countrymen and honest men, and their tender mercies would be kinder than these ghoulish aliens. But they wouldn't have listened to me. That old devil with the eyelids had not taken long to get rid of them. I thought he probably had some kind of graft with the constabulary. Most likely he had letters from Cabinet Ministers saying he was to be given every facility for plotting against Britain. That's the sort of owlish way we run our politics in the Old Country.

The three would be back for lunch, so I hadn't more than a couple of hours to wait. It was simply waiting on destruction, for I could see no way out of this mess. I wished that I had Scudder's courage, for I am free to confess I didn't feel any great fortitude. The only thing that kept me going was that I was pretty furious. It made me boil with rage to think of those three spies getting the pull on me like this. I hoped that at any rate I might be able to twist one of their necks before they downed me.

The more I thought of it the angrier I grew, and I had to get up and move about the room. I tried the shutters, but they were the kind that lock with a key, and I couldn't move them. From the outside came the faint clucking of hens in the warm sun. Then I groped among the sacks and boxes. I couldn't open the latter, and the sacks seemed to be full of things like dog-biscuits that smelt of cinnamon. But, as I circumnavigated the room, I found a handle in the wall which seemed worth investigating.

It was the door of a wall cupboard—what they call a 'press' in Scotland—and it was locked. I shook it, and it seemed rather flimsy. For want of something better to do I put out my strength on that door, getting some purchase on the handle by looping my braces round it. Presently the thing gave with a crash which I thought would bring in my warders to inquire. I waited for a bit, and then started to explore the cupboard shelves.

There was a multitude of queer things there. I found an odd vesta or two in my trouser pockets and struck a light. It was out in a second, but it showed me one thing. There was a little stock of electric torches on one shelf. I picked up one, and found it was in working order.

With the torch to help me I investigated further. There were bottles and cases of queer-smelling stuffs, chemicals no doubt for experiments, and there were coils of fine copper wire and yanks and yanks of thin oiled silk. There was a box of detonators, and a lot of cord for fuses. Then away at the back of the shelf I found a stout brown cardboard box, and inside it a wooden case. I managed to wrench it open, and within lay half a dozen little grey bricks, each a couple of inches square.

I took up one, and found that it crumbled easily in my hand. Then I smelt it and put my tongue to it. After that I sat down to think. I hadn't been a mining engineer for nothing, and I knew lentonite when I saw it.

With one of these bricks I could blow the house to smithereens. I had used the stuff in Rhodesia and knew its power. But the trouble was that my knowledge wasn't exact. I had forgotten the proper charge and the right way of preparing it, and I wasn't sure about the timing. I had only a vague notion, too, as to its power, for though I had used it I had not handled it with my own fingers.

But it was a chance, the only possible chance. It was a mighty risk, but against it was an absolute black certainty. If I used it the odds were, as I reckoned, about five to one in favour of my blowing myself into the tree-tops; but if I didn't I should very likely be occupying a six-foot hole in the garden by the evening. That was the way I had to look at it. The prospect was pretty dark either way, but anyhow there was a chance, both for myself and for my country.

The remembrance of little Scudder decided me. It was about the beastliest moment of my life, for I'm no good at these cold-blooded resolutions. Still I managed to rake up the pluck to set my teeth and choke back the horrid doubts that flooded in on me. I simply shut off my mind and pretended I was doing an experiment as simple as Guy Fawkes fireworks.

I got a detonator, and fixed it to a couple of feet of fuse. Then I took a quarter of a lentonite brick, and buried it near the door below one of the sacks in a crack of the floor, fixing the detonator in it. For all I knew half those boxes might be dynamite. If the cupboard held such deadly explosives, why not the boxes? In that case there would be a glorious skyward journey for me and the German servants and about an acre of surrounding country. There was also the risk that the detonation might set off the other bricks in the cupboard, for I had forgotten most that I knew about lentonite. But it didn't do to begin thinking about the possibilities. The odds were horrible, but I had to take them.

I ensconced myself just below the sill of the window, and lit the fuse. Then I waited for a moment or two. There was dead silence—only a shuffle of heavy boots in the passage, and the peaceful cluck of hens from the warm out-of-doors. I commended my soul to my Maker, and wondered where I would be in five seconds ...

A great wave of heat seemed to surge upwards from the floor, and hang for a blistering instant in the air. Then the wall opposite me flashed into a golden yellow and dissolved with a rending thunder that hammered my brain into a pulp. Something dropped on me, catching the point of my left shoulder.

And then I think I became unconscious.

My stupor can scarcely have lasted beyond a few seconds. I felt myself being choked by thick yellow fumes, and struggled out of the debris to my feet. Somewhere behind me I felt fresh air. The jambs of the window had fallen, and through the ragged rent the smoke was pouring out to the summer noon. I stepped over the broken lintel, and found myself standing in a yard in a dense and acrid fog. I felt very sick and ill, but I could move my limbs, and I staggered blindly forward away from the house.

A small mill-lade ran in a wooden aqueduct at the other side of the yard, and into this I fell. The cool water revived me, and I had just enough wits left to think of escape. I squirmed up the lade among the slippery green slime till I reached the mill-wheel. Then I wriggled through the axle hole into the old mill and tumbled on to a bed of chaff. A nail caught the seat of my trousers, and I left a wisp of heather-mixture behind me.

The mill had been long out of use. The ladders were rotten with age, and in the loft the rats had gnawed great holes in the floor. Nausea shook me, and a wheel in my head kept turning, while my left shoulder and arm seemed to be stricken with the palsy. I looked out of the window and saw a fog still hanging over the house and smoke escaping from an upper window. Please God I had set the place on fire, for I could hear confused cries coming from the other side.

But I had no time to linger, since this mill was obviously a bad hiding-place. Anyone looking for me would naturally follow the lade, and I made certain the search would begin as soon as they found that my body was not in the storeroom. From another window I saw that on the far side of the mill stood an old stone dovecot. If I could get there without leaving tracks I might find a hiding-place, for I argued that my enemies, if they thought I could move, would conclude I had made for open country, and would go seeking me on the moor.

I crawled down the broken ladder, scattering chaff behind me to cover my footsteps. I did the same on the mill floor, and on the threshold where the door hung on broken hinges. Peeping out, I saw that between me and the dovecot was a piece of bare cobbled ground, where no footmarks would show. Also it was mercifully hid by the mill buildings from any view from the house. I slipped across the space, got to the back of the dovecot and prospected a way of ascent.

That was one of the hardest jobs I ever took on. My shoulder and arm ached like hell, and I was so sick and giddy that I was always on the verge of falling. But I managed it somehow. By the use of out-jutting stones and gaps in the masonry and a tough ivy root I got to the top in the end. There was a little parapet behind which I found space to lie down. Then I proceeded to go off into an old-fashioned swoon.

I woke with a burning head and the sun glaring in my face. For a long time I lay motionless, for those horrible fumes seemed to have loosened my joints and dulled my brain. Sounds came to me from the house—men speaking throatily and the throbbing of a stationary car. There was a little gap in the parapet to which I wriggled, and from which I had some sort of prospect of the yard. I saw figures come out—a servant with his head bound up, and then a younger man in knickerbockers. They were looking for something, and moved towards the mill. Then one of them caught sight of the wisp of cloth on the nail, and cried out to the other. They both went back to the house, and brought two more to look at it. I saw the rotund figure of my late captor, and I thought I made out the man with the lisp. I noticed that all had pistols.

For half an hour they ransacked the mill. I could hear them kicking over the barrels and pulling up the rotten planking. Then they came outside, and stood just below the dovecot arguing fiercely. The servant with the bandage was being soundly rated. I heard them fiddling with the door of the dovecote and for one horrid moment I fancied they were coming up. Then they thought better of it, and went back to the house.

All that long blistering afternoon I lay baking on the rooftop. Thirst was my chief torment. My tongue was like a stick, and to make it worse I could hear the cool drip of water from the mill-lade. I watched the course of the little stream as it came in from the moor, and my fancy followed it to the top of the glen, where it must issue from an icy fountain fringed with cool ferns and mosses. I would have given a thousand pounds to plunge my face into that.

I had a fine prospect of the whole ring of moorland. I saw the car speed away with two occupants, and a man on a hill pony riding east. I judged they were looking for me, and I wished them joy of their quest.

But I saw something else more interesting. The house stood almost on the summit of a swell of moorland which crowned a sort of plateau, and there was no higher point nearer than the big hills six miles off. The actual summit, as I have mentioned, was a biggish clump of trees—firs mostly, with a few ashes and beeches. On the dovecot I was almost on a level with the tree-tops, and could see what lay beyond. The wood was not solid, but only a ring, and inside was an oval of green turf, for all the world like a big cricket-field.

I didn't take long to guess what it was. It was an aerodrome, and a secret one. The place had been most cunningly chosen. For suppose anyone were watching an aeroplane descending here, he would think it had gone over the hill beyond the trees. As the place was on the top of a rise in the midst of a big amphitheatre, any observer from any direction would conclude it had passed out of view behind the hill. Only a man very close at hand would realize that the aeroplane had not gone over but had descended in the midst of the wood. An observer with a telescope on one of the higher hills might have discovered the truth, but only herds went there, and herds do not carry spy-glasses. When I looked from the dovecot I could see far away a blue line which I knew was the sea, and I grew furious to think that our enemies had this secret conning-tower to rake our waterways.

Then I reflected that if that aeroplane came back the chances were ten to one that I would be discovered. So through the afternoon I lay and prayed for the coming of darkness, and glad I was when the sun went down over the big western hills and the twilight haze crept over the moor. The aeroplane was late. The gloaming was far advanced when I heard the beat of wings and saw it volplaning downward to its home in the wood. Lights twinkled for a bit and there was much coming and going from the house. Then the dark fell, and silence.

Thank God it was a black night. The moon was well on its last quarter and would not rise till late. My thirst was too great to allow me to tarry, so about nine o'clock, so far as I could judge, I started to descend. It wasn't easy, and half-way down I heard the back door of the house open, and saw the gleam of a lantern against the mill wall. For some agonizing minutes I hung by the ivy and prayed that whoever it was would not come round by the dovecot. Then the light disappeared, and I dropped as softly as I could on to the hard soil of the yard.

I crawled on my belly in the lee of a stone dyke till I reached the fringe of trees which surrounded the house. If I had known how to do it I would have tried to put that aeroplane out of action, but I realized that any attempt would probably be futile. I was pretty certain that there would be some kind of defence round the house, so I went through the wood on hands and knees, feeling carefully every inch before me. It was as well, for presently I came on a wire about two feet from the ground. If I had tripped over that, it would doubtless have rung some bell in the house and I would have been captured.

A hundred yards farther on I found another wire cunningly placed on the edge of a small stream. Beyond that lay the moor, and in five minutes I was deep in bracken and heather. Soon I was round the shoulder of the rise, in the little glen from which the mill-lade flowed. Ten minutes later my face was in the spring, and I was soaking down pints of the blessed water.

But I did not stop till I had put half a dozen miles between me and that accursed dwelling.

CHAPTER SEVEN

The Dry-Fly Fisherman

I sat down on a hill-top and took stock of my position. I wasn't feeling very happy, for my natural thankfulness at my escape was clouded by my severe bodily discomfort. Those lentonite fumes had fairly poisoned me, and the baking hours on the dovecot hadn't helped matters. I had a crushing headache, and felt as sick as a cat. Also my shoulder was in a bad way. At first I thought it was only a bruise, but it seemed to be swelling, and I had no use of my left arm.

My plan was to seek Mr Turnbull's cottage, recover my garments, and especially Scudder's note-book, and then make for the main line and get back to the south. It seemed to me that the sooner I got in touch with the Foreign Office man, Sir Walter Bullivant, the better. I didn't see how I could get more proof than I had got already. He must just take or leave my story, and anyway, with him I would be in better hands than those devilish Germans. I had begun to feel quite kindly towards the British police.

It was a wonderful starry night, and I had not much difficulty about the road. Sir Harry's map had given me the lie of the land, and all I had to do was to steer a point or two west of south-west to come to the stream where I had met the roadman. In all these travels I never knew the names of the places, but I believe this stream was no less than the upper waters of the river Tweed. I calculated I must be about eighteen miles distant, and that meant I could not get there before morning. So I must lie up a day somewhere, for I was too outrageous a figure to be seen in the sunlight. I had neither coat, waistcoat, collar, nor hat, my trousers were badly torn, and my face and hands were black with the explosion. I daresay I had other beauties, for my eyes felt as if they were furiously bloodshot. Altogether I was no spectacle for God-fearing citizens to see on a highroad.

Very soon after daybreak I made an attempt to clean myself in a hill burn, and then approached a herd's cottage, for I was feeling the need of food. The herd was away from home, and his wife was alone, with no neighbour for five miles. She was a decent old body, and a plucky one, for though she got a fright when she saw me, she had an axe handy, and would have used it on any evil-doer. I told her that I had had a fall—I didn't say how—and she saw by my looks that I was pretty sick. Like a true Samaritan she asked no questions, but gave me a bowl of milk with a dash of whisky in it, and let me sit for a little by her kitchen fire. She would have bathed my shoulder, but it ached so badly that I would not let her touch it.

I don't know what she took me for—a repentant burglar, perhaps; for when I wanted to pay her for the milk and tendered a sovereign which was the smallest coin I had, she shook her head and said something about 'giving it to them that had a right to it'. At this I protested so strongly that I think she believed me honest, for she took the money and gave me a warm new plaid for it, and an old hat of her man's. She showed me how to wrap the plaid around my shoulders, and when I left that cottage I was the living image of the kind of Scotsman you see in the illustrations to Burns's poems. But at any rate I was more or less clad.

It was as well, for the weather changed before midday to a thick drizzle of rain. I found shelter below an overhanging rock in the crook of a burn, where a drift of dead brackens made a tolerable bed. There I managed to sleep till nightfall, waking very cramped and wretched, with my shoulder gnawing like a toothache. I ate the oatcake and cheese the old wife had given me and set out again just before the darkening.

I pass over the miseries of that night among the wet hills. There were no stars to steer by, and I had to do the best I could from my memory of the map. Twice I lost my way, and I had some nasty falls into peat-bogs. I had only about ten miles to go as the crow flies, but my mistakes made it nearer twenty. The last bit was completed with set teeth and a very light and dizzy head. But I managed it, and in the early dawn I was knocking at Mr Turnbull's door. The mist lay close and thick, and from the cottage I could not see the highroad.

Mr Turnbull himself opened to me—sober and something more than sober. He was primly dressed in an ancient but well-tended suit of black; he had been shaved not later than the night before; he wore a linen collar; and in his left hand he carried a pocket Bible. At first he did not recognize me.

'Whae are ye that comes stravaigin' here on the Sabbath mornin'?' he asked.

I had lost all count of the days. So the Sabbath was the reason for this strange decorum.

My head was swimming so wildly that I could not frame a coherent answer. But he recognized me, and he saw that I was ill.

'Hae ye got my specs?' he asked.

I fetched them out of my trouser pocket and gave him them.

'Ye'll hae come for your jaicket and westcoat,' he said. 'Come in-bye. Losh, man, ye're terrible dune i' the legs. Haud up till I get ye to a chair.'

I perceived I was in for a bout of malaria. I had a good deal of fever in my bones, and the wet night had brought it out, while my shoulder and the effects of the fumes combined to make me feel pretty bad. Before I knew, Mr Turnbull was helping me off with my clothes, and putting me to bed in one of the two cupboards that lined the kitchen walls.

He was a true friend in need, that old roadman. His wife was dead years ago, and since his daughter's marriage he lived alone.

For the better part of ten days he did all the rough nursing I needed. I simply wanted to be left in peace while the fever took its course, and when my skin was cool again I found that the bout had more or less cured my shoulder. But it was a baddish go, and though I was out of bed in five days, it took me some time to get my legs again.

He went out each morning, leaving me milk for the day, and locking the door behind him; and came in in the evening to sit silent in the chimney corner. Not a soul came near the place. When I was getting better, he never bothered me with a question. Several times he fetched me a two days' old SCOTSMAN, and I noticed that the interest in the Portland Place murder seemed to have died down. There was no mention of it, and I could find very little about anything except a thing called the General Assembly—some ecclesiastical spree, I gathered.

One day he produced my belt from a lockfast drawer. 'There's a terrible heap o' siller in't,' he said. 'Ye'd better coont it to see it's a' there.'

He never even sought my name. I asked him if anybody had been around making inquiries subsequent to my spell at the road-making.

'Ay, there was a man in a motor-cawr. He speired whae had ta'en my place that day, and I let on I thocht him daft. But he keepit on at me, and syne I said he maun be thinkin' o' my gude-brither frae the Cleuch that whiles lent me a haun'. He was a wersh-lookin' sowl, and I couldna understand the half o' his English tongue.'

I was getting restless those last days, and as soon as I felt myself fit I decided to be off. That was not till the twelfth day of June, and as luck would have it a drover went past that morning taking some cattle to Moffat. He was a man named Hislop, a friend of Turnbull's, and he came in to his breakfast with us and offered to take me with him.

I made Turnbull accept five pounds for my lodging, and a hard job I had of it. There never was a more independent being. He grew positively rude when I pressed him, and shy and red, and took the money at last without a thank you. When I told him how much I owed him, he grunted something about 'ae guid turn deservin' anither'. You would have thought from our leave-taking that we had parted in disgust.

Hislop was a cheery soul, who chattered all the way over the pass and down the sunny vale of Annan. I talked of Galloway markets and sheep prices, and he made up his mind I was a 'pack-shepherd' from those parts—whatever that may be. My plaid and my old hat, as I have said, gave me a fine theatrical Scots look. But driving cattle is a mortally slow job, and we took the better part of the day to cover a dozen miles.

If I had not had such an anxious heart I would have enjoyed that time. It was shining blue weather, with a constantly changing prospect of brown hills and far green meadows, and a continual sound of larks and curlews and falling streams. But I had no mind for the summer, and little for Hislop's conversation, for as the fateful fifteenth of June drew near I was overweighed with the hopeless difficulties of my enterprise.

I got some dinner in a humble Moffat public-house, and walked the two miles to the junction on the main line. The night express for the south was not due till near midnight, and to fill up the time I went up on the hillside and fell asleep, for the walk had tired me. I all but slept too long, and had to run to the station and catch the train with two minutes to spare. The feel of the hard third-class cushions and the smell of stale tobacco cheered me up wonderfully. At any rate, I felt now that I was getting to grips with my job.

I was decanted at Crewe in the small hours and had to wait till six to get a train for Birmingham. In the afternoon I got to Reading, and changed into a local train which journeyed into the deeps of Berkshire. Presently I was in a land of lush water-meadows and slow reedy streams. About eight o'clock in the evening, a weary and travel-stained being—a cross between a farm-labourer and a vet—with a checked black-and-white plaid over his arm (for I did not dare to wear it south of the Border), descended at the little station of Artinswell. There were several people on the platform, and I thought I had better wait to ask my way till I was clear of the place.

The road led through a wood of great beeches and then into a shallow valley, with the green backs of downs peeping over the distant trees. After Scotland the air smelt heavy and flat, but infinitely sweet, for the limes and chestnuts and lilac bushes were domes of blossom. Presently I came to a bridge, below which a clear slow stream flowed between snowy beds of water-buttercups. A little above it was a mill; and the lasher made a pleasant cool sound in the scented dusk. Somehow the place soothed me and put me at my ease. I fell to whistling as I looked into the green depths, and the tune which came to my lips was 'Annie Laurie'.

A fisherman came up from the waterside, and as he neared me he too began to whistle. The tune was infectious, for he followed my suit. He was a huge man in untidy old flannels and a wide-brimmed hat, with a canvas bag slung on his shoulder. He nodded to me, and I thought I had never seen a shrewder or better-tempered face. He leaned his delicate ten-foot split-cane rod against the bridge, and looked with me at the water.

'Clear, isn't it?' he said pleasantly. 'I back our Kenner any day against the Test. Look at that big fellow. Four pounds if he's an ounce. But the evening rise is over and you can't tempt 'em.'

'I don't see him,' said I.

'Look! There! A yard from the reeds just above that stickle.'

'I've got him now. You might swear he was a black stone.'

'So,' he said, and whistled another bar of 'Annie Laurie'.

'Twisdon's the name, isn't it?' he said over his shoulder, his eyes still fixed on the stream.

'No,' I said. 'I mean to say, Yes.' I had forgotten all about my alias.

'It's a wise conspirator that knows his own name,' he observed, grinning broadly at a moor-hen that emerged from the bridge's shadow.

I stood up and looked at him, at the square, cleft jaw and broad, lined brow and the firm folds of cheek, and began to think that here at last was an ally worth having. His whimsical blue eyes seemed to go very deep.

Suddenly he frowned. 'I call it disgraceful,' he said, raising his voice. 'Disgraceful that an able-bodied man like you should dare to beg. You can get a meal from my kitchen, but you'll get no money from me.'

A dog-cart was passing, driven by a young man who raised his whip to salute the fisherman. When he had gone, he picked up his rod.

'That's my house,' he said, pointing to a white gate a hundred yards on. 'Wait five minutes and then go round to the back door.' And with that he left me.

I did as I was bidden. I found a pretty cottage with a lawn running down to the stream, and a perfect jungle of guelder-rose and lilac flanking the path. The back door stood open, and a grave butler was awaiting me.

'Come this way, Sir,' he said, and he led me along a passage and up a back staircase to a pleasant bedroom looking towards the river. There I found a complete outfit laid out for me—dress clothes with all the fixings, a brown flannel suit, shirts, collars, ties, shaving things and hair-brushes, even a pair of patent shoes. 'Sir Walter thought as how Mr Reggie's things would fit you, Sir,' said the butler. 'He keeps some clothes 'ere, for he comes regular on the week-ends. There's a bathroom next door, and I've prepared a 'ot bath. Dinner in 'alf an hour, Sir. You'll 'ear the gong.'

The grave being withdrew, and I sat down in a chintz-covered easy-chair and gaped. It was like a pantomime, to come suddenly out of beggardom into this orderly comfort. Obviously Sir Walter believed in me, though why he did I could not guess. I looked at myself in the mirror and saw a wild, haggard brown fellow, with a fortnight's ragged beard, and dust in ears and eyes, collarless, vulgarly shirted, with shapeless old tweed clothes and boots that had not been cleaned for the better part of a month. I made a fine tramp and a fair drover; and here I was ushered by a prim butler into this temple of gracious ease. And the best of it was that they did not even know my name.

I resolved not to puzzle my head but to take the gifts the gods had provided. I shaved and bathed luxuriously, and got into the dress clothes and clean crackling shirt, which fitted me not so badly. By the time I had finished the looking-glass showed a not unpersonable young man.

Sir Walter awaited me in a dusky dining-room where a little round table was lit with silver candles. The sight of him—so respectable and established and secure, the embodiment of law and government and all the conventions—took me aback and made me feel an interloper. He couldn't know the truth about me, or he wouldn't treat me like this. I simply could not accept his hospitality on false pretences.

'I'm more obliged to you than I can say, but I'm bound to make things clear,' I said. 'I'm an innocent man, but I'm wanted by the police. I've got to tell you this, and I won't be surprised if you kick me out.'

He smiled. 'That's all right. Don't let that interfere with your appetite. We can talk about these things after dinner.' I never ate a meal with greater relish, for I had had nothing all day but railway sandwiches. Sir Walter did me proud, for we drank a good champagne and had some uncommon fine port afterwards. It made me almost hysterical to be sitting there, waited on by a footman and a sleek butler, and remember that I had been living for three weeks like a brigand, with every man's hand against me. I told Sir Walter about tiger-fish in the Zambesi that bite off your fingers if you give them a chance, and we discussed sport up and down the globe, for he had hunted a bit in his day.

We went to his study for coffee, a jolly room full of books and trophies and untidiness and comfort. I made up my mind that if ever I got rid of this business and had a house of my own, I would create just such a room. Then when the coffee-cups were cleared away, and we had got our cigars alight, my host swung his long legs over the side of his chair and bade me get started with my yarn.

'I've obeyed Harry's instructions,' he said, 'and the bribe he offered me was that you would tell me something to wake me up. I'm ready, Mr Hannay.'

I noticed with a start that he called me by my proper name.

I began at the very beginning. I told of my boredom in London, and the night I had come back to find Scudder gibbering on my doorstep. I told him all Scudder had told me about Karolides and the Foreign Office conference, and that made him purse his lips and grin.

Then I got to the murder, and he grew solemn again. He heard all about the milkman and my time in Galloway, and my deciphering Scudder's notes at the inn.

'You've got them here?' he asked sharply, and drew a long breath when I whipped the little book from my pocket.

I said nothing of the contents. Then I described my meeting with Sir Harry, and the speeches at the hall. At that he laughed uproariously.

'Harry talked dashed nonsense, did he? I quite believe it. He's as good a chap as ever breathed, but his idiot of an uncle has stuffed his head with maggots. Go on, Mr Hannay.'

My day as roadman excited him a bit. He made me describe the two fellows in the car very closely, and seemed to be raking back in his memory. He grew merry again when he heard of the fate of that ass Jopley.

But the old man in the moorland house solemnized him. Again I had to describe every detail of his appearance.

'Bland and bald-headed and hooded his eyes like a bird ... He sounds a sinister wild-fowl! And you dynamited his hermitage, after he had saved you from the police. Spirited piece of work, that!' Presently I reached the end of my wanderings. He got up slowly, and looked down at me from the hearth-rug.

'You may dismiss the police from your mind,' he said. 'You're in no danger from the law of this land.'

'Great Scot!' I cried. 'Have they got the murderer?'

'No. But for the last fortnight they have dropped you from the list of possibles.'

'Why?' I asked in amazement.

'Principally because I received a letter from Scudder. I knew something of the man, and he did several jobs for me. He was half crank, half genius, but he was wholly honest. The trouble about him was his partiality for playing a lone hand. That made him pretty well useless in any Secret Service—a pity, for he had uncommon gifts. I think he was the bravest man in the world, for he was always shivering with fright, and yet nothing would choke him off. I had a letter from him on the 31st of May.'

'But he had been dead a week by then.'

'The letter was written and posted on the 23rd. He evidently did not anticipate an immediate decease. His communications usually took a week to reach me, for they were sent under cover to Spain and then to Newcastle. He had a mania, you know, for concealing his tracks.'

'What did he say?' I stammered.

'Nothing. Merely that he was in danger, but had found shelter with a good friend, and that I would hear from him before the 15th of June. He gave me no address, but said he was living near Portland Place. I think his object was to clear you if anything happened. When I got it I went to Scotland Yard, went over the details of the inquest, and concluded that you were the friend. We made inquiries about you, Mr Hannay, and found you were respectable. I thought I knew the motives for your disappearance—not only the police, the other one too—and when I got Harry's scrawl I guessed at the rest. I have been expecting you any time this past week.' You can imagine what a load this took off my mind. I felt a free man once more, for I was now up against my country's enemies only, and not my country's law.

'Now let us have the little note-book,' said Sir Walter.

It took us a good hour to work through it. I explained the cypher, and he was jolly quick at picking it up. He emended my reading of it on several points, but I had been fairly correct, on the whole. His face was very grave before he had finished, and he sat silent for a while.

'I don't know what to make of it,' he said at last. 'He is right about one thing—what is going to happen the day after tomorrow. How the devil can it have got known? That is ugly enough in itself. But all this about war and the Black Stone—it reads like some wild melodrama. If only I had more confidence in Scudder's judgement. The trouble about him was that he was too romantic. He had the artistic temperament, and wanted a story to be better than God meant it to be. He had a lot of odd biases, too. Jews, for example, made him see red. Jews and the high finance.

'The Black Stone,' he repeated. 'DER SCHWARZE STEIN. It's like a penny novelette. And all this stuff about Karolides. That is the weak part of the tale, for I happen to know that the virtuous Karolides is likely to outlast us both. There is no State in Europe that wants him gone. Besides, he has just been playing up to Berlin and Vienna and giving my Chief some uneasy moments. No! Scudder has gone off the track there. Frankly, Hannay, I don't believe that part of his story. There's some nasty business afoot, and he found out too much and lost his life over it. But I am ready to take my oath that it is ordinary spy work. A certain great European Power makes a hobby of her spy system, and her methods are not too particular. Since she pays by piecework her blackguards are not likely to stick at a murder or two. They want our naval dispositions for their collection at the Marineamt; but they will be pigeon-holed—nothing more.'

Just then the butler entered the room.

'There's a trunk-call from London, Sir Walter. It's Mr 'Eath, and he wants to speak to you personally.'

My host went off to the telephone.

He returned in five minutes with a whitish face. 'I apologize to the shade of Scudder,' he said. 'Karolides was shot dead this evening at a few minutes after seven.'

CHAPTER EIGHT

The Coming of the Black Stone

I came down to breakfast next morning, after eight hours of blessed dreamless sleep, to find Sir Walter decoding a telegram in the midst of muffins and marmalade. His fresh rosiness of yesterday seemed a thought tarnished.

'I had a busy hour on the telephone after you went to bed,' he said. 'I got my Chief to speak to the First Lord and the Secretary for War, and they are bringing Royer over a day sooner. This wire clinches it. He will be in London at five. Odd that the code word for a SOUS-CHEF D/ETAT MAJOR-GENERAL should be "Porker".'

He directed me to the hot dishes and went on.

'Not that I think it will do much good. If your friends were clever enough to find out the first arrangement they are clever enough to discover the change. I would give my head to know where the leak is. We believed there were only five men in England who knew about Royer's visit, and you may be certain there were fewer in France, for they manage these things better there.'

While I ate he continued to talk, making me to my surprise a present of his full confidence.

'Can the dispositions not be changed?' I asked.

'They could,' he said. 'But we want to avoid that if possible. They are the result of immense thought, and no alteration would be as good. Besides, on one or two points change is simply impossible. Still, something could be done, I suppose, if it were absolutely necessary. But you see the difficulty, Hannay. Our enemies are not going to be such fools as to pick Royer's pocket or any childish game like that. They know that would mean a row and put us on our guard. Their aim is to get the details without any one of us knowing, so that Royer will go back to Paris in the belief that the whole business is still deadly secret. If they can't do that they fail, for, once we suspect, they know that the whole thing must be altered.'

'Then we must stick by the Frenchman's side till he is home again,' I said. 'If they thought they could get the information in Paris they would try there. It means that they have some deep scheme on foot in London which they reckon is going to win out.'

'Royer dines with my Chief, and then comes to my house where four people will see him—Whittaker from the Admiralty, myself, Sir Arthur Drew, and General Winstanley. The First Lord is ill, and has gone to Sheringham. At my house he will get a certain document from Whittaker, and after that he will be motored to Portsmouth where a destroyer will take him to Havre. His journey is too important for the ordinary boat-train.

He will never be left unattended for a moment till he is safe on French soil. The same with Whittaker till he meets Royer. That is the best we can do, and it's hard to see how there can be any miscarriage. But I don't mind admitting that I'm horribly nervous. This murder of Karolides will play the deuce in the chancelleries of Europe.'

After breakfast he asked me if I could drive a car. 'Well, you'll be my chauffeur today and wear Hudson's rig. You're about his size. You have a hand in this business and we are taking no risks. There are desperate men against us, who will not respect the country retreat of an overworked official.'

When I first came to London I had bought a car and amused myself with running about the south of England, so I knew something of the geography. I took Sir Walter to town by the Bath Road and made good going. It was a soft breathless June morning, with a promise of sultriness later, but it was delicious enough swinging through the little towns with their freshly watered streets, and past the summer gardens of the Thames valley. I landed Sir Walter at his house in Queen Anne's Gate punctually by half-past eleven. The butler was coming up by train with the luggage.

The first thing he did was to take me round to Scotland Yard. There we saw a prim gentleman, with a clean-shaven, lawyer's face.

'I've brought you the Portland Place murderer,' was Sir Walter's introduction.

The reply was a wry smile. 'It would have been a welcome present, Bullivant. This, I presume, is Mr Richard Hannay, who for some days greatly interested my department.'

'Mr Hannay will interest it again. He has much to tell you, but not today. For certain grave reasons his tale must wait for four hours. Then, I can promise you, you will be entertained and possibly edified. I want you to assure Mr Hannay that he will suffer no further inconvenience.'

This assurance was promptly given. 'You can take up your life where you left off,' I was told. 'Your flat, which probably you no longer wish to occupy, is waiting for you, and your man is still there. As you were never publicly accused, we considered that there was no need of a public exculpation. But on that, of course, you must please yourself.'

'We may want your assistance later on, MacGillivray,' Sir Walter said as we left.

Then he turned me loose.

'Come and see me tomorrow, Hannay. I needn't tell you to keep deadly quiet. If I were you I would go to bed, for you must have considerable arrears of sleep to overtake. You had better lie low, for if one of your Black Stone friends saw you there might be trouble.'

I felt curiously at a loose end. At first it was very pleasant to be a free man, able to go where I wanted without fearing anything. I had only been a month under the ban of the law, and it was quite enough for me. I went to the Savoy and ordered very carefully a very good luncheon, and then smoked the best cigar the house could provide. But I was still feeling nervous. When I saw anybody look at me in the lounge, I grew shy, and wondered if they were thinking about the murder.

After that I took a taxi and drove miles away up into North London. I walked back through fields and lines of villas and terraces and then slums and mean streets, and it took me pretty nearly two hours. All the while my restlessness was growing worse. I felt that great things, tremendous things, were happening or about to happen, and I, who was the cog-wheel of the whole business, was out of it. Royer would be landing at Dover, Sir Walter would be making plans with the few people in England who were in the secret, and somewhere in the darkness the Black Stone would be working. I felt the sense of danger and impending calamity, and I had the curious feeling, too, that I alone could avert it, alone could grapple with it. But I was out of the game now. How could it be otherwise? It was not likely that Cabinet Ministers and Admiralty Lords and Generals would admit me to their councils.

I actually began to wish that I could run up against one of my three enemies. That would lead to developments. I felt that I wanted enormously to have a vulgar scrap with those gentry, where I could hit out and flatten something. I was rapidly getting into a very bad temper.

I didn't feel like going back to my flat. That had to be faced some time, but as I still had sufficient money I thought I would put it off till next morning, and go to a hotel for the night.

My irritation lasted through dinner, which I had at a restaurant in Jermyn Street. I was no longer hungry, and let several courses pass untasted. I drank the best part of a bottle of Burgundy, but it did nothing to cheer me. An abominable restlessness had taken possession of me. Here was I, a very ordinary fellow, with no particular brains, and yet I was convinced that somehow I was needed to help this business through—that without me it would all go to blazes. I told myself it was sheer silly conceit, that four or five of the cleverest people living, with all the might of the British Empire at their back, had the job in hand. Yet I couldn't be convinced. It seemed as if a voice kept speaking in my ear, telling me to be up and doing, or I would never sleep again.

The upshot was that about half-past nine I made up my mind to go to Queen Anne's Gate. Very likely I would not be admitted, but it would ease my conscience to try.

I walked down Jermyn Street, and at the corner of Duke Street passed a group of young men. They were in evening dress, had been dining somewhere, and were going on to a music-hall. One of them was Mr Marmaduke Jopley.

He saw me and stopped short.

'By God, the murderer!' he cried. 'Here, you fellows, hold him! That's Hannay, the man who did the Portland Place murder!' He gripped me by the arm, and the others crowded round. I wasn't looking for any trouble, but my ill-temper made me play the fool. A policeman came up, and I should have told him the truth, and, if he didn't believe it, demanded to be taken to Scotland Yard, or for that matter to the nearest police station. But a delay at that moment seemed to me unendurable, and the sight of Marmie's imbecile face was more than I could bear. I let out with my left, and had the satisfaction of seeing him measure his length in the gutter.

Then began an unholy row. They were all on me at once, and the policeman took me in the rear. I got in one or two good blows, for I think, with fair play, I could have licked the lot of them, but the policeman pinned me behind, and one of them got his fingers on my throat.

Through a black cloud of rage I heard the officer of the law asking what was the matter, and Marmie, between his broken teeth, declaring that I was Hannay the murderer.

'Oh, damn it all,' I cried, 'make the fellow shut up. I advise you to leave me alone, constable. Scotland Yard knows all about me, and you'll get a proper wigging if you interfere with me.'

'You've got to come along of me, young man,' said the policeman. 'I saw you strike that gentleman crool 'ard. You began it too, for he wasn't doing nothing. I seen you. Best go quietly or I'll have to fix you up.'

Exasperation and an overwhelming sense that at no cost must I delay gave me the strength of a bull elephant. I fairly wrenched the constable off his feet, floored the man who was gripping my collar, and set off at my best pace down Duke Street. I heard a whistle being blown, and the rush of men behind me.

I have a very fair turn of speed, and that night I had wings. In a jiffy I was in Pall Mall and had turned down towards St James's Park. I dodged the policeman at the Palace gates, dived through a press of carriages at the entrance to the Mall, and was making for the bridge before my pursuers had crossed the roadway. In the open ways of the Park I put on a spurt. Happily there were few people about and no one tried to stop me. I was staking all on getting to Queen Anne's Gate.

When I entered that quiet thoroughfare it seemed deserted. Sir Walter's house was in the narrow part, and outside it three or four motor-cars were drawn up. I slackened speed some yards off and walked briskly up to the door. If the butler refused me admission, or if he even delayed to open the door, I was done.

He didn't delay. I had scarcely rung before the door opened.

'I must see Sir Walter,' I panted. 'My business is desperately important.'

That butler was a great man. Without moving a muscle he held the door open, and then shut it behind me. 'Sir Walter is engaged, Sir, and I have orders to admit no one. Perhaps you will wait.'

The house was of the old-fashioned kind, with a wide hall and rooms on both sides of it. At the far end was an alcove with a telephone and a couple of chairs, and there the butler offered me a seat.

'See here,' I whispered. 'There's trouble about and I'm in it. But Sir Walter knows, and I'm working for him. If anyone comes and asks if I am here, tell him a lie.'

He nodded, and presently there was a noise of voices in the street, and a furious ringing at the bell. I never admired a man more than that butler. He opened the door, and with a face like a graven image waited to be questioned. Then he gave them it. He told them whose house it was, and what his orders were, and simply froze them off the doorstep. I could see it all from my alcove, and it was better than any play.

I hadn't waited long till there came another ring at the bell. The butler made no bones about admitting this new visitor.

While he was taking off his coat I saw who it was. You couldn't open a newspaper or a magazine without seeing that face—the grey beard cut like a spade, the firm fighting mouth, the blunt square nose, and the keen blue eyes. I recognized the First Sea Lord, the man, they say, that made the new British Navy.

He passed my alcove and was ushered into a room at the back of the hall. As the door opened I could hear the sound of low voices. It shut, and I was left alone again.

For twenty minutes I sat there, wondering what I was to do next. I was still perfectly convinced that I was wanted, but when or how I had no notion. I kept looking at my watch, and as the time crept on to half-past ten I began to think that the conference must soon end. In a quarter of an hour Royer should be speeding along the road to Portsmouth ...

Then I heard a bell ring, and the butler appeared. The door of the back room opened, and the First Sea

Lord came out. He walked past me, and in passing he glanced in my direction, and for a second we looked each other in the face.

Only for a second, but it was enough to make my heart jump. I had never seen the great man before, and he had never seen me. But in that fraction of time something sprang into his eyes, and that something was recognition. You can't mistake it. It is a flicker, a spark of light, a minute shade of difference which means one thing and one thing only. It came involuntarily, for in a moment it died, and he passed on. In a maze of wild fancies I heard the street door close behind him.

I picked up the telephone book and looked up the number of his house. We were connected at once, and I heard a servant's voice.

'Is his Lordship at home?' I asked.

'His Lordship returned half an hour ago,' said the voice, 'and has gone to bed. He is not very well tonight. Will you leave a message, Sir?'

I rang off and almost tumbled into a chair. My part in this business was not yet ended. It had been a close shave, but I had been in time.

Not a moment could be lost, so I marched boldly to the door of that back room and entered without knocking.

Five surprised faces looked up from a round table. There was Sir Walter, and Drew the War Minister, whom I knew from his photographs. There was a slim elderly man, who was probably Whittaker, the Admiralty official, and there was General Winstanley, conspicuous from the long scar on his forehead. Lastly, there was a short stout man with an iron-grey moustache and bushy eyebrows, who had been arrested in the middle of a sentence.

Sir Walter's face showed surprise and annoyance.

'This is Mr Hannay, of whom I have spoken to you,' he said apologetically to the company. 'I'm afraid, Hannay, this visit is ill-timed.'

I was getting back my coolness. 'That remains to be seen, Sir,' I said; 'but I think it may be in the nick of time. For God's sake, gentlemen, tell me who went out a minute ago?'

'Lord Alloa,' Sir Walter said, reddening with anger. 'It was not,' I cried; 'it was his living image, but it was not Lord Alloa. It was someone who recognized me, someone I have seen in the last month. He had scarcely left the doorstep when I rang up Lord Alloa's house and was told he had come in half an hour before and had gone to bed.'

'Who—who—' someone stammered.

'The Black Stone,' I cried, and I sat down in the chair so recently vacated and looked round at five badly scared gentlemen.

CHAPTER NINE

The Thirty-Nine Steps

'Nonsense!' said the official from the Admiralty.

Sir Walter got up and left the room while we looked blankly at the table. He came back in ten minutes with a long face. 'I have spoken to Alloa,' he said. 'Had him out of bed—very grumpy. He went straight home after Mulross's dinner.'

'But it's madness,' broke in General Winstanley. 'Do you mean to tell me that that man came here and sat beside me for the best part of half an hour and that I didn't detect the imposture? Alloa must be out of his mind.'

'Don't you see the cleverness of it?' I said. 'You were too interested in other things to have any eyes. You took Lord Alloa for granted. If it had been anybody else you might have looked more closely, but it was natural for him to be here, and that put you all to sleep.'

Then the Frenchman spoke, very slowly and in good English.

'The young man is right. His psychology is good. Our enemies have not been foolish!'

He bent his wise brows on the assembly.

'I will tell you a tale,' he said. 'It happened many years ago in Senegal. I was quartered in a remote station, and to pass the time used to go fishing for big barbel in the river. A little Arab mare used to carry my luncheon basket—one of the salted dun breed you got at Timbuctoo in the old days. Well, one morning I had good sport, and the mare was unaccountably restless. I could hear her whinnying and squealing and stamping her feet, and I kept soothing her with my voice while my mind was intent on fish. I could see her all the time, as I thought, out of a corner of my eye, tethered to a tree twenty yards away. After a couple of hours I began to think of food. I collected my fish in a tarpaulin bag, and moved down the stream towards the mare, trolling my line. When I got up to her I flung the tarpaulin on her back—'

He paused and looked round.

'It was the smell that gave me warning. I turned my head and found myself looking at a lion three feet off ... An old man-eater, that was the terror of the village ... What was left of the mare, a mass of blood and bones and hide, was behind him.'

'What happened?' I asked. I was enough of a hunter to know a true yarn when I heard it.

'I stuffed my fishing-rod into his jaws, and I had a pistol. Also my servants came presently with rifles. But he left his mark on me.' He held up a hand which lacked three fingers.

'Consider,' he said. 'The mare had been dead more than an hour, and the brute had been patiently watching me ever since. I never saw the kill, for I was accustomed to the mare's fretting, and I never marked her absence, for my consciousness of her was only of something tawny, and the lion filled that part. If I could blunder thus, gentlemen, in a land where men's senses are keen, why should we busy preoccupied urban folk not err also?'

Sir Walter nodded. No one was ready to gainsay him.

'But I don't see,' went on Winstanley. 'Their object was to get these dispositions without our knowing it. Now it only required one of us to mention to Alloa our meeting tonight for the whole fraud to be exposed.'

Sir Walter laughed dryly. 'The selection of Alloa shows their acumen. Which of us was likely to speak to him about tonight? Or was he likely to open the subject?'

I remembered the First Sea Lord's reputation for taciturnity and shortness of temper.

'The one thing that puzzles me,' said the General, 'is what good his visit here would do that spy fellow? He could not carry away several pages of figures and strange names in his head.'

'That is not difficult,' the Frenchman replied. 'A good spy is trained to have a photographic memory. Like your own Macaulay. You noticed he said nothing, but went through these papers again and again. I think we may assume that he has every detail stamped on his mind. When I was younger I could do the same trick.'

'Well, I suppose there is nothing for it but to change the plans,' said Sir Walter ruefully.

Whittaker was looking very glum. 'Did you tell Lord Alloa what has happened?' he asked. 'No? Well, I can't speak with absolute assurance, but I'm nearly certain we can't make any serious change unless we alter the geography of England.'

'Another thing must be said,' it was Royer who spoke. 'I talked freely when that man was here. I told something of the military plans of my Government. I was permitted to say so much. But that information would be worth many millions to our enemies. No, my friends, I see no other way. The man who came here and his confederates must be taken, and taken at once.'

'Good God,' I cried, 'and we have not a rag of a clue.'

'Besides,' said Whittaker, 'there is the post. By this time the news will be on its way.'

'No,' said the Frenchman. 'You do not understand the habits of the spy. He receives personally his reward, and he delivers personally his intelligence. We in France know something of the breed. There is still a chance, MES AMIS. These men must cross the sea, and there are ships to be searched and ports to be watched. Believe me, the need is desperate for both France and Britain.'

Royer's grave good sense seemed to pull us together. He was the man of action among fumblers. But I saw no hope in any face, and I felt none. Where among the fifty millions of these islands and within a dozen hours were we to lay hands on the three cleverest rogues in Europe?

Then suddenly I had an inspiration.

'Where is Scudder's book?' I cried to Sir Walter. 'Quick, man, I remember something in it.'

He unlocked the door of a bureau and gave it to me.

I found the place. THIRTY-NINE STEPS, I read, and again, THIRTY-NINE STEPS—I COUNTED THEM—HIGH TIDE 10.17 P.M.

The Admiralty man was looking at me as if he thought I had gone mad.

'Don't you see it's a clue,' I shouted. 'Scudder knew where these fellows laired—he knew where they were going to leave the country, though he kept the name to himself. Tomorrow was the day, and it was some place where high tide was at 10.17.'

'They may have gone tonight,' someone said.

'Not they. They have their own snug secret way, and they won't be hurried. I know Germans, and they are mad about working to a plan. Where the devil can I get a book of Tide Tables?'

Whittaker brightened up. 'It's a chance,' he said. 'Let's go over to the Admiralty.'

We got into two of the waiting motor-cars—all but Sir Walter, who went off to Scotland Yard—to 'mobilize MacGillivray', so he said. We marched through empty corridors and big bare chambers where the charwomen were busy, till we reached a little room lined with books and maps. A resident clerk was unearthed, who presently fetched from the library the Admiralty Tide Tables. I sat at the desk and the others stood round, for somehow or other I had got charge of this expedition.

It was no good. There were hundreds of entries, and so far as I could see 10.17 might cover fifty places. We had to find some way of narrowing the possibilities.

I took my head in my hands and thought. There must be some way of reading this riddle. What did Scudder mean by steps? I thought of dock steps, but if he had meant that I didn't think he would have mentioned the number. It must be some place where there were several staircases, and one marked out from the others by having thirty-nine steps.

Then I had a sudden thought, and hunted up all the steamer sailings. There was no boat which left for the Continent at 10.17 p.m.

Why was high tide so important? If it was a harbour it must be some little place where the tide mattered, or else it was a heavy-draught boat. But there was no regular steamer sailing at that hour, and somehow I didn't think they would travel by a big boat from a regular harbour. So it must be some little harbour where the tide was important, or perhaps no harbour at all.

But if it was a little port I couldn't see what the steps signified. There were no sets of staircases on any harbour that I had ever seen. It must be some place which a particular staircase identified, and where the tide was full at 10.17. On the whole it seemed to me that the place must be a bit of open coast. But the staircases kept puzzling me.

Then I went back to wider considerations. Whereabouts would a man be likely to leave for Germany, a man in a hurry, who wanted a speedy and a secret passage? Not from any of the big harbours. And not from the Channel or the West Coast or Scotland, for, remember, he was starting from London. I measured the distance on the map, and tried to put myself in the enemy's shoes. I should try for Ostend or Antwerp or Rotterdam, and I should sail from somewhere on the East Coast between Cromer and Dover.

All this was very loose guessing, and I don't pretend it was ingenious or scientific. I wasn't any kind of Sherlock Holmes. But I have always fancied I had a kind of instinct about questions like this. I don't know if I can explain myself, but I used to use my brains as far as they went, and after they came to a blank wall I guessed, and I usually found my guesses pretty right.

So I set out all my conclusions on a bit of Admiralty paper. They ran like this:

FAIRLY CERTAIN

(1) Place where there are several sets of stairs; one that matters distinguished by having thirty-nine steps.

(2) Full tide at 10.17 p.m. Leaving shore only possible at full tide.

(3) Steps not dock steps, and so place probably not harbour.

(4) No regular night steamer at 10.17. Means of transport must be tramp (unlikely), yacht, or fishing-boat.

There my reasoning stopped. I made another list, which I headed 'Guessed', but I was just as sure of the one as the other.

GUESSED

(1) Place not harbour but open coast.

(2) Boat small—trawler, yacht, or launch.

(3) Place somewhere on East Coast between Cromer and Dover.

It struck me as odd that I should be sitting at that desk with a Cabinet Minister, a Field-Marshal, two high Government officials, and a French General watching me, while from the scribble of a dead man I was trying to drag a secret which meant life or death for us.

Sir Walter had joined us, and presently MacGillivray arrived. He had sent out instructions to watch the ports and railway stations for the three men whom I had described to Sir Walter. Not that he or anybody else thought that that would do much good.

'Here's the most I can make of it,' I said. 'We have got to find a place where there are several staircases down to the beach, one of which has thirty-nine steps. I think it's a piece of open coast with biggish cliffs, somewhere between the Wash and the Channel. Also it's a place where full tide is at 10.17 tomorrow night.'

Then an idea struck me. 'Is there no Inspector of Coastguards or some fellow like that who knows the East Coast?'

Whittaker said there was, and that he lived in Clapham. He went off in a car to fetch him, and the rest of us sat about the little room and talked of anything that came into our heads. I lit a pipe and went over the whole thing again till my brain grew weary.

About one in the morning the coastguard man arrived. He was a fine old fellow, with the look of a naval officer, and was desperately respectful to the company. I left the War Minister to cross-examine him, for I felt he would think it cheek in me to talk.

'We want you to tell us the places you know on the East Coast where there are cliffs, and where several sets of steps run down to the beach.'

He thought for a bit. 'What kind of steps do you mean, Sir? There are plenty of places with roads cut down through the cliffs, and most roads have a step or two in them. Or do you mean regular staircases—all steps, so to speak?'

Sir Arthur looked towards me. 'We mean regular staircases,' I said.

He reflected a minute or two. 'I don't know that I can think of any. Wait a second. There's a place in Norfolk—Brattlesham—beside a golf-course, where there are a couple of staircases, to let the gentlemen get a lost ball.'

'That's not it,' I said.

'Then there are plenty of Marine Parades, if that's what you mean. Every seaside resort has them.'

I shook my head. 'It's got to be more retired than that,' I said.

'Well, gentlemen, I can't think of anywhere else. Of course, there's the Ruff—'

'What's that?' I asked.

'The big chalk headland in Kent, close to Bradgate. It's got a lot of villas on the top, and some of the houses have staircases down to a private beach. It's a very high-toned sort of place, and the residents there like to keep by themselves.'

I tore open the Tide Tables and found Bradgate. High tide there was at 10.17 P.m. on the 15th of June.

'We're on the scent at last,' I cried excitedly. 'How can I find out what is the tide at the Ruff?'

'I can tell you that, Sir,' said the coastguard man. 'I once was lent a house there in this very month, and I used to go out at night to the deep-sea fishing. The tide's ten minutes before Bradgate.'

I closed the book and looked round at the company.

'If one of those staircases has thirty-nine steps we have solved the mystery, gentlemen,' I said. 'I want the loan of your car, Sir Walter, and a map of the roads. If Mr MacGillivray will spare me ten minutes, I think we can prepare something for tomorrow.'

It was ridiculous in me to take charge of the business like this, but they didn't seem to mind, and after all I had been in the show from the start. Besides, I was used to rough jobs, and these eminent gentlemen were too clever not to see it. It was General Royer who gave me my commission. 'I for one,' he said, 'am content to leave the matter in Mr Hannay's hands.'

By half-past three I was tearing past the moonlit hedgerows of Kent, with MacGillivray's best man on the seat beside me.

CHAPTER TEN

Various Parties Converging on the Sea

A pink and blue June morning found me at Bradgate looking from the Griffin Hotel over a smooth sea to the lightship on the Cock sands which seemed the size of a bell-buoy. A couple of miles farther south and much nearer the shore a small destroyer was anchored. Scaife, MacGillivray's man, who had been in the Navy, knew the boat, and told me her name and her commander's, so I sent off a wire to Sir Walter.

After breakfast Scaife got from a house-agent a key for the gates of the staircases on the Ruff. I walked with him along the sands, and sat down in a nook of the cliffs while he investigated the half-dozen of them. I didn't want to be seen, but the place at this hour was quite deserted, and all the time I was on that beach I saw nothing but the sea-gulls.

It took him more than an hour to do the job, and when I saw him coming towards me, conning a bit of paper, I can tell you my heart was in my mouth. Everything depended, you see, on my guess proving right.

He read aloud the number of steps in the different stairs. 'Thirty-four, thirty-five, thirty-nine, forty-two, forty-seven,' and 'twenty-one' where the cliffs grew lower. I almost got up and shouted.

We hurried back to the town and sent a wire to MacGillivray. I wanted half a dozen men, and I directed them to divide themselves among different specified hotels. Then Scaife set out to prospect the house at the head of the thirty-nine steps.

He came back with news that both puzzled and reassured me. The house was called Trafalgar Lodge, and belonged to an old gentleman called Appleton—a retired stockbroker, the house-agent said. Mr Appleton was there a good deal in the summer time, and was in residence now—had been for the better part of a week. Scaife could pick up very little information about him, except that he was a decent old fellow, who paid his bills regularly, and was always good for a fiver for a local charity. Then Scaife seemed to have penetrated to the back door of the house, pretending he was an agent for sewing-machines. Only three servants were kept, a cook, a parlour-maid, and a housemaid, and they were just the sort that you would find in a respectable middle-class household. The cook was not the gossiping kind, and had pretty soon shut the door in his face, but Scaife said he was positive she knew nothing. Next door there was a new house building which would give good cover for observation, and the villa on the other side was to let, and its garden was rough and shrubby.

I borrowed Scaife's telescope, and before lunch went for a walk along the Ruff. I kept well behind the rows of villas, and found a good observation point on the edge of the golf-course. There I had a view of the line of turf along the cliff top, with seats placed at intervals, and the little square plots, railed in and planted with bushes, whence the staircases descended to the beach. I saw Trafalgar Lodge very plainly, a red-brick villa with a veranda, a tennis lawn behind, and in front the ordinary seaside flower-garden full of marguerites and scraggy geraniums. There was a flagstaff from which an enormous Union Jack hung limply in the still air.

Presently I observed someone leave the house and saunter along the cliff. When I got my glasses on him I saw it was an old man, wearing white flannel trousers, a blue serge jacket, and a straw hat. He carried field-glasses and a newspaper, and sat down on one of the iron seats and began to read. Sometimes he would lay down the paper and turn his glasses on the sea. He looked for a long time at the destroyer. I watched him for half an hour, till he got up and went back to the house for his luncheon, when I returned to the hotel for mine.

I wasn't feeling very confident. This decent common-place dwelling was not what I had expected. The man might be the bald archaeologist of that horrible moorland farm, or he might not. He was exactly the kind of satisfied old bird you will find in every suburb and every holiday place. If you wanted a type of the perfectly harmless person you would probably pitch on that.

But after lunch, as I sat in the hotel porch, I perked up, for I saw the thing I had hoped for and had dreaded to miss. A yacht came up from the south and dropped anchor pretty well opposite the Ruff. She seemed about a hundred and fifty tons, and I saw she belonged to the Squadron from the white ensign. So Scaife and I went down to the harbour and hired a boatman for an afternoon's fishing.

I spent a warm and peaceful afternoon. We caught between us about twenty pounds of cod and lythe, and out in that dancing blue sea I took a cheerier view of things. Above the white cliffs of the Ruff I saw the green and red of the villas, and especially the great flagstaff of Trafalgar Lodge. About four o'clock, when we had fished enough, I made the boatman row us round the yacht, which lay like a delicate white bird, ready at a moment to flee. Scaife said she must be a fast boat for her build, and that she was pretty heavily engined.

Her name was the ARIADNE, as I discovered from the cap of one of the men who was polishing brasswork. I spoke to him, and got an answer in the soft dialect of Essex. Another hand that came along passed me the time of day in an unmistakable English tongue. Our boatman had an argument with one of them about the weather, and for a few minutes we lay on our oars close to the starboard bow.

Then the men suddenly disregarded us and bent their heads to their work as an officer came along the deck. He was a pleasant, clean-looking young fellow, and he put a question to us about our fishing in very good English. But there could be no doubt about him. His close-cropped head and the cut of his collar and tie never came out of England.

That did something to reassure me, but as we rowed back to Bradgate my obstinate doubts would not be dismissed. The thing that worried me was the reflection that my enemies knew that I had got my knowledge from Scudder, and it was Scudder who had given me the clue to this place. If they knew that Scudder had this clue, would they not be certain to change their plans? Too much depended on their success for them to take any risks. The whole question was how much they understood about Scudder's knowledge. I had talked confidently last night about Germans always sticking to a scheme, but if they had any suspicions that I was on their track they would be fools not to cover it. I wondered if the man last night had seen that I recognized him. Somehow I did not think he had, and to that I had clung. But the whole business had never seemed so difficult as that afternoon when by all calculations I should have been rejoicing in assured success.

In the hotel I met the commander of the destroyer, to whom Scaife introduced me, and with whom I had a few words. Then I thought I would put in an hour or two watching Trafalgar Lodge.

I found a place farther up the hill, in the garden of an empty house. From there I had a full view of the court, on which two figures were having a game of tennis. One was the old man, whom I had already seen;

the other was a younger fellow, wearing some club colours in the scarf round his middle. They played with tremendous zest, like two city gents who wanted hard exercise to open their pores. You couldn't conceive a more innocent spectacle. They shouted and laughed and stopped for drinks, when a maid brought out two tankards on a salver. I rubbed my eyes and asked myself if I was not the most immortal fool on earth. Mystery and darkness had hung about the men who hunted me over the Scotch moor in aeroplane and motor-car, and notably about that infernal antiquarian. It was easy enough to connect those folk with the knife that pinned Scudder to the floor, and with fell designs on the world's peace. But here were two guileless citizens taking their innocuous exercise, and soon about to go indoors to a humdrum dinner, where they would talk of market prices and the last cricket scores and the gossip of their native Surbiton. I had been making a net to catch vultures and falcons, and lo and behold! two plump thrushes had blundered into it.

Presently a third figure arrived, a young man on a bicycle, with a bag of golf-clubs slung on his back. He strolled round to the tennis lawn and was welcomed riotously by the players. Evidently they were chaffing him, and their chaff sounded horribly English. Then the plump man, mopping his brow with a silk handkerchief, announced that he must have a tub. I heard his very words—'I've got into a proper lather,' he said. 'This will bring down my weight and my handicap, Bob. I'll take you on tomorrow and give you a stroke a hole.' You couldn't find anything much more English than that.

They all went into the house, and left me feeling a precious idiot. I had been barking up the wrong tree this time. These men might be acting; but if they were, where was their audience? They didn't know I was sitting thirty yards off in a rhododendron. It was simply impossible to believe that these three hearty fellows were anything but what they seemed—three ordinary, game-playing, suburban Englishmen, wearisome, if you like, but sordidly innocent.

And yet there were three of them; and one was old, and one was plump, and one was lean and dark; and their house chimed in with Scudder's notes; and half a mile off was lying a steam yacht with at least one German officer. I thought of Karolides lying dead and all Europe trembling on the edge of earthquake, and the men I had left behind me in London who were waiting anxiously for the events of the next hours. There was no doubt that hell was afoot somewhere. The Black Stone had won, and if it survived this June night would bank its winnings.

There seemed only one thing to do—go forward as if I had no doubts, and if I was going to make a fool of myself to do it handsomely. Never in my life have I faced a job with greater disinclination. I would rather in my then mind have walked into a den of anarchists, each with his Browning handy, or faced a charging lion with a popgun, than enter that happy home of three cheerful Englishmen and tell them that their game was up. How they would laugh at me!

But suddenly I remembered a thing I once heard in Rhodesia from old Peter Pienaar. I have quoted Peter already in this narrative. He was the best scout I ever knew, and before he had turned respectable he had been pretty often on the windy side of the law, when he had been wanted badly by the authorities. Peter once discussed with me the question of disguises, and he had a theory which struck me at the time. He said, barring absolute certainties like fingerprints, mere physical traits were very little use for identification if the fugitive really knew his business. He laughed at things like dyed hair and false beards and such childish follies. The only thing that mattered was what Peter called 'atmosphere'.

If a man could get into perfectly different surroundings from those in which he had been first observed, and—this is the important part—really play up to these surroundings and behave as if he had never been out of them, he would puzzle the cleverest detectives on earth. And he used to tell a story of how he once borrowed a black coat and went to church and shared the same hymn-book with the man that was looking for him. If that man had seen him in decent company before he would have recognized him; but he had only seen him snuffing the lights in a public-house with a revolver.

The recollection of Peter's talk gave me the first real comfort that I had had that day. Peter had been a wise old bird, and these fellows I was after were about the pick of the aviary. What if they were playing Peter's game? A fool tries to look different: a clever man looks the same and is different.

Again, there was that other maxim of Peter's which had helped me when I had been a roadman. 'If you are playing a part, you will never keep it up unless you convince yourself that you are it.' That would explain the game of tennis. Those chaps didn't need to act, they just turned a handle and passed into another life, which came as naturally to them as the first. It sounds a platitude, but Peter used to say that it was the big secret of all the famous criminals.

It was now getting on for eight o'clock, and I went back and saw Scaife to give him his instructions. I arranged with him how to place his men, and then I went for a walk, for I didn't feel up to any dinner. I went round the deserted golf-course, and then to a point on the cliffs farther north beyond the line of the villas.

On the little trim newly-made roads I met people in flannels coming back from tennis and the beach, and a coastguard from the wireless station, and donkeys and pierrots padding homewards. Out at sea in the blue dusk I saw lights appear on the ARIADNE and on the destroyer away to the south, and beyond the Cock sands the bigger lights of steamers making for the Thames. The whole scene was so peaceful and ordinary that I got more dashed in spirits every second. It took all my resolution to stroll towards Trafalgar Lodge about half-past nine.

On the way I got a piece of solid comfort from the sight of a greyhound that was swinging along at a nursemaid's heels. He reminded me of a dog I used to have in Rhodesia, and of the time when I took him hunting with me in the Pali hills. We were after rhebok, the dun kind, and I recollected how we had followed one beast, and both he and I had clean lost it. A greyhound works by sight, and my eyes are good enough, but that buck simply leaked out of the landscape. Afterwards I found out how it managed it. Against the grey rock of the kopjes it showed no more than a crow against a thundercloud. It didn't need to run away; all it had to do was to stand still and melt into the background.

Suddenly as these memories chased across my brain I thought of my present case and applied the moral. The Black Stone didn't need to bolt. They were quietly absorbed into the landscape. I was on the right track, and I jammed that down in my mind and vowed never to forget it. The last word was with Peter Pienaar.

Scaife's men would be posted now, but there was no sign of a soul. The house stood as open as a market-place for anybody to observe. A three-foot railing separated it from the cliff road; the windows on the ground-floor were all open, and shaded lights and the low sound of voices revealed where the occupants were finishing dinner. Everything was as public and above-board as a charity bazaar. Feeling the greatest fool on earth, I opened the gate and rang the bell.

A man of my sort, who has travelled about the world in rough places, gets on perfectly well with two classes, what you may call the upper and the lower. He understands them and they understand him. I was at home with herds and tramps and roadmen, and I was sufficiently at my ease with people like Sir Walter and the men I had met the night before. I can't explain why, but it is a fact. But what fellows like me don't understand is the great comfortable, satisfied middle-class world, the folk that live in villas and suburbs. He doesn't know how they look at things, he doesn't understand their conventions, and he is as shy of them as of a black mamba. When a trim parlour-maid opened the door, I could hardly find my voice.

I asked for Mr Appleton, and was ushered in. My plan had been to walk straight into the dining-room, and by a sudden appearance wake in the men that start of recognition which would confirm my theory. But when I found myself in that neat hall the place mastered me. There were the golf-clubs and tennis-rackets, the straw hats and caps, the rows of gloves, the sheaf of walking-sticks, which you will find in ten thousand British homes. A stack of neatly folded coats and waterproofs covered the top of an old oak chest; there was a grandfather clock ticking; and some polished brass warming-pans on the walls, and a barometer, and a print of Chiltern winning the St Leger. The place was as orthodox as an Anglican church. When the maid asked me for my name I gave it automatically, and was shown into the smoking-room, on the right side of the hall.

That room was even worse. I hadn't time to examine it, but I could see some framed group photographs above the mantelpiece, and I could have sworn they were English public school or college. I had only one glance, for I managed to pull myself together and go after the maid. But I was too late. She had already entered the dining-room and given my name to her master, and I had missed the chance of seeing how the three took it.

When I walked into the room the old man at the head of the table had risen and turned round to meet me. He was in evening dress—a short coat and black tie, as was the other, whom I called in my own mind the plump one. The third, the dark fellow, wore a blue serge suit and a soft white collar, and the colours of some club or school.

The old man's manner was perfect. 'Mr Hannay?' he said hesitatingly. 'Did you wish to see me? One moment, you fellows, and I'll rejoin you. We had better go to the smoking-room.'

Though I hadn't an ounce of confidence in me, I forced myself to play the game. I pulled up a chair and sat down on it.

'I think we have met before,' I said, 'and I guess you know my business.'

The light in the room was dim, but so far as I could see their faces, they played the part of mystification very well.

'Maybe, maybe,' said the old man. 'I haven't a very good memory, but I'm afraid you must tell me your errand, Sir, for I really don't know it.'

'Well, then,' I said, and all the time I seemed to myself to be talking pure foolishness—'I have come to tell you that the game's up. I have a warrant for the arrest of you three gentlemen.'

'Arrest,' said the old man, and he looked really shocked. 'Arrest! Good God, what for?'

'For the murder of Franklin Scudder in London on the 23rd day of last month.'

'I never heard the name before,' said the old man in a dazed voice.

One of the others spoke up. 'That was the Portland Place murder. I read about it. Good heavens, you must be mad, Sir! Where do you come from?'

'Scotland Yard,' I said.

After that for a minute there was utter silence. The old man was staring at his plate and fumbling with a nut, the very model of innocent bewilderment.

Then the plump one spoke up. He stammered a little, like a man picking his words.

'Don't get flustered, uncle,' he said. 'It is all a ridiculous mistake; but these things happen sometimes, and we can easily set it right. It won't be hard to prove our innocence. I can show that I was out of the country on the 23rd of May, and Bob was in a nursing home. You were in London, but you can explain what you were doing.'

'Right, Percy! Of course that's easy enough. The 23rd! That was the day after Agatha's wedding. Let me see. What was I doing? I came up in the morning from Woking, and lunched at the club with Charlie Symons. Then—oh yes, I dined with the Fishmongers. I remember, for the punch didn't agree with me, and I was seedy next morning. Hang it all, there's the cigar-box I brought back from the dinner.' He pointed to an object on the table, and laughed nervously.

'I think, Sir,' said the young man, addressing me respectfully, 'you will see you are mistaken. We want to assist the law like all Englishmen, and we don't want Scotland Yard to be making fools of themselves. That's so, uncle?'

'Certainly, Bob.' The old fellow seemed to be recovering his voice. 'Certainly, we'll do anything in our power to assist the authorities. But—but this is a bit too much. I can't get over it.'

'How Nellie will chuckle,' said the plump man. 'She always said that you would die of boredom because nothing ever happened to you. And now you've got it thick and strong,' and he began to laugh very pleasantly.

'By Jove, yes. Just think of it! What a story to tell at the club. Really, Mr Hannay, I suppose I should be angry, to show my innocence, but it's too funny! I almost forgive you the fright you gave me! You looked so glum, I thought I might have been walking in my sleep and killing people.'

It couldn't be acting, it was too confoundedly genuine. My heart went into my boots, and my first impulse was to apologize and clear out. But I told myself I must see it through, even though I was to be the laughing-stock of Britain. The light from the dinner-table candlesticks was not very good, and to cover my confusion I got up, walked to the door and switched on the electric light. The sudden glare made them blink, and I stood scanning the three faces.

Well, I made nothing of it. One was old and bald, one was stout, one was dark and thin. There was nothing in their appearance to prevent them being the three who had hunted me in Scotland, but there was nothing to identify them. I simply can't explain why I who, as a roadman, had looked into two pairs of eyes, and as Ned Ainslie into another pair, why I, who have a good memory and reasonable powers of observation, could find no satisfaction. They seemed exactly what they professed to be, and I could not have sworn to one of them.

There in that pleasant dining-room, with etchings on the walls, and a picture of an old lady in a bib above the mantelpiece, I could see nothing to connect them with the moorland desperadoes. There was a silver cigarette-box beside me, and I saw that it had been won by Percival Appleton, Esq., of the St Bede's Club, in a golf tournament. I had to keep a firm hold of Peter Pienaar to prevent myself bolting out of that house.

'Well,' said the old man politely, 'are you reassured by your scrutiny, Sir?'

I couldn't find a word.

'I hope you'll find it consistent with your duty to drop this ridiculous business. I make no complaint, but you'll see how annoying it must be to respectable people.'

I shook my head.

'O Lord,' said the young man. 'This is a bit too thick!'

'Do you propose to march us off to the police station?' asked the plump one. 'That might be the best way out of it, but I suppose you won't be content with the local branch. I have the right to ask to see your warrant, but I don't wish to cast any aspersions upon you. You are only doing your duty. But you'll admit it's horribly awkward. What do you propose to do?'

There was nothing to do except to call in my men and have them arrested, or to confess my blunder and clear out. I felt mesmerized by the whole place, by the air of obvious innocence—not innocence merely, but frank honest bewilderment and concern in the three faces.

'Oh, Peter Pienaar,' I groaned inwardly, and for a moment I was very near damning myself for a fool and asking their pardon.

'Meantime I vote we have a game of bridge,' said the plump one. 'It will give Mr Hannay time to think over things, and you know we have been wanting a fourth player. Do you play, Sir?'

I accepted as if it had been an ordinary invitation at the club. The whole business had mesmerized me. We went into the smoking-room where a card-table was set out, and I was offered things to smoke and drink. I took my place at the table in a kind of dream. The window was open and the moon was flooding the cliffs and sea with a great tide of yellow light. There was moonshine, too, in my head. The three had recovered their composure, and were talking easily—just the kind of slangy talk you will hear in any golf club-house. I must have cut a rum figure, sitting there knitting my brows with my eyes wandering.

My partner was the young dark one. I play a fair hand at bridge, but I must have been rank bad that night. They saw that they had got me puzzled, and that put them more than ever at their ease. I kept looking at their faces, but they conveyed nothing to me. It was not that they looked different; they were different. I clung desperately to the words of Peter Pienaar.

Then something awoke me.

The old man laid down his hand to light a cigar. He didn't pick it up at once, but sat back for a moment in his chair, with his fingers tapping on his knees.

It was the movement I remembered when I had stood before him in the moorland farm, with the pistols of his servants behind me.

A little thing, lasting only a second, and the odds were a thousand to one that I might have had my eyes on my cards at the time and missed it. But I didn't, and, in a flash, the air seemed to clear. Some shadow lifted from my brain, and I was looking at the three men with full and absolute recognition.

The clock on the mantelpiece struck ten o'clock.

The three faces seemed to change before my eyes and reveal their secrets. The young one was the murderer. Now I saw cruelty and ruthlessness, where before I had only seen good-humour. His knife, I made certain, had skewered Scudder to the floor. His kind had put the bullet in Karolides.

The plump man's features seemed to dislimn, and form again, as I looked at them. He hadn't a face, only a hundred masks that he could assume when he pleased. That chap must have been a superb actor. Perhaps he had been Lord Alloa of the night before; perhaps not; it didn't matter. I wondered if he was the fellow who had first tracked Scudder, and left his card on him. Scudder had said he lisped, and I could imagine how the adoption of a lisp might add terror.

But the old man was the pick of the lot. He was sheer brain, icy, cool, calculating, as ruthless as a steam hammer. Now that my eyes were opened I wondered where I had seen the benevolence. His jaw was like chilled steel, and his eyes had the inhuman luminosity of a bird's. I went on playing, and every second a greater hate welled up in my heart. It almost choked me, and I couldn't answer when my partner spoke. Only a little longer could I endure their company.

'Whew! Bob! Look at the time,' said the old man. 'You'd better think about catching your train. Bob's got to go to town tonight,' he added, turning to me. The voice rang now as false as hell. I looked at the clock, and it was nearly half-past ten.

'I am afraid he must put off his journey,' I said.

'Oh, damn,' said the young man. 'I thought you had dropped that rot. I've simply got to go. You can have my address, and I'll give any security you like.'

'No,' I said, 'you must stay.'

At that I think they must have realized that the game was desperate. Their only chance had been to convince me that I was playing the fool, and that had failed. But the old man spoke again.

'I'll go bail for my nephew. That ought to content you, Mr Hannay.' Was it fancy, or did I detect some halt in the smoothness of that voice?

There must have been, for as I glanced at him, his eyelids fell in that hawk-like hood which fear had stamped on my memory.

I blew my whistle.

In an instant the lights were out. A pair of strong arms gripped me round the waist, covering the pockets in which a man might be expected to carry a pistol.

'SCHNELL, FRANZ,' cried a voice, 'DAS BOOT, DAS BOOT!' As it spoke I saw two of my fellows emerge on the moonlit lawn.

The young dark man leapt for the window, was through it, and over the low fence before a hand could touch him. I grappled the old chap, and the room seemed to fill with figures. I saw the plump one collared, but my eyes were all for the out-of-doors, where Franz sped on over the road towards the railed entrance to the beach stairs. One man followed him, but he had no chance. The gate of the stairs locked behind the fugitive, and I stood staring, with my hands on the old boy's throat, for such a time as a man might take to descend those steps to the sea.

Suddenly my prisoner broke from me and flung himself on the wall. There was a click as if a lever had been pulled. Then came a low rumbling far, far below the ground, and through the window I saw a cloud of chalky dust pouring out of the shaft of the stairway.

Someone switched on the light.

The old man was looking at me with blazing eyes.

'He is safe,' he cried. 'You cannot follow in time ... He is gone ... He has triumphed ... DER SCHWARZE STEIN IST IN DER SIEGESKRONE.'

There was more in those eyes than any common triumph. They had been hooded like a bird of prey, and now they flamed with a hawk's pride. A white fanatic heat burned in them, and I realized for the first time the terrible thing I had been up against. This man was more than a spy; in his foul way he had been a patriot.

As the handcuffs clinked on his wrists I said my last word to him.

'I hope Franz will bear his triumph well. I ought to tell you that the ARIADNE for the last hour has been in our hands.'

Three weeks later, as all the world knows, we went to war. I joined the New Army the first week, and owing to my Matabele experience got a captain's commission straight off. But I had done my best service, I think, before I put on khaki.

GREENMANTLE

By

JOHN BUCHAN

To
Caroline Grosvenor

During the past year, in the intervals of an active life, I have amused myself with constructing this tale. It has been scribbled in every kind of odd place and moment—in England and abroad, during long journeys, in half-hours between graver tasks; and it bears, I fear, the mark of its gipsy begetting. But it has amused me to write, and I shall be well repaid if it amuses you—and a few others—to read.

Let no man or woman call its events improbable. The war has driven that word from our vocabulary, and melodrama has become the prosiest realism. Things unimagined before happen daily to our friends by sea and land. The one chance in a thousand is habitually taken, and as often as not succeeds. Coincidence, like some new Briareus, stretches a hundred long arms hourly across the earth. Some day, when the full history is written—sober history with ample documents—the poor romancer will give up business and fall to reading Miss Austen in a hermitage.

The characters of the tale, if you think hard, you will recall. Sandy you know well. That great spirit was last heard of at Basra, where he occupies the post that once was Harry Bullivant's. Richard Hannay is where he longed to be, commanding his battalion on the ugliest bit of front in the West. Mr John S. Blenkiron, full of honour and wholly cured of dyspepsia, has returned to the States, after vainly endeavouring to take Peter with him. As for Peter, he has attained the height of his ambition. He has shaved his beard and joined the Flying Corps.

CHAPTER ONE

A Mission is Proposed

I had just finished breakfast and was filling my pipe when I got Bullivant's telegram. It was at Furling, the big country house in Hampshire where I had come to convalesce after Loos, and Sandy, who was in the same case, was hunting for the marmalade. I flung him the flimsy with the blue strip pasted down on it, and he whistled.

'Hullo, Dick, you've got the battalion. Or maybe it's a staff billet. You'll be a blighted brass-hat, coming it heavy over the hard-working regimental officer. And to think of the language you've wasted on brass-hats in your time!'

I sat and thought for a bit, for the name 'Bullivant' carried me back eighteen months to the hot summer before the war. I had not seen the man since, though I had read about him in the papers. For more than a year I had been a busy battalion officer, with no other thought than to hammer a lot of raw stuff into good soldiers. I had succeeded pretty well, and there was no prouder man on earth than Richard Hannay when he took his Lennox Highlanders over the parapets on that glorious and bloody 25th day of September. Loos was no picnic, and we had had some ugly bits of scrapping before that, but the worst bit of the campaign I had seen was a tea-party to the show I had been in with Bullivant before the war started. [Major Hannay's narrative of this affair has been published under the title of *The Thirty-nine Steps.*]

The sight of his name on a telegram form seemed to change all my outlook on life. I had been hoping for the command of the battalion, and looking forward to being in at the finish with Brother Boche. But this message jerked my thoughts on to a new road. There might be other things in the war than straightforward fighting. Why on earth should the Foreign Office want to see an obscure Major of the New Army, and want to see him in double-quick time?

'I'm going up to town by the ten train,' I announced; 'I'll be back in time for dinner.'

'Try my tailor,' said Sandy. 'He's got a very nice taste in red tabs. You can use my name.'

An idea struck me. 'You're pretty well all right now. If I wire for you, will you pack your own kit and mine and join me?'

'Right-o! I'll accept a job on your staff if they give you a corps. If so be as you come down tonight, be a good chap and bring a barrel of oysters from Sweeting's.'

I travelled up to London in a regular November drizzle, which cleared up about Wimbledon to watery sunshine. I never could stand London during the war. It seemed to have lost its bearings and broken out into all manner of badges and uniforms which did not fit in with my notion of it. One felt the war more in its streets than in the field, or rather one felt the confusion of war without feeling the purpose. I dare say it was all right; but since August 1914 I never spent a day in town without coming home depressed to my boots.

I took a taxi and drove straight to the Foreign Office. Sir Walter did not keep me waiting long. But when his secretary took me to his room I would not have recognized the man I had known eighteen months before.

His big frame seemed to have dropped flesh and there was a stoop in the square shoulders. His face had lost its rosiness and was red in patches, like that of a man who gets too little fresh air. His hair was much greyer and very thin about the temples, and there were lines of overwork below the eyes. But the eyes were the same as before, keen and kindly and shrewd, and there was no change in the firm set of the jaw.

'We must on no account be disturbed for the next hour,' he told his secretary. When the young man had gone he went across to both doors and turned the keys in them.

'Well, Major Hannay,' he said, flinging himself into a chair beside the fire. 'How do you like soldiering?'

'Right enough,' I said, 'though this isn't just the kind of war I would have picked myself. It's a comfortless, bloody business. But we've got the measure of the old Boche now, and it's dogged as does it. I count on getting back to the front in a week or two.'

'Will you get the battalion?' he asked. He seemed to have followed my doings pretty closely.

'I believe I've a good chance. I'm not in this show for honour and glory, though. I want to do the best I can, but I wish to heaven it was over. All I think of is coming out of it with a whole skin.'

He laughed. 'You do yourself an injustice. What about the forward observation post at the Lone Tree? You forgot about the whole skin then.'

I felt myself getting red. 'That was all rot,' I said, 'and I can't think who told you about it. I hated the job, but I had to do it to prevent my subalterns going to glory. They were a lot of fire-eating young lunatics. If I had sent one of them he'd have gone on his knees to Providence and asked for trouble.'

Sir Walter was still grinning.

'I'm not questioning your caution. You have the rudiments of it, or our friends of the Black Stone would have gathered you in at our last merry meeting. I would question it as little as your courage. What exercises my mind is whether it is best employed in the trenches.'

'Is the War Office dissatisfied with me?' I asked sharply.

'They are profoundly satisfied. They propose to give you command of your battalion. Presently, if you escape a stray bullet, you will no doubt be a Brigadier. It is a wonderful war for youth and brains. But ... I take it you are in this business to serve your country, Hannay?'

'I reckon I am,' I said. 'I am certainly not in it for my health.'

He looked at my leg, where the doctors had dug out the shrapnel fragments, and smiled quizzically.

'Pretty fit again?' he asked.

'Tough as a sjambok. I thrive on the racket and eat and sleep like a schoolboy.'

He got up and stood with his back to the fire, his eyes staring abstractedly out of the window at the wintry park.

'It is a great game, and you are the man for it, no doubt. But there are others who can play it, for soldiering today asks for the average rather than the exception in human nature. It is like a big machine where the parts are standardized. You are fighting, not because you are short of a job, but because you want to help England. How if you could help her better than by commanding a battalion—or a brigade—or, if it comes to that, a division? How if there is a thing which you alone can do? Not some *embusque* business in an office, but a thing compared to which your fight at Loos was a Sunday-school picnic. You are not afraid of danger? Well, in this job you would not be fighting with an army around you, but alone. You are fond of tackling difficulties? Well, I can give you a task which will try all your powers. Have you anything to say?'

My heart was beginning to thump uncomfortably. Sir Walter was not the man to pitch a case too high.

'I am a soldier,' I said, 'and under orders.'

'True; but what I am about to propose does not come by any conceivable stretch within the scope of a soldier's duties. I shall perfectly understand if you decline. You will be acting as I should act myself—as any sane man would. I would not press you for worlds. If you wish it, I will not even make the proposal, but let you go here and now, and wish you good luck with your battalion. I do not wish to perplex a good soldier with impossible decisions.'

This piqued me and put me on my mettle.

'I am not going to run away before the guns fire. Let me hear what you propose.'

Sir Walter crossed to a cabinet, unlocked it with a key from his chain, and took a piece of paper from a drawer. It looked like an ordinary half-sheet of note-paper.

'I take it,' he said, 'that your travels have not extended to the East.'

'No,' I said, 'barring a shooting trip in East Africa.'

'Have you by any chance been following the present campaign there?'

'I've read the newspapers pretty regularly since I went to hospital. I've got some pals in the Mesopotamia show, and of course I'm keen to know what is going to happen at Gallipoli and Salonika. I gather that Egypt is pretty safe.'

'If you will give me your attention for ten minutes I will supplement your newspaper reading.'

Sir Walter lay back in an arm-chair and spoke to the ceiling. It was the best story, the clearest and the fullest, I had ever got of any bit of the war. He told me just how and why and when Turkey had left the rails. I heard about her grievances over our seizure of her ironclads, of the mischief the coming of the *Goeben* had wrought, of

Enver and his precious Committee and the way they had got a cinch on the old Turk. When he had spoken for a bit, he began to question me.

'You are an intelligent fellow, and you will ask how a Polish adventurer, meaning Enver, and a collection of Jews and gipsies should have got control of a proud race. The ordinary man will tell you that it was German organization backed up with German money and German arms. You will inquire again how, since Turkey is primarily a religious power, Islam has played so small a part in it all. The Sheikh-ul-Islam is neglected, and though the Kaiser proclaims a Holy War and calls himself Hadji Mohammed Guilliamo, and says the Hohenzollerns are descended from the Prophet, that seems to have fallen pretty flat. The ordinary man again will answer that Islam in Turkey is becoming a back number, and that Krupp guns are the new gods. Yet—I don't know. I do not quite believe in Islam becoming a back number.'

'Look at it in another way,' he went on. 'If it were Enver and Germany alone dragging Turkey into a European war for purposes that no Turk cared a rush about, we might expect to find the regular army obedient, and Constantinople. But in the provinces, where Islam is strong, there would be trouble. Many of us counted on that. But we have been disappointed. The Syrian army is as fanatical as the hordes of the Mahdi. The Senussi have taken a hand in the game. The Persian Moslems are threatening trouble. There is a dry wind blowing through the East, and the parched grasses wait the spark. And that wind is blowing towards the Indian border. Whence comes that wind, think you?'

Sir Walter had lowered his voice and was speaking very slow and distinct. I could hear the rain dripping from the eaves of the window, and far off the hoot of taxis in Whitehall.

'Have you an explanation, Hannay?' he asked again.

'It looks as if Islam had a bigger hand in the thing than we thought,' I said. 'I fancy religion is the only thing to knit up such a scattered empire.'

'You are right,' he said. 'You must be right. We have laughed at the Holy War, the jehad that old Von der Goltz prophesied. But I believe that stupid old man with the big spectacles was right. There is a jehad preparing. The question is, How?'

'I'm hanged if I know,' I said; 'but I'll bet it won't be done by a pack of stout German officers in *pickelhaubes*. I fancy you can't manufacture Holy Wars out of Krupp guns alone and a few staff officers and a battle cruiser with her boilers burst.'

'Agreed. They are not fools, however much we try to persuade ourselves of the contrary. But supposing they had got some tremendous sacred sanction—some holy thing, some book or gospel or some new prophet from the desert, something which would cast over the whole ugly mechanism of German war the glamour of the old torrential raids which crumpled the Byzantine Empire and shook the walls of Vienna? Islam is a fighting creed, and the mullah still stands in the pulpit with the Koran in one hand and a drawn sword in the other. Supposing there is some Ark of the Covenant which will madden the remotest Moslem peasant with dreams of Paradise? What then, my friend?'

'Then there will be hell let loose in those parts pretty soon.'

'Hell which may spread. Beyond Persia, remember, lies India.'

'You keep to suppositions. How much do you know?' I asked.

'Very little, except the fact. But the fact is beyond dispute. I have reports from agents everywhere—pedlars in South Russia, Afghan horse-dealers, Turcoman merchants, pilgrims on the road to Mecca, sheikhs in North Africa, sailors on the Black Sea coasters, sheep-skinned Mongols, Hindu fakirs, Greek traders in the Gulf, as well as respectable Consuls who use cyphers. They tell the same story. The East is waiting for a revelation. It has been promised one. Some star—man, prophecy, or trinket—is coming out of the West. The Germans know, and that is the card with which they are going to astonish the world.'

'And the mission you spoke of for me is to go and find out?'

He nodded gravely. 'That is the crazy and impossible mission.'

'Tell me one thing, Sir Walter,' I said. 'I know it is the fashion in this country if a man has a special knowledge to set him to some job exactly the opposite. I know all about Damaraland, but instead of being put on Botha's staff, as I applied to be, I was kept in Hampshire mud till the campaign in German South West Africa was over. I know a man who could pass as an Arab, but do you think they would send him to the East? They left him in my battalion—a lucky thing for me, for he saved my life at Loos. I know the fashion, but isn't this just carrying it a bit too far? There must be thousands of men who have spent years in the East and talk any language. They're the fellows for this job. I never saw a Turk in my life except a chap who did wrestling turns in a show at Kimberley. You've picked about the most useless man on earth.'

'You've been a mining engineer, Hannay,' Sir Walter said. 'If you wanted a man to prospect for gold in Barotseland you would of course like to get one who knew the country and the people and the language. But the first thing you would require in him would be that he had a nose for finding gold and knew his business. That is the position now. I believe that you have a nose for finding out what our enemies try to hide. I know that you are brave and cool and resourceful. That is why I tell you the story. Besides ...'

He unrolled a big map of Europe on the wall.

'I can't tell you where you'll get on the track of the secret, but I can put a limit to the quest. You won't find it east of the Bosporus—not yet. It is still in Europe. It may be in Constantinople, or in Thrace. It may be farther west. But it is moving eastwards. If you are in time you may cut into its march to Constantinople. That much I can tell you. The secret is known in Germany, too, to those whom it concerns. It is in Europe that the seeker must search—at present.'

'Tell me more,' I said. 'You can give me no details and no instructions. Obviously you can give me no help if I come to grief.'

He nodded. 'You would be beyond the pale.'

'You give me a free hand.'

'Absolutely. You can have what money you like, and you can get what help you like. You can follow any plan you fancy, and go anywhere you think fruitful. We can give no directions.'

'One last question. You say it is important. Tell me just how important.'

'It is life and death,' he said solemnly. 'I can put it no higher and no lower. Once we know what is the menace we can meet it. As long as we are in the dark it works unchecked and we may be too late. The war must be won or lost in Europe. Yes; but if the East blazes up, our effort will be distracted from Europe and the great *coup* may fail. The stakes are no less than victory and defeat, Hannay.'

I got out of my chair and walked to the window. It was a difficult moment in my life. I was happy in my soldiering; above all, happy in the company of my brother officers. I was asked to go off into the enemy's lands on a quest for which I believed I was manifestly unfitted—a business of lonely days and nights, of nerve-racking strain, of deadly peril shrouding me like a garment. Looking out on the bleak weather I shivered. It was too grim a business, too inhuman for flesh and blood. But Sir Walter had called it a matter of life and death, and I had told him that I was out to serve my country. He could not give me orders, but was I not under orders—higher orders than my Brigadier's? I thought myself incompetent, but cleverer men than me thought me competent, or at least competent enough for a sporting chance. I knew in my soul that if I declined I should never be quite at peace in the world again. And yet Sir Walter had called the scheme madness, and said that he himself would never have accepted.

How does one make a great decision? I swear that when I turned round to speak I meant to refuse. But my answer was Yes, and I had crossed the Rubicon. My voice sounded cracked and far away.

Sir Walter shook hands with me and his eyes blinked a little.

'I may be sending you to your death, Hannay—Good God, what a damned task-mistress duty is!—If so, I shall be haunted with regrets, but you will never repent. Have no fear of that. You have chosen the roughest road, but it goes straight to the hill-tops.'

He handed me the half-sheet of note-paper. On it were written three words—'*Kasredin*', '*cancer*', and '*v. I.*'

'That is the only clue we possess,' he said. 'I cannot construe it, but I can tell you the story. We have had our agents working in Persia and Mesopotamia for years—mostly young officers of the Indian Army. They carry their lives in their hands, and now and then one disappears, and the sewers of Baghdad might tell a tale. But they find out many things, and they count the game worth the candle. They have told us of the star rising in the West, but they could give us no details. All but one—the best of them. He had been working between Mosul and the Persian frontier as a muleteer, and had been south into the Bakhtiari hills. He found out something, but his enemies knew that he knew and he was pursued. Three months ago, just before Kut, he staggered into Delamain's camp with ten bullet holes in him and a knife slash on his forehead. He mumbled his name, but beyond that and the fact that there was a Something coming from the West he told them nothing. He died in ten minutes. They found this paper on him, and since he cried out the word "Kasredin" in his last moments, it must have had something to do with his quest. It is for you to find out if it has any meaning.'

I folded it up and placed it in my pocket-book.

'What a great fellow! What was his name?' I asked.

Sir Walter did not answer at once. He was looking out of the window. 'His name,' he said at last, 'was Harry Bullivant. He was my son. God rest his brave soul!'

CHAPTER TWO

The Gathering of the Missionaries

I wrote out a wire to Sandy, asking him to come up by the two-fifteen train and meet me at my flat.

'I have chosen my colleague,' I said.

'Billy Arbuthnot's boy? His father was at Harrow with me. I know the fellow—Harry used to bring him down to fish—tallish, with a lean, high-boned face and a pair of brown eyes like a pretty girl's. I know his record, too. There's a good deal about him in this office. He rode through Yemen, which no white man ever did before. The Arabs let him pass, for they thought him stark mad and argued that the hand of Allah was heavy enough on him without their efforts. He's blood-brother to every kind of Albanian bandit. Also he used to take a hand in Turkish politics, and got a huge reputation. Some Englishman was once complaining to old Mahmoud Shevkat about the scarcity of statesmen in Western Europe, and Mahmoud broke in with, "Have you not the Honourable Arbuthnot?" You say he's in your battalion. I was wondering what had become of him, for we tried to get hold of him here, but he had left no address. Ludovick Arbuthnot—yes, that's the man. Buried deep in the commissioned ranks of the New Army? Well, we'll get him out pretty quick!'

'I knew he had knocked about the East, but I didn't know he was that kind of swell. Sandy's not the chap to buck about himself.'

'He wouldn't,' said Sir Walter. 'He had always a more than Oriental reticence. I've got another colleague for you, if you like him.'

He looked at his watch. 'You can get to the Savoy Grill Room in five minutes in a taxi-cab. Go in from the Strand, turn to your left, and you will see in the alcove on the right-hand side a table with one large American gentleman sitting at it. They know him there, so he will have the table to himself. I want you to go and sit down beside him. Say you come from me. His name is Mr John Scantlebury Blenkiron, now a citizen of Boston, Mass., but born and raised in Indiana. Put this envelope in your pocket, but don't read its contents till you have talked to him. I want you to form your own opinion about Mr Blenkiron.'

I went out of the Foreign Office in as muddled a frame of mind as any diplomatist who ever left its portals. I was most desperately depressed. To begin with, I was in a complete funk. I had always thought I was about as brave as the average man, but there's courage and courage, and mine was certainly not the impassive kind. Stick me down in a trench and I could stand being shot at as well as most people, and my blood could get hot if it were given a chance. But I think I had too much imagination. I couldn't shake off the beastly forecasts that kept crowding my mind.

In about a fortnight, I calculated, I would be dead. Shot as a spy—a rotten sort of ending! At the moment I was quite safe, looking for a taxi in the middle of Whitehall, but the sweat broke on my forehead. I felt as I had felt in my adventure before the war. But this was far worse, for it was more cold-blooded and premeditated, and I didn't seem to have even a sporting chance. I watched the figures in khaki passing on the pavement, and thought what a nice safe prospect they had compared to mine. Yes, even if next week they were in the Hohenzollern, or the Hairpin trench at the Quarries, or that ugly angle at Hooge. I wondered why I had not been happier that morning before I got that infernal wire. Suddenly all the trivialities of English life seemed to me inexpressibly dear and terribly far away. I was very angry with Bullivant, till I remembered how fair he had been. My fate was my own choosing.

When I was hunting the Black Stone the interest of the problem had helped to keep me going. But now I could see no problem. My mind had nothing to work on but three words of gibberish on a sheet of paper and a mystery of which Sir Walter had been convinced, but to which he couldn't give a name. It was like the story I had read of Saint Teresa setting off at the age of ten with her small brother to convert the Moors. I sat huddled in the taxi with my chin on my breast, wishing that I had lost a leg at Loos and been comfortably tucked away for the rest of the war.

Sure enough I found my man in the Grill Room. There he was, feeding solemnly, with a napkin tucked under his chin. He was a big fellow with a fat, sallow, clean-shaven face. I disregarded the hovering waiter and pulled up a chair beside the American at the little table. He turned on me a pair of full sleepy eyes, like a ruminating ox.

'Mr Blenkiron?' I asked.

'You have my name, Sir,' he said. 'Mr John Scantlebury Blenkiron. I would wish you good morning if I saw anything good in this darned British weather.'

'I come from Sir Walter Bullivant,' I said, speaking low.

'So?' said he. 'Sir Walter is a very good friend of mine. Pleased to meet you, Mr—or I guess it's Colonel—'

'Hannay,' I said; 'Major Hannay.' I was wondering what this sleepy Yankee could do to help me.

'Allow me to offer you luncheon, Major. Here, waiter, bring the carte. I regret that I cannot join you in sampling the efforts of the management of this hotel. I suffer, Sir, from dyspepsia—duodenal dyspepsia. It gets me two hours after a meal and gives me hell just below the breast-bone. So I am obliged to adopt a diet. My nourishment is fish, Sir, and boiled milk and a little dry toast. It's a melancholy descent from the days when I could do justice to a lunch at Sherry's and sup off oyster-crabs and devilled bones.' He sighed from the depths of his capacious frame.

I ordered an omelette and a chop, and took another look at him. The large eyes seemed to be gazing steadily at me without seeing me. They were as vacant as an abstracted child's; but I had an uncomfortable feeling that they saw more than mine.

'You have been fighting, Major? The Battle of Loos? Well, I guess that must have been some battle. We in America respect the fighting of the British soldier, but we don't quite catch on to the de-vices of the British Generals. We opine that there is more bellicosity than science among your highbrows. That is so? My father fought at Chattanooga, but these eyes have seen nothing gorier than a Presidential election. Say, is there any way I could be let into a scene of real bloodshed?'

His serious tone made me laugh. 'There are plenty of your countrymen in the present show,' I said. 'The French Foreign Legion is full of young Americans, and so is our Army Service Corps. Half the chauffeurs you strike in France seem to come from the States.'

He sighed. 'I did think of some belligerent stunt a year back. But I reflected that the good God had not given John S. Blenkiron the kind of martial figure that would do credit to the tented field. Also I recollected that we Americans were nootrals—benevolent nootrals—and that it did not become me to be butting into the struggles of the effete monarchies of Europe. So I stopped at home. It was a big renunciation, Major, for I was lying sick during the Philippines business, and I have never seen the lawless passions of men let loose on a battlefield. And, as a stoodent of humanity, I hankered for the experience.'

'What have you been doing?' I asked. The calm gentleman had begun to interest me.

'Waal,' he said, 'I just waited. The Lord has blessed me with money to burn, so I didn't need to go scrambling like a wild cat for war contracts. But I reckoned I would get let into the game somehow, and I was. Being a nootral, I was in an advantageous position to take a hand. I had a pretty hectic time for a while, and then I reckoned I would leave God's country and see what was doing in Europe. I have counted myself out of the bloodshed business, but, as your poet sings, peace has its victories not less renowned than war, and I reckon that means that a nootral can have a share in a scrap as well as a belligerent.'

'That's the best kind of neutrality I've ever heard of,' I said.

'It's the right kind,' he replied solemnly. 'Say, Major, what are your lot fighting for? For your own skins and your Empire and the peace of Europe. Waal, those ideals don't concern us one cent. We're not Europeans, and there aren't any German trenches on Long Island yet. You've made the ring in Europe, and if we came butting in it wouldn't be the rules of the game. You wouldn't welcome us, and I guess you'd be right. We're that delicate-minded we can't interfere and that was what my friend, President Wilson, meant when he opined that America was too proud to fight. So we're nootrals. But likewise we're benevolent nootrals. As I follow events, there's a skunk been let loose in the world, and the odour of it is going to make life none too sweet till it is cleared away. It wasn't us that stirred up that skunk, but we've got to take a hand in disinfecting the planet. See? We can't fight, but, by God! some of us are going to sweat blood to sweep the mess up. Officially we do nothing except give off Notes like a leaky boiler gives off steam. But as individooal citizens we're in it up to the neck. So, in the spirit of Jefferson Davis and Woodrow Wilson, I'm going to be the nootralist kind of nootral till Kaiser will be sorry he didn't declare war on America at the beginning.'

I was completely recovering my temper. This fellow was a perfect jewel, and his spirit put purpose into me.

'I guess you British were the same kind of nootral when your Admiral warned off the German fleet from interfering with Dewey in Manila Bay in '98.' Mr

Blenkiron drank up the last drop of his boiled milk and lit a thin black cigar.

I leaned forward. 'Have you talked to Sir Walter?' I asked.

'I have talked to him, and he has given me to understand that there's a deal ahead which you're going to boss. There are no flies on that big man, and if he says it's good business then you can count me in.'

'You know that it's uncommonly dangerous?'

'I judged so. But it don't do to begin counting risks. I believe in an all-wise and beneficent Providence, but you have got to trust Him and give Him a chance. What's life anyhow? For me, it's living on a strict diet and having frequent pains in my stomach. It isn't such an almighty lot to give up, provided you get a good price in the deal. Besides, how big is the risk? About one o'clock in the morning, when you can't sleep, it will be the size of Mount Everest, but if you run out to meet it, it will be a hillock you can jump over. The grizzly looks very fierce when you're taking your ticket for the Rockies and wondering if you'll come back, but he's just an ordinary bear when you've got the sight of your rifle on him. I won't think about risks till I'm up to my neck in them and don't see the road out.'

I scribbled my address on a piece of paper and handed it to the stout philosopher. 'Come to dinner tonight at eight,' I said.

'I thank you, Major. A little fish, please, plain-boiled, and some hot milk. You will forgive me if I borrow your couch after the meal and spend the evening on my back. That is the advice of my noo doctor.'

I got a taxi and drove to my club. On the way I opened the envelope Sir Walter had given me. It contained a number of jottings, the dossier of Mr Blenkiron. He had done wonders for the Allies in the States. He had nosed out the Dumba plot, and had been instrumental in getting the portfolio of Dr Albert. Von Papen's spies had tried to murder him, after he had defeated an attempt to blow up one of the big gun factories. Sir Walter had written at the end: 'The best man we ever had. Better than Scudder. He would go through hell with a box of bismuth tablets and a pack of Patience cards.'

I went into the little back smoking-room, borrowed an atlas from the library, poked up the fire, and sat down to think. Mr Blenkiron had given me the fillip I needed. My mind was beginning to work now, and was running wide over the whole business. Not that I hoped to find anything by my cogitations. It wasn't thinking in an arm-chair that would solve the mystery. But I was getting a sort of grip on a plan of operations. And to my relief I had stopped thinking about the risks. Blenkiron had shamed me out of that. If a sedentary dyspeptic could show that kind of nerve, I wasn't going to be behind him.

I went back to my flat about five o'clock. My man Paddock had gone to the wars long ago, so I had shifted to one of the new blocks in Park Lane where they provide food and service. I kept the place on to have a home to go to when I got leave. It's a miserable business holidaying in an hotel.

Sandy was devouring tea-cakes with the serious resolution of a convalescent.

'Well, Dick, what's the news? Is it a brass hat or the boot?'

'Neither,' I said. 'But you and I are going to disappear from His Majesty's forces. Seconded for special service.'

'O my sainted aunt!' said Sandy. 'What is it? For Heaven's sake put me out of pain. Have we to tout deputations of suspicious neutrals over munition works or take the shivering journalist in a motor-car where he can imagine he sees a Boche?'

'The news will keep. But I can tell you this much. It's about as safe and easy as to go through the German lines with a walking-stick.'

'Come, that's not so dusty,' said Sandy, and began cheerfully on the muffins.

I must spare a moment to introduce Sandy to the reader, for he cannot be allowed to slip into this tale by a side-door. If you will consult the Peerage you will find that to Edward Cospatrick, fifteenth Baron Clanroyden, there was born in the year 1882, as his second son, Ludovick Gustavus Arbuthnot, commonly called the Honourable, etc. The said son was educated at Eton and New College, Oxford, was a captain in the Tweeddale Yeomanry, and served for some years as honorary attache at various embassies. The Peerage will stop short at this point, but that is by no means the end of the story. For the rest you must consult very different authorities. Lean brown men from the ends of the earth may be seen on the London pavements now and then in creased clothes, walking with the light outland step, slinking into clubs as if they could not remember whether or not they belonged to them. From them you may get news of Sandy. Better still, you will hear of him at little forgotten fishing ports where the Albanian mountains dip to the Adriatic. If you struck a Mecca pilgrimage the odds are you would meet a dozen of Sandy's friends in it. In shepherds' huts in the Caucasus you will find bits of his cast-off clothing, for he has a knack of shedding garments as he goes. In the caravanserais of Bokhara and Samarkand he is known, and there are shikaris in the Pamirs who still speak of him round their fires. If you were going to visit Petrograd or Rome or Cairo it would be no use asking him for introductions; if he gave them, they would lead you into strange haunts. But if Fate compelled you to go to Llasa or Yarkand or Seistan he could map out your road for you and pass the word to potent friends. We call ourselves insular, but the truth is that we are the only race on earth that can produce men capable of getting inside the skin of remote peoples. Perhaps the Scots are better than the English, but we're all a thousand per cent better than anybody else. Sandy was the wandering Scot carried to the pitch of genius. In old days he would have led a crusade or discovered a new road to the Indies. Today he merely roamed as the spirit moved him, till the war swept him up and dumped him down in my battalion.

I got out Sir Walter's half-sheet of note-paper. It was not the original—naturally he wanted to keep that—but it was a careful tracing. I took it that Harry Bullivant had not written down the words as a memo for his own use. People who follow his career have good memories. He must have written them in order that, if he perished and his body was found, his friends might get a clue. Wherefore, I argued, the words must be intelligible to somebody or other of our persuasion, and likewise they must be pretty well gibberish to any Turk or German that found them.

The first, '*Kasredin*', I could make nothing of. I asked Sandy.

'You mean Nasr-ed-din,' he said, still munching crumpets.

'What's that?' I asked sharply.

'He's the General believed to be commanding against us in Mesopotamia. I remember him years ago in Aleppo. He talked bad French and drank the sweetest of sweet champagne.'

I looked closely at the paper. The 'K' was unmistakable.

'Kasredin is nothing. It means in Arabic the House of Faith, and might cover anything from Hagia Sofia to a suburban villa. What's your next puzzle, Dick? Have you entered for a prize competition in a weekly paper?'

'*Cancer,*' I read out.

'It is the Latin for a crab. Likewise it is the name of a painful disease. It is also a sign of the Zodiac.'

'*V. I,*' I read.

'There you have me. It sounds like the number of a motor-car. The police would find out for you. I call this rather a difficult competition. What's the prize?'

I passed him the paper. 'Who wrote it? It looks as if he had been in a hurry.'

'Harry Bullivant,' I said.

Sandy's face grew solemn. 'Old Harry. He was at my tutor's. The best fellow God ever made. I saw his name in the casualty list before Kut. ... Harry didn't do things without a purpose. What's the story of this paper?'

'Wait till after dinner,' I said. 'I'm going to change and have a bath. There's an American coming to dine, and he's part of the business.'

Mr Blenkiron arrived punctual to the minute in a fur coat like a Russian prince's. Now that I saw him on his feet I could judge him better. He had a fat face, but was not too plump in figure, and very muscular wrists showed below his shirt-cuffs. I fancied that, if the occasion called, he might be a good man with his hands.

Sandy and I ate a hearty meal, but the American picked at his boiled fish and sipped his milk a drop at a time. When the servant had cleared away, he was as good as his word and laid himself out on my sofa. I offered him a good cigar, but he preferred one of his own lean black abominations. Sandy stretched his length in an easy chair and lit his pipe. 'Now for your story, Dick,' he said.

I began, as Sir Walter had begun with me, by telling them about the puzzle in the Near East. I pitched a pretty good yarn, for I had been thinking a lot about it, and the mystery of the business had caught my fancy. Sandy got very keen.

'It is possible enough. Indeed, I've been expecting it, though I'm hanged if I can imagine what card the Germans have got up their sleeve. It might be any one of twenty things. Thirty years ago there was a bogus prophecy that played the devil in Yemen. Or it might be a flag such as Ali Wad Helu had, or a jewel like Solomon's necklace in Abyssinia. You never know what will start off a jehad! But I rather think it's a man.'

'Where could he get his purchase?' I asked.

'It's hard to say. If it were merely wild tribesmen like the Bedouin he might have got a reputation as a saint and miracle-worker. Or he might be a fellow that preached a pure religion, like the chap that founded the Senussi. But I'm inclined to think he must be something extra special if he can put a spell on the whole Moslem world. The Turk and the Persian wouldn't follow the ordinary new theology game. He must be of the Blood. Your Mahdis and Mullahs and Imams were nobodies, but they had only a local prestige. To capture all Islam—and I gather that is what we fear—the man must be of the Koreish, the tribe of the Prophet himself.'

'But how could any impostor prove that? For I suppose he's an impostor.'

'He would have to combine a lot of claims. His descent must be pretty good to begin with, and there are families, remember, that claim the Koreish blood. Then he'd have to be rather a wonder on his own account—

saintly, eloquent, and that sort of thing. And I expect he'd have to show a sign, though what that could be I haven't a notion.'

'You know the East about as well as any living man. Do you think that kind of thing is possible?' I asked.

'Perfectly,' said Sandy, with a grave face.

'Well, there's the ground cleared to begin with. Then there's the evidence of pretty well every secret agent we possess. That all seems to prove the fact. But we have no details and no clues except that bit of paper.' I told them the story of it.

Sandy studied it with wrinkled brows. 'It beats me. But it may be the key for all that. A clue may be dumb in London and shout aloud at Baghdad.'

'That's just the point I was coming to. Sir Walter says this thing is about as important for our cause as big guns. He can't give me orders, but he offers the job of going out to find what the mischief is. Once he knows that, he says he can checkmate it. But it's got to be found out soon, for the mine may be sprung at any moment. I've taken on the job. Will you help?'

Sandy was studying the ceiling.

'I should add that it's about as safe as playing chuck-farthing at the Loos Cross-roads, the day you and I went in. And if we fail nobody can help us.'

'Oh, of course, of course,' said Sandy in an abstracted voice.

Mr Blenkiron, having finished his after-dinner recumbency, had sat up and pulled a small table towards him. From his pocket he had taken a pack of Patience cards and had begun to play the game called the Double Napoleon. He seemed to be oblivious of the conversation.

Suddenly I had a feeling that the whole affair was stark lunacy. Here were we three simpletons sitting in a London flat and projecting a mission into the enemy's citadel without an idea what we were to do or how we were to do it. And one of the three was looking at the ceiling, and whistling softly through his teeth, and another was playing Patience. The farce of the thing struck me so keenly that I laughed.

Sandy looked at me sharply.

'You feel like that? Same with me. It's idiocy, but all war is idiotic, and the most whole-hearted idiot is apt to win. We're to go on this mad trail wherever we think we can hit it. Well, I'm with you. But I don't mind admitting that I'm in a blue funk. I had got myself adjusted to this trench business and was quite happy.

And now you have hoicked me out, and my feet are cold.'

'I don't believe you know what fear is,' I said.

'There you're wrong, Dick,' he said earnestly. 'Every man who isn't a maniac knows fear. I have done some daft things, but I never started on them without wishing they were over. Once I'm in the show I get easier, and by the time I'm coming out I'm sorry to leave it. But at the start my feet are icy.'

'Then I take it you're coming?'

'Rather,' he said. 'You didn't imagine I would go back on you?'

'And you, sir?' I addressed Blenkiron.

His game of Patience seemed to be coming out. He was completing eight little heaps of cards with a contented grunt. As I spoke, he raised his sleepy eyes and nodded.

'Why, yes,' he said. 'You gentlemen mustn't think that I haven't been following your most engrossing conversation. I guess I haven't missed a syllable. I find that a game of Patience stimulates the digestion after meals and conduces to quiet reflection. John S. Blenkiron is with you all the time.'

He shuffled the cards and dealt for a new game.

I don't think I ever expected a refusal, but this ready assent cheered me wonderfully. I couldn't have faced the thing alone.

'Well, that's settled. Now for ways and means. We three have got to put ourselves in the way of finding out Germany's secret, and we have to go where it is known. Somehow or other we have to reach Constantinople, and to beat the biggest area of country we must go by different roads. Sandy, my lad, you've got to get into Turkey. You're the only one of us that knows that engaging people. You can't get in by Europe very easily, so you must try Asia. What about the coast of Asia Minor?'

'It could be done,' he said. 'You'd better leave that entirely to me. I'll find out the best way. I suppose the Foreign Office will help me to get to the jumping-off place?'

'Remember,' I said, 'it's no good getting too far east. The secret, so far as concerns us, is still west of Constantinople.'

'I see that. I'll blow in on the Bosporus by a short tack.'

'For you, Mr Blenkiron, I would suggest a straight journey. You're an American, and can travel through

Germany direct. But I wonder how far your activities in New York will allow you to pass as a neutral?'

'I have considered that, Sir,' he said. 'I have given some thought to the pecooliar psychology of the great German nation. As I read them they're as cunning as cats, and if you play the feline game they will outwit you every time. Yes, Sir, they are no slouches at sleuth-work. If I were to buy a pair of false whiskers and dye my hair and dress like a Baptist parson and go into Germany on the peace racket, I guess they'd be on my trail like a knife, and I should be shot as a spy inside of a week or doing solitary in the Moabite prison. But they lack the larger vision. They can be bluffed, Sir. With your approval I shall visit the Fatherland as John S. Blenkiron, once a thorn in the side of their brightest boys on the other side. But it will be a different John S. I reckon he will have experienced a change of heart. He will have come to appreciate the great, pure, noble soul of Germany, and he will be sorrowing for his past like a converted gun-man at a camp meeting. He will be a victim of the meanness and perfidy of the British Government. I am going to have a first-class row with your Foreign Office about my passport, and I am going to speak harsh words about them up and down this metropolis. I am going to be shadowed by your sleuths at my port of embarkation, and I guess I shall run up hard against the British Legations in Scandinavia. By that time our Teutonic friends will have begun to wonder what has happened to John S., and to think that maybe they have been mistaken in that child. So, when I get to Germany they will be waiting for me with an open mind. Then I judge my conduct will surprise and encourage them. I will confide to them valuable secret information about British preparations, and I will show up the British lion as the meanest kind of cur. You may trust me to make a good impression. After that I'll move eastwards, to see the demolition of the British Empire in those parts. By the way, where is the rendezvous?'

'This is the 17th day of November. If we can't find out what we want in two months we may chuck the job. On the 17th of January we should forgather in Constantinople. Whoever gets there first waits for the others. If by that date we're not all present, it will be considered that the missing man has got into trouble and must be given up. If ever we get there we'll be coming from different points and in different characters, so we want a rendezvous where all kinds of odd folk assemble. Sandy, you know Constantinople. You fix the meeting-place.'

'I've already thought of that,' he said, and going to the writing-table he drew a little plan on a sheet of paper. 'That lane runs down from the Kurdish Bazaar in Galata to the ferry of Ratchik. Half-way down on the left-hand side is a cafe kept by a Greek called Kuprasso. Behind the cafe is a garden, surrounded by high walls which were parts of the old Byzantine Theatre. At the end of the garden is a shanty called the Garden-house of Suliman the Red. It has been in its time a dancing-hall and a gambling hell and God knows what else. It's not a place for respectable people, but the ends of the earth converge there and no questions are asked. That's the best spot I can think of for a meeting-place.'

The kettle was simmering by the fire, the night was raw, and it seemed the hour for whisky-punch. I made a brew for Sandy and myself and boiled some milk for Blenkiron.

'What about language?' I asked. 'You're all right, Sandy?'

'I know German fairly well; and I can pass anywhere as a Turk. The first will do for eavesdropping and the second for ordinary business.'

'And you?' I asked Blenkiron.

'I was left out at Pentecost,' he said. 'I regret to confess I have no gift of tongues. But the part I have chosen for myself don't require the polyglot. Never forget I'm plain John S. Blenkiron, a citizen of the great American Republic.'

'You haven't told us your own line, Dick,' Sandy said.

'I am going to the Bosporus through Germany, and, not being a neutral, it won't be a very cushioned journey.'

Sandy looked grave.

'That sounds pretty desperate. Is your German good enough?'

'Pretty fair; quite good enough to pass as a native. But officially I shall not understand one word. I shall be a Boer from Western Cape Colony: one of Maritz's old lot who after a bit of trouble has got through Angola and reached Europe. I shall talk Dutch and nothing else. And, my hat! I shall be pretty bitter about the British. There's a powerful lot of good swear-words in the taal. I shall know all about Africa, and be panting to get another whack at the *verdommt rooinek*. With luck they may send me to the Uganda show or to Egypt, and I shall take care to go by Constantinople. If I'm to deal with the Mohammedan natives they're bound to show me what hand they hold. At least, that's the way I look at it.'

We filled our glasses—two of punch and one of milk—and drank to our next merry meeting. Then Sandy began to laugh, and I joined in. The sense of hopeless folly again descended on me. The best plans we could make were like a few buckets of water to ease the drought of the Sahara or the old lady who would have stopped the Atlantic with a broom. I thought with sympathy of little Saint Teresa.

CHAPTER THREE

Peter Pienaar

Our various departures were unassuming, all but the American's. Sandy spent a busy fortnight in his subterranean fashion, now in the British Museum, now running about the country to see old exploring companions, now at the War Office, now at the Foreign Office, but mostly in my flat, sunk in an arm-chair and meditating. He left finally on December 1st as a King's Messenger for Cairo. Once there I knew the King's Messenger would disappear, and some queer Oriental ruffian take his place. It would have been impertinence in me to inquire into his plans. He was the real professional, and I was only the dabbler.

Blenkiron was a different matter. Sir Walter told me to look out for squalls, and the twinkle in his eye gave me a notion of what was coming. The first thing the sportsman did was to write a letter to the papers signed with his name. There had been a debate in the House of Commons on foreign policy, and the speech of some idiot there gave him his cue. He declared that he had been heart and soul with the British at the start, but that he was reluctantly compelled to change his views. He said our blockade of Germany had broken all the laws of God and humanity, and he reckoned that Britain was now the worst exponent of Prussianism going. That letter made a fine racket, and the paper that printed it had a row with the Censor. But that was only the beginning of Mr Blenkiron's campaign. He got mixed up with some mountebanks called the League of Democrats against Aggression, gentlemen who thought that Germany was all right if we could only keep from hurting her feelings. He addressed a meeting under their auspices, which was broken up by the crowd, but not before John S. had got off his chest a lot of amazing stuff. I wasn't there, but a man who was told me that he never heard such clotted nonsense. He said that Germany was right in wanting the freedom of the seas, and that America would back her up, and that the British Navy was a bigger menace to the peace of the world than the Kaiser's army. He admitted that he had once thought differently, but he was an honest man and not afraid to face facts. The oration closed suddenly, when he got a brussels-sprout in the eye, at which my friend said he swore in a very unpacifist style.

After that he wrote other letters to the Press, saying that there was no more liberty of speech in England, and a lot of scallywags backed him up. Some Americans wanted to tar and feather him, and he got kicked out of the Savoy. There was an agitation to get him deported, and questions were asked in Parliament, and the Under-Secretary for Foreign Affairs said his department had the matter in hand. I was beginning to think that Blenkiron was carrying his tomfoolery too far, so I went to see Sir Walter, but he told me to keep my mind easy.

'Our friend's motto is "Thorough",' he said, 'and he knows very well what he is about. We have officially requested him to leave, and he sails from Newcastle on Monday. He will be shadowed wherever he goes, and we hope to provoke more outbreaks. He is a very capable fellow.'

The last I saw of him was on the Saturday afternoon when I met him in St james's Street and offered to shake hands. He told me that my uniform was a pollution, and made a speech to a small crowd about it. They hissed him and he had to get into a taxi. As he departed there was just the suspicion of a wink in his left eye. On Monday I read that he had gone off, and the papers observed that our shores were well quit of him.

I sailed on December 3rd from Liverpool in a boat bound for the Argentine that was due to put in at Lisbon. I had of course to get a Foreign Office passport to leave England, but after that my connection with the Government ceased. All the details of my journey were carefully thought out. Lisbon would be a good jumping-off place, for it was the rendezvous of scallywags from most parts of Africa. My kit was an old Gladstone bag, and my clothes were the relics of my South African wardrobe. I let my beard grow for some days before I sailed, and, since it grows fast, I went on board with the kind of hairy chin you will see on the young Boer. My name was now Brandt, Cornelis Brandt—at least so my passport said, and passports never lie.

There were just two other passengers on that beastly boat, and they never appeared till we were out of the Bay.

I was pretty bad myself, but managed to move about all the time, for the frowst in my cabin would have sickened a hippo. The old tub took two days and a night to waddle from Ushant to Finisterre. Then the weather changed and we came out of snow-squalls into something very like summer. The hills of Portugal were all blue and yellow like the Kalahari, and before we made the Tagus I was beginning to forget I had ever left Rhodesia. There was a Dutchman among the sailors with whom I used to patter the taal, and but for 'Good morning' and 'Good evening' in broken English to the captain, that was about all the talking I did on the cruise.

We dropped anchor off the quays of Lisbon on a shiny blue morning, pretty near warm enough to wear flannels. I had now got to be very wary. I did not leave the ship with the shore-going boat, but made a leisurely breakfast. Then I strolled on deck, and there, just casting anchor in the middle of the stream, was another ship with a blue and white funnel I knew so well. I calculated that a month before she had been smelling the mangrove swamps of Angola. Nothing could better answer my purpose. I proposed to board her, pretending I was looking for a friend, and come on shore from her, so that anyone in Lisbon who chose to be curious would think I had landed straight from Portuguese Africa.

I hailed one of the adjacent ruffians, and got into his rowboat, with my kit. We reached the vessel—they called her the *Henry the Navigator*—just as the first shore-boat was leaving. The crowd in it were all Portuguese, which suited my book.

But when I went up the ladder the first man I met was old Peter Pienaar.

Here was a piece of sheer monumental luck. Peter had opened his eyes and his mouth, and had got as far as '*Allemachtig*', when I shut him up.

'Brandt,' I said, 'Cornelis Brandt. That's my name now, and don't you forget it. Who is the captain here? Is it still old Sloggett?'

'*Ja,*' said Peter, pulling himself together. 'He was speaking about you yesterday.'

This was better and better. I sent Peter below to get hold of Sloggett, and presently I had a few words with that gentleman in his cabin with the door shut.

'You've got to enter my name in the ship's books. I came aboard at Mossamedes. And my name's Cornelis Brandt.'

At first Sloggett was for objecting. He said it was a felony. I told him that I dared say it was, but he had got to do it, for reasons which I couldn't give, but which were highly creditable to all parties. In the end he agreed, and I saw it done. I had a pull on old Sloggett, for I had known him ever since he owned a dissolute tug-boat at Delagoa Bay.

Then Peter and I went ashore and swaggered into Lisbon as if we owned De Beers. We put up at the big hotel opposite the railway station, and looked and behaved like a pair of lowbred South Africans home for a spree. It was a fine bright day, so I hired a motor-car and said I would drive it myself. We asked the name of some beauty-spot to visit, and were told Cintra and shown the road to it. I wanted a quiet place to talk, for I had a good deal to say to Peter Pienaar.

I christened that car the Lusitanian Terror, and it was a marvel that we did not smash ourselves up. There was something immortally wrong with its steering gear. Half a dozen times we slewed across the road, inviting destruction. But we got there in the end, and had luncheon in an hotel opposite the Moorish palace. There we left the car and wandered up the slopes of a hill, where, sitting among scrub very like the veld, I told Peter the situation of affairs.

But first a word must be said about Peter. He was the man that taught me all I ever knew of veld-craft, and a good deal about human nature besides. He was out of the Old Colony—Burgersdorp, I think—but he had come to the Transvaal when the Lydenburg goldfields started. He was prospector, transport-rider, and hunter in turns, but principally hunter. In those early days he was none too good a citizen. He was in Swaziland with Bob

Macnab, and you know what that means. Then he took to working off bogus gold propositions on Kimberley and Johannesburg magnates, and what he didn't know about salting a mine wasn't knowledge. After that he was in the Kalahari, where he and Scotty Smith were familiar names. An era of comparative respectability dawned for him with the Matabele War, when he did uncommon good scouting and transport work. Cecil Rhodes wanted to establish him on a stock farm down Salisbury way, but Peter was an independent devil and would call no man master. He took to big-game hunting, which was what God intended him for, for he could track a tsessebe in thick bush, and was far the finest shot I have seen in my life. He took parties to the Pungwe flats, and Barotseland, and up to Tanganyika. Then he made a speciality of the Ngami region, where I once hunted with him, and he was with me when I went prospecting in Damaraland.

When the Boer War started, Peter, like many of the very great hunters, took the British side and did most of our intelligence work in the North Transvaal. Beyers would have hanged him if he could have caught him, and there was no love lost between Peter and his own people for many a day. When it was all over and things had calmed down a bit, he settled in Bulawayo and used to go with me when I went on trek. At the time when I left Africa two years before, I had lost sight of him for months, and heard that he was somewhere on the Congo poaching elephants. He had always a great idea of making things hum so loud in Angola that the Union

Government would have to step in and annex it. After Rhodes Peter had the biggest notions south of the Line.

He was a man of about five foot ten, very thin and active, and as strong as a buffalo. He had pale blue eyes, a face as gentle as a girl's, and a soft sleepy voice. From his present appearance it looked as if he had been living hard lately. His clothes were of the cut you might expect to get at Lobito Bay, he was as lean as a rake, deeply browned with the sun, and there was a lot of grey in his beard. He was fifty-six years old, and used to be taken for forty. Now he looked about his age.

I first asked him what he had been up to since the war began. He spat, in the Kaffir way he had, and said he had been having hell's time.

'I got hung up on the Kafue,' he said. 'When I heard from old Letsitela that the white men were fighting I had a bright idea that I might get into German South West from the north. You see I knew that Botha couldn't long keep out of the war. Well, I got into German territory all right, and then a *skellum* of an officer came along, and commandeered all my mules, and wanted to commandeer me with them for his fool army. He was a very ugly man with a yellow face.' Peter filled a deep pipe from a kudu-skin pouch.

'Were you commandeered?' I asked.

'No. I shot him—not so as to kill, but to wound badly. It was all right, for he fired first on me. Got me too in the left shoulder. But that was the beginning of bad trouble. I trekked east pretty fast, and got over the border among the Ovamba. I have made many journeys, but that was the worst. Four days I went without water, and six without food. Then by bad luck I fell in with 'Nkitla—you remember, the half-caste chief. He said I owed him money for cattle which I bought when I came there with Carowab. It was a lie, but he held to it, and would give me no transport. So I crossed the Kalahari on my feet. Ugh, it was as slow as a vrouw coming from *nachtmaal*. It took weeks and weeks, and when I came to Lechwe's kraal, I heard that the fighting was over and that Botha had conquered the Germans. That, too, was a lie, but it deceived me, and I went north into Rhodesia, where I learned the truth. But by then I judged the war had gone too far for me to make any profit out of it, so I went into Angola to look for German refugees. By that time I was hating Germans worse than hell.'

'But what did you propose to do with them?' I asked.

'I had a notion they would make trouble with the Government in those parts. I don't specially love the Portugoose, but I'm for him against the Germans every day. Well, there was trouble, and I had a merry time for a month or two. But by and by it petered out, and I thought I had better clear for Europe, for South Africa was settling down just as the big show was getting really interesting. So here I am, Cornelis, my old friend. If I shave my beard will they let me join the Flying Corps?'

I looked at Peter sitting there smoking, as imperturbable as if he had been growing mealies in Natal all his life and had run home for a month's holiday with his people in Peckham.

'You're coming with me, my lad,' I said. 'We're going into Germany.'

Peter showed no surprise. 'Keep in mind that I don't like the Germans,' was all he said. 'I'm a quiet Christian man, but I've the devil of a temper.'

Then I told him the story of our mission. 'You and I have got to be Maritz's men. We went into Angola, and now we're trekking for the Fatherland to get a bit of our own back from the infernal English. Neither of us knows any German—publicly. We'd better plan out the fighting we were in—Kakamas will do for one, and Schuit Drift. You were a Ngamiland hunter before the war. They won't have your *dossier*, so you can tell any lie you like. I'd better be an educated Afrikander, one of Beyers's bright lads, and a pal of old Hertzog. We can let our imagination loose about that part, but we must stick to the same yarn about the fighting.'

'*Ja*, Cornelis,' said Peter. (He had called me Cornelis ever since I had told him my new name. He was a wonderful chap for catching on to any game.) 'But after we get into Germany, what then? There can't be much difficulty about the beginning. But once we're among the beer-swillers I don't quite see our line. We're to find out about something that's going on in Turkey? When I was a boy the predikant used to preach about Turkey. I wish I was better educated and remembered whereabouts in the map it was.'

'You leave that to me,' I said; 'I'll explain it all to you before we get there. We haven't got much of a spoor, but we'll cast about, and with luck will pick it up. I've seen you do it often enough when we hunted kudu on the Kafue.'

Peter nodded. 'Do we sit still in a German town?' he asked anxiously. 'I shouldn't like that, Cornelis.'

'We move gently eastward to Constantinople,' I said.

Peter grinned. 'We should cover a lot of new country. You can reckon on me, friend Cornelis. I've always had a hankering to see Europe.'

He rose to his feet and stretched his long arms.

'We'd better begin at once. God, I wonder what's happened to old Solly Maritz, with his bottle face? Yon was a fine battle at the drift when I was sitting up to my neck in the Orange praying that Brits' lads would take my head for a stone.'

Peter was as thorough a mountebank, when he got started, as Blenkiron himself. All the way back to Lisbon he yarned about Maritz and his adventures in German South West till I half believed they were true. He made a very good story of our doings, and by his constant harping on it I pretty soon got it into my memory. That was always Peter's way. He said if you were going to play a part, you must think yourself into it, convince yourself that you were it, till you really were it and didn't act but behaved naturally. The two men who had started that morning from the hotel door had been bogus enough, but the two men that returned were genuine desperadoes itching to get a shot at England.

We spent the evening piling up evidence in our favour. Some kind of republic had been started in Portugal, and ordinarily the cafes would have been full of politicians, but the war had quieted all these local squabbles, and the talk was of nothing but what was doing in France and Russia. The place we went to was a big, well-lighted show on a main street, and there were a lot of sharp-eyed fellows wandering about that I guessed were spies and police agents. I knew that Britain was the one country that doesn't bother about this kind of game, and that it would be safe enough to let ourselves go.

I talked Portuguese fairly well, and Peter spoke it like a Lourenco Marques bar-keeper, with a lot of Shangaan words to fill up. He started on curacao, which I reckoned was a new drink to him, and presently his tongue ran freely. Several neighbours pricked up their ears, and soon we had a small crowd round our table.

We talked to each other of Maritz and our doings. It didn't seem to be a popular subject in that cafe. One big blue-black fellow said that Maritz was a dirty swine who would soon be hanged. Peter quickly caught his knife-wrist with one hand and his throat with the other, and demanded an apology. He got it. The Lisbon *boulevardiers* have not lost any lions.

After that there was a bit of a squash in our corner. Those near to us were very quiet and polite, but the outer fringe made remarks. When Peter said that if Portugal, which he admitted he loved, was going to stick to England she was backing the wrong horse, there was a murmur of disapproval. One decent-looking old fellow, who had the air of a ship's captain, flushed all over his honest face, and stood up looking straight at Peter. I saw that we had struck an Englishman, and mentioned it to Peter in Dutch.

Peter played his part perfectly. He suddenly shut up, and, with furtive looks around him, began to jabber to me in a low voice. He was the very picture of the old stage conspirator.

The old fellow stood staring at us. 'I don't very well understand this damned lingo,' he said; 'but if so be you dirty Dutchmen are sayin' anything against England, I'll ask you to repeat it. And if so be as you repeats it I'll take either of you on and knock the face off him.'

He was a chap after my own heart, but I had to keep the game up. I said in Dutch to Peter that we mustn't get brawling in a public house. 'Remember the big thing,' I said darkly. Peter nodded, and the old fellow, after staring at us for a bit, spat scornfully, and walked out.

'The time is coming when the Englander will sing small,' I observed to the crowd. We stood drinks to one or two, and then swaggered into the street. At the door a hand touched my arm, and, looking down, I saw a little scrap of a man in a fur coat.

'Will the gentlemen walk a step with me and drink a glass of beer?' he said in very stiff Dutch.

'Who the devil are you?' I asked.

'*Gott strafe England!*' was his answer, and, turning back the lapel of his coat, he showed some kind of ribbon in his buttonhole.

'Amen,' said Peter. 'Lead on, friend. We don't mind if we do.'

He led us to a back street and then up two pairs of stairs to a very snug little flat. The place was filled with fine red lacquer, and I guessed that art-dealing was his nominal business. Portugal, since the republic broke up the convents and sold up the big royalist grandees, was full of bargains in the lacquer and curio line.

He filled us two long tankards of very good Munich beer.

'*Prosit*,' he said, raising his glass. 'You are from South Africa. What make you in Europe?'

We both looked sullen and secretive.

'That's our own business,' I answered. 'You don't expect to buy our confidence with a glass of beer.'

'So?' he said. 'Then I will put it differently. From your speech in the cafe I judge you do not love the English.'

Peter said something about stamping on their grandmothers, a Kaffir phrase which sounded gruesome in Dutch.

The man laughed. 'That is all I want to know. You are on the German side?'

'That remains to be seen,' I said. 'If they treat me fair I'll fight for them, or for anybody else that makes war on England. England has stolen my country and corrupted my people and made me an exile. We Afrikanders do not forget. We may be slow but we win in the end. We two are men worth a great price. Germany fights England in East Africa. We know the natives as no Englishmen can ever know them. They are too soft and easy and the Kaffirs laugh at them. But we can handle the blacks so that they will fight like devils for fear of us. What is the reward, little man, for our services? I will tell you. There will be no reward. We ask none. We fight for hate of England.'

Peter grunted a deep approval.

'That is good talk,' said our entertainer, and his close-set eyes flashed. 'There is room in Germany for such men as you. Where are you going now, I beg to know.'

'To Holland,' I said. 'Then maybe we will go to Germany. We are tired with travel and may rest a bit. This war will last long and our chance will come.'

'But you may miss your market,' he said significantly. 'A ship sails tomorrow for Rotterdam. If you take my advice, you will go with her.'

This was what I wanted, for if we stayed in Lisbon some real soldier of Maritz might drop in any day and blow the gaff.

'I recommend you to sail in the *Machado*,' he repeated. 'There is work for you in Germany—oh yes, much work; but if you delay the chance may pass. I will arrange your journey. It is my business to help the allies of my fatherland.'

He wrote down our names and an epitome of our doings contributed by Peter, who required two mugs of beer to help him through. He was a Bavarian, it seemed, and we drank to the health of Prince Rupprecht, the same blighter I was trying to do in at Loos. That was an irony which Peter unfortunately could not appreciate. If he could he would have enjoyed it.

The little chap saw us back to our hotel, and was with us the next morning after breakfast, bringing the steamer tickets. We got on board about two in the afternoon, but on my advice he did not see us off. I told him that, being British subjects and rebels at that, we did not want to run any risks on board, assuming a British cruiser caught us up and searched us. But Peter took twenty pounds off him for travelling expenses, it being his rule never to miss an opportunity of spoiling the Egyptians.

As we were dropping down the Tagus we passed the old *Henry the Navigator*.

'I met Sloggett in the street this morning,' said Peter, 'and he told me a little German man had been off in a boat at daybreak looking up the passenger list. Yon was a right notion of yours, Cornelis. I am glad we are going among Germans. They are careful people whom it is a pleasure to meet.'

CHAPTER FOUR

Adventures of Two Dutchmen on the Loose

The Germans, as Peter said, are a careful people. A man met us on the quay at Rotterdam. I was a bit afraid that something might have turned up in Lisbon to discredit us, and that our little friend might have warned his pals by telegram. But apparently all was serene.

Peter and I had made our plans pretty carefully on the voyage. We had talked nothing but Dutch, and had kept up between ourselves the role of Maritz's men, which Peter said was the only way to play a part well. Upon my soul, before we got to Holland I was not very clear in my own mind what my past had been. Indeed the danger was that the other side of my mind, which should be busy with the great problem, would get atrophied, and that I should soon be mentally on a par with the ordinary backveld desperado.

We had agreed that it would be best to get into Germany at once, and when the agent on the quay told us of a train at midday we decided to take it.

I had another fit of cold feet before we got over the frontier. At the station there was a King's Messenger whom I had seen in France, and a war correspondent who had been trotting round our part of the front before Loos. I heard a woman speaking pretty clean-cut English, which amid the hoarse Dutch jabber sounded like a lark among crows. There were copies of the English papers for sale, and English cheap editions. I felt pretty bad about the whole business, and wondered if I should ever see these homely sights again.

But the mood passed when the train started. It was a clear blowing day, and as we crawled through the flat pastures of Holland my time was taken up answering Peter's questions. He had never been in Europe before, and formed a high opinion of the farming. He said he reckoned that such land would carry four sheep a morgen. We were thick in talk when we reached the frontier station and jolted over a canal bridge into Germany.

I had expected a big barricade with barbed wire and entrenchments. But there was nothing to see on the German side but half a dozen sentries in the field-grey I had hunted at Loos. An under-officer, with the black-and-gold button of the Landsturm, hoicked us out of the train, and we were all shepherded into a big bare waiting-room where a large stove burned. They took us two at a time into an inner room for examination. I had explained to Peter all about this formality, but I was glad we went in together, for they made us strip to the skin, and I had to curse him pretty seriously to make him keep quiet. The men who did the job were fairly civil, but they were mighty thorough. They took down a list of all we had in our pockets and bags, and all the details from the passports the Rotterdam agent had given us.

We were dressing when a man in a lieutenant's uniform came in with a paper in his hand. He was a fresh-faced lad of about twenty, with short-sighted spectacled eyes.

'Herr Brandt,' he called out.

I nodded.

'And this is Herr Pienaar?' he asked in Dutch.

He saluted. 'Gentlemen, I apologize. I am late because of the slowness of the Herr Commandant's motor-car. Had I been in time you would not have been required to go through this ceremony. We have been advised of your coming, and I am instructed to attend you on your journey. The train for Berlin leaves in half an hour. Pray do me the honour to join me in a bock.'

With a feeling of distinction we stalked out of the ordinary ruck of passengers and followed the lieutenant to the station restaurant. He plunged at once into conversation, talking the Dutch of Holland, which Peter, who had forgotten his school-days, found a bit hard to follow. He was unfit for active service, because of his eyes and a weak heart, but he was a desperate fire-eater in that stuffy restaurant. By his way of it Germany could gobble up the French and the Russians whenever she cared, but she was aiming at getting all the Middle East in her hands first, so that she could come out conqueror with the practical control of half the world.

'Your friends the English,' he said grinning, 'will come last. When we have starved them and destroyed their commerce with our under-sea boats we will show them what our navy can do. For a year they have been wasting their time in brag and politics, and we have been building great ships—oh, so many! My cousin at Kiel—' and he looked over his shoulder.

But we never heard about that cousin at Kiel. A short sunburnt man came in and our friend sprang up and saluted, clicking his heels like a pair of tongs.

'These are the South African Dutch, Herr Captain,' he said.

The new-comer looked us over with bright intelligent eyes, and started questioning Peter in the taal. It was well that we had taken some pains with our story, for this man had been years in German South West, and knew every mile of the borders. Zorn was his name, and both Peter and I thought we remembered hearing him spoken of.

I am thankful to say that we both showed up pretty well. Peter told his story to perfection, not pitching it too high, and asking me now and then for a name or to verify some detail. Captain Zorn looked satisfied.

'You seem the right kind of fellows,' he said. 'But remember'—and he bent his brows on us—'we do not understand slimness in this land. If you are honest you will be rewarded, but if you dare to play a double game you will be shot like dogs. Your race has produced over many traitors for my taste.'

'I ask no reward,' I said gruffly. 'We are not Germans or Germany's slaves. But so long as she fights against England we will fight for her.'

'Bold words,' he said; 'but you must bow your stiff necks to discipline first. Discipline has been the weak point of you Boers, and you have suffered for it. You are no more a nation. In Germany we put discipline first and last, and therefore we will conquer the world. Off with you now. Your train starts in three minutes. We will see what von Stumm will make of you.'

That fellow gave me the best 'feel' of any German I had yet met. He was a white man and I could have worked with him. I liked his stiff chin and steady blue eyes.

My chief recollection of our journey to Berlin was its commonplaceness. The spectacled lieutenant fell asleep, and for the most part we had the carriage to ourselves. Now and again a soldier on leave would drop in, most of them tired men with heavy eyes. No wonder, poor devils, for they were coming back from the Yser or the Ypres salient. I would have liked to talk to them, but officially of course I knew no German, and the conversation I overheard did not signify much. It was mostly about regimental details, though one chap, who was in better spirits than the rest, observed that this was the last Christmas of misery, and that next year he would be holidaying at home with full pockets. The others assented, but without much conviction.

The winter day was short, and most of the journey was made in the dark. I could see from the window the lights of little villages, and now and then the blaze of ironworks and forges. We stopped at a town for dinner, where the platform was crowded with drafts waiting to go westward. We saw no signs of any scarcity of food, such as the English newspapers wrote about. We had an excellent dinner at the station restaurant, which, with a bottle of white wine, cost just three shillings apiece. The bread, to be sure, was poor, but I can put up with the absence of bread if I get a juicy fillet of beef and as good vegetables as you will see in the Savoy.

I was a little afraid of our giving ourselves away in our sleep, but I need have had no fear, for our escort slumbered like a hog with his mouth wide open. As we roared through the darkness I kept pinching myself to make myself feel that I was in the enemy's land on a wild mission. The rain came on, and we passed through dripping towns, with the lights shining from the wet streets. As we went eastward the lighting seemed to grow more generous. After the murk of London it was queer to slip through garish stations with a hundred arc lights glowing, and to see long lines of lamps running to the horizon. Peter dropped off early, but I kept awake till midnight, trying to focus thoughts that persistently strayed. Then I, too, dozed and did not awake till about five in the morning, when we ran into a great busy terminus as bright as midday. It was the easiest and most unsuspicious journey I ever made.

The lieutenant stretched himself and smoothed his rumpled uniform. We carried our scanty luggage to a *droschke*, for there seemed to be no porters. Our escort gave the address of some hotel and we rumbled out into brightly lit empty streets.

'A mighty dorp,' said Peter. 'Of a truth the Germans are a great people.'

The lieutenant nodded good-humouredly.

'The greatest people on earth,' he said, 'as their enemies will soon bear witness.'

I would have given a lot for a bath, but I felt that it would be outside my part, and Peter was not of the washing persuasion. But we had a very good breakfast of coffee and eggs, and then the lieutenant started on the telephone. He began by being dictatorial, then he seemed to be switched on to higher authorities, for he grew more polite, and at the end he fairly crawled. He made some arrangements, for he informed us that in the afternoon we would see some fellow whose title he could not translate into Dutch. I judged he was a great swell, for his voice became reverential at the mention of him.

He took us for a walk that morning after Peter and I had attended to our toilets. We were an odd pair of scallywags to look at, but as South African as a wait-a-bit bush. Both of us had ready-made tweed suits, grey flannel shirts with flannel collars, and felt hats with broader brims than they like in Europe. I had strong-nailed brown boots, Peter a pair of those mustard-coloured abominations which the Portuguese affect and which made him hobble like a Chinese lady. He had a scarlet satin tie which you could hear a mile off. My beard had grown to quite a respectable length, and I trimmed it like General Smuts'. Peter's was the kind of loose flapping thing the *taakhaar* loves, which has scarcely ever been shaved, and is combed once in a blue moon. I must say we made a pretty solid pair. Any South African would have set us down as a Boer from the back-veld who had bought a suit of clothes in the nearest store, and his cousin from some one-horse dorp who had been to school and thought himself the devil of a fellow. We fairly reeked of the sub-continent, as the papers call it.

It was a fine morning after the rain, and we wandered about in the streets for a couple of hours. They were busy enough, and the shops looked rich and bright with their Christmas goods, and one big store where I went to buy a pocket-knife was packed with customers. One didn't see very many young men, and most of the women wore mourning. Uniforms were everywhere, but their wearers generally looked like dug-outs or office fellows. We had a glimpse of the squat building which housed the General Staff and took off our hats to it. Then we stared at the Marinamt, and I wondered what plots were hatching there behind old Tirpitz's whiskers. The capital gave one an impression of ugly cleanness and a sort of dreary effectiveness. And yet I found it depressing—more depressing than London. I don't know how to put it, but the whole big concern seemed to have no soul in it, to be like a big factory instead of a city. You won't make a factory look like a house, though you decorate its front and plant rose-bushes all round it. The place depressed and yet cheered me. It somehow made the German people seem smaller.

At three o'clock the lieutenant took us to a plain white building in a side street with sentries at the door. A young staff officer met us and made us wait for five minutes in an ante-room. Then we were ushered into a big room with a polished floor on which Peter nearly sat down. There was a log fire burning, and seated at a table was a little man in spectacles with his hair brushed back from his brow like a popular violinist. He was the boss, for the lieutenant saluted him and announced our names. Then he disappeared, and the man at the table motioned us to sit down in two chairs before him.

'Herr Brandt and Herr Pienaar?' he asked, looking over his glasses.

But it was the other man that caught my eye. He stood with his back to the fire leaning his elbows on the mantelpiece. He was a perfect mountain of a fellow, six and a half feet if he was an inch, with shoulders on him like a shorthorn bull. He was in uniform and the black-and-white ribbon of the Iron Cross showed at a buttonhole. His tunic was all wrinkled and strained as if it could scarcely contain his huge chest, and mighty hands were clasped over his stomach. That man must have had the length of reach of a gorilla. He had a great, lazy, smiling face, with a square cleft chin which stuck out beyond the rest. His brow retreated and the stubby back of his head ran forward to meet it, while his neck below bulged out over his collar. His head was exactly the shape of a pear with the sharp end topmost.

He stared at me with his small bright eyes and I stared back. I had struck something I had been looking for for a long time, and till that moment I wasn't sure that it existed. Here was the German of caricature, the real German, the fellow we were up against. He was as hideous as a hippopotamus, but effective. Every bristle on his odd head was effective.

The man at the table was speaking. I took him to be a civilian official of sorts, pretty high up from his surroundings, perhaps an Under-Secretary. His Dutch was slow and careful, but good—too good for Peter. He had a paper before him and was asking us questions from it. They did not amount to much, being pretty well a repetition of those Zorn had asked us at the frontier. I answered fluently, for I had all our lies by heart.

Then the man on the hearthrug broke in. 'I'll talk to them, Excellency,' he said in German. 'You are too academic for those outland swine.'

He began in the taal, with the thick guttural accent that you get in German South West. 'You have heard of me,' he said. 'I am the Colonel von Stumm who fought the Hereros.'

Peter pricked up his ears. '*Ja*, Baas, you cut off the chief Baviaan's head and sent it in pickle about the country. I have seen it.'

The big man laughed. 'You see I am not forgotten,' he said to his friend, and then to us: 'So I treat my enemies, and so will Germany treat hers. You, too, if you fail me by a fraction of an inch.' And he laughed loud again.

There was something horrible in that boisterousness. Peter was watching him from below his eyelids, as I have seen him watch a lion about to charge.

He flung himself on a chair, put his elbows on the table, and thrust his face forward.

'You have come from a damned muddled show. If I had Maritz in my power I would have him flogged at a wagon's end. Fools and pig-dogs, they had the game in their hands and they flung it away. We could have raised a fire that would have burned the English into the sea, and for lack of fuel they let it die down. Then they try to fan it when the ashes are cold.'

He rolled a paper pellet and flicked it into the air. 'That is what I think of your idiot general,' he said, 'and of all you Dutch. As slow as a fat vrouw and as greedy as an aasvogel.'

We looked very glum and sullen.

'A pair of dumb dogs,' he cried. 'A thousand Brandenburgers would have won in a fortnight. Seitz hadn't much to boast of, mostly clerks and farmers and half-castes, and no soldier worth the name to lead them, but it took Botha and Smuts and a dozen generals to hunt him down. But Maritz!' His scorn came like a gust of wind.

'Maritz did all the fighting there was,' said Peter sulkily. 'At any rate he wasn't afraid of the sight of the khaki like your lot.'

'Maybe he wasn't,' said the giant in a cooing voice; 'maybe he had his reasons for that. You Dutchmen have always a feather-bed to fall on. You can always turn traitor. Maritz now calls himself Robinson, and has a pension from his friend Botha.'

'That,' said Peter, 'is a very damned lie.'

'I asked for information,' said Stumm with a sudden politeness. 'But that is all past and done with. Maritz matters no more than your old Cronjes and Krugers. The show is over, and you are looking for safety. For a new master perhaps? But, man, what can you bring? What can you offer? You and your Dutch are lying in the dust with the yoke on your necks. The Pretoria lawyers have talked you round. You see that map,' and he pointed to a big one on the wall. 'South Africa is coloured green. Not red for the English, or yellow for the Germans. Some day it will be yellow, but for a little it will be green—the colour of neutrals, of nothings, of boys and young ladies and chicken-hearts.'

I kept wondering what he was playing at.

Then he fixed his eyes on Peter. 'What do you come here for? The game's up in your own country. What can you offer us Germans? If we gave you ten million marks and sent you back you could do nothing. Stir up a village row, perhaps, and shoot a policeman. South Africa is counted out in this war. Botha is a cleverish man and has beaten you calves'-heads of rebels. Can you deny it?'

Peter couldn't. He was terribly honest in some things, and these were for certain his opinions.

'No,' he said, 'that is true, Baas.'

'Then what in God's name can you do?' shouted Stumm.

Peter mumbled some foolishness about nobbling Angola for Germany and starting a revolution among the natives. Stumm flung up his arms and cursed, and the Under-Secretary laughed.

It was high time for me to chip in. I was beginning to see the kind of fellow this Stumm was, and as he talked I thought of my mission, which had got overlaid by my Boer past. It looked as if he might be useful.

'Let me speak,' I said. 'My friend is a great hunter, but he fights better than he talks. He is no politician. You speak truth. South Africa is a closed door for the present, and the key to it is elsewhere. Here in Europe, and in the east, and in other parts of Africa. We have come to help you to find the key.'

Stumm was listening. 'Go on, my little Boer. It will be a new thing to hear a *taakhaar* on world-politics.'

'You are fighting,' I said, 'in East Africa; and soon you may fight in Egypt. All the east coast north of the Zambesi will be your battle-ground. The English run about the world with little expeditions. I do not know where the places are, though I read of them in the papers. But I know my Africa. You want to beat them here in Europe and on the seas. Therefore, like wise generals, you try to divide them and have them scattered throughout the globe while you stick at home. That is your plan?'

'A second Falkenhayn,' said Stumm, laughing.

'Well, England will not let East Africa go. She fears for Egypt and she fears, too, for India. If you press her there she will send armies and more armies till she is so weak in Europe that a child can crush her. That is England's way. She cares more for her Empire than for what may happen to her allies. So I say press and still press there, destroy the railway to the Lakes, burn her capital, pen up every Englishman in Mombasa island. At this moment it is worth for you a thousand Damaralands.'

The man was really interested and the Under-Secretary, too, pricked up his ears.

'We can keep our territory,' said the former; 'but as for pressing, how the devil are we to press? The accursed English hold the sea. We cannot ship men or guns there. South are the Portuguese and west the Belgians. You cannot move a mass without a lever.'

'The lever is there, ready for you,' I said.

'Then for God's sake show it me,' he cried.

I looked at the door to see that it was shut, as if what I had to say was very secret.

'You need men, and the men are waiting. They are black, but they are the stuff of warriors. All round your borders you have the remains of great fighting tribes, the Angoni, the Masai, the Manyumwezi, and above all the Somalis of the north, and the dwellers on the upper Nile. The British recruit their black regiments there, and so do you. But to get recruits is not enough. You must set whole nations moving, as the Zulu under Tchaka flowed over South Africa.'

'It cannot be done,' said the Under-Secretary.

'It can be done,' I said quietly. 'We two are here to do it.'

This kind of talk was jolly difficult for me, chiefly because of Stumm's asides in German to the official. I had, above all things, to get the credit of knowing no German, and, if you understand a language well, it is not very easy when you are interrupted not to show that you know it, either by a direct answer, or by referring to the interruption in what you say next. I had to be always on my guard, and yet it was up to me to be very persuasive and convince these fellows that I would be useful. Somehow or other I had to get into their confidence.

'I have been for years up and down in Africa—Uganda and the Congo and the Upper Nile. I know the ways of the Kaffir as no Englishman does. We Afrikanders see into the black man's heart, and though he may hate us he does our will. You Germans are like the English; you are too big folk to understand plain men. "Civilize," you cry. "Educate," say the English. The black man obeys and puts away his gods, but he worships them all the time in his soul. We must get his gods on our side, and then he will move mountains. We must do as John Laputa did with Sheba's necklace.'

'That's all in the air,' said Stumm, but he did not laugh.

'It is sober common sense,' I said. 'But you must begin at the right end. First find the race that fears its priests. It is waiting for you—the Mussulmans of Somaliland and the Abyssinian border and the Blue and White Nile. They would be like dried grasses to catch fire if you used the flint and steel of their religion. Look what the English suffered from a crazy Mullah who ruled only a dozen villages. Once get the flames going and they will lick up the pagans of the west and south. This is the way of Africa. How many thousands, think you, were in the Mahdi's army who never heard of the Prophet till they saw the black flags of the Emirs going into battle?'

Stumm was smiling. He turned his face to the official and spoke with his hand over his mouth, but I caught his words. They were: 'This is the man for Hilda.' The other pursed his lips and looked a little scared.

Stumm rang a bell and the lieutenant came in and clicked his heels. He nodded towards Peter. 'Take this man away with you. We have done with him. The other fellow will follow presently.'

Peter went out with a puzzled face and Stumm turned to me.

'You are a dreamer, Brandt,' he said. 'But I do not reject you on that account. Dreams sometimes come true, when an army follows the visionary. But who is going to kindle the flame?'

'You,' I said.

'What the devil do you mean?' he asked.

'That is your part. You are the cleverest people in the world. You have already half the Mussulman lands in your power. It is for you to show us how to kindle a holy war, for clearly you have the secret of it. Never fear but we will carry out your order.'

'We have no secret,' he said shortly, and glanced at the official, who stared out of the window.

I dropped my jaw and looked the picture of disappointment. 'I do not believe you,' I said slowly. 'You play a game with me. I have not come six thousand miles to be made a fool of.'

'Discipline, by God,' Stumm cried. 'This is none of your ragged commandos.' In two strides he was above me and had lifted me out of my seat. His great hands clutched my shoulders, and his thumbs gouged my armpits. I felt as if I were in the grip of a big ape. Then very slowly he shook me so that my teeth seemed loosened and my head swam. He let me go and I dropped limply back in the chair.

'Now, go! *Futsack!* And remember that I am your master. I, Ulric von Stumm, who owns you as a Kaffir owns his mongrel. Germany may have some use for you, my friend, when you fear me as you never feared your God.'

As I walked dizzily away the big man was smiling in his horrible way, and that little official was blinking and smiling too. I had struck a dashed queer country, so queer that I had had no time to remember that for the first time in my life I had been bullied without hitting back. When I realized it I nearly choked with anger. But I thanked heaven I had shown no temper, for I remembered my mission. Luck seemed to have brought me into useful company.

CHAPTER FIVE

Further Adventures of the Same

Next morning there was a touch of frost and a nip in the air which stirred my blood and put me in buoyant spirits. I forgot my precarious position and the long road I had still to travel. I came down to breakfast in great form, to find Peter's even temper badly ruffled. He had remembered Stumm in the night and disliked the memory; this he muttered to me as we rubbed shoulders at the dining-room door. Peter and I got no opportunity for private talk. The lieutenant was with us all the time, and at night we were locked in our rooms. Peter discovered this through trying to get out to find matches, for he had the bad habit of smoking in bed.

Our guide started on the telephone, and announced that we were to be taken to see a prisoners' camp. In the afternoon I was to go somewhere with Stumm, but the morning was for sight-seeing. 'You will see,' he told us, 'how merciful is a great people. You will also see some of the hated English in our power. That will delight you. They are the forerunners of all their nation.'

We drove in a taxi through the suburbs and then over a stretch of flat market-garden-like country to a low rise of wooded hills. After an hour's ride we entered the gate of what looked like a big reformatory or hospital. I believe it had been a home for destitute children. There were sentries at the gate and massive concentric circles of barbed wire through which we passed under an arch that was let down like a portcullis at nightfall. The lieutenant showed his permit, and we ran the car into a brick-paved yard and marched through a lot more sentries to the office of the commandant.

He was away from home, and we were welcomed by his deputy, a pale young man with a head nearly bald. There were introductions in German which our guide translated into Dutch, and a lot of elegant speeches about how Germany was foremost in humanity as well as martial valour. Then they stood us sandwiches and beer, and we formed a procession for a tour of inspection. There were two doctors, both mild-looking men in spectacles, and a couple of warders—under-officers of the good old burly, bullying sort I knew well. That was the cement which kept the German Army together. Her men were nothing to boast of on the average; no more were the officers, even in crack corps like the Guards and the Brandenburgers; but they seemed to have an inexhaustible supply of hard, competent N.C.O.s.

We marched round the wash-houses, the recreation-ground, the kitchens, the hospital—with nobody in it save one chap with the 'flu.' It didn't seem to be badly done. This place was entirely for officers, and I expect it was a show place where American visitors were taken. If half the stories one heard were true there were some pretty ghastly prisons away in South and East Germany.

I didn't half like the business. To be a prisoner has always seemed to me about the worst thing that could happen to a man. The sight of German prisoners used to give me a bad feeling inside, whereas I looked at dead Boches with nothing but satisfaction. Besides, there was the off-chance that I might be recognized. So I kept very much in the shadow whenever we passed anybody in the corridors. The few we met passed us incuriously. They saluted the deputy-commandant, but scarcely wasted a glance on us. No doubt they thought we were inquisitive Germans come to gloat over them. They looked fairly fit, but a little puffy about the eyes, like men who get too little exercise. They seemed thin, too. I expect the food, for all the commandant's talk, was nothing to boast of. In one room people were writing letters. It was a big place with only a tiny stove to warm it, and the windows were shut so that the atmosphere was a cold frowst. In another room a fellow was lecturing on something to a dozen hearers and drawing figures on a blackboard. Some were in ordinary khaki, others in any old thing they could pick up, and most wore greatcoats. Your blood gets thin when you have nothing to do but hope against hope and think of your pals and the old days.

I was moving along, listening with half an ear to the lieutenant's prattle and the loud explanations of the deputy-commandant, when I pitchforked into what might have been the end of my business. We were going through a sort of convalescent room, where people were sitting who had been in hospital. It was a big place, a little warmer than the rest of the building, but still abominably fuggy. There were about half a dozen men in the room, reading and playing games. They looked at us with lack-lustre eyes for a moment, and then returned to their occupations. Being convalescents I suppose they were not expected to get up and salute.

All but one, who was playing Patience at a little table by which we passed. I was feeling very bad about the thing, for I hated to see these good fellows locked away in this infernal German hole when they might have been giving the Boche his deserts at the front. The commandant went first with Peter, who had developed a great interest in prisons. Then came our lieutenant with one of the doctors; then a couple of warders; and then the second doctor and myself. I was absent-minded at the moment and was last in the queue.

The Patience-player suddenly looked up and I saw his face. I'm hanged if it wasn't Dolly Riddell, who was our brigade machine-gun officer at Loos. I had heard that the Germans had got him when they blew up a mine at the Quarries.

I had to act pretty quick, for his mouth was agape, and I saw he was going to speak. The doctor was a yard ahead of me.

I stumbled and spilt his cards on the floor. Then I kneeled to pick them up and gripped his knee. His head bent to help me and I spoke low in his ear.

'I'm Hannay all right. For God's sake don't wink an eye. I'm here on a secret job.'

The doctor had turned to see what was the matter. I got a few more words in. 'Cheer up, old man. We're winning hands down.'

Then I began to talk excited Dutch and finished the collection of the cards. Dolly was playing his part well, smiling as if he was amused by the antics of a monkey. The others were coming back, the deputy-commandant with an angry light in his dull eye. 'Speaking to the prisoners is forbidden,' he shouted.

I looked blankly at him till the lieutenant translated.

'What kind of fellow is he?' said Dolly in English to the doctor. 'He spoils my game and then jabbers High-Dutch at me.'

Officially I knew English, and that speech of Dolly's gave me my cue. I pretended to be very angry with the very damned Englishman, and went out of the room close by the deputy-commandant, grumbling like a sick jackal. After that I had to act a bit. The last place we visited was the close-confinement part where prisoners were kept as a punishment for some breach of the rules. They looked cheerless enough, but I pretended to gloat over the sight, and said so to the lieutenant, who passed it on to the others. I have rarely in my life felt such a cad.

On the way home the lieutenant discoursed a lot about prisoners and detention-camps, for at one time he had been on duty at Ruhleben. Peter, who had been in quod more than once in his life, was deeply interested and kept on questioning him. Among other things he told us was that they often put bogus prisoners among the rest, who acted as spies. If any plot to escape was hatched these fellows got into it and encouraged it. They never interfered till the attempt was actually made and then they had them on toast. There was nothing the Boche liked so much as an excuse for sending a poor devil to 'solitary'.

That afternoon Peter and I separated. He was left behind with the lieutenant and I was sent off to the station with my bag in the company of a Landsturm sergeant. Peter was very cross, and I didn't care for the look of things; but I brightened up when I heard I was going somewhere with Stumm. If he wanted to see me again he must think me of some use, and if he was going to use me he was bound to let me into his game. I liked Stumm about as much as a dog likes a scorpion, but I hankered for his society.

At the station platform, where the ornament of the Landsturm saved me all the trouble about tickets, I could not see my companion. I stood waiting, while a great crowd, mostly of soldiers, swayed past me and filled all the front carriages. An officer spoke to me gruffly and told me to stand aside behind a wooden rail. I obeyed, and suddenly found Stumm's eyes looking down at me.

'You know German?' he asked sharply.

'A dozen words,' I said carelessly. 'I've been to Windhuk and learned enough to ask for my dinner. Peter—my friend—speaks it a bit.'

'So,' said Stumm. 'Well, get into the carriage. Not that one! There, thickhead!'

I did as I was bid, he followed, and the door was locked behind us. The precaution was needless, for the sight of Stumm's profile at the platform end would have kept out the most brazen. I wondered if I had woken up his suspicions. I must be on my guard to show no signs of intelligence if he suddenly tried me in German, and that wouldn't be easy, for I knew it as well as I knew Dutch.

We moved into the country, but the windows were blurred with frost, and I saw nothing of the landscape. Stumm was busy with papers and let me alone. I read on a notice that one was forbidden to smoke, so to show my ignorance of German I pulled out my pipe. Stumm raised his head, saw what I was doing, and gruffly bade me put it away, as if he were an old lady that disliked the smell of tobacco.

In half an hour I got very bored, for I had nothing to read and my pipe was *verboten*. People passed now and then in the corridors, but no one offered to enter. No doubt they saw the big figure in uniform and thought he was the deuce of a staff swell who wanted solitude. I thought of stretching my legs in the corridor, and was just getting up to do it when somebody slid the door back and a big figure blocked the light.

He was wearing a heavy ulster and a green felt hat. He saluted Stumm, who looked up angrily, and smiled pleasantly on us both.

'Say, gentlemen,' he said, 'have you room in here for a little one? I guess I'm about smoked out of my car by your brave soldiers. I've gotten a delicate stomach ...'

Stumm had risen with a brow of wrath, and looked as if he were going to pitch the intruder off the train. Then he seemed to halt and collect himself, and the other's face broke into a friendly grin.

'Why, it's Colonel Stumm,' he cried. (He pronounced it like the first syllable in 'stomach'.) 'Very pleased to meet you again, Colonel. I had the honour of making your acquaintance at our Embassy. I reckon Ambassador Gerard didn't cotton to our conversation that night.' And the new-comer plumped himself down in the corner opposite me.

I had been pretty certain I would run across Blenkiron somewhere in Germany, but I didn't think it would be so soon. There he sat staring at me with his full, unseeing eyes, rolling out platitudes to Stumm, who was nearly bursting in his effort to keep civil. I looked moody and suspicious, which I took to be the right line.

'Things are getting a bit dead at Salonika,' said Mr Blenkiron, by way of a conversational opening.

Stumm pointed to a notice which warned officers to refrain from discussing military operations with mixed company in a railway carriage.

'Sorry,' said Blenkiron, 'I can't read that tombstone language of yours. But I reckon that that notice to trespassers, whatever it signifies, don't apply to you and me. I take it this gentleman is in your party.'

I sat and scowled, fixing the American with suspicious eyes.

'He is a Dutchman,' said Stumm; 'South African Dutch, and he is not happy, for he doesn't like to hear English spoken.'

'We'll shake on that,' said Blenkiron cordially. 'But who said I spoke English? It's good American. Cheer up, friend, for it isn't the call that makes the big wapiti, as they say out west in my country. I hate John Bull worse than a poison rattle. The Colonel can tell you that.'

I dare say he could, but at that moment, we slowed down at a station and Stumm got up to leave. 'Good day to you, Herr Blenkiron,' he cried over his shoulder. 'If you consider your comfort, don't talk English to strange travellers. They don't distinguish between the different brands.'

I followed him in a hurry, but was recalled by Blenkiron's voice.

'Say, friend,' he shouted, 'you've left your grip,' and he handed me my bag from the luggage rack. But he showed no sign of recognition, and the last I saw of him was sitting sunk in a corner with his head on his chest as if he were going to sleep. He was a man who kept up his parts well.

There was a motor-car waiting—one of the grey military kind—and we started at a terrific pace over bad forest roads. Stumm had put away his papers in a portfolio, and flung me a few sentences on the journey.

'I haven't made up my mind about you, Brandt,' he announced. 'You may be a fool or a knave or a good man. If you are a knave, we will shoot you.'

'And if I am a fool?' I asked.

'Send you to the Yser or the Dvina. You will be respectable cannon-fodder.'

'You cannot do that unless I consent,' I said.

'Can't we?' he said, smiling wickedly. 'Remember you are a citizen of nowhere. Technically, you are a rebel, and the British, if you go to them, will hang you, supposing they have any sense. You are in our power, my friend, to do precisely what we like with you.'

He was silent for a second, and then he said, meditatively:

'But I don't think you are a fool. You may be a scoundrel. Some kinds of scoundrel are useful enough. Other kinds are strung up with a rope. Of that we shall know more soon.'

'And if I am a good man?'

'You will be given a chance to serve Germany, the proudest privilege a mortal man can have.' The strange man said this with a ringing sincerity in his voice that impressed me.

The car swung out from the trees into a park lined with saplings, and in the twilight I saw before me a biggish house like an overgrown Swiss chalet. There was a kind of archway, with a sham portcullis, and a terrace with battlements which looked as if they were made of stucco. We drew up at a Gothic front door, where a thin middle-aged man in a shooting-jacket was waiting.

As we moved into the lighted hall I got a good look at our host. He was very lean and brown, with the stoop in the shoulder that one gets from being constantly on horseback. He had untidy grizzled hair and a ragged beard, and a pair of pleasant, short-sighted brown eyes.

'Welcome, my Colonel,' he said. 'Is this the friend you spoke of?'

'This is the Dutchman,' said Stumm. 'His name is Brandt. Brandt, you see before you Herr Gaudian.'

I knew the name, of course; there weren't many in my profession that didn't. He was one of the biggest railway engineers in the world, the man who had built the Baghdad and Syrian railways, and the new lines in German East. I suppose he was about the greatest living authority on tropical construction. He knew the East and he knew Africa; clearly I had been brought down for him to put me through my paces.

A blonde maidservant took me to my room, which had a bare polished floor, a stove, and windows that, unlike most of the German kind I had sampled, seemed made to open. When I had washed I descended to the hall, which was hung round with trophies of travel, like Dervish jibbahs and Masai shields and one or two good buffalo heads. Presently a bell was rung. Stumm appeared with his host, and we went in to supper.

I was jolly hungry and would have made a good meal if I hadn't constantly had to keep jogging my wits. The other two talked in German, and when a question was put to me Stumm translated. The first thing I had to do was to pretend I didn't know German and look listlessly round the room while they were talking. The second was to miss not a word, for there lay my chance. The third was to be ready to answer questions at any moment, and to show in the answering that I had not followed the previous conversation. Likewise, I must not prove myself a fool in these answers, for I had to convince them that I was useful. It took some doing, and I felt like a witness in the box under a stiff cross-examination, or a man trying to play three games of chess at once.

I heard Stumm telling Gaudian the gist of my plan. The engineer shook his head.

'Too late,' he said. 'It should have been done at the beginning. We neglected Africa. You know the reason why.'

Stumm laughed. 'The von Einem! Perhaps, but her charm works well enough.'

Gaudian glanced towards me while I was busy with an orange salad. 'I have much to tell you of that. But it can wait. Your friend is right in one thing. Uganda is a vital spot for the English, and a blow there will make their whole fabric shiver. But how can we strike? They have still the coast, and our supplies grow daily smaller.'

'We can send no reinforcements, but have we used all the local resources? That is what I cannot satisfy myself about. Zimmerman says we have, but Tressler thinks differently, and now we have this fellow coming out of the void with a story which confirms my doubt. He seems to know his job. You try him.'

Thereupon Gaudian set about questioning me, and his questions were very thorough. I knew just enough and no more to get through, but I think I came out with credit. You see I have a capacious memory, and in my time I had met scores of hunters and pioneers and listened to their yarns, so I could pretend to knowledge of a place even when I hadn't been there. Besides, I had once been on the point of undertaking a job up Tanganyika way, and I had got up that country-side pretty accurately.

'You say that with our help you can make trouble for the British on the three borders?' Gaudian asked at length.

'I can spread the fire if some one else will kindle it,' I said.

'But there are thousands of tribes with no affinities.'

'They are all African. You can bear me out. All African peoples are alike in one thing—they can go mad, and the madness of one infects the others. The English know this well enough.'

'Where would you start the fire?' he asked.

'Where the fuel is dryest. Up in the North among the Mussulman peoples. But there you must help me. I know nothing about Islam, and I gather that you do.'

'Why?' he asked.

'Because of what you have done already,' I answered.

Stumm had translated all this time, and had given the sense of my words very fairly. But with my last answer he took liberties. What he gave was: 'Because the Dutchman thinks that we have some big card in dealing with the Moslem world.' Then, lowering his voice and raising his eyebrows, he said some word like 'uhnmantl'.

The other looked with a quick glance of apprehension at me. 'We had better continue our talk in private, Herr Colonel,' he said. 'If Herr Brandt will forgive us, we will leave him for a little to entertain himself.' He pushed the cigar-box towards me and the two got up and left the room.

I pulled my chair up to the stove, and would have liked to drop off to sleep. The tension of the talk at supper had made me very tired. I was accepted by these men for exactly what I professed to be. Stumm might suspect me of being a rascal, but it was a Dutch rascal. But all the same I was skating on thin ice. I could not sink myself utterly in the part, for if I did I would get no good out of being there. I had to keep my wits going all the time, and join the appearance and manners of a backveld Boer with the mentality of a British intelligence-officer. Any moment the two parts might clash and I would be faced with the most alert and deadly suspicion.

There would be no mercy from Stumm. That large man was beginning to fascinate me, even though I hated him. Gaudian was clearly a good fellow, a white man and a gentleman. I could have worked with him for he belonged to my own totem. But the other was an incarnation of all that makes Germany detested, and yet he wasn't altogether the ordinary German, and I couldn't help admiring him. I noticed he neither smoked nor drank. His grossness was apparently not in the way of fleshly appetites. Cruelty, from all I had heard of him in German South West, was his hobby; but there were other things in him, some of them good, and he had that kind of crazy patriotism which becomes a religion. I wondered why he had not some high command in the field, for he had had the name of a good soldier. But probably he was a big man in his own line, whatever it was, for the Under-Secretary fellow had talked small in his presence, and so great a man as Gaudian clearly respected him. There must be no lack of brains inside that funny pyramidal head.

As I sat beside the stove I was casting back to think if I had got the slightest clue to my real job. There seemed to be nothing so far. Stumm had talked of a von Einem woman who was interested in his department, perhaps the same woman as the Hilda he had mentioned the day before to the Under-Secretary. There was not much in that. She was probably some minister's or ambassador's wife who had a finger in high politics. If I could have caught the word Stumm had whispered to Gaudian which made him start and look askance at me! But I had only heard a gurgle of something like 'uhnmantl', which wasn't any German word that I knew.

The heat put me into a half-doze and I began dreamily to wonder what other people were doing. Where had Blenkiron been posting to in that train, and what was he up to at this moment? He had been hobnobbing with ambassadors and swells—I wondered if he had found out anything. What was Peter doing? I fervently hoped he was behaving himself, for I doubted if Peter had really tumbled to the delicacy of our job. Where was Sandy, too? As like as not bucketing in the hold of some Greek coaster in the Aegean. Then I thought of my battalion somewhere on the line between Hulluch and La Bassee, hammering at the Boche, while I was five hundred miles or so inside the Boche frontier.

It was a comic reflection, so comic that it woke me up. After trying in vain to find a way of stoking that stove, for it was a cold night, I got up and walked about the room. There were portraits of two decent old fellows, probably Gaudian's parents. There were enlarged photographs, too, of engineering works, and a good picture of Bismarck. And close to the stove there was a case of maps mounted on rollers.

I pulled out one at random. It was a geological map of Germany, and with some trouble I found out where I was. I was an enormous distance from my goal and moreover I was clean off the road to the East. To go there I must first go to Bavaria and then into Austria. I noticed the Danube flowing eastwards and remembered that that was one way to Constantinople.

Then I tried another map. This one covered a big area, all Europe from the Rhine and as far east as Persia. I guessed that it was meant to show the Baghdad railway and the through routes from Germany to Mesopotamia. There were markings on it; and, as I looked closer, I saw that there were dates scribbled in blue pencil, as if to denote the stages of a journey. The dates began in Europe, and continued right on into Asia Minor and then south to Syria.

For a moment my heart jumped, for I thought I had fallen by accident on the clue I wanted. But I never got that map examined. I heard footsteps in the corridor, and very gently I let the map roll up and turned away. When the door opened I was bending over the stove trying to get a light for my pipe.

It was Gaudian, to bid me join him and Stumm in his study.

On our way there he put a kindly hand on my shoulder. I think he thought I was bullied by Stumm and wanted to tell me that he was my friend, and he had no other language than a pat on the back.

The soldier was in his old position with his elbows on the mantelpiece and his formidable great jaw stuck out.

'Listen to me,' he said. 'Herr Gaudian and I are inclined to make use of you. You may be a charlatan, in which case you will be in the devil of a mess and have yourself to thank for it. If you are a rogue you will have little scope for roguery. We will see to that. If you are a fool, you will yourself suffer for it. But if you are a good man, you will have a fair chance, and if you succeed we will not forget it. Tomorrow I go home and you will come with me and get your orders.'

I made shift to stand at attention and salute.

Gaudian spoke in a pleasant voice, as if he wanted to atone for Stumm's imperiousness. 'We are men who love our Fatherland, Herr Brandt,' he said. 'You are not of that Fatherland, but at least you hate its enemies. Therefore we are allies, and trust each other like allies. Our victory is ordained by God, and we are none of us more than His instruments.'

Stumm translated in a sentence, and his voice was quite solemn. He held up his right hand and so did

Gaudian, like a man taking an oath or a parson blessing his congregation.

Then I realized something of the might of Germany. She produced good and bad, cads and gentlemen, but she could put a bit of the fanatic into them all.

CHAPTER SIX

The Indiscretions of the Same

I was standing stark naked next morning in that icy bedroom, trying to bathe in about a quart of water, when Stumm entered. He strode up to me and stared me in the face. I was half a head shorter than him to begin with, and a man does not feel his stoutest when he has no clothes, so he had the pull on me every way.

'I have reason to believe that you are a liar,' he growled.

I pulled the bed-cover round me, for I was shivering with cold, and the German idea of a towel is a pocket-handkerchief. I own I was in a pretty blue funk.

'A liar!' he repeated. 'You and that swine Pienaar.'

With my best effort at surliness I asked what we had done.

'You lied, because you said you know no German. Apparently your friend knows enough to talk treason and blasphemy.'

This gave me back some heart.

'I told you I knew a dozen words. But I told you Peter could talk it a bit. I told you that yesterday at the station.' Fervently I blessed my luck for that casual remark.

He evidently remembered, for his tone became a trifle more civil.

'You are a precious pair. If one of you is a scoundrel, why not the other?'

'I take no responsibility for Peter,' I said. I felt I was a cad in saying it, but that was the bargain we had made at the start. 'I have known him for years as a great hunter and a brave man. I knew he fought well against the English. But more I cannot tell you. You have to judge him for yourself. What has he done?'

I was told, for Stumm had got it that morning on the telephone. While telling it he was kind enough to allow me to put on my trousers.

It was just the sort of thing I might have foreseen. Peter, left alone, had become first bored and then reckless. He had persuaded the lieutenant to take him out to supper at a big Berlin restaurant. There, inspired by the lights and music—novel things for a backveld hunter—and no doubt bored stiff by his company, he had proceeded to get drunk. That had happened in my experience with Peter about once in every three years, and it always happened for the same reason. Peter, bored and solitary in a town, went on the spree. He had a head like a rock, but he got to the required condition by wild mixing. He was quite a gentleman in his cups, and not in the least violent, but he was apt to be very free with his tongue. And that was what occurred at the Franciscana.

He had begun by insulting the Emperor, it seemed. He drank his health, but said he reminded him of a wart-hog, and thereby scarified the lieutenant's soul. Then an officer—some tremendous swell at an adjoining table had objected to his talking so loud, and Peter had replied insolently in respectable German. After that things became mixed. There was some kind of a fight, during which Peter calumniated the German army and all its female ancestry. How he wasn't shot or run through I can't imagine, except that the lieutenant loudly proclaimed that he was a crazy Boer. Anyhow the upshot was that Peter was marched off to gaol, and I was left in a pretty pickle.

'I don't believe a word of it,' I said firmly. I had most of my clothes on now and felt more courageous. 'It is all a plot to get him into disgrace and draft him off to the front.'

Stumm did not storm as I expected, but smiled.

'That was always his destiny,' he said, 'ever since I saw him. He was no use to us except as a man with a rifle. Cannon-fodder, nothing else. Do you imagine, you fool, that this great Empire in the thick of a world-war is going to trouble its head to lay snares for an ignorant *taakhaar*?'

'I wash my hands of him,' I said. 'If what you say of his folly is true I have no part in it. But he was my companion and I wish him well. What do you propose to do with him?'

'We will keep him under our eye,' he said, with a wicked twist of the mouth. 'I have a notion that there is more at the back of this than appears. We will investigate the antecedents of Herr Pienaar. And you, too, my friend. On you also we have our eye.'

I did the best thing I could have done, for what with anxiety and disgust I lost my temper.

'Look here, Sir,' I cried, 'I've had about enough of this. I came to Germany abominating the English and burning to strike a blow for you. But you haven't given me much cause to love you. For the last two days I've had nothing from you but suspicion and insult. The only decent man I've met is Herr Gaudian. It's because I believe that there are many in Germany like him that I'm prepared to go on with this business and do the best I can. But, by God, I wouldn't raise my little finger for your sake.'

He looked at me very steadily for a minute. 'That sounds like honesty,' he said at last in a civil voice. 'You had better come down and get your coffee.'

I was safe for the moment but in very low spirits. What on earth would happen to poor old Peter? I could do nothing even if I wanted, and, besides, my first duty was to my mission. I had made this very clear to him at Lisbon and he had agreed, but all the same it was a beastly reflection. Here was that ancient worthy left to the tender mercies of the people he most detested on earth. My only comfort was that they couldn't do very much with him. If they sent him to the front, which was the worst they could do, he would escape, for I would have backed him to get through any mortal lines. It wasn't much fun for me either. Only when I was to be deprived of it did I realize how much his company had meant to me. I was absolutely alone now, and I didn't like it. I seemed to have about as much chance of joining Blenkiron and Sandy as of flying to the moon.

After breakfast I was told to get ready. When I asked where I was going Stumm advised me to mind my own business, but I remembered that last night he had talked of taking me home with him and giving me my orders. I wondered where his home was.

Gaudian patted me on the back when we started and wrung my hand. He was a capital good fellow, and it made me feel sick to think that I was humbugging him. We got into the same big grey car, with Stumm's servant sitting beside the chauffeur. It was a morning of hard frost, the bare fields were white with rime, and the fir-trees powdered like a wedding-cake. We took a different road from the night before, and after a run of half a dozen miles came to a little town with a big railway station. It was a junction on some main line, and after five minutes' waiting we found our train. Once again we were alone in the carriage. Stumm must have had some colossal graft, for the train was crowded.

I had another three hours of complete boredom. I dared not smoke, and could do nothing but stare out of the window. We soon got into hilly country, where a good deal of snow was lying. It was the 23rd day of December, and even in war time one had a sort of feel of Christmas. You could see girls carrying evergreens, and when we stopped at a station the soldiers on leave had all the air of holiday making. The middle of Germany was a cheerier place than Berlin or the western parts. I liked the look of the old peasants, and the women in their neat Sunday best, but I noticed, too, how pinched they were. Here in the country, where no neutral tourists came, there was not the same stage-management as in the capital.

Stumm made an attempt to talk to me on the journey. I could see his aim. Before this he had cross-examined me, but now he wanted to draw me into ordinary conversation. He had no notion how to do it. He was either peremptory and provocative, like a drill-sergeant, or so obviously diplomatic that any fool would have been put on his guard. That is the weakness of the German. He has no gift for laying himself alongside different types of men. He is such a hard-shell being that he cannot put out feelers to his kind. He may have plenty of brains, as Stumm had, but he has the poorest notion of psychology of any of God's creatures. In

Germany only the Jew can get outside himself, and that is why, if you look into the matter, you will find that the Jew is at the back of most German enterprises.

After midday we stopped at a station for luncheon. We had a very good meal in the restaurant, and when we were finishing two officers entered. Stumm got up and saluted and went aside to talk to them. Then he came back and made me follow him to a waiting-room, where he told me to stay till he fetched me. I noticed that he called a porter and had the door locked when he went out.

It was a chilly place with no fire, and I kicked my heels there for twenty minutes. I was living by the hour now, and did not trouble to worry about this strange behaviour. There was a volume of time-tables on a shelf, and I turned the pages idly till I struck a big railway map. Then it occurred to me to find out where we were going. I had heard Stumm take my ticket for a place called Schwandorf, and after a lot of searching I found it. It was away south in Bavaria, and so far as I could make out less than fifty miles from the Danube. That cheered me enormously. If Stumm lived there he would most likely start me off on my travels by the railway which I saw running to Vienna and then on to the East. It looked as if I might get to Constantinople after all. But I feared it would be a useless achievement, for what could I do when I got there? I was being hustled out of Germany without picking up the slenderest clue.

The door opened and Stumm entered. He seemed to have got bigger in the interval and to carry his head higher. There was a proud light, too, in his eye.

'Brandt,' he said, 'you are about to receive the greatest privilege that ever fell to one of your race. His Imperial Majesty is passing through here, and has halted for a few minutes. He has done me the honour to receive me, and when he heard my story he expressed a wish to see you. You will follow me to his presence. Do not be afraid. The All-Highest is merciful and gracious. Answer his questions like a man.'

I followed him with a quickened pulse. Here was a bit of luck I had never dreamed of. At the far side of the station a train had drawn up, a train consisting of three big coaches, chocolate-coloured and picked out with gold. On the platform beside it stood a small group of officers, tall men in long grey-blue cloaks. They seemed to be mostly elderly, and one or two of the faces I thought I remembered from photographs in the picture papers.

As we approached they drew apart, and left us face to face with one man. He was a little below middle height, and all muffled in a thick coat with a fur collar. He wore a silver helmet with an eagle atop of it, and kept his left hand resting on his sword. Below the helmet was a face the colour of grey paper, from which shone curious sombre restless eyes with dark pouches beneath them. There was no fear of my mistaking him. These were the features which, since Napoleon, have been best known to the world.

I stood as stiff as a ramrod and saluted. I was perfectly cool and most desperately interested. For such a moment I would have gone through fire and water.

'Majesty, this is the Dutchman I spoke of,' I heard Stumm say.

'What language does he speak?' the Emperor asked.

'Dutch,' was the reply; 'but being a South African he also speaks English.'

A spasm of pain seemed to flit over the face before me. Then he addressed me in English.

'You have come from a land which will yet be our ally to offer your sword to our service? I accept the gift and hail it as a good omen. I would have given your race its freedom, but there were fools and traitors among you who misjudged me. But that freedom I shall yet give you in spite of yourselves. Are there many like you in your country?'

'There are thousands, sire,' I said, lying cheerfully. 'I am one of many who think that my race's life lies in your victory. And I think that that victory must be won not in Europe alone. In South Africa for the moment there is no chance, so we look to other parts of the continent.

You will win in Europe. You have won in the East, and it now remains to strike the English where they cannot fend the blow. If we take Uganda, Egypt will fall. By your permission I go there to make trouble for your enemies.'

A flicker of a smile passed over the worn face. It was the face of one who slept little and whose thoughts rode him like a nightmare. 'That is well,' he said. 'Some Englishman once said that he would call in the New World to redress the balance of the Old. We Germans will summon the whole earth to suppress the infamies of England. Serve us well, and you will not be forgotten.' Then he suddenly asked: 'Did you fight in the last South African War?'

'Yes, Sir,' I said. 'I was in the commando of that Smuts who has now been bought by England.'

'What were your countrymen's losses?' he asked eagerly.

I did not know, but I hazarded a guess. 'In the field some twenty thousand. But many more by sickness and in the accursed prison-camps of the English.'

Again a spasm of pain crossed his face.

'Twenty thousand,' he repeated huskily. 'A mere handful. Today we lose as many in a skirmish in the Polish marshes.'

Then he broke out fiercely. 'I did not seek the war ... It was forced on me ... I laboured for peace ... The blood of millions is on the heads of England and Russia, but England most of all. God will yet avenge it. He that takes the sword will perish by the sword. Mine was forced from the scabbard in self-defence, and I am guiltless. Do they know that among your people?'

'All the world knows it, sire,' I said.

He gave his hand to Stumm and turned away. The last I saw of him was a figure moving like a sleep-walker, with no spring in his step, amid his tall suite. I felt that I was looking on at a far bigger tragedy than any I had seen in action. Here was one that had loosed Hell, and the furies of Hell had got hold of him. He was no common man, for in his presence I felt an attraction which was not merely the mastery of one used to command. That would not have impressed me, for I had never owned a master. But here was a human being who, unlike Stumm and his kind, had the power of laying himself alongside other men. That was the irony of it. Stumm would not have cared a tinker's curse for all the massacres in history. But this man, the chief of a nation of Stumms, paid the price in war for the gifts that had made him successful in peace. He had imagination and nerves, and the one was white hot and the others were quivering. I would not have been in his shoes for the throne of the Universe ...

All afternoon we sped southward, mostly in a country of hills and wooded valleys. Stumm, for him, was very pleasant. His imperial master must have been gracious to him, and he passed a bit of it on to me. But he was anxious to see that I had got the right impression.

'The All-Highest is merciful, as I told you,' he said.

I agreed with him.

'Mercy is the prerogative of kings,' he said sententiously, 'but for us lesser folks it is a trimming we can well do without.'

I nodded my approval.

'I am not merciful,' he went on, as if I needed telling that. 'If any man stands in my way I trample the life out of him. That is the German fashion. That is what has made us great. We do not make war with lavender gloves and fine phrases, but with hard steel and hard brains. We Germans will cure the green-sickness of the world. The nations rise against us. Pouf! They are soft flesh, and flesh cannot resist iron. The shining ploughshare will cut its way through acres of mud.'

I hastened to add that these were also my opinions.

'What the hell do your opinions matter? You are a thick-headed boor of the veld ... Not but what,' he added, 'there is metal in you slow Dutchmen once we Germans have had the forging of it!'

The winter evening closed in, and I saw that we had come out of the hills and were in flat country. Sometimes a big sweep of river showed, and, looking out at one station I saw a funny church with a thing like an onion on top of its spire. It might almost have been a mosque, judging from the pictures I remembered of mosques. I wished to heaven I had given geography more attention in my time.

Presently we stopped, and Stumm led the way out. The train must have been specially halted for him, for it was a one-horse little place whose name I could not make out. The station-master was waiting, bowing and saluting, and outside was a motor-car with big head-lights. Next minute we were sliding through dark woods where the snow lay far deeper than in the north. There was a mild frost in the air, and the tyres slipped and skidded at the corners.

We hadn't far to go. We climbed a little hill and on the top of it stopped at the door of a big black castle. It looked enormous in the winter night, with not a light showing anywhere on its front. The door was opened by an old fellow who took a long time about it and got well cursed for his slowness. Inside the place was very noble and ancient. Stumm switched on the electric light, and there was a great hall with black tarnished portraits of men an women in old-fashioned clothes, and mighty horns of deer on the walls.

There seemed to be no superfluity of servants. The old fellow said that food was ready, and without more ado we went into the dining-room—another vast chamber with rough stone walls above the panelling—and found some cold meats on the table beside a big fire. The servant presently brought in a ham omelette, and on that and the cold stuff we dined. I remember there was nothing to drink but water. It puzzled me how Stumm kept his great body going on the very moderate amount of food he ate. He was the type you expect to swill beer by the bucket and put away a pie in a sitting.

When we had finished, he rang for the old man and told him that we should be in the study for the rest of the evening. 'You can lock up and go to bed when you like,' he said, 'but see you have coffee ready at seven sharp in the morning.'

Ever since I entered that house I had the uncomfortable feeling of being in a prison. Here was I alone in this great place with a fellow who could, and would, wring my neck if he wanted. Berlin and all the rest of it had seemed comparatively open country; I had felt that I could move freely and at the worst make a bolt for it. But here I was trapped, and I had to tell myself every minute that I was there as a friend and colleague. The fact is, I was afraid of Stumm, and I don't mind admitting it. He was a new thing in my experience and I didn't like it. If only he had drunk and guzzled a bit I should have been happier.

We went up a staircase to a room at the end of a long corridor. Stumm locked the door behind him and laid the key on the table. That room took my breath away, it was so unexpected. In place of the grim bareness of downstairs here was a place all luxury and colour and light. It was very large, but low in the ceiling, and the walls were full of little recesses with statues in them. A thick grey carpet of velvet pile covered the floor, and the chairs were low and soft and upholstered like a lady's boudoir. A pleasant fire burned on the hearth and there was a flavour of scent in the air, something like incense or burnt sandalwood. A French clock on the mantelpiece told me that it was ten minutes past eight. Everywhere on little tables and in cabinets was a profusion of knickknacks, and there was some beautiful embroidery framed on screens. At first sight you would have said it was a woman's drawing-room.

But it wasn't. I soon saw the difference. There had never been a woman's hand in that place. It was the room of a man who had a passion for frippery, who had a perverted taste for soft delicate things. It was the complement to his bluff brutality. I began to see the queer other side to my host, that evil side which gossip had spoken of as not unknown in the German army. The room seemed a horribly unwholesome place, and I was more than ever afraid of Stumm.

The hearthrug was a wonderful old Persian thing, all faint greens and pinks. As he stood on it he looked uncommonly like a bull in a china-shop. He seemed to bask in the comfort of it, and sniffed like a satisfied animal. Then he sat down at an escritoire, unlocked a drawer and took out some papers.

'We will now settle your business, friend Brandt,' he said. 'You will go to Egypt and there take your orders from one whose name and address are in this envelope. This card,' and he lifted a square piece of grey pasteboard with a big stamp at the corner and some code words stencilled on it, 'will be your passport. You will Show it to the man you seek. Keep it jealously, and never use it save under orders or in the last necessity. It is your badge as an accredited agent of the German Crown.'

I took the card and the envelope and put them in my pocket-book.

'Where do I go after Egypt?' I asked.

'That remains to be seen. Probably you will go up the Blue Nile. Riza, the man you will meet, will direct you. Egypt is a nest of our agents who work peacefully under the nose of the English Secret Service.'

'I am willing,' I said. 'But how do I reach Egypt?'

'You will travel by Holland and London. Here is your route,' and he took a paper from his pocket. 'Your passports are ready and will be given you at the frontier.'

This was a pretty kettle of fish. I was to be packed off to Cairo by sea, which would take weeks, and God knows how I would get from Egypt to Constantinople. I saw all my plans falling to pieces about my ears, and just when I thought they were shaping nicely.

Stumm must have interpreted the look on my face as fear.

'You have no cause to be afraid,' he said. 'We have passed the word to the English police to look out for a suspicious South African named Brandt, one of Maritz's rebels. It is not difficult to have that kind of a hint conveyed to the proper quarter. But the description will not be yours. Your name will be Van der Linden, a respectable Java merchant going home to his plantations after a visit to his native shores. You had better get your *dossier* by heart, but I guarantee you will be asked no questions. We manage these things well in Germany.'

I kept my eyes on the fire, while I did some savage thinking. I knew they would not let me out of their sight till they saw me in Holland, and, once there, there would be no possibility of getting back. When I left this house I would have no chance of giving them the slip. And yet I was well on my way to the East, the Danube could not be fifty miles off, and that way ran the road to

Constantinople. It was a fairly desperate position. If I tried to get away Stumm would prevent me, and the odds were that I would go to join Peter in some infernal prison-camp.

Those moments were some of the worst I ever spent. I was absolutely and utterly baffled, like a rat in a trap. There seemed nothing for it but to go back to London and tell Sir Walter the game was up. And that was about as bitter as death.

He saw my face and laughed. 'Does your heart fail you, my little Dutchman? You funk the English? I will tell you one thing for your comfort. There is nothing in the world to be feared except me. Fail, and you have cause to shiver. Play me false and you had far better never have been born.'

His ugly sneering face was close above mine. Then he put out his hands and gripped my shoulders as he had done the first afternoon.

I forget if I mentioned that part of the damage I got at Loos was a shrapnel bullet low down at the back of my neck. The wound had healed well enough, but I had pains there on a cold day. His fingers found the place and it hurt like hell.

There is a very narrow line between despair and black rage. I had about given up the game, but the sudden ache of my shoulders gave me purpose again. He must have seen the rage in my eyes, for his own became cruel.

'The weasel would like to bite,' he cried. 'But the poor weasel has found its master. Stand still, vermin. Smile, look pleasant, or I will make pulp of you. Do you dare to frown at me?'

I shut my teeth and said never a word. I was choking in my throat and could not have uttered a syllable if I had tried.

Then he let me go, grinning like an ape.

I stepped back a pace and gave him my left between the eyes.

For a second he did not realize what had happened, for I don't suppose anyone had dared to lift a hand to him since he was a child. He blinked at me mildly. Then his face grew as red as fire.

'God in heaven,' he said quietly. 'I am going to kill you,' and he flung himself on me like a mountain.

I was expecting him and dodged the attack. I was quite calm now, but pretty helpless. The man had a gorilla's reach and could give me at least a couple of stone. He wasn't soft either, but looked as hard as granite. I was only just from hospital and absurdly out of training. He would certainly kill me if he could, and I saw nothing to prevent him.

My only chance was to keep him from getting to grips, for he could have squeezed in my ribs in two seconds. I fancied I was lighter on my legs than him, and I had a good eye. Black Monty at Kimberley had taught me to fight a bit, but there is no art on earth which can prevent a big man in a narrow space from sooner or later cornering a lesser one. That was the danger.

Backwards and forwards we padded on the soft carpet. He had no notion of guarding himself, and I got in a good few blows.

Then I saw a queer thing. Every time I hit him he blinked and seemed to pause. I guessed the reason for that. He had gone through life keeping the crown of the causeway, and nobody had ever stood up to him. He wasn't a coward by a long chalk, but he was a bully, and had never been struck in his life. He was getting struck now in real earnest, and he didn't like it. He had lost his bearings and was growing as mad as a hatter.

I kept half an eye on the clock. I was hopeful now, and was looking for the right kind of chance. The risk was that I might tire sooner than him and be at his mercy.

Then I learned a truth I have never forgotten. If you are fighting a man who means to kill you, he will be apt to down you unless you mean to kill him too. Stumm did not know any rules to this game, and I forgot to allow for that. Suddenly, when I was watching his eyes, he launched a mighty kick at my stomach. If he had got me, this yarn would have had an abrupt ending. But by the mercy of God I was moving sideways when he let out, and his heavy boot just grazed my left thigh.

It was the place where most of the shrapnel had lodged, and for a second I was sick with pain and stumbled. Then I was on my feet again but with a new feeling in my blood. I had to smash Stumm or never sleep in my bed again.

I got a wonderful power from this new cold rage of mine. I felt I couldn't tire, and I danced round and dotted his face till it was streaming with blood. His bulky padded chest was no good to me, so I couldn't try for the mark.

He began to snort now and his breath came heavily. 'You infernal cad,' I said in good round English, 'I'm going to knock the stuffing out of you,' but he didn't know what I was saying.

Then at last he gave me my chance. He half tripped over a little table and his face stuck forward. I got him on the point of the chin, and put every ounce of weight I possessed behind the blow. He crumpled up in a heap and rolled over, upsetting a lamp and knocking a big china jar in two. His head, I remember, lay under the escritoire from which he had taken my passport.

I picked up the key and unlocked the door. In one of the gilded mirrors I smoothed my hair and tidied up my clothes. My anger had completely gone and I had no particular ill-will left against Stumm. He was a man of remarkable qualities, which would have brought him to the highest distinction in the Stone Age. But for all that he and his kind were back numbers.

I stepped out of the room, locked the door behind me, and started out on the second stage of my travels.

CHAPTER SEVEN

Christmastide

Everything depended on whether the servant was in the hall. I had put Stumm to sleep for a bit, but I couldn't flatter myself he would long be quiet, and when he came to he would kick the locked door to matchwood. I must get out of the house without a minute's delay, and if the door was shut and the old man gone to bed I was done.

I met him at the foot of the stairs, carrying a candle.

'Your master wants me to send off an important telegram. Where is the nearest office? There's one in the village, isn't there?' I spoke in my best German, the first time I had used the tongue since I crossed the frontier.

'The village is five minutes off at the foot of the avenue,' he said. 'Will you be long, sir?'

'I'll be back in a quarter of an hour,' I said. 'Don't lock up till I get in.'

I put on my ulster and walked out into a clear starry night. My bag I left lying on a settle in the hall. There was nothing in it to compromise me, but I wished I could have got a toothbrush and some tobacco out of it.

So began one of the craziest escapades you can well imagine. I couldn't stop to think of the future yet, but must take one step at a time. I ran down the avenue, my feet cracking on the hard snow, planning hard my programme for the next hour.

I found the village—half a dozen houses with one biggish place that looked like an inn. The moon was rising, and as I approached I saw that there was some kind of a store. A funny little two-seated car was purring before the door, and I guessed this was also the telegraph office.

I marched in and told my story to a stout woman with spectacles on her nose who was talking to a young man.

'It is too late,' she shook her head. 'The Herr Burgrave knows that well. There is no connection from here after eight o'clock. If the matter is urgent you must go to Schwandorf.'

'How far is that?' I asked, looking for some excuse to get decently out of the shop.

'Seven miles,' she said, 'but here is Franz and the post-wagon. Franz, you will be glad to give the gentleman a seat beside you.'

The sheepish-looking youth muttered something which I took to be assent, and finished off a glass of beer.

From his eyes and manner he looked as if he were half drunk.

I thanked the woman, and went out to the car, for I was in a fever to take advantage of this unexpected bit of luck. I could hear the post-mistress enjoining Franz not to keep the gentleman waiting, and presently he came out and flopped into the driver's seat. We started in a series of voluptuous curves, till his eyes got accustomed to the darkness.

At first we made good going along the straight, broad highway lined with woods on one side and on the other snowy fields melting into haze. Then he began to talk, and, as he talked, he slowed down. This by no means suited my book, and I seriously wondered whether I should pitch him out and take charge of the thing. He was obviously a weakling, left behind in the conscription, and I could have done it with one hand. But by a fortunate chance I left him alone.

'That is a fine hat of yours, mein Herr,' he said. He took off his own blue peaked cap, the uniform, I suppose, of the driver of the post-wagon, and laid it on his knee. The night air ruffled a shock of tow-coloured hair.

Then he calmly took my hat and clapped it on his head.

'With this thing I should be a gentleman,' he said.

I said nothing, but put on his cap and waited.

'That is a noble overcoat, mein Herr,' he went on. 'It goes well with the hat. It is the kind of garment I have always desired to own. In two days it will be the holy Christmas, when gifts are given. Would that the good God sent me such a coat as yours!'

'You can try it on to see how it looks,' I said good-humouredly.

He stopped the car with a jerk, and pulled off his blue coat. The exchange was soon effected. He was about my height, and my ulster fitted not so badly. I put on his overcoat, which had a big collar that buttoned round the neck.

The idiot preened himself like a girl. Drink and vanity had primed him for any folly. He drove so carelessly for a bit that he nearly put us into a ditch. We passed several cottages and at the last he slowed down.

'A friend of mine lives here,' he announced. 'Gertrud would like to see me in the fine clothes which the most amiable Herr has given me. Wait for me, I will not be long.' And he scrambled out of the car and lurched into the little garden.

I took his place and moved very slowly forward. I heard the door open and the sound of laughing and loud voices. Then it shut, and looking back I saw that my idiot had been absorbed into the dwelling of his Gertrud. I waited no longer, but sent the car forward at its best speed.

Five minutes later the infernal thing began to give trouble—a nut loose in the antiquated steering-gear. I unhooked a lamp, examined it, and put the mischief right, but I was a quarter of an hour doing it. The highway ran now in a thick forest and I noticed branches going off now and then to the right. I was just thinking of turning up one of them, for I had no anxiety to visit Schwandorf, when I heard behind me the sound of a great car driven furiously.

I drew in to the right side—thank goodness I remembered the rule of the road—and proceeded decorously, wondering what was going to happen. I could hear the brakes being clamped on and the car slowing down. Suddenly a big grey bonnet slipped past me and as I turned my head I heard a familiar voice.

It was Stumm, looking like something that has been run over. He had his jaw in a sling, so that I wondered if I had broken it, and his eyes were beautifully bunged up. It was that that saved me, that and his raging temper. The collar of the postman's coat was round my chin, hiding my beard, and I had his cap pulled well down on my brow. I remembered what Blenkiron had said—that the only way to deal with the Germans was naked bluff. Mine was naked enough, for it was all that was left to me.

'Where is the man you brought from Andersbach?' he roared, as well as his jaw would allow him.

I pretended to be mortally scared, and spoke in the best imitation I could manage of the postman's high cracked voice.

'He got out a mile back, Herr Burgrave,' I quavered. 'He was a rude fellow who wanted to go to Schwandorf, and then changed his mind.'

'Where, you fool? Say exactly where he got down or I will wring your neck.'

'In the wood this side of Gertrud's cottage ... on the left hand. I left him running among the trees.' I put all the terror I knew into my pipe, and it wasn't all acting.

'He means the Henrichs' cottage, Herr Colonel,' said the chauffeur. 'This man is courting the daughter.'

Stumm gave an order and the great car backed, and, as I looked round, I saw it turning. Then as it gathered speed it shot forward, and presently was lost in the shadows. I had got over the first hurdle.

But there was no time to be lost. Stumm would meet the postman and would be tearing after me any minute. I took the first turning, and bucketed along a narrow woodland road. The hard ground would show very few tracks, I thought, and I hoped the pursuit would think I had gone on to Schwandorf. But it wouldn't do to risk it, and I was determined very soon to get the car off the road, leave it, and take to the forest. I took out my watch and calculated I could give myself ten minutes.

I was very nearly caught. Presently I came on a bit of rough heath, with a slope away from the road and here and there a patch of black which I took to be a sandpit. Opposite one of these I slewed the car to the edge, got out, started it again and saw it pitch head-foremost into the darkness. There was a splash of water and then silence. Craning over I could see nothing but murk, and the marks at the lip where the wheels had passed. They would find my tracks in daylight but scarcely at this time of night.

Then I ran across the road to the forest. I was only just in time, for the echoes of the splash had hardly died away when I heard the sound of another car. I lay flat in a hollow below a tangle of snow-laden brambles and looked between the pine-trees at the moonlit road. It was Stumm's car again and to my consternation it stopped just a little short of the sandpit.

I saw an electric torch flashed, and Stumm himself got out and examined the tracks on the highway. Thank God, they would be still there for him to find, but had he tried half a dozen yards on he would have seen them turn towards the sandpit. If that had happened he would have beaten the adjacent woods and most certainly found me. There was a third man in the car, with my hat and coat on him. That poor devil of a postman had paid dear for his vanity.

They took a long time before they started again, and I was jolly well relieved when they went scouring down the road. I ran deeper into the woods till I found a track which—as I judged from the sky which I saw in a clearing—took me nearly due west. That wasn't the direction I wanted, so I bore off at right angles, and presently struck another road which I crossed in a hurry. After that I got entangled in some confounded kind of enclosure and had to climb paling after paling of rough stakes plaited with osiers. Then came a rise in the ground and I was on a low hill of pines which seemed to last for miles. All the time I was going at a good pace, and before I stopped to rest I calculated I had put six miles between me and the sandpit.

My mind was getting a little more active now; for the first part of the journey I had simply staggered from impulse to impulse. These impulses had been uncommon lucky, but I couldn't go on like that for ever. *Ek sal 'n plan maak*, says the old Boer when he gets into trouble, and it was up to me now to make a plan.

As soon as I began to think I saw the desperate business I was in for. Here was I, with nothing except what I stood up in—including a coat and cap that weren't mine—alone in mid-winter in the heart of South Germany. There was a man behind me looking for my blood, and soon there would be a hue-and-cry for me up and down the land. I had heard that the German police were pretty efficient, and I couldn't see that I stood the slimmest chance. If they caught me they would shoot me beyond doubt. I asked myself on what charge, and answered, 'For knocking about a German officer.' They couldn't have me up for espionage, for as far as I knew they had no evidence. I was simply a Dutchman that had got riled and had run amok. But if they cut down a cobbler for laughing at a second lieutenant—which is what happened at Zabern—I calculated that hanging would be too good for a man that had broken a colonel's jaw.

To make things worse my job was not to escape—though that would have been hard enough—but to get to Constantinople, more than a thousand miles off, and I reckoned I couldn't get there as a tramp. I had to be sent there, and now I had flung away my chance. If I had been a Catholic I would have said a prayer to St Teresa, for she would have understood my troubles.

My mother used to say that when you felt down on your luck it was a good cure to count your mercies. So I set about counting mine. The first was that I was well started on my journey, for I couldn't be above two score miles from the Danube. The second was that I had Stumm's pass. I didn't see how I could use it, but there it was. Lastly I had plenty of money—fifty-three English sovereigns and the equivalent of three pounds in German paper which I had changed at the hotel. Also I had squared accounts with old Stumm. That was the biggest mercy of all.

I thought I'd better get some sleep, so I found a dryish hole below an oak root and squeezed myself into it. The snow lay deep in these woods and I was sopping wet up to the knees. All the same I managed to sleep for some hours, and got up and shook myself just as the winter's dawn was breaking through the tree tops. Breakfast was the next thing, and I must find some sort of dwelling.

Almost at once I struck a road, a big highway running north and south. I trotted along in the bitter morning to get my circulation started, and presently I began to feel a little better. In a little I saw a church spire, which meant a village. Stumm wouldn't be likely to have got on my tracks yet, I calculated, but there was always the chance that he had warned all the villages round by telephone and that they might be on the look-out for me. But that risk had to be taken, for I must have food.

It was the day before Christmas, I remembered, and people would be holidaying. The village was quite a big place, but at this hour—just after eight o'clock—there was nobody in the street except a wandering dog. I chose the most unassuming shop I could find, where a little boy was taking down the shutters—one of those general stores where they sell everything. The boy fetched a very old woman, who hobbled in from the back, fitting on her spectacles.

'Gruss Gott,' she said in a friendly voice, and I took off my cap. I saw from my reflection in a saucepan that I looked moderately respectable in spite of my night in the woods.

I told her the story of how I was walking from Schwandorf to see my mother at an imaginary place called judenfeld, banking on the ignorance of villagers about any place five miles from their homes. I said my luggage had gone astray, and I hadn't time to wait for it, since my leave was short. The old lady was sympathetic and unsuspecting. She sold me a pound of chocolate, a box of biscuits, the better part of a ham, two tins of sardines and a rucksack to carry them. I also bought some soap, a comb and a cheap razor, and a small Tourists' Guide, published by a Leipzig firm. As I was leaving I saw what seemed like garments hanging up in the back shop, and turned to have a look at them. They were the kind of thing that Germans wear on their summer walking tours—long shooting capes made of a green stuff they call loden. I bought one, and a green felt hat and an alpenstock to keep it company. Then wishing the old woman and her belongings a merry Christmas, I departed and took the shortest cut out of the village. There were one or two people about now, but they did not seem to notice me.

I went into the woods again and walked for two miles till I halted for breakfast. I was not feeling quite so fit now, and I did not make much of my provisions, beyond eating a biscuit and some chocolate. I felt very thirsty and longed for hot tea. In an icy pool I washed and with infinite agony shaved my beard. That razor was the worst of its species, and my eyes were running all the time with the pain of the operation. Then I took off the postman's coat and cap, and buried them below some bushes. I was now a clean-shaven German pedestrian with a green cape and hat, and an absurd walking-stick with an iron-shod end—the sort of person who roams in thousands over the Fatherland in summer, but is a rarish bird in mid-winter.

The Tourists' Guide was a fortunate purchase, for it contained a big map of Bavaria which gave me my bearings. I was certainly not forty miles from the Danube—more like thirty. The road through the village I had left would have taken me to it. I had only to walk due south and I would reach it before night. So far as I could make out there were long tongues of forest running down to the river, and I resolved to keep to the woodlands. At the worst I would meet a forester or two, and I had a good enough story for them. On the highroad there might be awkward questions.

When I started out again I felt very stiff and the cold seemed to be growing intense. This puzzled me, for I had not minded it much up to now, and, being warm-blooded by nature, it never used to worry me. A sharp winter night on the high-veld was a long sight chillier than anything I had struck so far in Europe. But now my teeth were chattering and the marrow seemed to be freezing in my bones.

The day had started bright and clear, but a wrack of grey clouds soon covered the sky, and a wind from the east began to whistle. As I stumbled along through the snowy undergrowth I kept longing for bright warm places. I thought of those long days on the veld when the earth was like a great yellow bowl, with white roads running to the horizon and a tiny white farm basking in the heart of it, with its blue dam and patches of bright green lucerne. I thought of those baking days on the east coast, when the sea was like mother-of-pearl and the sky one burning turquoise. But most of all I thought of warm scented noons on trek, when one dozed in the shadow of the wagon and sniffed the wood-smoke from the fire where the boys were cooking dinner.

From these pleasant pictures I returned to the beastly present—the thick snowy woods, the lowering sky, wet clothes, a hunted present, and a dismal future. I felt miserably depressed, and I couldn't think of any mercies to count. It struck me that I might be falling sick.

About midday I awoke with a start to the belief that I was being pursued. I cannot explain how or why the feeling came, except that it is a kind of instinct that men get who have lived much in wild countries. My senses, which had been numbed, suddenly grew keen, and my brain began to work double quick.

I asked myself what I would do if I were Stumm, with hatred in my heart, a broken jaw to avenge, and pretty well limitless powers. He must have found the car in the sandpit and seen my tracks in the wood opposite. I didn't know how good he and his men might be at following a spoor, but I knew that any ordinary Kaffir could have nosed it out easily. But he didn't need to do that. This was a civilized country full of roads and railways. I must some time and somewhere come out of the woods. He could have all the roads watched, and the telephone would set everyone on my track within a radius of fifty miles. Besides, he would soon pick up my trail in the village I had visited that morning. From the map I learned that it was called Greif, and it was likely to live up to that name with me.

Presently I came to a rocky knoll which rose out of the forest. Keeping well in shelter I climbed to the top and cautiously looked around me. Away to the east I saw the vale of a river with broad fields and church-spires. West and south the forest rolled unbroken in a wilderness of snowy tree-tops. There was no sign of life anywhere, not even a bird, but I knew very well that behind me in the woods were men moving swiftly on my track, and that it was pretty well impossible for me to get away.

There was nothing for it but to go on till I dropped or was taken. I shaped my course south with a shade of west in it, for the map showed me that in that direction I would soonest strike the Danube. What I was going to do when I got there I didn't trouble to think. I had fixed the river as my immediate goal and the future must take care of itself.

I was now certain that I had fever on me. It was still in my bones, as a legacy from Africa, and had come out once or twice when I was with the battalion in Hampshire. The bouts had been short for I had known of their coming and dosed myself. But now I had no quinine, and it looked as if I were in for a heavy go. It made me feel desperately wretched and stupid, and I all but blundered into capture.

For suddenly I came on a road and was going to cross it blindly, when a man rode slowly past on a bicycle. Luckily I was in the shade of a clump of hollies and he was not looking my way, though he was not three yards off. I crawled forward to reconnoitre. I saw about half a mile of road running straight through the forest and every two hundred yards was a bicyclist. They wore uniform and appeared to be acting as sentries.

This could only have one meaning. Stumm had picketed all the roads and cut me off in an angle of the woods. There was no chance of getting across unobserved. As I lay there with my heart sinking, I had the horrible feeling that the pursuit might be following me from behind, and that at any moment I would be enclosed between two fires.

For more than an hour I stayed there with my chin in the snow. I didn't see any way out, and I was feeling so ill that I didn't seem to care. Then my chance came suddenly out of the skies.

The wind rose, and a great gust of snow blew from the east. In five minutes it was so thick that I couldn't see across the road. At first I thought it a new addition to my troubles, and then very slowly I saw the opportunity. I slipped down the bank and made ready to cross.

I almost blundered into one of the bicyclists. He cried out and fell off his machine, but I didn't wait to investigate. A sudden access of strength came to me and I darted into the woods on the farther side. I knew I would be soon swallowed from sight in the drift, and I knew that the falling snow would hide my tracks. So I put my best foot forward.

I must have run miles before the hot fit passed, and I stopped from sheer bodily weakness. There was no sound except the crush of falling snow, the wind seemed to have gone, and the place was very solemn and quiet. But Heavens! how the snow fell! It was partly screened by the branches, but all the same it was piling itself up deep everywhere. My legs seemed made of lead, my head burned, and there were fiery pains over all my body. I stumbled on blindly, without a notion of any direction, determined only to keep going to the last. For I knew that if I once lay down I would never rise again.

When I was a boy I was fond of fairy tales, and most of the stories I remembered had been about great German forests and snow and charcoal burners and woodmen's huts. Once I had longed to see these things, and now I was fairly in the thick of them. There had been wolves, too, and I wondered idly if I should fall in with a pack. I felt myself getting light-headed. I fell repeatedly and laughed sillily every time. Once I dropped into a hole and lay for some time at the bottom giggling. If anyone had found me then he would have taken me for a madman.

The twilight of the forest grew dimmer, but I scarcely noticed it. Evening was falling, and soon it would be night, a night without morning for me. My body was going on without the direction of my brain, for my mind was filled with craziness. I was like a drunk man who keeps running, for he knows that if he stops he will fall, and I had a sort of bet with myself not to lie down—not at any rate just yet. If I lay down I should feel the pain in my head worse. Once I had ridden for five days down country with fever on me and the flat bush trees had seemed to melt into one big mirage and dance quadrilles before my eyes. But then I had more or less kept my wits. Now I was fairly daft, and every minute growing dafter.

Then the trees seemed to stop and I was walking on flat ground. It was a clearing, and before me twinkled a little light. The change restored me to consciousness, and suddenly I felt with horrid intensity the fire in my head and bones and the weakness of my limbs. I longed to sleep, and I had a notion that a place to sleep was before me. I moved towards the light and presently saw through a screen of snow the outline of a cottage.

I had no fear, only an intolerable longing to lie down. Very slowly I made my way to the door and knocked. My weakness was so great that I could hardly lift my hand.

There were voices within, and a corner of the curtain was lifted from the window. Then the door opened and a woman stood before me, a woman with a thin, kindly face.

'Gruss Gott,' she said, while children peeped from behind her skirts.

'Gruss Gott,' I replied. I leaned against the door-post, and speech forsook me.

She saw my condition. 'Come in, Sir,' she said. 'You are sick and it is no weather for a sick man.'

I stumbled after her and stood dripping in the centre of the little kitchen, while three wondering children stared at me. It was a poor place, scantily furnished, but a good log-fire burned on the hearth. The shock of warmth gave me one of those minutes of self-possession which comes sometimes in the middle of a fever.

'I am sick, mother, and I have walked far in the storm and lost my way. I am from Africa, where the climate is hot, and your cold brings me fever. It will pass in a day or two if you can give me a bed.'

'You are welcome,' she said; 'but first I will make you coffee.'

I took off my dripping cloak, and crouched close to the hearth. She gave me coffee—poor washy stuff, but blessedly hot. Poverty was spelled large in everything I saw. I felt the tides of fever beginning to overflow my brain again, and I made a great attempt to set my affairs straight before I was overtaken. With difficulty I took out Stumm's pass from my pocket-book.

'That is my warrant,' I said. 'I am a member of the Imperial Secret Service and for the sake of my work I must move in the dark. If you will permit it, mother, I will sleep till I am better, but no one must know that I am here. If anyone comes, you must deny my presence.'

She looked at the big seal as if it were a talisman.

'Yes, yes,' she said, 'you will have the bed in the garret and be left in peace till you are well. We have no neighbours near, and the storm will shut the roads. I will be silent, I and the little ones.'

My head was beginning to swim, but I made one more effort.

'There is food in my rucksack—biscuits and ham and chocolate. Pray take it for your use. And here is some money to buy Christmas fare for the little ones.' And I gave her some of the German notes.

After that my recollection becomes dim. She helped me up a ladder to the garret, undressed me, and gave me a thick coarse nightgown. I seem to remember that she kissed my hand, and that she was crying. 'The good Lord has sent you,' she said. 'Now the little ones will have their prayers answered and the Christkind will not pass by our door.'

CHAPTER EIGHT

The Essen Barges

I lay for four days like a log in that garret bed. The storm died down, the thaw set in, and the snow melted. The children played about the doors and told stories at night round the fire. Stumm's myrmidons no doubt beset every road and troubled the lives of innocent wayfarers. But no one came near the cottage, and the fever worked itself out while I lay in peace.

It was a bad bout, but on the fifth day it left me, and I lay, as weak as a kitten, staring at the rafters and the little skylight. It was a leaky, draughty old place, but the woman of the cottage had heaped deerskins and blankets on my bed and kept me warm. She came in now and then, and once she brought me a brew of some bitter herbs which greatly refreshed me. A little thin porridge was all the food I could eat, and some chocolate made from the slabs in my rucksack.

I lay and dozed through the day, hearing the faint chatter of children below, and getting stronger hourly. Malaria passes as quickly as it comes and leaves a man little the worse, though this was one of the sharpest turns I ever had. As I lay I thought, and my thoughts followed curious lines. One queer thing was that Stumm and his doings seemed to have been shot back into a lumber-room of my brain and the door locked. He didn't seem to be a creature of the living present, but a distant memory on which I could look calmly. I thought a good deal about my battalion and the comedy of my present position. You see I was getting better, for I called it comedy now, not tragedy.

But chiefly I thought of my mission. All that wild day in the snow it had seemed the merest farce. The three words Harry Bullivant had scribbled had danced through my head in a crazy fandango. They were present to me now, but coolly and sanely in all their meagreness.

I remember that I took each one separately and chewed on it for hours. *Kasredin*—there was nothing to be got out of that. *Cancer*—there were too many meanings, all blind. *V. I.*—that was the worst gibberish of all.

Before this I had always taken the I as the letter of the alphabet. I had thought the v. must stand for von, and I had considered the German names beginning with I—Ingolstadt, Ingeburg, Ingenohl, and all the rest of them. I had made a list of about seventy at the British Museum before I left London.

Now I suddenly found myself taking the I as the numeral One. Idly, not thinking what I was doing, I put it into German.

Then I nearly fell out of the bed. Von Einem—the name I had heard at Gaudian's house, the name Stumm had spoken behind his hand, the name to which Hilda was probably the prefix. It was a tremendous discovery—the first real bit of light I had found. Harry Bullivant knew that some man or woman called von Einem was at the heart of the mystery. Stumm had spoken of the same personage with respect and in connection with the work I proposed to do in raising the Moslem Africans. If I found von Einem I would be getting very warm. What was the word that Stumm had whispered to Gaudian and scared that worthy? It had sounded like *uhnmantl.* If I could only get that clear, I would solve the riddle.

I think that discovery completed my cure. At any rate on the evening of the fifth day—it was Wednesday, the 29th of December—I was well enough to get up. When the dark had fallen and it was too late to fear a visitor, I came downstairs and, wrapped in my green cape, took a seat by the fire.

As we sat there in the firelight, with the three white-headed children staring at me with saucer eyes, and smiling when I looked their way, the woman talked. Her man had gone to the wars on the Eastern front, and the last she had heard from him he was in a Polish bog and longing for his dry native woodlands. The struggle meant little to her. It was an act of God, a thunderbolt out of the sky, which had taken a husband from her, and might soon make her a widow and her children fatherless. She knew nothing of its causes and purposes, and thought of the Russians as a gigantic nation of savages, heathens who had never been converted, and who would eat up German homes if the good Lord and the brave German soldiers did not stop them. I tried hard to find out if she had any notion of affairs in the West, but she hadn't, beyond the fact that there was trouble with the French. I doubt if she knew of England's share in it. She was a decent soul, with no bitterness against anybody, not even the Russians if they would spare her man.

That night I realized the crazy folly of war. When I saw the splintered shell of Ypres and heard hideous tales of German doings, I used to want to see the whole land of the Boche given up to fire and sword. I thought we could never end the war properly without giving the Huns some of their own medicine. But that woodcutter's cottage cured me of such nightmares. I was for punishing the guilty but letting the innocent go free. It was our business to thank God and keep our hands clean from the ugly blunders to which Germany's madness had driven her. What good would it do Christian folk to burn poor little huts like this and leave children's bodies by the wayside? To be able to laugh and to be merciful are the only things that make man better than the beasts.

The place, as I have said, was desperately poor. The woman's face had the skin stretched tight over the bones and that transparency which means under-feeding; I fancied she did not have the liberal allowance that soldiers' wives get in England. The children looked better nourished, but it was by their mother's sacrifice. I did my best to cheer them up. I told them long yarns about Africa and lions and tigers, and I got some pieces of wood and whittled them into toys. I am fairly good with a knife, and I carved very presentable likenesses of a monkey, a springbok, and a rhinoceros. The children went to bed hugging the first toys, I expect, they ever possessed.

It was clear to me that I must leave as soon as possible. I had to get on with my business, and besides, it was not fair to the woman. Any moment I might be found here, and she would get into trouble for harbouring me. I asked her if she knew where the Danube was, and her answer surprised me. 'You will reach it in an hour's walk,' she said. 'The track through the wood runs straight to the ferry.'

Next morning after breakfast I took my departure. It was drizzling weather, and I was feeling very lean. Before going I presented my hostess and the children with two sovereigns apiece. 'It is English gold,' I said, 'for I have to travel among our enemies and use our enemies' money. But the gold is good, and if you go to any town they will change it for you. But I advise you to put it in your stocking-foot and use it only if all else fails. You must keep your home going, for some day there will be peace and your man will come back from the wars.'

I kissed the children, shook the woman's hand, and went off down the clearing. They had cried 'Auf Wiedersehen,' but it wasn't likely I would ever see them again.

The snow had all gone, except in patches in the deep hollows. The ground was like a full sponge, and a cold rain drifted in my eyes. After half an hour's steady trudge the trees thinned, and presently I came out on a knuckle of open ground cloaked in dwarf junipers. And there before me lay the plain, and a mile off a broad brimming river.

I sat down and looked dismally at the prospect. The exhilaration of my discovery the day before had gone. I had stumbled on a worthless piece of knowledge, for I could not use it. Hilda von Einem, if such a person existed and possessed the great secret, was probably living in some big house in Berlin, and I was about as likely to get anything out of her as to be asked to dine with the Kaiser. Blenkiron might do something, but where on earth was Blenkiron? I dared say Sir Walter would value the information, but I could not get to Sir Walter. I was to go on to Constantinople, running away from the people who really pulled the ropes. But if I stayed I could do nothing, and I could not stay. I must go on and I didn't see how I could go on. Every course seemed shut to me, and I was in as pretty a tangle as any man ever stumbled into.

For I was morally certain that Stumm would not let the thing drop. I knew too much, and besides I had outraged his pride. He would beat the countryside till he got me, and he undoubtedly would get me if I waited much longer. But how was I to get over the border? My passport would be no good, for the number of that pass would long ere this have been wired to every police-station in Germany, and to produce it would be to ask for trouble. Without it I could not cross the borders by any railway. My studies of the Tourists' Guide had suggested that once I was in Austria I might find things slacker and move about easier. I thought of having a try at the Tyrol and I also thought of Bohemia. But these places were a long way off, and there were several thousand chances each day that I would be caught on the road.

This was Thursday, the 30th of December, the second last day of the year. I was due in Constantinople on the 17th of January. Constantinople! I had thought myself a long way from it in Berlin, but now it seemed as distant as the moon.

But that big sullen river in front of me led to it. And as I looked my attention was caught by a curious sight. On the far eastern horizon, where the water slipped round a corner of hill, there was a long trail of smoke. The streamers thinned out, and seemed to come from some boat well round the corner, but I could see at least two boats in view. Therefore there must be a long train of barges, with a tug in tow.

I looked to the west and saw another such procession coming into sight. First went a big river steamer—it can't have been much less than 1,000 tons—and after came a string of barges. I counted no less than six besides the tug. They were heavily loaded and their draught must have been considerable, but there was plenty of depth in the flooded river.

A moment's reflection told me what I was looking at. Once Sandy, in one of the discussions you have in hospital, had told us just how the Germans munitioned their Balkan campaign. They were pretty certain of dishing Serbia at the first go, and it was up to them to get through guns and shells to the old Turk, who was running pretty short in his first supply. Sandy said that they wanted the railway, but they wanted still more the river, and they could make certain of that in a week. He told us how endless strings of barges, loaded up at the big factories of Westphalia, were moving through the canals from the Rhine or the Elbe to the Danube. Once the first reached Turkey, there would be regular delivery, you see—as quick as the Turks could handle the stuff. And they didn't return empty, Sandy said, but came back full of Turkish cotton and Bulgarian beef and Rumanian corn. I don't know where Sandy got the knowledge, but there was the proof of it before my eyes.

It was a wonderful sight, and I could have gnashed my teeth to see those loads of munitions going snugly off to the enemy. I calculated they would give our poor chaps hell in Gallipoli. And then, as I looked, an idea came into my head and with it an eighth part of a hope.

There was only one way for me to get out of Germany, and that was to leave in such good company that I would be asked no questions. That was plain enough. If I travelled to Turkey, for instance, in the Kaiser's suite, I would be as safe as the mail; but if I went on my own I was done. I had, so to speak, to get my passport inside Germany, to join some caravan which had free marching powers. And there was the kind of caravan before me—the Essen barges.

It sounded lunacy, for I guessed that munitions of war would be as jealously guarded as old Hindenburg's health. All the safer, I replied to myself, once I get there. If you are looking for a deserter you don't seek him at the favourite regimental public-house. If you're after a thief, among the places you'd be apt to leave unsearched would be Scotland Yard.

It was sound reasoning, but how was I to get on board? Probably the beastly things did not stop once in a hundred miles, and Stumm would get me long before I struck a halting-place. And even if I did get a chance like that, how was I to get permission to travel?

One step was clearly indicated—to get down to the river bank at once. So I set off at a sharp walk across squelchy fields, till I struck a road where the ditches had overflowed so as almost to meet in the middle. The place was so bad that I hoped travellers might be few. And as I trudged, my thoughts were busy with my prospects as a stowaway. If I bought food, I might get a chance to lie snug on one of the barges. They would not break bulk till they got to their journey's end.

Suddenly I noticed that the steamer, which was now abreast me, began to move towards the shore, and as I came over a low rise, I saw on my left a straggling village with a church, and a small landing-stage. The houses stood about a quarter of a mile from the stream, and between them was a straight, poplar-fringed road.

Soon there could be no doubt about it. The procession was coming to a standstill. The big tug nosed her way in and lay up alongside the pier, where in that season of flood there was enough depth of water. She signalled to the barges and they also started to drop anchors, which showed that there must be at least two men aboard each. Some of them dragged a bit and it was rather a cock-eyed train that lay in mid-stream. The tug got out a gangway, and from where I lay I saw half a dozen men leave it, carrying something on their shoulders.

It could be only one thing—a dead body. Someone of the crew must have died, and this halt was to bury him. I watched the procession move towards the village and I reckoned they would take some time there, though they might have wired ahead for a grave to be dug. Anyhow, they would be long enough to give me a chance.

For I had decided upon the brazen course. Blenkiron had said you couldn't cheat the Boche, but you could bluff him. I was going to put up the most monstrous bluff. If the whole countryside was hunting for Richard

Hannay, Richard Hannay would walk through as a pal of the hunters. For I remembered the pass Stumm had given me. If that was worth a tinker's curse it should be good enough to impress a ship's captain.

Of course there were a thousand risks. They might have heard of me in the village and told the ship's party the story. For that reason I resolved not to go there but to meet the sailors when they were returning to the boat. Or the captain might have been warned and got the number of my pass, in which case Stumm would have his hands on me pretty soon. Or the captain might be an ignorant fellow who had never seen a Secret Service pass and did not know what it meant, and would refuse me transport by the letter of his instructions. In that case I might wait on another convoy.

I had shaved and made myself a fairly respectable figure before I left the cottage. It was my cue to wait for the men when they left the church, wait on that quarter-mile of straight highway. I judged the captain must be in the party. The village, I was glad to observe, seemed very empty. I have my own notions about the Bavarians as fighting men, but I am bound to say that, judging by my observations, very few of them stayed at home.

That funeral took hours. They must have had to dig the grave, for I waited near the road in a clump of cherry-trees, with my feet in two inches of mud and water, till I felt chilled to the bone. I prayed to God it would not bring back my fever, for I was only one day out of bed. I had very little tobacco left in my pouch, but I stood myself one pipe, and I ate one of the three cakes of chocolate I still carried.

At last, well after midday, I could see the ship's party returning. They marched two by two and I was thankful to see that they had no villagers with them. I walked to the road, turned up it, and met the vanguard, carrying my head as high as I knew how.

'Where's your captain?' I asked, and a man jerked his thumb over his shoulder. The others wore thick jerseys and knitted caps, but there was one man at the rear in uniform.

He was a short, broad man with a weather-beaten face and an anxious eye.

'May I have a word with you, Herr Captain?' I said, with what I hoped was a judicious blend of authority and conciliation.

He nodded to his companion, who walked on.

'Yes?' he asked rather impatiently.

I proffered him my pass. Thank Heaven he had seen the kind of thing before, for his face at once took on that curious look which one person in authority always wears when he is confronted with another. He studied it closely and then raised his eyes.

'Well, Sir?' he said. 'I observe your credentials. What can I do for you?'

'I take it you are bound for Constantinople?' I asked.

'The boats go as far as Rustchuk,' he replied. 'There the stuff is transferred to the railway.'

'And you reach Rustchuk when?'

'In ten days, bar accidents. Let us say twelve to be safe.'

'I want to accompany you,' I said. 'In my profession, Herr Captain, it is necessary sometimes to make journeys by other than the common route. That is now my desire. I have the right to call upon some other branch of our country's service to help me. Hence my request.'

Very plainly he did not like it.

'I must telegraph about it. My instructions are to let no one aboard, not even a man like you. I am sorry, Sir, but I must get authority first before I can fall in with your desire. Besides, my boat is ill-found. You had better wait for the next batch and ask Dreyser to take you. I lost Walter today. He was ill when he came aboard—a disease of the heart—but he would not be persuaded. And last night he died.'

'Was that him you have been burying?' I asked.

'Even so. He was a good man and my wife's cousin, and now I have no engineer. Only a fool of a boy from Hamburg. I have just come from wiring to my owners for a fresh man, but even if he comes by the quickest train he will scarcely overtake us before Vienna or even Buda.'

I saw light at last.

'We will go together,' I said, 'and cancel that wire. For behold, Herr Captain, I am an engineer, and will gladly keep an eye on your boilers till we get to Rustchuk.'

He looked at me doubtfully.

'I am speaking truth,' I said. 'Before the war I was an engineer in Damaraland. Mining was my branch, but I had a good general training, and I know enough to run a river-boat. Have no fear. I promise you I will earn my passage.'

His face cleared, and he looked what he was, an honest, good-humoured North German seaman.

'Come then in God's name,' he cried, 'and we will make a bargain. I will let the telegraph sleep. I require authority from the Government to take a passenger, but I need none to engage a new engineer.'

He sent one of the hands back to the village to cancel his wire. In ten minutes I found myself on board, and ten minutes later we were out in mid-stream and our tows were lumbering into line. Coffee was being made ready in the cabin, and while I waited for it I picked up the captain's binoculars and scanned the place I had left.

I saw some curious things. On the first road I had struck on leaving the cottage there were men on bicycles moving rapidly. They seemed to wear uniform. On the next parallel road, the one that ran through the village, I could see others. I noticed, too, that several figures appeared to be beating the intervening fields.

Stumm's cordon had got busy at last, and I thanked my stars that not one of the villagers had seen me. I had not got away much too soon, for in another half-hour he would have had me.

CHAPTER NINE

The Return of the Straggler

Before I turned in that evening I had done some good hours' work in the engine-room. The boat was oil-fired, and in very fair order, so my duties did not look as if they would be heavy. There was nobody who could be properly called an engineer; only, besides the furnace-men, a couple of lads from Hamburg who had been a year ago apprentices in a ship-building yard. They were civil fellows, both of them consumptive, who did what I told them and said little. By bedtime, if you had seen me in my blue jumper, a pair of carpet slippers, and a flat cap—all the property of the deceased Walter—you would have sworn I had been bred to the firing of river-boats, whereas I had acquired most of my knowledge on one run down the Zambesi, when the proper engineer got drunk and fell overboard among the crocodiles.

The captain—they called him Schenk—was out of his bearings in the job. He was a Frisian and a first-class deep-water seaman, but, since he knew the Rhine delta, and because the German mercantile marine was laid on the ice till the end of war, they had turned him on to this show. He was bored by the business, and didn't understand it very well. The river charts puzzled him, and though it was pretty plain going for hundreds of miles, yet he was in a perpetual fidget about the pilotage. You could see that he would have been far more in his element smelling his way through the shoals of the Ems mouth, or beating against a northeaster in the shallow Baltic. He had six barges in tow, but the heavy flood of the Danube made it an easy job except when it came to going slow. There were two men on each barge, who came aboard every morning to draw rations. That was a funny business, for we never lay to if we could help it. There was a dinghy belonging to each barge, and the men used to row to the next and get a lift in that barge's dinghy, and so forth. Six men would appear in the dinghy of the barge nearest us and carry off supplies for the rest. The men were mostly Frisians, slow-spoken, sandy-haired lads, very like the breed you strike on the Essex coast.

It was the fact that Schenk was really a deep-water sailor, and so a novice to the job, that made me get on with him. He was a good fellow and quite willing to take a hint, so before I had been twenty-four hours on board he was telling me all his difficulties, and I was doing my best to cheer him. And difficulties came thick, because the next night was New Year's Eve.

I knew that that night was a season of gaiety in Scotland, but Scotland wasn't in it with the Fatherland. Even Schenk, though he was in charge of valuable stores and was voyaging against time, was quite clear that the men must have permission for some kind of beano. Just before darkness we came abreast a fair-sized town, whose name I never discovered, and decided to lie to for the night. The arrangement was that one man should be left on guard in each barge, and the other get four hours' leave ashore. Then he would return and relieve his friend, who should proceed to do the same thing. I foresaw that there would be some fun when the first batch returned, but I did not dare to protest. I was desperately anxious to get past the Austrian frontier, for I had a half-notion we might be searched there, but Schenk took his *Sylvesterabend* business so seriously that I would have risked a row if I had tried to argue.

The upshot was what I expected. We got the first batch aboard about midnight, blind to the world, and the others straggled in at all hours next morning. I stuck to the boat for obvious reasons, but next day it became too serious, and I had to go ashore with the captain to try and round up the stragglers. We got them all in but two, and I am inclined to think these two had never meant to come back. If I had a soft job like a river-boat I shouldn't be inclined to run away in the middle of Germany with the certainty that my best fate would be to be scooped up for the trenches, but your Frisian has no more imagination than a haddock. The absentees were both watchmen from the barges, and I fancy the monotony of the life had got on their nerves.

The captain was in a raging temper, for he was short-handed to begin with. He would have started a press-gang, but there was no superfluity of men in that township: nothing but boys and grandfathers. As I was helping to run the trip I was pretty annoyed also, and I sluiced down the drunkards with icy Danube water, using all the worst language I knew in Dutch and

German. It was a raw morning, and as we raged through the river-side streets I remember I heard the dry crackle of wild geese going overhead, and wished I could get a shot at them. I told one fellow—he was the most troublesome—that he was a disgrace to a great Empire, and was only fit to fight with the filthy English.

'God in Heaven!' said the captain, 'we can delay no longer. We must make shift the best we can. I can spare one man from the deck hands, and you must give up one from the engine-room.'

That was arranged, and we were tearing back rather short in the wind when I espied a figure sitting on a bench beside the booking-office on the pier. It was a slim figure, in an old suit of khaki: some cast-off duds which had long lost the semblance of a uniform. It had a gentle face, and was smoking peacefully, looking out upon the river and the boats and us noisy fellows with meek philosophical eyes. If I had seen General French sitting there and looking like nothing on earth I couldn't have been more surprised.

The man stared at me without recognition. He was waiting for his cue.

I spoke rapidly in Sesutu, for I was afraid the captain might know Dutch.

'Where have you come from?' I asked.

'They shut me up in *tronk*,' said Peter, 'and I ran away. I am tired, Cornelis, and want to continue the journey by boat.'

'Remember you have worked for me in Africa,' I said. 'You are just home from Damaraland. You are a German who has lived thirty years away from home. You can tend a furnace and have worked in mines.'

Then I spoke to the captain.

'Here is a fellow who used to be in my employ, Captain Schenk. It's almighty luck we've struck him. He's old, and not very strong in the head, but I'll go bail he's a good worker. He says he'll come with us and I can use him in the engine-room.'

'Stand up,' said the Captain.

Peter stood up, light and slim and wiry as a leopard. A sailor does not judge men by girth and weight.

'He'll do,' said Schenk, and the next minute he was readjusting his crews and giving the strayed revellers the rough side of his tongue. As it chanced, I couldn't keep Peter with me, but had to send him to one of the barges, and I had time for no more than five words with him, when I told him to hold his tongue and live up to his reputation as a half-wit. That accursed *Sylvesterabend* had played havoc with the whole outfit, and the captain and I were weary men before we got things straight.

In one way it turned out well. That afternoon we passed the frontier and I never knew it till I saw a man in a strange uniform come aboard, who copied some figures on a schedule, and brought us a mail. With my dirty face and general air of absorption in duty, I must have been an unsuspicious figure. He took down the names of the men in the barges, and Peter's name was given as it appeared on the ship's roll—Anton Blum.

'You must feel it strange, Herr Brandt,' said the captain, 'to be scrutinized by a policeman, you who give orders, I doubt not, to many policemen.'

I shrugged my shoulders. 'It is my profession. It is my business to go unrecognized often by my own servants.' I could see that I was becoming rather a figure in the captain's eyes. He liked the way I kept the men up to their work, for I hadn't been a nigger-driver for nothing.

Late on that Sunday night we passed through a great city which the captain told me was Vienna. It seemed to last for miles and miles, and to be as brightly lit as a circus. After that, we were in big plains and the air grew perishing cold. Peter had come aboard once for his rations, but usually he left it to his partner, for he was lying very low. But one morning—I think it was the 5th of January, when we had passed Buda and were moving through great sodden flats just sprinkled with snow—the captain took it into his head to get me to overhaul the barge loads. Armed with a mighty type-written list, I made a tour of the barges, beginning with the hindmost. There was a fine old stock of deadly weapons—mostly machine-guns and some field-pieces, and enough shells to blow up the Gallipoli peninsula. All kinds of shell were there, from the big 14-inch crumps to rifle grenades and trench-mortars. It made me fairly sick to see all these good things preparing for our own fellows, and I wondered whether I would not be doing my best service if I engineered a big explosion. Happily I had the common sense to remember my job and my duty and to stick to it.

Peter was in the middle of the convoy, and I found him pretty unhappy, principally through not being allowed to smoke. His companion was an ox-eyed lad, whom I ordered to the look-out while Peter and I went over the lists.

'Cornelis, my old friend,' he said, 'there are some pretty toys here. With a spanner and a couple of clear hours I could make these maxims about as deadly as bicycles. What do you say to a try?'

'I've considered that,' I said, 'but it won't do. We're on a bigger business than wrecking munition convoys. I want to know how you got here.'

He smiled with that extraordinary Sunday-school docility of his.

'It was very simple, Cornelis. I was foolish in the cafe—but they have told you of that. You see I was angry and did not reflect. They had separated us, and I could see would treat me as dirt. Therefore, my bad temper came out, for, as I have told you, I do not like Germans.'

Peter gazed lovingly at the little bleak farms which dotted the Hungarian plain.

'All night I lay in *tronk* with no food. In the morning they fed me, and took me hundreds of miles in a train to a place which I think is called Neuburg. It was a great prison, full of English officers ... I asked myself many times on the journey what was the reason of this treatment, for I could see no sense in it. If they wanted to punish me for insulting them they had the chance to send me off to the trenches. No one could have objected. If they thought me useless they could have turned me back to Holland. I could not have stopped them. But they treated me as if I were a dangerous man, whereas all their conduct hitherto had shown that they thought me a fool. I could not understand it.

'But I had not been one night in that Neuburg place before I thought of the reason. They wanted to keep me under observation as a check upon you, Cornelis. I figured it out this way. They had given you some very important work which required them to let you into some big secret. So far, good. They evidently thought much of you, even yon Stumm man, though he was as rude as a buffalo. But they did not know you fully, and they wanted to check on you. That check they found in Peter Pienaar. Peter was a fool, and if there was anything to blab, sooner or later Peter would blab it. Then they would stretch out a long arm and nip you short, wherever you were. Therefore they must keep old Peter under their eye.'

'That sounds likely enough,' I said.

'It was God's truth,' said Peter. 'And when it was all clear to me I settled that I must escape. Partly because I am a free man and do not like to be in prison, but mostly because I was not sure of myself. Some day my temper would go again, and I might say foolish things for which Cornelis would suffer. So it was very certain that I must escape.

'Now, Cornelis, I noticed pretty soon that there were two kinds among the prisoners. There were the real prisoners, mostly English and French, and there were humbugs. The humbugs were treated, apparently, like the others, but not really, as I soon perceived. There was one man who passed as an English officer, another as a French Canadian, and the others called themselves Russians. None of the honest men suspected them, but they were there as spies to hatch plots for escape and get the poor devils caught in the act, and to worm out confidences which might be of value. That is the German notion of good business. I am not a British soldier to think all men are gentlemen. I know that amongst men there are desperate *skellums*, so I soon picked up this game. It made me very angry, but it was a good thing for my plan. I made my resolution to escape the day I arrived at Neuburg, and on Christmas Day I had a plan made.'

'Peter, you're an old marvel. Do you mean to say you were quite certain of getting away whenever you wanted?'

'Quite certain, Cornelis. You see, I have been wicked in my time and know something about the inside of prisons. You may build them like great castles, or they may be like a backveld *tronk*, only mud and corrugated iron, but there is always a key and a man who keeps it, and that man can be bested. I knew I could get away, but I did not think it would be so easy. That was due to the bogus prisoners, my friends, the spies.

'I made great pals with them. On Christmas night we were very jolly together. I think I spotted every one of them the first day. I bragged about my past and all I had done, and I told them I was going to escape. They backed me up and promised to help. Next morning I had a plan. In the afternoon, just after dinner, I had to go to the commandant's room. They treated me a little differently from the others, for I was not a prisoner of war, and I went there to be asked questions and to be cursed as a stupid Dutchman. There was no strict guard kept there, for the place was on the second floor, and distant by many yards from any staircase. In the corridor outside the commandant's room there was a window which had no bars, and four feet from the window the limb of a great tree. A man might reach that limb, and if he were active as a monkey might descend to the ground. Beyond that I knew nothing, but I am a good climber, Cornelis.

'I told the others of my plan. They said it was good, but no one offered to come with me. They were very noble; they declared that the scheme was mine and I should have the fruit of it, for if more than one tried, detection was certain. I agreed and thanked them—thanked them with tears in my eyes. Then one of them very secretly produced a map. We planned out my road, for I was going straight to Holland. It was a long road, and I had no money, for they had taken all my sovereigns when I was arrested, but they promised to get a subscription up among themselves to start me. Again I wept tears of gratitude. This was on Sunday, the day after Christmas, and I settled to make the attempt on the Wednesday afternoon.

'Now, Cornelis, when the lieutenant took us to see the British prisoners, you remember, he told us many things about the ways of prisons. He told us how they loved to catch a man in the act of escape, so that they could use him harshly with a clear conscience. I thought of that, and calculated that now my friends would have told everything to the commandant, and that they would be waiting to bottle me on the Wednesday. Till then I reckoned I would be slackly guarded, for they would look on me as safe in the net ...

'So I went out of the window next day. It was the Monday afternoon ...'

'That was a bold stroke,' I said admiringly.

'The plan was bold, but it was not skilful,' said Peter modestly. 'I had no money beyond seven marks, and I had but one stick of chocolate. I had no overcoat, and it was snowing hard. Further, I could not get down the tree, which had a trunk as smooth and branchless as a blue gum. For a little I thought I should be compelled to give in, and I was not happy.

'But I had leisure, for I did not think I would be missed before nightfall, and given time a man can do most things. By and by I found a branch which led beyond the outer wall of the yard and hung above the river. This I followed, and then dropped from it into the stream. It was a drop of some yards, and the water was very swift, so that I nearly drowned. I would rather swim the Limpopo, Cornelis, among all the crocodiles than that icy river. Yet I managed to reach the shore and get my breath lying in the bushes ...

'After that it was plain going, though I was very cold. I knew that I would be sought on the northern roads, as I had told my friends, for no one could dream of an ignorant Dutchman going south away from his kinsfolk. But I had learned enough from the map to know that our road lay south-east, and I had marked this big river.'

'Did you hope to pick me up?' I asked. 'No, Cornelis. I thought you would be travelling in first-class carriages while I should be plodding on foot. But I was set on getting to the place you spoke of (how do you call it? Constant Nople?), where our big business lay. I thought I might be in time for that.'

'You're an old Trojan, Peter,' I said; 'but go on. How did you get to that landing-stage where I found you?'

'It was a hard journey,' he said meditatively. 'It was not easy to get beyond the barbed-wire entanglements which surrounded Neuburg—yes, even across the river. But in time I reached the woods and was safe, for I did not think any German could equal me in wild country. The best of them, even their foresters, are but babes in veldcraft compared with such as me ... My troubles came only from hunger and cold. Then I met a Peruvian smouse, and sold him my clothes and bought from him these. [Peter meant a Polish-Jew pedlar.] I did not want to part with my own, which were better, but he gave me ten marks on the deal. After that I went into a village and ate heavily.'

'Were you pursued?' I asked.

'I do not think so. They had gone north, as I expected, and were looking for me at the railway stations which my friends had marked for me. I walked happily and put a bold face on it. If I saw a man or woman look at me suspiciously I went up to them at once and talked.

I told a sad tale, and all believed it. I was a poor Dutchman travelling home on foot to see a dying mother, and I had been told that by the Danube I should find the main railway to take me to Holland. There were kind people who gave me food, and one woman gave me half a mark, and wished me God speed ... Then on the last day of the year I came to the river and found many drunkards.'

'Was that when you resolved to get on one of the river-boats?'

'*Ja*, Cornelis. As soon as I heard of the boats I saw where my chance lay. But you might have knocked me over with a straw when I saw you come on shore. That was good fortune, my friend... I have been thinking much about the Germans, and I will tell you the truth. It is only boldness that can baffle them. They are a most diligent people. They will think of all likely difficulties, but not of all possible ones. They have not much imagination. They are like steam engines which must keep to prepared tracks. There they will hunt any man down, but let him trek for open country and they will be at a loss. Therefore boldness, my friend; for ever boldness. Remember as a nation they wear spectacles, which means that they are always peering.'

Peter broke off to gloat over the wedges of geese and the strings of wild swans that were always winging across those plains. His tale had bucked me up wonderfully. Our luck had held beyond all belief, and I had a kind of hope in the business now which had been wanting before. That afternoon, too, I got another fillip. I came on deck for a breath of air and found it pretty cold after the heat of the engine-room. So I called to one of the deck hands to fetch me up my cloak from the cabin—the same I had bought that first morning in the Greif village.

'*Der grune mantel?*' the man shouted up, and I cried, 'Yes'. But the words seemed to echo in my ears, and long after he had given me the garment I stood staring abstractedly over the bulwarks.

His tone had awakened a chord of memory, or, to be accurate, they had given emphasis to what before had been only blurred and vague. For he had spoken the words which Stumm had uttered behind his hand to Gaudian. I had heard something like 'Uhnmantl,' and could make nothing of it. Now I was as certain of those words as of my own existence. They had been '*Grune mantel*'. *Grune mantel*, whatever it might be, was the name which Stumm had not meant me to hear, which was some talisman for the task I had proposed, and which was connected in some way with the mysterious von Einem.

This discovery put me in high fettle. I told myself that, considering the difficulties, I had managed to find out a wonderful amount in a very few days. It only shows what a man can do with the slenderest evidence if he keeps chewing and chewing on it ...

Two mornings later we lay alongside the quays at Belgrade, and I took the opportunity of stretching my legs. Peter had come ashore for a smoke, and we wandered among the battered riverside streets, and looked at the broken arches of the great railway bridge which the Germans were working at like beavers. There was a big temporary pontoon affair to take the railway across, but I calculated that the main bridge would be ready inside a month. It was a clear, cold, blue day, and as one looked south one saw ridge after ridge of snowy hills. The upper streets of the city were still fairly whole, and there were shops open where food could be got. I remember hearing English spoken, and seeing some Red Cross nurses in the custody of Austrian soldiers coming from the railway station.

It would have done me a lot of good to have had a word with them. I thought of the gallant people whose capital this had been, how three times they had flung the Austrians back over the Danube, and then had only been beaten by the black treachery of their so-called allies. Somehow that morning in Belgrade gave both Peter and me a new purpose in our task. It was our business to put a spoke in the wheel of this monstrous bloody juggernaut that was crushing the life out of the little heroic nations.

We were just getting ready to cast off when a distinguished party arrived at the quay. There were all kinds of uniforms—German, Austrian, and Bulgarian, and amid them one stout gentleman in a fur coat and a black felt hat. They watched the barges up-anchor, and before we began to jerk into line I could hear their conversation. The fur coat was talking English.

'I reckon that's pretty good noos, General,' it said; 'if the English have run away from Gally-poly we can use these noo consignments for the bigger game. I guess it won't be long before we see the British lion moving out of Egypt with sore paws.'

They all laughed. 'The privilege of that spectacle may soon be ours,' was the reply.

I did not pay much attention to the talk; indeed I did not realize till weeks later that that was the first tidings of the great evacuation of Cape Helles. What rejoiced me was the sight of Blenkiron, as bland as a barber among those swells. Here were two of the missionaries within reasonable distance of their goal.

CHAPTER TEN

The Garden-House of Suliman the Red

We reached Rustchuk on January 10th, but by no means landed on that day. Something had gone wrong with the unloading arrangements, or more likely with the railway behind them, and we were kept swinging all day well out in the turbid river. On the top of this Captain Schenk got an ague, and by that evening was a blue and shivering wreck. He had done me well, and I reckoned I would stand by him. So I got his ship's papers, and the manifests of cargo, and undertook to see to the transshipment. It wasn't the first time I had tackled that kind of business, and I hadn't much to learn about steam cranes. I told him I was going on to Constantinople and would take Peter with me, and he was agreeable. He would have to wait at Rustchuk to get his return cargo, and could easily inspan a fresh engineer.

I worked about the hardest twenty-four hours of my life getting the stuff ashore. The landing officer was a Bulgarian, quite a competent man if he could have made the railways give him the trucks he needed. There was a collection of hungry German transport officers always putting in their oars, and being infernally insolent to everybody. I took the high and mighty line with them; and, as I had the Bulgarian commandant on my side, after about two hours' blasphemy got them quieted.

But the big trouble came the next morning when I had got nearly all the stuff aboard the trucks.

A young officer in what I took to be a Turkish uniform rode up with an aide-de-camp. I noticed the German guards saluting him, so I judged he was rather a swell. He came up to me and asked me very civilly in German for the way-bills. I gave him them and he looked carefully through them, marking certain items with a blue pencil. Then he coolly handed them to his aide-de-camp and spoke to him in Turkish.

'Look here, I want these back,' I said. 'I can't do without them, and we've no time to waste.'

'Presently,' he said, smiling, and went off.

I said nothing, reflecting that the stuff was for the Turks and they naturally had to have some say in its handling. The loading was practically finished when my gentleman returned. He handed me a neatly typed new set of way-bills. One glance at them showed that some of the big items had been left out.

'Here, this won't do,' I cried. 'Give me back the right set. This thing's no good to me.'

For answer he winked gently, smiled like a dusky seraph, and held out his hand. In it I saw a roll of money.

'For yourself,' he said. 'It is the usual custom.'

It was the first time anyone had ever tried to bribe me, and it made me boil up like a geyser. I saw his game clearly enough. Turkey would pay for the lot to Germany: probably had already paid the bill: but she would pay double for the things not on the way-bills, and pay to this fellow and his friends. This struck me as rather steep even for Oriental methods of doing business.

'Now look here, Sir,' I said, 'I don't stir from this place till I get the correct way-bills. If you won't give me them, I will have every item out of the trucks and make a new list. But a correct list I have, or the stuff stays here till Doomsday.'

He was a slim, foppish fellow, and he looked more puzzled than angry.

'I offer you enough,' he said, again stretching out his hand.

At that I fairly roared. 'If you try to bribe me, you infernal little haberdasher, I'll have you off that horse and chuck you in the river.'

He no longer misunderstood me. He began to curse and threaten, but I cut him short.

'Come along to the commandant, my boy,' I said, and I marched away, tearing up his typewritten sheets as I went and strewing them behind me like a paper chase.

We had a fine old racket in the commandant's office. I said it was my business, as representing the German Government, to see the stuff delivered to the consignee at Constantinople ship-shape and Bristol-fashion. I told him it wasn't my habit to proceed with cooked documents. He couldn't but agree with me, but there was that wrathful Oriental with his face as fixed as a Buddha.

'I am sorry, Rasta Bey,' he said; 'but this man is in the right.' 'I have authority from the Committee to receive the stores,' he said sullenly.

'Those are not my instructions,' was the answer. 'They are consigned to the Artillery commandant at Chataldja, General von Oesterzee.'

The man shrugged his shoulders. 'Very well. I will have a word to say to General von Oesterzee, and many to this fellow who flouts the Committee.' And he strode away like an impudent boy.

The harassed commandant grinned. 'You've offended his Lordship, and he is a bad enemy. All those damned Comitadjis are. You would be well advised not to go on to Constantinople.' 'And have that blighter in the red hat loot the trucks on the road? No, thank you. I am going to see them safe at Chataldja, or whatever they call the artillery depot.'

I said a good deal more, but that is an abbreviated translation of my remarks. My word for 'blighter' was *trottel*, but I used some other expressions which would have ravished my Young Turk friend to hear. Looking back, it seems pretty ridiculous to have made all this fuss about guns which were going to be used against my own people. But I didn't see that at the time. My professional pride was up in arms, and I couldn't bear to have a hand in a crooked deal.

'Well, I advise you to go armed,' said the commandant. 'You will have a guard for the trucks, of course, and I will pick you good men. They may hold you up all the same. I can't help you once you are past the frontier, but I'll send a wire to Oesterzee and he'll make trouble if anything goes wrong. I still think you would have been wiser to humour Rasta Bey.'

As I was leaving he gave me a telegram. 'Here's a wire for your Captain Schenk.' I slipped the envelope in my pocket and went Out.

Schenk was pretty sick, so I left a note for him. At one o'clock I got the train started, with a couple of German Landwehr in each truck and Peter and I in a horse-box. Presently I remembered Schenk's telegram, which still reposed in my pocket. I took it out and opened it, meaning to wire it from the first station we stopped at. But I changed my mind when I read it. It was from some official at Regensburg, asking him to put under arrest and send back by the first boat a man called

Brandt, who was believed to have come aboard at Absthafen on the 30th of December.

I whistled and showed it to Peter. The sooner we were at Constantinople the better, and I prayed we would get there before the fellow who sent this wire repeated it and got the commandant to send on the message and have us held up at Chataldja. For my back had fairly got stiffened about these munitions, and I was going to take any risk to see them safely delivered to their proper owner. Peter couldn't understand me at all. He still hankered after a grand destruction of the lot somewhere down the railway. But then, this wasn't the line of Peter's profession, and his pride was not at stake. We had a mortally slow journey. It was bad enough in Bulgaria, but when we crossed the frontier at a place called Mustafa Pasha we struck the real supineness of the East. Happily I found a German officer there who had some notion of hustling, and, after all, it was his interest to get the stuff moved. It was the morning of the 16th, after Peter and I had been living like pigs on black bread and condemned tin stuff, that we came in sight of a blue sea on our right hand and knew we couldn't be very far from the end.

It was jolly near the end in another sense. We stopped at a station and were stretching our legs on the platform when I saw a familiar figure approaching. It was Rasta, with half a dozen Turkish gendarmes.

I called Peter, and we clambered into the truck next our horse-box. I had been half expecting some move like this and had made a plan.

The Turk swaggered up and addressed us. 'You can get back to Rustchuk,' he said. 'I take over from you here. Hand me the papers.'

'Is this Chataldja?' I asked innocently.

'It is the end of your affair,' he said haughtily. 'Quick, or it will be the worse for you.'

'Now, look here, my son,' I said; 'you're a kid and know nothing. I hand over to General von Oesterzee and to no one else.'

'You are in Turkey,' he cried, 'and will obey the Turkish Government.'

'I'll obey the Government right enough,' I said; 'but if you're the Government I could make a better one with a bib and a rattle.'

He said something to his men, who unslung their rifles.

'Please don't begin shooting,' I said. 'There are twelve armed guards in this train who will take their orders from me. Besides, I and my friend can shoot a bit.'

'Fool!' he cried, getting very angry. 'I can order up a regiment in five minutes.'

'Maybe you can,' I said; 'but observe the situation. I am sitting on enough toluol to blow up this countryside. If you dare to come aboard I will shoot you. If you call in your regiment I will tell you what I'll do. I'll fire this stuff, and I reckon they'll be picking up the bits of you and your regiment off the Gallipoli Peninsula.'

He had put up a bluff—a poor one—and I had called it. He saw I meant what I said, and became silken.

'Good-bye, Sir,' he said. 'You have had a fair chance and rejected it. We shall meet again soon, and you will be sorry for your insolence.'

He strutted away and it was all I could do to keep from running after him. I wanted to lay him over my knee and spank him.

We got safely to Chataldja, and were received by von Oesterzee like long-lost brothers. He was the regular gunner-officer, not thinking about anything except his guns and shells. I had to wait about three hours while he was checking the stuff with the invoices, and then he gave me a receipt which I still possess. I told him about Rasta, and he agreed that I had done right. It didn't make him as mad as I expected, because, you see, he got his stuff safe in any case. It was only that the wretched Turks had to pay twice for the lot of it.

He gave Peter and me luncheon, and was altogether very civil and inclined to talk about the war. I would have liked to hear what he had to say, for it would have been something to get the inside view of Germany's Eastern campaign, but I did not dare to wait. Any moment there might arrive an incriminating wire from Rustchuk. Finally he lent us a car to take us the few miles to the city.

So it came about that at five past three on the 16th day of January, with only the clothes we stood up in, Peter and I entered Constantinople.

I was in considerable spirits, for I had got the final lap successfully over, and I was looking forward madly to meeting my friends; but, all the same, the first sight was a mighty disappointment. I don't quite know what I had expected—a sort of fairyland Eastern city, all white marble and blue water, and stately Turks in surplices, and veiled houris, and roses and nightingales, and some sort of string band discoursing sweet music. I had forgotten that winter is pretty much the same everywhere. It was a drizzling day, with a south-east wind blowing, and the streets were long troughs of mud. The first part I struck looked like a dingy colonial suburb—wooden houses and corrugated iron roofs, and endless dirty, sallow children. There was a cemetery, I remember, with Turks' caps stuck at the head of each grave. Then we got into narrow steep streets which descended to a kind of big canal. I saw what I took to be mosques and minarets, and they were about as impressive as factory chimneys. By and by we crossed a bridge, and paid a penny for the privilege. If I had known it was the famous Golden Horn I would have looked at it with more interest, but I saw nothing save a lot of moth-eaten barges and some queer little boats like gondolas. Then we came into busier streets, where ramshackle cabs drawn by lean horses spluttered through the mud. I saw one old fellow who looked like my notion of a Turk, but most of the population had the appearance of London old-clothes men. All but the soldiers, Turk and German, who seemed well-set-up fellows.

Peter had paddled along at my side like a faithful dog, not saying a word, but clearly not approving of this wet and dirty metropolis.

'Do you know that we are being followed, Cornelis?' he said suddenly, 'ever since we came into this evil-smelling dorp.'

Peter was infallible in a thing like that. The news scared me badly, for I feared that the telegram had come to Chataldja. Then I thought it couldn't be that, for if von Oesterzee had wanted me he wouldn't have taken the trouble to stalk me. It was more likely my friend Rasta.

I found the ferry of Ratchik by asking a soldier and a German sailor there told me where the Kurdish Bazaar was. He pointed up a steep street which ran past a high block of warehouses with every window broken. Sandy had said the left-hand side coming down, so it must be the right-hand side going up. We plunged into it, and it was the filthiest place of all. The wind whistled up it and stirred the garbage. It seemed densely inhabited, for at all the doors there were groups of people squatting, with their heads covered, though scarcely a window showed in the blank walls.

The street corkscrewed endlessly. Sometimes it seemed to stop; then it found a hole in the opposing masonry and edged its way in. Often it was almost pitch dark; then would come a greyish twilight where it opened out to the width of a decent lane. To find a house in that murk was no easy job, and by the time we had gone a quarter of a mile I began to fear we had missed it. It was no good asking any of the crowd we met. They didn't look as if they understood any civilized tongue.

At last we stumbled on it—a tumble-down coffee house, with A. Kuprasso above the door in queer amateur lettering. There was a lamp burning inside, and two or three men smoking at small wooden tables.

We ordered coffee, thick black stuff like treacle, which Peter anathematized. A negro brought it, and I told him in German I wanted to speak to Mr Kuprasso. He paid no attention, so I shouted louder at him, and the noise brought a man out of the back parts.

He was a fat, oldish fellow with a long nose, very like the Greek traders you see on the Zanzibar coast. I beckoned to him and he waddled forward, smiling oilily. Then I asked him what he would take, and he replied, in very halting German, that he would have a sirop.

'You are Mr Kuprasso,' I said. 'I wanted to show this place to my friend. He has heard of your garden-house and the fun there.'

'The Signor is mistaken. I have no garden-house.'

'Rot,' I said; 'I've been here before, my boy. I recall your shanty at the back and many merry nights there. What was it you called it? Oh, I remember—the Garden-House of Suliman the Red.'

He put his finger to his lip and looked incredibly sly. 'The Signor remembers that. But that was in the old happy days before war came. The place is long since shut. The people here are too poor to dance and sing.'

'All the same I would like to have another look at it,' I said, and I slipped an English sovereign into his hand.

He glanced at it in surprise and his manner changed. 'The Signor is a Prince, and I will do his will.' He clapped his hands and the negro appeared, and at his nod took his place behind a little side-counter.

'Follow me,' he said, and led us through a long, noisome passage, which was pitch dark and very unevenly paved. Then he unlocked a door and with a swirl the wind caught it and blew it back on us.

We were looking into a mean little yard, with on one side a high curving wall, evidently of great age, with bushes growing in the cracks of it. Some scraggy myrtles stood in broken pots, and nettles flourished in a corner. At one end was a wooden building like a dissenting chapel, but painted a dingy scarlet. Its windows and skylights were black with dirt, and its door, tied up with rope, flapped in the wind.

'Behold the Pavilion,' Kuprasso said proudly.

'That is the old place,' I observed with feeling. 'What times I've seen there! Tell me, Mr Kuprasso, do you ever open it now?'

He put his thick lips to my ear.

'If the Signor will be silent I will tell him. It is sometimes open—not often. Men must amuse themselves even in war. Some of the German officers come here for their pleasure, and but last week we had the ballet of Mademoiselle Cici. The police approve—but not often, for this is no time for too much gaiety. I will tell you a secret. Tomorrow afternoon there will be dancing—wonderful dancing! Only a few of my patrons know. Who, think you, will be here?'

He bent his head closer and said in a whisper—

'The Compagnie des Heures Roses.'

'Oh, indeed,' I said with a proper tone of respect, though I hadn't a notion what he meant.

'Will the Signor wish to come?'

'Sure,' I said. 'Both of us. We're all for the rosy hours.'

'Then the fourth hour after midday. Walk straight through the cafe and one will be there to unlock the door. You are new-comers here? Take the advice of Angelo Kuprasso and avoid the streets after nightfall. Stamboul is no safe place nowadays for quiet men.' I asked him to name a hotel, and he rattled off a list from which I chose one that sounded modest and in keeping with our get-up. It was not far off, only a hundred yards to the right at the top of the hill.

When we left his door the night had begun to drop. We hadn't gone twenty yards before Peter drew very near to me and kept turning his head like a hunted stag.

'We are being followed close, Cornelis,' he said calmly.

Another ten yards and we were at a cross-roads, where a little *place* faced a biggish mosque. I could see in the waning light a crowd of people who seemed to be moving towards us. I heard a high-pitched voice cry out a jabber of excited words, and it seemed to me that I had heard the voice before.

CHAPTER ELEVEN

The Companions of the Rosy Hours

We battled to a corner, where a jut of building stood out into the street. It was our only chance to protect our backs, to stand up with the rib of stone between us. It was only the work of seconds. One instant we were groping our solitary way in the darkness, the next we were pinned against a wall with a throaty mob surging round us.

It took me a moment or two to realize that we were attacked. Every man has one special funk in the back of his head, and mine was to be the quarry of an angry crowd. I hated the thought of it—the mess, the blind struggle, the sense of unleashed passions different from those of any single blackguard. It was a dark world to me, and I don't like darkness. But in my nightmares I had never imagined anything just like this. The narrow, fetid street, with the icy winds fanning the filth, the unknown tongue, the hoarse savage murmur, and my utter ignorance as to what it might all be about, made me cold in the pit of my stomach.

'We've got it in the neck this time, old man,' I said to Peter, who had out the pistol the commandant at Rustchuk had given him. These pistols were our only weapons. The crowd saw them and hung back, but if they chose to rush us it wasn't much of a barrier two pistols would make.

Rasta's voice had stopped. He had done his work, and had retired to the background. There were shouts from the crowd—'*Alleman*' and a word '*Khafiyeh*' constantly repeated. I didn't know what it meant at the time, but now I know that they were after us because we were Boches and spies. There was no love lost between the Constantinople scum and their new masters. It seemed an ironical end for Peter and me to be done in because we were Boches. And done in we should be. I had heard of the East as a good place for people to disappear in; there were no inquisitive newspapers or incorruptible police.

I wished to Heaven I had a word of Turkish. But I made my voice heard for a second in a pause of the din, and shouted that we were German sailors who had brought down big guns for Turkey, and were going home next day. I asked them what the devil they thought we had done? I don't know if any fellow there understood German; anyhow, it only brought a pandemonium of cries in which that ominous word *Khafiyeh* was predominant.

Then Peter fired over their heads. He had to, for a chap was pawing at his throat. The answer was a clatter of bullets on the wall above us. It looked as if they meant to take us alive, and that I was very clear should not happen. Better a bloody end in a street scrap than the tender mercies of that bandbox bravo.

I don't quite know what happened next. A press drove down at me and I fired. Someone squealed, and I looked the next moment to be strangled. And then, suddenly, the scrimmage ceased, and there was a wavering splash of light in that pit of darkness.

I never went through many worse minutes than these. When I had been hunted in the past weeks there had been mystery enough, but no immediate peril to face. When I had been up against a real, urgent, physical risk, like Loos, the danger at any rate had been clear. One knew what one was in for. But here was a threat I couldn't put a name to, and it wasn't in the future, but pressing hard at our throats.

And yet I couldn't feel it was quite real. The patter of the pistol bullets against the wall, like so many crackers, the faces felt rather than seen in the dark, the clamour which to me was pure gibberish, had all the madness of a nightmare. Only Peter, cursing steadily in Dutch by my side, was real. And then the light came, and made the scene more eerie!

It came from one or two torches carried by wild fellows with long staves who drove their way into the heart of the mob. The flickering glare ran up the steep walls and made monstrous shadows. The wind swung the flame into long streamers, dying away in a fan of sparks.

And now a new word was heard in the crowd. It was *Chinganeh*, shouted not in anger but in fear.

At first I could not see the newcomers. They were hidden in the deep darkness under their canopy of light, for they were holding their torches high at the full stretch of their arms. They were shouting, too, wild shrill cries ending sometimes in a gush of rapid speech. Their words did not seem to be directed against us, but against the crowd. A sudden hope came to me that for some unknown reason they were on our side.

The press was no longer heavy against us. It was thinning rapidly and I could hear the scuffle as men made off down the side streets. My first notion was that these were the Turkish police. But I changed my mind when the leader came out into a patch of light. He carried no torch, but a long stave with which he belaboured the heads of those who were too tightly packed to flee.

It was the most eldritch apparition you can conceive. A tall man dressed in skins, with bare legs and sandal-shod feet. A wisp of scarlet cloth clung to his shoulders, and, drawn over his head down close to his eyes, was a skull-cap of some kind of pelt with the tail waving behind it. He capered like a wild animal, keeping up a strange high monotone that fairly gave me the creeps.

I was suddenly aware that the crowd had gone. Before us was only this figure and his half-dozen companions, some carrying torches and all wearing clothes of skin. But only the one who seemed to be their leader wore the skull-cap; the rest had bare heads and long tangled hair.

The fellow was shouting gibberish at me. His eyes were glassy, like a man who smokes hemp, and his legs were never still for a second. You would think such a figure no better than a mountebank, and yet there was nothing comic in it. Fearful and sinister and uncanny it was; and I wanted to do anything but laugh.

As he shouted he kept pointing with his stave up the street which climbed the hillside.

'He means us to move,' said Peter. 'For God's sake let us get away from this witch-doctor.'

I couldn't make sense of it, but one thing was clear. These maniacs had delivered us for the moment from Rasta and his friends.

Then I did a dashed silly thing. I pulled out a sovereign and offered it to the leader. I had some kind of notion of showing gratitude, and as I had no words I had to show it by deed.

He brought his stick down on my wrist and sent the coin spinning in the gutter. His eyes blazed, and he made his weapon sing round my head. He cursed me—oh, I could tell cursing well enough, though I didn't follow a word; and he cried to his followers and they cursed me too. I had offered him a mortal insult and stirred up a worse hornet's nest than Rasta's push.

Peter and I, with a common impulse, took to our heels. We were not looking for any trouble with demoniacs. Up the steep, narrow lane we ran with that bedlamite crowd at our heels. The torches seemed to have gone out, for the place was black as pitch, and we tumbled over heaps of offal and splashed through running drains. The men were close behind us, and more than once I felt a stick on my shoulder. But fear lent us wings, and suddenly before us was a blaze of light and we saw the debouchment of our street in a main thoroughfare. The others saw it, too, for they slackened off. Just before we reached the light we stopped and looked round. There was no sound or sight behind us in the dark lane which dipped to the harbour.

'This is a queer country, Cornelis,' said Peter, feeling his limbs for bruises. 'Too many things happen in too short a time. I am breathless.'

The big street we had struck seemed to run along the crest of the hill. There were lamps in it, and crawling cabs, and quite civilized-looking shops. We soon found the hotel to which Kuprasso had directed us, a big place in a courtyard with a very tumble-down-looking portico, and green sun-shutters which rattled drearily in the winter's wind. It proved, as I had feared, to be packed to the door, mostly with German officers. With some trouble I got an interview with the proprietor, the usual

Greek, and told him that we had been sent there by Mr Kuprasso. That didn't affect him in the least, and we would have been shot into the street if I hadn't remembered about Stumm's pass.

So I explained that we had come from Germany with munitions and only wanted rooms for one night. I showed him the pass and blustered a good deal, till he became civil and said he would do the best he could for us.

That best was pretty poor. Peter and I were doubled up in a small room which contained two camp-beds and little else, and had broken windows through which the wind whistled. We had a Wretched dinner of stringy mutton, boiled with vegetables, and a white cheese strong enough to raise the dead. But I got a bottle of whisky, for which I paid a sovereign, and we managed to light the stove in our room, fasten the shutters, and warm our hearts with a brew of toddy. After that we went to bed and slept like logs for twelve hours. On the road from Rustchuk we had had uneasy slumbers.

I woke next morning and, looking out from the broken window, saw that it was snowing. With a lot of trouble I got hold of a servant and made him bring us some of the treacly Turkish coffee. We were both in pretty low spirits. 'Europe is a poor cold place,' said Peter, 'not worth fighting for. There is only one white man's land, and that is South Africa.' At the time I heartily agreed with him.

I remember that, sitting on the edge of my bed, I took stock of our position. It was not very cheering. We seemed to have been amassing enemies at a furious pace. First of all, there was Rasta, whom I had insulted and who wouldn't forget it in a hurry. He had his crowd of Turkish riff-raff and was bound to get us sooner or later. Then there was the maniac in the skin hat. He didn't like Rasta, and I made a guess that he and his weird friends were of some party hostile to the Young Turks. But, on the other hand, he didn't like us, and there would be bad trouble the next time we met him. Finally, there was Stumm and the German Government. It could only be a matter of hours at the best before he got the Rustchuk authorities on our trail. It would be easy to trace us from Chataldja, and once they had us we were absolutely done. There was a big black *dossier* against us, which by no conceivable piece of luck could be upset.

It was very clear to me that, unless we could find sanctuary and shed all our various pursuers during this day, we should be done in for good and all. But where on earth were we to find sanctuary? We had neither of us a word of the language, and there was no way I could see of taking on new characters. For that we wanted friends and help, and I could think of none anywhere. Somewhere, to be sure, there was Blenkiron, but how could we get in touch with him? As for Sandy, I had pretty well given him up. I always thought his enterprise the craziest of the lot and bound to fail. He was probably somewhere in Asia Minor, and a month or two later would get to Constantinople and hear in some pot-house the yarn of the two wretched Dutchmen who had disappeared so soon from men's sight.

That rendezvous at Kuprasso's was no good. It would have been all right if we had got here unsuspected, and could have gone on quietly frequenting the place till Blenkiron picked us up. But to do that we wanted leisure and secrecy, and here we were with a pack of hounds at our heels. The place was horribly dangerous already. If we showed ourselves there we should be gathered in by Rasta, or by the German military police, or by the madman in the skin cap. It was a stark impossibility to hang about on the off-chance of meeting Blenkiron.

I reflected with some bitterness that this was the 17th day of January, the day of our assignation. I had had high hopes all the way down the Danube of meeting with Blenkiron—for I knew he would be in time—of giving him the information I had had the good fortune to collect, of piecing it together with what he had found out, and of getting the whole story which Sir Walter hungered for. After that, I thought it wouldn't be hard to get away by Rumania, and to get home through Russia. I had hoped to be back with my battalion in February, having done as good a bit of work as anybody in the war. As it was, it looked as if my information would die with me, unless I could find Blenkiron before the evening.

I talked the thing over with Peter, and he agreed that we were fairly up against it. We decided to go to Kuprasso's that afternoon, and to trust to luck for the rest. It wouldn't do to wander about the streets, so we sat tight in our room all morning, and swopped old hunting yarns to keep our minds from the beastly present. We got some food at midday—cold mutton and the same cheese, and finished our whisky. Then I paid the bill, for I didn't dare to stay there another night. About half-past three we went into the street, without the foggiest notion where we would find our next quarters.

It was snowing heavily, which was a piece of luck for us. Poor old Peter had no greatcoat, so we went into a Jew's shop and bought a ready-made abomination, which looked as if it might have been meant for a dissenting parson. It was no good saving my money when the future was so black. The snow made the streets deserted, and we turned down the long lane which led to Ratchik ferry, and found it perfectly quiet. I do not think we met a soul till we got to Kuprasso's shop.

We walked straight through the cafe, which was empty, and down the dark passage, till we were stopped by the garden door. I knocked and it swung open. There was the bleak yard, now puddled with snow, and a blaze of light from the pavilion at the other end. There was a scraping of fiddles, too, and the sound of human talk. We paid the negro at the door, and passed from the bitter afternoon into a garish saloon.

There were forty or fifty people there, drinking coffee and sirops and filling the air with the fumes of latakia. Most of them were Turks in European clothes and the fez, but there were some German officers and what looked like German civilians—Army Service Corps clerks, probably, and mechanics from the Arsenal. A woman in cheap finery was tinkling at the piano, and there were several shrill females with the officers. Peter and I sat down modestly in the nearest corner, where old Kuprasso saw us and sent us coffee. A girl who looked like a Jewess came over to us and talked French, but I shook my head and she went off again.

Presently a girl came on the stage and danced, a silly affair, all a clashing of tambourines and wriggling. I have seen native women do the same thing better in a Mozambique kraal. Another sang a German song, a simple, sentimental thing about golden hair and rainbows, and the Germans present applauded. The place was so tinselly and common that, coming to it from weeks of rough travelling, it made me impatient. I forgot that, while for the others it might be a vulgar little dancing-hall, for us it was as perilous as a brigands' den.

Peter did not share my mood. He was quite interested in it, as he was interested in everything new. He had a genius for living in the moment.

I remember there was a drop-scene on which was daubed a blue lake with very green hills in the distance. As the tobacco smoke grew thicker and the fiddles went on squealing, this tawdry picture began to mesmerize me. I seemed to be looking out of a window at a lovely summer landscape where there were no wars or danger. I seemed to feel the warm sun and to smell the fragrance of blossom from the islands. And then I became aware that a queer scent had stolen into the atmosphere.

There were braziers burning at both ends to warm the room, and the thin smoke from these smelt like incense. Somebody had been putting a powder in the flames, for suddenly the place became very quiet. The fiddles still sounded, but far away like an echo. The lights went down, all but a circle on the stage, and into that circle stepped my enemy of the skin cap.

He had three others with him. I heard a whisper behind me, and the words were those which Kuprasso had used the day before. These bedlamites were called the Companions of the Rosy Hours, and Kuprasso had promised great dancing.

I hoped to goodness they would not see us, for they had fairly given me the horrors. Peter felt the same, and we both made ourselves very small in that dark corner. But the newcomers had no eyes for us.

In a twinkling the pavilion changed from a common saloon, which might have been in Chicago or Paris, to a place of mystery—yes, and of beauty. It became the Garden-House of Suliman the Red, whoever that sportsman may have been. Sandy had said that the ends of the earth converged there, and he had been right. I lost all consciousness of my neighbours—stout German, frock-coated Turk, frowsy Jewess—and saw only strange figures leaping in a circle of light, figures that came out of the deepest darkness to make a big magic.

The leader flung some stuff into the brazier, and a great fan of blue light flared up. He was weaving circles, and he was singing something shrill and high, whilst his companions made a chorus with their deep monotone. I can't tell you what the dance was. I had seen the Russian ballet just before the war, and one of the men in it reminded me of this man. But the dancing was the least part of it. It was neither sound nor movement nor scent that wrought the spell, but something far more potent. In an instant I found myself reft away from the present with its dull dangers, and looking at a world all young and fresh and beautiful. The gaudy drop-scene had vanished. It was a window I was looking from, and I was gazing at the finest landscape on earth, lit by the pure clean light of morning.

It seemed to be part of the veld, but like no veld I had ever seen. It was wider and wilder and more gracious. Indeed, I was looking at my first youth. I was feeling the kind of immortal light-heartedness which only a boy knows in the dawning of his days. I had no longer any fear of these magic-makers. They were kindly wizards, who had brought me into fairyland.

Then slowly from the silence there distilled drops of music. They came like water falling a long way into a cup, each the essential quality of pure sound. We, with our elaborate harmonies, have forgotten the charm of single notes. The African natives know it, and I remember a learned man once telling me that the Greeks had the same art. Those silver bells broke out of infinite space, so exquisite and perfect that no mortal words could have been fitted to them. That was the music, I expect, that the morning stars made when they sang together.

Slowly, very slowly, it changed. The glow passed from blue to purple, and then to an angry red. Bit by bit the notes spun together till they had made a harmony—a fierce, restless harmony. And I was conscious again of the skin-clad dancers beckoning out of their circle.

There was no mistake about the meaning now. All the daintiness and youth had fled, and passion was beating the air—terrible, savage passion, which belonged neither to day nor night, life nor death, but to the half-world between them. I suddenly felt the dancers as monstrous, inhuman, devilish. The thick scents that floated from the brazier seemed to have a tang of new-shed blood. Cries broke from the hearers—cries of anger and lust and terror. I heard a woman sob, and Peter, who is as tough as any mortal, took tight hold of my arm.

I now realized that these Companions of the Rosy Hours were the only thing in the world to fear. Rasta and Stumm seemed feeble simpletons by contrast. The window I had been looking out of was changed to a prison wall—I could see the mortar between the massive blocks. In a second these devils would be smelling out their enemies like some foul witch-doctors. I felt the burning eyes of their leader looking for me in the gloom. Peter was praying audibly beside me, and I could have choked him. His infernal chatter would reveal us, for it seemed to me that there was no one in the place except us and the magic-workers.

Then suddenly the spell was broken. The door was flung open and a great gust of icy wind swirled through the hall, driving clouds of ashes from the braziers. I heard loud voices without, and a hubbub began inside. For a moment it was quite dark, and then someone lit one of the flare lamps by the stage. It revealed nothing but the common squalor of a low saloon—white faces, sleepy eyes, and frowsy heads. The drop-piece was there in all its tawdriness.

The Companions of the Rosy Hours had gone. But at the door stood men in uniform, I heard a German a long way off murmur, 'Enver's bodyguards,' and I heard him distinctly; for, though I could not see clearly, my hearing was desperately acute. That is often the way when you suddenly come out of a swoon.

The place emptied like magic. Turk and German tumbled over each other, while Kuprasso wailed and wept. No one seemed to stop them, and then I saw the reason. Those Guards had come for us. This must be Stumm at last. The authorities had tracked us down, and it was all up with Peter and me.

A sudden revulsion leaves a man with a low vitality. I didn't seem to care greatly. We were done, and there was an end of it. It was Kismet, the act of God, and there was nothing for it but to submit. I hadn't a flicker of a thought of escape or resistance. The game was utterly and absolutely over.

A man who seemed to be a sergeant pointed to us and said something to Kuprasso, who nodded. We got heavily to our feet and stumbled towards them. With one on each side of us we crossed the yard, walked through the dark passage and the empty shop, and out into the snowy street. There was a closed carriage waiting which they motioned us to get into. It looked exactly like the Black Maria.

Both of us sat still, like truant schoolboys, with our hands on our knees. I didn't know where I was going and I didn't care. We seemed to be rumbling up the hill, and then I caught the glare of lighted streets.

'This is the end of it, Peter,' I said.

'*Ja*, Cornelis,' he replied, and that was all our talk.

By and by—hours later it seemed—we stopped. Someone opened the door and we got out, to find ourselves in a courtyard with a huge dark building around. The prison, I guessed, and I wondered if they would give us blankets, for it was perishing cold.

We entered a door, and found ourselves in a big stone hall. It was quite warm, which made me more hopeful about our cells. A man in some kind of uniform pointed to the staircase, up which we plodded wearily. My mind was too blank to take clear impressions, or in any way to forecast the future. Another warder met us and took us down a passage till we halted at a door. He stood aside and motioned us to enter.

I guessed that this was the governor's room, and we should be put through our first examination. My head was too stupid to think, and I made up my mind to keep perfectly mum. Yes, even if they tried thumbscrews. I had no kind of story, but I resolved not to give anything away. As I turned the handle I wondered idly what kind of sallow Turk or bulging-necked German we should find inside.

It was a pleasant room, with a polished wood floor and a big fire burning on the hearth. Beside the fire a man lay on a couch, with a little table drawn up beside him. On that table was a small glass of milk and a number of Patience cards spread in rows.

I stared blankly at the spectacle, till I saw a second figure. It was the man in the skin-cap, the leader of the dancing maniacs. Both Peter and I backed sharply at the sight and then stood stock still.

For the dancer crossed the room in two strides and gripped both of my hands.

'Dick, old man,' he cried, 'I'm most awfully glad to see you again!'

CHAPTER TWELVE

Four Missionaries See Light in their Mission

A spasm of incredulity, a vast relief, and that sharp joy which comes of reaction chased each other across my mind. I had come suddenly out of very black waters into an unbelievable calm. I dropped into the nearest chair and tried to grapple with something far beyond words.

'Sandy,' I said, as soon as I got my breath, 'you're an incarnate devil. You've given Peter and me the fright of our lives.'

'It was the only way, Dick. If I hadn't come mewing like a tom-cat at your heels yesterday, Rasta would have had you long before you got to your hotel. You two have given me a pretty anxious time, and it took some doing to get you safe here. However, that is all over now. Make yourselves at home, my children.'

'Over!' I cried incredulously, for my wits were still wool-gathering. 'What place is this?'

'You may call it my humble home'—it was Blenkiron's sleek voice that spoke. 'We've been preparing for you, Major, but it was only yesterday I heard of your friend.'

I introduced Peter.

'Mr Pienaar,' said Blenkiron, 'pleased to meet you. Well, as I was observing, you're safe enough here, but you've cut it mighty fine. Officially, a Dutchman called Brandt was to be arrested this afternoon and handed over to the German authorities. When Germany begins to trouble about that Dutchman she will find difficulty in getting the body; but such are the languid ways of an Oriental despotism. Meantime the Dutchman will be no more. He will have ceased upon the midnight without pain, as your poet sings.'

'But I don't understand,' I stammered. 'Who arrested us?'

'My men,' said Sandy. 'We have a bit of a graft here, and it wasn't difficult to manage it. Old Moellendorff will be nosing after the business tomorrow, but he will find the mystery too deep for him. That is the advantage of a Government run by a pack of adventurers. But, by Jove, Dick, we hadn't any time to spare. If Rasta had got you, or the Germans had had the job of lifting you, your goose would have been jolly well cooked. I had some unquiet hours this morning.'

The thing was too deep for me. I looked at Blenkiron, shuffling his Patience cards with his old sleepy smile, and Sandy, dressed like some bandit in melodrama, his lean face as brown as a nut, his bare arms all tattooed with crimson rings, and the fox pelt drawn tight over brow and ears. It was still a nightmare world, but the dream was getting pleasanter. Peter said not a word, but I could see his eyes heavy with his own thoughts.

Blenkiron hove himself from the sofa and waddled to a cupboard.

'You boys must be hungry,' he said. 'My duo-denum has been giving me hell as usual, and I don't eat no more than a squirrel. But I laid in some stores, for I guessed you would want to stoke up some after your travels.'

He brought out a couple of Strassburg pies, a cheese, a cold chicken, a loaf, and three bottles of champagne.

'Fizz,' said Sandy rapturously. 'And a dry Heidsieck too! We're in luck, Dick, old man.'

I never ate a more welcome meal, for we had starved in that dirty hotel. But I had still the old feeling of the hunted, and before I began I asked about the door.

'That's all right,' said Sandy. 'My fellows are on the stair and at the gate. If the *Metreb* are in possession, you may bet that other people will keep off. Your past is blotted out, clean vanished away, and you begin tomorrow morning with a new sheet. Blenkiron's the man you've got to thank for that. He was pretty certain you'd get here, but he was also certain that you'd arrive in a hurry with a good many inquirers behind you. So he arranged that you should leak away and start fresh.'

'Your name is Richard Hanau,' Blenkiron said, 'born in Cleveland, Ohio, of German parentage on both sides. One of our brightest mining-engineers, and the apple of Guggenheim's eye. You arrived this afternoon from Constanza, and I met you at the packet. The clothes for the part are in your bedroom next door. But I guess all that can wait, for I'm anxious to get to business. We're not here on a joy-ride, Major, so I reckon we'll leave out the dime-novel adventures. I'm just dying to hear them, but they'll keep. I want to know how our mutual inquiries have prospered.'

He gave Peter and me cigars, and we sat ourselves in armchairs in front of the blaze. Sandy squatted cross-legged on the hearthrug and lit a foul old briar pipe, which he extricated from some pouch among his skins. And so began that conversation which had never been out of my thoughts for four hectic weeks.

'If I presume to begin,' said Blenkiron, 'it's because I reckon my story is the shortest. I have to confess to you, gentlemen, that I have failed.'

He drew down the corners of his mouth till he looked a cross between a music-hall comedian and a sick child.

'If you were looking for something in the root of the hedge, you wouldn't want to scour the road in a high-speed automobile. And still less would you want to get a bird's-eye view in an aeroplane. That parable about fits my case. I have been in the clouds and I've been scorching on the pikes, but what I was wanting was in the ditch all the time, and I naturally missed it ... I had the wrong stunt, Major. I was too high up and refined. I've been processing through Europe like Barnum's Circus, and living with generals and transparencies. Not that I haven't picked up a lot of noos, and got some very interesting sidelights on high politics. But the thing I was after wasn't to be found on my beat, for those that knew it weren't going to tell. In that kind of society they don't get drunk and blab after their tenth cocktail. So I guess I've no contribution to make to quieting Sir Walter Bullivant's mind, except that he's dead right. Yes, Sir, he has hit the spot and rung the bell. There is a mighty miracle-working proposition being floated in these parts, but the promoters are keeping it to themselves. They aren't taking in more than they can help on the ground-floor.'

Blenkiron stopped to light a fresh cigar. He was leaner than when he left London and there were pouches below his eyes. I fancy his journey had not been as fur-lined as he made out. 'I've found out one thing, and that is, that the last dream Germany will part with is the control of the Near East. That is what your statesmen don't figure enough on. She'll give up Belgium and Alsace-Lorraine and Poland, but by God! she'll never give up the road to Mesopotamia till you have her by the throat and make her drop it. Sir Walter is a pretty bright-eyed citizen, and he sees it right enough. If the worst happens, Kaiser will fling overboard a lot of ballast in

Europe, and it will look like a big victory for the Allies, but he won't be beaten if he has the road to the East safe. Germany's like a scorpion: her sting's in her tail, and that tail stretches way down into Asia.

'I got that clear, and I also made out that it wasn't going to be dead easy for her to keep that tail healthy. Turkey's a bit of an anxiety, as you'll soon discover. But Germany thinks she can manage it, and I won't say she can't. It depends on the hand she holds, and she reckons it a good one. I tried to find out, but they gave me nothing but eyewash. I had to pretend to be satisfied, for the position of John S. wasn't so strong as to allow him to take liberties. If I asked one of the highbrows he looked wise and spoke of the might of German arms and German organization and German staff-work. I used to nod my head and get enthusiastic about these stunts, but it was all soft soap. She has a trick in hand—that much I know, but I'm darned if I can put a name to it. I pray to God you boys have been cleverer.'

His tone was quite melancholy, and I was mean enough to feel rather glad. He had been the professional with the best chance. It would be a good joke if the amateur succeeded where the expert failed.

I looked at Sandy. He filled his pipe again, and pushed back his skin cap from his brows. What with his long dishevelled hair, his high-boned face, and stained eyebrows he had the appearance of some mad mullah.

'I went straight to Smyrna,' he said. 'It wasn't difficult, for you see I had laid down a good many lines in former travels. I reached the town as a Greek money-lender from the Fayum, but I had friends there I could count on, and the same evening I was a Turkish gipsy, a member of the most famous fraternity in Western Asia. I had long been a member, and I'm blood-brother of the chief boss, so I stepped into the part ready made. But I found out that the Company of the Rosy Hours was not what I had known it in 1910. Then it had been all for the Young Turks and reform; now it hankered after the old regime and was the last hope of the Orthodox. It had no use for Enver and his friends, and it did not regard with pleasure the *beaux yeux* of the Teuton. It stood for Islam and the old ways, and might be described as a Conservative-Nationalist caucus. But it was uncommon powerful in the provinces, and Enver and Talaat daren't meddle with it. The dangerous thing about it was that it said nothing and apparently did nothing. It just bided its time and took notes.

'You can imagine that this was the very kind of crowd for my purpose. I knew of old its little ways, for with all its orthodoxy it dabbled a good deal in magic, and owed half its power to its atmosphere of the uncanny. The Companions could dance the heart out of the ordinary Turk. You saw a bit of one of our dances this afternoon, Dick—pretty good, wasn't it? They could go anywhere, and no questions asked. They knew what the ordinary man was thinking, for they were the best intelligence department in the Ottoman Empire—far better than Enver's *Khafiyeh*. And they were popular, too, for they had never bowed the knee to the *Nemseh*—the Germans who are squeezing out the life-blood of the Osmanli for their own ends. It would have been as much as the life of the Committee or its German masters was worth to lay a hand on us, for we clung together like leeches and we were not in the habit of sticking at trifles.

'Well, you may imagine it wasn't difficult for me to move where I wanted. My dress and the pass-word franked me anywhere. I travelled from Smyrna by the new railway to Panderma on the Marmora, and got there just before Christmas. That was after Anzac and Suvla had been evacuated, but I could hear the guns going hard at Cape Helles. From Panderma I started to cross to Thrace in a coasting steamer. And there an uncommon funny thing happened—I got torpedoed.

'It must have been about the last effort of a British submarine in those waters. But she got us all right. She gave us ten minutes to take to the boats, and then sent the blighted old packet and a fine cargo of 6-inch shells to the bottom. There weren't many passengers, so it was easy enough to get ashore in the ship's boats. The submarine sat on the surface watching us, as we wailed and howled in the true Oriental way, and I saw the captain quite close in the conning-tower. Who do you think it was? Tommy Elliot, who lives on the other side of the hill from me at home.

'I gave Tommy the surprise of his life. As we bumped past him, I started the "Flowers of the Forest"—the old version—on the antique stringed instrument I carried, and I sang the words very plain. Tommy's eyes bulged out of his head, and he shouted at me in English to know who the devil I was. I replied in the broadest Scots, which no man in the submarine or in our boat could have understood a word of. "Maister Tammy," I cried, "what for wad ye skail a dacent tinkler lad intil a cauld sea? I'll gie ye your kail through the reek for this ploy the next time I forgaither wi' ye on the tap o' Caerdon."

'Tommy spotted me in a second. He laughed till he cried, and as we moved off shouted to me in the same language to "pit a stoot hert tae a stey brae". I hope to Heaven he had the sense not to tell my father, or the old man will have had a fit. He never much approved of my wanderings, and thought I was safely anchored in the battalion.

'Well, to make a long story short, I got to Constantinople, and pretty soon found touch with Blenkiron. The rest you know. And now for business. I have been fairly lucky—but no more, for I haven't got to the bottom of the thing nor anything like it. But I've solved the first of Harry Bullivant's riddles. I know the meaning of *Kasredin.*

'Sir Walter was right, as Blenkiron has told us. There's a great stirring in Islam, something moving on the face of the waters. They make no secret of it. Those religious revivals come in cycles, and one was due about now. And they are quite clear about the details. A seer has arisen of the blood of the Prophet, who will restore the Khalifate to its old glories and Islam to its old purity. His sayings are everywhere in the Moslem world. All the orthodox believers have them by heart. That is why they are enduring grinding poverty and preposterous taxation, and that is why their young men are rolling up to the armies and dying without complaint in Gallipoli and Transcaucasia. They believe they are on the eve of a great deliverance.

'Now the first thing I found out was that the Young Turks had nothing to do with this. They are unpopular and unorthodox, and no true Turks. But Germany has. How, I don't know, but I could see quite plainly that in some subtle way Germany was regarded as a collaborator in the movement. It is that belief that is keeping the present regime going. The ordinary Turk loathes the Committee, but he has some queer perverted expectation from Germany. It is not a case of Enver and the rest carrying on their shoulders the unpopular Teuton; it is a case of the Teuton carrying the unpopular Committee. And Germany's graft is just this and nothing more—that she has some hand in the coming of the new deliverer.

'They talk about the thing quite openly. It is called the *Kaaba-i-hurriyeh*, the Palladium of Liberty. The prophet himself is known as Zimrud—"the Emerald"—and his four ministers are called also after jewels—Sapphire, Ruby, Pearl, and Topaz. You will hear their names as often in the talk of the towns and villages as you will hear the names of generals in England. But no one knew where Zimrud was or when he would reveal himself, though every week came his messages to the faithful. All that I could learn was that he and his followers were coming from the West.

'You will say, what about *Kasredin*? That puzzled me dreadfully, for no one used the phrase. The Home of the Spirit! It is an obvious cliche, just as in England some new sect might call itself the Church of Christ. Only no one seemed to use it.

'But by and by I discovered that there was an inner and an outer circle in this mystery. Every creed has an esoteric side which is kept from the common herd. I struck this side in Constantinople. Now there is a very famous Turkish *shaka* called *Kasredin*, one of those old half-comic miracle plays with an allegorical meaning which they call *orta oyun*, and which take a week to read. That tale tells of the coming of a prophet, and I found that the select of the faith spoke of the new revelation in terms of it. The curious thing is that in that tale the prophet is aided by one of the few women who play much part in the hagiology of Islam. That is the point of the tale, and it is partly a jest, but mainly a religious mystery. The prophet, too, is not called Emerald.'

'I know,' I said; 'he is called Greenmantle.'

Sandy scrambled to his feet, letting his pipe drop in the fireplace.

'Now how on earth did you find out that?' he cried.

Then I told them of Stumm and Gaudian and the whispered words I had not been meant to hear. Blenkiron was giving me the benefit of a steady stare, unusual from one who seemed always to have his eyes abstracted, and Sandy had taken to ranging up and down the room.

'Germany's in the heart of the plan. That is what I always thought. If we're to find the *Kaaba-i-hurriyeh* it is no good fossicking among the Committee or in the Turkish provinces. The secret's in Germany. Dick, you should not have crossed the Danube.'

'That's what I half feared,' I said. 'But on the other hand it is obvious that the thing must come east, and sooner rather than later. I take it they can't afford to delay too long before they deliver the goods. If we can stick it out here we must hit the trail ... I've got another bit of evidence. I have solved Harry Bullivant's third puzzle.'

Sandy's eyes were very bright and I had an audience on wires.

'Did you say that in the tale of *Kasredin* a woman is the ally of the prophet?'

'Yes,' said Sandy; 'what of that?'

'Only that the same thing is true of Greenmantle. I can give you her name.'

I fetched a piece of paper and a pencil from Blenkiron's desk and handed it to Sandy.

'Write down Harry Bullivant's third word.'

He promptly wrote down '*v. I.*'

Then I told them of the other name Stumm and Gaudian had spoken. I told of my discovery as I lay in the woodman's cottage.

'The "I" is not the letter of the alphabet, but the numeral. The name is Von Einem—Hilda von Einem.'

'Good old Harry,' said Sandy softly. 'He was a dashed clever chap. Hilda von Einem? Who and where is she? for if we find her we have done the trick.'

Then Blenkiron spoke. 'I reckon I can put you wise on that, gentlemen,' he said. 'I saw her no later than yesterday. She is a lovely lady. She happens also to be the owner of this house.'

Both Sandy and I began to laugh. It was too comic to have stumbled across Europe and lighted on the very headquarters of the puzzle we had set out to unriddle.

But Blenkiron did not laugh. At the mention of Hilda von Einem he had suddenly become very solemn, and the sight of his face pulled me up short.

'I don't like it, gentlemen,' he said. 'I would rather you had mentioned any other name on God's earth. I haven't been long in this city, but I have been long enough to size up the various political bosses. They haven't much to them. I reckon they wouldn't stand up against what we could show them in the U-nited States. But I have met the Frau von Einem, and that lady's a very different proposition. The man that will understand her has got to take a biggish size in hats.'

'Who is she?' I asked.

'Why, that is just what I can't tell you. She was a great excavator of Babylonish and Hittite ruins, and she married a diplomat who went to glory three years back. It isn't what she has been, but what she is, and that's a mighty clever woman.'

Blenkiron's respect did not depress me. I felt as if at last we had got our job narrowed to a decent compass, for I had hated casting about in the dark. I asked where she lived.

'That I don't know,' said Blenkiron. 'You won't find people unduly anxious to gratify your natural curiosity about Frau von Einem.'

'I can find that out,' said Sandy. 'That's the advantage of having a push like mine. Meantime, I've got to clear, for my day's work isn't finished. Dick, you and Peter must go to bed at once.' 'Why?' I asked in amazement. Sandy spoke like a medical adviser.

'Because I want your clothes—the things you've got on now. I'll take them off with me and you'll never see them again.'

'You've a queer taste in souvenirs,' I said.

'Say rather the Turkish police. The current in the Bosporus is pretty strong, and these sad relics of two misguided Dutchmen will be washed up tomorrow about Seraglio Point. In this game you must drop the curtain neat and pat at the end of each Scene, if you don't want trouble later with the missing heir and the family lawyer.'

CHAPTER THIRTEEN

I Move in Good Society

I walked out of that house next morning with Blenkiron's arm in mine, a different being from the friendless creature who had looked vainly the day before for sanctuary. To begin with, I was splendidly dressed. I had a navy-blue suit with square padded shoulders, a neat black bow-tie, shoes with a hump at the toe, and a brown bowler. Over that I wore a greatcoat lined with wolf fur. I had a smart malacca cane, and one of Blenkiron's cigars in my mouth. Peter had been made to trim his beard, and, dressed in unassuming pepper-and-salt, looked with his docile eyes and quiet voice a very respectable servant. Old Blenkiron had done the job in style, for, if you'll believe it, he had brought the clothes all the way from London. I realized now why he and Sandy had been fossicking in my wardrobe. Peter's suit had been of Sandy's procuring, and it was not the fit of mine. I had no difficulty about the accent. Any man brought up in the colonies can get his tongue round American, and I flattered myself I made a very fair shape at the lingo of the Middle West.

The wind had gone to the south and the snow was melting fast. There was a blue sky above Asia, and away to the north masses of white cloud drifting over the Black Sea. What had seemed the day before the dingiest of cities now took on a strange beauty, the beauty of unexpected horizons and tongues of grey water winding below cypress-studded shores. A man's temper has a lot to do with his appreciation of scenery. I felt a free man once more, and could use my eyes.

That street was a jumble of every nationality on earth. There were Turkish regulars in their queer conical khaki helmets, and wild-looking levies who had no kin with Europe. There were squads of Germans in flat forage-caps, staring vacantly at novel sights, and quick to salute any officer on the side-walk. Turks in closed carriages passed, and Turks on good Arab horses, and Turks who looked as if they had come out of the Ark. But it was the rabble that caught the eye—very wild, pinched, miserable rabble. I never in my life saw such swarms of beggars, and you walked down that street to the accompaniment of entreaties for alms in all the tongues of the Tower of Babel. Blenkiron and I behaved as if we were interested tourists. We would stop and laugh at one fellow and give a penny to a second, passing comments in high-pitched Western voices.

We went into a cafe and had a cup of coffee. A beggar came in and asked alms. Hitherto Blenkiron's purse had been closed, but now he took out some small nickels and planked five down on the table. The man cried down blessings and picked up three. Blenkiron very swiftly swept the other two into his pocket.

That seemed to me queer, and I remarked that I had never before seen a beggar who gave change. Blenkiron said nothing, and presently we moved on and came to the harbour-side.

There were a number of small tugs moored alongside, and one or two bigger craft—fruit boats, I judged, which used to ply in the Aegean. They looked pretty well moth-eaten from disuse. We stopped at one of them and watched a fellow in a blue nightcap splicing ropes. He raised his eyes once and looked at us, and then kept on with his business.

Blenkiron asked him where he came from, but he shook his head, not understanding the tongue. A Turkish policeman came up and stared at us suspiciously, till Blenkiron opened his coat, as if by accident, and displayed a tiny square of ribbon, at which he saluted.

Failing to make conversation with the sailor, Blenkiron flung him three of his black cigars.

'I guess you can smoke, friend, if you can't talk,' he said.

The man turned and caught the three neatly in the air. Then to my amazement he tossed one of them back.

The donor regarded it quizzically as it lay on the pavement.

'That boy's a connoisseur of tobacco,' he said. As we moved away I saw the Turkish policeman pick it up and put it inside his cap.

We returned by the long street on the crest of the hill. There was a man selling oranges on a tray, and Blenkiron stopped to look at them. I noticed that the man shuffled fifteen into a cluster. Blenkiron felt the oranges, as if to see that they were sound, and pushed two aside. The man instantly restored them to the group, never raising his eyes.

'This ain't the time of year to buy fruit,' said Blenkiron as we passed on. 'Those oranges are rotten as medlars.'

We were almost on our own doorstep before I guessed the meaning of the business.

'Is your morning's work finished?' I said.

'Our morning's walk?' he asked innocently.

'I said "work".'

He smiled blandly. 'I reckoned you'd tumble to it. Why, yes, except that I've some figuring still to do. Give me half an hour and I'll be at your service, Major.'

That afternoon, after Peter had cooked a wonderfully good luncheon, I had a heart-to-heart talk with Blenkiron.

'My business is to get noos,' he said; 'and before I start on a stunt I make considerable preparations. All the time in London when I was yelping at the British Government, I was busy with Sir Walter arranging things ahead. We used to meet in queer places and at all hours of the night. I fixed up a lot of connections in this city before I arrived, and especially a noos service with your Foreign Office by way of Rumania and Russia. In a day or two I guess our friends will know all about our discoveries.'

At that I opened my eyes very wide.

'Why, yes. You Britishers haven't any notion how wide-awake your Intelligence Service is. I reckon it's easy the best of all the belligerents. You never talked about it in peace time, and you shunned the theatrical ways of the Teuton. But you had the wires laid good and sure. I calculate there isn't much that happens in any corner of the earth that you don't know within twenty-four hours. I don't say your highbrows use the noos well. I don't take much stock in your political push. They're a lot of silver-tongues, no doubt, but it ain't oratory that is wanted in this racket. The William Jennings Bryan stunt languishes in war-time. Politics is like a chicken-coop, and those inside get to behave as if their little run were all the world. But if the politicians make mistakes it isn't from lack of good instruction to guide their steps. If I had a big proposition to handle and could have my pick of helpers I'd plump for the Intelligence Department of the British Admiralty. Yes, Sir, I take off my hat to your Government sleuths.'

'Did they provide you with ready-made spies here?' I asked in astonishment.

'Why, no,' he said. 'But they gave me the key, and I could make my own arrangements. In Germany I buried myself deep in the local atmosphere and never peeped out. That was my game, for I was looking for something in Germany itself, and didn't want any foreign cross-bearings. As you know, I failed where you succeeded. But so soon as I crossed the Danube I set about opening up my lines of communication, and I hadn't been two days in this metropolis before I had got my telephone exchange buzzing. Sometime I'll explain the thing to you, for it's a pretty little business. I've got the cutest cypher ... No, it ain't my invention. It's your Government's. Any one, babe, imbecile, or dotard, can carry my messages—you saw some of them today—but it takes some mind to set the piece, and it takes a lot of figuring at my end to work out the results. Some day you shall hear it all, for I guess it would please you.'

'How do you use it?' I asked.

'Well, I get early noos of what is going on in this cabbage-patch. Likewise I get authentic noos of the rest of Europe, and I can send a message to Mr X. in Petrograd and Mr Y. in London, or, if I wish, to Mr Z. in Noo York. What's the matter with that for a post-office? I'm the best informed man in Constantinople, for old General Liman only hears one side, and mostly lies at that, and Enver prefers not to listen at all. Also, I could give them points on what is happening at their very door, for our friend Sandy is a big boss in the best-run crowd of mountebanks that ever fiddled secrets out of men's hearts. Without their help I wouldn't have cut much ice in this city.'

'I want you to tell me one thing, Blenkiron,' I said. 'I've been playing a part for the past month, and it wears my nerves to tatters. Is this job very tiring, for if it is, I doubt I may buckle up.'

He looked thoughtful. 'I can't call our business an absolute rest-cure any time. You've got to keep your eyes skinned, and there's always the risk of the little packet of dynamite going off unexpected. But as these things go, I rate this stunt as easy. We've only got to be natural. We wear our natural clothes, and talk English, and sport a Teddy Roosevelt smile, and there isn't any call for theatrical talent. Where I've found the job tight was when I had got to be natural, and my naturalness was the same brand as that of everybody round about, and all the time I had to do unnatural things. It isn't easy to be going down town to business and taking cocktails with Mr Carl Rosenheim, and next hour being engaged trying to blow Mr Rosenheim's friends sky—high. And it isn't easy to keep up a part which is clean outside your ordinary life. I've never tried that. My line has always been to keep my normal personality. But you have, Major, and I guess you found it wearing.'

'Wearing's a mild word,' I said. 'But I want to know another thing. It seems to me that the line you've picked is as good as could be. But it's a cast-iron line. It commits us pretty deep and it won't be a simple job to drop it.'

'Why, that's just the point I was coming to,' he said. 'I was going to put you wise about that very thing. When I started out I figured on some situation like this. I argued that unless I had a very clear part with a big bluff in it I wouldn't get the confidences which I needed. We've got to be at the heart of the show, taking a real hand and not just looking on. So I settled I would be a big engineer—there was a time when there weren't many bigger in the United States than John S. Blenkiron. I talked large about what might be done in Mesopotamia in the way of washing the British down the river. Well, that talk caught on. They knew of my reputation as an hydraulic expert, and they were tickled to death to rope me in. I told them I wanted a helper, and I told them about my friend Richard Hanau, as good a German as ever supped sauerkraut, who was coming through Russia and Rumania as a benevolent neutral; but when he got to Constantinople would drop his neutrality and double his benevolence. They got reports on you by wire from the States—I arranged that before I left London. So you're going to be welcomed and taken to their bosoms just like John S. was. We've both got jobs we can hold down, and now you're in these pretty clothes you're the dead ringer of the brightest kind of American engineer ... But we can't go back on our tracks. If we wanted to leave for Constanza next week they'd be very polite, but they'd never let us. We've got to go on with this adventure and nose our way down into Mesopotamia, hoping that our luck will hold ... God knows how we will get out of it; but it's no good going out to meet trouble. As I observed before, I believe in an all-wise and beneficent Providence, but you've got to give him a chance.'

I am bound to confess the prospect staggered me. We might be let in for fighting—and worse than fighting—against our own side. I wondered if it wouldn't be better to make a bolt for it, and said SO.

He shook his head. 'I reckon not. In the first place we haven't finished our inquiries. We've got Greenmantle located right enough, thanks to you, but we still know mighty little about that holy man. In the second place it won't be as bad as you think. This show lacks cohesion, Sir. It is not going to last for ever. I calculate that before you and I strike the site of the garden that Adam and Eve frequented there will be a queer turn of affairs. Anyhow, it's good enough to gamble on.'

Then he got some sheets of paper and drew me a plan of the dispositions of the Turkish forces. I had no notion he was such a close student of war, for his exposition was as good as a staff lecture. He made out that the situation was none too bright anywhere. The troops released from Gallipoli wanted a lot of refitment, and would be slow in reaching the Transcaucasian frontier, where the Russians were threatening. The Army of Syria was pretty nearly a rabble under the lunatic Djemal. There wasn't the foggiest chance of a serious invasion of Egypt being undertaken. Only in Mesopotamia did things look fairly cheerful, owing to the blunders of British strategy. 'And you may take it from me,' he said, 'that if the old Turk mobilized a total of a million men, he has lost 40 per cent of them already. And if I'm anything of a prophet he's going pretty soon to lose more.'

He tore up the papers and enlarged on politics. 'I reckon I've got the measure of the Young Turks and their precious Committee. Those boys aren't any good. Enver's bright enough, and for sure he's got sand. He'll stick out a fight like a Vermont game-chicken, but he lacks the larger vision, Sir. He doesn't understand the intricacies of the job no more than a sucking-child, so the Germans play with him, till his temper goes and he bucks like a mule. Talaat is a sulky dog who wants to batter mankind with a club. Both these boys would have made good cow-punchers in the old days, and they might have got a living out West as the gun-men of a Labour Union. They're about the class of Jesse James or Bill the Kid, excepting that they're college-reared and can patter languages. But they haven't the organizing power to manage the Irish vote in a ward election. Their one notion is to get busy with their firearms, and people are getting tired of the Black Hand stunt. Their hold on the country is just the hold that a man with a Browning has over a crowd with walking-sticks. The cooler heads in the Committee are growing shy of them, and an old fox like David is lying low till his time comes. Now it doesn't want arguing that a gang of that kind has got to hang close together or they may hang separately. They've got no grip on the ordinary Turk, barring the fact that they are active and he is sleepy, and that they've got their guns loaded.'

'What about the Germans here?' I asked.

Blenkiron laughed. 'It is no sort of a happy family. But the Young Turks know that without the German boost they'll be strung up like Haman, and the Germans can't afford to neglect an ally. Consider what would happen if Turkey got sick of the game and made a separate peace. The road would be open for Russia to the Aegean. Ferdy of Bulgaria would take his depreciated goods to the other market, and not waste a day thinking about it. You'd have Rumania coming in on the Allies' side. Things would look pretty black for that control of the Near East on which Germany has banked her winnings. Kaiser says that's got to be prevented at all costs, but how is it going to be done?'

Blenkiron's face had become very solemn again. 'It won't be done unless Germany's got a trump card to play. Her game's mighty near bust, but it's still got a chance. And that chance is a woman and an old man. I reckon our landlady has a bigger brain than Enver and Liman. She's the real boss of the show. When I came here, I reported to her, and presently you've got to do the same. I am curious as to how she'll strike you, for I'm free to admit that she impressed me considerable.'

'It looks as if our job were a long way from the end,' I said.

'It's scarcely begun,' said Blenkiron.

That talk did a lot to cheer my spirits, for I realized that it was the biggest of big game we were hunting this time. I'm an economical soul, and if I'm going to be hanged I want a good stake for my neck.

Then began some varied experiences. I used to wake up in the morning, wondering where I should be at night, and yet quite pleased at the uncertainty. Greenmantle became a sort of myth with me. Somehow I couldn't fix any idea in my head of what he was like. The nearest I got was a picture of an old man in a turban coming out of a bottle in a cloud of smoke, which I remembered from a child's edition of the *Arabian Nights*. But if he was dim, the lady was dimmer. Sometimes I thought of her as a fat old German crone, sometimes as a harsh-featured woman like a schoolmistress with thin lips and eyeglasses. But I had to fit the East into the picture, so I made her young and gave her a touch of the languid houri in a veil. I was always wanting to pump Blenkiron on the subject, but he shut up like a rat-trap. He was looking for bad trouble in that direction, and was disinclined to speak about it beforehand.

We led a peaceful existence. Our servants were two of Sandy's lot, for Blenkiron had very rightly cleared out the Turkish caretakers, and they worked like beavers under Peter's eye, till I reflected I had never been so well looked after in my life. I walked about the city with Blenkiron, keeping my eyes open, and speaking very civil. The third night we were bidden to dinner at Moellendorff's, so we put on our best clothes and set out in an ancient cab. Blenkiron had fetched a dress suit of mine, from which my own tailor's label had been cut and a New York one substituted.

General Liman and Metternich the Ambassador had gone up the line to Nish to meet the Kaiser, who was touring in those parts, so Moellendorff was the biggest German in the city. He was a thin, foxy-faced fellow, cleverish but monstrously vain, and he was not very popular either with the Germans or the Turks. He was polite to both of us, but I am bound to say that I got a bad fright when I entered the room, for the first man I saw was Gaudian. I doubt if he would have recognized me even in the clothes I had worn in Stumm's company, for his eyesight was wretched. As it was, I ran no risk in dress-clothes, with my hair brushed back and a fine American accent. I paid him high compliments as a fellow engineer, and translated part of a very technical conversation between him and Blenkiron. Gaudian was in uniform, and I liked the look of his honest face better than ever.

But the great event was the sight of Enver. He was a slim fellow of Rasta's build, very foppish and precise in his dress, with a smooth oval face like a girl's, and rather fine straight black eyebrows. He spoke perfect German, and had the best kind of manners, neither pert nor overbearing. He had a pleasant trick, too, of appealing all round the table for confirmation, and so bringing everybody into the talk. Not that he spoke a great deal, but all he said was good sense, and he had a smiling way of saying it. Once or twice he ran counter to Moellendorff, and I could see there was no love lost between these two. I didn't think I wanted him as a friend—he was too cold-blooded and artificial; and I was pretty certain that I didn't want those steady black eyes as an enemy. But it was no good denying his quality. The little fellow was all cold courage, like the fine polished blue steel of a sword.

I fancy I was rather a success at that dinner. For one thing I could speak German, and so had a pull on Blenkiron. For another I was in a good temper, and really enjoyed putting my back into my part. They talked very high-flown stuff about what they had done and were going to do, and Enver was great on Gallipoli. I remember he said that he could have destroyed the whole British Army if it hadn't been for somebody's cold feet—at which Moellendorff looked daggers. They were so bitter about Britain and all her works that I gathered they were getting pretty panicky, and that made me as jolly as a sandboy. I'm afraid I was not free from bitterness myself on that subject. I said things about my own country that I sometimes wake in the night and sweat to think of.

Gaudian got on to the use of water power in war, and that gave me a chance.

'In my country,' I said, 'when we want to get rid of a mountain we wash it away. There's nothing on earth that will stand against water. Now, speaking with all respect, gentlemen, and as an absolute novice in the military art, I sometimes ask why this God-given weapon isn't more used in the present war. I haven't been to any of the fronts, but I've studied them some from maps and the newspapers. Take your German position in Flanders, where you've got the high ground. If I were a British general I reckon I would very soon make it no sort of position.'

Moellendorff asked, 'How?'

'Why, I'd wash it away. Wash away the fourteen feet of soil down to the stone. There's a heap of coalpits behind the British front where they could generate power, and I judge there's ample water supply from the rivers and canals. I'd guarantee to wash you away in twenty-four hours—yes, in spite of all your big guns. It beats me why the British haven't got on to this notion. They used to have some bright engineers.'

Enver was on the point like a knife, far quicker than Gaudian. He cross-examined me in a way that showed he knew how to approach a technical subject, though he mightn't have much technical knowledge. He was just giving me a sketch of the flooding in Mesopotamia when an aide-de-camp brought in a chit which fetched him to his feet.

'I have gossiped long enough,' he said. 'My kind host, I must leave you. Gentlemen all, my apologies and farewells.'

Before he left he asked my name and wrote it down. 'This is an unhealthy city for strangers, Mr Hanau,' he said in very good English. 'I have some small power of protecting a friend, and what I have is at your disposal.' This with the condescension of a king promising his favour to a subject.

The little fellow amused me tremendously, and rather impressed me too. I said so to Gaudian after he had left, but that decent soul didn't agree.

'I do not love him,' he said. 'We are allies—yes; but friends—no. He is no true son of Islam, which is a noble faith and despises liars and boasters and betrayers of their salt.'

That was the verdict of one honest man on this ruler in Israel. The next night I got another from Blenkiron on a greater than Enver. He had been out alone and had come back pretty late, with his face grey and drawn with pain. The food we ate—not at all bad of its kind—and the cold east wind played havoc with his dyspepsia. I can see him yet, boiling milk on a spirit-lamp, while Peter worked at a Primus stove to get him a hot-water bottle. He was using horrid language about his inside.

'My God, Major, if I were you with a sound stomach I'd fairly conquer the world. As it is, I've got to do my work with half my mind, while the other half is dwelling in my intestines. I'm like the child in the Bible that had a fox gnawing at its vitals.'

He got his milk boiling and began to sip it.

'I've been to see our pretty landlady,' he said. 'She sent for me and I hobbled off with a grip full of plans, for she's mighty set on Mesopotamy.'

'Anything about Greenmantle?' I asked eagerly.

'Why, no, but I have reached one conclusion. I opine that the hapless prophet has no sort of time with that lady. I opine that he will soon wish himself in Paradise. For if Almighty God ever created a female devil it's Madame von Einem.'

He sipped a little more milk with a grave face.

'That isn't my duodenal dyspepsia, Major. It's the verdict of a ripe experience, for I have a cool and penetrating judgement, even if I've a deranged stomach. And I give it as my considered conclusion that that woman's mad and bad—but principally bad.'

CHAPTER FOURTEEN

The Lady of the Mantilla

Since that first night I had never clapped eyes on Sandy. He had gone clean out of the world, and Blenkiron and I waited anxiously for a word of news. Our own business was in good trim, for we were presently going east towards Mesopotamia, but unless we learned more about Greenmantle our journey would be a grotesque failure. And learn about Greenmantle we could not, for nobody by word or deed suggested his existence, and it was impossible of course for us to ask questions. Our only hope was Sandy, for what we wanted to know was the prophet's whereabouts and his plans. I suggested to Blenkiron that we might do more to cultivate Frau von Einem, but he shut his jaw like a rat-trap.

'There's nothing doing for us in that quarter,' he said. 'That's the most dangerous woman on earth; and if she got any kind of notion that we were wise about her pet schemes I reckon you and I would very soon be in the Bosporus.'

This was all very well; but what was going to happen if the two of us were bundled off to Baghdad with instructions to wash away the British? Our time was getting pretty short, and I doubted if we could spin out more than three days more in Constantinople. I felt just as I had felt with Stumm that last night when I was about to be packed off to Cairo and saw no way of avoiding it. Even Blenkiron was getting anxious. He played Patience incessantly, and was disinclined to talk. I tried to find out something from the servants, but they either knew nothing or wouldn't speak—the former, I think. I kept my eyes lifting, too, as I walked about the streets, but there was no sign anywhere of the skin coats or the weird stringed instruments. The whole Company of the Rosy Hours seemed to have melted into the air, and I began to wonder if they had ever existed.

Anxiety made me restless, and restlessness made me want exercise. It was no good walking about the city. The weather had become foul again, and I was sick of the smells and the squalor and the flea-bitten crowds. So Blenkiron and I got horses, Turkish cavalry mounts with heads like trees, and went out through the suburbs into the open country.

It was a grey drizzling afternoon, with the beginnings of a sea fog which hid the Asiatic shores of the straits. It wasn't easy to find open ground for a gallop, for there were endless small patches of cultivation and the gardens of country houses. We kept on the high land above the sea, and when we reached a bit of downland came on squads of Turkish soldiers digging trenches. Whenever we let the horses go we had to pull up sharp for a digging party or a stretch of barbed wire. Coils of the beastly thing were lying loose everywhere, and Blenkiron nearly took a nasty toss over one. Then we were always being stopped by sentries and having to show our passes. Still the ride did us good and shook up our livers, and by the time we turned for home I was feeling more like a white man.

We jogged back in the short winter twilight, past the wooded grounds of white villas, held up every few minutes by transport-wagons and companies of soldiers. The rain had come on in real earnest, and it was two very bedraggled horsemen that crawled along the muddy lanes. As we passed one villa, shut in by a high white wall, a pleasant smell of wood smoke was wafted towards us, which made me sick for the burning veld. My ear, too, caught the twanging of a zither, which somehow reminded me of the afternoon in Kuprasso's garden-house.

I pulled up and proposed to investigate, but Blenkiron very testily declined.

'Zithers are as common here as fleas,' he said. 'You don't want to be fossicking around somebody's stables and find a horse-boy entertaining his friends. They don't like visitors in this country; and you'll be asking for trouble if you go inside those walls. I guess it's some old Buzzard's harem.' Buzzard was his own private peculiar name for the Turk, for he said he had had as a boy a natural history book with a picture of a bird called the turkey-buzzard, and couldn't get out of the habit of applying it to the Ottoman people.

I wasn't convinced, so I tried to mark down the place. It seemed to be about three miles out from the city, at the end of a steep lane on the inland side of the hill coming from the Bosporus. I fancied somebody of distinction lived there, for a little farther on we met a big empty motor-car snorting its way up, and I had a notion that the car belonged to the walled villa.

Next day Blenkiron was in grievous trouble with his dyspepsia. About midday he was compelled to lie down, and having nothing better to do I had out the horses again and took Peter with me. It was funny to see Peter in a Turkish army-saddle, riding with the long Boer stirrup and the slouch of the backveld.

That afternoon was unfortunate from the start. It was not the mist and drizzle of the day before, but a stiff northern gale which blew sheets of rain in our faces and numbed our bridle hands. We took the same road, but pushed west of the trench-digging parties and got to a shallow valley with a white village among the cypresses. Beyond that there was a very respectable road which brought us to the top of a crest that in clear weather must have given a fine prospect. Then we turned our horses, and I shaped our course so as to strike the top of the long lane that abutted on the down. I wanted to investigate the white villa.

But we hadn't gone far on our road back before we got into trouble. It arose out of a sheep-dog, a yellow mongrel brute that came at us like a thunderbolt. It took a special fancy to Peter, and bit savagely at his horse's heels and sent it capering off the road. I should have warned him, but I did not realize what was happening, till too late. For Peter, being accustomed to mongrels in Kaffir kraals, took a summary way with the pest. Since it despised his whip, he out with his pistol and put a bullet through its head.

The echoes of the shot had scarcely died away when the row began. A big fellow appeared running towards us, shouting wildly. I guessed he was the dog's owner, and proposed to pay no attention. But his cries summoned two other fellows—soldiers by the look of them—who closed in on us, unslinging their rifles as they ran. My first idea was to show them our heels, but I had no desire to be shot in the back, and they looked like men who wouldn't stop short of shooting. So we slowed down and faced them.

They made as savage-looking a trio as you would want to avoid. The shepherd looked as if he had been dug up, a dirty ruffian with matted hair and a beard like a bird's nest. The two soldiers stood staring with sullen faces, fingering their guns, while the other chap raved and stormed and kept pointing at Peter, whose mild eyes stared unwinkingly at his assailant.

The mischief was that neither of us had a word of Turkish. I tried German, but it had no effect. We sat looking at them and they stood storming at us, and it was fast getting dark. Once I turned my horse round as if to proceed, and the two soldiers jumped in front of me.

They jabbered among themselves, and then one said very slowly: 'He ... want ... pounds,' and he held up five fingers. They evidently saw by the cut of our jib that we weren't Germans.

'I'll be hanged if he gets a penny,' I said angrily, and the conversation languished.

The situation was getting serious, so I spoke a word to Peter. The soldiers had their rifles loose in their hands, and before they could lift them we had the pair covered with our pistols.

'If you move,' I said, 'you are dead.' They understood that all right and stood stock still, while the shepherd stopped his raving and took to muttering like a gramophone when the record is finished.

'Drop your guns,' I said sharply. 'Quick, or we shoot.'

The tone, if not the words, conveyed my meaning. Still staring at us, they let the rifles slide to the ground. The next second we had forced our horses on the top of them, and the three were off like rabbits. I sent a shot over their heads to encourage them. Peter dismounted and tossed the guns into a bit of scrub where they would take some finding.

This hold-up had wasted time. By now it was getting very dark, and we hadn't ridden a mile before it was black night. It was an annoying predicament, for I had completely lost my bearings and at the best I had only a foggy notion of the lie of the land. The best plan seemed to be to try and get to the top of a rise in the hope of seeing the lights of the city, but all the countryside was so pockety that it was hard to strike the right kind of rise.

We had to trust to Peter's instinct. I asked him where our line lay, and he sat very still for a minute sniffing the air. Then he pointed the direction. It wasn't what I would have taken myself, but on a point like that he was pretty near infallible.

Presently we came to a long slope which cheered me. But at the top there was no light visible anywhere—only a black void like the inside of a shell. As I stared into the gloom it seemed to me that there were patches of deeper darkness that might be woods.

'There is a house half-left in front of us,' said Peter.

I peered till my eyes ached and saw nothing.

'Well, for heaven's sake, guide me to it,' I said, and with Peter in front we set off down the hill.

It was a wild journey, for darkness clung as close to us as a vest. Twice we stepped into patches of bog, and once my horse saved himself by a hair from going head forward into a gravel pit. We got tangled up in strands of wire, and often found ourselves rubbing our noses against tree trunks. Several times I had to get down and make a gap in barricades of loose stones. But after a ridiculous amount of slipping and stumbling we finally struck what seemed the level of a road, and a piece of special darkness in front which turned out to be a high wall.

I argued that all mortal walls had doors, so we set to groping along it, and presently found a gap. There was an old iron gate on broken hinges, which we easily pushed open, and found ourselves on a back path to some house. It was clearly disused, for masses of rotting leaves covered it, and by the feel of it underfoot it was grass-grown.

We dismounted now, leading our horses, and after about fifty yards the path ceased and came out on a well-made carriage drive. So, at least, we guessed, for the place was as black as pitch. Evidently the house couldn't be far off, but in which direction I hadn't a notion.

Now, I didn't want to be paying calls on any Turk at that time of day. Our job was to find where the road opened into the lane, for after that our way to Constantinople was clear. One side the lane lay, and the other the house, and it didn't seem wise to take the risk of tramping up with horses to the front door. So I told Peter to wait for me at the end of the back-road, while I would prospect a bit. I turned to the right, my intention being if I saw the light of a house to return, and with Peter take the other direction.

I walked like a blind man in that nether-pit of darkness. The road seemed well kept, and the soft wet gravel muffled the sounds of my feet. Great trees overhung it, and several times I wandered into dripping bushes. And then I stopped short in my tracks, for I heard the sound of whistling.

It was quite close, about ten yards away. And the strange thing was that it was a tune I knew, about the last tune you would expect to hear in this part of the world. It was the Scots air: 'Ca' the yowes to the knowes,' which was a favourite of my father's.

The whistler must have felt my presence, for the air suddenly stopped in the middle of a bar. An unbounded curiosity seized me to know who the fellow could be. So I started in and finished it myself.

There was silence for a second, and then the unknown began again and stopped. Once more I chipped in and finished it. Then it seemed to me that he was coming nearer. The air in that dank tunnel was very still, and I thought I heard a light foot. I think I took a step backward. Suddenly there was a flash of an electric torch from a yard off, so quick that I could see nothing of the man who held it.

Then a low voice spoke out of the darkness—a voice I knew well—and, following it, a hand was laid on my arm. 'What the devil are you doing here, Dick?' it said, and there was something like consternation in the tone.

I told him in a hectic sentence, for I was beginning to feel badly rattled myself.

'You've never been in greater danger in your life,' said the voice. 'Great God, man, what brought you wandering here today of all days?'

You can imagine that I was pretty scared, for Sandy was the last man to put a case too high. And the next second I felt worse, for he clutched my arm and dragged me in a bound to the side of the road. I could see nothing, but I felt that his head was screwed round, and mine followed suit. And there, a dozen yards off, were the acetylene lights of a big motor-car.

It came along very slowly, purring like a great cat, while we pressed into the bushes. The headlights seemed to spread a fan far to either side, showing the full width of the drive and its borders, and about half the height of the over-arching trees. There was a figure in uniform sitting beside the chauffeur, whom I saw dimly in the reflex glow, but the body of the car was dark.

It crept towards us, passed, and my mind was just getting easy again when it stopped. A switch was snapped within, and the limousine was brightly lit up. Inside I saw a woman's figure.

The servant had got out and opened the door and a voice came from within—a clear soft voice speaking in some tongue I didn't understand. Sandy had started forward at the sound of it, and I followed him. It would never do for me to be caught skulking in the bushes.

I was so dazzled by the suddenness of the glare that at first I blinked and saw nothing. Then my eyes cleared and I found myself looking at the inside of a car upholstered in some soft dove-coloured fabric, and beautifully finished off in ivory and silver. The woman who sat in it had a mantilla of black lace over her head and shoulders, and with one slender jewelled hand she kept its fold over the greater part of her face. I saw only a pair of pale grey-blue eyes—these and the slim fingers.

I remember that Sandy was standing very upright with his hands on his hips, by no means like a servant in the presence of his mistress. He was a fine figure of a man at all times, but in those wild clothes, with his head thrown back and his dark brows drawn below his skull-cap, he looked like some savage king out of an older world. He was speaking Turkish, and glancing at me now and then as if angry and perplexed. I took the hint that he was not supposed to know any other tongue, and that he was asking who the devil I might be.

Then they both looked at me, Sandy with the slow unwinking stare of the gipsy, the lady with those curious, beautiful pale eyes. They ran over my clothes, my brand-new riding-breeches, my splashed boots, my wide-brimmed hat. I took off the last and made my best bow.

'Madam,' I said, 'I have to ask pardon for trespassing in your garden. The fact is, I and my servant—he's down the road with the horses and I guess you noticed him—the two of us went for a ride this afternoon, and got good and well lost. We came in by your back gate, and I was prospecting for your front door to find someone to direct us, when I bumped into this brigand-chief who didn't understand my talk. I'm American, and I'm here on a big Government proposition. I hate to trouble you, but if you'd send a man to show us how to strike the city I'd be very much in your debt.'

Her eyes never left my face. 'Will you come into the car?' she said in English. 'At the house I will give you a servant to direct you.'

She drew in the skirts of her fur cloak to make room for me, and in my muddy boots and sopping clothes I took the seat she pointed out. She said a word in Turkish to Sandy, switched off the light, and the car moved on.

Women had never come much my way, and I knew about as much of their ways as I knew about the Chinese language. All my life I had lived with men only, and rather a rough crowd at that. When I made my pile and came home I looked to see a little society, but I had first the business of the Black Stone on my hands, and then the war, so my education languished. I had never been in a motor-car with a lady before, and I felt like a fish on a dry sandbank. The soft cushions and the subtle scents filled me with acute uneasiness. I wasn't thinking now about Sandy's grave words, or about Blenkiron's warning, or about my job and the part this woman must play in it. I was thinking only that I felt mortally shy. The darkness made it worse. I was sure that my companion was looking at me all the time and laughing at me for a clown.

The car stopped and a tall servant opened the door. The lady was over the threshold before I was at the step. I followed her heavily, the wet squelching from my field-boots. At that moment I noticed that she was very tall.

She led me through a long corridor to a room where two pillars held lamps in the shape of torches. The place was dark but for their glow, and it was as warm as a hothouse from invisible stoves. I felt soft carpets underfoot, and on the walls hung some tapestry or rug of an amazingly intricate geometrical pattern, but with every strand as rich as jewels. There, between the pillars, she turned and faced me. Her furs were thrown back, and the black mantilla had slipped down to her shoulders.

'I have heard of you,' she said. 'You are called Richard Hanau, the American. Why have you come to this land?'

'To have a share in the campaign,' I said. 'I'm an engineer, and I thought I could help out with some business like Mesopotamia.'

'You are on Germany's side?' she asked.

'Why, yes,' I replied. 'We Americans are supposed to be nootrals, and that means we're free to choose any side we fancy. I'm for the Kaiser.'

Her cool eyes searched me, but not in suspicion. I could see she wasn't troubling with the question whether I was speaking the truth. She was sizing me up as a man. I cannot describe that calm appraising look. There was no sex in it, nothing even of that implicit sympathy with which one human being explores the existence of another. I was a chattel, a thing infinitely removed from intimacy. Even so I have myself looked at a horse which I thought of buying, scanning his shoulders and hocks and paces. Even so must the old lords of Constantinople have looked at the slaves which the chances of war brought to their markets, assessing their usefulness for some task or other with no thought of a humanity common to purchased and purchaser. And yet—not quite. This woman's eyes were weighing me, not for any special duty, but for my essential qualities. I felt that I was under the scrutiny of one who was a connoisseur in human nature.

I see I have written that I knew nothing about women. But every man has in his bones a consciousness of sex. I was shy and perturbed, but horribly fascinated. This slim woman, poised exquisitely like some statue between the pillared lights, with her fair cloud of hair, her long delicate face, and her pale bright eyes, had the glamour of a wild dream. I hated her instinctively, hated her intensely, but I longed to arouse her interest. To be valued coldly by those eyes was an offence to my manhood, and I felt antagonism rising within me. I am a strong fellow, well set up, and rather above the average height, and my irritation stiffened me from heel to crown. I flung my head back and gave her cool glance for cool glance, pride against pride.

Once, I remember, a doctor on board ship who dabbled in hypnotism told me that I was the most unsympathetic person he had ever struck. He said I was about as good a mesmeric subject as Table Mountain. Suddenly I began to realize that this woman was trying to cast some spell over me. The eyes grew large and luminous, and I was conscious for just an instant of some will battling to subject mine. I was aware, too, in the same moment of a strange scent which recalled that wild hour in Kuprasso's garden-house. It passed quickly, and for a second her eyes drooped. I seemed to read in them failure, and yet a kind of satisfaction, too, as if they had found more in me than they expected.

'What life have you led?' the soft voice was saying.

I was able to answer quite naturally, rather to my surprise. 'I have been a mining engineer up and down the world.'

'You have faced danger many times?'

'I have faced danger.'

'You have fought with men in battles?'

'I have fought in battles.'

Her bosom rose and fell in a kind of sigh. A smile—a very beautiful thing—flitted over her face. She gave me her hand. 'The horses are at the door now,' she said, 'and your servant is with them. One of my people will guide you to the city.'

She turned away and passed out of the circle of light into the darkness beyond ...

Peter and I jogged home in the rain with one of Sandy's skin-clad Companions loping at our side. We did not speak a word, for my thoughts were running like hounds on the track of the past hours. I had seen the mysterious Hilda von Einem, I had spoken to her, I had held her hand. She had insulted me with the subtlest of insults and yet I was not angry. Suddenly the game I was playing became invested with a tremendous solemnity. My old antagonists, Stumm and Rasta and the whole German Empire, seemed to shrink into the background, leaving only the slim woman with her inscrutable smile and devouring eyes. 'Mad and bad,' Blenkiron had called her, 'but principally bad.' I did not think they were the proper terms, for they belonged to the narrow world of our common experience. This was something beyond and above it, as a cyclone or an earthquake is outside the decent routine of nature. Mad and bad she might be, but she was also great.

Before we arrived our guide had plucked my knee and spoken some words which he had obviously got by heart. 'The Master says,' ran the message, 'expect him at midnight.'

CHAPTER FIFTEEN

An Embarrassed Toilet

I was soaked to the bone, and while Peter set off to look for dinner I went to my room to change. I had a rubdown and then got into pyjamas for some dumb-bell exercises with two chairs, for that long wet ride had stiffened my arm and shoulder muscles. They were a vulgar suit of primitive blue, which Blenkiron had looted from my London wardrobe. As Cornelis Brandt I had sported a flannel nightgown.

My bedroom opened off the sitting-room, and while I was busy with my gymnastics I heard the door open. I thought at first it was Blenkiron, but the briskness of the tread was unlike his measured gait. I had left the light burning there, and the visitor, whoever he was, had made himself at home. I slipped on a green dressing-gown Blenkiron had lent me, and sallied forth to investigate.

My friend Rasta was standing by the table, on which he had laid an envelope. He looked round at my entrance and saluted.

'I come from the Minister of War, sir,' he said, 'and bring you your passports for tomorrow. You will travel by ...' And then his voice tailed away and his black eyes narrowed to slits. He had seen something which switched him off the metals.

At that moment I saw it too. There was a mirror on the wall behind him, and as I faced him I could not help seeing my reflection. It was the exact image of the engineer on the Danube boat—blue jeans, loden cloak, and all. The accursed mischance of my costume had given him the clue to an identity which was otherwise buried deep in the Bosporus.

I am bound to say for Rasta that he was a man of quick action. In a trice he had whipped round to the other side of the table between me and the door, where he stood regarding me wickedly.

By this time I was at the table and stretched out a hand for the envelope. My one hope was nonchalance.

'Sit down, sir,' I said, 'and have a drink. It's a filthy night to move about in.'

'Thank you, no, Herr Brandt,' he said. 'You may burn these passports for they will not be used.'

'Whatever's the matter with you?' I cried. 'You've mistaken the house, my lad. I'm called Hanau—Richard Hanau—and my partner's Mr John S. Blenkiron. He'll be here presently. Never knew anyone of the name of Brandt, barring a tobacconist in Denver City.'

'You have never been to Rustchuk?' he said with a sneer.

'Not that I know of. But, pardon me, Sir, if I ask your name and your business here. I'm darned if I'm accustomed to be called by Dutch names or have my word doubted. In my country we consider that impolite as between gentlemen.'

I could see that my bluff was having its effect. His stare began to waver, and when he next spoke it was in a more civil tone.

'I will ask pardon if I'm mistaken, Sir, but you're the image of a man who a week ago was at Rustchuk, a man much wanted by the Imperial Government.'

'A week ago I was tossing in a dirty little hooker coming from Constanza. Unless Rustchuk's in the middle of the Black Sea I've never visited the township. I guess you're barking up the wrong tree. Come to think of it, I was expecting passports. Say, do you come from Enver Damad?'

'I have that honour,' he said.

'Well, Enver is a very good friend of mine. He's the brightest citizen I've struck this side of the Atlantic.'

The man was calming down, and in another minute his suspicions would have gone. But at that moment, by the crookedest kind of luck, Peter entered with a tray of dishes. He did not notice Rasta, and walked straight to the table and plumped down his burden on it. The Turk had stepped aside at his entrance, and I saw by the look in his eyes that his suspicions had become a certainty. For Peter, stripped to shirt and breeches, was the identical shabby little companion of the Rustchuk meeting.

I had never doubted Rasta's pluck. He jumped for the door and had a pistol out in a trice pointing at my head.

'*Bonne fortune*,' he cried. 'Both the birds at one shot.' His hand was on the latch, and his mouth was open to cry. I guessed there was an orderly waiting on the stairs.

He had what you call the strategic advantage, for he was at the door while I was at the other end of the table and Peter at the side of it at least two yards from him. The road was clear before him, and neither of us was armed. I made a despairing step forward, not knowing what I meant to do, for I saw no light. But Peter was before me.

He had never let go of the tray, and now, as a boy skims a stone on a pond, he skimmed it with its contents at Rasta's head. The man was opening the door with one hand while he kept me covered with the other, and he got the contrivance fairly in the face. A pistol shot cracked out, and the bullet went through the tray, but the noise was drowned in the crash of glasses and crockery. The next second Peter had wrenched the pistol from Rasta's hand and had gripped his throat.

A dandified Young Turk, brought up in Paris and finished in Berlin, may be as brave as a lion, but he cannot stand in a rough-and-tumble against a backveld hunter, though more than double his age. There was no need for me to help him. Peter had his own way, learned in a wild school, of knocking the sense out of a foe. He gagged him scientifically, and trussed him up with his own belt and two straps from a trunk in my bedroom.

'This man is too dangerous to let go,' he said, as if his procedure were the most ordinary thing in the world. 'He will be quiet now till we have time to make a plan.'

At that moment there came a knocking at the door. That is the sort of thing that happens in melodrama, just when the villain has finished off his job neatly. The correct thing to do is to pale to the teeth, and with a rolling, conscience-stricken eye glare round the horizon. But that was not Peter's way.

'We'd better tidy up if we're to have visitors,' he said calmly.

Now there was one of those big oak German cupboards against the wall which must have been brought in in sections, for complete it would never have got through the door. It was empty now, but for Blenkiron's hatbox. In it he deposited the unconscious Rasta, and turned the key. 'There's enough ventilation through the top,' he observed, 'to keep the air good.' Then he opened the door. A magnificent kavass in blue and silver stood outside. He saluted and proffered a card on which was written in pencil, 'Hilda von Einem'.

I would have begged for time to change my clothes, but the lady was behind him. I saw the black mantilla and the rich sable furs. Peter vanished through my bedroom and I was left to receive my guest in a room littered with broken glass and a senseless man in the cupboard.

There are some situations so crazily extravagant that they key up the spirit to meet them. I was almost laughing when that stately lady stepped over my threshold.

'Madam,' I said, with a bow that shamed my old dressing-gown and strident pyjamas. 'You find me at a disadvantage. I came home soaking from my ride, and was in the act of changing. My servant has just upset a tray of crockery, and I fear this room's no fit place for a lady. Allow me three minutes to make myself presentable.'

She inclined her head gravely and took a seat by the fire. I went into my bedroom, and as I expected found Peter lurking by the other door. In a hectic sentence I bade him get Rasta's orderly out of the place on any pretext, and tell him his master would return later. Then I hurried into decent garments, and came out to find my visitor in a brown study.

At the sound of my entrance she started from her dream and stood up on the hearthrug, slipping the long robe of fur from her slim body.

'We are alone?' she said. 'We will not be disturbed?'

Then an inspiration came to me. I remembered that Frau von Einem, according to Blenkiron, did not see eye to eye with the Young Turks; and I had a queer instinct that Rasta could not be to her liking. So I spoke the truth.

'I must tell you that there's another guest here tonight. I reckon he's feeling pretty uncomfortable. At present he's trussed up on a shelf in that cupboard.'

She did not trouble to look round.

'Is he dead?' she asked calmly.

'By no means,' I said, 'but he's fixed so he can't speak, and I guess he can't hear much.'

'He was the man who brought you this?' she asked, pointing to the envelope on the table which bore the big blue stamp of the Ministry of War.

'The same,' I said. 'I'm not perfectly sure of his name, but I think they call him Rasta.'

Not a flicker of a smile crossed her face, but I had a feeling that the news pleased her.

'Did he thwart you?' she asked.

'Why, yes. He thwarted me some. His head is a bit swelled, and an hour or two on the shelf will do him good.'

'He is a powerful man,' she said, 'a jackal of Enver's. You have made a dangerous enemy.'

'I don't value him at two cents,' said I, though I thought grimly that as far as I could see the value of him was likely to be about the price of my neck.

'Perhaps you are right,' she said with serious eyes. 'In these days no enemy is dangerous to a bold man. I have come tonight, Mr Hanau, to talk business with you, as they say in your country. I have heard well of you, and today I have seen you. I may have need of you, and you assuredly will have need of me....'

She broke off, and again her strange potent eyes fell on my face. They were like a burning searchlight which showed up every cranny and crack of the soul. I felt it was going to be horribly difficult to act a part under that compelling gaze. She could not mesmerize me, but she could strip me of my fancy dress and set me naked in the masquerade.

'What came you forth to seek?' she asked. 'You are not like the stout American Blenkiron, a lover of shoddy power and a devotee of a feeble science. There is something more than that in your face. You are on our side, but you are not of the Germans with their hankerings for a rococo Empire. You come from America, the land of pious follies, where men worship gold and words. I ask, what came you forth to seek?'

As she spoke I seemed to get a vision of a figure, like one of the old gods looking down on human nature from a great height, a figure disdainful and passionless, but with its own magnificence. It kindled my imagination, and I answered with the stuff I had often cogitated when I had tried to explain to myself just how a case could be made out against the Allied cause.

'I will tell you, Madam,' I said. 'I am a man who has followed a science, but I have followed it in wild places, and I have gone through it and come out at the other side. The world, as I see it, had become too easy and cushioned. Men had forgotten their manhood in soft speech, and imagined that the rules of their smug civilization were the laws of the universe. But that is not the teaching of science, and it is not the teaching of life. We have forgotten the greater virtues, and we were becoming emasculated humbugs whose gods were our own weaknesses. Then came war, and the air was cleared. Germany, in spite of her blunders and her grossness, stood forth as the scourge of cant. She had the courage to cut through the bonds of humbug and to laugh at the fetishes of the herd. Therefore I am on Germany's side. But I came here for another reason. I know nothing of the East, but as I read history it is from the desert that the purification comes. When mankind is smothered with shams and phrases and painted idols a wind blows out of the wild to cleanse and simplify life. The world needs space and fresh air. The civilization we have boasted of is a toy-shop and a blind alley, and I hanker for the open country.'

This confounded nonsense was well received. Her pale eyes had the cold light of the fanatic. With her bright hair and the long exquisite oval of her face she looked like some destroying fury of a Norse legend. At that moment I think I first really feared her; before I had half-hated and half-admired. Thank Heaven, in her absorption she did not notice that I had forgotten the speech of Cleveland, Ohio.

'You are of the Household of Faith,' she said. 'You will presently learn many things, for the Faith marches to victory. Meantime I have one word for you. You and your companion travel eastward.'

'We go to Mesopotamia,' I said. 'I reckon these are our passports,' and I pointed to the envelope.

She picked it up, opened it, and then tore it in pieces and tossed it in the fire.

'The orders are countermanded,' she said. 'I have need of you and you go with me. Not to the flats of the Tigris, but to the great hills. Tomorrow you will receive new passports.'

She gave me her hand and turned to go. At the threshold she paused, and looked towards the oak cupboard. 'Tomorrow I will relieve you of your prisoner. He will be safer in my hands.'

She left me in a condition of pretty blank bewilderment. We were to be tied to the chariot-wheels of this fury, and started on an enterprise compared to which fighting against our friends at Kut seemed tame and reasonable. On the other hand, I had been spotted by Rasta, and had got the envoy of the most powerful man in Constantinople locked in a cupboard. At all costs we had to keep Rasta safe, but I was very determined that he should not be handed over to the lady. I was going to be no party to cold-blooded murder, which I judged to be her expedient. It was a pretty kettle of fish, but in the meantime I must have food, for I had eaten nothing for nine hours. So I went in search of Peter.

I had scarcely begun my long deferred meal when Sandy entered. He was before his time, and he looked as solemn as a sick owl. I seized on him as a drowning man clutches a spar.

He heard my story of Rasta with a lengthening face.

'That's bad,' he said. 'You say he spotted you, and your subsequent doings of course would not disillusion him. It's an infernal nuisance, but there's only one way out of it. I must put him in charge of my own people. They will keep him safe and sound till he's wanted. Only he mustn't see me.' And he went out in a hurry.

I fetched Rasta from his prison. He had come to his senses by this time, and lay regarding me with stony, malevolent eyes.

'I'm very sorry, Sir,' I said, 'for what has happened. But you left me no alternative. I've got a big job on hand and I can't have it interfered with by you or anyone. You're paying the price of a suspicious nature. When you know a little more you'll want to apologize to me. I'm going to see that you are kept quiet and comfortable for a day or two. You've no cause to worry, for you'll suffer no harm. I give you my word of honour as an American citizen.'

Two of Sandy's miscreants came in and bore him off, and presently Sandy himself returned. When I asked him where he was being taken, Sandy said he didn't know. 'They've got their orders, and they'll carry them out to the letter. There's a big unknown area in Constantinople to hide a man, into which the *Khafiyeh* never enter.'

Then he flung himself in a chair and lit his old pipe.

'Dick,' he said, 'this job is getting very difficult and very dark. But my knowledge has grown in the last few days. I've found out the meaning of the second word that Harry Bullivant scribbled.'

'*Cancer*?' I asked.

'Yes. It means just what it reads and no more. Greenmantle is dying—has been dying for months. This afternoon they brought a German doctor to see him, and the man gave him a few hours of life. By now he may be dead.'

The news was a staggerer. For a moment I thought it cleared up things. 'Then that busts the show,' I said. 'You can't have a crusade without a prophet.'

'I wish I thought it did. It's the end of one stage, but the start of a new and blacker one. Do you think that woman will be beaten by such a small thing as the death of her prophet? She'll find a substitute—one of the four Ministers, or someone else. She's a devil incarnate, but she has the soul of a Napoleon. The big danger is only beginning.'

Then he told me the story of his recent doings. He had found out the house of Frau von Einem without much trouble, and had performed with his ragamuffins in the servants' quarters. The prophet had a large retinue, and the fame of his minstrels—for the Companions were known far and wide in the land of Islam—came speedily to the ears of the Holy Ones. Sandy, a leader in this most orthodox coterie, was taken into favour and brought to the notice of the four Ministers. He and his half-dozen retainers became inmates of the villa, and Sandy, from his knowledge of Islamic lore and his ostentatious piety, was admitted to the confidence of the household. Frau von Einem welcomed him as an ally, for the Companions had been the most devoted propagandists of the new revelation.

As he described it, it was a strange business. Greenmantle was dying and often in great pain, but he struggled to meet the demands of his protectress. The four Ministers, as Sandy saw them, were unworldly ascetics; the prophet himself was a saint, though a practical saint with some notions of policy; but the controlling brain and will were those of the lady. Sandy seemed to have won his favour, even his affection. He spoke of him with a kind of desperate pity.

'I never saw such a man. He is the greatest gentleman you can picture, with a dignity like a high mountain. He is a dreamer and a poet, too—a genius if I can judge these things. I think I can assess him rightly, for I know something of the soul of the East, but it would be too long a story to tell now. The West knows nothing of the true Oriental. It pictures him as lapped in colour and idleness and luxury and gorgeous dreams. But it is all wrong. The *Kaf* he yearns for is an austere thing. It is the austerity of the East that is its beauty and its terror ... It always wants the same things at the back of its head. The Turk and the Arab came out of big spaces, and they have the desire of them in their bones. They settle down and stagnate, and by the by they degenerate into that appalling subtlety which is their ruling passion gone crooked. And then comes a new revelation and a great simplifying. They want to live face to face with God without a screen of ritual and images and priestcraft. They want to prune life of its foolish fringes and get back to the noble bareness of the desert. Remember, it is always the empty desert and the empty sky that cast their spell over them—these, and the hot, strong, antiseptic sunlight which burns up all rot and decay. It isn't inhuman. It's the humanity of one part of the human race. It isn't ours, it isn't as good as ours, but it's jolly good all the same. There are times when it grips me so hard that I'm inclined to forswear the gods of my fathers!

'Well, Greenmantle is the prophet of this great simplicity. He speaks straight to the heart of Islam, and it's an honourable message. But for our sins it's been twisted into part of that damned German propaganda. His unworldliness has been used for a cunning political move, and his creed of space and simplicity for the furtherance of the last word in human degeneracy. My God, Dick, it's like seeing St Francis run by Messalina.'

'The woman has been here tonight,' I said. 'She asked me what I stood for, and I invented some infernal nonsense which she approved of. But I can see one thing. She and her prophet may run for different stakes, but it's the same course.'

Sandy started. 'She has been here!' he cried. 'Tell me, Dick, what do you think of her?'

'I thought she was about two parts mad, but the third part was uncommon like inspiration.'

'That's about right,' he said. 'I was wrong in comparing her to Messalina. She's something a dashed sight more complicated. She runs the prophet just because she shares his belief. Only what in him is sane and fine, in her is mad and horrible. You see, Germany also wants to simplify life.'

'I know,' I said. 'I told her that an hour ago, when I talked more rot to the second than any normal man ever achieved. It will come between me and my sleep for the rest of my days.'

'Germany's simplicity is that of the neurotic, not the primitive. It is megalomania and egotism and the pride of the man in the Bible that waxed fat and kicked. But the results are the same. She wants to destroy and simplify; but it isn't the simplicity of the ascetic, which is of the spirit, but the simplicity of the madman that grinds down all the contrivances of civilization to a featureless monotony. The prophet wants to save the souls of his people; Germany wants to rule the inanimate corpse of the world. But you can get the same language to cover both. And so you have the partnership of St Francis and Messalina. Dick, did you ever hear of a thing called the Superman?'

'There was a time when the papers were full of nothing else,' I answered. 'I gather it was invented by a sportsman called Nietzsche.'

'Maybe,' said Sandy. 'Old Nietzsche has been blamed for a great deal of rubbish he would have died rather than acknowledge. But it's a craze of the new, fatted Germany. It's a fancy type which could never really exist, any more than the Economic Man of the politicians. Mankind has a sense of humour which stops short of the final absurdity. There never has been, and there never could be a real Superman ... But there might be a Superwoman.'

'You'll get into trouble, my lad, if you talk like that,' I said.

'It's true all the same. Women have got a perilous logic which we never have, and some of the best of them don't see the joke of life like the ordinary man. They can be far greater than men, for they can go straight to the heart of things. There never was a man so near the divine as Joan of Arc. But I think, too, they can be more entirely damnable than anything that ever was breeched, for they don't stop still now and then and laugh at themselves ... There is no Superman. The poor old donkeys that fancy themselves in the part are either crackbrained professors who couldn't rule a Sunday-school class, or bristling soldiers with pint-pot heads who imagine that the shooting of a Duc d'Enghien made a

Napoleon. But there is a Superwoman, and her name's Hilda von Einem.'

'I thought our job was nearly over,' I groaned, 'and now it looks as if it hadn't well started. Bullivant said that all we had to do was to find out the truth.'

'Bullivant didn't know. No man knows except you and me. I tell you, the woman has immense power. The Germans have trusted her with their trump card, and she's going to play it for all she is worth. There's no crime that will stand in her way. She has set the ball rolling, and if need be she'll cut all her prophets' throats and run the show herself ... I don't know about your job, for honestly I can't quite see what you and Blenkiron are going to do. But I'm very clear about my own duty. She's let me into the business, and I'm going to stick to it in the hope that I'll find a chance of wrecking it ... We're moving eastward tomorrow—with a new prophet if the old one is dead.'

'Where are you going?' I asked.

'I don't know. But I gather it's a long journey, judging by the preparations. And it must be to a cold country, judging by the clothes provided.'

'Well, wherever it is, we're going with you. You haven't heard the end of our yarn. Blenkiron and I have been moving in the best circles as skilled American engineers who are going to play Old Harry with the

British on the Tigris. I'm a pal of Enver's now, and he has offered me his protection. The lamented Rasta brought our passports for the journey to Mesopotamia tomorrow, but an hour ago your lady tore them up and put them in the fire. We are going with her, and she vouchsafed the information that it was towards the great hills.'

Sandy whistled long and low. 'I wonder what the deuce she wants with you? This thing is getting dashed complicated, Dick ... Where, more by token, is Blenkiron? He's the fellow to know about high politics.'

The missing Blenkiron, as Sandy spoke, entered the room with his slow, quiet step. I could see by his carriage that for once he had no dyspepsia, and by his eyes that he was excited.

'Say, boys,' he said, 'I've got something pretty considerable in the way of noos. There's been big fighting on the Eastern border, and the Buzzards have taken a bad knock.'

His hands were full of papers, from which he selected a map and spread it on the table.

'They keep mum about this thing in the capital, but I've been piecing the story together these last days and I think I've got it straight. A fortnight ago old man Nicholas descended from his mountains and scuppered his enemies there—at Kuprikeui, where the main road eastwards crosses the Araxes. That was only the beginning of the stunt, for he pressed on on a broad front, and the gentleman called Kiamil, who commands in those parts, was not up to the job of holding him. The Buzzards were shepherded in from north and east and south, and now the Muscovite is sitting down outside the forts of Erzerum. I can tell you they're pretty miserable about the situation in the highest quarters ... Enver is sweating blood to get fresh divisions to Erzerum from Gally-poly, but it's a long road and it looks as if they would be too late for the fair ... You and I, Major, start for Mesopotamy tomorrow, and that's about the meanest bit of bad luck that ever happened to John S. We're missing the chance of seeing the goriest fight of this campaign.'

I picked up the map and pocketed it. Maps were my business, and I had been looking for one.

'We're not going to Mesopotamia,' I said. 'Our orders have been cancelled.'

'But I've just seen Enver, and he said he had sent round our passports.'

'They're in the fire,' I said. 'The right ones will come along tomorrow morning.'

Sandy broke in, his eyes bright with excitement.

'The great hills! ... We're going to Erzerum ... Don't you see that the Germans are playing their big card? They're sending Greenmantle to the point of danger in the hope that his coming will rally the Turkish defence. Things are beginning to move, Dick, old man. No more kicking the heels for us. We're going to be in it up to the neck, and Heaven help the best man ... I must be off now, for I've a lot to do. *Au revoir*. We meet some time in the hills.'

Blenkiron still looked puzzled, till I told him the story of that night's doings. As he listened, all the satisfaction went out of his face, and that funny, childish air of bewilderment crept in.

'It's not for me to complain, for it's in the straight line of our dooty, but I reckon there's going to be big trouble ahead of this caravan. It's Kismet, and we've got to bow. But I won't pretend that I'm not considerable scared at the prospect.'

'Oh, so am I,' I said. 'The woman frightens me into fits. We're up against it this time all right. All the same I'm glad we're to be let into the real star metropolitan performance. I didn't relish the idea of touring the provinces.'

'I guess that's correct. But I could wish that the good God would see fit to take that lovely lady to Himself. She's too much for a quiet man at my time of life. When she invites us to go in on the ground-floor I feel like taking the elevator to the roof-garden.'

CHAPTER SIXTEEN

The Battered Caravanserai

Two days later, in the evening, we came to Angora, the first stage in our journey.

The passports had arrived next morning, as Frau von Einem had promised, and with them a plan of our journey. More, one of the Companions, who spoke a little English, was detailed to accompany us—a wise precaution, for no one of us had a word of Turkish. These were the sum of our instructions. I heard nothing more of Sandy or Greenmantle or the lady. We were meant to travel in our own party.

We had the railway to Angora, a very comfortable German *Schlafwagen*, tacked to the end of a troop-train. There wasn't much to be seen of the country, for after we left the Bosporus we ran into scuds of snow, and except that we seemed to be climbing on to a big plateau I had no notion of the landscape. It was a marvel that we made such good time, for that line was congested beyond anything I have ever seen. The place was crawling with the Gallipoli troops, and every siding was packed with supply trucks. When we stopped—which we did on an average about once an hour—you could see vast camps on both sides of the line, and often we struck regiments on the march along the railway track. They looked a fine, hardy lot of ruffians, but many were deplorably ragged, and I didn't think much of their boots. I wondered how they would do the five hundred miles of road to Erzerum.

Blenkiron played Patience, and Peter and I took a hand at picquet, but mostly we smoked and yarned. Getting away from that infernal city had cheered us up wonderfully. Now we were out on the open road, moving to the sound of the guns. At the worst, we should not perish like rats in a sewer. We would be all together, too, and that was a comfort. I think we felt the relief which a man who has been on a lonely outpost feels when he is brought back to his battalion. Besides, the thing had gone clean beyond our power to direct. It was no good planning and scheming, for none of us had a notion what the next step might be. We were fatalists now, believing in Kismet, and that is a comfortable faith.

All but Blenkiron. The coming of Hilda von Einem into the business had put a very ugly complexion on it for him. It was curious to see how she affected the different members of our gang. Peter did not care a rush: man, woman, and hippogriff were the same to him; he met it all as calmly as if he were making plans to round up an old lion in a patch of bush, taking the facts as they came and working at them as if they were a sum in arithmetic. Sandy and I were impressed—it's no good denying it: horribly impressed—but we were too interested to be scared, and we weren't a bit fascinated. We hated her too much for that. But she fairly struck Blenkiron dumb. He said himself it was just like a rattlesnake and a bird.

I made him talk about her, for if he sat and brooded he would get worse. It was a strange thing that this man, the most imperturbable and, I think, about the most courageous I have ever met, should be paralysed by a slim woman. There was no doubt about it. The thought of her made the future to him as black as a thunder cloud. It took the power out of his joints, and if she was going to be much around, it looked as if Blenkiron might be counted out.

I suggested that he was in love with her, but this he vehemently denied.

'No, Sir; I haven't got no sort of affection for the lady. My trouble is that she puts me out of countenance, and I can't fit her in as an antagonist. I guess we Americans haven't got the right poise for dealing with that kind of female. We've exalted our womenfolk into little tin gods, and at the same time left them out of the real business of life. Consequently, when we strike one playing the biggest kind of man's game we can't place her. We aren't used to regarding them as anything except angels and children. I wish I had had you boys' upbringing.'

Angora was like my notion of some place such as Amiens in the retreat from Mons. It was one mass of troops and transport—the neck of the bottle, for more arrived every hour, and the only outlet was the single eastern road. The town was pandemonium into which distracted German officers were trying to introduce some order. They didn't worry much about us, for the heart of Anatolia wasn't a likely hunting-ground for suspicious characters. We took our passport to the commandant, who visaed them readily, and told us he'd do his best to get us transport. We spent the night in a sort of hotel, where all four crowded into one little bedroom, and next morning I had my work cut out getting a motor-car. It took four hours, and the use of every great name in the Turkish Empire, to raise a dingy sort of Studebaker, and another two to get the petrol and spare tyres. As for a chauffeur, love or money couldn't find him, and I was compelled to drive the thing myself.

We left just after midday and swung out into bare bleak downs patched with scrubby woodlands. There was no snow here, but a wind was blowing from the east which searched the marrow. Presently we climbed up into hills, and the road, though not badly engineered to begin with, grew as rough as the channel of a stream. No wonder, for the traffic was like what one saw on that awful stretch between Cassel and Ypres, and there were no gangs of Belgian roadmakers to mend it up. We found troops by the thousands striding along with their impassive Turkish faces, ox convoys, mule convoys, wagons drawn by sturdy little Anatolian horses, and, coming in the contrary direction, many shabby Red Crescent cars and wagons of the wounded. We had to crawl for hours on end, till we got past a block. Just before the darkening we seemed to outstrip the first press, and had a clear run for about ten miles over a low pass in the hills. I began to get anxious about the car, for it was a poor one at the best, and the road was guaranteed sooner or later to knock even a Rolls-Royce into scrap iron.

All the same it was glorious to be out in the open again. Peter's face wore a new look, and he sniffed the bitter air like a stag. There floated up from little wayside camps the odour of wood-smoke and dung-fires. That, and the curious acrid winter smell of great wind-blown spaces, will always come to my memory as I think of that day. Every hour brought me peace of mind and resolution. I felt as I had felt when the battalion first marched from Aire towards the firing-line, a kind of keying-up and wild expectation. I'm not used to cities, and lounging about Constantinople had slackened my fibre. Now, as the sharp wind buffeted us, I felt braced to any kind of risk. We were on the great road to the east and the border hills, and soon we should stand upon the farthest battle-front of the war. This was no commonplace intelligence job. That was all over, and we were going into the firing-zone, going to take part in what might be the downfall of our enemies. I didn't reflect that we were among those enemies, and would probably share their downfall if we were not shot earlier. The truth is, I had got out of the way of regarding the thing as a struggle between armies and nations. I hardly bothered to think where my sympathies lay. First and foremost it was a contest between the four of us and a crazy woman, and this personal antagonism made the strife of armies only a dimly-felt background.

We slept that night like logs on the floor of a dirty khan, and started next morning in a powder of snow. We were getting very high up now, and it was perishing cold. The Companion—his name sounded like Hussin—had travelled the road before and told me what the places were, but they conveyed nothing to me. All morning we wriggled through a big lot of troops, a brigade at least, who swung along at a great pace with a fine free stride that I don't think I have ever seen bettered. I must say I took a fancy to the Turkish fighting man: I remembered the testimonial our fellows gave him as a clean fighter, and I felt very bitter that Germany should have lugged him into this dirty business. They halted for a meal, and we stopped, too, and lunched off some brown bread and dried figs and a flask of very sour wine. I had a few words with one of the officers who spoke a little German. He told me they were marching straight for Russia, since there had been a great Turkish victory in the Caucasus. 'We have beaten the French and the British, and now it is Russia's turn,' he said stolidly, as if repeating a lesson. But he added that he was mortally sick of war.

In the afternoon we cleared the column and had an open road for some hours. The land now had a tilt eastward, as if we were moving towards the valley of a great river. Soon we began to meet little parties of men coming from the east with a new look in their faces. The first lots of wounded had been the ordinary thing you see on every front, and there had been some pretence at organization. But these new lots were very weary and broken; they were often barefoot, and they seemed to have lost their transport and to be starving. You would find a group stretched by the roadside in the last stages of exhaustion. Then would come a party limping along, so tired that they never turned their heads to look at us. Almost all were wounded, some badly, and most were horribly thin. I wondered how my Turkish friend behind would explain the sight to his men, if he believed in a great victory. They had not the air of the backwash of a conquering army.

Even Blenkiron, who was no soldier, noticed it.

'These boys look mighty bad,' he observed. 'We've got to hustle, Major, if we're going to get seats for the last act.'

That was my own feeling. The sight made me mad to get on faster, for I saw that big things were happening in the East. I had reckoned that four days would take us from Angora to Erzerum, but here was the second nearly over and we were not yet a third of the way. I pressed on recklessly, and that hurry was our undoing.

I have said that the Studebaker was a rotten old car. Its steering-gear was pretty dicky, and the bad surface and continual hairpin bends of the road didn't improve it. Soon we came into snow lying fairly deep, frozen hard and rutted by the big transport-wagons. We bumped and bounced horribly, and were shaken about like peas in a bladder. I began to be acutely anxious about the old boneshaker, the more as we seemed a long way short of the village I had proposed to spend the night in. Twilight was falling and we were still in an unfeatured waste, crossing the shallow glen of a stream. There was a bridge at the bottom of a slope—a bridge of logs and earth which had apparently been freshly strengthened for heavy traffic. As we approached it at a good pace the car ceased to answer to the wheel.

I struggled desperately to keep it straight, but it swerved to the left and we plunged over a bank into a marshy hollow. There was a sickening bump as we struck the lower ground, and the whole party were shot out into the frozen slush. I don't yet know how I escaped, for the car turned over and by rights I should have had my back broken. But no one was hurt. Peter was laughing, and Blenkiron, after shaking the snow out of his hair, joined him. For myself I was feverishly examining the machine. It was about as ugly as it could be, for the front axle was broken.

Here was a piece of hopeless bad luck. We were stuck in the middle of Asia Minor with no means of conveyance, for to get a new axle there was as likely as to find snowballs on the Congo. It was all but dark and there was no time to lose. I got out the petrol tins and spare tyres and cached them among some rocks on the hillside. Then we collected our scanty baggage from the derelict Studebaker. Our only hope was Hussin. He had got to find us some lodging for the night, and next day we would have a try for horses or a lift in some passing wagon. I had no hope of another car. Every automobile in Anatolia would now be at a premium.

It was so disgusting a mishap that we all took it quietly. It was too bad to be helped by hard swearing. Hussin and Peter set off on different sides of the road to prospect for a house, and Blenkiron and I sheltered under the nearest rock and smoked savagely.

Hussin was the first to strike oil. He came back in twenty minutes with news of some kind of dwelling a couple of miles up the stream. He went off to collect Peter, and, humping our baggage, Blenkiron and I plodded up the waterside. Darkness had fallen thick by this time, and we took some bad tosses among the bogs. When Hussin and Peter overtook us they found a better road, and presently we saw a light twinkle in the hollow ahead.

It proved to be a wretched tumble-down farm in a grove of poplars—a foul-smelling, muddy yard, a two-roomed hovel of a house, and a barn which was tolerably dry and which we selected for our sleeping-place. The owner was a broken old fellow whose sons were all at the war, and he received us with the profound calm of one who expects nothing but unpleasantness from life.

By this time we had recovered our tempers, and I was trying hard to put my new Kismet philosophy into practice. I reckoned that if risks were foreordained, so were difficulties, and both must be taken as part of the day's work. With the remains of our provisions and some curdled milk we satisfied our hunger and curled ourselves up among the pease straw of the barn. Blenkiron announced with a happy sigh that he had now been for two days quit of his dyspepsia.

That night, I remember, I had a queer dream. I seemed to be in a wild place among mountains, and I was being hunted, though who was after me I couldn't tell. I remember sweating with fright, for I seemed to be quite alone and the terror that was pursuing me was more than human. The place was horribly quiet and still, and there was deep snow lying everywhere, so that each step I took was heavy as lead. A very ordinary sort of nightmare, you will say. Yes, but there was one strange feature in this one. The night was pitch dark, but ahead of me in the throat of the pass there was one patch of light, and it showed a rum little hill with a rocky top: what we call in South Africa a *castrol* or saucepan. I had a notion that if I could get to that *castrol* I should be safe, and I panted through the drifts towards it with the avenger of blood at my heels. I woke, gasping, to find the winter morning struggling through the cracked rafters, and to hear Blenkiron say cheerily that his duodenum had behaved all night like a gentleman. I lay still for a bit trying to fix the dream, but it all dissolved into haze except the picture of the little hill, which was quite clear in every detail. I told myself it was a reminiscence of the veld, some spot down in the Wakkerstroom country, though for the life of me I couldn't place it.

I pass over the next three days, for they were one uninterrupted series of heart-breaks. Hussin and Peter scoured the country for horses, Blenkiron sat in the barn and played Patience, while I haunted the roadside near the bridge in the hope of picking up some kind of conveyance. My task was perfectly futile. The columns passed, casting wondering eyes on the wrecked car among the frozen rushes, but they could offer no help. My friend the Turkish officer promised to wire to Angora from some place or other for a fresh car, but, remembering the state of affairs at Angora, I had no hope from that quarter. Cars passed, plenty of them, packed with staff-officers, Turkish and German, but they were in far too big a hurry even to stop and speak. The only conclusion I reached from my roadside vigil was that things were getting very warm in the neighbourhood of Erzerum. Everybody on that road seemed to be in mad haste either to get there or to get away.

Hussin was the best chance, for, as I have said, the Companions had a very special and peculiar graft throughout the Turkish Empire. But the first day he came back empty-handed. All the horses had been commandeered for the war, he said; and though he was certain that some had been kept back and hidden away, he could not get on their track. The second day he returned with two—miserable screws and deplorably short in the wind from a diet of beans. There was no decent corn or hay left in the countryside. The third day he picked up a nice little Arab stallion: in poor condition, it is true, but perfectly sound. For these beasts we paid good money, for Blenkiron was well supplied and we had no time to spare for the interminable Oriental bargaining.

Hussin said he had cleaned up the countryside, and I believed him. I dared not delay another day, even though it meant leaving him behind. But he had no notion of doing anything of the kind. He was a good runner, he said, and could keep up with such horses as ours for ever. If this was the manner of our progress, I reckoned we would be weeks in getting to Erzerum.

We started at dawn on the morning of the fourth day, after the old farmer had blessed us and sold us some stale rye-bread. Blenkiron bestrode the Arab, being the heaviest, and Peter and I had the screws. My worst forebodings were soon realized, and Hussin, loping along at my side, had an easy job to keep up with us. We were about as slow as an ox-wagon. The brutes were unshod, and with the rough roads I saw that their feet would very soon go to pieces. We jogged along like a tinker's caravan, about five miles to the hour, as feckless a party as ever disgraced a highroad.

The weather was now a drizzle, which increased my depression. Cars passed us and disappeared in the mist, going at thirty miles an hour to mock our slowness. None of us spoke, for the futility of the business clogged our spirits. I bit hard on my lip to curb my restlessness, and I think I would have sold my soul there and then for anything that could move fast. I don't know any sorer trial than to be mad for speed and have to crawl at a snail's pace. I was getting ripe for any kind of desperate venture.

About midday we descended on a wide plain full of the marks of rich cultivation. Villages became frequent, and the land was studded with olive groves and scarred with water furrows. From what I remembered of the map I judged that we were coming to that champagne country near Siwas, which is the granary of Turkey, and the home of the true Osmanli stock.

Then at the turning of the road we came to the caravanserai.

It was a dingy, battered place, with the pink plaster falling in patches from its walls. There was a courtyard abutting on the road, and a flat-topped house with a big hole in its side. It was a long way from any battle-ground, and I guessed that some explosion had wrought the damage. Behind it, a few hundred yards off, a detachment of cavalry were encamped beside a stream, with their horses tied up in long lines of pickets.

And by the roadside, quite alone and deserted, stood a large new motor-car.

In all the road before and behind there was no man to be seen except the troops by the stream. The owners, whoever they were, must be inside the caravanserai.

I have said I was in the mood for some desperate deed, and lo and behold providence had given me the chance! I coveted that car as I have never coveted anything on earth. At the moment all my plans had narrowed down to a feverish passion to get to the battle-field. We had to find Greenmantle at Erzerum, and once there we should have Hilda von Einem's protection. It was a time of war, and a front of brass was the surest safety. But, indeed, I could not figure out any plan worth speaking of. I saw only one thing—a fast car which might be ours.

I said a word to the others, and we dismounted and tethered our horses at the near end of the courtyard. I heard the low hum of voices from the cavalrymen by the stream, but they were three hundred yards off and could not see us. Peter was sent forward to scout in the courtyard. In the building itself there was but one window looking on the road, and that was in the upper floor.

Meantime I crawled along beside the wall to where the car stood, and had a look at it. It was a splendid six-cylinder affair, brand new, with the tyres little worn. There were seven tins of petrol stacked behind as well as spare tyres, and, looking in, I saw map-cases and field-glasses strewn on the seats as if the owners had only got out for a minute to stretch their legs.

Peter came back and reported that the courtyard was empty.

'There are men in the upper room,' he said; 'more than one, for I heard their voices. They are moving about restlessly, and may soon be coming out.'

I reckoned that there was no time to be lost, so I told the others to slip down the road fifty yards beyond the caravanserai and be ready to climb in as I passed. I had to start the infernal thing, and there might be shooting.

I waited by the car till I saw them reach the right distance. I could hear voices from the second floor of the house and footsteps moving up and down. I was in a fever of anxiety, for any moment a man might come to the window. Then I flung myself on the starting handle and worked like a demon.

The cold made the job difficult, and my heart was in my mouth, for the noise in that quiet place must have woke the dead. Then, by the mercy of Heaven, the engine started, and I sprang to the driving seat, released the clutch, and opened the throttle. The great car shot forward, and I seemed to hear behind me shrill voices. A pistol bullet bored through my hat, and another buried itself in a cushion beside me.

In a second I was clear of the place and the rest of the party were embarking. Blenkiron got on the step and rolled himself like a sack of coals into the tonneau. Peter nipped up beside me, and Hussin scrambled in from the back over the folds of the hood. We had our baggage in our pockets and had nothing to carry.

Bullets dropped round us, but did no harm. Then I heard a report at my ear, and out of a corner of my eye saw Peter lower his pistol. Presently we were out of range, and, looking back, I saw three men gesticulating in the middle of the road.

'May the devil fly away with this pistol,' said Peter ruefully. 'I never could make good shooting with a little gun. Had I had my rifle...'

'What did you shoot for?' I asked in amazement. 'We've got the fellows' car, and we don't want to do them any harm.'

'It would have saved trouble had I had my rifle,' said Peter, quietly. 'The little man you call Rasta was there, and he knew you. I heard him cry your name. He is an angry little man, and I observe that on this road there is a telegraph.'

CHAPTER SEVENTEEN

Trouble by The Waters of Babylon

From that moment I date the beginning of my madness. Suddenly I forgot all cares and difficulties of the present and future and became foolishly light-hearted. We were rushing towards the great battle where men were busy at my proper trade. I realized how much I had loathed the lonely days in Germany, and still more the dawdling week in Constantinople. Now I was clear of it all, and bound for the clash of armies. It didn't trouble me that we were on the wrong side of the battle line. I had a sort of instinct that the darker and wilder things grew the better chance for us.

'Seems to me,' said Blenkiron, bending over me, 'that this joy-ride is going to come to an untimely end pretty soon. Peter's right. That young man will set the telegraph going, and we'll be held up at the next township.'

'He's got to get to a telegraph office first,' I answered. 'That's where we have the pull on him. He's welcome to the screws we left behind, and if he finds an operator before the evening I'm the worst kind of a Dutchman. I'm going to break all the rules and bucket this car for what she's worth. Don't you see that the nearer we get to Erzerum the safer we are?'

'I don't follow,' he said slowly. 'At Erzerum I reckon they'll be waiting for us with the handcuffs. Why in thunder couldn't those hairy ragamuffins keep the little cuss safe? Your record's a bit too precipitous, Major, for the most innocent-minded military boss.'

'Do you remember what you said about the Germans being open to bluff? Well, I'm going to put up the steepest sort of bluff. Of course they'll stop us. Rasta will do his damnedest. But remember that he and his friends are not very popular with the Germans, and Madame von Einem is. We're her proteges, and the bigger the German swell I get before the safer I'll feel. We've got our passports and our orders, and he'll be a bold man that will stop us once we get into the German zone. Therefore I'm going to hurry as fast as God will let me.'

It was a ride that deserved to have an epic written about it. The car was good, and I handled her well, though I say it who shouldn't. The road in that big central plain was fair, and often I knocked fifty miles an hour out of her. We passed troops by a circuit over the veld, where we took some awful risks, and once we skidded by some transport with our off wheels almost over the lip of a ravine. We went through the narrow streets of Siwas like a fire-engine, while I shouted out in German that we carried despatches for headquarters. We shot out of drizzling rain into brief spells of winter sunshine, and then into a snow blizzard which all but whipped the skin from our faces. And always before us the long road unrolled, with somewhere at the end of it two armies clinched in a death-grapple.

That night we looked for no lodging. We ate a sort of meal in the car with the hood up, and felt our way on in the darkness, for the headlights were in perfect order. Then we turned off the road for four hours' sleep, and I had a go at the map. Before dawn we started again, and came over a pass into the vale of a big river. The winter dawn showed its gleaming stretches, ice-bound among the sprinkled meadows. I called to Blenkiron:

'I believe that river is the Euphrates,' I said. 'So,' he said, acutely interested. 'Then that's the waters of Babylon. Great snakes, that I should have lived to see the fields where King Nebuchadnezzar grazed! Do you know the name of that big hill, Major?'

'Ararat, as like as not,' I cried, and he believed me.

We were among the hills now, great, rocky, black slopes, and, seen through side glens, a hinterland of snowy peaks. I remember I kept looking for the *castrol* I had seen in my dream. The thing had never left off haunting me, and I was pretty clear now that it did not belong to my South African memories. I am not a superstitious man, but the way that little *kranz* clung to my mind made me think it was a warning sent by Providence. I was pretty certain that when I clapped eyes on it I would be in for bad trouble.

All morning we travelled up that broad vale, and just before noon it spread out wider, the road dipped to the water's edge, and I saw before me the white roofs of a town. The snow was deep now, and lay down to the riverside, but the sky had cleared, and against a space of blue heaven some peaks to the south rose glittering like jewels. The arches of a bridge, spanning two forks of the stream, showed in front, and as I slowed down at the bend a sentry's challenge rang out from a block-house. We had reached the fortress of Erzingjan, the headquarters of a Turkish corps and the gate of Armenia.

I showed the man our passports, but he did not salute and let us move on. He called another fellow from the guardhouse, who motioned us to keep pace with him as he stumped down a side lane. At the other end was a big barracks with sentries outside. The man spoke to us in Turkish, which Hussin interpreted. There was somebody in that barracks who wanted badly to see us.

'By the waters of Babylon we sat down and wept,' quoted Blenkiron softly. 'I fear, Major, we'll soon be remembering Zion.'

I tried to persuade myself that this was merely the red tape of a frontier fortress, but I had an instinct that difficulties were in store for us. If Rasta had started wiring I was prepared to put up the brazenest bluff, for we were still eighty miles from Erzerum, and at all costs we were going to be landed there before night.

A fussy staff-officer met us at the door. At the sight of us he cried to a friend to come and look.

'Here are the birds safe. A fat man and two lean ones and a savage who looks like a Kurd. Call the guard and march them off. There's no doubt about their identity.'

'Pardon me, Sir,' I said, 'but we have no time to spare and we'd like to be in Erzerum before the dark. I would beg you to get through any formalities as soon as possible. This man,' and I pointed to the sentry, 'has our passports.'

'Compose yourself,' he said impudently; 'you're not going on just yet, and when you do it won't be in a stolen car.' He took the passports and fingered them casually. Then something he saw there made him cock his eyebrows.

'Where did you steal these?' he asked, but with less assurance in his tone.

I spoke very gently. 'You seem to be the victim of a mistake, sir. These are our papers. We are under orders to report ourselves at Erzerum without an hour's delay. Whoever hinders us will have to answer to General von Liman. We will be obliged if you will conduct us at once to the Governor.'

'You can't see General Posselt,' he said; 'this is my business. I have a wire from Siwas that four men stole a car belonging to one of Enver Damad's staff. It describes you all, and says that two of you are notorious spies wanted by the Imperial Government. What have you to say to that?'

'Only that it is rubbish. My good Sir, you have seen our passes. Our errand is not to be cried on the housetops, but five minutes with General Posselt will make things clear. You will be exceedingly sorry for it if you delay another minute.'

He was impressed in spite of himself, and after pulling his moustache turned on his heel and left us. Presently he came back and said very gruffly that the Governor would see us. We followed him along a corridor into a big room looking out on the river, where an oldish fellow sat in an arm-chair by a stove, writing letters with a fountain pen.

This was Posselt, who had been Governor of Erzerum till he fell sick and Ahmed Fevzi took his place. He had a peevish mouth and big blue pouches below his eyes. He was supposed to be a good engineer and to have made Erzerum impregnable, but the look on his face gave me the impression that his reputation at the moment was a bit unstable.

The staff-officer spoke to him in an undertone.

'Yes, yes, I know,' he said testily. 'Are these the men? They look a pretty lot of scoundrels. What's that you say? They deny it. But they've got the car. They can't deny that. Here, you,' and he fixed on Blenkiron, 'who the devil are you?'

Blenkiron smiled sleepily at him, not understanding one word, and I took up the parable.

'Our passports, Sir, give our credentials,' I said. He glanced through them, and his face lengthened.

'They're right enough. But what about this story of stealing a car?'

'It is quite true,' I said, 'but I would prefer to use a pleasanter word. You will see from our papers that every authority on the road is directed to give us the best transport. Our own car broke down, and after a long delay we got some wretched horses. It is vitally important that we should be in Erzerum without delay, so I took the liberty of appropriating an empty car we found outside an inn. I am sorry for the discomfort of the owners, but our business was too grave to wait.'

'But the telegram says you are notorious spies!'

I smiled. 'Who sent the telegram?'

'I see no reason why I shouldn't give you his name. It was Rasta Bey. You've picked an awkward fellow to make an enemy of.'

I did not smile but laughed. 'Rasta!' I cried. 'He's one of Enver's satellites. That explains many things. I should like a word with you alone, Sir.'

He nodded to the staff-officer, and when he had gone I put on my most Bible face and looked as important as a provincial mayor at a royal visit.

'I can speak freely,' I said, 'for I am speaking to a soldier of Germany. There is no love lost between Enver and those I serve. I need not tell you that. This Rasta thought he had found a chance of delaying us, so he invents this trash about spies. Those Comitadjis have spies on the brain ... Especially he hates Frau von Einem.'

He jumped at the name.

'You have orders from her?' he asked, in a respectful tone.

'Why, yes,' I answered, 'and those orders will not wait.'

He got up and walked to a table, whence he turned a puzzled face on me. 'I'm torn in two between the Turks and my own countrymen. If I please one I offend the other, and the result is a damnable confusion. You can go on to Erzerum, but I shall send a man with you to see that you report to headquarters there. I'm sorry, gentlemen, but I'm obliged to take no chances in this business. Rasta's got a grievance against you, but you can easily hide behind the lady's skirts. She passed through this town two days ago.'

Ten minutes later we were coasting through the slush of the narrow streets with a stolid German lieutenant sitting beside me.

The afternoon was one of those rare days when in the pauses of snow you have a spell of weather as mild as May. I remembered several like it during our winter's training in Hampshire. The road was a fine one, well engineered, and well kept too, considering the amount of traffic. We were little delayed, for it was sufficiently broad to let us pass troops and transport without slackening pace. The fellow at my side was good-humoured enough, but his presence naturally put the lid on our conversation. I didn't want to talk, however. I was trying to piece together a plan, and making very little of it, for I had nothing to go upon. We must find Hilda von Einem and Sandy, and between us we must wreck the Greenmantle business. That done, it didn't matter so much what happened to us. As I reasoned it out, the Turks must be in a bad way, and, unless they got a fillip from Greenmantle, would crumple up before the Russians. In the rout I hoped we might get a chance to change our sides. But it was no good looking so far forward; the first thing was to get to Sandy.

Now I was still in the mood of reckless bravado which I had got from bagging the car. I did not realize how thin our story was, and how easily Rasta might have a big graft at headquarters. If I had, I would have shot out the German lieutenant long before we got to Erzerum, and found some way of getting mixed up in the ruck of the population. Hussin could have helped me to that. I was getting so confident since our interview with Posselt that I thought I could bluff the whole outfit.

But my main business that afternoon was pure nonsense. I was trying to find my little hill. At every turn of the road I expected to see the *castrol* before us. You must know that ever since I could stand I have been crazy about high mountains. My father took me to Basutoland when I was a boy, and I reckon I have scrambled over almost every bit of upland south of the Zambesi, from the Hottentots Holland to the Zoutpansberg, and from the ugly yellow kopjes of Damaraland to the noble cliffs of Mont aux Sources. One of the things I had looked forward to in coming home was the chance of climbing the Alps. But now I was among peaks that I fancied were bigger than the Alps, and I could hardly keep my eyes on the road. I was pretty certain that my *castrol* was among them, for that dream had taken an almighty hold on my mind. Funnily enough, I was ceasing to think it a place of evil omen, for one soon forgets the atmosphere of nightmare. But I was convinced that it was a thing I was destined to see, and to see pretty soon.

Darkness fell when we were some miles short of the city, and the last part was difficult driving. On both sides of the road transport and engineers' stores were parked, and some of it strayed into the highway. I noticed lots of small details—machine-gun detachments, signalling parties, squads of stretcher-bearers—which mean the fringe of an army, and as soon as the night began the white fingers of searchlights began to grope in the skies.

And then, above the hum of the roadside, rose the voice of the great guns. The shells were bursting four or five miles away, and the guns must have been as many more distant. But in that upland pocket of plain in the frosty night they sounded most intimately near. They kept up their solemn litany, with a minute's interval between each—no *rafale* which rumbles like a drum, but the steady persistence of artillery exactly ranged on a target. I judged they must be bombarding the outer forts, and once there came a loud explosion and a red glare as if a magazine had suffered.

It was a sound I had not heard for five months, and it fairly crazed me. I remembered how I had first heard it on the ridge before Laventie. Then I had been half-afraid, half-solemnized, but every nerve had been quickened. Then it had been the new thing in my life that held me breathless with anticipation; now it was the old thing, the thing I had shared with so many good fellows, my proper work, and the only task for a man. At the sound of the guns I felt that I was moving in natural air once more. I felt that I was coming home.

We were stopped at a long line of ramparts, and a German sergeant stared at us till he saw the lieutenant beside me, when he saluted and we passed on. Almost at once we dipped into narrow twisting streets, choked with soldiers, where it was hard business to steer. There were few lights—only now and then the flare of a torch which showed the grey stone houses, with every window latticed and shuttered. I had put out my headlights and had only side lamps, so we had to pick our way gingerly through the labyrinth. I hoped we would strike Sandy's quarters soon, for we were all pretty empty, and a frost had set in which made our thick coats seem as thin as paper.

The lieutenant did the guiding. We had to present our passports, and I anticipated no more difficulty than in landing from the boat at Boulogne. But I wanted to get it over, for my hunger pinched me and it was fearsome cold. Still the guns went on, like hounds baying before a quarry. The city was out of range, but there were strange lights on the ridge to the east.

At last we reached our goal and marched through a fine old carved archway into a courtyard, and thence into a draughty hall.

'You must see the *Sektionschef*,' said our guide. I looked round to see if we were all there, and noticed that Hussin had disappeared. It did not matter, for he was not on the passports.

We followed as we were directed through an open door. There was a man standing with his back towards us looking at a wall map, a very big man with a neck that bulged over his collar. I would have known that neck among a million. At the sight of it I made a half-turn to bolt back. It was too late, for the door had closed behind us and there were two armed sentries beside it.

The man slewed round and looked into my eyes. I had a despairing hope that I might bluff it out, for I was in different clothes and had shaved my beard. But you cannot spend ten minutes in a death-grapple without your adversary getting to know you.

He went very pale, then recollected himself and twisted his features into the old grin.

'So,' he said, 'the little Dutchmen! We meet after many days.'

It was no good lying or saying anything. I shut my teeth and waited.

'And you, Herr Blenkiron? I never liked the look of you. You babbled too much, like all your damned Americans.'

'I guess your personal dislikes haven't got anything to do with the matter,' said Blenkiron, calmly. 'If you're the boss here, I'll thank you to cast your eye over these passports, for we can't stand waiting for ever.'

This fairly angered him. 'I'll teach you manners,' he cried, and took a step forward to reach for Blenkiron's shoulder—the game he had twice played with me.

Blenkiron never took his hands from his coat pockets. 'Keep your distance,' he drawled in a new voice. 'I've got you covered, and I'll make a hole in your bullet head if you lay a hand on me.'

With an effort Stumm recovered himself. He rang a bell and fell to smiling. An orderly appeared to whom he spoke in Turkish, and presently a file of soldiers entered the room.

'I'm going to have you disarmed, gentlemen,' he said. 'We can conduct our conversation more pleasantly without pistols.'

It was idle to resist. We surrendered our arms, Peter almost in tears with vexation. Stumm swung his legs over a chair, rested his chin on the back and looked at me.

'Your game is up, you know,' he said. 'These fools of Turkish police said the Dutchmen were dead, but I had the happier inspiration. I believed the good God had spared them for me. When I got Rasta's telegram I was certain, for your doings reminded me of a little trick you once played me on the Schwandorf road. But I didn't think to find this plump old partridge,' and he smiled at Blenkiron. 'Two eminent American engineers and their servant bound for Mesopotamia on business of high

Government importance! It was a good lie; but if I had been in Constantinople it would have had a short life. Rasta and his friends are no concern of mine. You can trick them as you please. But you have attempted to win the confidence of a certain lady, and her interests are mine. Likewise you have offended me, and I do not forgive. By God,' he cried, his voice growing shrill with passion, 'by the time I have done with you your mothers in their graves will weep that they ever bore you!'

It was Blenkiron who spoke. His voice was as level as the chairman's of a bogus company, and it fell on that turbid atmosphere like acid on grease.

'I don't take no stock in high-falutin'. If you're trying to scare me by that dime-novel talk I guess you've hit the wrong man. You're like the sweep that stuck in the chimney, a bit too big for your job. I reckon you've a talent for romance that's just wasted in soldiering. But if you're going to play any ugly games on me I'd like you to know that I'm an American citizen, and pretty well considered in my own country and in yours, and you'll sweat blood for it later. That's a fair warning, Colonel Stumm.'

I don't know what Stumm's plans were, but that speech of Blenkiron's put into his mind just the needed amount of uncertainty. You see, he had Peter and me right enough, but he hadn't properly connected Blenkiron with us, and was afraid either to hit out at all three, or to let Blenkiron go. It was lucky for us that the American had cut such a dash in the Fatherland.

'There is no hurry,' he said blandly. 'We shall have long happy hours together. I'm going to take you all home with me, for I am a hospitable soul. You will be safer with me than in the town gaol, for it's a trifle draughty. It lets things in, and it might let things out.'

Again he gave an order, and we were marched out, each with a soldier at his elbow. The three of us were bundled into the back seat of the car, while two men sat before us with their rifles between their knees, one got up behind on the baggage rack, and one sat beside Stumm's chauffeur. Packed like sardines we moved into the bleak streets, above which the stars twinkled in ribbons of sky.

Hussin had disappeared from the face of the earth, and quite right too. He was a good fellow, but he had no call to mix himself up in our troubles.

CHAPTER EIGHTEEN

Sparrows on the Housetops

'I've often regretted,' said Blenkiron, 'that miracles have left off happening.'

He got no answer, for I was feeling the walls for something in the nature of a window.

'For I reckon,' he went on, 'that it wants a good old-fashioned copper-bottomed miracle to get us out of this fix. It's plumb against all my principles. I've spent my life using the talents God gave me to keep things from getting to the point of rude violence, and so far I've succeeded. But now you come along, Major, and you hustle a respectable middle-aged citizen into an aboriginal mix-up. It's mighty indelicate. I reckon the next move is up to you, for I'm no good at the housebreaking stunt.'

'No more am I,' I answered; 'but I'm hanged if I'll chuck up the sponge. Sandy's somewhere outside, and he's got a hefty crowd at his heels.'

I simply could not feel the despair which by every law of common sense was due to the case. The guns had intoxicated me. I could still hear their deep voices, though yards of wood and stone separated us from the upper air.

What vexed us most was our hunger. Barring a few mouthfuls on the road we had eaten nothing since the morning, and as our diet for the past days had not been generous we had some leeway to make up. Stumm had never looked near us since we were shoved into the car. We had been brought to some kind of house and bundled into a place like a wine-cellar. It was pitch dark, and after feeling round the walls, first on my feet and then on Peter's back, I decided that there were no windows. It must have been lit and ventilated by some lattice in the ceiling. There was not a stick of furniture in the place: nothing but a damp earth floor and bare stone sides, The door was a relic of the Iron Age, and I could hear the paces of a sentry outside it.

When things get to the pass that nothing you can do can better them, the only thing is to live for the moment. All three of us sought in sleep a refuge from our empty stomachs. The floor was the poorest kind of bed, but we rolled up our coats for pillows and made the best of it. Soon I knew by Peter's regular breathing that he was asleep, and I presently followed him ...

I was awakened by a pressure below my left ear. I thought it was Peter, for it is the old hunter's trick of waking a man so that he makes no noise. But another voice spoke. It told me that there was no time to lose and to rise and follow, and the voice was the voice of Hussin.

Peter was awake, and we stirred Blenkiron out of heavy slumber. We were bidden take off our boots and hang them by their laces round our necks as country boys do when they want to go barefoot. Then we tiptoed to the door, which was ajar.

Outside was a passage with a flight of steps at one end which led to the open air. On these steps lay a faint shine of starlight, and by its help I saw a man huddled up at the foot of them. It was our sentry, neatly and scientifically gagged and tied up.

The steps brought us to a little courtyard about which the walls of the houses rose like cliffs. We halted while Hussin listened intently. Apparently the coast was clear and our guide led us to one side, which was clothed by a stout wooden trellis. Once it may have supported fig-trees, but now the plants were dead and only withered tendrils and rotten stumps remained.

It was child's play for Peter and me to go up that trellis, but it was the deuce and all for Blenkiron. He was in poor condition and puffed like a grampus, and he seemed to have no sort of head for heights. But he was as game as a buffalo, and started in gallantly till his arms gave out and he fairly stuck. So Peter and I went up on each side of him, taking an arm apiece, as I had once seen done to a man with vertigo in the Kloof Chimney on Table Mountain. I was mighty thankful when I got him panting on the top and Hussin had shinned up beside us.

We crawled along a broadish wall, with an inch or two of powdery snow on it, and then up a sloping buttress on to the flat roof of the house. It was a miserable business for Blenkiron, who would certainly have fallen if he could have seen what was below him, and Peter and I had to stand to attention all the time. Then began a more difficult job. Hussin pointed out a ledge which took us past a stack of chimneys to another building slightly lower, this being the route he fancied. At that I sat down resolutely and put on my boots, and the others followed. Frost-bitten feet would be a poor asset in this kind of travelling.

It was a bad step for Blenkiron, and we only got him past it by Peter and I spread-eagling ourselves against the wall and passing him in front of us with his face towards us. We had no grip, and if he had stumbled we should all three have been in the courtyard. But we got it over, and dropped as softly as possible on to the roof of the next house. Hussin had his finger on his lips, and I soon saw why. For there was a lighted window in the wall we had descended.

Some imp prompted me to wait behind and explore. The others followed Hussin and were soon at the far end of the roof, where a kind of wooden pavilion broke the line, while I tried to get a look inside. The window was curtained, and had two folding sashes which clasped in the middle. Through a gap in the curtain I saw a little lamp-lit room and a big man sitting at a table littered with papers.

I watched him, fascinated, as he turned to consult some document and made a marking on the map before him. Then he suddenly rose, stretched himself, cast a glance at the window, and went out of the room, making a great clatter in descending the wooden staircase. He left the door ajar and the lamp burning.

I guessed he had gone to have a look at his prisoners, in which case the show was up. But what filled my mind was an insane desire to get a sight of his map. It was one of those mad impulses which utterly cloud right reason, a thing independent of any plan, a crazy leap in the dark. But it was so strong that I would have pulled that window out by its frame, if need be, to get to that table.

There was no need, for the flimsy clasp gave at the first pull, and the sashes swung open. I scrambled in, after listening for steps on the stairs. I crumpled up the map and stuck it in my pocket, as well as the paper from which I had seen him copying. Very carefully I removed all marks of my entry, brushed away the snow from the boards, pulled back the curtain, got out and refastened the window. Still there was no sound of his return. Then I started off to catch up the others.

I found them shivering in the roof pavilion. 'We've got to move pretty fast,' I said, 'for I've just been burgling old Stumm's private cabinet. Hussin, my lad, d'you hear that? They may be after us any moment, so I pray Heaven we soon strike better going.'

Hussin understood. He led us at a smart pace from one roof to another, for here they were all of the same height, and only low parapets and screens divided them. We never saw a soul, for a winter's night is not the time you choose to saunter on your housetop. I kept my ears open for trouble behind us, and in about five minutes I heard it. A riot of voices broke out, with one louder than the rest, and, looking back, I saw lanterns waving. Stumm had realized his loss and found the tracks of the thief.

Hussin gave one glance behind and then hurried us on at break-neck pace, with old Blenkiron gasping and stumbling. The shouts behind us grew louder, as if some eye quicker than the rest had caught our movement in the starlit darkness. It was very evident that if they kept up the chase we should be caught, for Blenkiron was about as useful on a roof as a hippo.

Presently we came to a big drop, with a kind of ladder down it, and at the foot a shallow ledge running to the left into a pit of darkness. Hussin gripped my arm and pointed down it. 'Follow it,' he whispered, 'and you will reach a roof which spans a street. Cross it, and on the other side is a mosque. Turn to the right there and you will find easy going for fifty metres, well screened from the higher roofs. For Allah's sake keep in the shelter of the screen. Somewhere there I will join you.'

He hurried us along the ledge for a bit and then went back, and with snow from the corners covered up our tracks. After that he went straight on himself, taking strange short steps like a bird. I saw his game. He wanted to lead our pursuers after him, and he had to multiply the tracks and trust to Stumm's fellows not spotting that they all were made by one man.

But I had quite enough to think of in getting Blenkiron along that ledge. He was pretty nearly foundered, he was in a sweat of terror, and as a matter of fact he was taking one of the biggest risks of his life, for we had no rope and his neck depended on himself. I could hear him invoking some unknown deity called Holy Mike. But he ventured gallantly, and we got to the roof which ran across the street. That was easier, though ticklish enough, but it was no joke skirting the cupola of that infernal mosque. At last we found the parapet and breathed more freely, for we were now under shelter from the direction of danger. I spared a moment to look round, and thirty yards off, across the street, I saw a weird spectacle.

The hunt was proceeding along the roofs parallel to the one we were lodged on. I saw the flicker of the lanterns, waved up and down as the bearers slipped in the snow, and I heard their cries like hounds on a trail. Stumm was not among them: he had not the shape for that sort of business. They passed us and continued to our left, now hid by a jutting chimney, now clear to view against the sky line. The roofs they were on were perhaps six feet higher than ours, so even from our shelter we could mark their course. If Hussin were going to be hunted across Erzerum it was a bad look-out for us, for I hadn't the foggiest notion where we were or where we were going to.

But as we watched we saw something more. The wavering lanterns were now three or four hundred yards away, but on the roofs just opposite us across the street there appeared a man's figure. I thought it was one of the hunters, and we all crouched lower, and then I recognized the lean agility of Hussin. He must have doubled back, keeping in the dusk to the left of the pursuit, and taking big risks in the open places. But there he was now, exactly in front of us, and separated only by the width of the narrow street.

He took a step backward, gathered himself for a spring, and leaped clean over the gap. Like a cat he lighted on the parapet above us, and stumbled forward with the impetus right on our heads.

'We are safe for the moment,' he whispered, 'but when they miss me they will return. We must make good haste.'

The next half-hour was a maze of twists and turns, slipping down icy roofs and climbing icier chimney-stacks. The stir of the city had gone, and from the black streets below came scarcely a sound. But always the great tattoo of guns beat in the east. Gradually we descended to a lower level, till we emerged on the top of a shed in a courtyard. Hussin gave an odd sort of cry, like a demented owl, and something began to stir below us.

It was a big covered wagon, full of bundles of forage, and drawn by four mules. As we descended from the shed into the frozen litter of the yard, a man came out of the shade and spoke low to Hussin. Peter and I lifted Blenkiron into the cart, and scrambled in beside him, and I never felt anything more blessed than the warmth and softness of that place after the frosty roofs. I had forgotten all about my hunger, and only yearned for sleep. Presently the wagon moved out of the courtyard into the dark streets.

Then Blenkiron began to laugh, a deep internal rumble which shook him violently and brought down a heap of forage on his head. I thought it was hysterics, the relief from the tension of the past hour. But it wasn't. His body might be out of training, but there was never anything the matter with his nerves. He was consumed with honest merriment.

'Say, Major,' he gasped, 'I don't usually cherish dislikes for my fellow men, but somehow I didn't cotton to Colonel Stumm. But now I almost love him. You hit his jaw very bad in Germany, and now you've annexed his private file, and I guess it's important or he wouldn't have been so mighty set on steeple-chasing over those roofs. I haven't done such a thing since I broke into neighbour Brown's woodshed to steal his tame 'possum, and that's forty years back. It's the first piece of genooine amusement I've struck in this game, and I haven't laughed so much since old Jim Hooker told the tale of "Cousin Sally Dillard" when we were hunting ducks in Michigan and his wife's brother had an apoplexy in the night and died of it.'

To the accompaniment of Blenkiron's chuckles I did what Peter had done in the first minute, and fell asleep.

When I woke it was still dark. The wagon had stopped in a courtyard which seemed to be shaded by great trees. The snow lay deeper here, and by the feel of the air we had left the city and climbed to higher ground. There were big buildings on one side, and on the other what looked like the lift of a hill. No lights were shown, the place was in profound gloom, but I felt the presence near me of others besides Hussin and the driver.

We were hurried, Blenkiron only half awake, into an outbuilding, and then down some steps to a roomy cellar. There Hussin lit a lantern, which showed what had once been a storehouse for fruit. Old husks still strewed the floor and the place smelt of apples. Straw had been piled in corners for beds, and there was a rude table and a divan of boards covered with sheepskins.

'Where are we?' I asked Hussin.

'In the house of the Master,' he said. 'You will be safe here, but you must keep still till the Master comes.'

'Is the Frankish lady here?' I asked.

Hussin nodded, and from a wallet brought out some food—raisins and cold meat and a loaf of bread. We fell on it like vultures, and as we ate Hussin disappeared. I noticed that he locked the door behind him.

As soon as the meal was ended the others returned to their interrupted sleep. But I was wakeful now and my mind was sharp-set on many things. I got Blenkiron's electric torch and lay down on the divan to study Stumm's map.

The first glance showed me that I had lit on a treasure. It was the staff map of the Erzerum defences, showing the forts and the field trenches, with little notes scribbled in Stumm's neat small handwriting. I got out the big map which I had taken from Blenkiron, and made out the general lie of the land. I saw the horseshoe of Deve Boyun to the east which the Russian guns were battering. Stumm's was just like the kind of squared artillery map we used in France, 1 in 10,000, with spidery red lines showing the trenches, but with the difference that it was the Turkish trenches that were shown in detail and the Russian only roughly indicated. The thing was really a confidential plan of the whole Erzerum *enceinte*, and would be worth untold gold to the enemy. No wonder Stumm had been in a wax at its loss.

The Deve Boyun lines seemed to me monstrously strong, and I remembered the merits of the Turk as a fighter behind strong defences. It looked as if Russia were up against a second Plevna or a new Gallipoli.

Then I took to studying the flanks. South lay the Palantuken range of mountains, with forts defending the passes, where ran the roads to Mush and Lake Van. That side, too, looked pretty strong. North in the valley of the Euphrates I made out two big forts, Tafta and Kara Gubek, defending the road from Olti. On this part of the map Stumm's notes were plentiful, and I gave them all my attention. I remembered Blenkiron's news about the Russians advancing on a broad front, for it was clear that Stumm was taking pains about the flank of the fortress.

Kara Gubek was the point of interest. It stood on a rib of land between two peaks, which from the contour lines rose very steep. So long as it was held it was clear that no invader could move down the Euphrates glen. Stumm had appended a note to the peaks—'*not fortified*'; and about two miles to the north-east there was a red cross and the name '*Prjevalsky*'. I assumed that to be the farthest point yet reached by the right wing of the Russian attack.

Then I turned to the paper from which Stumm had copied the jottings on to his map. It was typewritten, and consisted of notes on different points. One was headed '*Kara Gubek*' and read: '*No time to fortify adjacent peaks. Difficult for enemy to get batteries there, but not impossible. This the real point of danger, for if Prjevalsky wins the Peaks Kara Gubek and Tafta must fall, and enemy will be on left rear of Deve Boyun main position.*'

I was soldier enough to see the tremendous importance of this note. On Kara Gubek depended the defence of Erzerum, and it was a broken reed if one knew where the weakness lay. Yet, searching the map again, I could not believe that any mortal commander would see any chance in the adjacent peaks, even if he thought them unfortified. That was information confined to the Turkish and German staff. But if it could be conveyed to the Grand Duke he would have Erzerum in his power in a day. Otherwise he would go on battering at the Deve Boyun ridge for weeks, and long ere he won it the Gallipoli divisions would arrive, he would be out-numbered by two to one, and his chance would have vanished.

My discovery set me pacing up and down that cellar in a perfect fever of excitement. I longed for wireless, a carrier pigeon, an aeroplane—anything to bridge over that space of half a dozen miles between me and the Russian lines. It was maddening to have stumbled on vital news and to be wholly unable to use it. How could three fugitives in a cellar, with the whole hornet's nest of Turkey and Germany stirred up against them, hope to send this message of life and death?

I went back to the map and examined the nearest Russian positions. They were carefully marked. Prjevalsky in the north, the main force beyond Deve

Boyun, and the southern columns up to the passes of the Palantuken but not yet across them. I could not know which was nearest to us till I discovered where we were. And as I thought of this I began to see the rudiments of a desperate plan. It depended on Peter, now slumbering like a tired dog on a couch of straw.

Hussin had locked the door and I must wait for information till he came back. But suddenly I noticed a trap in the roof, which had evidently been used for raising and lowering the cellar's stores. It looked ill-fitting and might be unbarred, so I pulled the table below it, and found that with a little effort I could raise the flap. I knew I was taking immense risks, but I was so keen on my plan that I disregarded them. After some trouble I got the thing prised open, and catching the edges of the hole with my fingers raised my body and got my knees on the edge.

It was the outbuilding of which our refuge was the cellar, and it was half filled with light. Not a soul was there, and I hunted about till I found what I wanted. This was a ladder leading to a sort of loft, which in turn gave access to the roof. Here I had to be very careful, for I might be overlooked from the high buildings. But by good luck there was a trellis for grape vines across the place, which gave a kind of shelter. Lying flat on my face I stared over a great expanse of country.

Looking north I saw the city in a haze of morning smoke, and, beyond, the plain of the Euphrates and the opening of the glen where the river left the hills. Up there, among the snowy heights, were Tafta and Kara Gubek. To the east was the ridge of Deve Boyun, where the mist was breaking before the winter's sun. On the roads up to it I saw transport moving, I saw the circle of the inner forts, but for a moment the guns were silent. South rose a great wall of white mountain, which I took to be the Palantuken. I could see the roads running to the passes, and the smoke of camps and horse-lines right under the cliffs.

I had learned what I needed. We were in the outbuildings of a big country house two or three miles south of the city. The nearest point of the Russian front was somewhere in the foothills of the Palantuken.

As I descended I heard, thin and faint and beautiful, like the cry of a wild bird, the muezzin from the minarets of Erzerum.

When I dropped through the trap the others were awake. Hussin was setting food on the table, and viewing my descent with anxious disapproval.

'It's all right,' I said; 'I won't do it again, for I've found out all I wanted. Peter, old man, the biggest job of your life is before you!'

CHAPTER NINETEEN

Greenmantle

Peter scarcely looked up from his breakfast.

'I'm willing, Dick,' he said. 'But you mustn't ask me to be friends with Stumm. He makes my stomach cold, that one.'

For the first time he had stopped calling me 'Cornelis'. The day of make-believe was over for all of us.

'Not to be friends with him,' I said, 'but to bust him and all his kind.'

'Then I'm ready,' said Peter cheerfully. 'What is it?'

I spread out the maps on the divan. There was no light in the place but Blenkiron's electric torch, for Hussin had put out the lantern. Peter got his nose into the things at once, for his intelligence work in the Boer War had made him handy with maps. It didn't want much telling from me to explain to him the importance of the one I had looted.

'That news is worth many a million pounds,' said he, wrinkling his brows, and scratching delicately the tip of his left ear. It was a way he had when he was startled.

'How can we get it to our friends?'

Peter cogitated. 'There is but one way. A man must take it. Once, I remember, when we fought the Matabele it was necessary to find out whether the chief Makapan was living. Some said he had died, others that he'd gone over the Portuguese border, but I believed he lived. No native could tell us, and since his kraal was well defended no runner could get through. So it was necessary to send a man.'

Peter lifted up his head and laughed. 'The man found the chief Makapan. He was very much alive, and made good shooting with a shot-gun. But the man brought the chief Makapan out of his kraal and handed him over to the Mounted Police. You remember Captain Arcoll, Dick—Jim Arcoll? Well, Jim laughed so much that he broke open a wound in his head, and had to have a doctor.'

'You were that man, Peter,' I said.

'*Ja*. I was the man. There are more ways of getting into kraals than there are ways of keeping people out.'

'Will you take this chance?'

'For certain, Dick. I am getting stiff with doing nothing, and if I sit in houses much longer I shall grow old. A man bet me five pounds on the ship that I could not get through a trench-line, and if there had been a trench-line handy I would have taken him on. I will be very happy, Dick, but I do not say I will succeed. It is new country to me, and I will be hurried, and hurry makes bad stalking.'

I showed him what I thought the likeliest place—in the spurs of the Palantuken mountains. Peter's way of doing things was all his own. He scraped earth and plaster out of a corner and sat down to make a little model of the landscape on the table, following the contours of the map. He did it extraordinarily neatly, for, like all great hunters, he was as deft as a weaver bird. He puzzled over it for a long time, and conned the map till he must have got it by heart. Then he took his field-glasses—a very good single Zeiss which was part of the spoils from Rasta's motor-car—and announced that he was going to follow my example and get on to the house-top. Presently his legs disappeared through the trap, and Blenkiron and I were left to our reflections.

Peter must have found something uncommon interesting, for he stayed on the roof the better part of the day. It was a dull job for us, since there was no light, and Blenkiron had not even the consolation of a game of Patience. But for all that he was in good spirits, for he had had no dyspepsia since we left Constantinople, and announced that he believed he was at last getting even with his darned duodenum. As for me I was pretty restless, for I could not imagine what was detaining Sandy. It was clear that our presence must have been kept secret from Hilda von Einem, for she was a pal of Stumm's, and he must by now have blown the gaff on Peter and me. How long could this secrecy last, I asked myself. We had now no sort of protection in the whole outfit. Rasta and the Turks wanted our blood: so did Stumm and the Germans; and once the lady found we were deceiving her she would want it most of all. Our only hope was Sandy, and he gave no sign of his existence. I began to fear that with him, too, things had miscarried.

And yet I wasn't really depressed, only impatient. I could never again get back to the beastly stagnation of that Constantinople week. The guns kept me cheerful. There was the devil of a bombardment all day, and the thought that our Allies were thundering there half a dozen miles off gave me a perfectly groundless hope. If they burst through the defence Hilda von Einem and her prophet and all our enemies would be overwhelmed in the deluge. And that blessed chance depended very much on old Peter, now brooding like a pigeon on the house-tops.

It was not till the late afternoon that Hussin appeared again. He took no notice of Peter's absence, but lit a lantern and set it on the table. Then he went to the door and waited. Presently a light step fell on the stairs, and Hussin drew back to let someone enter. He promptly departed and I heard the key turn in the lock behind him.

Sandy stood there, but a new Sandy who made Blenkiron and me jump to our feet. The pelts and skin-cap had gone, and he wore instead a long linen tunic clasped at the waist by a broad girdle. A strange green turban adorned his head, and as he pushed it back I saw that his hair had been shaved. He looked like some acolyte—a weary acolyte, for there was no spring in his walk or nerve in his carriage. He dropped numbly on the divan and laid his head in his hands. The lantern showed his haggard eyes with dark lines beneath them.

'Good God, old man, have you been sick?' I cried.

'Not sick,' he said hoarsely. 'My body is right enough, but the last few days I have been living in hell.'

Blenkiron nodded sympathetically. That was how he himself would have described the company of the lady.

I marched across to him and gripped both his wrists.

'Look at me,' I said, 'straight in the eyes.'

His eyes were like a sleep-walker's, unwinking, unseeing. 'Great heavens, man, you've been drugged!' I said.

'Drugged,' he cried, with a weary laugh. 'Yes, I have been drugged, but not by any physic. No one has been doctoring my food. But you can't go through hell without getting your eyes red-hot.'

I kept my grip on his wrists. 'Take your time, old chap, and tell us about it. Blenkiron and I are here, and old Peter's on the roof not far off. We'll look after you.'

'It does me good to hear your voice, Dick,' he said. 'It reminds me of clean, honest things.'

'They'll come back, never fear. We're at the last lap now. One more spurt and it's over. You've got to tell me what the new snag is. Is it that woman?'

He shivered like a frightened colt. 'Woman!' he cried. 'Does a woman drag a man through the nether-pit? She's a she-devil. Oh, it isn't madness that's wrong with her. She's as sane as you and as cool as Blenkiron. Her life is an infernal game of chess, and she plays with souls for pawns. She is evil—evil—evil.' And once more he buried his head in his hands.

It was Blenkiron who brought sense into this hectic atmosphere. His slow, beloved drawl was an antiseptic against nerves.

'Say, boy,' he said, 'I feel just like you about the lady. But our job is not to investigate her character. Her Maker will do that good and sure some day. We've got to figure how to circumvent her, and for that you've got to tell us what exactly's been occurring since we parted company.'

Sandy pulled himself together with a great effort.

'Greenmantle died that night I saw you. We buried him secretly by her order in the garden of the villa. Then came the trouble about his successor ... The four Ministers would be no party to a swindle. They were honest men, and vowed that their task now was to make a tomb for their master and pray for the rest of their days at his shrine. They were as immovable as a granite hill and she knew it.... Then they, too, died.'

'Murdered?' I gasped.

'Murdered ... all four in one morning. I do not know how, but I helped to bury them. Oh, she had Germans and Kurds to do her foul work, but their hands were clean compared to hers. Pity me, Dick, for I have seen honesty and virtue put to the shambles and have abetted the deed when it was done. It will haunt me to my dying day.'

I did not stop to console him, for my mind was on fire with his news.

'Then the prophet is gone, and the humbug is over,' I cried.

'The prophet still lives. She has found a successor.'

He stood up in his linen tunic.

'Why do I wear these clothes? Because I am Greenmantle. I am the *Kaaba-i-hurriyeh* for all Islam. In three days' time I will reveal myself to my people and wear on my breast the green ephod of the prophet.'

He broke off with an hysterical laugh. 'Only you see, I won't. I will cut my throat first.'

'Cheer up!' said Blenkiron soothingly. 'We'll find some prettier way than that.'

'There is no way,' he said; 'no way but death. We're done for, all of us. Hussin got you out of Stumm's clutches, but you're in danger every moment. At the best you have three days, and then you, too, will be dead.'

I had no words to reply. This change in the bold and unshakeable Sandy took my breath away.

'She made me her accomplice,' he went on. 'I should have killed her on the graves of those innocent men. But instead I did all she asked and joined in her game ... She was very candid, you know ... She cares no more than Enver for the faith of Islam. She can laugh at it. But she has her own dreams, and they consume her as a saint is consumed by his devotion. She has told me them, and if the day in the garden was hell, the days since have been the innermost fires of Tophet. I think—it is horrible to say it—that she has got some kind of crazy liking for me. When we have reclaimed the East I am to be by her side when she rides on her milk-white horse into Jerusalem ... And there have been moments—only moments, I swear to God—when I have been fired myself by her madness ...'

Sandy's figure seemed to shrink and his voice grew shrill and wild. It was too much for Blenkiron. He indulged in a torrent of blasphemy such as I believe had never before passed his lips.

'I'm blessed if I'll listen to this God-darned stuff. It isn't delicate. You get busy, Major, and pump some sense into your afflicted friend.'

I was beginning to see what had happened. Sandy was a man of genius—as much as anybody I ever struck—but he had the defects of such high-strung, fanciful souls. He would take more than mortal risks, and you couldn't scare him by any ordinary terror. But let his old conscience get cross-eyed, let him find himself in some situation which in his eyes involved his honour, and he might go stark crazy. The woman, who roused in me and Blenkiron only hatred, could catch his imagination and stir in him—for the moment only—an unwilling response. And then came bitter and morbid repentance, and the last desperation.

It was no time to mince matters. 'Sandy, you old fool,' I cried, 'be thankful you have friends to keep you from playing the fool. You saved my life at Loos, and I'm jolly well going to get you through this show. I'm bossing the outfit now, and for all your confounded prophetic manners, you've got to take your orders from me. You aren't going to reveal yourself to your people, and still less are you going to cut your throat. Greenmantle will avenge the murder of his ministers, and make that bedlamite woman sorry she was born. We're going to get clear away, and inside of a week we'll be having tea with the Grand Duke Nicholas.'

I wasn't bluffing. Puzzled as I was about ways and means I had still the blind belief that we should win out. And as I spoke two legs dangled through the trap and a dusty and blinking Peter descended in our midst.

I took the maps from him and spread them on the table.

'First, you must know that we've had an almighty piece of luck. Last night Hussin took us for a walk over the roofs of Erzerum, and by the blessing of Providence I got into Stumm's room, and bagged his staff map ... Look there ... d'you see his notes? That's the danger-point of the whole defence. Once the Russians get that fort, Kara Gubek, they've turned the main position. And it can be got; Stumm knows it can; for these two adjacent hills are not held ... It looks a mad enterprise on paper, but Stumm knows that it is possible enough. The question is: Will the Russians guess that? I say no, not unless someone tells them. Therefore, by hook or by crook, we've got to get that information through to them.'

Sandy's interest in ordinary things was beginning to flicker up again. He studied the map and began to measure distances.

'Peter's going to have a try for it. He thinks there's a sporting chance of his getting through the lines. If he does—if he gets this map to the Grand Duke's staff—then Stumm's goose is cooked. In three days the Cossacks will be in the streets of Erzerum.'

'What are the chances?' Sandy asked.

I glanced at Peter. 'We're hard-bitten fellows and can face the truth. I think the chances against success are about five to one.'

'Two to one,' said Peter modestly. 'Not worse than that. I don't think you're fair to me, Dick, my old friend.'

I looked at that lean, tight figure and the gentle, resolute face, and I changed my mind. 'I'm hanged if I think there are any odds,' I said. 'With anybody else it would want a miracle, but with Peter I believe the chances are level.'

'Two to one,' Peter persisted. 'If it was evens I wouldn't be interested.'

'Let me go,' Sandy cried. 'I talk the lingo, and can pass as a Turk, and I'm a million times likelier to get through. For God's sake, Dick, let me go.'

'Not you. You're wanted here. If you disappear the whole show's busted too soon, and the three of us left behind will be strung up before morning ... No, my son. You're going to escape, but it will be in company with Blenkiron and me. We've got to blow the whole Greenmantle business so high that the bits of it will never come to earth again ... First, tell me how many of your fellows will stick by you? I mean the Companions.'

'The whole half-dozen. They are very worried already about what has happened. She made me sound them in her presence, and they were quite ready to accept me as Greenmantle's successor. But they have their suspicions about what happened at the villa, and they've no love for the woman ... They'd follow me through hell if I bade them, but they would rather it was my own show.'

'That's all right,' I cried. 'It is the one thing I've been doubtful about. Now observe this map. Erzerum isn't invested by a long chalk. The Russians are round it in a broad half-moon. That means that all the west, south-west, and north-west is open and undefended by trench lines. There are flanks far away to the north and south in the hills which can be turned, and once we get round a flank there's nothing between us and our friends ... I've figured out our road,' and I traced it on the map. 'If we can make that big circuit to the west and get over that pass unobserved we're bound to strike a Russian column the next day. It'll be a rough road, but I fancy we've all ridden as bad in our time. But one thing we must have, and that's horses. Can we and your six ruffians slip off in the darkness on the best beasts in this township? If you can manage that, we'll do the trick.'

Sandy sat down and pondered. Thank heaven, he was thinking now of action and not of his own conscience.

'It must be done,' he said at last, 'but it won't be easy. Hussin's a great fellow, but as you know well, Dick, horses right up at the battle-front are not easy to come by. Tomorrow I've got some kind of infernal fast to observe, and the next day that woman will be coaching me for my part. We'll have to give Hussin time ... I wish to heaven it could be tonight.' He was silent again for a bit, and then he said: 'I believe the best time would be the third night, the eve of the Revelation. She's bound to leave me alone that night.'

'Right-o,' I said. 'It won't be much fun sitting waiting in this cold sepulchre; but we must keep our heads and risk nothing by being in a hurry. Besides, if Peter wins through, the Turk will be a busy man by the day after tomorrow.'

The key turned in the door and Hussin stole in like a shade. It was the signal for Sandy to leave.

'You fellows have given me a new lease of life,' he said. 'I've got a plan now, and I can set my teeth and stick it out.'

He went up to Peter and gripped his hand. 'Good luck. You're the bravest man I've ever met, and I've seen a few.' Then he turned abruptly and went out, followed by an exhortation from Blenkiron to 'Get busy about the quadrupeds.'

Then we set about equipping Peter for his crusade. It was a simple job, for we were not rich in properties. His get-up, with his thick fur-collared greatcoat, was not unlike the ordinary Turkish officer seen in a dim light. But Peter had no intention of passing for a Turk, or indeed of giving anybody the chance of seeing him, and he was more concerned to fit in with the landscape. So he stripped off the greatcoat and pulled a grey sweater of mine over his jacket, and put on his head a woollen helmet of the same colour. He had no need of the map for he had long since got his route by heart, and what was once fixed in that mind stuck like wax; but I made him take Stumm's plan and paper, hidden below his shirt. The big difficulty, I saw, would be getting to the Russians without getting shot, assuming he passed the Turkish trenches. He could only hope that he would strike someone with a smattering of English or German. Twice he ascended to the roof and came back cheerful, for there was promise of wild weather.

Hussin brought in our supper, and Peter made up a parcel of food. Blenkiron and I had both small flasks of brandy and I gave him mine.

Then he held out his hand quite simply, like a good child who is going off to bed. It was too much for Blenkiron. With large tears rolling down his face he announced that, if we all came through, he was going to fit him into the softest berth that money could buy. I don't think he was understood, for old Peter's eyes had now the faraway absorption of the hunter who has found game. He was thinking only of his job.

Two legs and a pair of very shabby boots vanished through the trap, and suddenly I felt utterly lonely and desperately sad. The guns were beginning to roar again in the east, and in the intervals came the whistle of the rising storm.

CHAPTER TWENTY

Peter Pienaar Goes to the Wars

This chapter is the tale that Peter told me—long after, sitting beside a stove in the hotel at Bergen, where we were waiting for our boat.

He climbed on the roof and shinned down the broken bricks of the outer wall. The outbuilding we were lodged in abutted on a road, and was outside the proper *enceinte* of the house. At ordinary times I have no doubt there were sentries, but Sandy and Hussin had probably managed to clear them off this end for a little. Anyhow he saw nobody as he crossed the road and dived into the snowy fields.

He knew very well that he must do the job in the twelve hours of darkness ahead of him. The immediate front of a battle is a bit too public for anyone to lie hidden in by day, especially when two or three feet of snow make everything kenspeckle. Now hurry in a job of this kind was abhorrent to Peter's soul, for, like all Boers, his tastes were for slowness and sureness, though he could hustle fast enough when haste was needed. As he pushed through the winter fields he reckoned up the things in his favour, and found the only one the dirty weather. There was a high, gusty wind, blowing scuds of snow but never coming to any great fall. The frost had gone, and the lying snow was as soft as butter. That was all to the good, he thought, for a clear, hard night would have been the devil.

The first bit was through farmlands, which were seamed with little snow-filled water-furrows. Now and then would come a house and a patch of fruit trees, but there was nobody abroad. The roads were crowded enough, but Peter had no use for roads. I can picture him swinging along with his bent back, stopping every now and then to sniff and listen, alert for the foreknowledge of danger. When he chose he could cover country like an antelope.

Soon he struck a big road full of transport. It was the road from Erzerum to the Palantuken pass, and he waited his chance and crossed it. After that the ground grew rough with boulders and patches of thorn-trees, splendid cover where he could move fast without worrying. Then he was pulled up suddenly on the bank of a river. The map had warned him of it, but not that it would be so big.

It was a torrent swollen with melting snow and rains in the hills, and it was running fifty yards wide. Peter thought he could have swum it, but he was very averse to a drenching. 'A wet man makes too much noise,' he said, and besides, there was the off-chance that the current would be too much for him. So he moved up stream to look for a bridge.

In ten minutes he found one, a new-made thing of trestles, broad enough to take transport wagons. It was guarded, for he heard the tramp of a sentry, and as he pulled himself up the bank he observed a couple of long wooden huts, obviously some kind of billets. These were on the near side of the stream, about a dozen yards from the bridge. A door stood open and a light showed in it, and from within came the sound of voices.... Peter had a sense of hearing like a wild animal, and he could detect even from the confused gabble that the voices were German.

As he lay and listened someone came over the bridge. It was an officer, for the sentry saluted. The man disappeared in one of the huts. Peter had struck the billets and repairing shop of a squad of German sappers.

He was just going ruefully to retrace his steps and try to find a good place to swim the stream when it struck him that the officer who had passed him wore clothes very like his own. He, too, had had a grey sweater and a Balaclava helmet, for even a German officer ceases to be dressy on a mid-winter's night in Anatolia. The idea came to Peter to walk boldly across the bridge and trust to the sentry not seeing the difference.

He slipped round a corner of the hut and marched down the road. The sentry was now at the far end, which was lucky, for if the worst came to the worst he could throttle him. Peter, mimicking the stiff German walk, swung past him, his head down as if to protect him from the wind.

The man saluted. He did more, for he offered conversation. The officer must have been a genial soul.

'It's a rough night, Captain,' he said in German. 'The wagons are late. Pray God, Michael hasn't got a shell in his lot. They've begun putting over some big ones.'

Peter grunted good night in German and strode on. He was just leaving the road when he heard a great halloo behind him.

The real officer must have appeared on his heels, and the sentry's doubts had been stirred. A whistle was blown, and, looking back, Peter saw lanterns waving in the gale. They were coming out to look for the duplicate.

He stood still for a second, and noticed the lights spreading out south of the road. He was just about to dive off it on the north side when he was aware of a difficulty. On that side a steep bank fell to a ditch, and the bank beyond bounded a big flood. He could see the dull ruffle of the water under the wind.

On the road itself he would soon be caught; south of it the search was beginning; and the ditch itself was no place to hide, for he saw a lantern moving up it. Peter dropped into it all the same and made a plan. The side below the road was a little undercut and very steep. He resolved to plaster himself against it, for he would be hidden from the road, and a searcher in the ditch would not be likely to explore the unbroken sides. It was always a maxim of Peter's that the best hiding-place was the worst, the least obvious to the minds of those who were looking for you.

He waited until the lights both in the road and the ditch came nearer, and then he gripped the edge with his left hand, where some stones gave him purchase, dug the toes of his boots into the wet soil and stuck like a limpet. It needed some strength to keep the position for long, but the muscles of his arms and legs were like whipcord.

The searcher in the ditch soon got tired, for the place was very wet, and joined his comrades on the road. They came along, running, flashing the lanterns into the trench, and exploring all the immediate countryside.

Then rose a noise of wheels and horses from the opposite direction. Michael and the delayed wagons were approaching. They dashed up at a great pace, driven wildly, and for one horrid second Peter thought they were going to spill into the ditch at the very spot where he was concealed. The wheels passed so close to the edge that they almost grazed his fingers. Somebody shouted an order and they pulled up a yard or two nearer the bridge. The others came up and there was a consultation.

Michael swore he had passed no one on the road.

'That fool Hannus has seen a ghost,' said the officer testily. 'It's too cold for this child's play.'

Hannus, almost in tears, repeated his tale. 'The man spoke to me in good German,' he cried.

'Ghost or no ghost he is safe enough up the road,' said the officer. 'Kind God, that was a big one!' He stopped and stared at a shell-burst, for the bombardment from the east was growing fiercer.

They stood discussing the fire for a minute and presently moved off. Peter gave them two minutes' law and then clambered back to the highway and set off along it at a run. The noise of the shelling and the wind, together with the thick darkness, made it safe to hurry.

He left the road at the first chance and took to the broken country. The ground was now rising towards a spur of the Palantuken, on the far slope of which were the Turkish trenches. The night had begun by being pretty nearly as black as pitch; even the smoke from the shell explosions, which is often visible in darkness, could not be seen. But as the wind blew the snow-clouds athwart the sky patches of stars came out. Peter had a compass, but he didn't need to use it, for he had a kind of 'feel' for landscape, a special sense which is born in savages and can only be acquired after long experience by the white man. I believe he could smell where the north lay. He had settled roughly which part of the line he would try, merely because of its nearness to the enemy.

But he might see reason to vary this, and as he moved he began to think that the safest place was where the shelling was hottest. He didn't like the notion, but it sounded sense.

Suddenly he began to puzzle over queer things in the ground, and, as he had never seen big guns before, it took him a moment to fix them. Presently one went off at his elbow with a roar like the Last Day. These were Austrian howitzers—nothing over eight-inch, I fancy, but to Peter they looked like leviathans. Here, too, he saw for the first time a big and quite recent shell-hole, for the Russian guns were searching out the position. He was so interested in it all that he poked his nose where he shouldn't have been, and dropped plump into the pit behind a gun-emplacement.

Gunners all the world over are the same—shy people, who hide themselves in holes and hibernate and mortally dislike being detected.

A gruff voice cried '*Wer da*?' and a heavy hand seized his neck.

Peter was ready with his story. He belonged to Michael's wagon-team and had been left behind. He wanted to be told the way to the sappers' camp. He was very apologetic, not to say obsequious.

'It is one of those Prussian swine from the Marta bridge,' said a gunner. 'Land him a kick to teach him sense. Bear to your right, manikin, and you will find a road. And have a care when you get there, for the Russkoes are registering on it.'

Peter thanked them and bore off to the right. After that he kept a wary eye on the howitzers, and was thankful when he got out of their area on to the slopes up the hill. Here was the type of country that was familiar to him, and he defied any Turk or Boche to spot him among the scrub and boulders. He was getting on very well, when once more, close to his ear, came a sound like the crack of doom.

It was the field-guns now, and the sound of a field-gun close at hand is bad for the nerves if you aren't expecting it. Peter thought he had been hit, and lay flat for a little to consider. Then he found the right explanation, and crawled forward very warily.

Presently he saw his first Russian shell. It dropped half a dozen yards to his right, making a great hole in the snow and sending up a mass of mixed earth, snow, and broken stones. Peter spat out the dirt and felt very solemn. You must remember that never in his life had he seen big shelling, and was now being landed in the thick of a first-class show without any preparation. He said he felt cold in his stomach, and very wishful to run away, if there had been anywhere to run to. But he kept on to the crest of the ridge, over which a big glow was broadening like sunrise. He tripped once over a wire, which he took for some kind of snare, and after that went very warily.

By and by he got his face between two boulders and looked over into the true battle-field.

He told me it was exactly what the predikant used to say that Hell would be like. About fifty yards down the slope lay the Turkish trenches—they were dark against the snow, and now and then a black figure like a devil showed for an instant and disappeared. The Turks clearly expected an infantry attack, for they were sending up calcium rockets and Very flares. The Russians were battering their line and spraying all the hinterland, not with shrapnel, but with good, solid high-explosives. The place would be as bright as day for a moment, all smothered in a scurry of smoke and snow and debris, and then a black pall would fall on it, when only the thunder of the guns told of the battle.

Peter felt very sick. He had not believed there could be so much noise in the world, and the drums of his ears were splitting. Now, for a man to whom courage is habitual, the taste of fear—naked, utter fear—is a horrible thing. It seems to wash away all his manhood. Peter lay on the crest, watching the shells burst, and confident that any moment he might be a shattered remnant. He lay and reasoned with himself, calling himself every name he could think of, but conscious that nothing would get rid of that lump of ice below his heart.

Then he could stand it no longer. He got up and ran for his life.

But he ran forward.

It was the craziest performance. He went hell-for-leather over a piece of ground which was being watered with H.E., but by the mercy of heaven nothing hit him. He took some fearsome tosses in shell-holes, but partly erect and partly on all fours he did the fifty yards and tumbled into a Turkish trench right on top of a dead man.

The contact with that body brought him to his senses. That men could die at all seemed a comforting, homely thing after that unnatural pandemonium. The next moment a crump took the parapet of the trench some yards to his left, and he was half buried in an avalanche.

He crawled out of that, pretty badly cut about the head. He was quite cool now and thinking hard about his next step. There were men all around him, sullen dark faces as he saw them when the flares went up. They were manning the parapets and waiting tensely for something else than the shelling. They paid no attention to him, for I fancy in that trench units were pretty well mixed up, and under a bad bombardment no one bothers about his neighbour. He found himself free to move as he pleased. The ground of the trench was littered with empty cartridge-cases, and there were many dead bodies.

The last shell, as I have said, had played havoc with the parapet. In the next spell of darkness Peter crawled through the gap and twisted among some snowy hillocks. He was no longer afraid of shells, any more than he was afraid of a veld thunderstorm. But he was wondering very hard how he should ever get to the Russians. The Turks were behind him now, but there was the biggest danger in front.

Then the artillery ceased. It was so sudden that he thought he had gone deaf, and could hardly realize the blessed relief of it. The wind, too, seemed to have fallen, or perhaps he was sheltered by the lee of the hill. There were a lot of dead here also, and that he couldn't understand, for they were new dead. Had the Turks attacked and been driven back? When he had gone about thirty yards he stopped to take his bearings. On the right were the ruins of a large building set on fire by the guns. There was a blur of woods and the debris of walls round it. Away to the left another hill ran out farther to the east, and the place he was in seemed to be a kind of cup between the spurs. Just before him was a little ruined building, with the sky seen through its rafters, for the smouldering ruin on the right gave a certain light. He wondered if the Russian firing-line lay there.

Just then he heard voices—smothered voices—not a yard away and apparently below the ground. He instantly jumped to what this must mean. It was a Turkish trench—a communication trench. Peter didn't know much about modern warfare, but he had read in the papers, or heard from me, enough to make him draw the right moral. The fresh dead pointed to the same conclusion. What he had got through were the Turkish support trenches, not their firing-line. That was still before him.

He didn't despair, for the rebound from panic had made him extra courageous. He crawled forward, an inch at a time, taking no sort of risk, and presently found himself looking at the parados of a trench. Then he lay quiet to think out the next step.

The shelling had stopped, and there was that queer kind of peace which falls sometimes on two armies not a quarter of a mile distant. Peter said he could hear nothing but the far-off sighing of the wind. There seemed to be no movement of any kind in the trench before him, which ran through the ruined building. The light of the burning was dying, and he could just make out the mound of earth a yard in front. He began to feel hungry, and got out his packet of food and had a swig at the brandy flask. That comforted him, and he felt a master of his fate again. But the next step was not so easy. He must find out what lay behind that mound of earth.

Suddenly a curious sound fell on his ears. It was so faint that at first he doubted the evidence of his senses. Then as the wind fell it came louder. It was exactly like some hollow piece of metal being struck by a stick, musical and oddly resonant.

He concluded it was the wind blowing a branch of a tree against an old boiler in the ruin before him. The trouble was that there was scarcely enough wind now for that in this sheltered cup.

But as he listened he caught the note again. It was a bell, a fallen bell, and the place before him must have been a chapel. He remembered that an Armenian monastery had been marked on the big map, and he guessed it was the burned building on his right.

The thought of a chapel and a bell gave him the notion of some human agency. And then suddenly the notion was confirmed. The sound was regular and concerted—dot, dash, dot—dash, dot, dot. The branch of a tree and the wind may play strange pranks, but they do not produce the longs and shorts of the Morse Code.

This was where Peter's intelligence work in the Boer War helped him. He knew the Morse, he could read it, but he could make nothing of the signalling. It was either in some special code or in a strange language.

He lay still and did some calm thinking. There was a man in front of him, a Turkish soldier, who was in the enemy's pay. Therefore he could fraternize with him, for they were on the same side. But how was he to approach him without getting shot in the process? Again, how could a man send signals to the enemy from a firing-line without being detected? Peter found an answer in the strange configuration of the ground. He had not heard a sound until he was a few yards from the place, and they would be inaudible to men in the reserve trenches and even in the communication trenches. If somebody moving up the latter caught the noise, it would be easy to explain it naturally. But the wind blowing down the cup would carry it far in the enemy's direction.

There remained the risk of being heard by those parallel with the bell in the firing trenches. Peter concluded that that trench must be very thinly held, probably only by a few observers, and the nearest might be a dozen yards off. He had read about that being the French fashion under a big bombardment.

The next thing was to find out how to make himself known to this ally. He decided that the only way was to surprise him. He might get shot, but he trusted to his strength and agility against a man who was almost certainly wearied. When he had got him safe, explanations might follow.

Peter was now enjoying himself hugely. If only those infernal guns kept silent he would play out the game in the sober, decorous way he loved. So very delicately he began to wriggle forward to where the sound was.

The night was now as black as ink around him, and very quiet, too, except for soughings of the dying gale. The snow had drifted a little in the lee of the ruined walls, and Peter's progress was naturally very slow. He could not afford to dislodge one ounce of snow. Still the tinkling went on, now in greater volume. Peter was in terror lest it should cease before he got his man.

Presently his hand clutched at empty space. He was on the lip of the front trench. The sound was now a yard to his right, and with infinite care he shifted his position. Now the bell was just below him, and he felt the big rafter of the woodwork from which it had fallen. He felt something else—a stretch of wire fixed in the ground with the far end hanging in the void. That would be the spy's explanation if anyone heard the sound and came seeking the cause.

Somewhere in the darkness before him and below was the man, not a yard off. Peter remained very still, studying the situation. He could not see, but he could feel the presence, and he was trying to decide the relative position of the man and bell and their exact distance from him. The thing was not so easy as it looked, for if he jumped for where he believed the figure was, he might miss it and get a bullet in the stomach. A man who played so risky a game was probably handy with his firearms. Besides, if he should hit the bell, he would make a hideous row and alarm the whole front.

Fate suddenly gave him the right chance. The unseen figure stood up and moved a step, till his back was against the parados. He actually brushed against Peter's elbow, who held his breath.

There is a catch that the Kaffirs have which would need several diagrams to explain. It is partly a neck hold, and partly a paralysing backward twist of the right arm, but if it is practised on a man from behind, it locks him as sure as if he were handcuffed. Peter slowly got his body raised and his knees drawn under him, and reached for his prey.

He got him. A head was pulled backward over the edge of the trench, and he felt in the air the motion of the left arm pawing feebly but unable to reach behind.

'Be still,' whispered Peter in German; 'I mean you no harm. We are friends of the same purpose. Do you speak German?' '*Nein*,' said a muffled voice.

'English?'

'Yes,' said the voice.

'Thank God,' said Peter. 'Then we can understand each other. I've watched your notion of signalling, and a very good one it is. I've got to get through to the Russian lines somehow before morning, and I want you to help me. I'm English—a kind of English, so we're on the same side. If I let go your neck, will you be good and talk reasonably?'

The voice assented. Peter let go, and in the same instant slipped to the side. The man wheeled round and flung out an arm but gripped vacancy.

'Steady, friend,' said Peter; 'you mustn't play tricks with me or I'll be angry.'

'Who are you? Who sent you?' asked the puzzled voice.

Peter had a happy thought. 'The Companions of the Rosy Hours,' he said.

'Then are we friends indeed,' said the voice. 'Come out of the darkness, friend, and I will do you no harm. I am a good Turk, and I fought beside the English in Kordofan and learned their tongue. I live only to see the ruin of Enver, who has beggared my family and slain my twin brother. Therefore I serve the *Muscov ghiaours*.'

'I don't know what the Musky jaws are, but if you mean the Russians I'm with you. I've got news for them which will make Enver green. The question is, how I'm to get to them, and that is where you shall help me, my friend.'

'How?'

'By playing that little tune of yours again. Tell them to expect within the next half-hour a deserter with an important message. Tell them, for God's sake, not to fire at anybody till they've made certain it isn't me.'

The man took the blunt end of his bayonet and squatted beside the bell. The first stroke brought out a clear, searching note which floated down the valley. He struck three notes at slow intervals. For all the world, Peter said, he was like a telegraph operator calling up a station.

'Send the message in English,' said Peter.

'They may not understand it,' said the man.

'Then send it any way you like. I trust you, for we are brothers.'

After ten minutes the man ceased and listened. From far away came the sound of a trench-gong, the kind of thing they used on the Western Front to give the gas-alarm.

'They say they will be ready,' he said. 'I cannot take down messages in the darkness, but they have given me the signal which means "Consent".'

'Come, that is pretty good,' said Peter. 'And now I must be moving. You take a hint from me. When you hear big firing up to the north get ready to beat a quick retreat, for it will be all up with that city of yours. And tell your folk, too, that they're making a bad mistake letting those fool Germans rule their land. Let them hang Enver and his little friends, and we'll be happy once more.'

'May Satan receive his soul!' said the Turk. 'There is wire before us, but I will show you a way through. The guns this evening made many rents in it. But haste, for a working party may be here presently to repair it. Remember there is much wire before the other lines.'

Peter, with certain directions, found it pretty easy to make his way through the entanglement. There was one bit which scraped a hole in his back, but very soon he had come to the last posts and found himself in open country. The place, he said, was a graveyard of the unburied dead that smelt horribly as he crawled among them. He had no inducements to delay, for he thought he could hear behind him the movement of the Turkish working party, and was in terror that a flare might reveal him and a volley accompany his retreat.

From one shell-hole to another he wormed his way, till he struck an old ruinous communication trench which led in the right direction. The Turks must have been forced back in the past week, and the Russians were now in the evacuated trenches. The thing was half full of water, but it gave Peter a feeling of safety, for it enabled him to get his head below the level of the ground. Then it came to an end and he found before him a forest of wire.

The Turk in his signal had mentioned half an hour, but Peter thought it was nearer two hours before he got through that noxious entanglement. Shelling had made little difference to it. The uprights were all there, and the barbed strands seemed to touch the ground. Remember, he had no wire-cutter; nothing but his bare hands. Once again fear got hold of him. He felt caught in a net, with monstrous vultures waiting to pounce on him from above. At any moment a flare might go up and a dozen rifles find their mark. He had altogether forgotten about the message which had been sent, for no message could dissuade the ever-present death he felt around him. It was, he said, like following an old lion into bush when there was but one narrow way in, and no road out.

The guns began again—the Turkish guns from behind the ridge—and a shell tore up the wire a short way before him. Under cover of the burst he made good a few yards, leaving large portions of his clothing in the strands. Then, quite suddenly, when hope had almost died in his heart, he felt the ground rise steeply. He lay very still, a star-rocket from the Turkish side lit up the place, and there in front was a rampart with the points of bayonets showing beyond it. It was the Russian hour for stand-to.

He raised his cramped limbs from the ground and shouted 'Friend! English!'

A face looked down at him, and then the darkness again descended.

'Friend,' he said hoarsely. 'English.'

He heard speech behind the parapet. An electric torch was flashed on him for a second. A voice spoke, a friendly voice, and the sound of it seemed to be telling him to come over.

He was now standing up, and as he got his hands on the parapet he seemed to feel bayonets very near him. But the voice that spoke was kindly, so with a heave he scrambled over and flopped into the trench. Once more the electric torch was flashed, and revealed to the eyes of the onlookers an indescribably dirty, lean, middle-aged man with a bloody head, and scarcely a rag of shirt on his back. The said man, seeing friendly faces around him, grinned cheerfully.

'That was a rough trek, friends,' he said; 'I want to see your general pretty quick, for I've got a present for him.'

He was taken to an officer in a dug-out, who addressed him in French, which he did not understand. But the sight of Stumm's plan worked wonders. After that he was fairly bundled down communication trenches and then over swampy fields to a farm among trees. There he found staff officers, who looked at him and looked at his map, and then put him on a horse and hurried him eastwards. At last he came to a big ruined house, and was taken into a room which seemed to be full of maps and generals.

The conclusion must be told in Peter's words.

'There was a big man sitting at a table drinking coffee, and when I saw him my heart jumped out of my skin. For it was the man I hunted with on the Pungwe in '98—him whom the Kaffirs called "Buck's Horn", because of his long curled moustaches. He was a prince even then, and now he is a very great general. When I saw him, I ran forward and gripped his hand and cried, "*Hoe gat het, Mynheer*?" and he knew me and shouted in Dutch, "Damn, if it isn't old Peter Pienaar!" Then he gave me coffee and ham and good bread, and he looked at my map.

'"What is this?" he cried, growing red in the face.

'"It is the staff-map of one Stumm, a German *skellum* who commands in yon city," I said.

'He looked at it close and read the markings, and then he read the other paper which you gave me, Dick. And then he flung up his arms and laughed. He took a loaf and tossed it into the air so that it fell on the head of another general. He spoke to them in their own tongue, and they, too, laughed, and one or two ran out as if on some errand. I have never seen such merrymaking. They were clever men, and knew the worth of what you gave me.

'Then he got to his feet and hugged me, all dirty as I was, and kissed me on both cheeks.

'"Before God, Peter," he said, "you're the mightiest hunter since Nimrod. You've often found me game, but never game so big as this!"'

CHAPTER TWENTY-ONE

The Little Hill

It was a wise man who said that the biggest kind of courage was to be able to sit still. I used to feel that when we were getting shelled in the reserve trenches outside Vermelles. I felt it before we went over the parapets at Loos, but I never felt it so much as on the last two days in that cellar. I had simply to set my teeth and take a pull on myself. Peter had gone on a crazy errand which I scarcely believed could come off. There were no signs of Sandy; somewhere within a hundred yards he was fighting his own battles, and I was tormented by the thought that he might get jumpy again and wreck everything. A strange Companion brought us food, a man who spoke only Turkish and could tell us nothing; Hussin, I judged, was busy about the horses. If I could only have done something to help on matters I could have scotched my anxiety, but there was nothing to be done, nothing but wait and brood. I tell you I began to sympathize with the general behind the lines in a battle, the fellow who makes the plan which others execute. Leading a charge can be nothing like so nerve-shaking a business as sitting in an easy-chair and waiting on the news of it.

It was bitter cold, and we spent most of the day wrapped in our greatcoats and buried deep in the straw. Blenkiron was a marvel. There was no light for him to play Patience by, but he never complained. He slept a lot of the time, and when he was awake talked as cheerily as if he were starting out on a holiday. He had one great comfort, his dyspepsia was gone. He sang hymns constantly to the benign Providence that had squared his duodenum.

My only occupation was to listen for the guns. The first day after Peter left they were very quiet on the front nearest us, but in the late evening they started a terrific racket. The next day they never stopped from dawn to dusk, so that it reminded me of that tremendous forty-eight hours before Loos. I tried to read into this some proof that Peter had got through, but it would not work. It looked more like the opposite, for this desperate hammering must mean that the frontal assault was still the Russian game.

Two or three times I climbed on the housetop for fresh air. The day was foggy and damp, and I could see very little of the countryside. Transport was still bumping southward along the road to the Palantuken, and the slow wagon-loads of wounded returning. One thing I noticed, however; there was a perpetual coming and going between the house and the city. Motors and mounted messengers were constantly arriving and departing, and I concluded that Hilda von Einem was getting ready for her part in the defence of Erzerum.

These ascents were all on the first day after Peter's going. The second day, when I tried the trap, I found it closed and heavily weighted. This must have been done by our friends, and very right, too. If the house were becoming a place of public resort, it would never do for me to be journeying roof-ward.

Late on the second night Hussin reappeared. It was after supper, when Blenkiron had gone peacefully to sleep and I was beginning to count the hours till the morning. I could not close an eye during these days and not much at night.

Hussin did not light a lantern. I heard his key in the lock, and then his light step close to where we lay.

'Are you asleep?' he said, and when I answered he sat down beside me.

'The horses are found,' he said, 'and the Master bids me tell you that we start in the morning three hours before dawn.'

It was welcome news. 'Tell me what is happening,' I begged; 'we have been lying in this tomb for three days and heard nothing.'

'The guns are busy,' he said. 'The Allemans come to this place every hour, I know not for what. Also there has been a great search for you. The searchers have been here, but they were sent away empty.... Sleep, my lord, for there is wild work before us.'

I did not sleep much, for I was strung too high with expectation, and I envied Blenkiron his now eupeptic slumbers. But for an hour or so I dropped off, and my old nightmare came back. Once again I was in the throat of a pass, hotly pursued, straining for some sanctuary which I knew I must reach. But I was no longer alone. Others were with me: how many I could not tell, for when I tried to see their faces they dissolved in mist. Deep snow was underfoot, a grey sky was over us, black peaks were on all sides, but ahead in the mist of the pass was that curious *castrol* which I had first seen in my dream on the Erzerum road.

I saw it distinct in every detail. It rose to the left of the road through the pass, above a hollow where great boulders stood out in the snow. Its sides were steep, so that the snow had slipped off in patches, leaving stretches of glistening black shale. The *kranz* at the top did not rise sheer, but sloped at an angle of forty-five, and on the very summit there seemed a hollow, as if the earth within the rock-rim had been beaten by weather into a cup.

That is often the way with a South African *castrol*, and I knew it was so with this. We were straining for it, but the snow clogged us, and our enemies were very close behind.

Then I was awakened by a figure at my side. 'Get ready, my lord,' it said; 'it is the hour to ride.'

Like sleep-walkers we moved into the sharp air. Hussin led us out of an old postern and then through a place like an orchard to the shelter of some tall evergreen trees. There horses stood, champing quietly from their nosebags. 'Good,' I thought; 'a feed of oats before a big effort.'

There were nine beasts for nine riders. We mounted without a word and filed through a grove of trees to where a broken paling marked the beginning of cultivated land. There for the matter of twenty minutes Hussin chose to guide us through deep, clogging snow. He wanted to avoid any sound till we were well beyond earshot of the house. Then we struck a by-path which presently merged in a hard highway, running, as I judged, south-west by west. There we delayed no longer, but galloped furiously into the dark.

I had got back all my exhilaration. Indeed I was intoxicated with the movement, and could have laughed out loud and sung. Under the black canopy of the night perils are either forgotten or terribly alive. Mine were forgotten. The darkness I galloped into led me to freedom and friends. Yes, and success, which I had not dared to hope and scarcely even to dream of.

Hussin rode first, with me at his side. I turned my head and saw Blenkiron behind me, evidently mortally unhappy about the pace we set and the mount he sat. He used to say that horse-exercise was good for his liver, but it was a gentle amble and a short gallop that he liked, and not this mad helter-skelter. His thighs were too round to fit a saddle leather. We passed a fire in a hollow, the bivouac of some Turkish unit, and all the horses shied violently. I knew by Blenkiron's oaths that he had lost his stirrups and was sitting on his horse's neck.

Beside him rode a tall figure swathed to the eyes in wrappings, and wearing round his neck some kind of shawl whose ends floated behind him. Sandy, of course, had no European ulster, for it was months since he had worn proper clothes. I wanted to speak to him, but somehow I did not dare. His stillness forbade me. He was a wonderful fine horseman, with his firm English hunting seat, and it was as well, for he paid no attention to his beast. His head was still full of unquiet thoughts.

Then the air around me began to smell acrid and raw, and I saw that a fog was winding up from the hollows.

'Here's the devil's own luck,' I cried to Hussin. 'Can you guide us in a mist?'

'I do not know.' He shook his head. 'I had counted on seeing the shape of the hills.'

'We've a map and compass, anyhow. But these make slow travelling. Pray God it lifts!'

Presently the black vapour changed to grey, and the day broke. It was little comfort. The fog rolled in waves to the horses' ears, and riding at the head of the party I could but dimly see the next rank.

'It is time to leave the road,' said Hussin, 'or we may meet inquisitive folk.'

We struck to the left, over ground which was for all the world like a Scotch moor. There were pools of rain on it, and masses of tangled snow-laden junipers, and long reefs of wet slaty stone. It was bad going, and the fog made it hopeless to steer a good course. I had out the map and the compass, and tried to fix our route so as to round the flank of a spur of the mountains which separated us from the valley we were aiming at.

'There's a stream ahead of us,' I said to Hussin. 'Is it fordable?'

'It is only a trickle,' he said, coughing. 'This accursed mist is from Eblis.' But I knew long before we reached it that it was no trickle. It was a hill stream coming down in spate, and, as I soon guessed, in a deep ravine. Presently we were at its edge, one long whirl of yeasty falls and brown rapids. We could as soon get horses over it as to the topmost cliffs of the Palantuken.

Hussin stared at it in consternation. 'May Allah forgive my folly, for I should have known. We must return to the highway and find a bridge. My sorrow, that I should have led my lords so ill.'

Back over that moor we went with my spirits badly damped. We had none too long a start, and Hilda von Einem would rouse heaven and earth to catch us up. Hussin was forcing the pace, for his anxiety was as great as mine.

Before we reached the road the mist blew back and revealed a wedge of country right across to the hills beyond the river. It was a clear view, every object standing out wet and sharp in the light of morning. It showed the bridge with horsemen drawn up across it, and it showed, too, cavalry pickets moving along the road.

They saw us at the same instant. A word was passed down the road, a shrill whistle blew, and the pickets put their horses at the bank and started across the moor.

'Did I not say this mist was from Eblis?' growled Hussin, as we swung round and galloped back on our tracks. 'These cursed Zaptiehs have seen us, and our road is cut.'

I was for trying the stream at all costs, but Hussin pointed out that it would do us no good. The cavalry beyond the bridge was moving up the other bank. 'There is a path through the hills that I know, but it must be travelled on foot. If we can increase our lead and the mist cloaks us, there is yet a chance.'

It was a weary business plodding up to the skirts of the hills. We had the pursuit behind us now, and that put an edge on every difficulty. There were long banks of broken screes, I remember, where the snow slipped in wreaths from under our feet. Great boulders had to be circumvented, and patches of bog, where the streams from the snows first made contact with the plains, mired us to our girths. Happily the mist was down again, but this, though it hindered the chase, lessened the chances of Hussin finding the path.

He found it nevertheless. There was the gully and the rough mule-track leading upwards. But there also had been a landslip, quite recent from the marks. A large scar of raw earth had broken across the hillside, which with the snow above it looked like a slice cut out of an iced chocolate-cake.

We stared blankly for a second, till we recognized its hopelessness.

'I'm trying for the crags,' I said. 'Where there once was a way another can be found.'

'And be picked off at their leisure by these marksmen,' said Hussin grimly. 'Look!'

The mist had opened again, and a glance behind showed me the pursuit closing up on us. They were now less than three hundred yards off. We turned our horses and made off east-ward along the skirts of the cliffs.

Then Sandy spoke for the first time. 'I don't know how you fellows feel, but I'm not going to be taken. There's nothing much to do except to find a place and put up a fight. We can sell our lives dearly.'

'That's about all,' said Blenkiron cheerfully. He had suffered such tortures on that gallop that he welcomed any kind of stationary fight.

'Serve out the arms,' said Sandy.

The Companions all carried rifles slung across their shoulders. Hussin, from a deep saddle-bag, brought out rifles and bandoliers for the rest of us. As I laid mine across my saddle-bow I saw it was a German Mauser of the latest pattern.

'It's hell-for-leather till we find a place for a stand,' said Sandy. 'The game's against us this time.'

Once more we entered the mist, and presently found better going on a long stretch of even slope. Then came a rise, and on the crest of it I saw the sun. Presently we dipped into bright daylight and looked down on a broad glen, with a road winding up it to a pass in the range. I had expected this. It was one way to the Palantuken pass, some miles south of the house where we had been lodged.

And then, as I looked southward, I saw what I had been watching for for days. A little hill split the valley, and on its top was a *kranz* of rocks. It was the *castrol* of my persistent dream.

On that I promptly took charge. 'There's our fort,' I cried. 'If we once get there we can hold it for a week. Sit down and ride for it.'

We bucketed down that hillside like men possessed, even Blenkiron sticking on manfully among the twists and turns and slithers. Presently we were on the road and were racing past marching infantry and gun teams and empty wagons. I noted that most seemed to be moving downward and few going up. Hussin screamed some words in Turkish that secured us a passage, but indeed our crazy speed left them staring. Out of a corner of my eye I saw that Sandy had flung off most of his wrappings and seemed to be all a dazzle of rich colour. But I had thought for nothing except the little hill, now almost fronting us across the shallow glen.

No horses could breast that steep. We urged them into the hollow, and then hastily dismounted, humped the packs, and began to struggle up the side of the *castrol*. It was strewn with great boulders, which gave a kind of cover that very soon was needed. For, snatching a glance back, I saw that our pursuers were on the road above us and were getting ready to shoot.

At normal times we would have been easy marks, but, fortunately, wisps and streamers of mist now clung about that hollow. The rest could fend for themselves, so

I stuck to Blenkiron and dragged him, wholly breathless, by the least exposed route. Bullets spattered now and then against the rocks, and one sang unpleasantly near my head. In this way we covered three-fourths of the distance, and had only the bare dozen yards where the gradient eased off up to the edge of the *kranz*.

Blenkiron got hit in the leg, our only casualty. There was nothing for it but to carry him, so I swung him on my shoulders, and with a bursting heart did that last lap. It was hottish work, and the bullets were pretty thick about us, but we all got safely to the *kranz*, and a short scramble took us over the edge. I laid Blenkiron inside the *castrol* and started to prepare our defence.

We had little time to do it. Out of the thin fog figures were coming, crouching in cover. The place we were in was a natural redoubt, except that there were no loopholes or sandbags. We had to show our heads over the rim to shoot, but the danger was lessened by the superb field of fire given by those last dozen yards of glacis. I posted the men and waited, and Blenkiron, with a white face, insisted on taking his share, announcing that he used to be handy with a gun.

I gave the order that no man was to shoot till the enemy had come out of the rocks on to the glacis. The thing ran right round the top, and we had to watch all sides to prevent them getting us in flank or rear. Hussin's rifle cracked out presently from the back, so my precautions had not been needless.

We were all three fair shots, though none of us up to Peter's miraculous standard, and the Companions, too, made good practice. The Mauser was the weapon I knew best, and I didn't miss much. The attackers never had a chance, for their only hope was to rush us by numbers, and, the whole party being not above two dozen, they were far too few. I think we killed three, for their bodies were left lying, and wounded at least six, while the rest fell back towards the road. In a quarter of an hour it was all over.

'They are dogs of Kurds,' I heard Hussin say fiercely. 'Only a Kurdish *giaour* would fire on the livery of the Kaaba.'

Then I had a good look at Sandy. He had discarded shawls and wrappings, and stood up in the strangest costume man ever wore in battle. Somehow he had procured field-boots and an old pair of riding-breeches. Above these, reaching well below his middle, he had a wonderful silken jibbah or ephod of a bright emerald. I cal it silk, but it was like no silk I have ever known, so exquisite in the mesh, with such a sheen and depth in it. Some strange pattern was woven on the breast, which in the dim light I could not trace. I'll warrant no rarer or costlier garment was ever exposed to lead on a bleak winter hill.

Sandy seemed unconscious of his garb. His eye, listless no more, scanned the hollow. 'That's only the overture,' he cried. 'The opera will soon begin. We must put a breastwork up in these gaps or they'll pick us off from a thousand yards.'

I had meantime roughly dressed Blenkiron's wound with a linen rag which Hussin provided. It was from a ricochet bullet which had chipped into his left shin. Then I took a hand with the others in getting up earthworks to complete the circuit of the defence. It was no easy job, for we wrought only with our knives and had to dig deep down below the snowy gravel. As we worked I took stock of our refuge.

The *castrol* was a rough circle about ten yards in diameter, its interior filled with boulders and loose stones, and its parapet about four feet high. The mist had cleared for a considerable space, and I could see the immediate surroundings. West, beyond the hollow, was the road we had come, where now the remnants of the pursuit were clustered. North, the hill fell steeply to the valley bottom, but to the south, after a dip there was a ridge which shut the view. East lay another fork of the stream, the chief fork I guessed, and it was evidently followed by the main road to the pass, for I saw it crowded with transport. The two roads seemed to converge somewhere farther south of my sight.

I guessed we could not be very far from the front, for the noise of guns sounded very near, both the sharp crack of the field-pieces, and the deeper boom of the howitzers. More, I could hear the chatter of the machine-guns, a magpie note among the baying of hounds. I even saw the bursting of Russian shells, evidently trying to reach the main road. One big fellow—an eight-inch—landed not ten yards from a convoy to the east of us, and another in the hollow through which we had come. These were clearly ranging shots, and I wondered if the Russians had observation-posts on the heights to mark them. If so, they might soon try a curtain, and we should be very near its edge. It would be an odd irony if we were the target of friendly shells.

'By the Lord Harry,' I heard Sandy say, 'if we had a brace of machine-guns we could hold this place against a division.'

'What price shells?' I asked. 'If they get a gun up they can blow us to atoms in ten minutes.'

'Please God the Russians keep them too busy for that,' was his answer.

With anxious eyes I watched our enemies on the road. They seemed to have grown in numbers. They were signalling, too, for a white flag fluttered. Then the mist rolled down on us again, and our prospect was limited to ten yards of vapour.

'Steady,' I cried; 'they may try to rush us at any moment. Every man keep his eye on the edge of the fog, and shoot at the first sign.'

For nearly half an hour by my watch we waited in that queer white world, our eyes smarting with the strain of peering. The sound of the guns seemed to be hushed, and everything grown deathly quiet. Blenkiron's squeal, as he knocked his wounded leg against a rock, made every man start.

Then out of the mist there came a voice.

It was a woman's voice, high, penetrating, and sweet, but it spoke in no tongue I knew. Only Sandy understood. He made a sudden movement as if to defend himself against a blow.

The speaker came into clear sight on the glacis a yard or two away. Mine was the first face she saw.

'I come to offer terms,' she said in English. 'Will you permit me to enter?'

I could do nothing except take off my cap and say, 'Yes, ma'am.'

Blenkiron, snuggled up against the parapet, was cursing furiously below his breath.

She climbed up the *kranz* and stepped over the edge as lightly as a deer. Her clothes were strange—spurred boots and breeches over which fell a short green kirtle. A little cap skewered with a jewelled pin was on her head, and a cape of some coarse country cloth hung from her shoulders. She had rough gauntlets on her hands, and she carried for weapon a riding-whip. The fog-crystals clung to her hair, I remember, and a silvery film of fog lay on her garments.

I had never before thought of her as beautiful. Strange, uncanny, wonderful, if you like, but the word beauty had too kindly and human a sound for such a face. But as she stood with heightened colour, her eyes like stars, her poise like a wild bird's, I had to confess that she had her own loveliness. She might be a devil, but she was also a queen. I considered that there might be merits in the prospect of riding by her side into Jerusalem.

Sandy stood rigid, his face very grave and set. She held out both hands to him, speaking softly in Turkish. I noticed that the six Companions had disappeared from the *castrol* and were somewhere out of sight on the farther side.

I do not know what she said, but from her tone, and above all from her eyes, I judged that she was pleading—pleading for his return, for his partnership in her great adventure; pleading, for all I knew, for his love.

His expression was like a death-mask, his brows drawn tight in a little frown and his jaw rigid.

'Madam,' he said, 'I ask you to tell your business quick and to tell it in English. My friends must hear it as well as me.'

'Your friends!' she cried. 'What has a prince to do with these hirelings? Your slaves, perhaps, but not your friends.'

'My friends,' Sandy repeated grimly. 'You must know, Madam, that I am a British officer.'

That was beyond doubt a clean staggering stroke. What she had thought of his origin God knows, but she had never dreamed of this. Her eyes grew larger and more lustrous, her lips parted as if to speak, but her voice failed her. Then by an effort she recovered herself, and out of that strange face went all the glow of youth and ardour. It was again the unholy mask I had first known.

'And these others?' she asked in a level voice.

'One is a brother officer of my regiment. The other is an American friend. But all three of us are on the same errand. We came east to destroy Greenmantle and your devilish ambitions. You have yourself destroyed your prophets, and now it is your turn to fail and disappear. Make no mistake, Madam; that folly is over. I will tear this sacred garment into a thousand pieces and scatter them on the wind. The people wait today for the revelation, but none will come. You may kill us if you can, but we have at least crushed a lie and done service to our country.'

I would not have taken my eyes from her face for a king's ransom. I have written that she was a queen, and of that there is no manner of doubt. She had the soul of a conqueror, for not a flicker of weakness or disappointment marred her air. Only pride and the stateliest resolution looked out of her eyes.

'I said I came to offer terms. I will still offer them, though they are other than I thought. For the fat American, I will send him home safely to his own country. I do not make war on such as he. He is Germany's foe, not mine. You,' she said, turning fiercely on me, 'I will hang before dusk.'

Never in my life had I been so pleased. I had got my revenge at last. This woman had singled me out above the others as the object of her wrath, and I almost loved her for it.

She turned to Sandy, and the fierceness went out of her face.

'You seek the truth,' she said. 'So also do I, and if we use a lie it is only to break down a greater. You are of my household in spirit, and you alone of all men I have seen are fit to ride with me on my mission. Germany may fail, but I shall not fail. I offer you the greatest career that mortal has known. I offer you a task which will need every atom of brain and sinew and courage. Will you refuse that destiny?'

I do not know what effect this vapouring might have had in hot scented rooms, or in the languor of some rich garden; but up on that cold hill-top it was as unsubstantial as the mist around us. It sounded not even impressive, only crazy.

'I stay with my friends,' said Sandy.

'Then I will offer more. I will save your friends. They, too, shall share in my triumph.'

This was too much for Blenkiron. He scrambled to his feet to speak the protest that had been wrung from his soul, forgot his game leg, and rolled back on the ground with a groan.

Then she seemed to make a last appeal. She spoke in Turkish now, and I do not know what she said, but I judged it was the plea of a woman to her lover. Once more she was the proud beauty, but there was a tremor in her pride—I had almost written tenderness. To listen to her was like horrid treachery, like eavesdropping on something pitiful. I know my cheeks grew scarlet and Blenkiron turned away his head.

Sandy's face did not move. He spoke in English.

'You can offer me nothing that I desire,' he said. 'I am the servant of my country, and her enemies are mine. I can have neither part nor lot with you. That is my answer, Madam von Einem.'

Then her steely restraint broke. It was like a dam giving before a pent-up mass of icy water. She tore off one of her gauntlets and hurled it in his face. Implacable hate looked out of her eyes.

'I have done with you,' she cried. 'You have scorned me, but you have dug your own grave.'

She leaped on the parapet and the next second was on the glacis. Once more the mist had fled, and across the hollow I saw a field-gun in place and men around it who were not Turkish. She waved her hand to them, and hastened down the hillside.

But at that moment I heard the whistle of a long-range Russian shell. Among the boulders there was the dull shock of an explosion and a mushroom of red earth. It all passed in an instant of time: I saw the gunners on the road point their hands and I heard them cry; I heard too, a kind of sob from Blenkiron—all this before I realized myself what had happened. The next thing I saw was Sandy, already beyond the glacis, leaping with great bounds down the hill. They were shooting at him, but he heeded them not. For the space of a minute he was out of sight, and his whereabouts was shown only by the patter of bullets.

Then he came back—walking quite slowly up the last slope, and he was carrying something in his arms. The enemy fired no more; they realized what had happened.

He laid his burden down gently in a corner of the *castrol.* The cap had fallen off, and the hair was breaking loose. The face was very white but there was no wound or bruise on it.

'She was killed at once,' I heard him saying. 'Her back was broken by a shell-fragment. Dick, we must bury her here ... You see, she ... she liked me. I can make her no return but this.'

We set the Companions to guard, and with infinite slowness, using our hands and our knives, we made a shallow grave below the eastern parapet. When it was done we covered her face with the linen cloak which Sandy had worn that morning. He lifted the body and laid it reverently in its place.

'I did not know that anything could be so light,' he said.

It wasn't for me to look on at that kind of scene. I went to the parapet with Blenkiron's field-glasses and had a stare at our friends on the road. There was no Turk there, and I guessed why, for it would not be easy to use the men of Islam against the wearer of the green ephod. The enemy were German or Austrian, and they had a field-gun. They seemed to have got it laid on our fort; but they were waiting. As I looked I saw behind them a massive figure I seemed to recognize. Stumm had come to see the destruction of his enemies.

To the east I saw another gun in the fields just below the main road. They had got us on both sides, and there was no way of escape. Hilda von Einem was to have a noble pyre and goodly company for the dark journey.

Dusk was falling now, a clear bright dusk where the stars pricked through a sheen of amethyst. The artillery were busy all around the horizon, and towards the pass on the other road, where Fort Palantuken stood, there was the dust and smoke of a furious bombardment. It seemed to me, too, that the guns on the other fronts had come nearer. Deve Boyun was hidden by a spur of hill, but up in the north, white clouds, like the streamers of evening, were hanging over the Euphrates glen. The whole firmament hummed and twanged like a taut string that has been struck ...

As I looked, the gun to the west fired—the gun where Stumm was. The shell dropped ten yards to our right. A second later another fell behind us.

Blenkiron had dragged himself to the parapet. I don't suppose he had ever been shelled before, but his face showed curiosity rather than fear.

'Pretty poor shooting, I reckon,' he said.

'On the contrary,' I said, 'they know their business. They're bracketing ...'

The words were not out of my mouth when one fell right among us. It struck the far rim of the *castrol*, shattering the rock, but bursting mainly outside. We all ducked, and barring some small scratches no one was a penny the worse. I remember that much of the debris fell on Hilda von Einem's grave.

I pulled Blenkiron over the far parapet, and called on the rest to follow, meaning to take cover on the rough side of the hill. But as we showed ourselves shots rang out from our front, shots fired from a range of a few hundred yards. It was easy to see what had happened. Riflemen had been sent to hold us in rear. They would not assault so long as we remained in the *castrol*, but they would block any attempt to find safety outside it. Stumm and his gun had us at their mercy.

We crouched below the parapet again. 'We may as well toss for it,' I said. 'There's only two ways—to stay here and be shelled or try to break through those fellows behind. Either's pretty unhealthy.'

But I knew there was no choice. With Blenkiron crippled we were pinned to the *castrol*. Our numbers were up all right.

CHAPTER TWENTY-TWO

The Guns of the North

But no more shells fell.

The night grew dark and showed a field of glittering stars, for the air was sharpening again towards frost. We waited for an hour, crouching just behind the far parapets, but never came that ominous familiar whistle.

Then Sandy rose and stretched himself. 'I'm hungry,' he said. 'Let's have out the food, Hussin. We've eaten nothing since before daybreak. I wonder what is the meaning of this respite?'

I fancied I knew.

'It's Stumm's way,' I said. 'He wants to torture us. He'll keep us hours on tenterhooks, while he sits over yonder exulting in what he thinks we're enduring. He has just enough imagination for that ... He would rush us if he had the men. As it is, he's going to blow us to pieces, but do it slowly and smack his lips over it.'

Sandy yawned. 'We'll disappoint him, for we won't be worried, old man. We three are beyond that kind of fear.'

'Meanwhile we're going to do the best we can,' I said. 'He's got the exact range for his whizz-bangs. We've got to find a hole somewhere just outside the *castrol*, and some sort of head-cover. We're bound to get damaged whatever happens, but we'll stick it out to the end. When they think they have finished with us and rush the place, there may be one of us alive to put a bullet through old Stumm. What do you say?'

They agreed, and after our meal Sandy and I crawled out to prospect, leaving the others on guard in case there should be an attack. We found a hollow in the glacis a little south of the *castrol*, and, working very quietly, managed to enlarge it and cut a kind of shallow cave in the hill. It would be no use against a direct hit, but it would give some cover from flying fragments. As I read the situation, Stumm could land as many shells as he pleased in the *castrol* and wouldn't bother to attend to the flanks. When the bad shelling began there would be shelter for one or two in the cave.

Our enemies were watchful. The riflemen on the east burnt Very flares at intervals, and Stumm's lot sent up a great star-rocket. I remember that just before midnight hell broke loose round Fort Palantuken. No more Russian shells came into our hollow, but all the road to the east was under fire, and at the Fort itself there was a shattering explosion and a queer scarlet glow which looked as if a magazine had been hit. For about two hours the firing was intense, and then it died down. But it was towards the north that I kept turning my head. There seemed to be something different in the sound there, something sharper in the report of the guns, as if shells were dropping in a narrow valley whose rock walls doubled the echo. Had the Russians by any blessed chance worked round that flank?

I got Sandy to listen, but he shook his head. 'Those guns are a dozen miles off,' he said. 'They're no nearer than three days ago. But it looks as if the sportsmen on the south might have a chance. When they break through and stream down the valley, they'll be puzzled to account for what remains of us ... We're no longer three adventurers in the enemy's country. We're the advance guard of the Allies. Our pals don't know about us, and we're going to be cut off, which has happened to advance guards before now. But all the same, we're in our own battle-line again. Doesn't that cheer you, Dick?'

It cheered me wonderfully, for I knew now what had been the weight on my heart ever since I accepted Sir Walter's mission. It was the loneliness of it. I was fighting far away from my friends, far away from the true fronts of battle. It was a side-show which, whatever its importance, had none of the exhilaration of the main effort. But now we had come back to familiar ground. We were like the Highlanders cut off at Cite St Auguste on the first day of Loos, or those Scots Guards at Festubert of whom I had heard. Only, the others did not know of it, would never hear of it. If Peter succeeded he might tell the tale, but most likely he was lying dead somewhere in the no-man's-land between the lines. We should never be heard of again any more, but our work remained. Sir Walter would know that, and he would tell our few belongings that we had gone out in our country's service.

We were in the *castrol* again, sitting under the parapets. The same thoughts must have been in Sandy's mind, for he suddenly laughed.

'It's a queer ending, Dick. We simply vanish into the infinite. If the Russians get through they will never recognize what is left of us among so much of the wreckage of battle. The snow will soon cover us, and when the spring comes there will only be a few bleached bones. Upon my soul it is the kind of death I always wanted.' And he quoted softly to himself a verse of an old Scots ballad:

'Mony's the ane for him maks mane,
But nane sall ken whar he is gane.
Ower his white banes, when they are bare,
The wind sall blaw for evermair.'

'But our work lives,' I cried, with a sudden great gasp of happiness. 'It's the job that matters, not the men that do it. And our job's done. We have won, old chap—won hands down—and there is no going back on that. We have won anyway; and if Peter has had a slice of luck, we've scooped the pool ... After all, we never expected to come out of this thing with our lives.'

Blenkiron, with his leg stuck out stiffly before him, was humming quietly to himself, as he often did when he felt cheerful. He had only one song, 'John Brown's Body'; usually only a line at a time, but now he got as far as the whole verse:

'He captured Harper's Ferry, with his nineteen men so true,
And he frightened old Virginny till she trembled through and through.
They hung him for a traitor, themselves the traitor crew,
But his soul goes marching along.'

'Feeling good?' I asked.

'Fine. I'm about the luckiest man on God's earth, Major. I've always wanted to get into a big show, but I didn't see how it would come the way of a homely citizen like me, living in a steam-warmed house and going down town to my office every morning. I used to envy my old dad that fought at Chattanooga, and never forgot to tell you about it. But I guess Chattanooga was like a scrap in a Bowery bar compared to this. When I meet the old man in Glory he'll have to listen some to me.'

It was just after Blenkiron spoke that we got a reminder of Stumm's presence. The gun was well laid, for a shell plumped on the near edge of the castro. It made an end of one of the Companions who was on guard there, badly wounded another, and a fragment gashed my thigh. We took refuge in the shallow cave, but some wild shooting from the east side brought us back to the parapets, for we feared an attack. None came, nor any more shells, and once again the night was quiet.

I asked Blenkiron if he had any near relatives.

'Why, no, except a sister's son, a college-boy who has no need of his uncle. It's fortunate that we three have no wives. I haven't any regrets, neither, for I've had a mighty deal out of life. I was thinking this morning that it was a pity I was going out when I had just got my duo-denum to listen to reason. But I reckon that's another of my mercies. The good God took away the pain in my stomach so that I might go to Him with a clear head and a thankful heart.'

'We're lucky fellows,' said Sandy; 'we've all had our whack. When I remember the good times I've had I could sing a hymn of praise. We've lived long enough to know ourselves, and to shape ourselves into some kind of decency. But think of those boys who have given their lives freely when they scarcely knew what life meant. They were just at the beginning of the road, and they didn't know what dreary bits lay before them. It was all sunshiny and bright-coloured, and yet they gave it up without a moment's doubt. And think of the men with wives and children and homes that were the biggest things in life to them. For fellows like us to shirk would be black cowardice. It's small credit for us to stick it out. But when those others shut their teeth and went forward, they were blessed heroes....'

After that we fell silent. A man's thoughts at a time like that seem to be double-powered, and the memory becomes very sharp and clear. I don't know what was in the others' minds, but I know what filled my own...

I fancy it isn't the men who get most out of the world and are always buoyant and cheerful that most fear to die. Rather it is the weak-engined souls who go about with dull eyes, that cling most fiercely to life. They have not the joy of being alive which is a kind of earnest of immortality ... I know that my thoughts were chiefly about the jolly things that I had seen and done; not regret, but gratitude. The panorama of blue noons on the veld unrolled itself before me, and hunter's nights in the bush, the taste of food and sleep, the bitter stimulus of dawn, the joy of wild adventure, the voices of old staunch friends. Hitherto the war had seemed to make a break with all that had gone before, but now the war was only part of the picture. I thought of my battalion, and the good fellows there, many of whom had fallen on the Loos parapets. I had never looked to come out of that myself. But I had been spared, and given the chance of a greater business, and I had succeeded. That was the tremendous fact, and my mood was humble gratitude to God and exultant pride. Death was a small price to pay for it. As Blenkiron would have said, I had got good value in the deal.

The night was getting bitter cold, as happens before dawn. It was frost again, and the sharpness of it woke our hunger. I got out the remnants of the food and wine and we had a last meal. I remember we pledged each other as we drank.

'We have eaten our Passover Feast,' said Sandy. 'When do you look for the end?'

'After dawn,' I said. 'Stumm wants daylight to get the full savour of his revenge.'

Slowly the sky passed from ebony to grey, and black shapes of hill outlined themselves against it. A wind blew down the valley, bringing the acrid smell of burning, but something too of the freshness of morn. It stirred strange thoughts in me, and woke the old morning vigour of the blood which was never to be mine again. For the first time in that long vigil I was torn with a sudden regret.

'We must get into the cave before it is full light,' I said. 'We had better draw lots for the two to go.'

The choice fell on one of the Companions and Blenkiron. 'You can count me out,' said the latter. 'If it's your wish to find a man to be alive when our friends come up to count their spoil, I guess I'm the worst of the lot. I'd prefer, if you don't mind, to stay here. I've made my peace with my Maker, and I'd like to wait quietly on His call. I'll play a game of Patience to pass the time.'

He would take no denial, so we drew again, and the lot fell to Sandy.

'If I'm the last to go,' he said, 'I promise I don't miss. Stumm won't be long in following me.'

He shook hands with his cheery smile, and he and the Companion slipped over the parapet in the final shadows before dawn.

Blenkiron spread his Patience cards on a flat rock, and dealt out the Double Napoleon. He was perfectly calm, and hummed to himself his only tune. For myself I was drinking in my last draught of the hill air. My contentment was going. I suddenly felt bitterly loath to die.

Something of the same kind must have passed through Blenkiron's head. He suddenly looked up and asked, 'Sister Anne, Sister Anne, do you see anybody coming?'

I stood close to the parapet, watching every detail of the landscape as shown by the revealing daybreak. Up on the shoulders of the Palantuken, snowdrifts lipped over the edges of the cliffs. I wondered when they would come down as avalanches. There was a kind of croft on one hillside, and from a hut the smoke of breakfast was beginning to curl. Stumm's gunners were awake and apparently holding council. Far down on the main road a convoy was moving—I heard the creak of the wheels two miles away, for the air was deathly still.

Then, as if a spring had been loosed, the world suddenly leaped to a hideous life. With a growl the guns opened round all the horizon. They were especially fierce to the south, where a *rafale* beat as I had never heard it before. The one glance I cast behind me showed the gap in the hills choked with fumes and dust.

But my eyes were on the north. From Erzerum city tall tongues of flame leaped from a dozen quarters. Beyond, towards the opening of the Euphrates glen, there was the sharp crack of field-guns. I strained eyes and ears, mad with impatience, and I read the riddle.

'Sandy,' I yelled, 'Peter has got through. The Russians are round the flank. The town is burning. Glory to God, we've won, we've won!'

And as I spoke the earth seemed to split beside me, and I was flung forward on the gravel which covered Hilda von Einem's grave.

As I picked myself up, and to my amazement found myself uninjured, I saw Blenkiron rubbing the dust out of his eyes and arranging a disordered card. He had stopped humming, and was singing aloud:

'He captured Harper's Ferry, with his nineteen men so true
And he frightened old Virginny ...'

'Say, Major,' he cried, 'I believe this game of mine is coming out.'

I was now pretty well mad. The thought that old Peter had won, that we had won beyond our wildest dreams, that if we died there were those coming who would exact the uttermost vengeance, rode my brain like a fever. I sprang on the parapet and waved my hand to Stumm, shouting defiance. Rifle shots cracked out from behind, and I leaped back just in time for the next shell.

The charge must have been short, for it was a bad miss, landing somewhere on the glacis. The next was better and crashed on the near parapet, carving a great hole in the rocky *kranz*. This time my arm hung limp, broken by a fragment of stone, but I felt no pain.

Blenkiron seemed to bear a charmed life, for he was smothered in dust, but unhurt. He blew the dust away from his cards very gingerly and went on playing.

'Sister Anne,' he asked, 'do you see anybody coming?'

Then came a dud which dropped neatly inside on the soft ground.

I was determined to break for the open and chance the rifle fire, for if Stumm went on shooting the *castrol* was certain death. I caught Blenkiron round the middle, scattering his cards to the winds, and jumped over the parapet.

'Don't apologize, Sister Anne,' said he. 'The game was as good as won. But for God's sake drop me, for if you wave me like the banner of freedom I'll get plugged sure and good.'

My one thought was to get cover for the next minutes, for I had an instinct that our vigil was near its end. The defences of Erzerum were crumbling like sand-castles, and it was a proof of the tenseness of my nerves that I seemed to be deaf to the sound. Stumm had seen us cross the parapet, and he started to sprinkle all the surroundings of the *castrol.* Blenkiron and I lay like a working-party between the lines caught by machine-guns, taking a pull on ourselves as best we could. Sandy had some kind of cover, but we were on the bare farther slope, and the riflemen on that side might have had us at their mercy.

But no shots came from them. As I looked east, the hillside, which a little before had been held by our enemies, was as empty as the desert. And then I saw on the main road a sight which for a second time made me yell like a maniac. Down that glen came a throng of men and galloping limbers—a crazy, jostling crowd, spreading away beyond the road to the steep slopes, and leaving behind it many black dots to darken the snows. The gates of the South had yielded, and our friends were through them.

At that sight I forgot all about our danger. I didn't give a cent for Stumm's shells. I didn't believe he could hit me. The fate which had mercifully preserved us for the first taste of victory would see us through to the end.

I remember bundling Blenkiron along the hill to find Sandy. But our news was anticipated. For down our own side-glen came the same broken tumult of men. More; for at their backs, far up at the throat of the pass, I saw horsemen—the horsemen of the pursuit. Old Nicholas had flung his cavalry in.

Sandy was on his feet, with his lips set and his eye abstracted. If his face hadn't been burned black by weather it would have been pale as a dish-clout. A man like him doesn't make up his mind for death and then be given his life again without being wrenched out of his bearings. I thought he didn't understand what had happened, so I beat him on the shoulders.

'Man, d'you see?' I cried. 'The Cossacks! The Cossacks! God! How they're taking that slope! They're into them now. By heaven, we'll ride with them! We'll get the gun horses!'

A little knoll prevented Stumm and his men from seeing what was happening farther up the glen, till the first wave of the rout was on them. He had gone on bombarding the *castrol* and its environs while the world was cracking over his head. The gun team was in the hollow below the road, and down the hill among the boulders we crawled, Blenkiron as lame as a duck, and me with a limp left arm.

The poor beasts were straining at their pickets and sniffing the morning wind, which brought down the thick fumes of the great bombardment and the indescribable babbling cries of a beaten army. Before we reached them that maddened horde had swept down on them, men panting and gasping in their flight, many of them bloody from wounds, many tottering in the first stages of collapse and death. I saw the horses seized by a dozen hands, and a desperate fight for their possession. But as we halted there our eyes were fixed on the battery on the road above us, for round it was now sweeping the van of the retreat.

I had never seen a rout before, when strong men come to the end of their tether and only their broken shadows stumble towards the refuge they never find. No more had Stumm, poor devil. I had no ill-will left for him, though coming down that hill I was rather hoping that the two of us might have a final scrap. He was a brute and a bully, but, by God! he was a man. I heard his great roar when he saw the tumult, and the next I saw was his monstrous figure working at the gun. He swung it south and turned it on the fugitives.

But he never fired it. The press was on him, and the gun was swept sideways. He stood up, a foot higher than any of them, and he seemed to be trying to check the rush with his pistol. There is power in numbers, even though every unit is broken and fleeing. For a second to that wild crowd Stumm was the enemy, and they had strength enough to crush him. The wave flowed round and then across him. I saw the butt-ends of rifles crash on his head and shoulders, and the next second the stream had passed over his body.

That was God's judgement on the man who had set himself above his kind.

Sandy gripped my shoulder and was shouting in my ear:

'They're coming, Dick. Look at the grey devils ... Oh, God be thanked, it's our friends!'

The next minute we were tumbling down the hillside, Blenkiron hopping on one leg between us. I heard dimly Sandy crying, 'Oh, well done our side!' and Blenkiron declaiming about Harper's Ferry, but I had no voice at all and no wish to shout. I know the tears were in my eyes, and that if I had been left alone I would have sat down and cried with pure thankfulness. For sweeping down the glen came a cloud of grey cavalry on little wiry horses, a cloud which stayed not for the rear of the fugitives, but swept on like a flight of rainbows, with the steel of their lance-heads glittering in the winter sun. They were riding for Erzerum.

Remember that for three months we had been with the enemy and had never seen the face of an Ally in arms. We had been cut off from the fellowship of a great cause, like a fort surrounded by an army. And now we were delivered, and there fell around us the warm joy of comradeship as well as the exultation of victory.

We flung caution to the winds, and went stark mad. Sandy, still in his emerald coat and turban, was scrambling up the farther slope of the hollow, yelling greetings in every language known to man. The leader saw him, with a word checked his men for a moment—it was marvellous to see the horses reined in in such a break-neck ride—and from the squadron half a dozen troopers swung loose and wheeled towards us. Then a man in a grey overcoat and a sheepskin cap was on the ground beside us wringing our hands.

'You are safe, my old friends'—it was Peter's voice that spoke—'I will take you back to our army, and get you breakfast.'

'No, by the Lord, you won't,' cried Sandy. 'We've had the rough end of the job and now we'll have the fun. Look after Blenkiron and these fellows of mine. I'm going to ride knee by knee with your sportsmen for the city.'

Peter spoke a word, and two of the Cossacks dismounted. The next I knew I was mixed up in the cloud of greycoats, galloping down the road up which the morning before we had strained to the *castrol.*

That was the great hour of my life, and to live through it was worth a dozen years of slavery. With a broken left arm I had little hold on my beast, so I trusted my neck to him and let him have his will. Black with dirt and smoke, hatless, with no kind of uniform, I was a wilder figure than any Cossack. I soon was separated from Sandy, who had two hands and a better horse, and seemed resolute to press forward to the very van. That would have been suicide for me, and I had all I could do to keep my place in the bunch I rode with.

But, Great God! what an hour it was! There was loose shooting on our flank, but nothing to trouble us, though the gun team of some Austrian howitzer, struggling madly at a bridge, gave us a bit of a tussle. Everything flitted past me like smoke, or like the mad finale of a dream just before waking. I knew the living movement under me, and the companionship of men, but all dimly, for at heart I was alone, grappling with the realization of a new world. I felt the shadows of the Palantuken glen fading, and the great burst of light as we emerged on the wider valley. Somewhere before us was a pall of smoke seamed with red flames, and beyond the darkness of still higher hills. All that time I was dreaming, crooning daft catches of song to myself, so happy, so deliriously happy that I dared not try to think. I kept muttering a kind of prayer made up of Bible words to Him who had shown me His goodness in the land of the living.

But as we drew out from the skirts of the hills and began the long slope to the city, I woke to clear consciousness. I felt the smell of sheepskin and lathered horses, and above all the bitter smell of fire. Down in the trough lay Erzerum, now burning in many places, and from the east, past the silent forts, horsemen were closing in on it. I yelled to my comrades that we were nearest, that we would be first in the city, and they nodded happily and shouted their strange war-cries. As we topped the last ridge I saw below me the van of our charge—a dark mass on the snow—while the broken enemy on both sides were flinging away their arms and scattering in the fields.

In the very front, now nearing the city ramparts, was one man. He was like the point of the steel spear soon to be driven home. In the clear morning air I could see that he did not wear the uniform of the invaders. He was turbaned and rode like one possessed, and against the snow I caught the dark sheen of emerald. As he rode it seemed that the fleeing Turks were stricken still, and sank by the roadside with eyes strained after his unheeding figure ...

Then I knew that the prophecy had been true, and that their prophet had not failed them. The long-looked for revelation had come. Greenmantle had appeared at last to an awaiting people.

MR STANDFAST

By

JOHN BUCHAN

TO THAT MOST GALLANT COMPANY
THE OFFICERS AND MEN
OF THE
SOUTH AFRICAN INFANTRY BRIGADE
on the Western Front

PART I

CHAPTER ONE

The Wicket-Gate

I spent one-third of my journey looking out of the window of a first-class carriage, the next in a local motor-car following the course of a trout stream in a shallow valley, and the last tramping over a ridge of downland through great beech-woods to my quarters for the night. In the first part I was in an infamous temper; in the second I was worried and mystified; but the cool twilight of the third stage calmed and heartened me, and I reached the gates of Fosse Manor with a mighty appetite and a quiet mind.

As we slipped up the Thames valley on the smooth Great Western line I had reflected ruefully on the thorns in the path of duty. For more than a year I had never been out of khaki, except the months I spent in hospital. They gave me my battalion before the Somme, and I came out of that weary battle after the first big September fighting with a crack in my head and a D.S.O. I had received a C.B. for the Erzerum business, so what with these and my Matabele and South African medals and the Legion of Honour, I had a chest like the High Priest's breastplate. I rejoined in January, and got a brigade on the eve of Arras. There we had a star turn, and took about as many prisoners as we put infantry over the top. After that we were hauled out for a month, and subsequently planted in a bad bit on the Scarpe with a hint that we would soon be used for a big push. Then suddenly I was ordered home to report to the War Office, and passed on by them to Bullivant and his merry men. So here I was sitting in a railway carriage in a grey tweed suit, with a neat new suitcase on the rack labelled C.B. The initials stood for Cornelius Brand, for that was my name now. And an old boy in the corner was asking me questions and wondering audibly why I wasn't fighting, while a young blood of a second lieutenant with a wound stripe was eyeing me with scorn.

The old chap was one of the cross-examining type, and after he had borrowed my matches he set to work to find out all about me. He was a tremendous fire-eater, and a bit of a pessimist about our slow progress in the west. I told him I came from South Africa and was a mining engineer.

'Been fighting with Botha?' he asked.

'No,' I said. 'I'm not the fighting kind.'

The second lieutenant screwed up his nose.

'Is there no conscription in South Africa?'

'Thank God there isn't,' I said, and the old fellow begged permission to tell me a lot of unpalatable things.

I knew his kind and didn't give much for it. He was the sort who, if he had been under fifty, would have crawled on his belly to his tribunal to get exempted, but being over age was able to pose as a patriot. But I didn't like the second lieutenant's grin, for he seemed a good class of lad. I looked steadily out of the window for the rest of the way, and wasn't sorry when I got to my station.

I had had the queerest interview with Bullivant and Macgillivray. They asked me first if I was willing to serve again in the old game, and I said I was. I felt as bitter as sin, for I had got fixed in the military groove, and had made good there. Here was I—a brigadier and still under forty, and with another year of the war there was no saying where I might end. I had started out without any ambition, only a great wish to see the business finished. But now I had acquired a professional interest in the thing, I had a nailing good brigade, and I had got the hang of our new kind of war as well as any fellow from Sandhurst and Camberley. They were asking me to scrap all I had learned and start again in a new job. I had to agree, for discipline's discipline, but I could have knocked their heads together in my vexation.

What was worse they wouldn't, or couldn't, tell me anything about what they wanted me for. It was the old game of running me in blinkers. They asked me to take it on trust and put myself unreservedly in their hands. I would get my instructions later, they said.

I asked if it was important.

Bullivant narrowed his eyes. 'If it weren't, do you suppose we could have wrung an active brigadier out of the War Office? As it was, it was like drawing teeth.'

'Is it risky?' was my next question.

'In the long run—damnably,' was the answer.

'And you can't tell me anything more?'

'Nothing as yet. You'll get your instructions soon enough. You know both of us, Hannay, and you know we wouldn't waste the time of a good man on folly. We are going to ask you for something which will make a big call on your patriotism. It will be a difficult and arduous task, and it may be a very grim one before you get to the end of it, but we believe you can do it, and that no one else can ... You know us pretty well. Will you let us judge for you?'

I looked at Bullivant's shrewd, kind old face and Macgillivray's steady eyes. These men were my friends and wouldn't play with Me.

'All right,' I said. 'I'm willing. What's the first step?'

'Get out of uniform and forget you ever were a soldier. Change your name. Your old one, Cornelis Brandt, will do, but you'd better spell it "Brand" this time. Remember that you are an engineer just back from South Africa, and that you don't care a rush about the war. You can't understand what all the fools are fighting about, and you think we might have peace at once by a little friendly business talk. You needn't be pro-German—if you like you can be rather severe on the Hun. But you must be in deadly earnest about a speedy peace.'

I expect the corners of my mouth fell, for Bullivant burst out laughing.

'Hang it all, man, it's not so difficult. I feel sometimes inclined to argue that way myself, when my dinner doesn't agree with me. It's not so hard as to wander round the Fatherland abusing Britain, which was your last job.'

'I'm ready,' I said. 'But I want to do one errand on my own first. I must see a fellow in my brigade who is in a shell-shock hospital in the Cotswolds. Isham's the name of the place.'

The two men exchanged glances. 'This looks like fate,' said Bullivant. 'By all means go to Isham. The place where your work begins is only a couple of miles off. I want you to spend next Thursday night as the guest of two maiden ladies called Wymondham at Fosse Manor. You will go down there as a lone South African visiting a sick friend. They are hospitable souls and entertain many angels unawares.'

'And I get my orders there?'

'You get your orders, and you are under bond to obey them.' And Bullivant and Macgillivray smiled at each other.

I was thinking hard about that odd conversation as the small Ford car, which I had wired for to the inn, carried me away from the suburbs of the county town into a land of rolling hills and green water-meadows. It was a gorgeous afternoon and the blossom of early June was on every tree. But I had no eyes for landscape and the summer, being engaged in reprobating Bullivant and cursing my fantastic fate. I detested my new part and looked forward to naked shame. It was bad enough for anyone to have to pose as a pacifist, but for me, strong as a bull and as sunburnt as a gipsy and not looking my forty years, it was a black disgrace. To go into Germany as an anti-British Afrikander was a stoutish adventure, but to lounge about at home talking rot was a very different-sized job. My stomach rose at the thought of it, and I had pretty well decided to wire to Bullivant and cry off. There are some things that no one has a right to ask of any white man.

When I got to Isham and found poor old Blaikie I didn't feel happier. He had been a friend of mine in Rhodesia, and after the German South-West affair was over had come home to a Fusilier battalion, which was in my brigade at Arras. He had been buried by a big crump just before we got our second objective, and was dug out without a scratch on him, but as daft as a hatter. I had heard he was mending, and had promised his family to look him up the first chance I got. I found him sitting on a garden seat, staring steadily before him like a lookout at sea. He knew me all right and cheered up for a second, but very soon he was back at his staring, and every word he uttered was like the careful speech of a drunken man. A bird flew out of a bush, and I could see him holding himself tight to keep from screaming. The best I could do was to put a hand on his shoulder and stroke him as one strokes a frightened horse. The sight of the price my old friend had paid didn't put me in love with pacificism.

We talked of brother officers and South Africa, for I wanted to keep his thoughts off the war, but he kept edging round to it.

'How long will the damned thing last?' he asked.

'Oh, it's practically over,' I lied cheerfully. 'No more fighting for you and precious little for me. The Boche is done in all right ... What you've got to do, my lad, is to sleep fourteen hours in the twenty-four and spend half the rest catching trout. We'll have a shot at the grouse-bird together this autumn and we'll get some of the old gang to join us.'

Someone put a tea-tray on the table beside us, and I looked up to see the very prettiest girl I ever set eyes on. She seemed little more than a child, and before the war would probably have still ranked as a flapper. She wore the neat blue dress and apron of a V.A.D. and her white cap was set on hair like spun gold. She smiled demurely as she arranged the tea-things, and I thought I had never seen eyes at once so merry and so grave. I stared after her as she walked across the lawn, and I remember noticing that she moved with the free grace of an athletic boy.

'Who on earth's that?' I asked Blaikie.

'That? Oh, one of the sisters,' he said listlessly. 'There are squads of them. I can't tell one from another.'

Nothing gave me such an impression of my friend's sickness as the fact that he should have no interest in something so fresh and jolly as that girl. Presently my time was up and I had to go, and as I looked back I saw him sunk in his chair again, his eyes fixed on vacancy, and his hands gripping his knees.

The thought of him depressed me horribly. Here was I condemned to some rotten buffoonery in inglorious safety, while the salt of the earth like Blaikie was paying the ghastliest price. From him my thoughts flew to old Peter Pienaar, and I sat down on a roadside wall and read his last letter. It nearly made me howl. Peter, you must know, had shaved his beard and joined the Royal Flying Corps the summer before when we got back from the Greenmantle affair. That was the only kind of reward he wanted, and, though he was absurdly over age, the authorities allowed it. They were wise not to stickle about rules, for Peter's eyesight and nerve were as good as those of any boy of twenty. I knew he would do well, but

I was not prepared for his immediately blazing success. He got his pilot's certificate in record time and went out to France; and presently even we foot-sloggers, busy shifting ground before the Somme, began to hear rumours of his doings. He developed a perfect genius for air-fighting. There were plenty better trick-flyers, and plenty who knew more about the science of the game, but there was no one with quite Peter's genius for an actual scrap. He was as full of dodges a couple of miles up in the sky as he had been among the rocks of the Berg. He apparently knew how to hide in the empty air as cleverly as in the long grass of the Lebombo Flats. Amazing yarns began to circulate among the infantry about this new airman, who could take cover below one plane of an enemy squadron while all the rest were looking for him. I remember talking about him with the South Africans when we were out resting next door to them after the bloody Delville Wood business. The day before we had seen a good battle in the clouds when the Boche plane had crashed, and a Transvaal machine-gun officer brought the report that the British airman had been Pienaar. 'Well done, the old *takhaar*!' he cried, and started to yarn about Peter's methods. It appeared that Peter had a theory that every man has a blind spot, and that he knew just how to find that blind spot in the world of air. The best cover, he maintained, was not in cloud or a wisp of fog, but in the unseeing patch in the eye of your enemy. I recognized that talk for the real thing. It was on a par with Peter's doctrine of 'atmosphere' and 'the double bluff' and all the other principles that his queer old mind had cogitated out of his rackety life.

By the end of August that year Peter's was about the best-known figure in the Flying Corps. If the reports had mentioned names he would have been a national hero, but he was only 'Lieutenant Blank', and the newspapers, which expatiated on his deeds, had to praise the Service and not the man. That was right enough, for half the magic of our Flying Corps was its freedom from advertisement. But the British Army knew all about him, and the men in the trenches used to discuss him as if he were a crack football-player. There was a very big German airman called Lensch, one of the Albatross heroes, who about the end of August claimed to have destroyed thirty-two Allied machines. Peter had then only seventeen planes to his credit, but he was rapidly increasing his score. Lensch was a mighty man of valour and a good sportsman after his fashion. He was amazingly quick at manoeuvring his machine in the actual fight, but Peter was supposed to be better at forcing the kind of fight he wanted. Lensch, if you like, was the tactician and Peter the strategist. Anyhow the two were out to get each other. There were plenty of fellows who saw the campaign as a struggle not between Hun and Briton, but between Lensch and Pienaar.

The 15th September came, and I got knocked out and went to hospital. When I was fit to read the papers again and receive letters, I found to my consternation that Peter had been downed. It happened at the end of

October when the southwest gales badly handicapped our airwork. When our bombing or reconnaissance jobs behind the enemy lines were completed, instead of being able to glide back into safety, we had to fight our way home slowly against a head-wind exposed to Archies and Hun planes. Somewhere east of Bapaume on a return journey Peter fell in with Lensch—at least the German Press gave Lensch the credit. His petrol tank was shot to bits and he was forced to descend in a wood near Morchies. 'The celebrated British airman, Pinner,' in the words of the German communique, was made prisoner.

I had no letter from him till the beginning of the New Year, when I was preparing to return to France. It was a very contented letter. He seemed to have been fairly well treated, though he had always a low standard of what he expected from the world in the way of comfort. I inferred that his captors had not identified in the brilliant airman the Dutch miscreant who a year before had broken out of a German jail. He had discovered the pleasures of reading and had perfected himself in an art which he had once practised indifferently. Somehow or other he had got a *Pilgrim's Progress*, from which he seemed to extract enormous pleasure. And then at the end, quite casually, he mentioned that he had been badly wounded and that his left leg would never be much use again.

After that I got frequent letters, and I wrote to him every week and sent him every kind of parcel I could think of. His letters used to make me both ashamed and happy. I had always banked on old Peter, and here he was behaving like an early Christian martyr—never a word of complaint, and just as cheery as if it were a winter morning on the high veld and we were off to ride down springbok. I knew what the loss of a leg must mean to him, for bodily fitness had always been his pride. The rest of life must have unrolled itself before him very drab and dusty to the grave. But he wrote as if he were on the top of his form and kept commiserating me on the discomforts of my job. The picture of that patient, gentle old fellow, hobbling about his compound and puzzling over his *Pilgrim's Progress*, a cripple for life after five months of blazing glory, would have stiffened the back of a jellyfish.

This last letter was horribly touching, for summer had come and the smell of the woods behind his prison reminded Peter of a place in the Woodbush, and one could read in every sentence the ache of exile. I sat on that stone wall and considered how trifling were the crumpled leaves in my bed of life compared with the thorns Peter and Blaikie had to lie on. I thought of Sandy far off in Mesopotamia, and old Blenkiron groaning with dyspepsia somewhere in America, and I considered that they were the kind of fellows who did their jobs without complaining. The result was that when I got up to go on I had recovered a manlier temper. I wasn't going to shame my friends or pick and choose my duty. I would trust myself to Providence, for, as Blenkiron used to say, Providence was all right if you gave him a chance.

It was not only Peter's letter that steadied and calmed me. Isham stood high up in a fold of the hills away from the main valley, and the road I was taking brought me over the ridge and back to the stream-side. I climbed through great beechwoods, which seemed in the twilight like some green place far below the sea, and then over a short stretch of hill pasture to the rim of the vale. All about me were little fields enclosed with walls of grey stone and full of dim sheep. Below were dusky woods around what I took to be Fosse Manor, for the great Roman Fosse Way, straight as an arrow, passed over the hills to the south and skirted its grounds. I could see the stream slipping among its water-meadows and could hear the plash of the weir. A tiny village settled in a crook of the hill, and its church-tower sounded seven with a curiously sweet chime. Otherwise there was no noise but the twitter of small birds and the night wind in the tops of the beeches.

In that moment I had a kind of revelation. I had a vision of what I had been fighting for, what we all were fighting for. It was peace, deep and holy and ancient, peace older than the oldest wars, peace which would endure when all our swords were hammered into ploughshares. It was more; for in that hour England first took hold of me. Before my country had been South Africa, and when I thought of home it had been the wide sun-steeped spaces of the veld or some scented glen of the Berg. But now I realized that I had a new home. I understood what a precious thing this little England was, how old and kindly and comforting, how wholly worth striving for. The freedom of an acre of her soil was cheaply bought by the blood of the best of us. I knew what it meant to be a poet, though for the life of me I could not have made a line of verse. For in that hour I had a prospect as if from a hilltop which made all the present troubles of the road seem of no account. I saw not only victory after war, but a new and happier world after victory, when I should inherit something of this English peace and wrap myself in it till the end of my days.

Very humbly and quietly, like a man walking through a cathedral, I went down the hill to the Manor lodge, and came to a door in an old red-brick facade, smothered in magnolias which smelt like hot lemons in the June dusk. The car from the inn had brought on my baggage, and presently I was dressing in a room which looked out on a water-garden. For the first time for more than a year I put on a starched shirt and a dinner-jacket, and as I dressed I could have sung from pure lightheartedness. I was in for some arduous job, and sometime that evening in that place I should get my marching orders. Someone would arrive—perhaps Bullivant—and read me the riddle. But whatever it was, I was ready for it, for my whole being had found a new purpose. Living in the trenches, you are apt to get your horizon narrowed down to the front line of enemy barbed wire on one side and the nearest rest billets on the other. But now I seemed to see beyond the fog to a happy country.

High-pitched voices greeted my ears as I came down the broad staircase, voices which scarcely accorded with the panelled walls and the austere family portraits; and when I found my hostesses in the hall I thought their looks still less in keeping with the house. Both ladies were on the wrong side of forty, but their dress was that of young girls. Miss Doria Wymondham was tall and thin with a mass of nondescript pale hair confined by a black velvet fillet. Miss Claire Wymondham was shorter and plumper and had done her best by ill-applied cosmetics to make herself look like a foreign *demi-mondaine*. They greeted me with the friendly casualness which I had long ago discovered was the right English manner towards your guests; as if they had just strolled in and billeted themselves, and you were quite glad to see them but mustn't be asked to trouble yourself further. The next second they were cooing like pigeons round a picture which a young man was holding up in the lamplight.

He was a tallish, lean fellow of round about thirty years, wearing grey flannels and shoes dusty from the country roads. His thin face was sallow as if from living indoors, and he had rather more hair on his head than most of us. In the glow of the lamp his features were very clear, and I examined them with interest, for, remember, I was expecting a stranger to give me orders. He had a long, rather strong chin and an obstinate mouth with peevish lines about its corners. But the remarkable feature was his eyes. I can best describe them by saying that they looked hot—not fierce or angry, but so restless that they seemed to ache physically and to want sponging with cold water.

They finished their talk about the picture—which was couched in a jargon of which I did not understand one word—and Miss Doria turned to me and the young man.

'My cousin Launcelot Wake—Mr Brand.'

We nodded stiffly and Mr Wake's hand went up to smooth his hair in a self-conscious gesture.

'Has Barnard announced dinner? By the way, where is Mary?'

'She came in five minutes ago and I sent her to change,' said Miss Claire. 'I won't have her spoiling the evening with that horrid uniform. She may masquerade as she likes out-of-doors, but this house is for civilized people.'

The butler appeared and mumbled something. 'Come along,' cried Miss Doria, 'for I'm sure you are starving, Mr Brand. And Launcelot has bicycled ten miles.'

The dining-room was very unlike the hall. The panelling had been stripped off, and the walls and ceiling were covered with a dead-black satiny paper on which hung the most monstrous pictures in large dull-gold frames. I could only see them dimly, but they seemed to be a mere riot of ugly colour. The young man nodded towards them. 'I see you have got the Degousses hung at last,' he said.

'How exquisite they are!' cried Miss Claire. 'How subtle and candid and brave! Doria and I warm our souls at their flame.'

Some aromatic wood had been burned in the room, and there was a queer sickly scent about. Everything in that place was strained and uneasy and abnormal—the candle shades on the table, the mass of faked china fruit in the centre dish, the gaudy hangings and the nightmarish walls. But the food was magnificent. It was the best dinner I had eaten since 1914.

'Tell me, Mr Brand,' said Miss Doria, her long white face propped on a much-beringed hand. 'You are one of us? You are in revolt against this crazy war?'

'Why, yes,' I said, remembering my part. 'I think a little common-sense would settle it right away.'

'With a little common-sense it would never have started,' said Mr Wake.

'Launcelot's a C.O., you know,' said Miss Doria.

I did not know, for he did not look any kind of soldier ... I was just about to ask him what he commanded, when I remembered that the letters stood also for 'Conscientious Objector,' and stopped in time.

At that moment someone slipped into the vacant seat on my right hand. I turned and saw the V.A.D. girl who had brought tea to Blaikie that afternoon at the hospital.

'He was exempted by his Department,' the lady went on, 'for he's a Civil Servant, and so he never had a chance of testifying in court, but no one has done better work for our cause. He is on the committee of the L.D.A., and questions have been asked about him in Parliament.'

The man was not quite comfortable at this biography. He glanced nervously at me and was going to begin some kind of explanation, when Miss Doria cut him short. 'Remember our rule, Launcelot. No turgid war controversy within these walls.'

I agreed with her. The war had seemed closely knit to the Summer landscape for all its peace, and to the noble old chambers of the Manor. But in that demented modish dining-room it was shriekingly incongruous.

Then they spoke of other things. Mostly of pictures or common friends, and a little of books. They paid no heed to me, which was fortunate, for I know nothing about these matters and didn't understand half the language. But once Miss Doria tried to bring me in.

They were talking about some Russian novel—a name like Leprous Souls—and she asked me if I had read it. By a curious chance I had. It had drifted somehow into our dug-out on the Scarpe, and after we had all stuck in the second chapter it had disappeared in the mud to which it naturally belonged. The lady praised its 'poignancy' and 'grave beauty'. I assented and congratulated myself on my second escape—for if the question had been put to me I should have described it as God-forgotten twaddle.

I turned to the girl, who welcomed me with a smile. I had thought her pretty in her V.A.D. dress, but now, in a filmy black gown and with her hair no longer hidden by a cap, she was the most ravishing thing you ever saw. And I observed something else. There was more than good looks in her young face. Her broad, low brow and her laughing eyes were amazingly intelligent. She had an uncanny power of making her eyes go suddenly grave and deep, like a glittering river narrowing into a pool.

'We shall never be introduced,' she said, 'so let me reveal myself. I'm Mary Lamington and these are my aunts ... Did you really like Leprous Souls?'

It was easy enough to talk to her. And oddly enough her mere presence took away the oppression I had felt in that room. For she belonged to the out-of-doors and to the old house and to the world at large. She belonged to the war, and to that happier world beyond it—a world which must be won by going through the struggle and not by shirking it, like those two silly ladies.

I could see Wake's eyes often on the girl, while he boomed and oraculated and the Misses Wymondham prattled. Presently the conversation seemed to leave the flowery paths of art and to verge perilously near forbidden topics. He began to abuse our generals in the field. I could not choose but listen. Miss Lamington's brows were slightly bent, as if in disapproval, and my own temper began to rise.

He had every kind of idiotic criticism—incompetence, faint-heartedness, corruption. Where he got the stuff I can't imagine, for the most grousing Tommy, with his leave stopped, never put together such balderdash. Worst of all he asked me to agree with him.

It took all my sense of discipline. 'I don't know much about the subject,' I said, 'but out in South Africa I did hear that the British leading was the weak point. I expect there's a good deal in what you say.'

It may have been fancy, but the girl at my side seemed to whisper 'Well done!'

Wake and I did not remain long behind before joining the ladies; I purposely cut it short, for I was in mortal fear lest I should lose my temper and spoil everything. I stood up with my back against the mantelpiece for as long as a man may smoke a cigarette, and I let him yarn to me, while I looked steadily at his face. By this time I was very clear that Wake was not the fellow to give me my instructions. He wasn't playing a game. He was a perfectly honest crank, but not a fanatic, for he wasn't sure of himself. He had somehow lost his self-respect and was trying to argue himself back into it. He had considerable brains, for the reasons he gave for differing from most of his countrymen were good so far as they went. I shouldn't have cared to take him on in public argument. If you had told me about such a fellow a week before I should have been sick at the thought of him. But now I didn't dislike him. I was bored by him and I was also tremendously sorry for him. You could see he was as restless as a hen.

When we went back to the hall he announced that he must get on the road, and commandeered Miss Lamington to help him find his bicycle. It appeared he was staying at an inn a dozen miles off for a couple of days' fishing, and the news somehow made me like him better. Presently the ladies of the house departed to bed for their beauty sleep and I was left to my own devices.

For some time I sat smoking in the hall wondering when the messenger would arrive. It was getting late and there seemed to be no preparation in the house to receive anybody. The butler came in with a tray of drinks and I asked him if he expected another guest that night.

'I 'adn't 'eard of it, sir,' was his answer. 'There 'asn't been a telegram that I know of, and I 'ave received no instructions.'

I lit my pipe and sat for twenty minutes reading a weekly paper. Then I got up and looked at the family portraits. The moon coming through the lattice invited me out-of-doors as a cure for my anxiety. It was after eleven o'clock, and I was still without any knowledge of my next step. It is a maddening business to be screwed up for an unpleasant job and to have the wheels of the confounded thing tarry.

Outside the house beyond a flagged terrace the lawn fell away, white in the moonshine, to the edge of the stream, which here had expanded into a miniature lake. By the water's edge was a little formal garden with grey stone parapets which now gleamed like dusky marble. Great wafts of scent rose from it, for the lilacs were scarcely over and the may was in full blossom. Out from the shade of it came suddenly a voice like a nightingale.

It was singing the old song 'Cherry Ripe', a common enough thing which I had chiefly known from barrel-organs. But heard in the scented moonlight it seemed to hold all the lingering magic of an elder England and of this hallowed countryside. I stepped inside the garden bounds and saw the head of the girl Mary.

She was conscious of my presence, for she turned towards me.

'I was coming to look for you,' she said, 'now that the house is quiet. I have something to say to you, General Hannay.'

She knew my name and must be somehow in the business. The thought entranced me.

'Thank God I can speak to you freely,' I cried. 'Who and what are you—living in that house in that kind of company?'

'My good aunts!' She laughed softly. 'They talk a great deal about their souls, but they really mean their nerves. Why, they are what you call my camouflage, and a very good one too.'

'And that cadaverous young prig?'

'Poor Launcelot! Yes—camouflage too—perhaps something a little more. You must not judge him too harshly.'

'But ... but—' I did not know how to put it, and stammered in my eagerness. 'How can I tell that you are the right person for me to speak to? You see I am under orders, and I have got none about you.'

'I will give You Proof,' she said. 'Three days ago Sir Walter Bullivant and Mr Macgillivray told you to come here tonight and to wait here for further instructions. You met them in the little smoking-room at the back of the Rota Club. You were bidden take the name of Cornelius Brand, and turn yourself from a successful general into a pacifist South African engineer. Is that correct?'

'Perfectly.'

'You have been restless all evening looking for the messenger to give you these instructions. Set your mind at ease. No messenger is coming. You will get your orders from me.'

'I could not take them from a more welcome source,' I said.

'Very prettily put. If you want further credentials I can tell you much about your own doings in the past three years. I can explain to you who don't need the explanation, every step in the business of the Black Stone. I think I could draw a pretty accurate map of your journey to Erzerum. You have a letter from Peter Pienaar in your pocket—I can tell you its contents. Are you willing to trust me?'

'With all my heart,' I said.

'Good. Then my first order will try you pretty hard. For I have no orders to give you except to bid you go and steep yourself in a particular kind of life. Your first duty is to get "atmosphere", as your friend Peter used to say. Oh, I will tell you where to go and how to behave. But I can't bid you do anything, only live idly with open eyes and ears till you have got the "feel" of the situation.'

She stopped and laid a hand on my arm.

'It won't be easy. It would madden me, and it will be a far heavier burden for a man like you. You have got to sink down deep into the life of the half-baked, the people whom this war hasn't touched or has touched in the wrong way, the people who split hairs all day and are engrossed in what you and I would call selfish little fads. Yes. People like my aunts and Launcelot, only for the most part in a different social grade. You won't live in an old manor like this, but among gimcrack little "arty" houses. You will hear everything you regard as sacred laughed at and condemned, and every kind of nauseous folly acclaimed, and you must hold your tongue and pretend to agree. You will have nothing in the world to do except to let the life soak into you, and, as I have said, keep your eyes and ears open.'

'But you must give me some clue as to what I should be looking for?'

'My orders are to give you none. Our chiefs—yours and mine—want you to go where you are going without any kind of *parti pris*. Remember we are still in the intelligence stage of the affair. The time hasn't yet come for a plan of campaign, and still less for action.'

'Tell me one thing,' I said. 'Is it a really big thing we're after?'

'A—really—big—thing,' she said slowly and very gravely. 'You and I and some hundred others are hunting the most dangerous man in all the world. Till we succeed everything that Britain does is crippled. If we fail or succeed too late the Allies may never win the victory which is their right. I will tell you one thing to cheer you. It is in some sort a race against time, so your purgatory won't endure too long.'

I was bound to obey, and she knew it, for she took my willingness for granted.

From a little gold satchel she selected a tiny box, and opening it extracted a thing like a purple wafer with a white St Andrew's Cross on it.

'What kind of watch have you? Ah, a hunter. Paste that inside the lid. Some day you may be called on to show it ... One other thing. Buy tomorrow a copy of the *Pilgrim's Progress* and get it by heart. You will receive letters and messages some day and the style of our friends is apt to be reminiscent of John Bunyan ... The car will be at the door tomorrow to catch the ten-thirty, and I will give you the address of the rooms that have been taken for you ... Beyond that I have nothing to say, except to beg you to play the part well and keep your temper. You behaved very nicely at dinner.'

I asked one last question as we said good night in the hall. 'Shall I see you again?'

'Soon, and often,' was the answer. 'Remember we are colleagues.'

I went upstairs feeling extraordinarily comforted. I had a perfectly beastly time ahead of me, but now it was all glorified and coloured with the thought of the girl who had sung 'Cherry Ripe' in the garden. I commended the wisdom of that old serpent Bullivant in the choice of his intermediary, for I'm hanged if I would have taken such orders from anyone else.

CHAPTER TWO

'The Village Named Morality'

UP on the high veld our rivers are apt to be strings of pools linked by muddy trickles—the most stagnant kind of watercourse you would look for in a day's journey. But presently they reach the edge of the plateau and are tossed down into the flats in noble ravines, and roll thereafter in full and sounding currents to the sea. So with the story I am telling. It began in smooth reaches, as idle as a mill-pond; yet the day soon came when I was in the grip of a torrent, flung breathless from rock to rock by a destiny which I could not control. But for the present I was in a backwater, no less than the Garden City of Biggleswick, where Mr Cornelius Brand, a South African gentleman visiting England on holiday, lodged in a pair of rooms in the cottage of Mr Tancred Jimson.

The house—or 'home' as they preferred to name it at Biggleswick—was one of some two hundred others which ringed a pleasant Midland common. It was badly built and oddly furnished; the bed was too short, the windows did not fit, the doors did not stay shut; but it was as clean as soap and water and scrubbing could make it. The three-quarters of an acre of garden were mainly devoted to the culture of potatoes, though under the parlour window Mrs Jimson had a plot of sweet-smelling herbs, and lines of lank sunflowers fringed the path that led to the front door. It was Mrs Jimson who received me as I descended from the station fly—a large red woman with hair bleached by constant exposure to weather, clad in a gown which, both in shape and material, seemed to have been modelled on a chintz curtain. She was a good kindly soul, and as proud as Punch of her house.

'We follow the simple life here, Mr Brand,' she said. 'You must take us as you find us.'

I assured her that I asked for nothing better, and as I unpacked in my fresh little bedroom with a west wind blowing in at the window I considered that I had seen worse quarters.

I had bought in London a considerable number of books, for I thought that, as I would have time on my hands, I might as well do something about my education. They were mostly English classics, whose names I knew but which I had never read, and they were all in a little flat-backed series at a shilling apiece. I arranged them on top of a chest of drawers, but I kept the *Pilgrim's Progress* beside my bed, for that was one of my working tools and I had got to get it by heart.

Mrs Jimson, who came in while I was unpacking to see if the room was to my liking, approved my taste. At our midday dinner she wanted to discuss books with me, and was so full of her own knowledge that I was able to conceal my ignorance.

'We are all labouring to express our personalities,' she informed me. 'Have you found your medium, Mr

Brand? is it to be the pen or the pencil? Or perhaps it is music? You have the brow of an artist, the frontal "bar of Michelangelo", you remember!'

I told her that I concluded I would try literature, but before writing anything I would read a bit more.

It was a Saturday, so Jimson came back from town in the early afternoon. He was a managing clerk in some shipping office, but you wouldn't have guessed it from his appearance. His city clothes were loose dark-grey flannels, a soft collar, an orange tie, and a soft black hat. His wife went down the road to meet him, and they returned hand-in-hand, swinging their arms like a couple of schoolchildren. He had a skimpy red beard streaked with grey, and mild blue eyes behind strong glasses. He was the most friendly creature in the world, full of rapid questions, and eager to make me feel one of the family. Presently he got into a tweed Norfolk jacket, and started to cultivate his garden. I took off my coat and lent him a hand, and when he stopped to rest from his labours—which was every five minutes, for he had no kind of physique—he would mop his brow and rub his spectacles and declaim about the good smell of the earth and the joy of getting close to Nature.

Once he looked at my big brown hands and muscular arms with a kind of wistfulness. 'You are one of the doers, Mr Brand,' he said, 'and I could find it in my heart to envy you. You have seen Nature in wild forms in far countries. Some day I hope you will tell us about your life. I must be content with my little corner, but happily there are no territorial limits for the mind. This modest dwelling is a watch-tower from which I look over all the world.'

After that he took me for a walk. We met parties of returning tennis-players and here and there a golfer. There seemed to be an abundance of young men, mostly rather weedy-looking, but with one or two well-grown ones who should have been fighting. The names of some of them Jimson mentioned with awe. An unwholesome youth was Aronson, the great novelist; a sturdy, bristling fellow with a fierce moustache was Letchford, the celebrated leader-writer of the Critic. Several were pointed out to me as artists who had gone one better than anybody else, and a vast billowy creature was described as the leader of the new Orientalism in England. I noticed that these people, according to Jimson, were all 'great', and that they all dabbled in something 'new'. There were quantities of young women, too, most of them rather badly dressed and inclining to untidy hair. And there were several decent couples taking the air like house-holders of an evening all the world Over. Most of these last were Jimson's friends, to whom he introduced me. They were his own class—modest folk, who sought for a coloured background to their prosaic city lives and found it in this odd settlement.

At supper I was initiated into the peculiar merits of Biggleswick.

'It is one great laboratory of thought,' said Mrs Jimson. 'It is glorious to feel that you are living among the eager, vital people who are at the head of all the newest movements, and that the intellectual history of England is being made in our studies and gardens. The war to us seems a remote and secondary affair. As someone has said, the great fights of the world are all fought in the mind.'

A spasm of pain crossed her husband's face. 'I wish I could feel it far away. After all, Ursula, it is the sacrifice of the young that gives people like us leisure and peace to think. Our duty is to do the best which is permitted to us, but that duty is a poor thing compared with what our young soldiers are giving! I may be quite wrong about the war ... I know I can't argue with Letchford. But I will not pretend to a superiority I do not feel.'

I went to bed feeling that in Jimson I had struck a pretty sound fellow. As I lit the candles on my dressing-table I observed that the stack of silver which I had taken out of my pockets when I washed before supper was top-heavy. It had two big coins at the top and sixpences and shillings beneath. Now it is one of my oddities that ever since I was a small boy I have arranged my loose coins symmetrically, with the smallest uppermost. That made me observant and led me to notice a second point. The English classics on the top of the chest of drawers were not in the order I had left them. Izaak Walton had got to the left of Sir Thomas Browne, and the poet Burns was wedged disconsolately between two volumes of Hazlitt.

Moreover a receipted bill which I had stuck in the *Pilgrim's Progress* to mark my place had been moved. Someone had been going through my belongings.

A moment's reflection convinced me that it couldn't have been Mrs Jimson. She had no servant and did the housework herself, but my things had been untouched when I left the room before supper, for she had come to tidy up before I had gone downstairs. Someone had been here while we were at supper, and had examined elaborately everything I possessed. Happily I had little luggage, and no papers save the new books and a bill or two in the name of Cornelius Brand. The inquisitor, whoever he was, had found nothing ... The incident gave me a good deal of comfort. It had been hard to believe that any mystery could exist in this public place, where people lived brazenly in the open, and wore their hearts on their sleeves and proclaimed their opinions from the rooftops. Yet mystery there must be, or an inoffensive stranger with a kit-bag would not have received these strange attentions. I made a practice after that of sleeping with my watch below my pillow, for inside the case was Mary Lamington's label. Now began a period of pleasant idle receptiveness. Once a week it was my custom to go up to London for the day to receive letters and instructions, if any should come. I had moved from my chambers in Park Lane, which I leased under my proper name, to a small flat in Westminster taken in the name of Cornelius Brand. The letters addressed to Park Lane were forwarded to Sir Walter, who sent them round under cover to my new address. For the rest I used to spend my mornings reading in the garden, and I discovered for the first time what a pleasure was to be got from old books. They recalled and amplified that vision I had seen from the Cotswold ridge, the revelation of the priceless heritage which is England. I imbibed a mighty quantity of history, but especially I liked the writers, like Walton, who got at the very heart of the English countryside. Soon, too, I found the *Pilgrim's Progress* not a duty but a delight. I discovered new jewels daily in the honest old story, and my letters to Peter began to be as full of it as Peter's own epistles. I loved, also, the songs of the Elizabethans, for they reminded me of the girl who had sung to me in the June night.

In the afternoons I took my exercise in long tramps along the good dusty English roads. The country fell away from Biggleswick into a plain of wood and pasture-land, with low hills on the horizon. The Place was sown with villages, each with its green and pond and ancient church. Most, too, had inns, and there I had many a draught of cool nutty ale, for the inn at Biggleswick was a reformed place which sold nothing but washy cider. Often, tramping home in the dusk, I was so much in love with the land that I could have sung with the pure joy of it. And in the evening, after a bath, there would be supper, when a rather fagged Jimson struggled between sleep and hunger, and the lady, with an artistic mutch on her untidy head, talked ruthlessly of culture.

Bit by bit I edged my way into local society. The Jimsons were a great help, for they were popular and had a nodding acquaintance with most of the inhabitants. They regarded me as a meritorious aspirant towards a higher life, and I was paraded before their friends with the suggestion of a vivid, if Philistine, past. If I had any gift for writing, I would make a book about the inhabitants of Biggleswick. About half were respectable citizens who came there for country air and low rates, but even these had a touch of queerness and had picked up the jargon of the place. The younger men were mostly Government clerks or writers or artists. There were a few widows with flocks of daughters, and on the outskirts were several bigger houses—mostly houses which had been there before the garden city was planted. One of them was brand-new, a staring villa with sham-antique timbering, stuck on the top of a hill among raw gardens. It belonged to a man called Moxon Ivery, who was a kind of academic pacificist and a great god in the place. Another, a quiet Georgian manor house, was owned by a London publisher, an ardent Liberal whose particular branch of business compelled him to keep in touch with the new movements. I used to see him hurrying to the station swinging a little black bag and returning at night with the fish for dinner.

I soon got to know a surprising lot of people, and they were the rummiest birds you can imagine. For example, there were the Weekeses, three girls who lived with their mother in a house so artistic that you broke your head whichever way you turned in it. The son of the family was a conscientious objector who had refused to do any sort of work whatever, and had got quodded for his pains. They were immensely proud of him and used to relate his sufferings in Dartmoor with a gusto which I thought rather heartless. Art was their great subject, and I am afraid they found me pretty heavy going. It was their fashion never to admire anything that was obviously beautiful, like a sunset or a pretty woman, but to find surprising loveliness in things which I thought hideous. Also they talked a language that was beyond me. This kind of conversation used to happen.—MISS WEEKES: 'Don't you admire Ursula Jimson?' SELF: 'Rather!' MISS W.: 'She is so John-esque in her lines.' SELF: 'Exactly!' MISS W.: 'And Tancred, too—he is so full of nuances.' SELF: 'Rather!' MISS W.: 'He suggests one of Degousse's countrymen.' SELF: 'Exactly!'

They hadn't much use for books, except some Russian ones, and I acquired merit in their eyes for having read Leprous Souls. If you talked to them about that divine countryside, you found they didn't give a rap for it and had never been a mile beyond the village. But they admired greatly the sombre effect of a train going into Marylebone station on a rainy day.

But it was the men who interested me most. Aronson, the novelist, proved on acquaintance the worst kind of blighter. He considered himself a genius whom it was the duty of the country to support, and he sponged on his wretched relatives and anyone who would lend him money. He was always babbling about his sins, and pretty squalid they were. I should like to have flung him among a few good old-fashioned full-blooded sinners of my acquaintance; they would have scared him considerably. He told me that he sought 'reality' and 'life' and 'truth', but it was hard to see how he could know much about them, for he spent half the day in bed smoking cheap cigarettes, and the rest sunning himself in the admiration of half-witted girls. The creature was tuberculous in mind and body, and the only novel of his I read, pretty well turned my stomach. Mr Aronson's strong point was jokes about the war. If he heard of any acquaintance who had joined up or was even doing war work his merriment knew no bounds. My fingers used to itch to box the little wretch's ears.

Letchford was a different pair of shoes. He was some kind of a man, to begin with, and had an excellent brain and the worst manners conceivable. He contradicted everything you said, and looked out for an argument as other people look for their dinner. He was a double-engined, high-speed pacificist, because he was the kind of cantankerous fellow who must always be in a minority. If Britain had stood out of the war he would have been a raving militarist, but since she was in it he had got to find reasons why she was wrong. And jolly good reasons they were, too. I couldn't have met his arguments if I had wanted to, so I sat docilely at his feet. The world was all crooked for Letchford, and God had created him with two left hands. But the fellow had merits. He had a couple of jolly children whom he adored, and he would walk miles with me on a Sunday, and spout poetry about the beauty and greatness of England. He was forty-five; if he had been thirty and in my battalion I could have made a soldier out of him.

There were dozens more whose names I have forgotten, but they had one common characteristic. They were puffed up with spiritual pride, and I used to amuse myself with finding their originals in the *Pilgrim's Progress*. When I tried to judge them by the standard of old Peter, they fell woefully short. They shut out the war from their lives, some out of funk, some out of pure levity of mind, and some because they were really convinced that the thing was all wrong. I think I grew rather popular in my role of the seeker after truth, the honest colonial who was against the war by instinct and was looking for instruction in the matter. They regarded me as a convert from an alien world of action which they secretly dreaded, though they affected to despise it. Anyhow they talked to me very freely, and before long I had all the pacifist arguments by heart. I made out that there were three schools. One objected to war altogether, and this had few adherents except Aronson and Weekes, C.O., now languishing in Dartmoor. The second thought that the Allies' cause was tainted, and that Britain had contributed as much as Germany to the catastrophe. This included all the adherents of the L.D.A.—or League of Democrats against Aggression—a very proud body. The third and much the largest, which embraced everybody else, held that we had fought long enough and that the business could now be settled by negotiation, since Germany had learned her lesson. I was myself a modest member of the last school, but I was gradually working my way up to the second, and I hoped with luck to qualify for the first. My acquaintances approved my progress. Letchford said I had a core of fanaticism in my slow nature, and that I would end by waving the red flag.

Spiritual pride and vanity, as I have said, were at the bottom of most of them, and, try as I might, I could find nothing very dangerous in it all. This vexed me, for I began to wonder if the mission which I had embarked on so solemnly were not going to be a fiasco. Sometimes they worried me beyond endurance. When the news of Messines came nobody took the slightest interest, while I was aching to tooth every detail of the great fight. And when they talked on military affairs, as Letchford and others did sometimes, it was difficult to keep from sending them all to the devil, for their amateur cocksureness would have riled Job. One had got to batten down the recollection of our fellows out there who were sweating blood to keep these fools snug. Yet I found it impossible to be angry with them for long, they were so babyishly innocent. Indeed, I couldn't help liking them, and finding a sort of quality in them. I had spent three years among soldiers, and the British regular, great follow that he is, has his faults. His discipline makes him in a funk of red-tape and any kind of superior authority. Now these people were quite honest and in a perverted way courageous. Letchford was, at any rate. I could no more have done what he did and got hunted off platforms by the crowd and hooted at by women in the streets than I could have written his leading articles.

All the same I was rather low about my job. Barring the episode of the ransacking of my effects the first night, I had not a suspicion of a clue or a hint of any mystery. The place and the people were as open and bright as a Y.M.C.A. hut. But one day I got a solid wad of comfort. In a corner of Letchford's paper, the *Critic*, I found a letter which was one of the steepest pieces of invective I had ever met with. The writer gave tongue like a beagle pup about the prostitution, as he called it, of American republicanism to the vices of European aristocracies. He declared that Senator La Follette was a much-misunderstood patriot, seeing that he alone spoke for the toiling millions who had no other friend. He was mad with President Wilson, and he prophesied a great awakening when Uncle Sam got up against John Bull in Europe and found out the kind of standpatter he was. The letter was signed 'John S. Blenkiron' and dated 'London, 3 July'.

The thought that Blenkiron was in England put a new complexion on my business. I reckoned I would see him soon, for he wasn't the man to stand still in his tracks. He had taken up the role he had played before he left in December 1915, and very right too, for not more than half a dozen people knew of the Erzerum affair, and to the British public he was only the man who had been fired out of the Savoy for talking treason. I had felt a bit lonely before, but now somewhere within the four corners of the island the best companion God ever made was writing nonsense with his tongue in his old cheek.

There was an institution in Biggleswick which deserves mention. On the south of the common, near the station, stood a red-brick building called the Moot Hall, which was a kind of church for the very undevout population. Undevout in the ordinary sense, I mean, for I had already counted twenty-seven varieties of religious conviction, including three Buddhists, a Celestial Hierarch, five Latter-day Saints, and about ten varieties of Mystic whose names I could never remember. The hall had been the gift of the publisher I have spoken of, and twice a week it was used for lectures and debates. The place was managed by a committee and was surprisingly popular, for it gave all the bubbling intellects a chance of airing their views. When you asked where somebody was and were told he was 'at Moot,' the answer was spoken in the respectful tone in which you would mention a sacrament.

I went there regularly and got my mind broadened to cracking point. We had all the stars of the New Movements. We had Doctor Chirk, who lectured on 'God', which, as far as I could make out, was a new name he had invented for himself. There was a woman, a terrible woman, who had come back from Russia with what she called a 'message of healing'. And to my joy, one night there was a great buck nigger who had a lot to say about 'Africa for the Africans'. I had a few words with him in Sesutu afterwards, and rather spoiled his visit. Some of the people were extraordinarily good, especially one jolly old fellow who talked about English folk songs and dances, and wanted us to set up a

Maypole. In the debates which generally followed I began to join, very coyly at first, but presently with some confidence. If my time at Biggleswick did nothing else it taught me to argue on my feet.

The first big effort I made was on a full-dress occasion, when Launcelot Wake came down to speak. Mr Ivery was in the chair—the first I had seen of him—a plump middle-aged man, with a colourless face and nondescript features. I was not interested in him till he began to talk, and then I sat bolt upright and took notice. For he was the genuine silver-tongue, the sentences flowing from his mouth as smooth as butter and as neatly dovetailed as a parquet floor. He had a sort of man-of-the-world manner, treating his opponents with condescending geniality, deprecating all passion and exaggeration and making you feel that his urbane statement must be right, for if he had wanted he could have put the case so much higher. I watched him, fascinated, studying his face carefully; and the thing that struck me was that there was nothing in it—nothing, that is to say, to lay hold on. It was simply nondescript, so almightily commonplace that that very fact made it rather remarkable.

Wake was speaking of the revelations of the Sukhomhnov trial in Russia, which showed that Germany had not been responsible for the war. He was jolly good at the job, and put as clear an argument as a first-class lawyer. I had been sweating away at the subject and had all the ordinary case at my fingers' ends, so when I got a chance of speaking I gave them a long harangue, with some good quotations I had cribbed out of the *Vossische Zeitung*, which Letchford lent me. I felt it was up to me to be extra violent, for I wanted to establish my character with Wake, seeing that he was a friend of Mary and Mary would know that I was playing the game. I got tremendously applauded, far more than the chief speaker, and after the meeting Wake came up to me with his hot eyes, and wrung my hand. 'You're coming on well, Brand,' he said, and then he introduced me to Mr Ivery. 'Here's a second and a better Smuts,' he said.

Ivery made me walk a bit of the road home with him. 'I am struck by your grip on these difficult problems, Mr Brand,' he told me. 'There is much I can tell you, and you may be of great value to our cause.' He asked me a lot of questions about my past, which I answered with easy mendacity. Before we parted he made me promise to come one night to supper.

Next day I got a glimpse of Mary, and to my vexation she cut me dead. She was walking with a flock of bare-headed girls, all chattering hard, and though she saw me quite plainly she turned away her eyes. I had been waiting for my cue, so I did not lift my hat, but passed on as if we were strangers. I reckoned it was part of the game, but that trifling thing annoyed me, and I spent a morose evening.

The following day I saw her again, this time talking sedately with Mr Ivery, and dressed in a very pretty summer gown, and a broad-brimmed straw hat with flowers in it. This time she stopped with a bright smile and held out her hand. 'Mr Brand, isn't it?' she asked with a pretty hesitation. And then, turning to her companion—'This is Mr Brand. He stayed with us last month in Gloucestershire.'

Mr Ivery announced that he and I were already acquainted. Seen in broad daylight he was a very personable fellow, somewhere between forty-five and fifty, with a middle-aged figure and a curiously young face. I noticed that there were hardly any lines on it, and it was rather that of a very wise child than that of a man. He had a pleasant smile which made his jaw and cheeks expand like indiarubber. 'You are coming to sup with me, Mr Brand,' he cried after me. 'On Tuesday after Moot. I have already written.' He whisked Mary away from me, and I had to content myself with contemplating her figure till it disappeared round a bend of the road.

Next day in London I found a letter from Peter. He had been very solemn of late, and very reminiscent of old days now that he concluded his active life was over. But this time he was in a different mood. '*I think,*' he wrote, '*that you and I will meet again soon, my old friend. Do you remember when we went after the big black-maned lion in the Rooirand and couldn't get on his track, and then one morning we woke up and said we would get him today?—*

and we did, but he very near got you first. I've had a feel these last days that we're both going down into the Valley to meet with Apolyon, and that the devil will give us a bad time, but anyhow we'll be together.'

I had the same kind of feel myself, though I didn't see how Peter and I were going to meet, unless I went out to the Front again and got put in the bag and sent to the same Boche prison. But I had an instinct that my time in Biggleswick was drawing to a close, and that presently I would be in rougher quarters. I felt quite affectionate towards the place, and took all my favourite walks, and drank my own health in the brew of the village inns, with a consciousness of saying goodbye. Also I made haste to finish my English classics, for I concluded I wouldn't have much time in the future for miscellaneous reading.

The Tuesday came, and in the evening I set out rather late for the Moot Hall, for I had been getting into decent clothes after a long, hot stride. When I reached the place it was pretty well packed, and I could only find a seat on the back benches. There on the platform was Ivery, and beside him sat a figure that thrilled every inch of me with affection and a wild anticipation. 'I have now the privilege,' said the chairman, 'of introducing to you the speaker whom we so warmly welcome, our fearless and indefatigable American friend, Mr Blenkiron.'

It was the old Blenkiron, but almightily changed. His stoutness had gone, and he was as lean as Abraham

Lincoln. Instead of a puffy face, his cheek-bones and jaw stood out hard and sharp, and in place of his former pasty colour his complexion had the clear glow of health. I saw now that he was a splendid figure of a man, and when he got to his feet every movement had the suppleness of an athlete in training. In that moment I realized that my serious business had now begun. My senses suddenly seemed quicker, my nerves tenser, my brain more active. The big game had started, and he and I were playing it together.

I watched him with strained attention. It was a funny speech, stuffed with extravagance and vehemence, not very well argued and terribly discursive. His main point was that Germany was now in a fine democratic mood and might well be admitted into a brotherly partnership—that indeed she had never been in any other mood, but had been forced into violence by the plots of her enemies. Much of it, I should have thought, was in stark defiance of the Defence of the Realm Acts, but if any wise Scotland Yard officer had listened to it he would probably have considered it harmless because of its contradictions. It was full of a fierce earnestness, and it was full of humour—long-drawn American metaphors at which that most critical audience roared with laughter. But it was not the kind of thing that they were accustomed to, and I could fancy what Wake would have said of it. The conviction grew upon me that Blenkiron was deliberately trying to prove himself an honest idiot. If so, it was a huge success. He produced on one the impression of the type of sentimental revolutionary who ruthlessly knifes his opponent and then weeps and prays over his tomb.

Just at the end he seemed to pull himself together and to try a little argument. He made a great point of the Austrian socialists going to Stockholm, going freely and with their Government's assent, from a country which its critics called an autocracy, while the democratic western peoples held back. 'I admit I haven't any real water-tight proof,' he said, 'but I will bet my bottom dollar that the influence which moved the Austrian Government to allow this embassy of freedom was the influence of Germany herself. And that is the land from which the Allied Pharisees draw in their skirts lest their garments be defiled!'

He sat down amid a good deal of applause, for his audience had not been bored, though I could see that some of them thought his praise of Germany a bit steep. It was all right in Biggleswick to prove Britain in the wrong, but it was a slightly different thing to extol the enemy. I was puzzled about his last point, for it was not of a piece with the rest of his discourse, and I was trying to guess at his purpose. The chairman referred to it in his concluding remarks. 'I am in a position,' he said, 'to bear out all that the lecturer has said. I can go further. I can assure him on the best authority that his surmise is correct, and that Vienna's decision to send delegates to Stockholm was largely dictated by representations from Berlin. I am given to understand that the fact has in the last few days been admitted in the Austrian Press.'

A vote of thanks was carried, and then I found myself shaking hands with Ivery while Blenkiron stood a yard off, talking to one of the Misses Weekes. The next moment I was being introduced.

'Mr Brand, very pleased to meet you,' said the voice I knew so well. 'Mr Ivery has been telling me about you, and I guess we've got something to say to each other. We're both from noo countries, and we've got to teach the old nations a little horse-sense.'

Mr Ivery's car—the only one left in the neighbourhood—carried us to his villa, and presently we were seated in a brightly-lit dining-room. It was not a pretty house, but it had the luxury of an expensive hotel, and the supper we had was as good as any London restaurant. Gone were the old days of fish and toast and boiled milk. Blenkiron squared his shoulders and showed himself a noble trencherman.

'A year ago,' he told our host, 'I was the meanest kind of dyspeptic. I had the love of righteousness in my heart, but I had the devil in my stomach. Then I heard stories about the Robson Brothers, the star surgeons way out west in White Springs, Nebraska. They were reckoned the neatest hands in the world at carving up a man and removing devilments from his intestines. Now, sir, I've always fought pretty shy of surgeons, for I considered that our Maker never intended His handiwork to be reconstructed like a bankrupt Dago railway. But by that time I was feeling so almighty wretched that I could have paid a man to put a bullet through my head. "There's no other way," I said to myself. "Either you forget your religion and your miserable cowardice and get cut up, or it's you for the Golden Shore." So I set my teeth and journeyed to White Springs, and the Brothers had a look at my duodenum. They saw that the darned thing wouldn't do, so they sidetracked it and made a noo route for my noo-trition traffic. It was the cunningest piece of surgery since the Lord took a rib out of the side of our First Parent. They've got a mighty fine way of charging, too, for they take five per cent of a man's income, and it's all one to them whether he's a Meat King or a clerk on twenty dollars a week. I can tell you I took some trouble to be a very rich man last year.'

All through the meal I sat in a kind of stupor. I was trying to assimilate the new Blenkiron, and drinking in the comfort of his heavenly drawl, and I was puzzling my head about Ivery. I had a ridiculous notion that I had seen him before, but, delve as I might into my memory, I couldn't place him. He was the incarnation of the commonplace, a comfortable middle-class sentimentalist, who patronized pacificism out of vanity, but was very careful not to dip his hands too far. He was always damping down Blenkiron's volcanic utterances. 'Of course, as you know, the other side have an argument which I find rather hard to meet ...' 'I can sympathize with patriotism, and even with jingoism, in certain moods, but I always come back to this difficulty.' 'Our opponents are not ill-meaning so much as ill-judging,'—

these were the sort of sentences he kept throwing in. And he was full of quotations from private conversations he had had with every sort of person—including members of the Government. I remember that he expressed great admiration for Mr Balfour.

Of all that talk, I only recalled one thing clearly, and I recalled it because Blenkiron seemed to collect his wits and try to argue, just as he had done at the end of his lecture. He was speaking about a story he had heard from someone, who had heard it from someone else, that Austria in the last week of July 1914 had accepted Russia's proposal to hold her hand and negotiate, and that the Kaiser had sent a message to the Tsar saying he agreed. According to his story this telegram had been received in Petrograd, and had been re-written, like Bismarck's Ems telegram, before it reached the Emperor. He expressed his disbelief in the yarn. 'I reckon if it had been true,' he said, 'we'd have had the right text out long ago. They'd have kept a copy in Berlin. All the same I did hear a sort of rumour that some kind of message of that sort was published in a German paper.'

Mr Ivery looked wise. 'You are right,' he said. 'I happen to know that it has been published. You will find it in the *Wiener Zeitung*.'

'You don't say?' he said admiringly. 'I wish I could read the old tombstone language. But if I could they wouldn't let me have the papers.'

'Oh yes they would.' Mr Ivery laughed pleasantly. 'England has still a good share of freedom. Any respectable person can get a permit to import the enemy press. I'm not considered quite respectable, for the authorities have a narrow definition of patriotism, but happily I have respectable friends.'

Blenkiron was staying the night, and I took my leave as the clock struck twelve. They both came into the hall to see me off, and, as I was helping myself to a drink, and my host was looking for my hat and stick, I suddenly heard Blenkiron's whisper in my ear. 'London ... the day after tomorrow,' he said. Then he took a formal farewell. 'Mr Brand, it's been an honour for me, as an American citizen, to make your acquaintance, sir. I will consider myself fortunate if we have an early reunion. I am stopping at Claridge's Ho-tel, and I hope to be privileged to receive you there.'

CHAPTER THREE

The Reflections of a Cured Dyspeptic

Thirty-five hours later I found myself in my rooms in Westminster. I thought there might be a message for me there, for I didn't propose to go and call openly on Blenkiron at Claridge's till I had his instructions. But there was no message—only a line from Peter, saying he had hopes of being sent to Switzerland. That made me realize that he must be pretty badly broken up.

Presently the telephone bell rang. It was Blenkiron who spoke. 'Go down and have a talk with your brokers about the War Loan. Arrive there about twelve o'clock and don't go upstairs till you have met a friend. You'd better have a quick luncheon at your club, and then come to Traill's bookshop in the Haymarket at two. You can get back to Biggleswick by the 5.16.'

I did as I was bid, and twenty minutes later, having travelled by Underground, for I couldn't raise a taxi, I approached the block of chambers in Leadenhall Street where dwelt the respected firm who managed my investments. It was still a few minutes before noon, and as I slowed down a familiar figure came out of the bank next door.

Ivery beamed recognition. 'Up for the day, Mr Brand?' he asked. 'I have to see my brokers,' I said, 'read the South African papers in my club, and get back by the 5.16. Any chance of your company?'

'Why, yes—that's my train. *Au revoir.* We meet at the station.' He bustled off, looking very smart with his neat clothes and a rose in his button-hole.

I lunched impatiently, and at two was turning over some new books in Traill's shop with an eye on the street-door behind me. It seemed a public place for an assignation. I had begun to dip into a big illustrated book on flower-gardens when an assistant came up. 'The manager's compliments, sir, and he thinks there are some old works of travel upstairs that might interest you.' I followed him obediently to an upper floor lined with every kind of volume and with tables littered with maps and engravings. 'This way, sir,' he said, and opened a door in the wall concealed by bogus book-backs. I found myself in a little study, and Blenkiron sitting in an armchair smoking.

He got up and seized both my hands. 'Why, Dick, this is better than good noos. I've heard all about your exploits since we parted a year ago on the wharf at Liverpool. We've both been busy on our own jobs, and there was no way of keeping you wise about my doings, for after I thought I was cured I got worse than hell inside, and, as I told you, had to get the doctor-men to dig into me. After that I was playing a pretty dark game, and had to get down and out of decent society. But, holy Mike! I'm a new man. I used to do my work with a sick heart and a taste in my mouth like a graveyard, and now I can eat and drink what I like and frolic round like a colt. I wake up every morning whistling and thank the good God that I'm alive. It was a bad day for Kaiser when I got on the cars for White Springs.'

'This is a rum place to meet,' I said, 'and you brought me by a roundabout road.'

He grinned and offered me a cigar.

'There were reasons. It don't do for you and me to advertise our acquaintance in the street. As for the shop, I've owned it for five years. I've a taste for good reading, though you wouldn't think it, and it tickles me to hand it out across the counter ... First, I want to hear about Biggleswick.'

'There isn't a great deal to it. A lot of ignorance, a large slice of vanity, and a pinch or two of wrong-headed honesty—these are the ingredients of the pie. Not much real harm in it. There's one or two dirty literary gents who should be in a navvies' battalion, but they're about as dangerous as yellow Kaffir dogs. I've learned a lot and got all the arguments by heart, but you might plant a Biggleswick in every shire and it wouldn't help the Boche. I can see where the danger lies all the same. These fellows talked academic anarchism, but the genuine article is somewhere about and to find it you've got to look in the big industrial districts. We had faint echoes of it in Biggleswick. I mean that the really dangerous fellows are those who want to close up the war at once and so get on with their blessed class war, which cuts across nationalities. As for being spies and that sort of thing, the Biggleswick lads are too callow.'

'Yes,' said Blenkiron reflectively. 'They haven't got as much sense as God gave to geese. You're sure you didn't hit against any heavier metal?'

'Yes. There's a man called Launcelot Wake, who came down to speak once. I had met him before. He has the makings of a fanatic, and he's the more dangerous because you can see his conscience is uneasy. I can fancy him bombing a Prime Minister merely to quiet his own doubts.'

'So,' he said. 'Nobody else?'

I reflected. 'There's Mr Ivery, but you know him better than I. I shouldn't put much on him, but I'm not precisely certain, for I never had a chance of getting to know him.'

'Ivery,' said Blenkiron in surprise. 'He has a hobby for half-baked youth, just as another rich man might fancy orchids or fast trotters. You sure can place him right enough.'

'I dare say. Only I don't know enough to be positive.'

He sucked at his cigar for a minute or so. 'I guess, Dick, if I told you all I've been doing since I reached these shores you would call me a romancer. I've been way down among the toilers. I did a spell as unskilled dilooted labour in the Barrow shipyards. I was barman in a hotel on the Portsmouth Road, and I put in a black month driving a taxicab in the city of London. For a while I was the accredited correspondent of the Noo York Sentinel and used to go with the rest of the bunch to the pow-wows of under-secretaries of State and War Office generals. They censored my stuff so cruel that the paper fired me. Then I went on a walking-tour round England and sat for a fortnight in a little farm in Suffolk. By and by I came back to Claridge's and this bookshop, for I had learned most of what I wanted.

'I had learned,' he went on, turning his curious, full, ruminating eyes on me, 'that the British working-man is about the soundest piece of humanity on God's earth. He grumbles a bit and jibs a bit when he thinks the Government are giving him a crooked deal, but he's gotten the patience of Job and the sand of a gamecock. And he's gotten humour too, that tickles me to death. There's not much trouble in that quarter for it's he and his kind that's beating the Hun ... But I picked up a thing or two besides that.'

He leaned forward and tapped me on the knee. 'I reverence the British Intelligence Service. Flies don't settle on it to any considerable extent. It's got a mighty fine mesh, but there's one hole in that mesh, and it's our job to mend it. There's a high-powered brain in the game against us. I struck it a couple of years ago when I was hunting Dumba and Albert, and I thought it was in Noo York, but it wasn't. I struck its working again at home last year and located its head office in Europe. So I tried Switzerland and Holland, but only bits of it were there. The centre of the web where the old spider sits is right here in England, and for six months I've been shadowing that spider. There's a gang to help, a big gang, and a clever gang, and partly an innocent gang. But there's only one brain, and it's to match that that the Robson Brothers settled my duodenum.'

I was listening with a quickened pulse, for now at last I was getting to business.

'What is he—international socialist, or anarchist, or what?' I asked.

'Pure-blooded Boche agent, but the biggest-sized brand in the catalogue—bigger than Steinmeier or old Bismarck's Staubier. Thank God I've got him located ... I must put you wise about some things.'

He lay back in his rubbed leather armchair and yarned for twenty minutes. He told me how at the beginning of the war Scotland Yard had had a pretty complete register of enemy spies, and without making any fuss had just tidied them away. After that, the covey having been broken up, it was a question of picking off stray birds. That had taken some doing. There had been all kinds of inflammatory stuff around, Red Masons and international anarchists, and, worst of all, international finance-touts, but they had mostly been ordinary cranks and rogues, the tools of the Boche agents rather than agents themselves. However, by the middle of 1915 most of the stragglers had been gathered in. But there remained loose ends, and towards the close of last year somebody was very busy combining these ends into a net. Funny cases cropped up of the leakage of vital information. They began to be bad about October 1916, when the Hun submarines started on a special racket. The enemy suddenly appeared possessed of a knowledge which we thought to be shared only by half a dozen officers. Blenkiron said he was not surprised at the leakage, for there's always a lot of people who hear things they oughtn't to. What surprised him was that it got so quickly to the enemy.

Then after last February, when the Hun submarines went in for frightfulness on a big scale, the thing grew desperate. Leakages occurred every week, and the business was managed by people who knew their way about, for they avoided all the traps set for them, and when bogus news was released on purpose, they never sent it. A convoy which had been kept a deadly secret would be attacked at the one place where it was helpless. A carefully prepared defensive plan would be checkmated before it could be tried. Blenkiron said that there was no evidence that a single brain was behind it all, for there was no similarity in the cases, but he had a strong impression all the time that it was the work of one man.

We managed to close some of the bolt-holes, but we couldn't put our hands near the big ones. 'By this time,' said he, 'I reckoned I was about ready to change my methods. I had been working by what the highbrows call induction, trying to argue up from the deeds to the doer. Now I tried a new lay, which was to calculate down from the doer to the deeds. They call it deduction. I opined that somewhere in this island was a gentleman whom we will call Mr X, and that, pursuing the line of business he did, he must have certain characteristics. I considered very carefully just what sort of personage he must be. I had noticed that his device was apparently the Double Bluff. That is to say, when he had two courses open to him, A and B, he pretended he was going to take B, and so got us guessing that he would try A. Then he took B after all. So I reckoned that his camouflage must correspond to this little idiosyncrasy. Being a Boche agent, he wouldn't pretend to be a hearty patriot, an honest old blood-and-bones Tory. That would be only the Single Bluff. I considered that he would be a pacifist, cunning enough just to keep inside the law, but with the eyes of the police on him. He would write books which would not be allowed to be exported. He would get himself disliked in the popular papers, but all the mugwumps would admire his moral courage. I drew a mighty fine picture to myself of just the man I expected to find. Then I started out to look for him.'

Blenkiron's face took on the air of a disappointed child. 'It was no good. I kept barking up the wrong tree and wore myself out playing the sleuth on white-souled innocents.'

'But you've found him all right,' I cried, a sudden suspicion leaping into my brain.

'He's found,' he said sadly, 'but the credit does not belong to John S. Blenkiron. That child merely muddied the pond. The big fish was left for a young lady to hook.'

'I know,' I cried excitedly. 'Her name is Miss Mary Lamington.'

He shook a disapproving head. 'You've guessed right, my son, but you've forgotten your manners. This is a rough business and we won't bring in the name of a gently reared and pure-minded young girl. If we speak to her at all we call her by a pet name out of the *Pilgrim's Progress* ... Anyhow she hooked the fish, though he isn't landed. D'you see any light?'

'Ivery,' I gasped.

'Yes. Ivery. Nothing much to look at, you say. A common, middle-aged, pie-faced, golf-playing high-brow, that you wouldn't keep out of a Sunday school. A touch of the drummer, too, to show he has no dealings with your effete aristocracy. A languishing silver-tongue that adores the sound of his own voice. As mild, you'd say, as curds and cream.'

Blenkiron got out of his chair and stood above me. 'I tell you, Dick, that man makes my spine cold. He hasn't a drop of good red blood in him. The dirtiest apache is a Christian gentleman compared to Moxon Ivery. He's as cruel as a snake and as deep as hell. But, by God, he's got a brain below his hat. He's hooked and we're playing him, but Lord knows if he'll ever be landed!'

'Why on earth don't you put him away?' I asked.

'We haven't the proof—legal proof, I mean; though there's buckets of the other kind. I could put up a morally certain case, but he'd beat me in a court of law. And half a hundred sheep would get up in Parliament and bleat about persecution. He has a graft with every collection of cranks in England, and with all the geese that cackle about the liberty of the individual when the Boche is ranging about to enslave the world. No, sir, that's too dangerous a game! Besides, I've a better in hand, Moxon Ivery is the best-accredited member of this State. His *dossier* is the completest thing outside the Recording Angel's little note-book. We've taken up his references in every corner of the globe and they're all as right as Morgan's balance sheet. From these it appears he's been a high-toned citizen ever since he was in short-clothes. He was raised in Norfolk, and there are people living who remember his father. He was educated at Melton School and his name's in the register. He was in business in Valparaiso, and there's enough evidence to write three volumes of his innocent life there. Then he came home with a modest competence two years before the war, and has been in the public eye ever since. He was Liberal candidate for a London constitooency and he has decorated the board of every institootion formed for the amelioration of mankind. He's got enough alibis to choke a boa constrictor, and they're water-tight and copper-bottomed, and they're mostly damned lies ... But you can't beat him at that stunt. The man's the superbest actor that ever walked the earth. You can see it in his face. It isn't a face, it's a mask. He could make himself look like Shakespeare or Julius Caesar or Billy Sunday or Brigadier-General Richard Hannay if he wanted to. He hasn't got any personality either—he's got fifty, and there's no one he could call his own. I reckon when the devil gets the handling of him at last he'll have to put sand on his claws to keep him from slipping through.'

Blenkiron was settled in his chair again, with one leg hoisted over the side.

'We've closed a fair number of his channels in the last few months. No, he don't suspect me. The world knows nothing of its greatest men, and to him I'm only a Yankee peace-crank, who gives big subscriptions to loony societies and will travel a hundred miles to let off steam before any kind of audience. He's been to see me at Claridge's and I've arranged that he shall know all my record. A darned bad record it is too, for two years ago I was violent pro-British before I found salvation and was requested to leave England. When I was home last I was officially anti-war, when I wasn't stretched upon a bed of pain. Mr Moxon Ivery don't take any stock in John S.

Blenkiron as a serious proposition. And while I've been here I've been so low down in the social scale and working in so many devious ways that he can't connect me up ... As I was saying, we've cut most of his wires, but the biggest we haven't got at. He's still sending stuff out, and mighty compromising stuff it is. Now listen close, Dick, for we're coming near your own business.'

It appeared that Blenkiron had reason to suspect that the channel still open had something to do with the North. He couldn't get closer than that, till he heard from his people that a certain Abel Gresson had turned up in Glasgow from the States. This Gresson he discovered was the same as one Wrankester, who as a leader of the Industrial Workers of the World had been mixed up in some ugly cases of sabotage in Colorado. He kept his news to himself, for he didn't want the police to interfere, but he had his own lot get into touch with Gresson and shadow him closely. The man was very discreet but very mysterious, and he would disappear for a week at a time, leaving no trace. For some unknown reason—he couldn't explain why—Blenkiron had arrived at the conclusion that Gresson was in touch with Ivery, so he made experiments to prove it.

'I wanted various cross-bearings to make certain, and I got them the night before last. My visit to Biggleswick was good business.'

'I don't know what they meant,' I said, 'but I know where they came in. One was in your speech when you spoke of the Austrian socialists, and Ivery took you up about them. The other was after supper when he quoted the *Wiener Zeitung*.'

'You're no fool, Dick,' he said, with his slow smile. 'You've hit the mark first shot. You know me and you could follow my process of thought in those remarks. Ivery, not knowing me so well, and having his head full of just that sort of argument, saw nothing unusual. Those bits of noos were pumped into Gresson that he might pass them on. And he did pass them on—to Ivery. They completed my chain.'

'But they were commonplace enough things which he might have guessed for himself.'

'No, they weren't. They were the nicest tit-bits of political noos which all the cranks have been reaching after.'

'Anyhow, they were quotations from German papers. He might have had the papers themselves earlier than you thought.'

'Wrong again. The paragraph never appeared in the *Wiener Zeitung*. But we faked up a torn bit of that noospaper, and a very pretty bit of forgery it was, and Gresson, who's a kind of a scholar, was allowed to have it. He passed it on. Ivery showed it me two nights ago. Nothing like it ever sullied the columns of Boche journalism. No, it was a perfectly final proof ... Now, Dick, it's up to you to get after Gresson.'

'Right,' I said. 'I'm jolly glad I'm to start work again. I'm getting fat from lack of exercise. I suppose you want me to catch Gresson out in some piece of blackguardism and have him and Ivery snugly put away.'

'I don't want anything of the kind,' he said very slowly and distinctly. 'You've got to attend very close to your instructions, I cherish these two beauties as if they were my own white-headed boys. I wouldn't for the world interfere with their comfort and liberty. I want them to go on corresponding with their friends. I want to give them every facility.'

He burst out laughing at my mystified face.

'See here, Dick. How do we want to treat the Boche? Why, to fill him up with all the cunningest lies and get him to act on them. Now here is Moxon Ivery, who has always given them good information. They trust him absolutely, and we would be fools to spoil their confidence. Only, if we can find out Moxon's methods, we can arrange to use them ourselves and send noos in his name which isn't quite so genooine. Every word he dispatches goes straight to the Grand High Secret General Staff, and old Hindenburg and Ludendorff put towels round their heads and cipher it out. We want to encourage them to go on doing it. We'll arrange to send true stuff that don't matter, so as they'll continue to trust him, and a few selected falsehoods that'll matter like hell. It's a game you can't play for ever, but with luck I propose to play it long enough to confuse Fritz's little plans.'

His face became serious and wore the air that our corps commander used to have at the big pow-wow before a push.

'I'm not going to give you instructions, for you're man enough to make your own. But I can give you the general hang of the situation. You tell Ivery you're going North to inquire into industrial disputes at first hand. That will seem to him natural and in line with your recent behaviour. He'll tell his people that you're a guileless colonial who feels disgruntled with Britain, and may come in useful. You'll go to a man of mine in Glasgow, a red-hot agitator who chooses that way of doing his bit for his country. It's a darned hard way and darned dangerous. Through him you'll get in touch with Gresson, and you'll keep alongside that bright citizen. Find out what he is doing, and get a chance of following him. He must never suspect you, and for that purpose you must be very near the edge of the law yourself. You go up there as an unabashed pacifist and you'll live with folk that will turn your stomach. Maybe you'll have to break some of these two-cent rules the British Government have invented to defend the realm, and it's up to you not to get caught out ... Remember, you'll get no help from me. You've got to wise up about Gresson with the whole forces of the British State arrayed officially against you. I guess it's a steep proposition, but you're man enough to make good.'

As we shook hands, he added a last word. 'You must take your own time, but it's not a case for slouching. Every day that passes Ivery is sending out the worst kind of poison. The Boche is blowing up for a big campaign in the field, and a big effort to shake the nerve and confuse the judgement of our civilians. The whole earth's war-weary, and we've about reached the danger-point. There's pretty big stakes hang on you, Dick, for things are getting mighty delicate.'

I purchased a new novel in the shop and reached St Pancras in time to have a cup of tea at the buffet. Ivery was at the bookstall buying an evening paper. When we got into the carriage he seized my *Punch* and kept laughing and calling my attention to the pictures. As I looked at him, I thought that he made a perfect picture of the citizen turned countryman, going back of an evening to his innocent home. Everything was right—his neat tweeds, his light spats, his spotted neckcloth, and his Aquascutum.

Not that I dared look at him much. What I had learned made me eager to search his face, but I did not dare show any increased interest. I had always been a little off-hand with him, for I had never much liked him, so I had to keep on the same manner. He was as merry as a grig, full of chat and very friendly and amusing. I remember he picked up the book I had brought off that morning to read in the train—the second volume of Hazlitt's *Essays*, the last of my English classics—and discoursed so wisely about books that I wished I had spent more time in his company at Biggleswick.

'Hazlitt was the academic Radical of his day,' he said. 'He is always lashing himself into a state of theoretical fury over abuses he has never encountered in person. Men who are up against the real thing save their breath for action.'

That gave me my cue to tell him about my journey to the North. I said I had learned a lot in Biggleswick, but I wanted to see industrial life at close quarters. 'Otherwise I might become like Hazlitt,' I said.

He was very interested and encouraging. 'That's the right way to set about it,' he said. 'Where were you thinking of going?'

I told him that I had half thought of Barrow, but decided to try Glasgow, since the Clyde seemed to be a warm corner.

'Right,' he said. 'I only wish I was coming with you. It'll take you a little while to understand the language. You'll find a good deal of senseless bellicosity among the workmen, for they've got parrot-cries about the war as they used to have parrot-cries about their labour politics.

But there's plenty of shrewd brains and sound hearts too. You must write and tell me your conclusions.'

It was a warm evening and he dozed the last part of the journey. I looked at him and wished I could see into the mind at the back of that mask-like face. I counted for nothing in his eyes, not even enough for him to want to make me a tool, and I was setting out to try to make a tool of him. It sounded a forlorn enterprise. And all the while I was puzzled with a persistent sense of recognition. I told myself it was idiocy, for a man with a face like that must have hints of resemblance to a thousand people. But the idea kept nagging at me till we reached our destination.

As we emerged from the station into the golden evening I saw Mary Lamington again. She was with one of the Weekes girls, and after the Biggleswick fashion was bareheaded, so that the sun glinted from her hair. Ivery swept his hat off and made her a pretty speech, while I faced her steady eyes with the expressionlessness of the stage conspirator.

'A charming child,' he observed as we passed on. 'Not without a touch of seriousness, too, which may yet be touched to noble issues.'

I considered, as I made my way to my final supper with the Jimsons, that the said child was likely to prove a sufficiently serious business for Mr Moxon Ivery before the game was out.

CHAPTER FOUR

Andrew Amos

I took the train three days later from King's Cross to Edinburgh. I went to the Pentland Hotel in Princes Street and left there a suit-case containing some clean linen and a change of clothes. I had been thinking the thing out, and had come to the conclusion that I must have a base somewhere and a fresh outfit. Then in well-worn tweeds and with no more luggage than a small trench kit-bag, I descended upon the city of Glasgow.

I walked from the station to the address which Blenkiron had given me. It was a hot summer evening, and the streets were filled with bareheaded women and weary-looking artisans. As I made my way down the Dumbarton Road I was amazed at the number of able-bodied fellows about, considering that you couldn't stir a mile on any British front without bumping up against a Glasgow battalion. Then I realized that there were such things as munitions and ships, and I wondered no more.

A stout and dishevelled lady at a close-mouth directed me to Mr Amos's dwelling. 'Twa stairs up. Andra will be in noo, havin' his tea. He's no yin for overtime. He's generally hame on the chap of six.' I ascended the stairs with a sinking heart, for like all South Africans I have a horror of dirt. The place was pretty filthy, but at each landing there were two doors with well-polished handles and brass plates. On one I read the name of Andrew Amos.

A man in his shirt-sleeves opened to me, a little man, without a collar, and with an unbuttoned waistcoat. That was all I saw of him in the dim light, but he held out a paw like a gorilla's and drew me in.

The sitting-room, which looked over many chimneys to a pale yellow sky against which two factory stalks stood out sharply, gave me light enough to observe him fully. He was about five feet four, broad-shouldered, and with a great towsy head of grizzled hair. He wore spectacles, and his face was like some old-fashioned Scots minister's, for he had heavy eyebrows and whiskers which joined each other under his jaw, while his chin and enormous upper lip were clean-shaven. His eyes were steely grey and very solemn, but full of smouldering energy. His voice was enormous and would have shaken the walls if he had not had the habit of speaking with half-closed lips. He had not a sound tooth in his head.

A saucer full of tea and a plate which had once contained ham and eggs were on the table. He nodded towards them and asked me if I had fed.

'Ye'll no eat onything? Well, some would offer ye a dram, but this house is staunch teetotal. I doot ye'll have to try the nearest public if ye're thirsty.'

I disclaimed any bodily wants, and produced my pipe, at which he started to fill an old clay. 'Mr Brand's your name?' he asked in his gusty voice. 'I was expectin' ye, but Dod! man ye're late!'

He extricated from his trousers pocket an ancient silver watch, and regarded it with disfavour. 'The dashed thing has stoppit. What do ye make the time, Mr Brand?'

He proceeded to prise open the lid of his watch with the knife he had used to cut his tobacco, and, as he examined the works, he turned the back of the case towards me. On the inside I saw pasted Mary Lamington's purple-and-white wafer.

I held my watch so that he could see the same token. His keen eyes, raised for a second, noted it, and he shut his own with a snap and returned it to his pocket. His manner lost its wariness and became almost genial.

'Ye've come up to see Glasgow, Mr Brand? Well, it's a steerin' bit, and there's honest folk bides in it, and some not so honest. They tell me ye're from South Africa. That's a long gait away, but I ken something aboot South Africa, for I had a cousin's son oot there for his lungs. He was in a shop in Main Street, Bloomfountain. They called him Peter Dobson. Ye would maybe mind of him.'

Then he discoursed of the Clyde. He was an incomer, he told me, from the Borders, his native place being the town of Galashiels, or, as he called it, 'Gawly'. 'I began as a powerloom tuner in Stavert's mill. Then my father dee'd and I took up his trade of jiner. But it's no world nowadays for the sma' independent business, so I cam to the Clyde and learned a shipwright's job. I may say I've become a leader in the trade, for though I'm no an official of the Union, and not likely to be, there's no man's word carries more weight than mine. And the Goavernment kens that, for they've sent me on commissions up and down the land to look at wuds and report on the nature of the timber. Bribery, they think it is, but Andrew Amos is not to be bribit. He'll have his say about any Goavernment on earth, and tell them to their face what he thinks of them. Ay, and he'll fight the case of the workingman against his oppressor, should it be the Goavernment or the fatted calves they ca' Labour Members. Ye'll have heard tell o' the shop stewards, Mr Brand?'

I admitted I had, for I had been well coached by Blenkiron in the current history of industrial disputes.

'Well, I'm a shop steward. We represent the rank and file against office-bearers that have lost the confidence o' the workingman. But I'm no socialist, and I would have ye keep mind of that. I'm yin o' the old Border radicals, and I'm not like to change. I'm for individual liberty and equal rights and chances for all men. I'll no more bow down before a Dagon of a Goavernment official than before the Baal of a feckless Tweedside laird. I've to keep my views to mysel', for thae young lads are all drucken-daft with their wee books about Cawpital and Collectivism and a wheen long senseless words I wouldna fyle my tongue with. Them and their socialism! There's more gumption in a page of John Stuart Mill than in all that foreign trash. But, as I say, I've got to keep a quiet sough, for the world is gettin' socialism now like the measles. It all comes of a defective eddication.'

'And what does a Border radical say about the war?' I asked.

He took off his spectacles and cocked his shaggy brows at me. 'I'll tell ye, Mr Brand. All that was bad in all that I've ever wrestled with since I cam to years o' discretion—Tories and lairds and manufacturers and publicans and the Auld Kirk—all that was bad, I say, for there were orra bits of decency, ye'll find in the Germans full measure pressed down and running over. When the war started, I considered the subject calmly for three days, and then I said: "Andra Amos, ye've found the enemy at last. The ones ye fought before were in a manner o' speakin' just misguided friends. It's either you or the Kaiser this time, my man!"'

His eyes had lost their gravity and had taken on a sombre ferocity. 'Ay, and I've not wavered. I got a word early in the business as to the way I could serve my country best. It's not been an easy job, and there's plenty of honest folk the day will give me a bad name. They think I'm stirrin' up the men at home and desertin' the cause o' the lads at the front. Man, I'm keepin' them straight. If I didna fight their battles on a sound economic isshue, they would take the dorts and be at the mercy of the first blagyird that preached revolution. Me and my like are safety-valves, if ye follow me. And dinna you make ony mistake, Mr Brand. The men that are agitating for a rise in wages are not for peace. They're fighting for the lads overseas as much as for themselves. There's not yin in a thousand that wouldna sweat himself blind to beat the Germans. The Goavernment has made mistakes, and maun be made to pay for them. If it were not so, the men would feel like a moose in a trap, for they would have no way to make their grievance felt. What for should the big man double his profits and the small man be ill set to get his ham and egg on Sabbath mornin'? That's the meaning o' Labour unrest, as they call it, and it's a good thing, says I, for if Labour didna get its leg over the traces now and then, the spunk o' the land would be dead in it, and Hindenburg could squeeze it like a rotten aipple.'

I asked if he spoke for the bulk of the men.

'For ninety per cent in ony ballot. I don't say that there's not plenty of riff-raff—the pint-and-a-dram gentry and the soft-heads that are aye reading bits of newspapers, and muddlin' their wits with foreign whigmaleeries. But the average man on the Clyde, like the average man in ither places, hates just three things, and that's the Germans, the profiteers, as they call them, and the Irish. But he hates the Germans first.'

'The Irish!' I exclaimed in astonishment.

'Ay, the Irish,' cried the last of the old Border radicals. 'Glasgow's stinkin' nowadays with two things, money and Irish. I mind the day when I followed Mr Gladstone's Home Rule policy, and used to threep about the noble, generous, warm-hearted sister nation held in a foreign bondage. My Goad! I'm not speakin' about Ulster, which is a dour, ill-natured den, but our own folk all the same. But the men that will not do a hand's turn to help the war and take the chance of our necessities to set up a bawbee rebellion are hateful to Goad and man. We treated them like pet lambs and that's the thanks we get. They're coming over here in thousands to tak the jobs of the lads that are doing their duty. I was speakin' last week to a widow woman that keeps a wee dairy down the Dalmarnock Road. She has two sons, and both in the airmy, one in the Cameronians and one a prisoner in Germany. She was telling me that she could not keep goin' any more, lacking the help of the boys, though she had worked her fingers to the bone. "Surely it's a crool job, Mr Amos," she says, "that the Goavernment should tak baith my laddies, and I'll maybe never see them again, and let the Irish gang free and tak the bread frae our mouth. At the gasworks across the road they took on a hundred Irish last week, and every yin o' them as young and well set up as you would ask to see. And my wee Davie, him that's in Germany, had aye a weak chest, and Jimmy was troubled wi' a bowel complaint. That's surely no justice!". ...'

He broke off and lit a match by drawing it across the seat of his trousers. 'It's time I got the gas lichtit. There's some men coming here at half-ten.'

As the gas squealed and flickered in the lighting, he sketched for me the coming guests. 'There's Macnab and Niven, two o' my colleagues. And there's Gilkison of the Boiler-fitters, and a lad Wilkie—he's got consumption, and writes wee bits in the papers. And there's a queer chap o' the name o' Tombs—they tell me he comes frae Cambridge, and is a kind of a professor there—anyway he's more stuffed wi' havers than an egg wi' meat. He telled me he was here to get at the heart o' the workingman, and I said to him that he would hae to look a bit further than the sleeve o' the workin'-man's jaicket. There's no muckle in his head, poor soul. Then there'll be Tam Norie, him that edits our weekly paper—*Justice for All.* Tam's a humorist and great on Robert Burns, but he hasna the balance o' a dwinin' teetotum ... Ye'll understand, Mr Brand, that I keep my mouth shut in such company, and don't express my own views more than is absolutely necessary. I criticize whiles, and that gives me a name of whunstane common-sense, but I never let my tongue wag. The feck o' the lads comin' the night are not the real workingman—they're just the froth on the pot, but it's the froth that will be useful to you. Remember they've heard tell o' ye already, and ye've some sort o' reputation to keep up.'

'Will Mr Abel Gresson be here?' I asked.

'No,' he said. 'Not yet. Him and me havena yet got to the point o' payin' visits. But the men that come will be Gresson's friends and they'll speak of ye to him. It's the best kind of introduction ye could seek.'

The knocker sounded, and Mr Amos hastened to admit the first comers. These were Macnab and Wilkie: the one a decent middle-aged man with a fresh-washed face and a celluloid collar, the other a round-shouldered youth, with lank hair and the large eyes and luminous skin which are the marks of phthisis. 'This is Mr Brand boys, from South Africa,' was Amos's presentation. Presently came Niven, a bearded giant, and Mr Norie, the editor, a fat dirty fellow smoking a rank cigar. Gilkison of the Boiler-fitters, when he arrived, proved to be a pleasant young man in spectacles who spoke with an educated voice and clearly belonged to a slightly different social scale. Last came Tombs, the Cambridge professor, a lean youth with a sour mouth and eyes that reminded me of Launcelot Wake.

'Ye'll no be a mawgnate, Mr Brand, though ye come from South Africa,' said Mr Norie with a great guffaw.

'Not me. I'm a working engineer,' I said. 'My father was from Scotland, and this is my first visit to my native country, as my friend Mr Amos was telling you.'

The consumptive looked at me suspiciously. 'We've got two—three of the comrades here that the cawpitalist Government expelled from the Transvaal. If ye're our way of thinking, ye will maybe ken them.'

I said I would be overjoyed to meet them, but that at the time of the outrage in question I had been working on a mine a thousand miles further north.

Then ensued an hour of extraordinary talk. Tombs in his sing-song namby-pamby University voice was concerned to get information. He asked endless questions, chiefly of Gilkison, who was the only one who really understood his language. I thought I had never seen anyone quite so fluent and so futile, and yet there was a kind of feeble violence in him like a demented sheep. He was engaged in venting some private academic spite against society, and I thought that in a revolution he would be the class of lad I would personally conduct to the nearest lamp-post. And all the while Amos and Macnab and Niven carried on their own conversation about the affairs of their society, wholly impervious to the tornado raging around them.

It was Mr Norie, the editor, who brought me into the discussion.

'Our South African friend is very blate,' he said in his boisterous way. 'Andra, if this place of yours wasn't so damned teetotal and we had a dram apiece, we might get his tongue loosened. I want to hear what he's got to say about the war. You told me this morning he was sound in the faith.'

'I said no such thing,' said Mr Amos. 'As ye ken well, Tam Norie, I don't judge soundness on that matter as you judge it. I'm for the war myself, subject to certain conditions that I've often stated. I know nothing of Mr Brand's opinions, except that he's a good democrat, which is more than I can say of some o' your friends.'

'Hear to Andra,' laughed Mr Norie. 'He's thinkin' the inspector in the Socialist State would be a waur kind of awristocrat then the Duke of Buccleuch. Weel, there's maybe something in that. But about the war he's wrong. Ye ken my views, boys. This war was made by the cawpitalists, and it has been fought by the workers, and it's the workers that maun have the ending of it. That day's comin' very near. There are those that want to spin it out till Labour is that weak it can be pit in chains for the rest o' time. That's the manoeuvre we're out to prevent. We've got to beat the Germans, but it's the workers that has the right to judge when the enemy's beaten and not the cawpitalists. What do you say, Mr Brand?'

Mr Norie had obviously pinned his colours to the fence, but he gave me the chance I had been looking for. I let them have my views with a vengeance, and these views were that for the sake of democracy the war must be ended. I flatter myself I put my case well, for I had got up every rotten argument and I borrowed largely from Launcelot Wake's armoury. But I didn't put it too well, for I had a very exact notion of the impression I wanted to produce. I must seem to be honest and in earnest, just a bit of a fanatic, but principally a hard-headed businessman who knew when the time had come to make a deal. Tombs kept interrupting me with imbecile questions, and I had to sit on him. At the end Mr Norie hammered with his pipe on the table.

'That'll sort ye, Andra. Ye're entertain' an angel unawares. What do ye say to that, my man?'

Mr Amos shook his head. 'I'll no deny there's something in it, but I'm not convinced that the Germans have got enough of a wheepin'.' Macnab agreed with him; the others were with me. Norie was for getting me to write an article for his paper, and the consumptive wanted me to address a meeting.

'Wull ye say a' that over again the morn's night down at our hall in Newmilns Street? We've got a lodge meeting o' the I.W.B., and I'll make them pit ye in the programme.' He kept his luminous eyes, like a sick dog's, fixed on me, and I saw that I had made one ally. I told him I had come to Glasgow to learn and not to teach, but I would miss no chance of testifying to my faith.

'Now, boys, I'm for my bed,' said Amos, shaking the dottle from his pipe. 'Mr Tombs, I'll conduct ye the morn over the Brigend works, but I've had enough clavers for one evening. I'm a man that wants his eight hours' sleep.'

The old fellow saw them to the door, and came back to me with the ghost of a grin in his face.

'A queer crowd, Mr Brand! Macnab didna like what ye said. He had a laddie killed in Gallypoly, and he's no lookin' for peace this side the grave. He's my best friend in Glasgow. He's an elder in the Gaelic kirk in the Cowcaddens, and I'm what ye call a free-thinker, but we're wonderful agreed on the fundamentals. Ye spoke your bit verra well, I must admit. Gresson will hear tell of ye as a promising recruit.'

'It's a rotten job,' I said.

'Ay, it's a rotten job. I often feel like vomiting over it mysel'. But it's no for us to complain. There's waur jobs oot in France for better men ... A word in your ear, Mr Brand. Could ye not look a bit more sheepish? Ye stare folk ower straight in the een, like a Hieland sergeant-major up at Maryhill Barracks.' And he winked slowly and grotesquely with his left eye.

He marched to a cupboard and produced a black bottle and glass. 'I'm blue-ribbon myself, but ye'll be the better of something to tak the taste out of your mouth. There's Loch Katrine water at the pipe there ... As I was saying, there's not much ill in that lot. Tombs is a black offence, but a dominie's a dominie all the world over.

They may crack about their Industrial Workers and the braw things they're going to do, but there's a wholesome dampness about the tinder on Clydeside. They should try Ireland.'

'Supposing,' I said, 'there was a really clever man who wanted to help the enemy. You think he could do little good by stirring up trouble in the shops here?'

'I'm positive.'

'And if he were a shrewd fellow, he'd soon tumble to that?'

'Ay.'

'Then if he still stayed on here he would be after bigger game—something really dangerous and damnable?'

Amos drew down his brows and looked me in the face. 'I see what ye're ettlin' at. Ay! That would be my conclusion. I came to it weeks syne about the man ye'll maybe meet the morn's night.'

Then from below the bed he pulled a box from which he drew a handsome flute. 'Ye'll forgive me, Mr Brand, but I aye like a tune before I go to my bed. Macnab says his prayers, and I have a tune on the flute, and the principle is just the same.'

So that singular evening closed with music—very sweet and true renderings of old Border melodies like 'My Peggy is a young thing', and 'When the kye come hame'. I fell asleep with a vision of Amos, his face all puckered up at the mouth and a wandering sentiment in his eye, recapturing in his dingy world the emotions of a boy.

The widow-woman from next door, who acted as house-keeper, cook, and general factotum to the establishment, brought me shaving water next morning, but I had to go without a bath. When I entered the kitchen I found no one there, but while I consumed the inevitable ham and egg, Amos arrived back for breakfast. He brought with him the morning's paper.

'The *Herald* says there's been a big battle at Eepers,' he announced.

I tore open the sheet and read of the great attack of 31 July which was spoiled by the weather. 'My God!' I cried. 'They've got St Julien and that dirty Frezenberg ridge ... and Hooge ... and Sanctuary Wood. I know every inch of the damned place....'

'Mr Brand,' said a warning voice, 'that'll never do. If our friends last night heard ye talk like that ye might as well tak the train back to London ... They're speakin' about ye in the yards this morning. Ye'll get a good turnout at your meeting the night, but they're Sayin' that the polis will interfere. That mightna be a bad thing, but I trust ye to show discretion, for ye'll not be muckle use to onybody if they jyle ye in Duke Street. I hear Gresson will be there with a fraternal message from his lunatics in America ... I've arranged that ye go down to Tam Norie this afternoon and give him a hand with his bit paper. Tam will tell ye the whole clash o' the West country, and I look to ye to keep him off the drink. He's aye arguin' that writin' and drinkin' gang thegither, and quotin' Robert Burns, but the creature has a wife and five bairns dependin' on him.'

I spent a fantastic day. For two hours I sat in Norie's dirty den, while he smoked and orated, and, when he remembered his business, took down in shorthand my impressions of the Labour situation in South Africa for his rag. They were fine breezy impressions, based on the most whole-hearted ignorance, and if they ever reached the Rand I wonder what my friends there made of Cornelius Brand, their author. I stood him dinner in an indifferent eating-house in a street off the Broomielaw, and thereafter had a drink with him in a public-house, and was introduced to some of his less reputable friends.

About tea-time I went back to Amos's lodgings, and spent an hour or so writing a long letter to Mr Ivery. I described to him everybody I had met, I gave highly coloured views of the explosive material on the Clyde, and I deplored the lack of clearheadedness in the progressive forces. I drew an elaborate picture of Amos, and deduced from it that the Radicals were likely to be a bar to true progress. 'They have switched their old militancy,' I wrote, 'on to another track, for with them it is a matter of conscience to be always militant.' I finished up with some very crude remarks on economics culled from the table-talk of the egregious Tombs. It was the kind of letter which I hoped would establish my character in his mind as an industrious innocent.

Seven o'clock found me in Newmilns Street, where I was seized upon by Wilkie. He had put on a clean collar for the occasion and had partially washed his thin face. The poor fellow had a cough that shook him like the walls of a power-house when the dynamos are going.

He was very apologetic about Amos. 'Andra belongs to a past worrld,' he said. 'He has a big reputation in his society, and he's a fine fighter, but he has no kind of Vision, if ye understand me. He's an auld Gladstonian, and that's done and damned in Scotland. He's not a Modern, Mr Brand, like you and me. But tonight ye'll meet one or two chaps that'll be worth your while to ken. Ye'll maybe no go quite as far as them, but ye're on the same road. I'm hoping for the day when we'll have oor Councils of Workmen and Soldiers like the Russians all over the land and dictate our terms to the pawrasites in Pawrliament. They tell me, too, the boys in the trenches are comin' round to our side.'

We entered the hall by a back door, and in a little waiting-room I was introduced to some of the speakers.

They were a scratch lot as seen in that dingy place. The chairman was a shop-steward in one of the Societies, a fierce little rat of a man, who spoke with a cockney accent and addressed me as 'Comrade'. But one of them roused my liveliest interest. I heard the name of Gresson, and turned to find a fellow of about thirty-five, rather sprucely dressed, with a flower in his buttonhole. 'Mr Brand,' he said, in a rich American voice which recalled Blenkiron's. 'Very pleased to meet you, sir. We have come from remote parts of the globe to be present at this gathering.' I noticed that he had reddish hair, and small bright eyes, and a nose with a droop like a Polish Jew's.

As soon as we reached the platform I saw that there was going to be trouble. The hall was packed to the door, and in all the front half there was the kind of audience I expected to see—working-men of the political type who before the war would have thronged to party meetings. But not all the crowd at the back had come to listen. Some were scallawags, some looked like better-class clerks out for a spree, and there was a fair quantity of khaki. There were also one or two gentlemen not strictly sober.

The chairman began by putting his foot in it. He said we were there tonight to protest against the continuation of the war and to form a branch of the new British Council of Workmen and Soldiers. He told them with a fine mixture of metaphors that we had got to take the reins into our own hands, for the men who were running the war had their own axes to grind and were marching to oligarchy through the blood of the workers. He added that we had no quarrel with Germany half as bad as we had with our own capitalists. He looked forward to the day when British soldiers would leap from their trenches and extend the hand of friendship to their German comrades.

'No me!' said a solemn voice. 'I'm not seekin' a bullet in my wame,'—at which there was laughter and cat-calls.

Tombs followed and made a worse hash of it. He was determined to speak, as he would have put it, to democracy in its own language, so he said 'hell' several times, loudly but without conviction. Presently he slipped into the manner of the lecturer, and the audience grew restless. 'I propose to ask myself a question—' he began, and from the back of the hall came—'And a damned sully answer ye'll get.' After that there was no more Tombs.

I followed with extreme nervousness, and to my surprise got a fair hearing. I felt as mean as a mangy dog on a cold morning, for I hated to talk rot before soldiers—especially before a couple of Royal Scots Fusiliers, who, for all I knew, might have been in my own brigade. My line was the plain, practical, patriotic man, just come from the colonies, who looked at things with fresh eyes, and called for a new deal. I was very moderate, but to justify my appearance there I had to put in a wild patch or two, and I got these by impassioned attacks on the Ministry of Munitions. I mixed up a little mild praise of the Germans, whom I said I had known all over the world for decent fellows. I received little applause, but no marked dissent, and sat down with deep thankfulness.

The next speaker put the lid on it. I believe he was a noted agitator, who had already been deported. Towards him there was no lukewarmness, for one half of the audience cheered wildly when he rose, and the other half hissed and groaned. He began with whirlwind abuse of the idle rich, then of the middle-classes (he called them the 'rich man's flunkeys'), and finally of the Government. All that was fairly well received, for it is the fashion of the Briton to run down every Government and yet to be very averse to parting from it. Then he started on the soldiers and slanged the officers ('gentry pups' was his name for them), and the generals, whom he accused of idleness, of cowardice, and of habitual intoxication. He told us that our own kith and kin were sacrificed in every battle by leaders who had not the guts to share their risks. The Scots Fusiliers looked perturbed, as if they were in doubt of his meaning. Then he put it more plainly. 'Will any soldier deny that the men are the barrage to keep the officers' skins whole?'

'That's a bloody lee,' said one of the Fusilier jocks.

The man took no notice of the interruption, being carried away by the torrent of his own rhetoric, but he had not allowed for the persistence of the interrupter.

The jock got slowly to his feet, and announced that he wanted satisfaction. 'If ye open your dirty gab to blagyird honest men, I'll come up on the platform and wring your neck.'

At that there was a fine old row, some crying out 'Order', some 'Fair play', and some applauding. A Canadian at the back of the hall started a song, and there was an ugly press forward. The hall seemed to be moving up from the back, and already men were standing in all the passages and right to the edge of the platform. I did not like the look in the eyes of these new-comers, and among the crowd I saw several who were obviously plain-clothes policemen.

The chairman whispered a word to the speaker, who continued when the noise had temporarily died down. He kept off the army and returned to the Government, and for a little sluiced out pure anarchism. But he got his foot in it again, for he pointed to the Sinn Feiners as examples of manly independence. At that, pandemonium broke loose, and he never had another look in. There were several fights going on in the hall between the public and courageous supporters of the orator.

Then Gresson advanced to the edge of the platform in a vain endeavour to retrieve the day. I must say he did it uncommonly well. He was clearly a practised speaker, and for a moment his appeal 'Now, boys, let's cool down a bit and talk sense,' had an effect. But the mischief had been done, and the crowd was surging round the lonely redoubt where we sat. Besides, I could see that for all his clever talk the meeting did not like the look of him. He was as mild as a turtle dove, but they wouldn't stand for it. A missile hurtled past my nose, and I saw a rotten cabbage envelop the baldish head of the ex-deportee. Someone reached out a long arm and grabbed a chair, and with it took the legs from Gresson. Then the lights suddenly went out, and we retreated in good order by the platform door with a yelling crowd at our heels.

It was here that the plain-clothes men came in handy. They held the door while the ex-deportee was smuggled out by some side entrance. That class of lad would soon cease to exist but for the protection of the law which he would abolish. The rest of us, having less to fear, were suffered to leak into Newmilns Street. I found myself next to Gresson, and took his arm. There was something hard in his coat pocket.

Unfortunately there was a big lamp at the point where we emerged, and there for our confusion were the Fusilier jocks. Both were strung to fighting pitch, and were determined to have someone's blood. Of me they took no notice, but Gresson had spoken after their ire had been roused, and was marked out as a victim. With a howl of joy they rushed for him.

I felt his hand steal to his side-pocket. 'Let that alone, you fool,' I growled in his ear.

'Sure, mister,' he said, and the next second we were in the thick of it.

It was like so many street fights I have seen—an immense crowd which surged up around us, and yet left a clear ring. Gresson and I got against the wall on the side-walk, and faced the furious soldiery. My intention was to do as little as possible, but the first minute convinced me that my companion had no idea how to use his fists, and I was mortally afraid that he would get busy with the gun in his pocket. It was that fear that brought me into the scrap. The jocks were sportsmen every bit of them, and only one advanced to the combat. He hit Gresson a clip on the jaw with his left, and but for the wall would have laid him out. I saw in the lamplight the vicious gleam in the American's eye and the twitch of his hand to his pocket. That decided me to interfere and I got in front of him.

This brought the second jock into the fray. He was a broad, thickset fellow, of the adorable bandy-legged stocky type that I had seen go through the Railway Triangle at Arras as though it were blotting-paper. He had some notion of fighting, too, and gave me a rough time, for I had to keep edging the other fellow off Gresson.

'Go home, you fool,' I shouted. 'Let this gentleman alone. I don't want to hurt you.'

The only answer was a hook-hit which I just managed to guard, followed by a mighty drive with his right which I dodged so that he barked his knuckles on the wall. I heard a yell of rage, and observed that Gresson seemed to have kicked his assailant on the shin. I began to long for the police.

Then there was that swaying of the crowd which betokens the approach of the forces of law and order. But they were too late to prevent trouble. In self-defence I had to take my jock seriously, and got in my blow when he had overreached himself and lost his balance. I never hit anyone so unwillingly in my life. He went over like a poled ox, and measured his length on the causeway.

I found myself explaining things politely to the constables. 'These men objected to this gentleman's speech at the meeting, and I had to interfere to protect him. No, no! I don't want to charge anybody. It was all a misunderstanding.' I helped the stricken jock to rise and offered him ten bob for consolation.

He looked at me sullenly and spat on the ground. 'Keep your dirty money,' he said. 'I'll be even with ye yet, my man—you and that red-headed scab. I'll mind the looks of ye the next time I see ye.'

Gresson was wiping the blood from his cheek with a silk handkerchief. 'I guess I'm in your debt, Mr Brand,' he said. 'You may bet I won't forget it.'

I returned to an anxious Amos. He heard my story in silence and his only comment was—'Well done the Fusiliers!'

'It might have been worse, I'll not deny,' he went on. 'Ye've established some kind of a claim upon Gresson, which may come in handy ... Speaking about Gresson, I've news for ye. He's sailing on Friday as purser in the *Tobermory*. The *Tobermory's* a boat that wanders every month up the West Highlands as far as Stornoway. I've arranged for ye to take a trip on that boat, Mr Brand.'

I nodded. 'How did you find out that?' I asked.

'It took me some finding,' he said dryly, 'but I've ways and means. Now I'll not trouble ye with advice, for ye ken your job as well as me. But I'm going north myself the morn to look after some of the Ross-shire wuds, and I'll be in the way of getting telegrams at the Kyle. Ye'll keep that in mind. Keep in mind, too, that I'm a great reader of the *Pilgrim's Progress* and that I've a cousin of the name of Ochterlony.'

CHAPTER FIVE

Various Doings in the West

The *Tobermory* was no ship for passengers. Its decks were littered with a hundred oddments, so that a man could barely walk a step without tacking, and my bunk was simply a shelf in the frowsty little saloon, where the odour of ham and eggs hung like a fog. I joined her at Greenock and took a turn on deck with the captain after tea, when he told me the names of the big blue hills to the north. He had a fine old copper-coloured face and side-whiskers like an archbishop, and, having spent all his days beating up the western seas, had as many yarns in his head as Peter himself.

'On this boat,' he announced, 'we don't ken what a day may bring forth. I may put into Colonsay for twa hours and bide there three days. I get a telegram at Oban and the next thing I'm awa ayont Barra. Sheep's the difficult business. They maun be fetched for the sales, and they're dooms slow to lift. So ye see it's not what ye call a pleasure trip, Maister Brand.'

Indeed it wasn't, for the confounded tub wallowed like a fat sow as soon as we rounded a headland and got the weight of the south-western wind. When asked my purpose, I explained that I was a colonial of Scots extraction, who was paying his first visit to his fatherland and wanted to explore the beauties of the West

Highlands. I let him gather that I was not rich in this world's goods.

'Ye'll have a passport?' he asked. 'They'll no let ye go north o' Fort William without one.'

Amos had said nothing about passports, so I looked blank.

'I could keep ye on board for the whole voyage,' he went on, 'but ye wouldna be permitted to land. If ye're seekin' enjoyment, it would be a poor job sittin' on this deck and admirin' the works o' God and no allowed to step on the pier-head. Ye should have applied to the military gentlemen in Glesca. But ye've plenty o' time to make up your mind afore we get to Oban. We've a heap o' calls to make Mull and Islay way.'

The purser came up to inquire about my ticket, and greeted me with a grin.

'Ye're acquaint with Mr Gresson, then?' said the captain. 'Weel, we're a cheery wee ship's company, and that's the great thing on this kind o' job.'

I made but a poor supper, for the wind had risen to half a gale, and I saw hours of wretchedness approaching. The trouble with me is that I cannot be honestly sick and get it over. Queasiness and headache beset me and there is no refuge but bed. I turned into my bunk, leaving the captain and the mate smoking shag not six feet from my head, and fell into a restless sleep. When I woke the place was empty, and smelt vilely of stale tobacco and cheese. My throbbing brows made sleep impossible, and I tried to ease them by staggering upon deck. I saw a clear windy sky, with every star as bright as a live coal, and a heaving waste of dark waters running to ink-black hills. Then a douche of spray caught me and sent me down the companion to my bunk again, where I lay for hours trying to make a plan of campaign.

I argued that if Amos had wanted me to have a passport he would have provided one, so I needn't bother my head about that. But it was my business to keep alongside Gresson, and if the boat stayed a week in some port and he went off ashore, I must follow him. Having no passport I would have to be always dodging trouble, which would handicap my movements and in all likelihood make me more conspicuous than I wanted. I guessed that Amos had denied me the passport for the very reason that he wanted Gresson to think me harmless. The area of danger would, therefore, be the passport country, somewhere north of Fort William.

But to follow Gresson I must run risks and enter that country. His suspicions, if he had any, would be lulled if I left the boat at Oban, but it was up to me to follow overland to the north and hit the place where the *Tobermory* made a long stay. The confounded tub had no plans; she wandered about the West Highlands looking for sheep and things; and the captain himself could give me no time-table of her voyage. It was incredible that

Gresson should take all this trouble if he did not know that at some place—and the right place—he would have time to get a spell ashore. But I could scarcely ask Gresson for that information, though I determined to cast a wary fly over him. I knew roughly the *Tobermory's* course—through the Sound of Islay to Colonsay; then up the east side of Mull to Oban; then through the Sound of Mull to the islands with names like cocktails, Rum and Eigg and Coll; then to Skye; and then for the Outer Hebrides. I thought the last would be the place, and it seemed madness to leave the boat, for the Lord knew how I should get across the Minch. This consideration upset all my plans again, and I fell into a troubled sleep without coming to any conclusion.

Morning found us nosing between Jura and Islay, and about midday we touched at a little port, where we unloaded some cargo and took on a couple of shepherds who were going to Colonsay. The mellow afternoon and the good smell of salt and heather got rid of the dregs of my queasiness, and I spent a profitable hour on the pier-head with a guide-book called *Baddely's Scotland*, and one of Bartholomew's maps. I was beginning to think that Amos might be able to tell me something, for a talk with the captain had suggested that the *Tobermory* would not dally long in the neighbourhood of Rum and Eigg. The big droving season was scarcely on yet, and sheep for the Oban market would be lifted on the return journey. In that case Skye was the first place to watch, and if I could get wind of any big cargo waiting there I would be able to make a plan. Amos was somewhere near the Kyle, and that was across the narrows from Skye. Looking at the map, it seemed to me that, in spite of being passportless, I might be able somehow to make my way up through Morvern and Arisaig to the latitude of Skye. The difficulty would be to get across the strip of sea, but there must be boats to beg, borrow or steal.

I was poring over Baddely when Gresson sat down beside me. He was in a good temper, and disposed to talk, and to my surprise his talk was all about the beauties of the countryside. There was a kind of apple-green light over everything; the steep heather hills cut into the sky like purple amethysts, while beyond the straits the western ocean stretched its pale molten gold to the sunset. Gresson waxed lyrical over the scene. 'This just about puts me right inside, Mr Brand. I've got to get away from that little old town pretty frequent or I begin to moult like a canary. A man feels a man when he gets to a place that smells as good as this. Why in hell do we ever get messed up in those stone and lime cages? I reckon some day I'll pull my freight for a clean location and settle down there and make little poems. This place would about content me. And there's a spot out in California in the Coast ranges that I've been keeping my eye on,' The odd thing was that I believe he meant it. His ugly face was lit up with a serious delight.

He told me he had taken this voyage before, so I got out Baddely and asked for advice. 'I can't spend too much time on holidaying,' I told him, 'and I want to see all the beauty spots. But the best of them seem to be in the area that this fool British Government won't let you into without a passport. I suppose I shall have to leave you at Oban.'

'Too bad,' he said sympathetically. 'Well, they tell me there's some pretty sights round Oban.' And he thumbed the guide-book and began to read about Glencoe.

I said that was not my purpose, and pitched him a yarn about Prince Charlie and how my mother's great-grandfather had played some kind of part in that show. I told him I wanted to see the place where the Prince landed and where he left for France. 'So far as I can make out that won't take me into the passport country, but I'll have to do a bit of footslogging. Well, I'm used to padding the hoof. I must get the captain to put me off in Morvern, and then I can foot it round the top of Lochiel and get back to Oban through Appin. How's that for a holiday trek?'

He gave the scheme his approval. 'But if it was me, Mr Brand, I would have a shot at puzzling your gallant policemen. You and I don't take much stock in Governments and their two-cent laws, and it would be a good game to see just how far you could get into the forbidden land. A man like you could put up a good bluff on those hayseeds. I don't mind having a bet ...'

'No,' I said. 'I'm out for a rest, and not for sport. If there was anything to be gained I'd undertake to bluff my way to the Orkney Islands. But it's a wearing job and I've better things to think about.'

'So? Well, enjoy yourself your own way. I'll be sorry when you leave us, for I owe you something for that rough-house, and beside there's darned little company in the old moss-back captain.'

That evening Gresson and I swopped yarns after supper to the accompaniment of the 'Ma Goad!' and 'Is't possible?' of captain and mate. I went to bed after a glass or two of weak grog, and made up for the last night's vigil by falling sound asleep. I had very little kit with me, beyond what I stood up in and could carry in my waterproof pockets, but on Amos's advice I had brought my little nickel-plated revolver. This lived by day in my hip pocket, but at night I put it behind my pillow. But when I woke next morning to find us casting anchor in the bay below rough low hills, which I knew to be the island of Colonsay, I could find no trace of the revolver. I searched every inch of the bunk and only shook out feathers from the mouldy ticking. I remembered perfectly putting the thing behind my head before I went to sleep, and now it had vanished utterly. Of course I could not advertise my loss, and I didn't greatly mind it, for this was not a job where I could do much shooting. But it made me think a good deal about Mr Gresson. He simply could not suspect me; if he had bagged my gun, as I was pretty certain he had, it must be because he wanted it for himself and not that he might disarm me.

Every way I argued it I reached the same conclusion. In Gresson's eyes I must seem as harmless as a child.

We spent the better part of a day at Colonsay, and Gresson, so far as his duties allowed, stuck to me like a limpet. Before I went ashore I wrote out a telegram for Amos. I devoted a hectic hour to the *Pilgrim's Progress*, but I could not compose any kind of intelligible message with reference to its text. We had all the same edition—the one in the *Golden Treasury* series—so I could have made up a sort of cipher by referring to lines and pages, but that would have taken up a dozen telegraph forms and seemed to me too elaborate for the purpose. So I sent this message:

Ochterlony, Post Office, Kyle,

I hope to spend part of holiday near you and to see you if boat's programme permits. Are any good cargoes waiting in your neighbourhood? Reply Post Office, Oban.

It was highly important that Gresson should not see this, but it was the deuce of a business to shake him off. I went for a walk in the afternoon along the shore and passed the telegraph office, but the confounded fellow was with me all the time. My only chance was just before we sailed, when he had to go on board to check some cargo. As the telegraph office stood full in view of the ship's deck I did not go near it. But in the back end of the clachan I found the schoolmaster, and got him to promise to send the wire. I also bought off him a couple of well-worn sevenpenny novels.

The result was that I delayed our departure for ten minutes and when I came on board faced a wrathful Gresson. 'Where the hell have you been?' he asked. 'The weather's blowing up dirty and the old man's mad to get off. Didn't you get your legs stretched enough this afternoon?'

I explained humbly that I had been to the schoolmaster to get something to read, and produced my dingy red volumes. At that his brow cleared. I could see that his suspicions were set at rest.

We left Colonsay about six in the evening with the sky behind us banking for a storm, and the hills of Jura to starboard an angry purple. Colonsay was too low an island to be any kind of breakwater against a western gale, so the weather was bad from the start. Our course was north by east, and when we had passed the butt-end of the island we nosed about in the trough of big seas, shipping tons of water and rolling like a buffalo. I know as much about boats as about Egyptian hieroglyphics, but even my landsman's eyes could tell that we were in for a rough night. I was determined not to get queasy again, but when I went below the smell of tripe and onions promised to be my undoing; so I dined off a slab of chocolate and a cabin biscuit, put on my waterproof, and resolved to stick it out on deck.

I took up position near the bows, where I was out of reach of the oily steamer smells. It was as fresh as the top of a mountain, but mighty cold and wet, for a gusty drizzle had set in, and I got the spindrift of the big waves. There I balanced myself, as we lurched into the twilight, hanging on with one hand to a rope which descended from the stumpy mast. I noticed that there was only an indifferent rail between me and the edge, but that interested me and helped to keep off sickness. I swung to the movement of the vessel, and though I was mortally cold it was rather pleasant than otherwise. My notion was to get the nausea whipped out of me by the weather, and, when I was properly tired, to go down and turn in.

I stood there till the dark had fallen. By that time I was an automaton, the way a man gets on sentry-go, and I could have easily hung on till morning. My thoughts ranged about the earth, beginning with the business I had set out on, and presently—by way of recollections of Blenkiron and Peter—reaching the German forest where, in the Christmas of 1915, I had been nearly done in by fever and old Stumm. I remembered the bitter cold of that wild race, and the way the snow seemed to burn like fire when I stumbled and got my face into it. I reflected that sea-sickness was kitten's play to a good bout of malaria.

The weather was growing worse, and I was getting more than spindrift from the seas. I hooked my arm round the rope, for my fingers were numbing. Then I fell to dreaming again, principally about Fosse Manor and Mary Lamington. This so ravished me that I was as good as asleep. I was trying to reconstruct the picture as I had last seen her at Biggleswick station ...

A heavy body collided with me and shook my arm from the rope. I slithered across the yard of deck, engulfed in a whirl of water. One foot caught a stanchion of the rail, and it gave with me, so that for an instant I was more than half overboard. But my fingers clawed wildly and caught in the links of what must have been the anchor chain. They held, though a ton's weight seemed to be tugging at my feet ... Then the old tub rolled back, the waters slipped off, and I was sprawling on a wet deck with no breath in me and a gallon of brine in my windpipe.

I heard a voice cry out sharply, and a hand helped me to my feet. It was Gresson, and he seemed excited.

'God, Mr Brand, that was a close call! I was coming up to find you, when this damned ship took to lying on her side. I guess I must have cannoned into you, and I was calling myself bad names when I saw you rolling into the Atlantic. If I hadn't got a grip on the rope I would have been down beside you. Say, you're not hurt? I reckon you'd better come below and get a glass of rum under your belt. You're about as wet as mother's dish-clouts.'

There's one advantage about campaigning. You take your luck when it comes and don't worry about what might have been. I didn't think any more of the business, except that it had cured me of wanting to be sea-sick. I went down to the reeking cabin without one qualm in my stomach, and ate a good meal of welsh-rabbit and bottled Bass, with a tot of rum to follow up with. Then I shed my wet garments, and slept in my bunk till we anchored off a village in Mull in a clear blue morning.

It took us four days to crawl up that coast and make Oban, for we seemed to be a floating general store for every hamlet in those parts. Gresson made himself very pleasant, as if he wanted to atone for nearly doing me in. We played some poker, and I read the little books I had got in Colonsay, and then rigged up a fishing-line, and caught saithe and lythe and an occasional big haddock. But I found the time pass slowly, and I was glad that about noon one day we came into a bay blocked with islands and saw a clean little town sitting on the hills and the smoke of a railway engine.

I went ashore and purchased a better brand of hat in a tweed store. Then I made a bee-line for the post office, and asked for telegrams. One was given to me, and as I opened it I saw Gresson at my elbow.

It read thus:

Brand, Post office, Oban. Page 117, paragraph 3. Ochterlony.

I passed it to Gresson with a rueful face.

'There's a piece of foolishness,' I said. 'I've got a cousin who's a Presbyterian minister up in Ross-shire, and before I knew about this passport humbug I wrote to him and offered to pay him a visit. I told him to wire me here if it was convenient, and the old idiot has sent me the wrong telegram. This was likely as not meant for some other brother parson, who's got my message instead.'

'What's the guy's name?' Gresson asked curiously, peering at the signature.

'Ochterlony. David Ochterlony. He's a great swell at writing books, but he's no earthly use at handling the telegraph. However, it don't signify, seeing I'm not going near him.' I crumpled up the pink form and tossed it on the floor. Gresson and I walked to the *Tobermory* together.

That afternoon, when I got a chance, I had out my *Pilgrim's Progress*. Page 117, paragraph 3, read:

'*Then I saw in my dream, that a little off the road, over against the Silver-mine, stood Demas (gentlemanlike) to call to passengers to come and see: who said to Christian and his fellow, Ho, turn aside hither and I will show you a thing.*

At tea I led the talk to my own past life. I yarned about my experiences as a mining engineer, and said I could never get out of the trick of looking at country with the eye of the prospector. 'For instance,' I said, 'if this had been Rhodesia, I would have said there was a good chance of copper in these little kopjes above the town. They're not unlike the hills round the Messina mine.' I told the captain that after the war I was thinking of turning my attention to the West Highlands and looking out for minerals.

'Ye'll make nothing of it,' said the captain. 'The costs are ower big, even if ye found the minerals, for ye'd have to import a' your labour. The West Hielandman is no fond o' hard work. Ye ken the psalm o' the crofter?

O that the peats would cut themselves,
The fish chump on the shore,
And that I in my bed might lie
Henceforth for ever more!'

'Has it ever been tried?' I asked.

'Often. There's marble and slate quarries, and there was word o' coal in Benbecula. And there's the iron mines at Ranna.'

'Where's that?' I asked.

'Up forenent Skye. We call in there, and generally bide a bit. There's a heap of cargo for Ranna, and we usually get a good load back. But as I tell ye, there's few Hielanders working there. Mostly Irish and lads frae Fife and Falkirk way.'

I didn't pursue the subject, for I had found Demas's silver-mine. If the *Tobermory* lay at Ranna for a week, Gresson would have time to do his own private business. Ranna would not be the spot, for the island was bare to the world in the middle of a much-frequented channel. But Skye was just across the way, and when I looked in my map at its big, wandering peninsulas I concluded that my guess had been right, and that Skye was the place to make for.

That night I sat on deck with Gresson, and in a wonderful starry silence we watched the lights die out of the houses in the town, and talked of a thousand things. I noticed—what I had had a hint of before—that my companion was no common man. There were moments when he forgot himself and talked like an educated gentleman: then he would remember, and relapse into the lingo of Leadville, Colorado. In my character of the ingenuous inquirer I set him posers about politics and economics, the kind of thing I might have been supposed to pick up from unintelligent browsing among little books. Generally he answered with some slangy catchword, but occasionally he was interested beyond his discretion, and treated me to a harangue like an equal. I discovered another thing, that he had a craze for poetry, and a capacious memory for it. I forgot how we drifted into the subject, but I remember he quoted some queer haunting stuff which he said was Swinburne, and verses by people I had heard of from Letchford at Biggleswick. Then he saw by my silence that he had gone too far, and fell back into the jargon of the West. He wanted to know about my plans, and we went down into the cabin and had a look at the map. I explained my route, up Morvern and round the head of Lochiel, and back to Oban by the east side of Loch Linnhe.

'Got you,' he said. 'You've a hell of a walk before you. That bug never bit me, and I guess I'm not envying you any. And after that, Mr Brand?'

'Back to Glasgow to do some work for the cause,' I said lightly.

'Just so,' he said with a grin. 'It's a great life if you don't weaken.'

We steamed out of the bay next morning at dawn, and about nine o'clock I got on shore at a little place called Lochaline. My kit was all on my person, and my waterproof's pockets were stuffed with chocolates and biscuits I had bought in Oban. The captain was discouraging. 'Ye'll get your bellyful o' Hieland hills, Mr Brand, afore ye win round the loch head. Ye'll be wishin' yerself back on the *Tobermory*.' But Gresson speeded me joyfully on my way, and said he wished he were coming with me. He even accompanied me the first hundred yards, and waved his hat after me till I was round the turn of the road.

The first stage in that journey was pure delight. I was thankful to be rid of the infernal boat, and the hot summer scents coming down the glen were comforting after the cold, salt smell of the sea. The road lay up the side of a small bay, at the top of which a big white house stood among gardens. Presently I had left the coast and was in a glen where a brown salmon-river swirled through acres of bog-myrtle. It had its source in a loch, from which the mountain rose steeply—a place so glassy in that August forenoon that every scar and wrinkle of the hillside were faithfully reflected. After that I crossed a low pass to the head of another sea-lock, and, following the map, struck over the shoulder of a great hill and ate my luncheon far up on its side, with a wonderful vista of wood and water below me.

All that morning I was very happy, not thinking about Gresson or Ivery, but getting my mind clear in those wide spaces, and my lungs filled with the brisk hill air. But I noticed one curious thing. On my last visit to Scotland, when I covered more moorland miles a day than any man since Claverhouse, I had been fascinated by the land, and had pleased myself with plans for settling down in it. But now, after three years of war and general rocketing, I felt less drawn to that kind of landscape. I wanted something more green and peaceful and habitable, and it was to the Cotswolds that my memory turned with longing.

I puzzled over this till I realized that in all my Cotswold pictures a figure kept going and coming—a young girl with a cloud of gold hair and the strong, slim grace of a boy, who had sung 'Cherry Ripe' in a moonlit garden. Up on that hillside I understood very clearly that I, who had been as careless of women as any monk, had fallen wildly in love with a child of half my age. I was loath to admit it, though for weeks the conclusion had been forcing itself on me. Not that I didn't revel in my madness, but that it seemed too hopeless a business, and I had no use for barren philandering. But, seated on a rock munching chocolate and biscuits, I faced up to the fact and resolved to trust my luck. After all we were comrades in a big job, and it was up to me to be man enough to win her. The thought seemed to brace any courage that was in me. No task seemed too hard with her approval to gain and her companionship somewhere at the back of it. I sat for a long time in a happy dream, remembering all the glimpses I had had of her, and humming her song to an audience of one black-faced sheep.

On the highroad half a mile below me, I saw a figure on a bicycle mounting the hill, and then getting off to mop its face at the summit. I turned my Ziess glasses on to it, and observed that it was a country policeman. It caught sight of me, stared for a bit, tucked its machine into the side of the road, and then very slowly began to climb the hillside. Once it stopped, waved its hand and shouted something which I could not hear. I sat finishing my luncheon, till the features were revealed to me of a fat oldish man, blowing like a grampus, his cap well on the back of a bald head, and his trousers tied about the shins with string.

There was a spring beside me and I had out my flask to round off my meal.

'Have a drink,' I said.

His eye brightened, and a smile overran his moist face.

'Thank you, sir. It will be very warrm coming up the brae.'

'You oughtn't to,' I said. 'You really oughtn't, you know. Scorching up hills and then doubling up a mountain are not good for your time of life.'

He raised the cap of my flask in solemn salutation. 'Your very good health.' Then he smacked his lips, and had several cupfuls of water from the spring.

'You will haf come from Achranich way, maybe?' he said in his soft sing-song, having at last found his breath.

'Just so. Fine weather for the birds, if there was anybody to shoot them.'

'Ah, no. There will be few shots fired today, for there are no gentlemen left in Morvern. But I wass asking you, if you come from Achranich, if you haf seen anybody on the road.'

From his pocket he extricated a brown envelope and a bulky telegraph form. 'Will you read it, sir, for I haf forgot my spectacles?'

It contained a description of one Brand, a South African and a suspected character, whom the police were warned to stop and return to Oban. The description wasn't bad, but it lacked any one good distinctive detail. Clearly the policeman took me for an innocent pedestrian, probably the guest of some moorland shooting-box, with my brown face and rough tweeds and hobnailed shoes.

I frowned and puzzled a little. 'I did see a fellow about three miles back on the hillside. There's a public-house just where the burn comes in, and I think he was making for it. Maybe that was your man. This wire says "South African"; and now I remember the fellow had the look of a colonial.'

The policeman sighed. 'No doubt it will be the man. Perhaps he will haf a pistol and will shoot.'

'Not him,' I laughed. 'He looked a mangy sort of chap, and he'll be scared out of his senses at the sight of you. But take my advice and get somebody with you before you tackle him. You're always the better of a witness.'

'That is so,' he said, brightening. 'Ach, these are the bad times! in old days there wass nothing to do but watch the doors at the flower-shows and keep the yachts from poaching the sea-trout. But now it is spies, spies, and "Donald, get out of your bed, and go off twenty mile to find a German." I wass wishing the war wass by, and the Germans all dead.'

'Hear, hear!' I cried, and on the strength of it gave him another dram.

I accompanied him to the road, and saw him mount his bicycle and zig-zag like a snipe down the hill towards Achranich. Then I set off briskly northward. It was clear that the faster I moved the better.

As I went I paid disgusted tribute to the efficiency of the Scottish police. I wondered how on earth they had marked me down. Perhaps it was the Glasgow meeting, or perhaps my association with Ivery at Biggleswick. Anyhow there was somebody somewhere mighty quick at compiling a *dossier*. Unless I wanted to be bundled back to Oban I must make good speed to the Arisaig coast.

Presently the road fell to a gleaming sea-loch which lay like the blue blade of a sword among the purple of the hills. At the head there was a tiny clachan, nestled among birches and rowans, where a tawny burn wound to the sea. When I entered the place it was about four o'clock in the afternoon, and peace lay on it like a garment. In the wide, sunny street there was no sign of life, and no sound except of hens clucking and of bees busy among the roses. There was a little grey box of a kirk, and close to the bridge a thatched cottage which bore the sign of a post and telegraph office.

For the past hour I had been considering that I had better prepare for mishaps. If the police of these parts had been warned they might prove too much for me, and Gresson would be allowed to make his journey unmatched. The only thing to do was to send a wire to Amos and leave the matter in his hands. Whether that was possible or not depended upon this remote postal authority.

I entered the little shop, and passed from bright sunshine to a twilight smelling of paraffin and black-striped peppermint balls. An old woman with a mutch sat in an arm-chair behind the counter. She looked up at me over her spectacles and smiled, and I took to her on the instant. She had the kind of old wise face that God loves.

Beside her I noticed a little pile of books, one of which was a Bible. Open on her lap was a paper, the *United Free Church Monthly*. I noticed these details greedily, for I had to make up my mind on the part to play.

'It's a warm day, mistress,' I said, my voice falling into the broad Lowland speech, for I had an instinct that she was not of the Highlands.

She laid aside her paper. 'It is that, sir. It is grand weather for the hairst, but here that's no till the hinner end o' September, and at the best it's a bit scart o' aits.'

'Ay. It's a different thing down Annandale way,' I said.

Her face lit up. 'Are ye from Dumfries, sir?'

'Not just from Dumfries, but I know the Borders fine.'

'Ye'll no beat them,' she cried. 'Not that this is no a guid place and I've muckle to be thankfu' for since John Sanderson—that was ma man—brought me here forty-seeven year syne come Martinmas. But the aulder I get the mair I think o' the bit whaur I was born. It was twae miles from Wamphray on the Lockerbie road, but they tell me the place is noo just a rickle o' stanes.'

'I was wondering, mistress, if I could get a cup of tea in the village.'

'Ye'll hae a cup wi' me,' she said. 'It's no often we see onybody frae the Borders hereaways. The kettle's just on the boil.'

She gave me tea and scones and butter, and black-currant jam, and treacle biscuits that melted in the mouth. And as we ate we talked of many things—chiefly of the war and of the wickedness of the world.

'There's nae lads left here,' she said. 'They a' joined the Camerons, and the feck o' them fell at an awfu' place called Lowse. John and me never had no boys, jist the one lassie that's married on Donald Frew, the Strontian carrier. I used to vex mysel' about it, but now I thank the Lord that in His mercy He spared me sorrow. But I wad hae liked to have had one laddie fechtin' for his country. I whiles wish I was a Catholic and could pit up prayers for the sodgers that are deid. It maun be a great consolation.'

I whipped out the *Pilgrim's Progress* from my pocket. 'That is the grand book for a time like this.'

'Fine I ken it,' she said. 'I got it for a prize in the Sabbath School when I was a lassie.'

I turned the pages. I read out a passage or two, and then I seemed struck with a sudden memory.

'This is a telegraph office, mistress. Could I trouble you to send a telegram? You see I've a cousin that's a minister in Ross-shire at the Kyle, and him and me are great correspondents. He was writing about something in the *Pilgrim's Progress* and I think I'll send him a telegram in answer.'

'A letter would be cheaper,' she said.

'Ay, but I'm on holiday and I've no time for writing.'

She gave me a form, and I wrote:

Ochterlony. Post Office, Kyle.—Demas will be at his mine within the week. Strive with him, lest I faint by the way.

'Ye're unco lavish wi' the words, sir,' was her only comment.

We parted with regret, and there was nearly a row when I tried to pay for the tea. I was bidden remember her to one David Tudhole, farmer in Nether Mirecleuch, the next time I passed by Wamphray.

The village was as quiet when I left it as when I had entered. I took my way up the hill with an easier mind, for I had got off the telegram, and I hoped I had covered my tracks. My friend the postmistress would, if questioned, be unlikely to recognize any South African suspect in the frank and homely traveller who had spoken with her of Annandale and the *Pilgrim's Progress.*

The soft mulberry gloaming of the west coast was beginning to fall on the hills. I hoped to put in a dozen miles before dark to the next village on the map, where I might find quarters. But ere I had gone far I heard the sound of a motor behind me, and a car slipped past bearing three men. The driver favoured me with a sharp glance, and clapped on the brakes. I noted that the two men in the tonneau were carrying sporting rifles.

'Hi, you, sir,' he cried. 'Come here.' The two rifle-bearers—solemn gillies—brought their weapons to attention.

'By God,' he said, 'it's the man. What's your name? Keep him covered, Angus.'

The gillies duly covered me, and I did not like the look of their wavering barrels. They were obviously as surprised as myself.

I had about half a second to make my plans. I advanced with a very stiff air, and asked him what the devil he meant. No Lowland Scots for me now. My tone was that of an adjutant of a Guards' battalion.

My inquisitor was a tall man in an ulster, with a green felt hat on his small head. He had a lean, well-bred face, and very choleric blue eyes. I set him down as a soldier, retired, Highland regiment or cavalry, old style.

He produced a telegraph form, like the policeman.

'Middle height—strongly built—grey tweeds—brown hat—speaks with a colonial accent—much sunburnt. What's your name, sir?'

I did not reply in a colonial accent, but with the hauteur of the British officer when stopped by a French sentry. I asked him again what the devil he had to do with my business. This made him angry and he began to stammer.

'I'll teach you what I have to do with it. I'm a deputy-lieutenant of this county, and I have Admiralty instructions to watch the coast. Damn it, sir, I've a wire here from the Chief Constable describing you. You're Brand, a very dangerous fellow, and we want to know what the devil you're doing here.'

As I looked at his wrathful eye and lean head, which could not have held much brains, I saw that I must change my tone. If I irritated him he would get nasty and refuse to listen and hang me up for hours. So my voice became respectful.

'I beg your pardon, sir, but I've not been accustomed to be pulled up suddenly, and asked for my credentials. My name is Blaikie, Captain Robert Blaikie, of the Scots Fusiliers. I'm home on three weeks' leave, to get a little peace after Hooge. We were only hauled out five days ago.' I hoped my old friend in the shell-shock hospital at Isham would pardon my borrowing his identity.

The man looked puzzled. 'How the devil am I to be satisfied about that? Have you any papers to prove it?'

'Why, no. I don't carry passports about with me on a walking tour. But you can wire to the depot, or to my London address.'

He pulled at his yellow moustache. 'I'm hanged if I know what to do. I want to get home for dinner. I tell you what, sir, I'll take you on with me and put you up for the night. My boy's at home, convalescing, and if he says you're pukka I'll ask your pardon and give you a dashed good bottle of port. I'll trust him and I warn you he's a keen hand.'

There was nothing to do but consent, and I got in beside him with an uneasy conscience. Supposing the son knew the real Blaikie! I asked the name of the boy's battalion, and was told the 10th Seaforths. That wasn't pleasant hearing, for they had been brigaded with us on the Somme. But Colonel Broadbury—for he told me his name—volunteered another piece of news which set my mind at rest. The boy was not yet twenty, and had only been out seven months. At Arras he had got a bit of shrapnel in his thigh, which had played the deuce with the sciatic nerve, and he was still on crutches.

We spun over ridges of moorland, always keeping northward, and brought up at a pleasant white-washed house close to the sea. Colonel Broadbury ushered me into a hall where a small fire of peats was burning, and on a couch beside it lay a slim, pale-faced young man. He had dropped his policeman's manner, and behaved like a gentleman. 'Ted,' he said, 'I've brought a friend home for the night. I went out to look for a suspect and found a British officer. This is Captain Blaikie, of the Scots Fusiliers.'

The boy looked at me pleasantly. 'I'm very glad to meet you, sir. You'll excuse me not getting up, but I've got a game leg.' He was the copy of his father in features, but dark and sallow where the other was blond. He had just the same narrow head, and stubborn mouth, and honest, quick-tempered eyes. It is the type that makes dashing regimental officers, and earns V.C.s, and gets done in wholesale. I was never that kind. I belonged to the school of the cunning cowards.

In the half-hour before dinner the last wisp of suspicion fled from my host's mind. For Ted Broadbury and I were immediately deep in 'shop'. I had met most of his senior officers, and I knew all about their doings at Arras, for his brigade had been across the river on my left. We fought the great fight over again, and yarned about technicalities and slanged the Staff in the way young officers have, the father throwing in questions that showed how mighty proud he was of his son. I had a bath before dinner, and as he led me to the bathroom he apologized very handsomely for his bad manners. 'Your coming's been a godsend for Ted. He was moping a bit in this place. And, though I say it that shouldn't, he's a dashed good boy.'

I had my promised bottle of port, and after dinner I took on the father at billiards. Then we settled in the smoking-room, and I laid myself out to entertain the pair. The result was that they would have me stay a week, but I spoke of the shortness of my leave, and said I must get on to the railway and then back to Fort William for my luggage.

So I spent that night between clean sheets, and ate a Christian breakfast, and was given my host's car to set me a bit on the road. I dismissed it after half a dozen miles, and, following the map, struck over the hills to the west. About midday I topped a ridge, and beheld the Sound of Sleat shining beneath me. There were other things in the landscape. In the valley on the right a long goods train was crawling on the Mallaig railway. And across the strip of sea, like some fortress of the old gods, rose the dark bastions and turrets of the hills of Skye.

CHAPTER SIX

The Skirts of the Coolin

Obviously I must keep away from the railway. If the police were after me in Morvern, that line would be warned, for it was a barrier I must cross if I were to go farther north. I observed from the map that it turned up the coast, and concluded that the place for me to make for was the shore south of that turn, where Heaven might send me some luck in the boat line. For I was pretty certain that every porter and station-master on that tin-pot outfit was anxious to make better acquaintance with my humble self.

I lunched off the sandwiches the Broadburys had given me, and in the bright afternoon made my way down the hill, crossed at the foot of a small fresh-water lochan, and pursued the issuing stream through midge-infested woods of hazels to its junction with the sea. It was rough going, but very pleasant, and I fell into the same mood of idle contentment that I had enjoyed the previous morning. I never met a soul. Sometimes a roe deer broke out of the covert, or an old blackcock startled me with his scolding. The place was bright with heather, still in its first bloom, and smelt better than the myrrh of Arabia. It was a blessed glen, and I was as happy as a king, till I began to feel the coming of hunger, and reflected that the Lord alone knew when I might get a meal. I had still some chocolate and biscuits, but I wanted something substantial.

The distance was greater than I thought, and it was already twilight when I reached the coast. The shore was open and desolate—great banks of pebbles to which straggled alders and hazels from the hillside scrub. But as I marched northward and turned a little point of land I saw before me in a crook of the bay a smoking cottage. And, plodding along by the water's edge, was the bent figure of a man, laden with nets and lobster pots. Also, beached on the shingle was a boat.

I quickened my pace and overtook the fisherman. He was an old man with a ragged grey beard, and his rig was seaman's boots and a much-darned blue jersey. He was deaf, and did not hear me when I hailed him. When he caught sight of me he never stopped, though he very solemnly returned my good evening. I fell into step with him, and in his silent company reached the cottage.

He halted before the door and unslung his burdens. The place was a two-roomed building with a roof of thatch, and the walls all grown over with a yellow-flowered creeper. When he had straightened his back, he looked seaward and at the sky, as if to prospect the weather. Then he turned on me his gentle, absorbed eyes. 'It will haf been a fine day, sir. Wass you seeking the road to anywhere?'

'I was seeking a night's lodging,' I said. 'I've had a long tramp on the hills, and I'd be glad of a chance of not going farther.'

'We will haf no accommodation for a gentleman,' he said gravely.

'I can sleep on the floor, if you can give me a blanket and a bite of supper.'

'Indeed you will not,' and he smiled slowly. 'But I will ask the wife. Mary, come here!'

An old woman appeared in answer to his call, a woman whose face was so old that she seemed like his mother. In highland places one sex ages quicker than the other.

'This gentleman would like to bide the night. I wass telling him that we had a poor small house, but he says he will not be minding it.'

She looked at me with the timid politeness that you find only in outland places.

'We can do our best, indeed, sir. The gentleman can have Colin's bed in the loft, but he will haf to be doing with plain food. Supper is ready if you will come in now.'

I had a scrub with a piece of yellow soap at an adjacent pool in the burn and then entered a kitchen blue with peat-reek. We had a meal of boiled fish, oatcakes and skim-milk cheese, with cups of strong tea to wash it down. The old folk had the manners of princes. They pressed food on me, and asked me no questions, till for very decency's sake I had to put up a story and give some account of myself.

I found they had a son in the Argylls and a young boy in the Navy. But they seemed disinclined to talk of them or of the war. By a mere accident I hit on the old man's absorbing interest. He was passionate about the land. He had taken part in long-forgotten agitations, and had suffered eviction in some ancient landlords' quarrel farther north. Presently he was pouring out to me all the woes of the crofter—woes that seemed so antediluvian and forgotten that I listened as one would listen to an old song. 'You who come from a new country will not haf heard of these things,' he kept telling me, but by that peat fire I made up for my defective education. He told me of evictions in the year. One somewhere in Sutherland, and of harsh doings in the Outer Isles. It was far more than a political grievance. It was the lament of the conservative for vanished days and manners. 'Over in Skye wass the fine land for black cattle, and every man had his bit herd on the hillside. But the lairds said it wass better for sheep, and then they said it wass not good for sheep, so they put it under deer, and now there is no black cattle anywhere in Skye.' I tell you it was like sad music on the bagpipes hearing that old fellow. The war and all things modern meant nothing to him; he lived among the tragedies of his youth and his prime.

I'm a Tory myself and a bit of a land-reformer, so we agreed well enough. So well, that I got what I wanted without asking for it. I told him I was going to Skye, and he offered to take me over in his boat in the morning. 'It will be no trouble. Indeed no. I will be going that way myself to the fishing.'

I told him that after the war, every acre of British soil would have to be used for the men that had earned the right to it. But that did not comfort him. He was not thinking about the land itself, but about the men who had been driven from it fifty years before. His desire was not for reform, but for restitution, and that was past the power of any Government. I went to bed in the loft in a sad, reflective mood, considering how in speeding our newfangled plough we must break down a multitude of molehills and how desirable and unreplaceable was the life of the moles.

In brisk, shining weather, with a wind from the south-east, we put off next morning. In front was a brown line of low hills, and behind them, a little to the north, that black toothcomb of mountain range which I had seen the day before from the Arisaig ridge.

'That is the Coolin,' said the fisherman. 'It is a bad place where even the deer cannot go. But all the rest of Skye wass the fine land for black cattle.'

As we neared the coast, he pointed out many places. 'Look there, Sir, in that glen. I haf seen six cot houses smoking there, and now there is not any left. There were three men of my own name had crofts on the machars beyond the point, and if you go there you will only find the marks of their bit gardens. You will know the place by the gean trees.'

When he put me ashore in a sandy bay between green ridges of bracken, he was still harping upon the past. I got him to take a pound—for the boat and not for the night's hospitality, for he would have beaten me with an oar if I had suggested that. The last I saw of him, as I turned round at the top of the hill, he had still his sail down, and was gazing at the lands which had once been full of human dwellings and now were desolate.

I kept for a while along the ridge, with the Sound of Sleat on my right, and beyond it the high hills of Knoydart and Kintail. I was watching for the *Tobermory*, but saw no sign of her. A steamer put out from Mallaig, and there were several drifters crawling up the channel and once I saw the white ensign and a destroyer bustled northward, leaving a cloud of black smoke in her wake. Then, after consulting the map, I struck across country, still keeping the higher ground, but, except at odd minutes, being out of sight of the sea. I concluded that my business was to get to the latitude of Ranna without wasting time.

So soon as I changed my course I had the Coolin for company. Mountains have always been a craze of mine, and the blackness and mystery of those grim peaks went to my head. I forgot all about Fosse Manor and the Cotswolds. I forgot, too, what had been my chief feeling since I left Glasgow, a sense of the absurdity of my mission. It had all seemed too far-fetched and whimsical. I was running apparently no great personal risk, and I had always the unpleasing fear that Blenkiron might have been too clever and that the whole thing might be a mare's nest. But that dark mountain mass changed my outlook. I began to have a queer instinct that that was the place, that something might be concealed there, something pretty damnable. I remember I sat on a top for half an hour raking the hills with my glasses. I made out ugly precipices, and glens which lost themselves in primeval blackness. When the sun caught them—for it was a gleamy day—it brought out no colours, only degrees of shade. No mountains I had ever seen—not the Drakensberg or the red kopjes of Damaraland or the cold, white peaks around Erzerum—ever looked so unearthly and uncanny.

Oddly enough, too, the sight of them set me thinking about Ivery. There seemed no link between a smooth, sedentary being, dwelling in villas and lecture-rooms, and that shaggy tangle of precipices. But I felt there was, for I had begun to realize the bigness of my opponent. Blenkiron had said that he spun his web wide. That was intelligible enough among the half-baked youth of Biggleswick, and the pacifist societies, or even the toughs on the Clyde. I could fit him in all right to that picture. But that he should be playing his game among those mysterious black crags seemed to make him bigger and more desperate, altogether a different kind of proposition. I didn't exactly dislike the idea, for my objection to my past weeks had been that I was out of my proper job, and this was more my line of country. I always felt that I was a better bandit than a detective. But a sort of awe mingled with my satisfaction. I began to feel about Ivery as I had felt about the three devils of the Black Stone who had hunted me before the war, and as I never felt about any other Hun. The men we fought at the Front and the men I had run across in the Greenmantle business, even old Stumm himself, had been human miscreants. They were formidable enough, but you could gauge and calculate their capacities. But this Ivery was like a poison gas that hung in the air and got into unexpected crannies and that you couldn't fight in an upstanding way. Till then, in spite of Blenkiron's solemnity, I had regarded him simply as a problem. But now he seemed an intimate and omnipresent enemy, intangible, too, as the horror of a haunted house. Up on that sunny hillside, with the sea winds round me and the whaups calling, I got a chill in my spine when I thought of him.

I am ashamed to confess it, but I was also horribly hungry. There was something about the war that made me ravenous, and the less chance of food the worse I felt. If I had been in London with twenty restaurants open to me, I should as likely as not have gone off my feed. That was the cussedness of my stomach. I had still a little chocolate left, and I ate the fisherman's buttered scones for luncheon, but long before the evening my thoughts were dwelling on my empty interior.

I put up that night in a shepherd's cottage miles from anywhere. The man was called Macmorran, and he had come from Galloway when sheep were booming. He was a very good imitation of a savage, a little fellow with red hair and red eyes, who might have been a Pict. He lived with a daughter who had once been in service in Glasgow, a fat young woman with a face entirely covered with freckles and a pout of habitual discontent. No wonder, for that cottage was a pretty mean place. It was so thick with peat-reek that throat and eyes were always smarting. It was badly built, and must have leaked like a sieve in a storm. The father was a surly fellow, whose conversation was one long growl at the world, the high prices, the difficulty of moving his sheep, the meanness of his master, and the godforsaken character of Skye. 'Here's me no seen baker's bread for a month, and no company but a wheen ignorant Hielanders that yatter Gawlic. I wish I was back in the Glenkens. And I'd gang the morn if I could get paid what I'm awed.'

However, he gave me supper—a braxy ham and oatcake, and I bought the remnants off him for use next day. I did not trust his blankets, so I slept the night by the fire in the ruins of an arm-chair, and woke at dawn with a foul taste in my mouth. A dip in the burn refreshed me, and after a bowl of porridge I took the road again. For I was anxious to get to some hill-top that looked over to Ranna.

Before midday I was close under the eastern side of the Coolin, on a road which was more a rockery than a path. Presently I saw a big house ahead of me that looked like an inn, so I gave it a miss and struck the highway that led to it a little farther north. Then I bore off to the east, and was just beginning to climb a hill which I judged stood between me and the sea, when I heard wheels on the road and looked back.

It was a farmer's gig carrying one man. I was about half a mile off, and something in the cut of his jib seemed familiar. I got my glasses on him and made out a short, stout figure clad in a mackintosh, with a woollen comforter round its throat. As I watched, it made a movement as if to rub its nose on its sleeve. That was the pet trick of one man I knew. Inconspicuously I slipped through the long heather so as to reach the road ahead of the gig. When I rose like a wraith from the wayside the horse started, but not the driver.

'So ye're there,' said Amos's voice. 'I've news for ye. The *Tobermory* will be in Ranna by now. She passed Broadford two hours syne. When I saw her I yoked this beast and came up on the chance of foregathering with ye.'

'How on earth did you know I would be here?' I asked in some surprise.

'Oh, I saw the way your mind was workin' from your telegram. And says I to mysel'—that man Brand, says I, is not the chiel to be easy stoppit. But I was feared ye might be a day late, so I came up the road to hold the fort. Man, I'm glad to see ye. Ye're younger and soopler than me, and yon Gresson's a stirrin' lad.'

'There's one thing you've got to do for me,' I said. 'I can't go into inns and shops, but I can't do without food. I see from the map there's a town about six miles on. Go there and buy me anything that's tinned—biscuits and tongue and sardines, and a couple of bottles of whisky if you can get them. This may be a long job, so buy plenty.'

'Whaur'll I put them?' was his only question.

We fixed on a cache, a hundred yards from the highway in a place where two ridges of hill enclosed the view so that only a short bit of road was visible.

'I'll get back to the Kyle,' he told me, 'and a'body there kens Andra Amos, if ye should find a way of sendin' a message or comin' yourself. Oh, and I've got a word to ye from a lady that we ken of. She says, the sooner ye're back in Vawnity Fair the better she'll be pleased, always provided ye've got over the Hill Difficulty.'

A smile screwed up his old face and he waved his whip in farewell. I interpreted Mary's message as an incitement to speed, but I could not make the pace. That was Gresson's business. I think I was a little nettled, till I cheered myself by another interpretation. She might be anxious for my safety, she might want to see me again, anyhow the mere sending of the message showed I was not forgotten. I was in a pleasant muse as I breasted the hill, keeping discreetly in the cover of the many gullies. At the top I looked down on Ranna and the sea.

There lay the *Tobermory* busy unloading. It would be some time, no doubt, before Gresson could leave. There was no row-boat in the channel yet, and I might have to wait hours. I settled myself snugly between two rocks, where I could not be seen, and where I had a clear view of the sea and shore. But presently I found that I wanted some long heather to make a couch, and I emerged to get some. I had not raised my head for a second when I flopped down again. For I had a neighbour on the hill-top.

He was about two hundred yards off, just reaching the crest, and, unlike me, walking quite openly. His eyes were on Ranna, so he did not notice me, but from my cover I scanned every line of him. He looked an ordinary countryman, wearing badly cut, baggy knickerbockers of the kind that gillies affect. He had a face like a Portuguese Jew, but I had seen that type before among people with Highland names; they might be Jews or not, but they could speak Gaelic. Presently he disappeared. He had followed my example and selected a hiding-place.

It was a clear, hot day, but very pleasant in that airy place. Good scents came up from the sea, the heather was warm and fragrant, bees droned about, and stray seagulls swept the ridge with their wings. I took a look now and then towards my neighbour, but he was deep in his hidey-hole. Most of the time I kept my glasses on Ranna, and watched the doings of the *Tobermory.* She was tied up at the jetty, but seemed in no hurry to unload. I watched the captain disembark and walk up to a house on the hillside. Then some idlers sauntered down towards her and stood talking and smoking close to her side. The captain returned and left again. A man with papers in his hand appeared, and a woman with what looked like a telegram. The mate went ashore in his best clothes. Then at last, after midday, Gresson appeared. He joined the captain at the piermaster's office, and presently emerged on the other side of the jetty where some small boats were beached. A man from the *Tobermory* came in answer to his call, a boat was launched, and began to make its way into the channel. Gresson sat in the stern, placidly eating his luncheon.

I watched every detail of that crossing with some satisfaction that my forecast was turning out right. About half-way across, Gresson took the oars, but soon surrendered them to the *Tobermory* man, and lit a pipe. He got out a pair of binoculars and raked my hillside. I tried to see if my neighbour was making any signal, but all was quiet. Presently the boat was hid from me by the bulge of the hill, and I caught the sound of her scraping on the beach.

Gresson was not a hill-walker like my neighbour. It took him the best part of an hour to get to the top, and he reached it at a point not two yards from my hiding-place. I could hear by his labouring breath that he was very blown. He walked straight over the crest till he was out of sight of Ranna, and flung himself on the ground. He was now about fifty yards from me, and I made shift to lessen the distance. There was a grassy trench skirting the north side of the hill, deep and thickly overgrown with heather. I wound my way along it till I was about twelve yards from him, where I stuck, owing to the trench dying away. When I peered out of the cover I saw that the other man had joined him and that the idiots were engaged in embracing each other.

I dared not move an inch nearer, and as they talked in a low voice I could hear nothing of what they said. Nothing except one phrase, which the strange man repeated twice, very emphatically. 'Tomorrow night,' he said, and I noticed that his voice had not the Highland inflection which I looked for. Gresson nodded and glanced at his watch, and then the two began to move downhill towards the road I had travelled that morning.

I followed as best I could, using a shallow dry watercourse of which sheep had made a track, and which kept me well below the level of the moor. It took me down the hill, but some distance from the line the pair were taking, and I had to reconnoitre frequently to watch their movements. They were still a quarter of a mile or so from the road, when they stopped and stared, and I stared with them. On that lonely highway travellers were about as rare as roadmenders, and what caught their eye was a farmer's gig driven by a thick-set elderly man with a woollen comforter round his neck.

I had a bad moment, for I reckoned that if Gresson recognized Amos he might take fright. Perhaps the driver of the gig thought the same, for he appeared to be very drunk. He waved his whip, he jiggoted the reins, and he made an effort to sing. He looked towards the figures on the hillside, and cried out something. The gig narrowly missed the ditch, and then to my relief the horse bolted. Swaying like a ship in a gale, the whole outfit lurched out of sight round the corner of hill where lay my cache. If Amos could stop the beast and deliver the goods there, he had put up a masterly bit of buffoonery.

The two men laughed at the performance, and then they parted. Gresson retraced his steps up the hill. The other man—I called him in my mind the Portuguese Jew—started off at a great pace due west, across the road, and over a big patch of bog towards the northern butt of the Coolin. He had some errand, which Gresson knew about, and he was in a hurry to perform it. It was clearly my job to get after him.

I had a rotten afternoon. The fellow covered the moorland miles like a deer, and under the hot August sun I toiled on his trail. I had to keep well behind, and as much as possible in cover, in case he looked back; and that meant that when he had passed over a ridge I had to double not to let him get too far ahead, and when we were in an open place I had to make wide circuits to keep hidden. We struck a road which crossed a low pass and skirted the flank of the mountains, and this we followed till we were on the western side and within sight of the sea. It was gorgeous weather, and out on the blue water I saw cool sails moving and little breezes ruffling the calm, while I was glowing like a furnace. Happily I was in fair training, and I needed it. The Portuguese Jew must have done a steady six miles an hour over abominable country.

About five o'clock we came to a point where I dared not follow. The road ran flat by the edge of the sea, so that several miles of it were visible. Moreover, the man had begun to look round every few minutes. He was getting near something and wanted to be sure that no one was in his neighbourhood. I left the road accordingly, and took to the hillside, which to my undoing was one long cascade of screes and tumbled rocks. I saw him drop over a rise which seemed to mark the rim of a little bay into which descended one of the big corries of the mountains. It must have been a good half-hour later before I, at my greater altitude and with far worse going, reached the same rim. I looked into the glen and my man had disappeared.

He could not have crossed it, for the place was wider than I had thought. A ring of black precipices came down to within half a mile of the shore, and between them was a big stream—long, shallow pools at the sea end and a chain of waterfalls above. He had gone to earth like a badger somewhere, and I dared not move in case he might be watching me from behind a boulder.

But even as I hesitated he appeared again, fording the stream, his face set on the road we had come. Whatever his errand was he had finished it, and was posting back to his master. For a moment I thought I should follow him, but another instinct prevailed. He had not come to this wild place for the scenery. Somewhere down in the glen there was something or somebody that held the key of the mystery. It was my business to stay there till I had unlocked it. Besides, in two hours it would be dark, and I had had enough walking for one day.

I made my way to the stream side and had a long drink. The corrie behind me was lit up with the westering sun, and the bald cliffs were flushed with pink and gold. On each side of the stream was turf like a lawn, perhaps a hundred yards wide, and then a tangle of long heather and boulders right up to the edge of the great rocks. I had never seen a more delectable evening, but I could not enjoy its peace because of my anxiety about the Portuguese Jew. He had not been there more than half an hour, just about long enough for a man to travel to the first ridge across the burn and back. Yet he had found time to do his business. He might have left a letter in some prearranged place—in which case I would stay there till the man it was meant for turned up. Or he might have met someone, though I didn't think that possible. As I scanned the acres of rough moor and then looked at the sea lapping delicately on the grey sand I had the feeling that a knotty problem was before me. It was too dark to try to track his steps. That must be left for the morning, and I prayed that there would be no rain in the night.

I ate for supper most of the braxy ham and oatcake I had brought from Macmorran's cottage. It took some self-denial, for I was ferociously hungry, to save a little for breakfast next morning. Then I pulled heather and bracken and made myself a bed in the shelter of a rock which stood on a knoll above the stream. My bed-chamber was well hidden, but at the same time, if anything should appear in the early dawn, it gave me a prospect. With my waterproof I was perfectly warm, and, after smoking two pipes, I fell asleep.

My night's rest was broken. First it was a fox which came and barked at my ear and woke me to a pitch-black night, with scarcely a star showing. The next time it was nothing but a wandering hill-wind, but as I sat up and listened I thought I saw a spark of light near the edge of the sea. It was only for a second, but it disquieted me. I got out and climbed on the top of the rock, but all was still save for the gentle lap of the tide and the croak of some night bird among the crags. The third time I was suddenly quite wide awake, and without any reason, for I had not been dreaming. Now I have slept hundreds of times alone beside my horse on the veld, and I never knew any cause for such awakenings but the one, and that was the presence near me of some human being. A man who is accustomed to solitude gets this extra sense which announces like an alarm-clock the approach of one of his kind.

But I could hear nothing. There was a scraping and rustling on the moor, but that was only the wind and the little wild things of the hills. A fox, perhaps, or a blue hare. I convinced my reason, but not my senses, and for long I lay awake with my ears at full cock and every nerve tense. Then I fell asleep, and woke to the first flush of dawn.

The sun was behind the Coolin and the hills were black as ink, but far out in the western seas was a broad band of gold. I got up and went down to the shore. The mouth of the stream was shallow, but as I moved south I came to a place where two small capes enclosed an inlet. It must have been a fault in the volcanic rock, for its depth was portentous. I stripped and dived far into its cold abysses, but I did not reach the bottom. I came to the surface rather breathless, and struck out to sea, where I floated on my back and looked at the great rampart of crag. I saw that the place where I had spent the night was only a little oasis of green at the base of one of the grimmest corries the imagination could picture. It was as desert as Damaraland. I noticed, too, how sharply the cliffs rose from the level. There were chimneys and gullies by which a man might have made his way to the summit, but no one of them could have been scaled except by a mountaineer.

I was feeling better now, with all the frowsiness washed out of me, and I dried myself by racing up and down the heather. Then I noticed something. There were marks of human feet at the top of the deep-water inlet—not mine, for they were on the other side. The short sea-turf was bruised and trampled in several places, and there were broken stems of bracken. I thought that some fisherman had probably landed there to stretch his legs.

But that set me thinking of the Portuguese Jew. After breakfasting on my last morsels of food—a knuckle of braxy and a bit of oatcake—I set about tracking him from the place where he had first entered the glen. To get my bearings, I went back over the road I had come myself, and after a good deal of trouble I found his spoor. It was pretty clear as far as the stream, for he had been walking—or rather running—over ground with many patches of gravel on it. After that it was difficult, and I lost it entirely in the rough heather below the crags. All that I could make out for certain was that he had crossed the stream, and that his business, whatever it was, had been with the few acres of tumbled wilderness below the precipices.

I spent a busy morning there, but found nothing except the skeleton of a sheep picked clean by the ravens. It was a thankless job, and I got very cross over it. I had an ugly feeling that I was on a false scent and wasting my time. I wished to Heaven I had old Peter with me. He could follow spoor like a Bushman, and would have riddled the Portuguese Jew's track out of any jungle on earth. That was a game I had never learned, for in the old days I had always left it to my natives. I chucked the attempt, and lay disconsolately on a warm patch of grass and smoked and thought about Peter. But my chief reflections were that I had breakfasted at five, that it was now eleven, that I was intolerably hungry, that there was nothing here to feed a grasshopper, and that I should starve unless I got supplies.

It was a long road to my cache, but there were no two ways of it. My only hope was to sit tight in the glen, and it might involve a wait of days. To wait I must have food, and, though it meant relinquishing guard for a matter of six hours, the risk had to be taken. I set off at a brisk pace with a very depressed mind.

From the map it seemed that a short cut lay over a pass in the range. I resolved to take it, and that short cut, like most of its kind, was unblessed by Heaven. I will not dwell upon the discomforts of the journey. I found myself slithering among screes, climbing steep chimneys, and travelling precariously along razor-backs. The shoes were nearly rent from my feet by the infernal rocks, which were all pitted as if by some geological small-pox. When at last I crossed the divide, I had a horrible business getting down from one level to another in a gruesome corrie, where each step was composed of smooth boiler-plates. But at last I was among the bogs on the east side, and came to the place beside the road where I had fixed my cache.

The faithful Amos had not failed me. There were the provisions—a couple of small loaves, a dozen tins, and a bottle of whisky. I made the best pack I could of them in my waterproof, swung it on my stick, and started back, thinking that I must be very like the picture of Christian on the title-page of *Pilgrim's Progress.*

I was liker Christian before I reached my destination—Christian after he had got up the Hill Difficulty. The morning's walk had been bad, but the afternoon's was worse, for I was in a fever to get back, and, having had enough of the hills, chose the longer route I had followed the previous day. I was mortally afraid of being seen, for I cut a queer figure, so I avoided every stretch of road where I had not a clear view ahead. Many weary detours I made among moss-hags and screes and the stony channels of burns. But I got there at last, and it was almost with a sense of comfort that I flung my pack down beside the stream where I had passed the night.

I ate a good meal, lit my pipe, and fell into the equable mood which follows upon fatigue ended and hunger satisfied. The sun was westering, and its light fell upon the rock-wall above the place where I had abandoned my search for the spoor.

As I gazed at it idly I saw a curious thing.

It seemed to be split in two and a shaft of sunlight came through between. There could be no doubt about it. I saw the end of the shaft on the moor beneath, while all the rest lay in shadow. I rubbed my eyes, and got out my glasses. Then I guessed the explanation. There was a rock tower close against the face of the main precipice and indistinguishable from it to anyone looking direct at the face. Only when the sun fell on it obliquely could it be discovered. And between the tower and the cliff there must be a substantial hollow.

The discovery brought me to my feet, and set me running towards the end of the shaft of sunlight. I left the heather, scrambled up some yards of screes, and had a difficult time on some very smooth slabs, where only the friction of tweed and rough rock gave me a hold. Slowly I worked my way towards the speck of sunlight, till I found a handhold, and swung myself into the crack. On one side was the main wall of the hill, on the other a tower some ninety feet high, and between them a long crevice varying in width from three to six feet. Beyond it there showed a small bright patch of sea.

There was more, for at the point where I entered it there was an overhang which made a fine cavern, low at the entrance but a dozen feet high inside, and as dry as tinder. Here, thought I, is the perfect hiding-place. Before going farther I resolved to return for food. It was not very easy descending, and I slipped the last twenty feet, landing on my head in a soft patch of screes. At the burnside I filled my flask from the whisky bottle, and put half a loaf, a tin of sardines, a tin of tongue, and a packet of chocolate in my waterproof pockets. Laden as I was, it took me some time to get up again, but I managed it, and stored my belongings in a corner of the cave. Then I set out to explore the rest of the crack.

It slanted down and then rose again to a small platform. After that it dropped in easy steps to the moor beyond the tower. If the Portuguese Jew had come here, that was the way by which he had reached it, for he would not have had the time to make my ascent. I went very cautiously, for I felt I was on the eve of a big discovery. The platform was partly hidden from my end by a bend in the crack, and it was more or less screened by an outlying bastion of the tower from the other side. Its surface was covered with fine powdery dust, as were the steps beyond it. In some excitement I knelt down and examined it.

Beyond doubt there was spoor here. I knew the Portuguese Jew's footmarks by this time, and I made them out clearly, especially in one corner. But there were other footsteps, quite different. The one showed the rackets of rough country boots, the others were from un-nailed soles. Again I longed for Peter to make certain, though I was pretty sure of my conclusions. The man I had followed had come here, and he had not stayed long. Someone else had been here, probably later, for the un-nailed shoes overlaid the rackets. The first man might have left a message for the second. Perhaps the second was that human presence of which I had been dimly conscious in the night-time.

I carefully removed all traces of my own footmarks, and went back to my cave. My head was humming with my discovery. I remembered Gresson's word to his friend: 'Tomorrow night.' As I read it, the Portuguese Jew had taken a message from Gresson to someone, and that someone had come from somewhere and picked it up. The message contained an assignation for this very night. I had found a point of observation, for no one was likely to come near my cave, which was reached from the moor by such a toilsome climb. There I should bivouac and see what the darkness brought forth. I remember reflecting on the amazing luck which had so far attended me. As I looked from my refuge at the blue haze of twilight creeping over the waters, I felt my pulses quicken with a wild anticipation.

Then I heard a sound below me, and craned my neck round the edge of the tower. A man was climbing up the rock by the way I had come.

CHAPTER SEVEN

I Hear of the Wild Birds

I saw an old green felt hat, and below it lean tweed-clad shoulders. Then I saw a knapsack with a stick slung through it, as the owner wriggled his way on to a shelf. Presently he turned his face upward to judge the remaining distance. It was the face of a young man, a face sallow and angular, but now a little flushed with the day's sun and the work of climbing. It was a face that I had first seen at Fosse Manor.

I felt suddenly sick and heartsore. I don't know why, but I had never really associated the intellectuals of Biggleswick with a business like this. None of them but Ivery, and he was different. They had been silly and priggish, but no more—I would have taken my oath on it. Yet here was one of them engaged in black treason against his native land. Something began to beat in my temples when I remembered that Mary and this man had been friends, that he had held her hand, and called her by her Christian name. My first impulse was to wait till he got up and then pitch him down among the boulders and let his German accomplices puzzle over his broken neck.

With difficulty I kept down that tide of fury. I had my duty to do, and to keep on terms with this man was part of it. I had to convince him that I was an accomplice, and that might not be easy. I leaned over the edge, and, as he got to his feet on the ledge above the boiler-plates, I whistled so that he turned his face to me.

'Hullo, Wake,'I said.

He started, stared for a second, and recognized me. He did not seem over-pleased to see me.

'Brand!' he cried. 'How did you get here?'

He swung himself up beside me, straightened his back and unbuckled his knapsack. 'I thought this was my own private sanctuary, and that nobody knew it but me. Have you spotted the cave? It's the best bedroom in Skye.' His tone was, as usual, rather acid.

That little hammer was beating in my head. I longed to get my hands on his throat and choke the smug treason in him. But I kept my mind fixed on one purpose—to persuade him that I shared his secret and was on his side. His off-hand self-possession seemed only the clever screen of the surprised conspirator who was hunting for a plan.

We entered the cave, and he flung his pack into a corner. 'Last time I was here,' he said, 'I covered the floor with heather. We must get some more if we would sleep soft.' In the twilight he was a dim figure, but he seemed a new man from the one I had last seen in the Moot Hall at Biggleswick. There was a wiry vigour in his body and a purpose in his face. What a fool I had been to set him down as no more than a conceited fidneur!

He went out to the shelf again and sniffed the fresh evening. There was a wonderful red sky in the west, but in the crevice the shades had fallen, and only the bright patches at either end told of the sunset.

'Wake,' I said, 'you and I have to understand each other. I'm a friend of Ivery and I know the meaning of this place. I discovered it by accident, but I want you to know that I'm heart and soul with you. You may trust me in tonight's job as if I were Ivery himself.'

He swung round and looked at me sharply. His eyes were hot again, as I remembered them at our first meeting.

'What do you mean? How much do you know?'

The hammer was going hard in my forehead, and I had to pull myself together to answer.

'I know that at the end of this crack a message was left last night, and that someone came out of the sea and picked it up. That someone is coming again when darkness falls, and there will be another message.'

He had turned his head away. 'You are talking nonsense. No submarine could land on this coast.'

I could see that he was trying me.

'This morning,' I said, 'I swam in the deep-water inlet below us. It is the most perfect submarine shelter in Britain.'

He still kept his face from me, looking the way he had come. For a moment he was silent, and then he spoke in the bitter, drawling voice which had annoyed me at Fosse Manor.

'How do you reconcile this business with your principles, Mr Brand? You were always a patriot, I remember, though you didn't see eye to eye with the Government.'

It was not quite what I expected and I was unready. I stammered in my reply. 'It's because I am a patriot that I want peace. I think that ... I mean ...'

'Therefore you are willing to help the enemy to win?'

'They have already won. I want that recognized and the end hurried on.' I was getting my mind clearer and continued fluently.

'The longer the war lasts, the worse this country is ruined. We must make the people realize the truth, and—'

But he swung round suddenly, his eyes blazing.

'You blackguard!' he cried, 'you damnable blackguard!' And he flung himself on me like a wild-cat.

I had got my answer. He did not believe me, he knew me for a spy, and he was determined to do me in. We were beyond finesse now, and back at the old barbaric game. It was his life or mine. The hammer beat furiously in my head as we closed, and a fierce satisfaction rose in my heart.

He never had a chance, for though he was in good trim and had the light, wiry figure of the mountaineer, he hadn't a quarter of my muscular strength. Besides, he was wrongly placed, for he had the outside station. Had he been on the inside he might have toppled me over the edge by his sudden assault. As it was, I grappled him and forced him to the ground, squeezing the breath out of his body in the process. I must have hurt him considerably, but he never gave a cry. With a good deal of trouble I lashed his hands behind his back with the belt of my waterproof, carried him inside the cave and laid him in the dark end of it. Then I tied his feet with the strap of his own knapsack. I would have to gag him, but that could wait.

I had still to contrive a plan of action for the night, for I did not know what part he had been meant to play in it. He might be the messenger instead of the Portuguese Jew, in which case he would have papers about his person. If he knew of the cave, others might have the same knowledge, and I had better shift him before they came. I looked at my wrist-watch, and the luminous dial showed that the hour was half past nine.

Then I noticed that the bundle in the corner was sobbing. It was a horrid sound and it worried me. I had a little pocket electric torch and I flashed it on Wake's face. If he was crying, it was with dry eyes.

'What are you going to do with me?' he asked.

'That depends,' I said grimly.

'Well, I'm ready. I may be a poor creature, but I'm damned if I'm afraid of you, or anything like you.' That was a brave thing to say, for it was a lie; his teeth were chattering.

'I'm ready for a deal,' I said.

'You won't get it,' was his answer. 'Cut my throat if you mean to, but for God's sake don't insult me ... I choke when I think about you. You come to us and we welcome you, and receive you in our houses, and tell you our inmost thoughts, and all the time you're a bloody traitor. You want to sell us to Germany. You may win now, but by God! your time will come! That is my last word to you ... you swine!'

The hammer stopped beating in my head. I saw myself suddenly as a blind, preposterous fool. I strode over to Wake, and he shut his eyes as if he expected a blow. Instead I unbuckled the straps which held his legs and arms.

'Wake, old fellow,' I said, 'I'm the worst kind of idiot. I'll eat all the dirt you want. I'll give you leave to knock me black and blue, and I won't lift a hand. But not now. Now we've another job on hand. Man, we're on the same side and I never knew it. It's too bad a case for apologies, but if it's any consolation to you I feel the lowest dog in Europe at this moment.'

He was sitting up rubbing his bruised shoulders. 'What do you mean?' he asked hoarsely.

'I mean that you and I are allies. My name's not Brand. I'm a soldier—a general, if you want to know. I went to Biggleswick under orders, and I came chasing up here on the same job. Ivery's the biggest German agent in Britain and I'm after him. I've struck his communication lines, and this very night, please God, we'll get the last clue to the riddle. Do you hear? We're in this business together, and you've got to lend a hand.'

I told him briefly the story of Gresson, and how I had tracked his man here. As I talked we ate our supper, and I wish I could have watched Wake's face. He asked questions, for he wasn't convinced in a hurry. I think it was my mention of Mary Lamington that did the trick. I don't know why, but that seemed to satisfy him. But he wasn't going to give himself away.

'You may count on me,' he said, 'for this is black, blackguardly treason. But you know my politics, and I don't change them for this. I'm more against your accursed war than ever, now that I know what war involves.'

'Right-o,' I said, 'I'm a pacifist myself. You won't get any heroics about war from me. I'm all for peace, but we've got to down those devils first.'

It wasn't safe for either of us to stick in that cave, so we cleared away the marks of our occupation, and hid our packs in a deep crevice on the rock. Wake announced his intention of climbing the tower, while there was still a faint afterglow of light. 'It's broad on the top, and I can keep a watch out to sea if any light shows. I've been up it before. I found the way two years ago. No, I won't fall asleep and tumble off. I slept most of the afternoon on the top of Sgurr Vhiconnich, and I'm as wakeful as a bat now.'

I watched him shin up the face of the tower, and admired greatly the speed and neatness with which he climbed. Then I followed the crevice southward to the hollow just below the platform where I had found the footmarks. There was a big boulder there, which partly shut off the view of it from the direction of our cave. The place was perfect for my purpose, for between the boulder and the wall of the tower was a narrow gap, through which I could hear all that passed on the platform. I found a stance where I could rest in comfort and keep an eye through the crack on what happened beyond.

There was still a faint light on the platform, but soon that disappeared and black darkness settled down on the hills. It was the dark of the moon, and, as had happened the night before, a thin wrack blew over the sky, hiding the stars. The place was very still, though now and then would come the cry of a bird from the crags that beetled above me, and from the shore the pipe of a tern or oyster-catcher. An owl hooted from somewhere up on the tower. That I reckoned was Wake, so I hooted back and was answered. I unbuckled my wrist-watch and pocketed it, lest its luminous dial should betray me; and I noticed that the hour was close on eleven. I had already removed my shoes, and my jacket was buttoned at the collar so as to show no shirt. I did not think that the coming visitor would trouble to explore the crevice beyond the platform, but I wanted to be prepared for emergencies.

Then followed an hour of waiting. I felt wonderfully cheered and exhilarated, for Wake had restored my confidence in human nature. In that eerie place we were wrapped round with mystery like a fog. Some unknown figure was coming out of the sea, the emissary of that Power we had been at grips with for three years. It was as if the war had just made contact with our own shores, and never, not even when I was alone in the South German forest, had I felt so much the sport of a whimsical fate. I only wished Peter could have been with me. And so my thoughts fled to Peter in his prison camp, and I longed for another sight of my old friend as a girl longs for her lover.

Then I heard the hoot of an owl, and presently the sound of careful steps fell on my ear. I could see nothing, but I guessed it was the Portuguese Jew, for I could hear the grinding of heavily nailed boots on the gritty rock.

The figure was very quiet. It appeared to be sitting down, and then it rose and fumbled with the wall of the tower just beyond the boulder behind which I sheltered. It seemed to move a stone and to replace it. After that came silence, and then once more the hoot of an owl. There were steps on the rock staircase, the steps of a man who did not know the road well and stumbled a little. Also they were the steps of one without nails in his boots.

They reached the platform and someone spoke. It was the Portuguese Jew and he spoke in good German.

'*Die voegelein schweigen im Walde,*' he said.

The answer came from a clear, authoritative voice.

'*Warte nur, balde ruhest du auch.*'

Clearly some kind of password, for sane men don't talk about little birds in that kind of situation. It sounded to me like indifferent poetry.

Then followed a conversation in low tones, of which I only caught odd phrases. I heard two names—Chelius and what sounded like a Dutch word, Bommaerts. Then to my joy I caught *Elfenbein*, and when uttered it seemed to be followed by a laugh. I heard too a phrase several times repeated, which seemed to me to be pure gibberish—*Die Stubenvogel verstehn*. It was spoken by the man from the sea. And then the word *Wildvogel*. The pair seemed demented about birds.

For a second an electric torch was flashed in the shelter of the rock, and I could see a tanned, bearded face looking at some papers. The light disappeared, and again the Portuguese Jew was fumbling with the stones at the base of the tower. To my joy he was close to my crack, and I could hear every word. 'You cannot come here very often,' he said, 'and it may be hard to arrange a meeting. See, therefore, the place I have made to put the *Viageffutter*. When I get a chance I will come here, and you will come also when you are able. Often there will be nothing, but sometimes there will be much.'

My luck was clearly in, and my exultation made me careless. A stone, on which a foot rested, slipped and though I checked myself at once, the confounded thing rolled down into the hollow, making a great clatter. I plastered myself in the embrasure of the rock and waited with a beating heart. The place was pitch dark, but they had an electric torch, and if they once flashed it on me I was gone. I heard them leave the platform and climb down into the hollow. There they stood listening, while I held my breath. Then I heard '*Nix, mein freund,*' and the two went back, the naval officer's boots slipping on the gravel.

They did not leave the platform together. The man from the sea bade a short farewell to the Portuguese Jew, listening, I thought, impatiently to his final message as if eager to be gone. It was a good half-hour before the latter took himself off, and I heard the sound of his nailed boots die away as he reached the heather of the moor.

I waited a little longer, and then crawled back to the cave. The owl hooted, and presently Wake descended lightly beside me; he must have known every foothold and handhold by heart to do the job in that inky blackness. I remember that he asked no question of me, but he used language rare on the lips of conscientious objectors about the men who had lately been in the crevice. We, who four hours earlier had been at death grips, now curled up on the hard floor like two tired dogs, and fell sound asleep.

I woke to find Wake in a thundering bad temper. The thing he remembered most about the night before was our scrap and the gross way I had insulted him. I didn't blame him, for if any man had taken me for a German spy I would have been out for his blood, and it was no good explaining that he had given me grounds for suspicion. He was as touchy about his blessed principles as an old maid about her age. I was feeling rather extra buckish myself and that didn't improve matters. His face was like a gargoyle as we went down to the beach to bathe, so I held my tongue. He was chewing the cud of his wounded pride.

But the salt water cleared out the dregs of his distemper. You couldn't be peevish swimming in that jolly, shining sea. We raced each other away beyond the inlet to the outer water, which a brisk morning breeze was curling. Then back to a promontory of heather, where the first beams of the sun coming over the Coolin dried our skins. He sat hunched up staring at the mountains while I prospected the rocks at the edge. Out in the Minch two destroyers were hurrying southward, and I wondered where in that waste of blue was the craft which had come here in the night watches.

I found the spoor of the man from the sea quite fresh on a patch of gravel above the tide-mark.

'There's our friend of the night,' I said.

'I believe the whole thing was a whimsy,' said Wake, his eyes on the chimneys of Sgurr Dearg. 'They were only two natives—poachers, perhaps, or tinkers.'

'They don't speak German in these parts.'

'It was Gaelic probably.'

'What do you make of this, then?' and I quoted the stuff about birds with which they had greeted each other.

Wake looked interested. 'That's *Uber allen Gipfeln*. Have you ever read Goethe?'

'Never a word. And what do you make of that?' I pointed to a flat rock below tide-mark covered with a tangle of seaweed. It was of a softer stone than the hard stuff in the hills and somebody had scraped off half the seaweed and a slice of the side. 'That wasn't done yesterday morning, for I had my bath here.'

Wake got up and examined the place. He nosed about in the crannies of the rocks lining the inlet, and got into the water again to explore better. When he joined me he was smiling. 'I apologize for my scepticism,' he said. 'There's been some petrol-driven craft here in the night. I can smell it, for I've a nose like a retriever. I daresay you're on the right track. Anyhow, though you seem to know a bit about German, you could scarcely invent immortal poetry.'

We took our belongings to a green crook of the burn, and made a very good breakfast. Wake had nothing in his pack but plasmon biscuits and raisins, for that, he said, was his mountaineering provender, but he was not averse to sampling my tinned stuff. He was a different-sized fellow out in the hills from the anaemic intellectual of Biggleswick. He had forgotten his beastly self-consciousness, and spoke of his hobby with a serious passion. It seemed he had scrambled about everywhere in Europe, from the Caucasus to the Pyrenees. I could see he must be good at the job, for he didn't brag of his exploits. It was the mountains that he loved, not wriggling his body up hard places. The Coolin, he said, were his favourites, for on some of them you could get two thousand feet of good rock. We got our glasses on the face of Sgurr Alasdair, and he sketched out for me various ways of getting to its grim summit. The Coolin and the Dolomites for him, for he had grown tired of the Chamonix aiguilles. I remember he described with tremendous gusto the joys of early dawn in Tyrol, when you ascended through acres of flowery meadows to a tooth of clean white limestone against a clean blue sky. He spoke, too, of the little wild hills in the Bavarian Wettersteingebirge, and of a guide he had picked up there and trained to the job.

'They called him Sebastian Buchwieser. He was the jolliest boy you ever saw, and as clever on crags as a chamois. He is probably dead by now, dead in a filthy jaeger battalion. That's you and your accursed war.'

'Well, we've got to get busy and end it in the right way,' I said. 'And you've got to help, my lad.'

He was a good draughtsman, and with his assistance I drew a rough map of the crevice where we had roosted for the night, giving its bearings carefully in relation to the burn and the sea. Then I wrote down all the details about Gresson and the Portuguese Jew, and described the latter in minute detail. I described, too, most precisely the cache where it had been arranged that the messages should be placed. That finished my stock of paper, and I left the record of the oddments overheard of the conversation for a later time. I put the thing in an old leather cigarette-case I possessed, and handed it to Wake.

'You've got to go straight off to the Kyle and not waste any time on the way. Nobody suspects you, so you can travel any road you please. When you get there you ask for Mr Andrew Amos, who has some Government job in the neighbourhood. Give him that paper from me. He'll know what to do with it all right. Tell him I'll get somehow to the Kyle before midday the day after tomorrow. I must cover my tracks a bit, so I can't come with you, and I want that thing in his hands just as fast as your legs will take you. If anyone tries to steal it from you, for God's sake eat it. You can see for yourself that it's devilish important.'

'I shall be back in England in three days,' he said. 'Any message for your other friends?'

'Forget all about me. You never saw me here. I'm still Brand, the amiable colonial studying social movements. If you meet Ivery, say you heard of me on the Clyde, deep in sedition. But if you see Miss Lamington you can tell her I'm past the Hill Difficulty. I'm coming back as soon as God will let me, and I'm going to drop right into the Biggleswick push. Only this time I'll be a little more advanced in my views ... You needn't get cross. I'm not saying anything against your principles. The main point is that we both hate dirty treason.'

He put the case in his waistcoat pocket. 'I'll go round Garsbheinn,' he said, 'and over by Camasunary. I'll be at the Kyle long before evening. I meant anyhow to sleep at Broadford tonight ... Goodbye, Brand, for I've forgotten your proper name. You're not a bad fellow, but you've landed me in melodrama for the first time in my sober existence. I have a grudge against you for mixing up the Coolin with a shilling shocker. You've spoiled their sanctity.'

'You've the wrong notion of romance,' I said. 'Why, man, last night for an hour you were in the front line—the place where the enemy forces touch our own. You were over the top—you were in No-man's-land.'

He laughed. 'That is one way to look at it'; and then he stalked off and I watched his lean figure till it was round the turn of the hill.

All that morning I smoked peacefully by the burn, and let my thoughts wander over the whole business. I had got precisely what Blenkiron wanted, a post office for the enemy. It would need careful handling, but I could see the juiciest lies passing that way to the *Grosses Haupiquartier*. Yet I had an ugly feeling at the back of my head that it had been all too easy, and that Ivery was not the man to be duped in this way for long. That set me thinking about the queer talk on the crevice. The poetry stuff I dismissed as the ordinary password, probably changed every time. But who were Chelius and Bommaerts, and what in the name of goodness were the Wild Birds and the Cage Birds? Twice in the past three years I had had two such riddles to solve—Scudder's scribble in his pocket-book, and Harry Bullivant's three words. I remembered how it had only been by constant chewing at them that I had got a sort of meaning, and I wondered if fate would some day expound this puzzle also.

Meantime I had to get back to London as inconspicuously as I had come. It might take some doing, for the police who had been active in Morvern might be still on the track, and it was essential that I should keep out of trouble and give no hint to Gresson and his friends that I had been so far north. However, that was for Amos to advise me on, and about noon I picked up my waterproof with its bursting pockets and set off on a long detour up the coast. All that blessed day I scarcely met a soul. I passed a distillery which seemed to have quit business, and in the evening came to a little town on the sea where I had a bed and supper in a superior kind of public-house.

Next day I struck southward along the coast, and had two experiences of interest. I had a good look at Ranna, and observed that the *Tobermory* was no longer there. Gresson had only waited to get his job finished; he could probably twist the old captain any way he wanted. The second was that at the door of a village smithy I saw the back of the Portuguese Jew. He was talking Gaelic this time—good Gaelic it sounded, and in that knot of idlers he would have passed for the ordinariest kind of gillie.

He did not see me, and I had no desire to give him the chance, for I had an odd feeling that the day might come when it would be good for us to meet as strangers.

That night I put up boldly in the inn at Broadford, where they fed me nobly on fresh sea-trout and I first tasted an excellent liqueur made of honey and whisky. Next morning I was early afoot, and well before midday was in sight of the narrows of the Kyle, and the two little stone clachans which face each other across the strip of sea.

About two miles from the place at a turn of the road I came upon a farmer's gig, drawn up by the wayside, with the horse cropping the moorland grass. A man sat on the bank smoking, with his left arm hooked in the reins. He was an oldish man, with a short, square figure, and a woollen comforter enveloped his throat.

CHAPTER EIGHT

The Adventures of a Bagman

'Ye're punctual to time, Mr Brand,' said the voice of Amos. 'But losh! man, what have ye done to your breeks! And your buits? Ye're no just very respectable in your appearance.'

I wasn't. The confounded rocks of the Coolin had left their mark on my shoes, which moreover had not been cleaned for a week, and the same hills had rent my jacket at the shoulders, and torn my trousers above the right knee, and stained every part of my apparel with peat and lichen.

I cast myself on the bank beside Amos and lit my pipe. 'Did you get my message?' I asked.

'Ay. It's gone on by a sure hand to the destination we ken of. Ye've managed well, Mr Brand, but I wish ye were back in London.' He sucked at his pipe, and the shaggy brows were pulled so low as to hide the wary eyes. Then he proceeded to think aloud.

'Ye canna go back by Mallaig. I don't just understand why, but they're lookin' for you down that line. It's a vexatious business when your friends, meanin' the polis, are doing their best to upset your plans and you no able to enlighten them. I could send word to the Chief Constable and get ye through to London without a stop like a load of fish from Aiberdeen, but that would be spoilin' the fine character ye've been at such pains to construct. Na, na! Ye maun take the risk and travel by Muirtown without ony creedentials.'

'It can't be a very big risk,' I interpolated.

'I'm no so sure. Gresson's left the *Tobermory.* He went by here yesterday, on the Mallaig boat, and there was a wee blackavised man with him that got out at the Kyle. He's there still, stoppin' at the hotel. They ca' him Linklater and he travels in whisky. I don't like the looks of him.'

'But Gresson does not suspect me?'

'Maybe no. But ye wouldna like him to see ye hereaways. Yon gentry don't leave muckle to chance. Be very certain that every man in Gresson's lot kens all about ye, and has your description down to the mole on your chin.'

'Then they've got it wrong,' I replied.

'I was speakin' feeguratively,' said Amos. 'I was considerin' your case the feck of yesterday, and I've brought the best I could do for ye in the gig. I wish ye were more respectable clad, but a good topcoat will hide defeecencies.'

From behind the gig's seat he pulled out an ancient Gladstone bag and revealed its contents. There was a bowler of a vulgar and antiquated style; there was a ready-made overcoat of some dark cloth, of the kind that a clerk wears on the road to the office; there was a pair of detachable celluloid cuffs, and there was a linen collar and dickie. Also there was a small handcase, such as bagmen carry on their rounds.

'That's your luggage,' said Amos with pride. 'That wee bag's full of samples. Ye'll mind I took the precaution of measurin' ye in Glasgow, so the things'll fit. Ye've got a new name, Mr Brand, and I've taken a room for ye in the hotel on the strength of it. Ye're Archibald McCaskie, and ye're travellin' for the firm o' Todd, Sons & Brothers, of Edinburgh. Ye ken the folk? They publish wee releegious books, that ye've bin trying to sell for Sabbath-school prizes to the Free Kirk ministers in Skye.'

The notion amused Amos, and he relapsed into the sombre chuckle which with him did duty for a laugh.

I put my hat and waterproof in the bag and donned the bowler and the top-coat. They fitted fairly well. Likewise the cuffs and collar, though here I struck a snag, for I had lost my scarf somewhere in the Coolin, and Amos, pelican-like, had to surrender the rusty black tie which adorned his own person. It was a queer rig, and I felt like nothing on earth in it, but Amos was satisfied.

'Mr McCaskie, sir,' he said, 'ye're the very model of a publisher's traveller. Ye'd better learn a few biographical details, which ye've maybe forgotten. Ye're an Edinburgh man, but ye were some years in London, which explains the way ye speak. Ye bide at 6, Russell Street, off the Meadows, and ye're an elder in the Nethergate U.F. Kirk. Have ye ony special taste ye could lead the crack on to, if ye're engaged in conversation?'

I suggested the English classics.

'And very suitable. Ye can try poalitics, too. Ye'd better be a Free-trader but convertit by Lloyd George. That's a common case, and ye'll need to be by-ordinar common ... If I was you, I would daunder about here for a bit, and no arrive at your hotel till after dark. Then ye can have your supper and gang to bed. The Muirtown train leaves at half-seven in the morning ... Na, ye can't come with me. It wouldna do for us to be seen thegither. If I meet ye in the street I'll never let on I know ye.'

Amos climbed into the gig and jolted off home. I went down to the shore and sat among the rocks, finishing about tea-time the remains of my provisions. In the mellow gloaming I strolled into the clachan and got a boat to put me over to the inn. It proved to be a comfortable place, with a motherly old landlady who showed me to my room and promised ham and eggs and cold salmon for supper. After a good wash, which I needed, and an honest attempt to make my clothes presentable, I descended to the meal in a coffee-room lit by a single dim parafin lamp.

The food was excellent, and, as I ate, my spirits rose. In two days I should be back in London beside Blenkiron and somewhere within a day's journey of Mary. I could picture no scene now without thinking how Mary fitted into it. For her sake I held Biggleswick delectable, because I had seen her there. I wasn't sure if this was love, but it was something I had never dreamed of before, something which I now hugged the thought of. It made the whole earth rosy and golden for me, and life so well worth living that I felt like a miser towards the days to come.

I had about finished supper, when I was joined by another guest. Seen in the light of that infamous lamp, he seemed a small, alert fellow, with a bushy, black moustache, and black hair parted in the middle. He had fed already and appeared to be hungering for human society.

In three minutes he had told me that he had come down from Portree and was on his way to Leith. A minute later he had whipped out a card on which I read 'J. J. Linklater', and in the corner the name of Hatherwick Bros. His accent betrayed that he hailed from the west.

'I've been up among the distilleries,' he informed me. 'It's a poor business distillin' in these times, wi' the teetotallers yowlin' about the nation's shame and the way to lose the war. I'm a temperate man mysel', but I would think shame to spile decent folks' business. If the Government want to stop the drink, let them buy us out. They've permitted us to invest good money in the trade, and they must see that we get it back. The other way will wreck public credit. That's what I say. Supposin' some Labour Government takes the notion that soap's bad for the nation? Are they goin' to shut up Port Sunlight? Or good clothes? Or lum hats? There's no end to their daftness if they once start on that track. A lawfu' trade's a lawfu' trade, says I, and it's contrary to public policy to pit it at the mercy of wheen cranks. D'ye no agree, sir? By the way, I havena got your name?'

I told him and he rambled on.

'We're blenders and do a very high-class business, mostly foreign. The war's hit us wi' our export trade, of course, but we're no as bad as some. What's your line, Mr McCaskie?'

When he heard he was keenly interested.

'D'ye say so? Ye're from Todd's! Man, I was in the book business mysel', till I changed it for something a wee bit more lucrative. I was on the road for three years for Andrew Matheson. Ye ken the name—Paternoster Row—I've forgotten the number. I had a kind of ambition to start a book-sellin' shop of my own and to make Linklater o' Paisley a big name in the trade. But I got the offer from Hatherwick's, and I was wantin' to get married, so filthy lucre won the day. And I'm no sorry I changed. If it hadna been for this war, I would have been makin' four figures with my salary and commissions ... My pipe's out. Have you one of those rare and valuable curiosities called a spunk, Mr McCaskie?'

He was a merry little grig of a man, and he babbled on, till I announced my intention of going to bed. If this was Amos's bagman, who had been seen in company with Gresson, I understood how idle may be the suspicions of a clever man. He had probably foregathered with Gresson on the Skye boat, and wearied that saturnine soul with his cackle.

I was up betimes, paid my bill, ate a breakfast of porridge and fresh haddock, and walked the few hundred yards to the station. It was a warm, thick morning, with no sun visible, and the Skye hills misty to their base. The three coaches on the little train were nearly filled when I had bought my ticket, and I selected a third-class smoking carriage which held four soldiers returning from leave.

The train was already moving when a late passenger hurried along the platform and clambered in beside me. A cheery 'Mornin', Mr McCaskie,' revealed my fellow guest at the hotel.

We jolted away from the coast up a broad glen and then on to a wide expanse of bog with big hills showing towards the north. It was a drowsy day, and in that atmosphere of shag and crowded humanity I felt my eyes closing. I had a short nap, and woke to find that Mr Linklater had changed his seat and was now beside me.

'We'll no get a Scotsman till Muirtown,' he said. 'Have ye nothing in your samples ye could give me to read?'

I had forgotten about the samples. I opened the case and found the oddest collection of little books, all in gay bindings. Some were religious, with names like *Dew of Hermon* and *Cool Siloam*; some were innocent narratives, *How Tommy saved his Pennies*, *A Missionary Child in China*, and *Little Susie and her Uncle*. There was a *Life of David Livingstone*, a child's book on sea-shells, and a richly gilt edition of the poems of one James Montgomery. I offered the selection to Mr Linklater, who grinned and chose the Missionary Child. 'It's not the reading I'm accustomed to,' he said. 'I like strong meat—Hall Caine and Jack London. By the way, how d'ye square this business of yours wi' the booksellers? When I was in Matheson's there would have been trouble if we had dealt direct wi' the public like you.'

The confounded fellow started to talk about the details of the book trade, of which I knew nothing. He wanted to know on what terms we sold 'juveniles', and what discount we gave the big wholesalers, and what class of book we put out 'on sale'. I didn't understand a word of his jargon, and I must have given myself away badly, for he asked me questions about firms of which I had never heard, and I had to make some kind of answer. I told myself that the donkey was harmless, and that his opinion of me mattered nothing, but as soon as I decently could I pretended to be absorbed in the *Pilgrim's Progress*, a gaudy copy of which was among the samples. It opened at the episode of Christian and Hopeful in the Enchanted Ground, and in that stuffy carriage I presently followed the example of Heedless and Too-Bold and fell sound asleep. I was awakened by the train rumbling over the points of a little moorland junction. Sunk in a pleasing lethargy, I sat with my eyes closed, and then covertly took a glance at my companion. He had abandoned the Missionary Child and was reading a little dun-coloured book, and marking passages with a pencil. His face was absorbed, and it was a new face, not the vacant, good-humoured look of the garrulous bagman, but something shrewd, purposeful, and formidable. I remained hunched up as if still sleeping, and tried to see what the book was. But my eyes, good as they are, could make out nothing of the text or title, except that I had a very strong impression that that book was not written in the English tongue.

I woke abruptly, and leaned over to him. Quick as lightning he slid his pencil up his sleeve and turned on me with a fatuous smile.

'What d'ye make o' this, Mr McCaskie? It's a wee book I picked up at a roup along with fifty others. I paid five shillings for the lot. It looks like Gairman, but in my young days they didna teach us foreign languages.'

I took the thing and turned over the pages, trying to keep any sign of intelligence out of my face. It was German right enough, a little manual of hydrography with no publisher's name on it. It had the look of the kind of textbook a Government department might issue to its officials.

I handed it back. 'It's either German or Dutch. I'm not much of a scholar, barring a little French and the Latin I got at Heriot's Hospital ... This is an awful slow train, Mr Linklater.'

The soldiers were playing nap, and the bagman proposed a game of cards. I remembered in time that I was an elder in the Nethergate U.F. Church and refused with some asperity. After that I shut my eyes again, for I wanted to think out this new phenomenon.

The fellow knew German—that was clear. He had also been seen in Gresson's company. I didn't believe he suspected me, though I suspected him profoundly. It was my business to keep strictly to my part and give him no cause to doubt me. He was clearly practising his own part on me, and I must appear to take him literally on his professions. So, presently, I woke up and engaged him in a disputatious conversation about the morality of selling strong liquors. He responded readily, and put the case for alcohol with much point and vehemence. The discussion interested the soldiers, and one of them, to show he was on Linklater's side, produced a flask and offered him a drink. I concluded by observing morosely that the bagman had been a better man when he peddled books for Alexander Matheson, and that put the closure on the business.

That train was a record. It stopped at every station, and in the afternoon it simply got tired and sat down in the middle of a moor and reflected for an hour. I stuck my head out of the window now and then, and smelt the rooty fragrance of bogs, and when we halted on a bridge I watched the trout in the pools of the brown river. Then I slept and smoked alternately, and began to get furiously hungry.

Once I woke to hear the soldiers discussing the war. There was an argument between a lance-corporal in the Camerons and a sapper private about some trivial incident on the Somme.

'I tell ye I was there,' said the Cameron. 'We were relievin' the Black Watch, and Fritz was shelling the road, and we didna get up to the line till one o'clock in the mornin'. Frae Frickout Circus to the south end o' the High Wood is every bit o' five mile.'

'Not abune three,' said the sapper dogmatically.

'Man, I've trampit it.'

'Same here. I took up wire every nicht for a week.'

The Cameron looked moodily round the company. 'I wish there was anither man here that kent the place. He wad bear me out. These boys are no good, for they didna join till later. I tell ye it's five mile.'

'Three,' said the sapper.

Tempers were rising, for each of the disputants felt his veracity assailed. It was too hot for a quarrel and I was so drowsy that I was heedless.

'Shut up, you fools,' I said. 'The distance is six kilometres, so you're both wrong.'

My tone was so familiar to the men that it stopped the wrangle, but it was not the tone of a publisher's traveller. Mr Linklater cocked his ears.

'What's a kilometre, Mr McCaskie?' he asked blandly.

'Multiply by five and divide by eight and you get the miles.'

I was on my guard now, and told a long story of a nephew who had been killed on the Somme, and how I had corresponded with the War Office about his case. 'Besides,' I said, 'I'm a great student o' the newspapers, and I've read all the books about the war. It's a difficult time this for us all, and if you can take a serious interest in the campaign it helps a lot. I mean working out the places on the map and reading Haig's dispatches.'

'Just so,' he said dryly, and I thought he watched me with an odd look in his eyes.

A fresh idea possessed me. This man had been in Gresson's company, he knew German, he was obviously something very different from what he professed to be. What if he were in the employ of our own Secret Service? I had appeared out of the void at the Kyle, and I had made but a poor appearance as a bagman, showing no knowledge of my own trade. I was in an area interdicted to the ordinary public; and he had good reason to keep an eye on my movements. He was going south, and so was I; clearly we must somehow part company.

'We change at Muirtown, don't we?' I asked. 'When does the train for the south leave?'

He consulted a pocket timetable. 'Ten-thirty-three. There's generally four hours to wait, for we're due in at six-fifteen. But this auld hearse will be lucky if it's in by nine.'

His forecast was correct. We rumbled out of the hills into haughlands and caught a glimpse of the North Sea. Then we were hung up while a long goods train passed down the line. It was almost dark when at last we crawled into Muirtown station and disgorged our load of hot and weary soldiery.

I bade an ostentatious farewell to Linklater. 'Very pleased to have met you. I'll see you later on the Edinburgh train. I'm for a walk to stretch my legs, and a bite o' supper.' I was very determined that the ten-thirty for the south should leave without me.

My notion was to get a bed and a meal in some secluded inn, and walk out next morning and pick up a slow train down the line. Linklater had disappeared towards the guard's van to find his luggage, and the soldiers were sitting on their packs with that air of being utterly and finally lost and neglected which characterizes the British fighting-man on a journey. I gave up my ticket and, since I had come off a northern train, walked unhindered into the town.

It was market night, and the streets were crowded. Blue-jackets from the Fleet, country-folk in to shop, and every kind of military detail thronged the pavements. Fish-hawkers were crying their wares, and there was a tatterdemalion piper making the night hideous at a corner. I took a tortuous route and finally fixed on a modest-looking public-house in a back street. When I inquired for a room I could find no one in authority, but a slatternly girl informed me that there was one vacant bed, and that I could have ham and eggs in the bar. So, after hitting my head violently against a cross-beam, I stumbled down some steps and entered a frowsty little place smelling of spilt beer and stale tobacco.

The promised ham and eggs proved impossible—there were no eggs to be had in Muirtown that night—but I was given cold mutton and a pint of indifferent ale. There was nobody in the place but two farmers drinking hot whisky and water and discussing with sombre interest the rise in the price of feeding-stuffs. I ate my supper, and was just preparing to find the whereabouts of my bedroom when through the street door there entered a dozen soldiers.

In a second the quiet place became a babel. The men were strictly sober; but they were in that temper of friendliness which demands a libation of some kind. One was prepared to stand treat; he was the leader of the lot, and it was to celebrate the end of his leave that he was entertaining his pals. From where I sat I could not see him, but his voice was dominant. 'What's your fancy, jock? Beer for you, Andra? A pint and a dram for me. This is better than vongblong and vongrooge, Davie. Man, when I'm sittin' in those estamints, as they ca' them, I often long for a guid Scots public.'

The voice was familiar. I shifted my seat to get a view of the speaker, and then I hastily drew back. It was the Scots Fusilier I had clipped on the jaw in defending Gresson after the Glasgow meeting.

But by a strange fatality he had caught sight of me.

'Whae's that i' the corner?' he cried, leaving the bar to stare at me. Now it is a queer thing, but if you have once fought with a man, though only for a few seconds, you remember his face, and the scrap in Glasgow had been under a lamp. The jock recognized me well enough.

'By God!' he cried, 'if this is no a bit o' luck! Boys, here's the man I feucht wi' in Glesca. Ye mind I telled ye about it. He laid me oot, and it's my turn to do the same wi' him. I had a notion I was gaun to mak' a nicht o't. There's naebody can hit Geordie Hamilton without Geordie gettin' his ain back some day. Get up, man, for I'm gaun to knock the heid off ye.'

I duly got up, and with the best composure I could muster looked him in the face.

'You're mistaken, my friend. I never clapped eyes on you before, and I never was in Glasgow in my life.'

'That's a damned lee,' said the Fusilier. 'Ye're the man, and if ye're no, ye're like enough him to need a hidin'!'

'Confound your nonsense!' I said. 'I've no quarrel with you, and I've better things to do than be scrapping with a stranger in a public-house.'

'Have ye sae? Well, I'll learn ye better. I'm gaun to hit ye, and then ye'll hae to fecht whether ye want it or no. Tam, haud my jacket, and see that my drink's no skailed.'

This was an infernal nuisance, for a row here would bring in the police, and my dubious position would be laid bare. I thought of putting up a fight, for I was certain I could lay out the jock a second time, but the worst of that was that I did not know where the thing would end. I might have to fight the lot of them, and that meant a noble public shindy. I did my best to speak my opponent fair. I said we were all good friends and offered to stand drinks for the party. But the Fusilier's blood was up and he was spoiling for a row, ably abetted by his comrades. He had his tunic off now and was stamping in front of me with doubled fists.

I did the best thing I could think of in the circumstances. My seat was close to the steps which led to the other part of the inn. I grabbed my hat, darted up them, and before they realized what I was doing had bolted the door behind me. I could hear pandemonium break loose in the bar.

I slipped down a dark passage to another which ran at right angles to it, and which seemed to connect the street door of the inn itself with the back premises. I could hear voices in the little hall, and that stopped me short.

One of them was Linklater's, but he was not talking as Linklater had talked. He was speaking educated

English. I heard another with a Scots accent, which I took to be the landlord's, and a third which sounded like some superior sort of constable's, very prompt and official. I heard one phrase, too, from Linklater—'He calls himself McCaskie.' Then they stopped, for the turmoil from the bar had reached the front door. The Fusilier and his friends were looking for me by the other entrance.

The attention of the men in the hall was distracted, and that gave me a chance. There was nothing for it but the back door. I slipped through it into a courtyard and almost tumbled over a tub of water. I planted the thing so that anyone coming that way would fall over it. A door led me into an empty stable, and from that into a lane. It was all absurdly easy, but as I started down the lane I heard a mighty row and the sound of angry voices. Someone had gone into the tub and I hoped it was Linklater. I had taken a liking to the Fusilier jock.

There was the beginning of a moon somewhere, but that lane was very dark. I ran to the left, for on the right it looked like a cul-de-sac. This brought me into a quiet road of two-storied cottages which showed at one end the lights of a street. So I took the other way, for I wasn't going to have the whole population of Muirtown on the hue-and-cry after me. I came into a country lane, and I also came into the van of the pursuit, which must have taken a short cut. They shouted when they saw me, but I had a small start, and legged it down that road in the belief that I was making for open country.

That was where I was wrong. The road took me round to the other side of the town, and just when I was beginning to think I had a fair chance I saw before me the lights of a signal-box and a little to the left of it the lights of the station. In half an hour's time the Edinburgh train would be leaving, but I had made that impossible. Behind me I could hear the pursuers, giving tongue like hound puppies, for they had attracted some pretty drunken gentlemen to their party. I was badly puzzled where to turn, when I noticed outside the station a long line of blurred lights, which could only mean a train with the carriage blinds down. It had an engine attached and seemed to be waiting for the addition of a couple of trucks to start. It was a wild chance, but the only one I saw. I scrambled across a piece of waste ground, climbed an embankment and found myself on the metals. I ducked under the couplings and got on the far side of the train, away from the enemy.

Then simultaneously two things happened. I heard the yells of my pursuers a dozen yards off, and the train jolted into motion. I jumped on the footboard, and looked into an open window. The compartment was packed with troops, six a side and two men sitting on the floor, and the door was locked. I dived headforemost through the window and landed on the neck of a weary warrior who had just dropped off to sleep.

While I was falling I made up my mind on my conduct. I must be intoxicated, for I knew the infinite sympathy of the British soldier towards those thus overtaken. They pulled me to my feet, and the man I had descended on rubbed his skull and blasphemously demanded explanations.

'Gen'lmen,' I hiccoughed, 'I 'pologize. I was late for this bl-blighted train and I mus' be in E'inburgh 'morrow or I'll get the sack. I 'pologize. If I've hurt my friend's head, I'll kiss it and make it well.'

At this there was a great laugh. 'Ye'd better accept, Pete,' said one. 'It's the first time anybody ever offered to kiss your ugly heid.'

A man asked me who I was, and I appeared to be searching for a card-case.

'Losht,' I groaned. 'Losht, and so's my wee bag and I've bashed my po' hat. I'm an awful sight, gen'lmen—an awful warning to be in time for trains. I'm John Johnstone, managing clerk to Messrs Watters, Brown & Elph'stone, 923 Charl'tte Street, E'inburgh. I've been up north seein' my mamma.'

'Ye should be in France,' said one man.

'Wish't I was, but they wouldn't let me. "Mr Johnstone," they said, "ye're no dam good. Ye've varicose veins and a bad heart," they said. So I says, "Good mornin', gen'lmen. Don't blame me if the country's ru'ned". That's what I said.'

I had by this time occupied the only remaining space left on the floor. With the philosophy of their race the men had accepted my presence, and were turning again to their own talk. The train had got up speed, and as I judged it to be a special of some kind I looked for few stoppings. Moreover it was not a corridor carriage, but one of the old-fashioned kind, so I was safe for a time from the unwelcome attention of conductors. I stretched my legs below the seat, rested my head against the knees of a brawny gunner, and settled down to make the best of it.

My reflections were not pleasant. I had got down too far below the surface, and had the naked feeling you get in a dream when you think you have gone to the theatre in your nightgown. I had had three names in two days, and as many characters. I felt as if I had no home or position anywhere, and was only a stray dog with everybody's hand and foot against me. It was an ugly sensation, and it was not redeemed by any acute fear or any knowledge of being mixed up in some desperate drama. I knew I could easily go on to Edinburgh, and when the police made trouble, as they would, a wire to Scotland Yard would settle matters in a couple of hours. There wasn't a suspicion of bodily danger to restore my dignity. The worst that could happen would be that Ivery would hear of my being befriended by the authorities, and the part I had settled to play would be impossible. He would certainly hear. I had the greatest respect for his intelligence service.

Yet that was bad enough. So far I had done well. I had put Gresson off the scent. I had found out what Bullivant wanted to know, and I had only to return unostentatiously to London to have won out on the game. I told myself all that, but it didn't cheer my spirits. I was feeling mean and hunted and very cold about the feet.

But I have a tough knuckle of obstinacy in me which makes me unwilling to give up a thing till I am fairly choked off it. The chances were badly against me. The Scottish police were actively interested in my movements and would be ready to welcome me at my journey's end. I had ruined my hat, and my clothes, as Amos had observed, were not respectable. I had got rid of a four-days' beard the night before, but had cut myself in the process, and what with my weather-beaten face and tangled hair looked liker a tinker than a decent bagman. I thought with longing of my portmanteau in the Pentland Hotel, Edinburgh, and the neat blue serge suit and the clean linen that reposed in it. It was no case for a subtle game, for I held no cards. Still I was determined not to chuck in my hand till I was forced to. If the train stopped anywhere I would get out, and trust to my own wits and the standing luck of the British Army for the rest.

The chance came just after dawn, when we halted at a little junction. I got up yawning and tried to open the door, till I remembered it was locked. Thereupon I stuck my legs out of the window on the side away from the platform, and was immediately seized upon by a sleepy Seaforth who thought I contemplated suicide.

'Let me go,' I said. 'I'll be back in a jiffy.'

'Let him gang, jock,' said another voice. 'Ye ken what a man's like when he's been on the bash. The cauld air'll sober him.'

I was released, and after some gymnastics dropped on the metals and made my way round the rear of the train. As I clambered on the platform it began to move, and a face looked out of one of the back carriages. It was Linklater and he recognized me. He tried to get out, but the door was promptly slammed by an indignant porter. I heard him protest, and he kept his head out till the train went round the curve. That cooked my goose all right. He would wire to the police from the next station.

Meantime in that clean, bare, chilly place there was only one traveller. He was a slim young man, with a kit-bag and a gun-case. His clothes were beautiful, a green Homburg hat, a smart green tweed overcoat, and boots as brightly polished as a horse chestnut. I caught his profile as he gave up his ticket and to my amazement I recognized it.

The station-master looked askance at me as I presented myself, dilapidated and dishevelled, to the official gaze. I tried to speak in a tone of authority.

'Who is the man who has just gone out?'

'Whaur's your ticket?'

'I had no time to get one at Muirtown, and as you see I have left my luggage behind me. Take it out of that pound and I'll come back for the change. I want to know if that was Sir Archibald Roylance.'

He looked suspiciously at the note. 'I think that's the name. He's a captain up at the Fleein' School. What was ye wantin' with him?'

I charged through the booking-office and found my man about to enter a big grey motor-car.

'Archie,' I cried and beat him on the shoulders.

He turned round sharply. 'What the devil—! Who are you?' And then recognition crept into his face and he gave a joyous shout. 'My holy aunt! The General disguised as Charlie Chaplin! Can I drive you anywhere, sir?'

CHAPTER NINE

I Take the Wings of a Dove

'Drive me somewhere to breakfast, Archie,' I said, 'for I'm perishing hungry.'

He and I got into the tonneau, and the driver swung us out of the station road up a long incline of hill. Sir Archie had been one of my subalterns in the old Lennox Highlanders, and had left us before the Somme to join the Flying Corps. I had heard that he had got his wings and had done well before Arras, and was now training pilots at home. He had been a light-hearted youth, who had endured a good deal of rough-tonguing from me for his sins of omission. But it was the casual class of lad I was looking for now.

I saw him steal amused glances at my appearance.

'Been seein' a bit of life, sir?' he inquired respectfully.

'I'm being hunted by the police,' I said.

'Dirty dogs! But don't worry, sir; we'll get you off all right. I've been in the same fix myself. You can lie snug in my little log hut, for that old image Gibbons won't blab. Or, tell you what, I've got an aunt who lives near here and she's a bit of a sportsman. You can hide in her moated grange till the bobbies get tired.'

I think it was Archie's calm acceptance of my position as natural and becoming that restored my good temper. He was far too well bred to ask what crime I had committed, and I didn't propose to enlighten him much. But as we swung up the moorland road I let him know that I was serving the Government, but that it was necessary that I should appear to be unauthenticated and that therefore I must dodge the police. He whistled his appreciation.

'Gad, that's a deep game. Sort of camouflage? Speaking from my experience it is easy to overdo that kind of stunt. When I was at Misieux the French started out to camouflage the caravans where they keep their pigeons, and they did it so damned well that the poor little birds couldn't hit 'em off, and spent the night out.'

We entered the white gates of a big aerodrome, skirted a forest of tents and huts, and drew up at a shanty on the far confines of the place. The hour was half past four, and the world was still asleep. Archie nodded towards one of the hangars, from the mouth of which projected the propeller end of an aeroplane.

'I'm by way of flyin' that bus down to Farnton tomorrow,' he remarked. 'It's the new Shark-Gladas. Got a mouth like a tree.'

An idea flashed into my mind.

'You're going this morning,' I said.

'How did you know?' he exclaimed. 'I'm due to go today, but the grouse up in Caithness wanted shootin' so badly that I decided to wangle another day's leave. They can't expect a man to start for the south of England when he's just off a frowsy journey.'

'All the same you're going to be a stout fellow and start in two hours' time. And you're going to take me with you.'

He stared blankly, and then burst into a roar of laughter. 'You're the man to go tiger-shootin' with. But what price my commandant? He's not a bad chap, but a trifle shaggy about the fetlocks. He won't appreciate the joke.'

'He needn't know. He mustn't know. This is an affair between you and me till it's finished. I promise you I'll make it all square with the Flying Corps. Get me down to Farnton before evening, and you'll have done a good piece of work for the country.'

'Right-o! Let's have a tub and a bit of breakfast, and then I'm your man. I'll tell them to get the bus ready.'

In Archie's bedroom I washed and shaved and borrowed a green tweed cap and a brand-new Aquascutum. The latter covered the deficiencies of my raiment, and when I commandeered a pair of gloves I felt almost respectable. Gibbons, who seemed to be a jack-of-all-trades, cooked us some bacon and an omelette, and as he ate Archie yarned. In the battalion his conversation had been mostly of race-meetings and the forsaken delights of town, but now he had forgotten all that, and, like every good airman I have ever known, wallowed enthusiastically in 'shop'. I have a deep respect for the Flying Corps, but it is apt to change its jargon every month, and its conversation is hard for the layman to follow. He was desperately keen about the war, which he saw wholly from the viewpoint of the air. Arras to him was over before the infantry crossed the top, and the tough bit of the Somme was October, not September. He calculated that the big air-fighting had not come along yet, and all he hoped for was to be allowed out to France to have his share in it. Like all good airmen, too, he was very modest about himself. 'I've done a bit of steeple-chasin' and huntin' and I've good hands for a horse, so I can handle a bus fairly well. It's all a matter of hands, you know. There ain't half the risk of the infantry down below you, and a million times the fun. Jolly glad I changed, sir.'

We talked of Peter, and he put him about top. Voss, he thought, was the only Boche that could compare with him, for he hadn't made up his mind about Lensch. The Frenchman Guynemer he ranked high, but in a different way. I remember he had no respect for Richthofen and his celebrated circus.

At six sharp we were ready to go. A couple of mechanics had got out the machine, and Archie put on his coat and gloves and climbed into the pilot's seat, while I squeezed in behind in the observer's place. The aerodrome was waking up, but I saw no officers about. We were scarcely seated when Gibbons called our attention to a motor-car on the road, and presently we heard a shout and saw men waving in our direction.

'Better get off, my lad,' I said. 'These look like my friends.'

The engine started and the mechanics stood clear. As we taxied over the turf I looked back and saw several figures running in our direction. The next second we had left the bumpy earth for the smooth highroad of the air.

I had flown several dozen times before, generally over the enemy lines when I wanted to see for myself how the land lay. Then we had flown low, and been nicely dusted by the Hun Archies, not to speak of an occasional machine-gun. But never till that hour had I realized the joy of a straight flight in a swift plane in perfect weather. Archie didn't lose time. Soon the hangars behind looked like a child's toys, and the world ran away from us till it seemed like a great golden bowl spilling over with the quintessence of light. The air was cold and my hands numbed, but I never felt them. As we throbbed and tore southward, sometimes bumping in eddies, sometimes swimming evenly in a stream of motionless ether, my head and heart grew as light as a boy's. I forgot all about the vexations of my job and saw only its joyful comedy. I didn't think that anything on earth could worry me again. Far to the left was a wedge of silver and beside it a cluster of toy houses. That must be Edinburgh, where reposed my portmanteau, and where a most efficient police force was now inquiring for me. At the thought I laughed so loud that Archie must have heard me. He turned round, saw my grinning face, and grinned back. Then he signalled to me to strap myself in. I obeyed, and he proceeded to practise 'stunts'—the loop, the spinning nose-dive, and others I didn't know the names of. It was glorious fun, and he handled his machine as a good rider coaxes a nervous horse over a stiff hurdle. He had that extra something in his blood that makes the great pilot.

Presently the chessboard of green and brown had changed to a deep purple with faint silvery lines like veins in a rock. We were crossing the Border hills, the place where I had legged it for weary days when I was mixed up in the Black Stone business. What a marvellous element was this air, which took one far above the fatigues of humanity! Archie had done well to change. Peter had been the wise man. I felt a tremendous pity for my old friend hobbling about a German prison-yard, when he had once flown a hawk. I reflected that I had wasted my life hitherto. And then I remembered that all this glory had only one use in war and that was to help the muddy British infantryman to down his Hun opponent. He was the fellow, after all, that decided battles, and the thought comforted me.

A great exhilaration is often the precursor of disaster, and mine was to have a sudden downfall. It was getting on for noon and we were well into England—I guessed from the rivers we had passed that we were somewhere in the north of Yorkshire—when the machine began to make odd sounds, and we bumped in perfectly calm patches of air. We dived and then climbed, but the confounded thing kept sputtering. Archie passed back a slip of paper on which he had scribbled: 'Engine conked. Must land at Micklegill. Very sorry.' So we dropped to a lower elevation where we could see clearly the houses and roads and the long swelling ridges of a moorland country. I could never have found my way about, but Archie's practised eye knew every landmark. We were trundling along very slowly now, and even I was soon able to pick up the hangars of a big aerodrome.

We made Micklegill, but only by the skin of our teeth. We were so low that the smoky chimneys of the city of Bradfield seven miles to the east were half hidden by a ridge of down. Archie achieved a clever descent in the lee of a belt of firs, and got out full of imprecations against the Gladas engine. 'I'll go up to the camp and report,' he said, 'and send mechanics down to tinker this darned gramophone. You'd better go for a walk, sir. I don't want to answer questions about you till we're ready to start. I reckon it'll be an hour's job.'

The cheerfulness I had acquired in the upper air still filled me. I sat down in a ditch, as merry as a sand-boy, and lit a pipe. I was possessed by a boyish spirit of casual adventure, and waited on the next turn of fortune's wheel with only a pleasant amusement.

That turn was not long in coming. Archie appeared very breathless.

'Look here, sir, there's the deuce of a row up there. They've been wirin' about you all over the country, and they know you're with me. They've got the police, and they'll have you in five minutes if you don't leg it. I lied like billy-o and said I had never heard of you, but they're comin' to see for themselves. For God's sake get off ... You'd better keep in cover down that hollow and round the back of these trees. I'll stay here and try to brazen it out. I'll get strafed to blazes anyhow ... I hope you'll get me out of the scrape, sir.'

'Don't you worry, my lad,' I said. 'I'll make it all square when I get back to town. I'll make for Bradfield, for this place is a bit conspicuous. Goodbye, Archie. You're a good chap and I'll see you don't suffer.'

I started off down the hollow of the moor, trying to make speed atone for lack of strategy, for it was hard to know how much my pursuers commanded from that higher ground. They must have seen me, for I heard whistles blown and men's cries. I struck a road, crossed it, and passed a ridge from which I had a view of Bradfield six miles off. And as I ran I began to reflect that this kind of chase could not last long. They were bound to round me up in the next half-hour unless I could puzzle them. But in that bare green place there was no cover, and it looked as if my chances were pretty much those of a hare coursed by a good greyhound on a naked moor.

Suddenly from just in front of me came a familiar sound. It was the roar of guns—the slam of field-batteries and the boom of small howitzers. I wondered if I had gone off my head. As I plodded on the rattle of machine-guns was added, and over the ridge before me I saw the dust and fumes of bursting shells. I concluded that I was not mad, and that therefore the Germans must have landed. I crawled up the last slope, quite forgetting the pursuit behind me.

And then I'm blessed if I did not look down on a veritable battle.

There were two sets of trenches with barbed wire and all the fixings, one set filled with troops and the other empty. On these latter shells were bursting, but there was no sign of life in them. In the other lines there seemed the better part of two brigades, and the first trench was stiff with bayonets. My first thought was that Home Forces had gone dotty, for this kind of show could have no sort of training value. And then I saw other things—cameras and camera-men on platforms on the flanks, and men with megaphones behind them on wooden scaffoldings. One of the megaphones was going full blast all the time.

I saw the meaning of the performance at last. Some movie-merchant had got a graft with the Government, and troops had been turned out to make a war film. It occurred to me that if I were mixed up in that push I might get the cover I was looking for. I scurried down the hill to the nearest camera-man.

As I ran, the first wave of troops went over the top. They did it uncommon well, for they entered into the spirit of the thing, and went over with grim faces and that slow, purposeful lope that I had seen in my own fellows at Arras. Smoke grenades burst among them, and now and then some resourceful mountebank would roll over. Altogether it was about the best show I have ever seen. The cameras clicked, the guns banged, a background of boy scouts applauded, and the dust rose in billows to the sky.

But all the same something was wrong. I could imagine that this kind of business took a good deal of planning from the point of view of the movie-merchant, for his purpose was not the same as that of the officer in command. You know how a photographer finicks about and is dissatisfied with a pose that seems all right to his sitter. I should have thought the spectacle enough to get any cinema audience off their feet, but the man on the scaffolding near me judged differently. He made his megaphone boom like the swan-song of a dying buffalo. He wanted to change something and didn't know how to do it. He hopped on one leg; he took the megaphone from his mouth to curse; he waved it like a banner and yelled at some opposite number on the other flank. And then his patience forsook him and he skipped down the ladder, dropping his megaphone, past the camera-men, on to the battlefield.

That was his undoing. He got in the way of the second wave and was swallowed up like a leaf in a torrent. For a moment I saw a red face and a loud-checked suit, and the rest was silence. He was carried on over the hill, or rolled into an enemy trench, but anyhow he was lost to my ken.

I bagged his megaphone and hopped up the steps to the platform. At last I saw a chance of first-class cover, for with Archie's coat and cap I made a very good appearance as a movie-merchant. Two waves had gone over the top, and the cinema-men, working like beavers, had filmed the lot. But there was still a fair amount of troops to play with, and I determined to tangle up that outfit so that the fellows who were after me would have better things to think about.

My advantage was that I knew how to command men. I could see that my opposite number with the megaphone was helpless, for the mistake which had swept my man into a shell-hole had reduced him to impotence. The troops seemed to be mainly in charge of N.C.O.s (I could imagine that the officers would try to shirk this business), and an N.C.O. is the most literal creature on earth. So with my megaphone I proceeded to change the battle order.

I brought up the third wave to the front trenches. In about three minutes the men had recognized the professional touch and were moving smartly to my orders. They thought it was part of the show, and the obedient cameras clicked at everything that came into their orbit. My aim was to deploy the troops on too narrow a front so that they were bound to fan outward, and I had to be quick about it, for I didn't know when the hapless movie-merchant might be retrieved from the battle-field and dispute my authority.

It takes a long time to straighten a thing out, but it does not take long to tangle it, especially when the thing is so delicate a machine as disciplined troops. In about eight minutes I had produced chaos. The flanks spread out, in spite of all the shepherding of the N.C.O.s, and the fringe engulfed the photographers. The cameras on their little platforms went down like ninepins. It was solemn to see the startled face of a photographer, taken unawares, supplicating the purposeful infantry, before he was swept off his feet into speechlessness.

It was no place for me to linger in, so I chucked away the megaphone and got mixed up with the tail of the third wave. I was swept on and came to anchor in the enemy trenches, where I found, as I expected, my profane and breathless predecessor, the movie-merchant. I had nothing to say to him, so I stuck to the trench till it ended against the slope of the hill.

On that flank, delirious with excitement, stood a knot of boy scouts. My business was to get to Bradfield as quick as my legs would take me, and as inconspicuously as the gods would permit. Unhappily I was far too great an object of interest to that nursery of heroes. Every boy scout is an amateur detective and hungry for knowledge. I was followed by several, who plied me with questions, and were told that I was off to Bradfield to hurry up part of the cinema outfit. It sounded lame enough, for that cinema outfit was already past praying for.

We reached the road and against a stone wall stood several bicycles. I selected one and prepared to mount.

'That's Mr Emmott's machine,' said one boy sharply. 'He told me to keep an eye on it.'

'I must borrow it, sonny,' I said. 'Mr Emmott's my very good friend and won't object.'

From the place where we stood I overlooked the back of the battle-field and could see an anxious congress of officers. I could see others, too, whose appearance I did not like. They had not been there when I operated on the megaphone. They must have come downhill from the aerodrome and in all likelihood were the pursuers I had avoided. The exhilaration which I had won in the air and which had carried me into the tomfoolery of the past half-hour was ebbing. I had the hunted feeling once more, and grew middle-aged and cautious. I had a baddish record for the day, what with getting Archie into a scrape and busting up an official cinema show—neither consistent with the duties of a brigadier-general. Besides, I had still to get to London.

I had not gone two hundred yards down the road when a boy scout, pedalling furiously, came up abreast me.

'Colonel Edgeworth wants to see you,' he panted. 'You're to come back at once.'

'Tell him I can't wait now,' I said. 'I'll pay my respects to him in an hour.'

'He said you were to come at once,' said the faithful messenger. 'He's in an awful temper with you, and he's got bobbies with him.'

I put on pace and left the boy behind. I reckoned I had the better part of two miles' start and could beat anything except petrol. But my enemies were bound to have cars, so I had better get off the road as soon as possible. I coasted down a long hill to a bridge which spanned a small discoloured stream that flowed in a wooded glen. There was nobody for the moment on the hill behind me, so I slipped into the covert, shoved the bicycle under the bridge, and hid Archie's aquascutum in a bramble thicket. I was now in my own disreputable tweeds and I hoped that the shedding of my most conspicuous garment would puzzle my pursuers if they should catch up with me.

But this I was determined they should not do. I made good going down that stream and out into a lane which led from the downs to the market-gardens round the city. I thanked Heaven I had got rid of the aquascutum, for the August afternoon was warm and my pace was not leisurely. When I was in secluded ground I ran, and when anyone was in sight I walked smartly.

As I went I reflected that Bradfield would see the end of my adventures. The police knew that I was there and would watch the stations and hunt me down if I lingered in the place. I knew no one there and had no chance of getting an effective disguise. Indeed I very soon began to wonder if I should get even as far as the streets. For at the moment when I had got a lift on the back of a fishmonger's cart and was screened by its flapping canvas, two figures passed on motor-bicycles, and one of them was the inquisitive boy scout. The main road from the aerodrome was probably now being patrolled by motor-cars. It looked as if there would be a degrading arrest in one of the suburbs.

The fish-cart, helped by half a crown to the driver, took me past the outlying small-villadom, between long lines of workmen's houses, to narrow cobbled lanes and the purlieus of great factories. As soon as I saw the streets well crowded I got out and walked. In my old clothes I must have appeared like some second-class bookie or seedy horse-coper. The only respectable thing I had about me was my gold watch. I looked at the time and found it half past five.

I wanted food and was casting about for an eating-house when I heard the purr of a motor-cycle and across the road saw the intelligent boy scout. He saw me, too, and put on the brake with a sharpness which caused him to skid and all but come to grief under the wheels of a wool-wagon. That gave me time to efface myself by darting up a side street. I had an unpleasant sense that I was about to be trapped, for in a place I knew nothing of I had not a chance to use my wits.

I remember trying feverishly to think, and I suppose that my preoccupation made me careless. I was now in a veritable slum, and when I put my hand to my vest pocket I found that my watch had gone. That put the top stone on my depression. The reaction from the wild burnout of the forenoon had left me very cold about the feet. I was getting into the under-world again and there was no chance of a second Archie Roylance turning up to rescue me. I remember yet the sour smell of the factories and the mist of smoke in the evening air. It is a smell I have never met since without a sort of dulling of spirit.

Presently I came out into a market-place. Whistles were blowing, and there was a great hurrying of people back from the mills. The crowd gave me a momentary sense of security, and I was just about to inquire my way to the railway station when someone jostled my arm.

A rough-looking fellow in mechanic's clothes was beside me.

'Mate,' he whispered. 'I've got summat o' yours here.' And to my amazement he slipped my watch into my hand.

'It was took by mistake. We're friends o' yours. You're right enough if you do what I tell you. There's a peeler over there got his eye on you. Follow me and I'll get you off.'

I didn't much like the man's looks, but I had no choice, and anyhow he had given me back my watch. He sidled into an alley between tall houses and I sidled after him. Then he took to his heels, and led me a twisting course through smelly courts into a tanyard and then by a narrow lane to the back-quarters of a factory. Twice we doubled back, and once we climbed a wall and followed the bank of a blue-black stream with a filthy scum on it. Then we got into a very mean quarter of the town, and emerged in a dingy garden, strewn with tin cans and broken flowerpots. By a back door we entered one of the cottages and my guide very carefully locked it behind him.

He lit the gas and drew the blinds in a small parlour and looked at me long and quizzically. He spoke now in an educated voice.

'I ask no questions,' he said, 'but it's my business to put my services at your disposal. You carry the passport.'

I stared at him, and he pulled out his watch and showed a white-and-purple cross inside the lid.

'I don't defend all the people we employ,' he said, grinning. 'Men's morals are not always as good as their patriotism. One of them pinched your watch, and when he saw what was inside it he reported to me. We soon picked up your trail, and observed you were in a bit of trouble. As I say, I ask no questions. What can we do for you?'

'I want to get to London without any questions asked. They're looking for me in my present rig, so I've got to change it.'

'That's easy enough,' he said. 'Make yourself comfortable for a little and I'll fix you up. The night train goes at eleven-thirty.... You'll find cigars in the cupboard and there's this week's *Critic* on that table. It's got a good article on Conrad, if you care for such things.'

I helped myself to a cigar and spent a profitable half-hour reading about the vices of the British Government. Then my host returned and bade me ascend to his bedroom. 'You're Private Henry Tomkins of the 12th Gloucesters, and you'll find your clothes ready for you. I'll send on your present togs if you give me an address.'

I did as I was bid, and presently emerged in the uniform of a British private, complete down to the shapeless boots and the dropsical puttees. Then my friend took me in hand and finished the transformation. He started on my hair with scissors and arranged a lock which, when well oiled, curled over my forehead. My hands were hard and rough and only needed some grubbiness and hacking about the nails to pass muster. With my cap on the side of my head, a pack on my back, a service rifle in my hands, and my pockets bursting with penny picture papers, I was the very model of the British soldier returning from leave. I had also a packet of Woodbine cigarettes and a hunch of bread-and-cheese for the journey. And I had a railway warrant made out in my name for London.

Then my friend gave me supper—bread and cold meat and a bottle of Bass, which I wolfed savagely, for I had had nothing since breakfast. He was a curious fellow, as discreet as a tombstone, very ready to speak about general subjects, but never once coming near the intimate business which had linked him and me and Heaven knew how many others by means of a little purple-and-white cross in a watch-case. I remember we talked about the topics that used to be popular at Biggleswick—the big political things that begin with capital letters. He took Amos's view of the soundness of the British working-man, but he said something which made me think. He was convinced that there was a tremendous lot of German spy work about, and that most of the practitioners were innocent. 'The ordinary

Briton doesn't run to treason, but he's not very bright. A clever man in that kind of game can make better use of a fool than a rogue.'

As he saw me off he gave me a piece of advice. 'Get out of these clothes as soon as you reach London. Private Tomkins will frank you out of Bradfield, but it mightn't be a healthy alias in the metropolis.'

At eleven-thirty I was safe in the train, talking the jargon of the returning soldier with half a dozen of my own type in a smoky third-class carriage. I had been lucky in my escape, for at the station entrance and on the platform I had noticed several men with the unmistakable look of plainclothes police. Also—though this may have been my fancy—I thought I caught in the crowd a glimpse of the bagman who had called himself Linklater.

CHAPTER TEN

The Advantages of an Air Raid

The train was abominably late. It was due at eight-twenty-seven, but it was nearly ten when we reached St Pancras. I had resolved to go straight to my rooms in Westminster, buying on the way a cap and waterproof to conceal my uniform should anyone be near my door on my arrival. Then I would ring up Blenkiron and tell him all my adventures. I breakfasted at a coffee-stall, left my pack and rifle in the cloak-room, and walked out into the clear sunny morning.

I was feeling very pleased with myself. Looking back on my madcap journey, I seemed to have had an amazing run of luck and to be entitled to a little credit too. I told myself that persistence always pays and that nobody is beaten till he is dead. All Blenkiron's instructions had been faithfully carried out. I had found Ivery's post office. I had laid the lines of our own special communications with the enemy, and so far as I could see I had left no clue behind me. Ivery and Gresson took me for a well-meaning nincompoop. It was true that I had aroused profound suspicion in the breasts of the Scottish police. But that mattered nothing, for Cornelius Brand, the suspect, would presently disappear, and there was nothing against that rising soldier, Brigadier-General Richard Hannay, who would soon be on his way to France. After all this piece of service had not been so very unpleasant. I laughed when I remembered my grim forebodings in Gloucestershire. Bullivant had said it would be damnably risky in the long run, but here was the end and I had never been in danger of anything worse than making a fool of myself.

I remember that, as I made my way through Bloomsbury, I was not thinking so much of my triumphant report to Blenkiron as of my speedy return to the Front. Soon I would be with my beloved brigade again. I had missed Messines and the first part of Third Ypres, but the battle was still going on, and I had yet a chance. I might get a division, for there had been talk of that before I left. I knew the Army Commander thought a lot of me. But on the whole I hoped I would be left with the brigade. After all I was an amateur soldier, and I wasn't certain of my powers with a bigger command.

In Charing Cross Road I thought of Mary, and the brigade seemed suddenly less attractive. I hoped the war wouldn't last much longer, though with Russia heading straight for the devil I didn't know how it was going to stop very soon. I was determined to see Mary before I left, and I had a good excuse, for I had taken my orders from her. The prospect entranced me, and I was mooning along in a happy dream, when I collided violently with in agitated citizen.

Then I realized that something very odd was happening.

There was a dull sound like the popping of the corks of flat soda-water bottles. There was a humming, too, from very far up in the skies. People in the street were either staring at the heavens or running wildly for shelter. A motor-bus in front of me emptied its contents in a twinkling; a taxi pulled up with a jar and the driver and fare dived into a second-hand bookshop. It took me a moment or two to realize the meaning of it all, and I had scarcely done this when I got a very practical proof. A hundred yards away a bomb fell on a street island, shivering every window-pane in a wide radius, and sending splinters of stone flying about my head. I did what I had done a hundred times before at the Front, and dropped flat on my face.

The man who says he doesn't mind being bombed or shelled is either a liar or a maniac. This London air raid seemed to me a singularly unpleasant business. I think it was the sight of the decent civilized life around one and the orderly streets, for what was perfectly natural in a rubble-heap like Ypres or Arras seemed an outrage here. I remember once being in billets in a Flanders village where I had the Maire's house and sat in a room upholstered in cut velvet, with wax flowers on the mantelpiece and oil paintings of three generations on the walls. The Boche took it into his head to shell the place with a long-range naval gun, and I simply loathed it. It was horrible to have dust and splinters blown into that snug, homely room, whereas if I had been in a ruined barn I wouldn't have given the thing two thoughts. In the same way bombs dropping in central London seemed a grotesque indecency. I hated to see plump citizens with wild eyes, and nursemaids with scared children, and miserable women scuttling like rabbits in a warren.

The drone grew louder, and, looking up, I could see the enemy planes flying in a beautiful formation, very leisurely as it seemed, with all London at their mercy. Another bomb fell to the right, and presently bits of our own shrapnel were clattering viciously around me. I thought it about time to take cover, and ran shamelessly for the best place I could see, which was a Tube station. Five minutes before the street had been crowded; now I left behind me a desert dotted with one bus and three empty taxicabs.

I found the Tube entrance filled with excited humanity. One stout lady had fainted, and a nurse had become hysterical, but on the whole people were behaving well. Oddly enough they did not seem inclined to go down the stairs to the complete security of underground; but preferred rather to collect where they could still get a glimpse of the upper world, as if they were torn between fear of their lives and interest in the spectacle. That crowd gave me a good deal of respect for my countrymen. But several were badly rattled, and one man a little way off, whose back was turned, kept twitching his shoulders as if he had the colic.

I watched him curiously, and a movement of the crowd brought his face into profile. Then I gasped with amazement, for I saw that it was Ivery.

And yet it was not Ivery. There were the familiar nondescript features, the blandness, the plumpness, but all, so to speak, in ruins. The man was in a blind funk. His features seemed to be dislimning before my eyes. He was growing sharper, finer, in a way younger, a man without grip on himself, a shapeless creature in process of transformation. He was being reduced to his rudiments. Under the spell of panic he was becoming a new man.

And the crazy thing was that I knew the new man better than the old.

My hands were jammed close to my sides by the crowd; I could scarcely turn my head, and it was not the occasion for one's neighbours to observe one's expression. If it had been, mine must have been a study. My mind was far away from air raids, back in the hot summer weather of 1914. I saw a row of villas perched on a headland above the sea. In the garden of one of them two men were playing tennis, while I was crouching behind an adjacent bush. One of these was a plump young man who wore a coloured scarf round his waist and babbled of golf handicaps ... I saw him again in the villa dining-room, wearing a dinner-jacket, and lisping a little.... I sat opposite him at bridge, I beheld him collared by two of Macgillivray's men, when his comrade had rushed for the thirty-nine steps that led to the sea ... I saw, too, the sitting-room of my old flat in Portland Place and heard little Scudder's quick, anxious voice talking about the three men he feared most on earth, one of whom lisped in his speech. I had thought that all three had long ago been laid under the turf ...

He was not looking my way, and I could devour his face in safety. There was no shadow of doubt. I had always put him down as the most amazing actor on earth, for had he not played the part of the First Sea Lord and deluded that officer's daily colleagues? But he could do far more than any human actor, for he could take on a new personality and with it a new appearance, and live steadily in the character as if he had been born in it ... My mind was a blank, and I could only make blind gropings at conclusions ... How had he escaped the death of a spy and a murderer, for I had last seen him in the hands of justice? ... Of course he had known me from the first day in Biggleswick ... I had thought to play with him, and he had played most cunningly and damnably with me. In that sweating sardine-tin of refugees I shivered in the bitterness of my chagrin.

And then I found his face turned to mine, and I knew that he recognized me. More, I knew that he knew that I had recognized him—not as Ivery, but as that other man. There came into his eyes a curious look of comprehension, which for a moment overcame his funk.

I had sense enough to see that that put the final lid on it. There was still something doing if he believed that I was blind, but if he once thought that I knew the truth he would be through our meshes and disappear like a fog.

My first thought was to get at him and collar him and summon everybody to help me by denouncing him for what he was. Then I saw that that was impossible. I was a private soldier in a borrowed uniform, and he could easily turn the story against me. I must use surer weapons. I must get to Bullivant and Macgillivray and set their big machine to work. Above all I must get to Blenkiron.

I started to squeeze out of that push, for air raids now seemed far too trivial to give a thought to. Moreover the guns had stopped, but so sheeplike is human nature that the crowd still hung together, and it took me a good fifteen minutes to edge my way to the open air. I found that the trouble was over, and the street had resumed its usual appearance. Buses and taxis were running, and voluble knots of people were recounting their experiences. I started off for Blenkiron's bookshop, as the nearest harbour of refuge.

But in Piccadilly Circus I was stopped by a military policeman. He asked my name and battalion, and I gave him them, while his suspicious eye ran over my figure. I had no pack or rifle, and the crush in the Tube station had not improved my appearance. I explained that I was going back to France that evening, and he asked for my warrant. I fancy my preoccupation made me nervous and I lied badly. I said I had left it with my kit in the house of my married sister, but I fumbled in giving the address. I could see that the fellow did not believe a word of it.

Just then up came an A.P.M. He was a pompous dug-out, very splendid in his red tabs and probably bucked up at having just been under fire. Anyhow he was out to walk in the strict path of duty.

'Tomkins!' he said. 'Tomkins! We've got some fellow of that name on our records. Bring him along, Wilson.'

'But, sir,' I said, 'I must—I simply must meet my friend. It's urgent business, and I assure you I'm all right. If you don't believe me, I'll take a taxi and we'll go down to Scotland Yard and I'll stand by what they say.'

His brow grew dark with wrath. 'What infernal nonsense is this? Scotland Yard! What the devil has Scotland Yard to do with it? You're an imposter. I can see it in your face. I'll have your depot rung up, and you'll be in jail in a couple of hours. I know a deserter when I see him. Bring him along, Wilson. You know what to do if he tries to bolt.'

I had a momentary thought of breaking away, but decided that the odds were too much against me. Fuming with impatience, I followed the A.P.M. to his office on the first floor in a side street. The precious minutes were slipping past; Ivery, now thoroughly warned, was making good his escape; and I, the sole repository of a deadly secret, was tramping in this absurd procession.

The A.P.M. issued his orders. He gave instructions that my depot should be rung up, and he bade Wilson remove me to what he called the guard-room. He sat down at his desk, and busied himself with a mass of buff dockets.

In desperation I renewed my appeal. 'I implore you to telephone to Mr Macgillivray at Scotland Yard. It's a matter of life and death, Sir. You're taking a very big responsibility if you don't.'

I had hopelessly offended his brittle dignity. 'Any more of your insolence and I'll have you put in irons. I'll attend to you soon enough for your comfort. Get out of this till I send for you.'

As I looked at his foolish, irritable face I realized that I was fairly UP against it. Short of assault and battery on everybody I was bound to submit. I saluted respectfully and was marched away.

The hours I spent in that bare anteroom are like a nightmare in my recollection. A sergeant was busy at a desk with more buff dockets and an orderly waited on a stool by a telephone. I looked at my watch and observed that it was one o'clock. Soon the slamming of a door announced that the A.P.M. had gone to lunch. I tried conversation with the fat sergeant, but he very soon shut me up. So I sat hunched up on the wooden form and chewed the cud of my vexation.

I thought with bitterness of the satisfaction which had filled me in the morning. I had fancied myself the devil of a fine fellow, and I had been no more than a mountebank. The adventures of the past days seemed merely childish. I had been telling lies and cutting capers over half Britain, thinking I was playing a deep game, and I had only been behaving like a schoolboy. On such occasions a man is rarely just to himself, and the intensity of my self-abasement would have satisfied my worst enemy. It didn't console me that the futility of it all was not my blame. I was looking for excuses. It was the facts that cried out against me, and on the facts I had been an idiotic failure.

For of course Ivery had played with me, played with me since the first day at Biggleswick. He had applauded my speeches and flattered me, and advised me to go to the Clyde, laughing at me all the time. Gresson, too, had known. Now I saw it all. He had tried to drown me between Colonsay and Mull. It was Gresson who had set the police on me in Morvern. The bagman Linklater had been one of Gresson's creatures. The only meagre consolation was that the gang had thought me dangerous enough to attempt to murder me, and that they knew nothing about my doings in Skye. Of that I was positive. They had marked me down, but for several days I had slipped clean out of their ken.

As I went over all the incidents, I asked if everything was yet lost. I had failed to hoodwink Ivery, but I had found out his post office, and if he only believed I hadn't recognized him for the miscreant of the Black Stone he would go on in his old ways and play into Blenkiron's hands. Yes, but I had seen him in undress, so to speak, and he knew that I had so seen him. The only thing now was to collar him before he left the country, for there was ample evidence to hang him on. The law must stretch out its long arm and collect him and Gresson and the Portuguese Jew, try them by court martial, and put them decently underground.

But he had now had more than an hour's warning, and I was entangled with red-tape in this damned A.P.M.'s office. The thought drove me frantic, and I got up and paced the floor. I saw the orderly with rather a scared face making ready to press the bell, and I noticed that the fat sergeant had gone to lunch.

'Say, mate,' I said, 'don't you feel inclined to do a poor fellow a good turn? I know I'm for it all right, and I'll take my medicine like a lamb. But I want badly to put a telephone call through.'

'It ain't allowed,' was the answer. 'I'd get 'ell from the old man.'

'But he's gone out,' I urged. 'I don't want you to do anything wrong, mate, I leave you to do the talkin' if you'll only send my message. I'm flush of money, and I don't mind handin' you a quid for the job.'

He was a pinched little man with a weak chin, and he obviously wavered.

''Oo d'ye want to talk to?' he asked.

'Scotland Yard,' I said, 'the home of the police. Lord bless you, there can't be no harm in that. Ye've only got to ring up Scotland Yard—I'll give you the number—and give the message to Mr Macgillivray. He's the head bummer of all the bobbies.'

'That sounds a bit of all right,' he said. 'The old man 'e won't be back for 'alf an hour, nor the sergeant neither. Let's see your quid though.'

I laid a pound note on the form beside me. 'It's yours, mate, if you get through to Scotland Yard and speak the piece I'm goin' to give you.'

He went over to the instrument. 'What d'you want to say to the bloke with the long name?'

'Say that Richard Hannay is detained at the A.P.M.'s office in Claxton Street. Say he's got important news—say urgent and secret news—and ask Mr Macgillivray to do something about it at once.'

'But 'Annay ain't the name you gave.'

'Lord bless you, no. Did you never hear of a man borrowin' another name? Anyhow that's the one I want you to give.'

'But if this Mac man comes round 'ere, they'll know 'e's bin rung up, and I'll 'ave the old man down on me.'

It took ten minutes and a second pound note to get him past this hurdle. By and by he screwed up courage and rang up the number. I listened with some nervousness while he gave my message—he had to repeat it twice—and waited eagerly on the next words.

'No, sir,' I heard him say, ''e don't want you to come round 'ere. 'E thinks as 'ow—I mean to say, 'e wants—'

I took a long stride and twitched the receiver from him.

'Macgillivray,' I said, 'is that you? Richard Hannay! For the love of God come round here this instant and deliver me from the clutches of a tomfool A.P.M. I've got the most deadly news. There's not a second to waste. For God's sake come quick!' Then I added: 'Just tell your fellows to gather Ivery in at once. You know his lairs.'

I hung up the receiver and faced a pale and indignant orderly. 'It's all right,' I said. 'I promise you that you won't get into any trouble on my account. And there's your two quid.'

The door in the next room opened and shut. The A.P.M. had returned from lunch ...

Ten minutes later the door opened again. I heard Macgillivray's voice, and it was not pitched in dulcet tones. He had run up against minor officialdom and was making hay with it.

I was my own master once more, so I forsook the company of the orderly. I found a most rattled officer trying to save a few rags of his dignity and the formidable figure of Macgillivray instructing him in manners.

'Glad to see you, Dick,' he said. 'This is General Hannay, sir. It may comfort you to know that your folly may have made just the difference between your country's victory and defeat. I shall have a word to say to your superiors.'

It was hardly fair. I had to put in a word for the old fellow, whose red tabs seemed suddenly to have grown dingy.

'It was my blame wearing this kit. We'll call it a misunderstanding and forget it. But I would suggest that civility is not wasted even on a poor devil of a defaulting private soldier.'

Once in Macgillivray's car, I poured out my tale. 'Tell me it's a nightmare,' I cried. 'Tell me that the three men we collected on the Ruff were shot long ago.'

'Two,' he replied, 'but one escaped. Heaven knows how he managed it, but he disappeared clean out of the world.'

'The plump one who lisped in his speech?'

Macgillivray nodded.

'Well, we're in for it this time. Have you issued instructions?'

'Yes. With luck we shall have our hands on him within an hour. We've our net round all his haunts.'

'But two hours' start! It's a big handicap, for you're dealing with a genius.'

'Yet I think we can manage it. Where are you bound for?'

I told him my rooms in Westminster and then to my old flat in Park Lane. 'The day of disguises is past. In half an hour I'll be Richard Hannay. It'll be a comfort to get into uniform again. Then I'll look up Blenkiron.'

He grinned. 'I gather you've had a riotous time. We've had a good many anxious messages from the north about a certain Mr Brand. I couldn't discourage our men, for I fancied it might have spoiled your game. I heard that last night they had lost touch with you in Bradfield, so I rather expected to see you here today. Efficient body of men the Scottish police.'

'Especially when they have various enthusiastic amateur helpers.'

'So?' he said. 'Yes, of course. They would have. But I hope presently to congratulate you on the success of your mission.'

'I'll bet you a pony you don't,' I said.

'I never bet on a professional subject. Why this pessimism?'

'Only that I know our gentleman better than you. I've been twice up against him. He's the kind of wicked that don't cease from troubling till they're stone-dead. And even then I'd want to see the body cremated and take the ashes into mid-ocean and scatter them. I've got a feeling that he's the biggest thing you or I will ever tackle.'

CHAPTER ELEVEN

The Valley of Humiliation

I collected some baggage and a pile of newly arrived letters from my rooms in Westminster and took a taxi to my Park Lane flat. Usually I had gone back to that old place with a great feeling of comfort, like a boy from school who ranges about his room at home and examines his treasures. I used to like to see my hunting trophies on the wall and to sink into my own armchairs But now I had no pleasure in the thing. I had a bath, and changed into uniform, and that made me feel in better fighting trim. But I suffered from a heavy conviction of abject failure, and had no share in Macgillivray's optimism. The awe with which the Black Stone gang had filled me three years before had revived a thousandfold. Personal humiliation was the least part of my trouble. What worried me was the sense of being up against something inhumanly formidable and wise and strong. I believed I was willing to own defeat and chuck up the game.

Among the unopened letters was one from Peter, a very bulky one which I sat down to read at leisure. It was a curious epistle, far the longest he had ever written me, and its size made me understand his loneliness. He was still at his German prison-camp, but expecting every day to go to Switzerland. He said he could get back to England or South Africa, if he wanted, for they were clear that he could never be a combatant again; but he thought he had better stay in Switzerland, for he would be unhappy in England with all his friends fighting. As usual he made no complaints, and seemed to be very grateful for his small mercies. There was a doctor who was kind to him, and some good fellows among the prisoners.

But Peter's letter was made up chiefly of reflection. He had always been a bit of a philosopher, and now, in his isolation, he had taken to thinking hard, and poured out the results to me on pages of thin paper in his clumsy handwriting. I could read between the lines that he was having a stiff fight with himself. He was trying to keep his courage going in face of the bitterest trial he could be called on to face—a crippled old age. He had always known a good deal about the Bible, and that and the *Pilgrim's Progress* were his chief aids in reflection. Both he took quite literally, as if they were newspaper reports of actual recent events.

He mentioned that after much consideration he had reached the conclusion that the three greatest men he had ever heard of or met were Mr Valiant-for-Truth, the Apostle Paul, and a certain Billy Strang who had been with him in Mashonaland in '92. Billy I knew all about; he had been Peter's hero and leader till a lion got him in the Blaauwberg. Peter preferred Valiant-for-Truth to Mr Greatheart, I think, because of his superior truculence, for, being very gentle himself, he loved a bold speaker. After that he dropped into a vein of self-examination. He regretted that he fell far short of any of the three. He thought that he might with luck resemble Mr Standfast, for like him he had not much trouble in keeping wakeful, and was also as 'poor as a howler', and didn't care for women. He only hoped that he could imitate him in making a good end.

Then followed some remarks of Peter's on courage, which came to me in that London room as if spoken by his living voice. I have never known anyone so brave, so brave by instinct, or anyone who hated so much to be told so. It was almost the only thing that could make him angry. All his life he had been facing death, and to take risks seemed to him as natural as to get up in the morning and eat his breakfast. But he had started out to consider the very thing which before he had taken for granted, and here is an extract from his conclusions. I paraphrase him, for he was not grammatical.

It's easy enough to be brave if you're feeling well and have food inside you. And it's not so difficult even if you're short of a meal and seedy, for that makes you inclined to gamble. I mean by being brave playing the game by the right rules without letting it worry you that you may very likely get knocked on the head. It's the wisest way to save your skin. It doesn't do to think about death if you're facing a charging lion or trying to bluff a lot of savages. If you think about it you'll get it; if you don't, the odds are you won't. That kind of courage is only good nerves and experience ... Most courage is experience. Most people are a little scared at new things ...

You want a bigger heart to face danger which you go out to look for, and which doesn't come to you in the ordinary way of business. Still, that's pretty much the same thing—good nerves and good health, and a natural liking for rows. You see, Dick, in all that game there's a lot of fun. There's excitement and the fun of using your wits and skill, and you know that the bad bits can't last long. When Arcoll sent me to Makapan's kraal I didn't altogether fancy the job, but at the worst it was three parts sport, and I got so excited that I never thought of the risk till it was over ...

But the big courage is the cold-blooded kind, the kind that never lets go even when you're feeling empty inside, and your blood's thin, and there's no kind of fun or profit to be had, and the trouble's not over in an hour or two but lasts for months and years. One of the men here was speaking about that kind, and he called it 'Fortitude'. I reckon fortitude's the biggest thing a man can have—just to go on enduring when there's no guts or heart left in you. Billy had it when he trekked solitary from Garungoze to the Limpopo with fever and a broken arm just to show the Portugooses that he wouldn't be downed by them. But the head man at the job was the Apostle Paul ...

Peter was writing for his own comfort, for fortitude was all that was left to him now. But his words came pretty straight to me, and I read them again and again, for I needed the lesson. Here was I losing heart just because I had failed in the first round and my pride had taken a knock. I felt honestly ashamed of myself, and that made me a far happier man. There could be no question of dropping the business, whatever its difficulties. I had a queer religious feeling that Ivery and I had our fortunes intertwined, and that no will of mine could keep us apart. I had faced him before the war and won; I had faced him again and lost; the third time or the twentieth time we would reach a final decision. The whole business had hitherto appeared to me a trifle unreal, at any rate my own connection with it. I had been docilely obeying orders, but my real self had been standing aside and watching my doings with a certain aloofness. But that hour in the Tube station had brought me into the serum, and I saw the affair not as Bullivant's or even Blenkiron's, but as my own. Before I had been itching to get back to the Front; now I wanted to get on to Ivery's trail, though it should take me through the nether pit. Peter was right; fortitude was the thing a man must possess if he would save his soul.

The hours passed, and, as I expected, there came no word from Macgillivray. I had some dinner sent up to me at seven o'clock, and about eight I was thinking of looking up Blenkiron. Just then came a telephone call asking me to go round to Sir Walter Bullivant's house in Queen Anne's Gate.

Ten minutes later I was ringing the bell, and the door was opened to me by the same impassive butler who had admitted me on that famous night three years before. Nothing had changed in the pleasant green-panelled hall; the alcove was the same as when I had watched from it the departure of the man who now called himself Ivery; the telephone book lay in the very place from which I had snatched it in order to ring up the First Sea Lord. And in the back room, where that night five anxious officials had conferred, I found Sir Walter and Blenkiron.

Both looked worried, the American feverishly so. He walked up and down the hearthrug, sucking an unlit black cigar.

'Say, Dick,' he said, 'this is a bad business. It wasn't no fault of yours. You did fine. It was us—me and Sir Walter and Mr Macgillivray that were the quitters.'

'Any news?' I asked.

'So far the cover's drawn blank,' Sir Walter replied. 'It was the devil's own work that our friend looked your way today. You're pretty certain he saw that you recognized him?'

'Absolutely. As sure as that he knew I recognized him in your hall three years ago when he was swaggering as Lord Alloa.'

'No,' said Blenkiron dolefully, 'that little flicker of recognition is just the one thing you can't be wrong about. Land alive! I wish Mr Macgillivray would come.'

The bell rang, and the door opened, but it was not Macgillivray. It was a young girl in a white ball-gown, with a cluster of blue cornflowers at her breast. The sight of her fetched Sir Walter out of his chair so suddenly that he upset his coffee cup.

'Mary, my dear, how did you manage it? I didn't expect you till the late train.'

'I was in London, you see, and they telephoned on your telegram. I'm staying with Aunt Doria, and I cut her theatre party. She thinks I'm at the Shandwick's dance, so I needn't go home till morning ... Good evening, General Hannay. You got over the Hill Difficulty.'

'The next stage is the Valley of Humiliation,' I answered.

'So it would appear,' she said gravely, and sat very quietly on the edge of Sir Walter's chair with her small, cool hand upon his.

I had been picturing her in my recollection as very young and glimmering, a dancing, exquisite child. But now I revised that picture. The crystal freshness of morning was still there, but I saw how deep the waters were. It was the clean fineness and strength of her that entranced me. I didn't even think of her as pretty, any more than a man thinks of the good looks of the friend he worships.

We waited, hardly speaking a word, till Macgillivray came. The first sight of his face told his story.

'Gone?' asked Blenkiron sharply. The man's lethargic calm seemed to have wholly deserted him.

'Gone,' repeated the newcomer. 'We have just tracked him down. Oh, he managed it cleverly. Never a sign of disturbance in any of his lairs. His dinner ordered at Biggleswick and several people invited to stay with him for the weekend—one a member of the Government. Two meetings at which he was to speak arranged for next week. Early this afternoon he flew over to France as a passenger in one of the new planes. He had been mixed up with the Air Board people for months—of course as another man with another face. Miss Lamington discovered that just too late. The bus went out of its course and came down in Normandy. By this time our man's in Paris or beyond it.'

Sir Walter took off his big tortoiseshell spectacles and laid them carefully on the table.

'Roll up the map of Europe,' he said. 'This is our Austerlitz. Mary, my dear, I am feeling very old.'

Macgillivray had the sharpened face of a bitterly disappointed man. Blenkiron had got very red, and I could see that he was blaspheming violently under his breath. Mary's eyes were quiet and solemn. She kept on patting Sir Walter's hand. The sense of some great impending disaster hung heavily on me, and to break the spell I asked for details.

'Tell me just the extent of the damage,' I asked. 'Our neat plan for deceiving the Boche has failed. That is bad. A dangerous spy has got beyond our power. That's worse. Tell me, is there still a worst? What's the limit of mischief he can do?'

Sir Walter had risen and joined Blenkiron on the hearthrug. His brows were furrowed and his mouth hard as if he were suffering pain.

'There is no limit,' he said. 'None that I can see, except the long-suffering of God. You know the man as Ivery, and you knew him as that other whom you believed to have been shot one summer morning and decently buried. You feared the second—at least if you didn't, I did—most mortally. You realized that we feared Ivery, and you knew enough about him to see his fiendish cleverness. Well, you have the two men combined in one man. Ivery was the best brain Macgillivray and I ever encountered, the most cunning and patient and long-sighted. Combine him with the other, the chameleon who can blend himself with his environment, and has as many personalities as there are types and traits on the earth. What kind of enemy is that to have to fight?'

'I admit it's a steep proposition. But after all how much ill can he do? There are pretty strict limits to the activity of even the cleverest spy.'

'I agree. But this man is not a spy who buys a few wretched subordinates and steals a dozen private letters. He's a genius who has been living as part of our English life. There's nothing he hasn't seen. He's been on terms of intimacy with all kinds of politicians. We know that. He did it as Ivery. They rather liked him, for he was clever and flattered them, and they told him things. But God knows what he saw and heard in his other personalities. For all I know he may have breakfasted at Downing Street with letters of introduction from President Wilson, or visited the Grand Fleet as a distinguished neutral. Then think of the women; how they talk. We're the leakiest society on earth, and we safeguard ourselves by keeping dangerous people out of it. We trust to our outer barrage. But anyone who has really slipped inside has a million chances. And this, remember, is one man in ten millions, a man whose brain never sleeps for a moment, who is quick to seize the slightest hint, who can piece a plan together out of a dozen bits of gossip. It's like—it's as if the Chief of the Intelligence Department were suddenly to desert to the enemy ... The ordinary spy knows only bits of unconnected facts. This man knows our life and our way of thinking and everything about us.'

'Well, but a treatise on English life in time of war won't do much good to the Boche.'

Sir Walter shook his head. 'Don't you realize the explosive stuff that is lying about? Ivery knows enough to make the next German peace offensive really deadly—not the blundering thing which it has been up to now, but something which gets our weak spots on the raw. He knows enough to wreck our campaign in the field. And the awful thing is that we don't know just what he knows or what he is aiming for. This war's a packet of surprises. Both sides are struggling for the margin, the little fraction of advantage, and between evenly matched enemies it's just the extra atom of foreknowledge that tells.'

'Then we've got to push off and get after him,' I said cheerfully.

'But what are you going to do?' asked Macgillivray. 'If it were merely a question of destroying an organization it might be managed, for an organization presents a big front. But it's a question of destroying this one man, and his front is a razor edge. How are you going to find him? It's like looking for a needle in a haystack, and such a needle! A needle which can become a piece of straw or a tin-tack when it chooses!'

'All the same we've got to do it,' I said, remembering old Peter's lesson on fortitude, though I can't say I was feeling very stout-hearted.

Sir Walter flung himself wearily into an arm-chair. 'I wish I could be an optimist,' he said, 'but it looks as if we must own defeat. I've been at this work for twenty years, and, though I've been often beaten, I've always held certain cards in the game. Now I'm hanged if I've any. It looks like a knock-out, Hannay. It's no good deluding ourselves. We're men enough to look facts in the face and tell ourselves the truth. I don't see any ray of light in the business. We've missed our shot by a hairsbreadth and that's the same as missing by miles.'

I remember he looked at Mary as if for confirmation, but she did not smile or nod. Her face was very grave and her eyes looked steadily at him. Then they moved and met mine, and they seemed to give me my marching orders.

'Sir Walter,' I said, 'three years ago you and I sat in this very room. We thought we were done to the world, as we think now. We had just that one miserable little clue to hang on to—a dozen words scribbled in a notebook by a dead man. You thought I was mad when I asked for Scudder's book, but we put our backs into the job and in twenty-four hours we had won out. Remember that then we were fighting against time. Now we have a reasonable amount of leisure. Then we had nothing but a sentence of gibberish. Now we have a great body of knowledge, for Blenkiron has been brooding over Ivery like an old hen, and he knows his ways of working and his breed of confederate. You've got something to work on now. Do you mean to tell me that, when the stakes are so big, you're going to chuck in your hand?'

Macgillivray raised his head. 'We know a good deal about Ivery, but Ivery's dead. We know nothing of the man who was gloriously resurrected this evening in Normandy.'

'Oh, yes we do. There are many faces to the man, but only one mind, and you know plenty about that mind.'

'I wonder,' said Sir Walter. 'How can you know a mind which has no characteristics except that it is wholly and supremely competent? Mere mental powers won't give us a clue. We want to know the character which is behind all the personalities. Above all we want to know its foibles. If we had only a hint of some weakness we might make a plan.'

'Well, let's set down all we know,' I cried, for the more I argued the keener I grew. I told them in some detail the story of the night in the Coolin and what I had heard there.

'There's the two names Chelius and Bommaerts. The man spoke them in the same breath as Elfenbein, so they must be associated with Ivery's gang. You've got to get the whole Secret Service of the Allies busy to fit a meaning to these two words. Surely to goodness you'll find something! Remember those names don't belong to the Ivery part, but to the big game behind all the different disguises ... Then there's the talk about the Wild Birds and the Cage Birds. I haven't a guess at what it means. But it refers to some infernal gang, and among your piles of records there must be some clue. You set the intelligence of two hemispheres busy on the job. You've got all the machinery, and it's my experience that if even one solitary man keeps chewing on at a problem he discovers something.'

My enthusiasm was beginning to strike sparks from Macgillivray. He was looking thoughtful now, instead of despondent.

'There might be something in that,' he said, 'but it's a far-out chance.'

'Of course it's a far-out chance, and that's all we're ever going to get from Ivery. But we've taken a bad chance before and won ... Then you've all that you know about Ivery here. Go through his *dossier* with a small-tooth comb and I'll bet you find something to work on. Blenkiron, you're a man with a cool head. You admit we've a sporting chance.'

'Sure, Dick. He's fixed things so that the lines are across the track, but we'll clear somehow. So far as John S. Blenkiron is concerned he's got just one thing to do in this world, and that's to follow the yellow dog and have him neatly and cleanly tidied up. I've got a stack of personal affronts to settle. I was easy fruit and he hasn't been very respectful. You can count me in, Dick.'

'Then we're agreed,' I cried. 'Well, gentlemen, it's up to you to arrange the first stage. You've some pretty solid staff work to put in before you get on the trail.'

'And you?' Sir Walter asked.

'I'm going back to my brigade. I want a rest and a change. Besides, the first stage is office work, and I'm no use for that. But I'll be waiting to be summoned, and I'll come like a shot as soon as you hoick me out. I've got a presentiment about this thing. I know there'll be a finish and that I'll be in at it, and I think it will be a desperate, bloody business too.'

I found Mary's eyes fixed upon me, and in them I read the same thought. She had not spoken a word, but had sat on the edge of a chair, swinging a foot idly, one hand playing with an ivory fan. She had given me my old orders and I looked to her for confirmation of the new.

'Miss Lamington, you are the wisest of the lot of us. What do you say?'

She smiled—that shy, companionable smile which I had been picturing to myself through all the wanderings of the past month.

'I think you are right. We've a long way to go yet, for the Valley of Humiliation comes only half-way in the *Pilgrim's Progress*. The next stage was Vanity Fair. I might be of some use there, don't you think?'

I remember the way she laughed and flung back her head like a gallant boy.

'The mistake we've all been making,' she said, 'is that our methods are too terre-a-terre. We've a poet to deal with, a great poet, and we must fling our imaginations forward to catch up with him. His strength is his unexpectedness, you know, and we won't beat him by plodding only. I believe the wildest course is the wisest, for it's the most likely to intersect his ... Who's the poet among us?'

'Peter,' I said. 'But he's pinned down with a game leg in Germany. All the same we must rope him in.'

By this time we had all cheered up, for it is wonderful what a tonic there is in a prospect of action. The butler brought in tea, which it was Bullivant's habit to drink after dinner. To me it seemed fantastic to watch a slip of a girl pouring it out for two grizzled and distinguished servants of the State and one battered soldier—as decorous a family party as you would ask to see—and to reflect that all four were engaged in an enterprise where men's lives must be reckoned at less than thistledown.

After that we went upstairs to a noble Georgian drawing-room and Mary played to us. I don't care two straws for music from an instrument—unless it be the pipes or a regimental band—but I dearly love the human voice. But she would not sing, for singing to her, I fancy, was something that did not come at will, but flowed only like a bird's note when the mood favoured. I did not want it either. I was content to let 'Cherry Ripe' be the one song linked with her in my memory.

It was Macgillivray who brought us back to business.

'I wish to Heaven there was one habit of mind we could definitely attach to him and to no one else.' (At this moment 'He' had only one meaning for us.)

'You can't do nothing with his mind,' Blenkiron drawled. 'You can't loose the bands of Orion, as the Bible says, or hold Leviathan with a hook. I reckoned I could and made a mighty close study of his de-vices. But the darned cuss wouldn't stay put. I thought I had tied him down to the double bluff, and he went and played the triple bluff on me. There's nothing doing that line.'

A memory of Peter recurred to me.

'What about the "blind spot"?' I asked, and I told them old Peter's pet theory. 'Every man that God made has his weak spot somewhere, some flaw in his character which leaves a dull patch in his brain. We've got to find that out, and I think I've made a beginning.'

Macgillivray in a sharp voice asked my meaning.

'He's in a funk ... of something. Oh, I don't mean he's a coward. A man in his trade wants the nerve of a buffalo. He could give us all points in courage. What I mean is that he's not clean white all through. There are yellow streaks somewhere in him ... I've given a good deal of thought to this courage business, for I haven't got a great deal of it myself. Not like Peter, I mean. I've got heaps of soft places in me. I'm afraid of being drowned for one thing, or of getting my eyes shot out. Ivery's afraid of bombs—at any rate he's afraid of bombs in a big city. I once read a book which talked about a thing called agoraphobia. Perhaps it's that ... Now if we know that weak spot it helps us in our work. There are some places he won't go to, and there are some things he can't do—not well, anyway. I reckon that's useful.'

'Ye-es,' said Macgillivray. 'Perhaps it's not what you'd call a burning and a shining light.'

'There's another chink in his armour,' I went on. 'There's one person in the world he can never practise his transformations on, and that's me. I shall always know him again, though he appeared as Sir Douglas Haig. I can't explain why, but I've got a feel in my bones about it. I didn't recognize him before, for I thought he was dead, and the nerve in my brain which should have been looking for him wasn't working. But I'm on my guard now, and that nerve's functioning at full power. Whenever and wherever and howsoever we meet again on the face of the earth, it will be "Dr Livingstone, I presume" between him and me.'

'That is better,' said Macgillivray. 'If we have any luck, Hannay, it won't be long till we pull you out of His Majesty's Forces.'

Mary got up from the piano and resumed her old perch on the arm of Sir Walter's chair.

'There's another blind spot which you haven't mentioned.' It was a cool evening, but I noticed that her cheeks had suddenly flushed.

'Last week Mr Ivery asked me to marry him,' she said.

PART II

CHAPTER TWELVE

I Become a Combatant Once More

I returned to France on 13 September, and took over my old brigade on the 19th of the same month. We were shoved in at the Polygon Wood on the 26th, and after four days got so badly mauled that we were brought out to refit. On 7 October, very much to my surprise, I was given command of a division and was on the fringes of the Ypres fighting during the first days of November. From that front we were hurried down to Cambrai in support, but came in only for the last backwash of that singular battle. We held a bit of the St Quentin sector till just before Christmas, when we had a spell of rest in billets, which endured, so far as I was concerned, till the beginning of January, when I was sent off on the errand which I shall presently relate.

That is a brief summary of my military record in the latter part of 1917. I am not going to enlarge on the fighting. Except for the days of the Polygon Wood it was neither very severe nor very distinguished, and you will find it in the history books. What I have to tell of here is my own personal quest, for all the time I was living with my mind turned two ways. In the morasses of the Haanebeek flats, in the slimy support lines at Zonnebeke, in the tortured uplands about Flesquieres, and in many other odd places I kept worrying at my private conundrum. At night I would lie awake thinking of it, and many a toss I took into shell-holes and many a time I stepped off the duckboards, because my eyes were on a different landscape. Nobody ever chewed a few wretched clues into such a pulp as I did during those bleak months in Flanders and Picardy.

For I had an instinct that the thing was desperately grave, graver even than the battle before me. Russia had gone headlong to the devil, Italy had taken it between the eyes and was still dizzy, and our own prospects were none too bright. The Boche was getting uppish and with some cause, and I foresaw a rocky time ahead till America could line up with us in the field. It was the chance for the Wild Birds, and I used to wake in a sweat to think what devilry Ivery might be engineering. I believe I did my proper job reasonably well, but I put in my most savage thinking over the other. I remember how I used to go over every hour of every day from that June night in the Cotswolds till my last meeting with Bullivant in London, trying to find a new bearing. I should probably have got brain-fever, if I hadn't had to spend most of my days and nights fighting a stiffish battle with a very watchful Hun. That kept my mind balanced, and I dare say it gave an edge to it; for during those months I was lucky enough to hit on a better scent than Bullivant and Macgillivray and Blenkiron, pulling a thousand wires in their London offices.

I will set down in order of time the various incidents in this private quest of mine. The first was my meeting with Geordie Hamilton. It happened just after I rejoined the brigade, when I went down to have a look at our Scots Fusilier battalion. The old brigade had been roughly handled on 31st July, and had had to get heavy drafts to come anywhere near strength. The Fusiliers especially were almost a new lot, formed by joining our remnants to the remains of a battalion in another division and bringing about a dozen officers from the training unit at home.

I inspected the men and my eyes caught sight of a familiar face. I asked his name and the colonel got it from the sergeant-major. It was Lance-Corporal George Hamilton.

Now I wanted a new batman, and I resolved then and there to have my old antagonist. That afternoon he reported to me at brigade headquarters. As I looked at that solid bandy-legged figure, standing as stiff to attention as a tobacconist's sign, his ugly face hewn out of brown oak, his honest, sullen mouth, and his blue eyes staring into vacancy, I knew I had got the man I wanted.

'Hamilton,' I said, 'you and I have met before.'

'Sirr?' came the mystified answer.

'Look at me, man, and tell me if you don't recognize me.'

He moved his eyes a fraction, in a respectful glance.

'Sirr, I don't mind of you.'

'Well, I'll refresh your memory. Do you remember the hall in Newmilns Street and the meeting there? You had a fight with a man outside, and got knocked down.'

He made no answer, but his colour deepened.

'And a fortnight later in a public-house in Muirtown you saw the same man, and gave him the chase of his life.'

I could see his mouth set, for visions of the penalties laid down by the King's Regulations for striking an officer must have crossed his mind. But he never budged.

'Look me in the face, man,' I said. 'Do you remember me now?'

He did as he was bid.

'Sirr, I mind of you.'

'Have you nothing more to say?'

He cleared his throat. 'Sirr, I did not ken I was hittin' an officer.'

'Of course you didn't. You did perfectly right, and if the war was over and we were both free men, I would give you a chance of knocking me down here and now. That's got to wait. When you saw me last I was serving my country, though you didn't know it. We're serving together now, and you must get your revenge out of the Boche. I'm going to make you my servant, for you and I have a pretty close bond between us. What do you say to that?'

This time he looked me full in the face. His troubled eye appraised me and was satisfied. 'I'm proud to be servant to ye, sirr,' he said. Then out of his chest came a strangled chuckle, and he forgot his discipline. 'Losh, but ye're the great lad!' He recovered himself promptly, saluted, and marched off.

The second episode befell during our brief rest after the Polygon Wood, when I had ridden down the line one afternoon to see a friend in the Heavy Artillery. I was returning in the drizzle of evening, clanking along the greasy path between the sad poplars, when I struck a Labour company repairing the ravages of a Boche strafe that morning. I wasn't very certain of my road and asked one of the workers. He straightened himself and saluted, and I saw beneath a disreputable cap the features of the man who had been with me in the Coolin crevice.

I spoke a word to his sergeant, who fell him out, and he walked a bit of the way with me.

'Great Scot, Wake, what brought you here?' I asked.

'Same thing as brought you. This rotten war.'

I had dismounted and was walking beside him, and I noticed that his lean face had lost its pallor and that his eyes were less hot than they used to be.

'You seem to thrive on it,' I said, for I did not know what to say. A sudden shyness possessed me. Wake must have gone through some violent cyclones of feeling before it came to this. He saw what I was thinking and laughed in his sharp, ironical way.

'Don't flatter yourself you've made a convert. I think as I always thought. But I came to the conclusion that since the fates had made me a Government servant I might as well do my work somewhere less cushioned than a chair in the Home Office ... Oh, no, it wasn't a matter of principle. One kind of work's as good as another, and I'm a better clerk than a navvy. With me it was self-indulgence: I wanted fresh air and exercise.'

I looked at him—mud to the waist, and his hands all blistered and cut with unaccustomed labour. I could realize what his associates must mean to him, and how he would relish the rough tonguing of non-coms.

'You're a confounded humbug,' I said. 'Why on earth didn't you go into an O.T.C. and come out with a commission? They're easy enough to get.'

'You mistake my case,' he said bitterly. 'I experienced no sudden conviction about the justice of the war. I stand where I always stood. I'm a non-combatant, and I wanted a change of civilian work ... No, it wasn't any idiotic tribunal sent me here. I came of my own free will, and I'm really rather enjoying myself.'

'It's a rough job for a man like you,' I said.

'Not so rough as the fellows get in the trenches. I watched a battalion marching back today and they looked like ghosts who had been years in muddy graves. White faces and dazed eyes and leaden feet. Mine's a cushy job. I like it best when the weather's foul. It cheats me into thinking I'm doing my duty.'

I nodded towards a recent shell-hole. 'Much of that sort of thing?'

'Now and then. We had a good dusting this morning. I can't say I liked it at the time, but I like to look back on it. A sort of moral anodyne.'

'I wonder what on earth the rest of your lot make of you?'

'They don't make anything. I'm not remarkable for my *bonhomie*. They think I'm a prig—which I am. It doesn't amuse me to talk about beer and women or listen to a gramophone or grouse about my last meal. But I'm quite content, thank you. Sometimes I get a seat in a corner of a Y.M.C.A. hut, and I've a book or two. My chief affliction is the padre. He was up at Keble in my time, and, as one of my colleagues puts it, wants to be "too bloody helpful".... What are you doing, Hannay? I see you're some kind of general. They're pretty thick on the ground here.'

'I'm a sort of general. Soldiering in the Salient isn't the softest of jobs, but I don't believe it's as tough as yours is for you. D'you know, Wake, I wish I had you in my brigade. Trained or untrained, you're a dashed stout-hearted fellow.'

He laughed with a trifle less acidity than usual. 'Almost thou persuadest me to be combatant. No, thank you. I haven't the courage, and besides there's my jolly old principles. All the same I'd like to be near you. You're a good chap, and I've had the honour to assist in your education ... I must be getting back, or the sergeant will think I've bolted.'

We shook hands, and the last I saw of him was a figure saluting stiffly in the wet twilight.

The third incident was trivial enough, though momentous in its results. Just before I got the division I had a bout of malaria. We were in support in the Salient, in very uncomfortable trenches behind Wieltje, and I spent three days on my back in a dug-out. Outside was a blizzard of rain, and the water now and then came down the stairs through the gas curtain and stood in pools at my bed foot. It wasn't the merriest place to convalesce in, but I was as hard as nails at the time and by the third day I was beginning to sit up and be bored.

I read all my English papers twice and a big stack of German ones which I used to have sent up by a friend in the G.H.Q. Intelligence, who knew I liked to follow what the Boche was saying. As I dozed and ruminated in the way a man does after fever, I was struck by the tremendous display of one advertisement in the English press. It was a thing called 'Gussiter's Deep-breathing System,' which, according to its promoter, was a cure for every ill, mental, moral, or physical, that man can suffer. Politicians, generals, admirals, and music-hall artists all testified to the new life it had opened up for them. I remember wondering what these sportsmen got for their testimonies, and thinking I would write a spoof letter myself to old Gussiter.

Then I picked up the German papers, and suddenly my eye caught an advertisement of the same kind in the *Frankfurter Zeitung*. It was not Gussiter this time, but one Weissmann, but his game was identical—'deep breathing'. The Hun style was different from the English—all about the Goddess of Health, and the Nymphs of the Mountains, and two quotations from Schiller. But the principle was the same.

That made me ponder a little, and I went carefully through the whole batch. I found the advertisement in the *Frankfurter* and in one or two rather obscure *Volkstimmes* and *Volkszeitungs*. I found it too in *Der Grosse Krieg*, the official German propagandist picture-paper. They were the same all but one, and that one had a bold variation, for it contained four of the sentences used in the ordinary English advertisement.

This struck me as fishy, and I started to write a letter to Macgillivray pointing out what seemed to be a case of trading with the enemy, and advising him to get on to Mr Gussiter's financial backing. I thought he might find a Hun syndicate behind him. And then I had another notion, which made me rewrite my letter.

I went through the papers again. The English ones which contained the advertisement were all good, solid, bellicose organs; the kind of thing no censorship would object to leaving the country. I had before me a small sheaf of pacifist prints, and they had not the advertisement. That might be for reasons of circulation, or it might not. The German papers were either Radical or Socialist publications, just the opposite of the English lot, except the *Grosse Krieg*. Now we have a free press, and Germany has, strictly speaking, none. All her journalistic indiscretions are calculated. Therefore the Boche has no objection to his rags getting to enemy countries. He wants it. He likes to see them quoted in columns headed 'Through German Glasses', and made the text of articles showing what a good democrat he is becoming.

As I puzzled over the subject, certain conclusions began to form in my mind. The four identical sentences seemed to hint that 'Deep Breathing' had Boche affiliations. Here was a chance of communicating with the enemy which would defy the argus-eyed gentlemen who examine the mails. What was to hinder Mr A at one end writing an advertisement with a good cipher in it, and the paper containing it getting into Germany by Holland in three days? Herr B at the other end replied in the *Frankfurter*, and a few days later shrewd editors and acute Intelligence officers—and Mr A—were reading it in London, though only Mr A knew what it really meant.

It struck me as a bright idea, the sort of simple thing that doesn't occur to clever people, and very rarely to the Boche. I wished I was not in the middle of a battle, for I would have had a try at investigating the cipher myself. I wrote a long letter to Macgillivray putting my case, and then went to sleep. When I awoke I reflected that it was a pretty thin argument, and would have stopped the letter, if it hadn't gone off early by a ration party.

After that things began very slowly to happen. The first was when Hamilton, having gone to Boulogne to fetch some mess-stores, returned with the startling news that he had seen Gresson. He had not heard his name, but described him dramatically to me as the wee red-headed devil that kicked Ecky Brockie's knee yon time in Glesca, sirr,' I recognized the description.

Gresson, it appeared, was joy-riding. He was with a party of Labour delegates who had been met by two officers and carried off in chars-a-bancs. Hamilton reported from inquiries among his friends that this kind of visitor came weekly. I thought it a very sensible notion on the Government's part, but I wondered how Gresson had been selected. I had hoped that Macgillivray had weeks ago made a long arm and quodded him. Perhaps they had too little evidence to hang him, but he was the blackest sort of suspect and should have been interned.

A week later I had occasion to be at G.H.Q. on business connected with my new division. My friends in the Intelligence allowed me to use the direct line to London, and I called up Macgillivray. For ten minutes I had an exciting talk, for I had had no news from that quarter since I left England. I heard that the Portuguese Jew had escaped—had vanished from his native heather when they went to get him. They had identified him as a German professor of Celtic languages, who had held a chair in a Welsh college—a dangerous fellow, for he was an upright, high-minded, raging fanatic. Against Gresson they had no evidence at all, but he was kept under strict observation. When I asked about his crossing to France, Macgillivray replied that that was part of their scheme. I inquired if the visit had given them any clues, but I never got an answer, for the line had to be cleared at that moment for the War Office. I hunted up the man who had charge of these Labour visits, and made friends with him. Gresson, he said, had been a quiet, well-mannered, and most appreciative guest. He had wept tears on Vimy Ridge, and—strictly against orders—had made a speech to some troops he met on the Arras road about how British Labour was remembering the Army in its prayers and sweating blood to make guns. On the last day he had had a misadventure, for he got very sick on the road—some kidney trouble that couldn't stand the jolting of the car—and had to be left at a village and picked up by the party on its way back. They found him better, but still shaky. I cross-examined the particular officer in charge about that halt, and learned that Gresson had been left alone in a peasant's cottage, for he said he only needed to lie down. The place was the hamlet of Eaucourt Sainte-Anne.

For several weeks that name stuck in my head. It had a pleasant, quaint sound, and I wondered how Gresson had spent his hours there. I hunted it up on the map, and promised myself to have a look at it the next time we came out to rest. And then I forgot about it till I heard the name mentioned again.

On 23rd October I had the bad luck, during a tour of my first-line trenches, to stop a small shell-fragment with my head. It was a close, misty day and I had taken off my tin hat to wipe my brow when the thing happened. I got a long, shallow scalp wound which meant nothing but bled a lot, and, as we were not in for any big move, the M.O. sent me back to a clearing station to have it seen to. I was three days in the place and, being perfectly well, had leisure to look about me and reflect, so that I recall that time as a queer, restful interlude in the infernal racket of war. I remember yet how on my last night there a gale made the lamps swing and flicker, and turned the grey-green canvas walls into a mass of mottled shadows. The floor canvas was muddy from the tramping of many feet bringing in the constant dribble of casualties from the line. In my tent there was no one very bad at the time, except a boy with his shoulder half-blown off by a whizz-bang, who lay in a drugged sleep at the far end. The majority were influenza, bronchitis, and trench-fever—waiting to be moved to the base, or convalescent and about to return to their units.

A small group of us dined off tinned chicken, stewed fruit, and radon cheese round the smoky stove, where two screens manufactured from packing cases gave some protection against the draughts which swept like young tornadoes down the tent. One man had been reading a book called the *Ghost Stories of an Antiquary*, and the talk turned on the unexplainable things that happen to everybody once or twice in a lifetime. I contributed a yarn about the men who went to look for Kruger's treasure in the bushveld and got scared by a green wildebeeste. It is a good yarn and I'll write it down some day. A tall Highlander, who kept his slippered feet on the top of the stove, and whose costume consisted of a kilt, a

British warm, a grey hospital dressing-gown, and four pairs of socks, told the story of the Camerons at First Ypres, and of the Lowland subaltern who knew no Gaelic and suddenly found himself encouraging his men with some ancient Highland rigmarole. The poor chap had a racking bronchial cough, which suggested that his country might well use him on some warmer battle-ground than Flanders. He seemed a bit of a scholar and explained the Cameron business in a lot of long words.

I remember how the talk meandered on as talk does when men are idle and thinking about the next day. I didn't pay much attention, for I was reflecting on a change I meant to make in one of my battalion commands, when a fresh voice broke in. It belonged to a Canadian captain from Winnipeg, a very silent fellow who smoked shag tobacco.

'There's a lot of ghosts in this darned country,' he said.

Then he started to tell about what happened to him when his division was last back in rest billets. He had a staff job and put up with the divisional command at an old French chateau. They had only a little bit of the house; the rest was shut up, but the passages were so tortuous that it was difficult to keep from wandering into the unoccupied part. One night, he said, he woke with a mighty thirst, and, since he wasn't going to get cholera by drinking the local water in his bedroom, he started out for the room they messed in to try to pick up a whisky-and-soda. He couldn't find it, though he knew the road like his own name. He admitted he might have taken a wrong turning, but he didn't think so. Anyway he landed in a passage which he had never seen before, and, since he had no candle, he tried to retrace his steps. Again he went wrong, and groped on till he saw a faint light which he thought must be the room of the G.S.O., a good fellow and a friend of his. So he barged in, and found a big, dim salon with two figures in it and a lamp burning between them, and a queer, unpleasant smell about. He took a step forward, and then he saw that the figures had no faces. That fairly loosened his joints with fear, and he gave a cry. One of the two ran towards him, the lamp went out, and the sickly scent caught suddenly at his throat. After that he knew nothing till he awoke in his own bed next morning with a splitting headache. He said he got the General's permission and went over all the unoccupied part of the house, but he couldn't find the room. Dust lay thick on everything, and there was no sign of recent human presence.

I give the story as he told it in his drawling voice. 'I reckon that was the genuine article in ghosts. You don't believe me and conclude I was drunk? I wasn't. There isn't any drink concocted yet that could lay me out like that. I just struck a crack in the old universe and pushed my head outside. It may happen to you boys any day.'

The Highlander began to argue with him, and I lost interest in the talk. But one phrase brought me to attention. 'I'll give you the name of the darned place, and next time you're around you can do a bit of prospecting for yourself. It's called the Chateau of Eaucourt Sainte-Anne, about seven kilometres from Douvecourt. If I was purchasing real estate in this country I guess I'd give that location a miss.'

After that I had a grim month, what with the finish of Third Ypres and the hustles to Cambrai. By the middle of December we had shaken down a bit, but the line my division held was not of our choosing, and we had to keep a wary eye on the Boche doings. It was a weary job, and I had no time to think of anything but the military kind of intelligence—fixing the units against us from prisoners' stories, organizing small raids, and keeping the Royal Flying Corps busy. I was keen about the last, and I made several trips myself over the lines with Archie Roylance, who had got his heart's desire and by good luck belonged to the squadron just behind me. I said as little as possible about this, for G.H.Q. did not encourage divisional generals to practise such methods, though there was one famous army commander who made a hobby of them. It was on one of these trips that an incident occurred which brought my spell of waiting on the bigger game to an end.

One dull December day, just after luncheon, Archie and I set out to reconnoitre. You know the way that fogs in Picardy seem suddenly to reek out of the ground and envelop the slopes like a shawl. That was our luck this time. We had crossed the lines, flying very high, and received the usual salute of Hun Archies. After a mile or two the ground seemed to climb up to us, though we hadn't descended, and presently we were in the heart of a cold, clinging mist. We dived for several thousand feet, but the confounded thing grew thicker and no sort of landmark could be found anywhere. I thought if we went on at this rate we should hit a tree or a church steeple and be easy fruit for the enemy.

The same thought must have been in Archie's mind, for he climbed again. We got into a mortally cold zone, but the air was no clearer. Thereupon he decided to head for home, and passed me word to work out a compass course on the map. That was easier said than done, but I had a rough notion of the rate we had travelled since we had crossed the lines and I knew our original direction, so I did the best I could. On we went for a bit, and then I began to get doubtful. So did Archie. We dropped low down, but we could hear none of the row that's always going on for a mile on each side of the lines. The world was very eerie and deadly still, so still that Archie and I could talk through the speaking-tube.

'We've mislaid this blamed battle,'he shouted.

'I think your rotten old compass has soured on us,' I replied.

We decided that it wouldn't do to change direction, so we held on the same course. I was getting as nervous as a kitten, chiefly owing to the silence. It's not what you expect in the middle of a battle-field ... I looked at the compass carefully and saw that it was really crocked. Archie must have damaged it on a former flight and forgotten to have it changed.

He had a very scared face when I pointed this out.

'Great God!' he croaked—for he had a fearsome cold—'we're either about Calais or near Paris or miles the wrong side of the Boche line. What the devil are we to do?'

And then to put the lid on it his engine went wrong. It was the same performance as on the Yorkshire moors, and seemed to be a speciality of the Shark-Gladas type. But this time the end came quick. We dived steeply, and I could see by Archie's grip on the stick that he was going to have his work cut out to save our necks. Save them he did, but not by much for we jolted down on the edge of a ploughed field with a series of bumps that shook the teeth in my head. It was the same dense, dripping fog, and we crawled out of the old bus and bolted for cover like two ferreted rabbits.

Our refuge was the lee of a small copse.

'It's my opinion,' said Archie solemnly, 'that we're somewhere about La Cateau. Tim Wilbraham got left there in the Retreat, and it took him nine months to make the Dutch frontier. It's a giddy prospect, sir.'

I sallied out to reconnoitre. At the other side of the wood was a highway, and the fog so blanketed sound that I could not hear a man on it till I saw his face. The first one I saw made me lie flat in the covert ... For he was a German soldier, field-grey, forage cap, red band and all, and he had a pick on his shoulder.

A second's reflection showed me that this was not final proof. He might be one of our prisoners. But it was no place to take chances. I went back to Archie, and the pair of us crossed the ploughed field and struck the road farther on. There we saw a farmer's cart with a woman and child in it. They looked French, but melancholy, just what you would expect from the inhabitants of a countryside in enemy occupation.

Then we came to the park wall of a great house, and saw dimly the outlines of a cottage. Here sooner or later we would get proof of our whereabouts, so we lay and shivered among the poplars of the roadside. No one seemed abroad that afternoon. For a quarter of an hour it was as quiet as the grave. Then came a sound of whistling, and muffled steps.

'That's an Englishman,' said Archie joyfully. 'No Boche could make such a beastly noise.'

He was right. The form of an Army Service Corps private emerged from the mist, his cap on the back of his head, his hands in his pockets, and his walk the walk of a free man. I never saw a welcomer sight than that jam-merchant.

We stood up and greeted him. 'What's this place?' I shouted.

He raised a grubby hand to his forelock. ''Ockott Saint Anny, sir,' he said. 'Beg pardon, sir, but you ain't whurt, sir?'

Ten minutes later I was having tea in the mess of an M.T. workshop while Archie had gone to the nearest Signals to telephone for a car and give instructions about his precious bus. It was almost dark, but I gulped my tea and hastened out into the thick dusk. For I wanted to have a look at the Chateau.

I found a big entrance with high stone pillars, but the iron gates were locked and looked as if they had not been opened in the memory of man. Knowing the way of such places, I hunted for the side entrance and found a muddy road which led to the back of the house. The front was evidently towards a kind of park; at the back was a nest of outbuildings and a section of moat which looked very deep and black in the winter twilight. This was crossed by a stone bridge with a door at the end of it.

Clearly the Chateau was not being used for billets. There was no sign of the British soldier; there was no sign of anything human. I crept through the fog as noiselessly as if I trod on velvet, and I hadn't even the company of my own footsteps. I remembered the Canadian's ghost story, and concluded I would be imagining the same sort of thing if I lived in such a place.

The door was bolted and padlocked. I turned along the side of the moat, hoping to reach the house front, which was probably modern and boasted a civilized entrance. There must be somebody in the place, for one chimney was smoking. Presently the moat petered out, and gave place to a cobbled causeway, but a wall, running at right angles with the house, blocked my way. I had half a mind to go back and hammer at the door, but I reflected that major-generals don't pay visits to deserted chateaux at night without a reasonable errand. I should look a fool in the eyes of some old concierge. The daylight was almost gone, and I didn't wish to go groping about the house with a candle.

But I wanted to see what was beyond the wall—one of those whims that beset the soberest men. I rolled a dissolute water-butt to the foot of it, and gingerly balanced myself on its rotten staves. This gave me a grip on the flat brick top, and I pulled myself up.

I looked down on a little courtyard with another wall beyond it, which shut off any view of the park. On the right was the Chateau, on the left more outbuildings; the whole place was not more than twenty yards each way. I was just about to retire by the road I had come, for in spite of my fur coat it was uncommon chilly on that perch, when I heard a key turn in the door in the Chateau wall beneath me.

A lantern made a blur of light in the misty darkness. I saw that the bearer was a woman, an oldish woman, round-shouldered like most French peasants. In one hand she carried a leather bag, and she moved so silently that she must have worn rubber boots. The light was held level with her head and illumined her face. It was the evillest thing I have ever beheld, for a horrible scar had puckered the skin of the forehead and drawn up the eyebrows so that it looked like some diabolical Chinese mask.

Slowly she padded across the yard, carrying the bag as gingerly as if it had been an infant. She stopped at the door of one of the outhouses and set down the lantern and her burden on the ground. From her apron she drew something which looked like a gas-mask, and put it over her head. She also put on a pair of long gauntlets. Then she unlocked the door, picked up the lantern and went in. I heard the key turn behind her.

Crouching on that wall, I felt a very ugly tremor run down my spine. I had a glimpse of what the Canadian's ghost might have been. That hag, hooded like some venomous snake, was too much for my stomach. I dropped off the wall and ran—yes, ran till I reached the highroad and saw the cheery headlights of a transport wagon, and heard the honest speech of the British soldier. That restored me to my senses, and made me feel every kind of a fool.

As I drove back to the line with Archie, I was black ashamed of my funk. I told myself that I had seen only an old countrywoman going to feed her hens. I convinced my reason, but I did not convince the whole of me. An insensate dread of the place hung around me, and I could only retrieve my self-respect by resolving to return and explore every nook of it.

CHAPTER THIRTEEN

The Adventure of the Picardy Chateau

I looked up Eaucourt Sainte-Anne on the map, and the more I studied its position the less I liked it. It was the knot from which sprang all the main routes to our Picardy front. If the Boche ever broke us, it was the place for which old Hindenburg would make. At all hours troops and transport trains were moving through that insignificant hamlet. Eminent generals and their staffs passed daily within sight of the Chateau. It was a convenient halting-place for battalions coming back to rest. Supposing, I argued, our enemies wanted a key-spot for some assault upon the morale or the discipline or health of the British Army, they couldn't find a better than Eaucourt Sainte-Anne. It was the ideal centre of espionage. But when I guardedly sounded my friends of the Intelligence they didn't seem to be worrying about it.

From them I got a chit to the local French authorities, and, as soon as we came out of the line, towards the end of December, I made straight for the country town of Douvecourt. By a bit of luck our divisional quarters were almost next door. I interviewed a tremendous swell in a black uniform and black kid gloves, who received me affably and put his archives and registers at my disposal. By this time I talked French fairly well, having a natural turn for languages, but half the rapid speech of the *sous-prifet* was lost on me. By and by he left me with the papers and a clerk, and I proceeded to grub up the history of the Chateau.

It had belonged since long before Agincourt to the noble house of the D'Eaucourts, now represented by an ancient Marquise who dwelt at Biarritz. She had never lived in the place, which a dozen years before had been falling to ruins, when a rich American leased it and partially restored it. He had soon got sick of it—his daughter had married a blackguard French cavalry officer with whom he quarrelled, said the clerk—and since then there had been several tenants. I wondered why a house so unattractive should have let so readily, but the clerk explained that the cause was the partridge-shooting. It was about the best in France, and in 1912 had shown the record bag.

The list of the tenants was before me. There was a second American, an Englishman called Halford, a Paris Jew-banker, and an Egyptian prince. But the space for 1913 was blank, and I asked the clerk about it. He told me that it had been taken by a woollen manufacturer from Lille, but he had never shot the partridges, though he had spent occasional nights in the house. He had a five years' lease, and was still paying rent to the Marquise. I asked the name, but the clerk had forgotten. 'It will be written there,' he said.

'But, no,' I said. 'Somebody must have been asleep over this register. There's nothing after 1912.'

He examined the page and blinked his eyes. 'Someone indeed must have slept. No doubt it was young Louis who is now with the guns in Champagne. But the name will be on the Commissary's list. It is, as I remember, a sort of Flemish.'

He hobbled off and returned in five minutes.

'Bommaerts,' he said, 'Jacques Bommaerts. A young man with no wife but with money—Dieu de Dieu, what oceans of it!'

That clerk got twenty-five francs, and he was cheap at the price. I went back to my division with a sense of awe on me. It was a marvellous fate that had brought me by odd routes to this out-of-the-way corner. First, the accident of Hamilton's seeing Gresson; then the night in the Clearing Station; last the mishap of Archie's plane getting lost in the fog. I had three grounds of suspicion—Gresson's sudden illness, the Canadian's ghost, and that horrid old woman in the dusk. And now I had one tremendous fact. The place was leased by a man called Bommaerts, and that was one of the two names I had heard whispered in that far-away cleft in the Coolin by the stranger from the sea.

A sensible man would have gone off to the contre-espionage people and told them his story. I couldn't do this; I felt that it was my own private find and I was going to do the prospecting myself. Every moment of leisure I had I was puzzling over the thing. I rode round by the Chateau one frosty morning and examined all the entrances. The main one was the grand avenue with the locked gates. That led straight to the front of the house where the terrace was—or you might call it the back, for the main door was on the other side. Anyhow the drive came up to the edge of the terrace and then split into two, one branch going to the stables by way of the outbuildings where I had seen the old woman, the other circling round the house, skirting the moat, and joining the back road just before the bridge. If I had gone to the right instead of the left that first evening with Archie, I should have circumnavigated the place without any trouble.

Seen in the fresh morning light the house looked commonplace enough. Part of it was as old as Noah, but most was newish and jerry-built, the kind of flat-chested, thin French Chateau, all front and no depth, and full of draughts and smoky chimneys. I might have gone in and ransacked the place, but I knew I should find nothing. It was borne in on me that it was only when evening fell that that house was interesting and that I must come, like Nicodemus, by night. Besides I had a private account to settle with my conscience. I had funked the place in the foggy twilight, and it does not do to let a matter like that slide. A man's courage is like a horse that refuses a fence; you have got to take him by the head and cram him at it again. If you don't, he will funk worse next time. I hadn't enough courage to be able to take chances with it, though I was afraid of many things, the thing I feared most mortally was being afraid.

I did not get a chance till Christmas Eve. The day before there had been a fall of snow, but the frost set in and the afternoon ended in a green sunset with the earth crisp and crackling like a shark's skin. I dined early, and took with me Geordie Hamilton, who added to his many accomplishments that of driving a car. He was the only man in the B.E.F. who guessed anything of the game I was after, and I knew that he was as discreet as a tombstone. I put on my oldest trench cap, slacks, and a pair of scaife-soled boots, that I used to change into in the evening. I had a useful little electric torch, which lived in my pocket, and from which a cord led to a small bulb of light that worked with a switch and could be hung on my belt. That left my arms free in case of emergencies. Likewise I strapped on my pistol.

There was little traffic in the hamlet of Eaucourt Sainte-Anne that night. Few cars were on the road, and the M.T. detachment, judging from the din, seemed to be busy on a private spree. It was about nine o'clock when we turned into the side road, and at the entrance to it I saw a solid figure in khaki mounting guard beside two bicycles. Something in the man's gesture, as he saluted, struck me as familiar, but I had no time to hunt for casual memories. I left the car just short of the bridge, and took the road which would bring me to the terraced front of the house.

Once I turned the corner of the Chateau and saw the long ghostly facade white in the moonlight, I felt less confident. The eeriness of the place smote me. In that still, snowy world it loomed up immense and mysterious with its rows of shuttered windows, each with that air which empty houses have of concealing some wild story. I longed to have old Peter with me, for he was the man for this kind of escapade. I had heard that he had been removed to Switzerland and I pictured him now in some mountain village where the snow lay deep. I would have given anything to have had Peter with a whole leg by my side.

I stepped on the terrace and listened. There was not a sound in the world, not even the distant rumble of a cart. The pile towered above me like a mausoleum, and I reflected that it must take some nerve to burgle an empty house. It would be good enough fun to break into a bustling dwelling and pinch the plate when the folk were at dinner, but to burgle emptiness and silence meant a fight with the terrors in a man's soul. It was worse in my case, for I wasn't cheered with prospects of loot. I wanted to get inside chiefly to soothe my conscience.

I hadn't much doubt I would find a way, for three years of war and the frequent presence of untidy headquarters' staffs have loosened the joints of most Picardy houses. There's generally a window that doesn't latch or a door that doesn't bar. But I tried window after window on the terrace without result. The heavy green sun-shutters were down over each, and when I broke the hinges of one there was a long bar within to hold it firm. I was beginning to think of shinning up a rain-pipe and trying the second floor, when a shutter I had laid hold on swung back in my hand. It had been left unfastened, and, kicking the snow from my boots, I entered a room.

A gleam of moonlight followed me and I saw I was in a big salon with a polished wood floor and dark lumps of furniture swathed in sheets. I clicked the bulb at my belt, and the little circle of light showed a place which had not been dwelt in for years. At the far end was another door, and as I tiptoed towards it something caught my eye on the parquet. It was a piece of fresh snow like that which clumps on the heel of a boot. I had not brought it there. Some other visitor had passed this way, and not long before me.

Very gently I opened the door and slipped in. In front of me was a pile of furniture which made a kind of screen, and behind that I halted and listened. There was somebody in the room. I heard the sound of human breathing and soft movements; the man, whoever he was, was at the far end from me, and though there was a dim glow of Moon through a broken shutter I could see nothing of what he was after. I was beginning to enjoy myself now. I knew of his presence and he did not know of mine, and that is the sport of stalking.

An unwary movement of my hand caused the screen to creak. Instantly the movements ceased and there was utter silence. I held my breath, and after a second or two the tiny sounds began again. I had a feeling, though my eyes could not assure me, that the man before me was at work, and was using a very small shaded torch. There was just the faintest moving shimmer on the wall beyond, though that might come from the crack of moonlight.

Apparently he was reassured, for his movements became more distinct. There was a jar as if a table had been pushed back. Once more there was silence, and I heard only the intake of breath. I have very quick ears, and to me it sounded as if the man was rattled. The breathing was quick and anxious.

Suddenly it changed and became the ghost of a whistle—the kind of sound one makes with the lips and teeth without ever letting the tune break out clear. We all do it when we are preoccupied with something—shaving, or writing letters, or reading the newspaper. But I did not think my man was preoccupied. He was whistling to quiet fluttering nerves.

Then I caught the air. It was 'Cherry Ripe'.

In a moment, from being hugely at my ease, I became the nervous one. I had been playing peep-bo with the unseen, and the tables were turned. My heart beat against my ribs like a hammer. I shuffled my feet, and again there fell the tense silence.

'Mary,' I said—and the word seemed to explode like a bomb in the stillness—'Mary! It's me—Dick Hannay.'

There was no answer but a sob and the sound of a timid step.

I took four paces into the darkness and caught in my arms a trembling girl ...

Often in the last months I had pictured the kind of scene which would be the culminating point of my life. When our work was over and war had been forgotten, somewhere—perhaps in a green Cotswold meadow or in a room of an old manor—I would talk with Mary. By that time we should know each other well and I would have lost my shyness. I would try to tell her that I loved her, but whenever I thought of what I should say my heart sank, for I knew I would make a fool of myself. You can't live my kind of life for forty years wholly among men and be of any use at pretty speeches to women. I knew I should stutter and blunder, and I used despairingly to invent impossible situations where I might make my love plain to her without words by some piece of melodramatic sacrifice.

But the kind Fates had saved me the trouble. Without a syllable save Christian names stammered in that eerie darkness we had come to complete understanding. The fairies had been at work unseen, and the thoughts of each of us had been moving towards the other, till love had germinated like a seed in the dark. As I held her in my arms I stroked her hair and murmured things which seemed to spring out of some ancestral memory. Certainly my tongue had never used them before, nor my mind imagined them ... By and by she slipped her arms round my neck and with a half sob strained towards me. She was still trembling.

'Dick,' she said, and to hear that name on her lips was the sweetest thing I had ever known. 'Dick, is it really you? Tell me I'm not dreaming.'

'It's me, sure enough, Mary dear. And now I have found you I will never let you go again. But, my precious child, how on earth did you get here?'

She disengaged herself and let her little electric torch wander over my rough habiliments.

'You look a tremendous warrior, Dick. I have never seen you like this before. I was in Doubting Castle and very much afraid of Giant Despair, till you came.'

'I think I call it the Interpreter's House,' I said.

'It's the house of somebody we both know,' she went on. 'He calls himself Bommaerts here. That was one of the two names, you remember. I have seen him since in Paris. Oh, it is a long story and you shall hear it all soon. I knew he came here sometimes, so I came here too. I have been nursing for the last fortnight at the Douvecourt Hospital only four miles away.'

'But what brought you alone at night?'

'Madness, I think. Vanity, too. You see I had found out a good deal, and I wanted to find out the one vital thing which had puzzled Mr Blenkiron. I told myself it was foolish, but I couldn't keep away. And then my courage broke down, and before you came I would have screamed at the sound of a mouse. If I hadn't whistled I would have cried.'

'But why alone and at this hour?'

'I couldn't get off in the day. And it was safest to come alone. You see he is in love with me, and when he heard I was coming to Douvecourt forgot his caution and proposed to meet me here. He said he was going on a long journey and wanted to say goodbye. If he had found me alone—well, he would have said goodbye. If there had been anyone with me, he would have suspected, and he mustn't suspect me. Mr Blenkiron says that would be fatal to his great plan. He believes I am like my aunts, and that I think him an apostle of peace working by his own methods against the stupidity and wickedness of all the Governments. He talks more bitterly about Germany than about England. He had told me how he had to disguise himself and play many parts on his mission, and of course I have applauded him. Oh, I have had a difficult autumn.'

'Mary,' I cried, 'tell me you hate him.'

'No,' she said quietly. 'I do not hate him. I am keeping that for later. I fear him desperately. Some day when we have broken him utterly I will hate him, and drive all likeness of him out of my memory like an unclean thing. But till then I won't waste energy on hate. We want to hoard every atom of our strength for the work of beating him.'

She had won back her composure, and I turned on my light to look at her. She was in nurses' outdoor uniform, and I thought her eyes seemed tired. The priceless gift that had suddenly come to me had driven out all recollection of my own errand. I thought of Ivery only as a would-be lover of Mary, and forgot the manufacturer from Lille who had rented his house for the partridge-shooting. 'And you, Dick,' she asked; 'is it part of a general's duties to pay visits at night to empty houses?'

'I came to look for traces of M. Bommaerts. I, too, got on his track from another angle, but that story must wait.'

'You observe that he has been here today?'

She pointed to some cigarette ash spilled on the table edge, and a space on its surface cleared from dust. 'In a place like this the dust would settle again in a few hours, and that is quite clean. I should say he has been here just after luncheon.'

'Great Scott!' I cried, 'what a close shave! I'm in the mood at this moment to shoot him at sight. You say you saw him in Paris and knew his lair. Surely you had a good enough case to have him collared.'

She shook her head. 'Mr Blenkiron—he's in Paris too—wouldn't hear of it. He hasn't just figured the thing out yet, he says. We've identified one of your names, but we're still in doubt about Chelius.'

'Ah, Chelius! Yes, I see. We must get the whole business complete before we strike. Has old Blenkiron had any luck?'

'Your guess about the "Deep-breathing" advertisement was very clever, Dick. It was true, and it may give us Chelius. I must leave Mr Blenkiron to tell you how. But the trouble is this. We know something of the doings of someone who may be Chelius, but we can't link them with Ivery. We know that Ivery is Bommaerts, and our hope is to link Bommaerts with Chelius. That's why I came here. I was trying to burgle this escritoire in an amateur way. It's a bad piece of fake Empire and deserves smashing.'

I could see that Mary was eager to get my mind back to business, and with some difficulty I clambered down from the exultant heights. The intoxication of the thing was on me—the winter night, the circle of light in that dreary room, the sudden coming together of two souls from the ends of the earth, the realization of my wildest hopes, the gilding and glorifying of all the future. But she had always twice as much wisdom as me, and we were in the midst of a campaign which had no use for day-dreaming. I turned my attention to the desk.

It was a flat table with drawers, and at the back a half-circle of more drawers with a central cupboard. I tilted it up and most of the drawers slid out, empty of anything but dust. I forced two open with my knife and they held empty cigar boxes. Only the cupboard remained, and that appeared to be locked. I wedged a key from my pocket into its keyhole, but the thing would not budge.

'It's no good,' I said. 'He wouldn't leave anything he valued in a place like this. That sort of fellow doesn't take risks. If he wanted to hide something there are a hundred holes in this Chateau which would puzzle the best detective.'

'Can't you open it?' she asked. 'I've a fancy about that table. He was sitting here this afternoon and he may be coming back.'

I solved the problem by turning up the escritoire and putting my knee through the cupboard door. Out of it tumbled a little dark-green attache case.

'This is getting solemn,' said Mary. 'Is it locked?'

It was, but I took my knife and cut the lock out and spilled the contents on the table. There were some papers, a newspaper or two, and a small bag tied with black cord. The last I opened, while Mary looked over my shoulder. It contained a fine yellowish powder.

'Stand back,' I said harshly. 'For God's sake, stand back and don't breathe.'

With trembling hands I tied up the bag again, rolled it in a newspaper, and stuffed it into my pocket. For I remembered a day near Peronne when a Boche plane had come over in the night and had dropped little bags like this. Happily they were all collected, and the men who found them were wise and took them off to the nearest laboratory. They proved to be full of anthrax germs ...

I remembered how Eaucourt Sainte-Anne stood at the junction of a dozen roads where all day long troops passed to and from the lines. From such a vantage ground an enemy could wreck the health of an army ...

I remembered the woman I had seen in the courtyard of this house in the foggy dusk, and I knew now why she had worn a gas-mask.

This discovery gave me a horrid shock. I was brought down with a crash from my high sentiment to something earthly and devilish. I was fairly well used to Boche filthiness, but this seemed too grim a piece of the utterly damnable. I wanted to have Ivery by the throat and force the stuff into his body, and watch him decay slowly into the horror he had contrived for honest men.

'Let's get out of this infernal place,' I said.

But Mary was not listening. She had picked up one of the newspapers and was gloating over it. I looked and saw that it was open at an advertisement of Weissmann's 'Deep-breathing' system.

'Oh, look, Dick,' she cried breathlessly.

The column of type had little dots made by a red pencil below certain words.

'It's it,' she whispered, 'it's the cipher—I'm almost sure it's the cipher!'

'Well, he'd be likely to know it if anyone did.'

'But don't you see it's the cipher which Chelius uses—the man in Switzerland? Oh, I can't explain now, for it's very long, but I think—I think—I have found out what we have all been wanting. Chelius ...'

'Whisht!' I said. 'What's that?'

There was a queer sound from the out-of-doors as if a sudden wind had risen in the still night.

'It's only a car on the main road,' said Mary.

'How did you get in?' I asked.

'By the broken window in the next room. I cycled out here one morning, and walked round the place and found the broken catch.'

'Perhaps it is left open on purpose. That may be the way M. Bommaerts visits his country home ... Let's get off, Mary, for this place has a curse on it. It deserves fire from heaven.'

I slipped the contents of the attache case into my pockets. 'I'm going to drive you back,' I said. 'I've got a car out there.'

'Then you must take my bicycle and my servant too. He's an old friend of yours—one Andrew Amos.'

'Now how on earth did Andrew get over here?'

'He's one of us,' said Mary, laughing at my surprise. 'A most useful member of our party, at present disguised as an *infirmier* in Lady Manorwater's Hospital at Douvecourt. He is learning French, and ...'

'Hush!' I whispered. 'There's someone in the next room.'

I swept her behind a stack of furniture, with my eyes glued on a crack of light below the door. The handle turned and the shadows raced before a big electric lamp of the kind they have in stables. I could not see the bearer, but I guessed it was the old woman.

There was a man behind her. A brisk step sounded on the parquet, and a figure brushed past her. It wore the horizon-blue of a French officer, very smart, with those French riding-boots that show the shape of the leg, and a handsome fur-lined pelisse. I would have called him a young man, not more than thirty-five. The face was brown and clean-shaven, the eyes bright and masterful ... Yet he did not deceive me. I had not boasted idly to Sir Walter when I said that there was one man alive who could never again be mistaken by me.

I had my hand on my pistol, as I motioned Mary farther back into the shadows. For a second I was about to shoot. I had a perfect mark and could have put a bullet through his brain with utter certitude. I think if I had been alone I might have fired. Perhaps not. Anyhow now I could not do it. It seemed like potting at a sitting rabbit. I was obliged, though he was my worst enemy, to give him a chance, while all the while my sober senses kept calling me a fool.

I stepped into the light.

'Hullo, Mr Ivery,' I said. 'This is an odd place to meet again!'

In his amazement he fell back a step, while his hungry eyes took in my face. There was no mistake about the recognition. I saw something I had seen once before in him, and that was fear. Out went the light and he sprang for the door.

I fired in the dark, but the shot must have been too high. In the same instant I heard him slip on the smooth parquet and the tinkle of glass as the broken window swung open. Hastily I reflected that his car must be at the moat end of the terrace, and that therefore to reach it he must pass outside this very room. Seizing the damaged escritoire, I used it as a ram, and charged the window nearest me. The panes and shutters went with a crash, for I had driven the thing out of its rotten frame. The next second I was on the moonlit snow.

I got a shot at him as he went over the terrace, and again I went wide. I never was at my best with a pistol. Still I reckoned I had got him, for the car which was waiting below must come back by the moat to reach the highroad. But I had forgotten the great closed park gates. Somehow or other they must have been opened, for as soon as the car started it headed straight for the grand avenue. I tried a couple of long-range shots after it, and one must have damaged either Ivery or his chauffeur, for there came back a cry of pain.

I turned in deep chagrin to find Mary beside me. She was bubbling with laughter.

'Were you ever a cinema actor, Dick? The last two minutes have been a really high-class performance. "Featuring Mary Lamington." How does the jargon go?'

'I could have got him when he first entered,' I said ruefully.

'I know,' she said in a graver tone. 'Only of course you couldn't ... Besides, Mr Blenkiron doesn't want it—yet.'

She put her hand on my arm. 'Don't worry about it. It wasn't written it should happen that way. It would have been too easy. We have a long road to travel yet before we clip the wings of the Wild Birds.'

'Look,' I cried. 'The fire from heaven!'

Red tongues of flame were shooting up from the out-buildings at the farther end, the place where I had first seen the woman. Some agreed plan must have been acted on, and Ivery was destroying all traces of his infamous yellow powder. Even now the concierge with her odds and ends of belongings would be slipping out to some refuge in the village.

In the still dry night the flames rose, for the place must have been made ready for a rapid burning. As I hurried Mary round the moat I could see that part of the main building had caught fire. The hamlet was awakened, and before we reached the corner of the highroad sleepy British soldiers were hurrying towards the scene, and the Town Major was mustering the fire brigade. I knew that Ivery had laid his plans well, and that they hadn't a chance—that long before dawn the Chateau of Eaucourt Sainte-Anne would be a heap of ashes and that in a day or two the lawyers of the aged

Marquise at Biarritz would be wrangling with the insurance company.

At the corner stood Amos beside two bicycles, solid as a graven image. He recognized me with a gap-toothed grin.

'It's a cauld night, General, but the home fires keep burnin'. I havena seen such a cheery lowe since Dickson's mill at Gawly.'

We packed, bicycles and all, into my car with Amos wedged in the narrow seat beside Hamilton. Recognizing a fellow countryman, he gave thanks for the lift in the broadest Doric. 'For,' said he, 'I'm not what you would call a practised hand wi' a velocipede, and my feet are dinnled wi' standin' in the snaw.'

As for me, the miles to Douvecourt passed as in a blissful moment of time. I wrapped Mary in a fur rug, and after that we did not speak a word. I had come suddenly into a great possession and was dazed with the joy of it.

CHAPTER FOURTEEN

Mr Blenkiron Discourses on Love and War

Three days later I got my orders to report at Paris for special service. They came none too soon, for I chafed at each hour's delay. Every thought in my head was directed to the game which we were playing against Ivery. He was the big enemy, compared to whom the ordinary Boche in the trenches was innocent and friendly. I had almost lost interest in my division, for I knew that for me the real battle-front was not in Picardy, and that my job was not so easy as holding a length of line. Also I longed to be at the same work as Mary.

I remember waking up in billets the morning after the night at the Chateau with the feeling that I had become extraordinarily rich. I felt very humble, too, and very kindly towards all the world—even to the Boche, though I can't say I had ever hated him very wildly. You find hate more among journalists and politicians at home than among fighting men. I wanted to be quiet and alone to think, and since that was impossible I went about my work in a happy abstraction. I tried not to look ahead, but only to live in the present, remembering that a war was on, and that there was desperate and dangerous business before me, and that my hopes hung on a slender thread. Yet for all that I had sometimes to let my fancies go free, and revel in delicious dreams.

But there was one thought that always brought me back to hard ground, and that was Ivery. I do not think I hated anybody in the world but him. It was his relation to Mary that stung me. He had the insolence with all his toad-like past to make love to that clean and radiant girl. I felt that he and I stood as mortal antagonists, and the thought pleased me, for it helped me to put some honest detestation into my job. Also I was going to win. Twice I had failed, but the third time I should succeed. It had been like ranging shots for a gun—first short, second over, and I vowed that the third should be dead on the mark.

I was summoned to G.H.Q., where I had half an hour's talk with the greatest British commander. I can see yet his patient, kindly face and that steady eye which no vicissitude of fortune could perturb. He took the biggest view, for he was statesman as well as soldier, and knew that the whole world was one battle-field and every man and woman among the combatant nations was in the battle-line. So contradictory is human nature, that talk made me wish for a moment to stay where I was. I wanted to go on serving under that man. I realized suddenly how much I loved my work, and when I got back to my quarters that night and saw my men swinging in from a route march I could have howled like a dog at leaving them. Though I say it who shouldn't, there wasn't a better division in the Army.

One morning a few days later I picked up Mary in Amiens. I always liked the place, for after the dirt of the

Somme it was a comfort to go there for a bath and a square meal, and it had the noblest church that the hand of man ever built for God. It was a clear morning when we started from the boulevard beside the railway station; and the air smelt of washed streets and fresh coffee, and women were going marketing and the little trams ran clanking by, just as in any other city far from the sound of guns. There was very little khaki or horizon-blue about, and I remember thinking how completely Amiens had got out of the war-zone. Two months later it was a different story.

To the end I shall count that day as one of the happiest in my life. Spring was in the air, though the trees and fields had still their winter colouring. A thousand good fresh scents came out of the earth, and the larks were busy over the new furrows. I remember that we ran up a little glen, where a stream spread into pools among sallows, and the roadside trees were heavy with mistletoe. On the tableland beyond the Somme valley the sun shone like April. At Beauvais we lunched badly in an inn—badly as to food, but there was an excellent Burgundy at two francs a bottle. Then we slipped down through little flat-chested townships to the Seine, and in the late afternoon passed through St Germains forest. The wide green spaces among the trees set my fancy dwelling on that divine English countryside where Mary and I would one day make our home. She had been in high spirits all the journey, but when I spoke of the Cotswolds her face grew grave.

'Don't let us speak of it, Dick,' she said. 'It's too happy a thing and I feel as if it would wither if we touched it. I don't let myself think of peace and home, for it makes me too homesick ... I think we shall get there some day, you and I ... but it's a long road to the Delectable Mountains, and Faithful, you know, has to die first ... There is a price to be paid.'

The words sobered me.

'Who is our Faithful?' I asked.

'I don't know. But he was the best of the Pilgrims.'

Then, as if a veil had lifted, her mood changed, and when we came through the suburbs of Paris and swung down the Champs Elysees she was in a holiday humour. The lights were twinkling in the blue January dusk, and the warm breath of the city came to greet us. I knew little of the place, for I had visited it once only on a four days' Paris leave, but it had seemed to me then the most habitable of cities, and now, coming from the battle-field with Mary by my side, it was like the happy ending of a dream.

I left her at her cousin's house near the Rue St Honore, and deposited myself, according to instructions, at the Hotel Louis Quinze. There I wallowed in a hot bath, and got into the civilian clothes which had been sent on from London. They made me feel that I had taken leave of my division for good and all this time.

Blenkiron had a private room, where we were to dine; and a more wonderful litter of books and cigar boxes I have never seen, for he hadn't a notion of tidiness. I could hear him grunting at his toilet in the adjacent bedroom, and I noticed that the table was laid for three. I went downstairs to get a paper, and on the way ran into Launcelot Wake.

He was no longer a private in a Labour Battalion. Evening clothes showed beneath his overcoat. 'Hullo, Wake, are you in this push too?'

'I suppose so,' he said, and his manner was not cordial. 'Anyhow I was ordered down here. My business is to do as I am told.'

'Coming to dine?' I asked.

'No. I'm dining with some friends at the Crillon.'

Then he looked me in the face, and his eyes were hot as I first remembered them. 'I hear I've to congratulate you, Hannay,' and he held out a limp hand.

I never felt more antagonism in a human being.

'You don't like it?' I said, for I guessed what he meant.

'How on earth can I like it?' he cried angrily. 'Good Lord, man, you'll murder her soul. You an ordinary, stupid, successful fellow and she—she's the most precious thing God ever made. You can never understand a fraction of her preciousness, but you'll clip her wings all right. She can never fly now ...'

He poured out this hysterical stuff to me at the foot of the staircase within hearing of an elderly French widow with a poodle. I had no impulse to be angry, for I was far too happy.

'Don't, Wake,' I said. 'We're all too close together to quarrel. I'm not fit to black Mary's shoes. You can't put me too low or her too high. But I've at least the sense to know it. You couldn't want me to be humbler than I felt.'

He shrugged his shoulders, as he went out to the street. 'Your infernal magnanimity would break any man's temper.'

I went upstairs to find Blenkiron, washed and shaven, admiring a pair of bright patent-leather shoes.

'Why, Dick, I've been wearying bad to see you. I was nervous you would be blown to glory, for I've been reading awful things about your battles in the noospapers. The war correspondents worry me so I can't take breakfast.'

He mixed cocktails and clinked his glass on mine. 'Here's to the young lady. I was trying to write her a pretty little sonnet, but the darned rhymes wouldn't fit. I've gotten a heap of things to say to you when we've finished dinner.'

Mary came in, her cheeks bright from the weather, and Blenkiron promptly fell abashed. But she had a way to meet his shyness, for, when he began an embarrassed speech of good wishes, she put her arms round his neck and kissed him. Oddly enough, that set him completely at his ease.

It was pleasant to eat off linen and china again, pleasant to see old Blenkiron's benignant face and the way he tucked into his food, but it was delicious for me to sit at a meal with Mary across the table. It made me feel that she was really mine, and not a pixie that would vanish at a word. To Blenkiron she bore herself like an affectionate but mischievous daughter, while the desperately refined manners that afflicted him whenever women were concerned mellowed into something like his everyday self. They did most of the talking, and I remember he fetched from some mysterious hiding-place a great box of chocolates, which you could no longer buy in Paris, and the two ate them like spoiled children. I didn't want to talk, for it was pure happiness for me to look on. I loved to watch her, when the servants had gone, with her elbows on the table like a schoolboy, her crisp gold hair a little rumpled, cracking walnuts with gusto, like some child who has been allowed down from the nursery for dessert and means to make the most of it.

With his first cigar Blenkiron got to business.

'You want to know about the staff-work we've been busy on at home. Well, it's finished now, thanks to you, Dick. We weren't getting on very fast till you took to peroosing the press on your sick-bed and dropped us that hint about the "Deep-breathing" ads.'

'Then there was something in it?' I asked.

'There was black hell in it. There wasn't any Gussiter, but there was a mighty fine little syndicate of crooks with old man Gresson at the back of them. First thing, I started out to get the cipher. It took some looking for, but there's no cipher on earth can't be got hold of somehow if you know it's there, and in this case we were helped a lot by the return messages in the German papers. It was bad stuff when we read it, and explained the darned leakages in important noos we've been up against. At first I figured to keep the thing going and turn Gussiter into a corporation with John S. Blenkiron as president. But it wouldn't do, for at the first hint of tampering with their communications the whole bunch got skeery and sent out SOS signals. So we tenderly plucked the flowers.'

'Gresson, too?' I asked.

He nodded. 'I guess your seafaring companion's now under the sod. We had collected enough evidence to hang him ten times over ... But that was the least of it. For your little old cipher, Dick, gave us a line on Ivery.'

I asked how, and Blenkiron told me the story. He had about a dozen cross-bearings proving that the organization of the 'Deep-breathing' game had its headquarters in Switzerland. He suspected Ivery from the first, but the man had vanished out of his ken, so he started working from the other end, and instead of trying to deduce the Swiss business from Ivery he tried to deduce Ivery from the Swiss business. He went to Berne and made a conspicuous public fool of himself for several weeks. He called himself an agent of the American propaganda there, and took some advertising space in the press and put in spread-eagle announcements of his mission, with the result that the Swiss Government threatened to turn him out of the country if he tampered that amount with their neutrality. He also wrote a lot of rot in the Geneva newspapers, which he paid to have printed, explaining how he was a pacifist, and was going to convert Germany to peace by 'inspirational advertisement of pure-minded war aims'. All this was in keeping with his English reputation, and he wanted to make himself a bait for Ivery.

But Ivery did not rise to the fly, and though he had a dozen agents working for him on the quiet he could never hear of the name Chelius. That was, he reckoned, a very private and particular name among the Wild Birds. However, he got to know a good deal about the Swiss end of the 'Deep-breathing' business. That took some doing and cost a lot of money. His best people were a girl who posed as a mannequin in a milliner's shop in Lyons and a concierge in a big hotel at St Moritz. His most important discovery was that there was a second cipher in the return messages sent from Switzerland, different from the one that the Gussiter lot used in England. He got this cipher, but though he could read it he couldn't make anything out of it. He concluded that it was a very secret means of communication between the inner circle of the Wild Birds, and that Ivery must be at the back of it ... But he was still a long way from finding out anything that mattered.

Then the whole situation changed, for Mary got in touch with Ivery. I must say she behaved like a shameless minx, for she kept on writing to him to an address he had once given her in Paris, and suddenly she got an answer. She was in Paris herself, helping to run one of the railway canteens, and staying with her French cousins, the de Mezieres. One day he came to see her. That showed the boldness of the man, and his cleverness, for the whole secret police of France were after him and they never got within sight or sound. Yet here he was coming openly in the afternoon to have tea with an English girl. It showed another thing, which made me blaspheme. A man so resolute and single-hearted in his job must have been pretty badly in love to take a risk like that.

He came, and he called himself the Capitaine Bommaerts, with a transport job on the staff of the

French G.Q.G. He was on the staff right enough too. Mary said that when she heard that name she nearly fell down. He was quite frank with her, and she with him. They are both peacemakers, ready to break the laws of any land for the sake of a great ideal. Goodness knows what stuff they talked together. Mary said she would blush to think of it till her dying day, and I gathered that on her side it was a mixture of Launcelot Wake at his most pedantic and schoolgirl silliness.

He came again, and they met often, unbeknown to the decorous Madame de Mezieres. They walked together in the Bois de Boulogne, and once, with a beating heart, she motored with him to Auteuil for luncheon. He spoke of his house in Picardy, and there were moments, I gathered, when he became the declared lover, to be rebuffed with a hoydenish shyness. Presently the pace became too hot, and after some anguished arguments with Bullivant on the long-distance telephone she went off to Douvecourt to Lady Manorwater's hospital. She went there to escape from him, but mainly, I think, to have a look—trembling in every limb, mind you—at the Chateau of Eaucourt Sainte-Anne.

I had only to think of Mary to know just what Joan of Arc was. No man ever born could have done that kind of thing. It wasn't recklessness. It was sheer calculating courage.

Then Blenkiron took up the tale. The newspaper we found that Christmas Eve in the Chateau was of tremendous importance, for Bommaerts had pricked out in the advertisement the very special second cipher of the Wild Birds. That proved that Ivery was at the back of the Swiss business. But Blenkiron made doubly sure.

'I considered the time had come,' he said, 'to pay high for valuable noos, so I sold the enemy a very pretty de-vice. If you ever gave your mind to ciphers and illicit correspondence, Dick, you would know that the one kind of document you can't write on in invisible ink is a coated paper, the kind they use in the weeklies to print photographs of leading actresses and the stately homes of England. Anything wet that touches it corrugates the surface a little, and you can tell with a microscope if someone's been playing at it. Well, we had the good fortune to discover just how to get over that little difficulty—how to write on glazed paper with a quill so as the cutest analyst couldn't spot it, and likewise how to detect the writing. I decided to sacrifice that invention, casting my bread upon the waters and looking for a good-sized bakery in return ... I had it sold to the enemy. The job wanted delicate handling, but the tenth man from me—he was an Austrian Jew—did the deal and scooped fifty thousand dollars out of it. Then I lay low to watch how my friend would use the de-vice, and I didn't wait long.'

He took from his pocket a folded sheet of *L'Illustration*. Over a photogravure plate ran some words in a large sprawling hand, as if written with a brush.

'That page when I got it yesterday,' he said, 'was an unassuming picture of General Petain presenting military medals. There wasn't a scratch or a ripple on its surface. But I got busy with it, and see there!'

He pointed out two names. The writing was a set of key-words we did not know, but two names stood out which I knew too well. They were 'Bommaerts' and 'Chelius'.

'My God!' I cried, 'that's uncanny. It only shows that if you chew long enough—'

'Dick,' said Mary, 'you mustn't say that again. At the best it's an ugly metaphor, and you're making it a platitude.'

'Who is Ivery anyhow?' I asked. 'Do you know more about him than we knew in the summer? Mary, what did Bommaerts pretend to be?'

'An Englishman.' Mary spoke in the most matter-of-fact tone, as if it were a perfectly usual thing to be made love to by a spy, and that rather soothed my annoyance. 'When he asked me to marry him he proposed to take me to a country-house in Devonshire. I rather think, too, he had a place in Scotland. But of course he's a German.'

'Ye-es,' said Blenkiron slowly, 'I've got on to his record, and it isn't a pretty story. It's taken some working out, but I've got all the links tested now ... He's a Boche and a large-sized nobleman in his own state. Did you ever hear of the Graf von Schwabing?'

I shook my head.

'I think I have heard Uncle Charlie speak of him,' said Mary, wrinkling her brows. 'He used to hunt with the Pytchley.'

'That's the man. But he hasn't troubled the Pytchley for the last eight years. There was a time when he was the last thing in smartness in the German court—officer in the Guards, ancient family, rich, darned clever—all the fixings. Kaiser liked him, and it's easy to see why. I guess a man who had as many personalities as the Graf was amusing after-dinner company. Specially among the Germans, who in my experience don't excel in the lighter vein. Anyway, he was William's white-headed boy, and there wasn't a mother with a daughter who wasn't out gunning for Otto von Schwabing. He was about as popular in London and Noo York—and in Paris, too. Ask Sir Walter about him, Dick. He says he had twice the brains of Kuhlmann, and better manners than the Austrian fellow he used to yarn about ... Well, one day there came an almighty court scandal, and the bottom dropped out of the Graf's World. It was a pretty beastly story, and I don't gather that Schwabing was as deep in it as some others. But the trouble was that those others had to be shielded at all costs, and Schwabing was made the scapegoat. His name came out in the papers and he had to go .'

'What was the case called?' I asked.

Blenkiron mentioned a name, and I knew why the word Schwabing was familiar. I had read the story long ago in Rhodesia.

'It was some smash,' Blenkiron went on. 'He was drummed out of the Guards, out of the clubs, out of the country ... Now, how would you have felt, Dick, if you had been the Graf? Your life and work and happiness crossed out, and all to save a mangy princeling. "Bitter as hell," you say. Hungering for a chance to put it across the lot that had outed you? You wouldn't rest till you had William sobbing on his knees asking your pardon, and you not thinking of granting it? That's the way you'd feel, but that wasn't the Graf's way, and what's more it isn't the German way. He went into exile hating humanity, and with a heart all poison and snakes, but itching to get back. And I'll tell you why. It's because his kind of German hasn't got any other home on this earth. Oh, yes, I know there's stacks of good old Teutons come and squat in our little country and turn into fine Americans. You can do a lot with them if you catch them young and teach them the Declaration of Independence and make them study our Sunday papers. But you can't deny there's something comic in the rough about all Germans, before you've civilized them. They're a pecooliar people, a darned pecooliar people, else they wouldn't staff all the menial and indecent occupations on the globe. But that pecooliarity, which is only skin-deep in the working Boche, is in the bone of the grandee. Your German aristocracy can't consort on terms of equality with any other Upper Ten Thousand. They swagger and bluff about the world, but they know very well that the world's sniggering at them. They're like a boss from Salt Creek Gully who's made his pile and bought a dress suit and dropped into a Newport evening party. They don't know where to put their hands or how to keep their feet still ... Your copper-bottomed English nobleman has got to keep jogging himself to treat them as equals instead of sending them down to the servants' hall. Their fine fixings are just the high light that reveals the everlasting jay. They can't be gentlemen, because they aren't sure of themselves. The world laughs at them, and they know it and it riles them like hell ... That's why when a Graf is booted out of the Fatherland, he's got to creep back somehow or be a wandering Jew for the rest of time.'

Blenkiron lit another cigar and fixed me with his steady, ruminating eye.

'For eight years the man has slaved, body and soul, for the men who degraded him. He's earned his restoration and I daresay he's got it in his pocket. If merit was rewarded he should be covered with Iron Crosses and Red Eagles ... He had a pretty good hand to start out with. He knew other countries and he was a dandy at languages. More, he had an uncommon gift for living a part. That is real genius, Dick, however much it gets up against us. Best of all he had a first-class outfit of brains. I can't say I ever struck a better, and I've come across some bright citizens in my time ... And now he's going to win out, unless we get mighty busy.'

There was a knock at the door and the solid figure of Andrew Amos revealed itself.

'It's time ye was home, Miss Mary. It chappit half-eleven as I came up the stairs. It's comin' on to rain, so I've brought an umbrelly.'

'One word,' I said. 'How old is the man?'

'Just gone thirty-six,' Blenkiron replied.

I turned to Mary, who nodded. 'Younger than you, Dick,' she said wickedly as she got into her big Jaeger coat.

'I'm going to see you home,' I said.

'Not allowed. You've had quite enough of my society for one day. Andrew's on escort duty tonight.'

Blenkiron looked after her as the door closed.

'I reckon you've got the best girl in the world.'

'Ivery thinks the same,' I said grimly, for my detestation of the man who had made love to Mary fairly choked me.

'You can see why. Here's this degenerate coming out of his rotten class, all pampered and petted and satiated with the easy pleasures of life. He has seen nothing of women except the bad kind and the overfed specimens of his own country. I hate being impolite about females, but I've always considered the German variety uncommon like cows. He has had desperate years of intrigue and danger, and consorting with every kind of scallawag. Remember, he's a big man and a poet, with a brain and an imagination that takes every grade without changing gears. Suddenly he meets something that is as fresh and lovely as a spring flower, and has wits too, and the steeliest courage, and yet is all youth and gaiety. It's a new experience for him, a kind of revelation, and he's big enough to value her as she should be valued ... No, Dick, I can understand you getting cross, but I reckon it an item to the man's credit.'

'It's his blind spot all the same,' I said.

'His blind spot,' Blenkiron repeated solemnly, 'and, please God, we're going to remember that.'

Next morning in miserable sloppy weather Blenkiron carted me about Paris. We climbed five sets of stairs to a flat away up in Montmartre, where I was talked to by a fat man with spectacles and a slow voice and told various things that deeply concerned me. Then I went to a room in the Boulevard St Germain, with a little cabinet opening off it, where I was shown papers and maps and some figures on a sheet of paper that made me open my eyes. We lunched in a modest cafe tucked away behind the Palais Royal, and our companions were two Alsatians who spoke German better than a Boche and had no names—only numbers. In the afternoon I went to a low building beside the Invalides and saw many generals, including more than one whose features were familiar in two hemispheres. I told them everything about myself, and I was examined like a convict, and all particulars about my appearance and manner of speech written down in a book. That was to prepare the way for me, in case of need, among the vast army of those who work underground and know their chief but do not know each other.

The rain cleared before night, and Blenkiron and I walked back to the hotel through that lemon-coloured dusk that you get in a French winter. We passed a company of American soldiers, and Blenkiron had to stop and stare. I could see that he was stiff with pride, though he wouldn't show it.

'What d'you think of that bunch?' he asked.

'First-rate stuff,' I said.

'The men are all right,' he drawled critically. 'But some of the officer-boys are a bit puffy. They want fining down.'

'They'll get it soon enough, honest fellows. You don't keep your weight long in this war.'

'Say, Dick,' he said shyly, 'what do you truly think of our Americans? You've seen a lot of them, and I'd value your views.' His tone was that of a bashful author asking for an opinion on his first book.

'I'll tell you what I think. You're constructing a great middle-class army, and that's the most formidable fighting machine on earth. This kind of war doesn't want the Berserker so much as the quiet fellow with a trained mind and a lot to fight for. The American ranks are filled with all sorts, from cow-punchers to college boys, but mostly with decent lads that have good prospects in life before them and are fighting because they feel they're bound to, not because they like it. It was the same stock that pulled through your Civil War. We have a middle-class division, too—Scottish Territorials, mostly clerks and shopmen and engineers and farmers' sons. When I first struck them my only crab was that the officers weren't much better than the men. It's still true, but the men are super-excellent, and consequently so are the officers. That division gets top marks in the Boche calendar for sheer fighting devilment ... And, please God, that's what your American army's going to be. You can wash out the old idea of a regiment of scallawags commanded by dukes. That was right enough, maybe, in the days when you hurrooshed into battle waving a banner, but it don't do with high explosives and a couple of million men on each side and a battle front of five hundred miles. The hero of this war is the plain man out of the middle class, who wants to get back to his home and is going to use all the brains and grit he possesses to finish the job soon.'

'That sounds about right,' said Blenkiron reflectively. 'It pleases me some, for you've maybe guessed that I respect the British Army quite a little. Which part of it do you put top?'

'All of it's good. The French are keen judges and they give front place to the Scots and the Australians. For myself I think the backbone of the Army is the old-fashioned English county regiments that hardly ever get into the papers Though I don't know, if I had to pick, but I'd take the South Africans. There's only a brigade of them, but they're hell's delight in a battle. But then you'll say I'm prejudiced.'

'Well,' drawled Blenkiron, you're a mighty Empire anyhow. I've sojourned up and down it and I can't guess how the old-time highbrows in your little island came to put it together. But I'll let you into a secret, Dick. I read this morning in a noospaper that there was a natural affinity between Americans and the men of the British Dominions. Take it from me, there isn't—at least not with this American. I don't understand them one little bit. When I see your lean, tall Australians with the sun at the back of their eyes, I'm looking at men from another planet. Outside you and Peter, I never got to fathom a South African. The Canadians live over the fence from us, but you mix up a Canuck with a Yank in your remarks and you'll get a bat in the eye ... But most of us Americans have gotten a grip on your Old Country. You'll find us mighty respectful to other parts of your Empire, but we say anything we damn well please about England. You see, we know her that well and like her that well, we can be free with her.

'It's like,' he concluded as we reached the hotel, 'it's like a lot of boys that are getting on in the world and are a bit jealous and stand-offish with each other. But they're all at home with the old man who used to warm them up with a hickory cane, even though sometimes in their haste they call him a stand-patter.'

That night at dinner we talked solid business—Blenkiron and I and a young French Colonel from the IIIeme Section at G.Q.G. Blenkiron, I remember, got very hurt about being called a business man by the Frenchman, who thought he was paying him a compliment.

'Cut it out,' he said. 'It is a word that's gone bad with me. There's just two kind of men, those who've gotten sense and those who haven't. A big percentage of us Americans make our living by trading, but we don't think because a man's in business or even because he's made big money that he's any natural good at every job. We've made a college professor our President, and do what he tells us like little boys, though he don't earn more than some of us pay our works' manager. You English have gotten business on the brain, and think a fellow's a dandy at handling your Government if he happens to have made a pile by some flat-catching ramp on your Stock Exchange. It makes me tired. You're about the best business nation on earth, but for God's sake don't begin to talk about it or you'll lose your power. And don't go confusing real business with the ordinary gift of raking in the dollars. Any man with sense could make money if he wanted to, but he mayn't want. He may prefer the fun of the job and let other people do the looting. I reckon the biggest business on the globe today is the work behind your lines and the way you feed and supply and transport your army. It beats the Steel Corporation and the Standard Oil to a frazzle. But the man at the head of it all don't earn more than a thousand dollars a month ... Your nation's getting to worship Mammon, Dick. Cut it out. There's just the one difference in humanity—sense or no sense, and most likely you won't find any more sense in the man that makes a billion selling bonds than in his brother Tim that lives in a shack and sells corn-cobs. I'm not speaking out of sinful jealousy, for there was a day when I was reckoned a railroad king, and I quit with a bigger pile than kings usually retire on. But I haven't the sense of old Peter, who never even had a bank account ... And it's sense that wins in this war.'

The Colonel, who spoke good English, asked a question about a speech which some politician had made.

'There isn't all the sense I'd like to see at the top,' said Blenkiron. 'They're fine at smooth words. That wouldn't matter, but they're thinking smooth thoughts. What d'you make of the situation, Dick?'

'I think it's the worst since First Ypres,' I said. 'Everybody's cock-a-whoop, but God knows why.'

'God knows why,' Blenkiron repeated. 'I reckon it's a simple calculation, and you can't deny it any more than a mathematical law. Russia is counted out. The Boche won't get food from her for a good many months, but he can get more men, and he's got them. He's fighting only on one foot, and he's been able to bring troops and guns west so he's as strong as the Allies now on paper. And he's stronger in reality. He's got better railways behind him, and he's fighting on inside lines and can concentrate fast against any bit of our front. I'm no soldier, but that's so, Dick?'

The Frenchman smiled and shook his head. 'All the same they will not pass. They could not when they were two to one in 1914, and they will not now. If we Allies could not break through in the last year when we had many more men, how will the Germans succeed now with only equal numbers?'

Blenkiron did not look convinced. 'That's what they all say. I talked to a general last week about the coming offensive, and he said he was praying for it to hurry up, for he reckoned Fritz would get the fright of his life. It's a good spirit, maybe, but I don't think it's sound on the facts. We've got two mighty great armies of fine fighting-men, but, because we've two commands, we're bound to move ragged like a peal of bells. The Hun's got one army and forty years of stiff tradition, and, what's more, he's going all out this time. He's going to smash our front before America lines up, or perish in the attempt ... Why do you suppose all the peace racket in Germany has died down, and the very men that were talking democracy in the summer are now hot for fighting to a finish? I'll tell you. It's because old Ludendorff has promised them complete victory this spring if they spend enough men, and the Boche is a good gambler and is out to risk it. We're not up against a local attack this time. We're standing up to a great nation going bald-headed for victory or destruction. If we're broken, then America's got to fight a new campaign by herself when she's ready, and the Boche has time to make Russia his feeding-ground and diddle our blockade. That puts another five years on to the war, maybe another ten. Are we free and independent peoples going to endure that much? ... I tell you we're tossing to quit before Easter.'

He turned towards me, and I nodded assent.

'That's more or less my view,' I said. 'We ought to hold, but it'll be by our teeth and nails. For the next six months we'll be fighting without any margin.'

'But, my friends, you put it too gravely,' cried the Frenchman. 'We may lose a mile or two of ground—yes. But serious danger is not possible. They had better chances at Verdun and they failed. Why should they succeed now?'

'Because they are staking everything,' Blenkiron replied. 'It is the last desperate struggle of a wounded beast, and in these struggles sometimes the hunter perishes. Dick's right. We've got a wasting margin and every extra ounce of weight's going to tell. The battle's in the field, and it's also in every corner of every Allied land. That's why within the next two months we've got to get even with the Wild Birds.'

The French Colonel—his name was de Valliere—smiled at the name, and Blenkiron answered my unspoken question.

'I'm going to satisfy some of your curiosity, Dick, for I've put together considerable noos of the menagerie. Germany has a good army of spies outside her borders. We shoot a batch now and then, but the others go on working like beavers and they do a mighty deal of harm. They're beautifully organized, but they don't draw on such good human material as we, and I reckon they don't pay in results more than ten cents on a dollar of trouble. But there they are. They're the intelligence officers and their business is just to forward noos. They're the birds in the cage, the—what is it your friend called them?'

'*Die Stubenvogel,*' I said.

'Yes, but all the birds aren't caged. There's a few outside the bars and they don't collect noos. They do things. If there's anything desperate they're put on the job, and they've got power to act without waiting on instructions from home. I've investigated till my brain's tired and I haven't made out more than half a dozen whom I can say for certain are in the business. There's your pal, the Portuguese Jew, Dick. Another's a woman in Genoa, a princess of some sort married to a Greek financier. One's the editor of a pro-Ally up-country paper in the Argentine. One passes as a Baptist minister in Colorado. One was a police spy in the Tzar's Government and is now a red-hot revolutionary in the Caucasus. And the biggest, of course, is Moxon Ivery, who in happier times was the Graf von Schwabing. There aren't above a hundred people in the world know of their existence, and these hundred call them the Wild Birds.'

'Do they work together?' I asked.

'Yes. They each get their own jobs to do, but they're apt to flock together for a big piece of devilment. There were four of them in France a year ago before the battle of the Aisne, and they pretty near rotted the French Army. That's so, Colonel?'

The soldier nodded grimly. 'They seduced our weary troops and they bought many politicians. Almost they succeeded, but not quite. The nation is sane again, and is judging and shooting the accomplices at its leisure. But the principals we have never caught.'

'You hear that, Dick, said Blenkiron. 'You're satisfied this isn't a whimsy of a melodramatic old Yank? I'll tell you more. You know how Ivery worked the submarine business from England. Also, it was the Wild Birds that wrecked Russia. It was Ivery that paid the Bolshevists to sedooce the Army, and the Bolshevists took his money for their own purpose, thinking they were playing a deep game, when all the time he was grinning like Satan, for they were playing his. It was Ivery or some other of the bunch that doped the brigades that broke at Caporetto. If I started in to tell you the history of their doings you wouldn't go to bed, and if you did you wouldn't sleep ... There's just this to it. Every finished subtle devilry that the Boche has wrought among the Allies since August 1914 has been the work of the Wild Birds and more or less organized by Ivery. They're worth half a dozen army corps to Ludendorff. They're the mightiest poison merchants the world ever saw, and they've the nerve of hell ...'

'I don't know,' I interrupted. 'Ivery's got his soft spot. I saw him in the Tube station.'

'Maybe, but he's got the kind of nerve that's wanted. And now I rather fancy he's whistling in his flock.'

Blenkiron consulted a notebook. 'Pavia—that's the Argentine man—started last month for Europe. He transhipped from a coasting steamer in the West Indies and we've temporarily lost track of him, but he's left his hunting-ground. What do you reckon that means?'

'It means,' Blenkiron continued solemnly, 'that Ivery thinks the game's nearly over. The play's working up for the big climax ... And that climax is going to be damnation for the Allies, unless we get a move on.'

'Right,' I said. 'That's what I'm here for. What's the move?'

'The Wild Birds mustn't ever go home, and the man they call Ivery or Bommaerts or Chelius has to decease. It's a cold-blooded proposition, but it's him or the world that's got to break. But before he quits this earth we're bound to get wise about some of his plans, and that means that we can't just shoot a pistol at his face. Also we've got to find him first. We reckon he's in Switzerland, but that is a state with quite a lot of diversified scenery to lose a man in ... Still I guess we'll find him. But it's the kind of business to plan out as carefully as a battle. I'm going back to Berne on my old stunt to boss the show, and I'm giving the orders. You're an obedient child, Dick, so I don't reckon on any trouble that way.'

Then Blenkiron did an ominous thing. He pulled up a little table and started to lay out Patience cards. Since his duodenum was cured he seemed to have dropped that habit, and from his resuming it I gathered that his mind was uneasy. I can see that scene as if it were yesterday—the French colonel in an armchair smoking a cigarette in a long amber holder, and Blenkiron sitting primly on the edge of a yellow silk ottoman, dealing his cards and looking guiltily towards me.

'You'll have Peter for company,' he said. 'Peter's a sad man, but he has a great heart, and he's been mighty useful to me already. They're going to move him to England very soon. The authorities are afraid of him, for he's apt to talk wild, his health having made him peevish about the British. But there's a deal of red-tape in the world, and the orders for his repatriation are slow in coming.' The speaker winked very slowly and deliberately with his left eye.

I asked if I was to be with Peter, much cheered at the prospect.

'Why, yes. You and Peter are the collateral in the deal. But the big game's not with you.'

I had a presentiment of something coming, something anxious and unpleasant.

'Is Mary in it?' I asked.

He nodded and seemed to pull himself together for an explanation.

'See here, Dick. Our main job is to get Ivery back to Allied soil where we can handle him. And there's just the one magnet that can fetch him back. You aren't going to deny that.'

I felt my face getting very red, and that ugly hammer began beating in my forehead. Two grave, patient eyes met my glare.

'I'm damned if I'll allow it!' I cried. 'I've some right to a say in the thing. I won't have Mary made a decoy. It's too infernally degrading.'

'It isn't pretty, but war isn't pretty, and nothing we do is pretty. I'd have blushed like a rose when I was young and innocent to imagine the things I've put my hand to in the last three years. But have you any other way, Dick? I'm not proud, and I'll scrap the plan if you can show me another ... Night after night I've hammered the thing out, and I can't hit on a better ... Heigh-ho, Dick, this isn't like you,' and he grinned ruefully. 'You're making yourself a fine argument in favour of celibacy—in time of war, anyhow. What is it the poet sings?—

White hands cling to the bridle rein,
Slipping the spur from the booted heel—'

I was as angry as sin, but I felt all the time I had no case. Blenkiron stopped his game of Patience, sending the cards flying over the carpet, and straddled on the hearthrug.

'You're never going to be a piker. What's dooty, if you won't carry it to the other side of Hell? What's the use of yapping about your country if you're going to keep anything back when she calls for it? What's the good of meaning to win the war if you don't put every cent you've got on your stake? You'll make me think you're like the jacks in your English novels that chuck in their hand and say it's up to God, and call that "seeing it through" ... No, Dick, that kind of dooty don't deserve a blessing. You dursn't keep back anything if you want to save your soul.

'Besides,' he went on, 'what a girl it is! She can't scare and she can't soil. She's white-hot youth and innocence, and she'd take no more harm than clean steel from a muck-heap.'

I knew I was badly in the wrong, but my pride was all raw.

'I'm not going to agree till I've talked to Mary.'

'But Miss Mary has consented,' he said gently. 'She made the plan.'

Next day, in clear blue weather that might have been May, I drove Mary down to Fontainebleau. We lunched in the inn by the bridge and walked into the forest. I hadn't slept much, for I was tortured by what I thought was anxiety for her, but which was in truth jealousy of Ivery. I don't think that I would have minded her risking her life, for that was part of the game we were both in, but I jibbed at the notion of Ivery coming near her again. I told myself it was honourable pride, but I knew deep down in me that it was jealousy.

I asked her if she had accepted Blenkiron's plan, and she turned mischievous eyes on me.

'I knew I should have a scene with you, Dick. I told Mr Blenkiron so ... Of course I agreed. I'm not even very much afraid of it. I'm a member of the team, you know, and I must play up to my form. I can't do a man's work, so all the more reason why I should tackle the thing I can do.'

'But,' I stammered, 'it's such a ... such a degrading business for a child like you. I can't bear ... It makes me hot to think of it.'

Her reply was merry laughter.

'You're an old Ottoman, Dick. You haven't doubled Cape Turk yet, and I don't believe you're round Seraglio Point. Why, women aren't the brittle things men used to think them. They never were, and the war has made them like whipcord. Bless you, my dear, we're the tougher sex now. We've had to wait and endure, and we've been so beaten on the anvil of patience that we've lost all our megrims.'

She put her hands on my shoulders and looked me in the eyes.

'Look at me, Dick, look at your someday-to-be espoused saint. I'm nineteen years of age next August. Before the war I should have only just put my hair up. I should have been the kind of shivering debutante who blushes when she's spoken to, and oh! I should have thought such silly, silly things about life ... Well, in the last two years I've been close to it, and to death. I've nursed the dying. I've seen souls in agony and in triumph. England has allowed me to serve her as she allows her sons. Oh, I'm a robust young woman now, and indeed I think women were always robuster than men ... Dick, dear Dick, we're lovers, but we're comrades too—always comrades, and comrades trust each other.'

I hadn't anything to say, except contrition, for I had my lesson. I had been slipping away in my thoughts from the gravity of our task, and Mary had brought me back to it. I remember that as we walked through the woodland we came to a place where there were no signs of war. Elsewhere there were men busy felling trees, and anti-aircraft guns, and an occasional transport wagon, but here there was only a shallow grassy vale, and in the distance, bloomed over like a plum in the evening haze, the roofs of an old dwelling-house among gardens.

Mary clung to my arm as we drank in the peace of it.

'That is what lies for us at the end of the road, Dick,' she said softly.

And then, as she looked, I felt her body shiver. She returned to the strange fancy she had had in the St Germains woods three days before.

'Somewhere it's waiting for us and we shall certainly find it ... But first we must go through the Valley of the Shadow ... And there is the sacrifice to be made ... the best of us.'

CHAPTER FIFTEEN

St Anton

Ten days later the porter Joseph Zimmer of Arosa, clad in the tough and shapeless trousers of his class, but sporting an old velveteen shooting-coat bequeathed to him by a former German master—speaking the guttural tongue of the Grisons, and with all his belongings in one massive rucksack, came out of the little station of St Anton and blinked in the frosty sunshine. He looked down upon the little old village beside its icebound lake, but his business was with the new village of hotels and villas which had sprung up in the last ten years south of the station. He made some halting inquiries of the station people, and a cab-driver outside finally directed him to the place he sought—the cottage of the Widow Summermatter, where resided an English intern, one Peter Pienaar.

The porter Joseph Zimmer had had a long and roundabout journey. A fortnight before he had worn the uniform of a British major-general. As such he had been the inmate of an expensive Paris hotel, till one morning, in grey tweed clothes and with a limp, he had taken the Paris-Mediterranean Express with a ticket for an officers' convalescent home at Cannes. Thereafter he had declined in the social scale. At Dijon he had been still an Englishman, but at Pontarlier he had become an American bagman of Swiss parentage, returning to wind up his father's estate. At Berne he limped excessively, and at Zurich, at a little back-street hotel, he became frankly the peasant. For he met a friend there from whom he acquired clothes with that odd rank smell, far stronger than Harris tweed, which marks the raiment of most Swiss guides and all Swiss porters. He also acquired a new name and an old aunt, who a little later received him with open arms and explained to her friends that he was her brother's son from Arosa who three winters ago had hurt his leg wood-cutting and had been discharged from the levy.

A kindly Swiss gentleman, as it chanced, had heard of the deserving Joseph and interested himself to find him employment. The said philanthropist made a hobby of the French and British prisoners returned from Germany, and had in mind an officer, a crabbed South African with a bad leg, who needed a servant. He was, it seemed, an ill-tempered old fellow who had to be billeted alone, and since he could speak German, he would be happier with a Swiss native. Joseph haggled somewhat over the wages, but on his aunt's advice he accepted the job, and, with a very complete set of papers and a store of ready-made reminiscences (it took him some time to swot up the names of the peaks and passes he had traversed) set out for St Anton, having dispatched beforehand a monstrously ill-spelt letter announcing his coming. He could barely read and write, but he was good at maps, which he had studied carefully, and he noticed with satisfaction that the valley of St Anton gave easy access to Italy.

As he journeyed south the reflections of that porter would have surprised his fellow travellers in the stuffy third-class carriage. He was thinking of a conversation he had had some days before in a cafe at Dijon with a young Englishman bound for Modane ...

We had bumped up against each other by chance in that strange flitting when all went to different places at different times, asking nothing of each other's business. Wake had greeted me rather shamefacedly and had proposed dinner together.

I am not good at receiving apologies, and Wake's embarrassed me more than they embarrassed him. 'I'm a bit of a cad sometimes,' he said. 'You know I'm a better fellow than I sounded that night, Hannay.'

I mumbled something about not talking rot—the conventional phrase. What worried me was that the man was suffering. You could see it in his eyes. But that evening I got nearer Wake than ever before, and he and I became true friends, for he laid bare his soul before me. That was his trouble, that he could lay bare his soul, for ordinary healthy folk don't analyse their feelings. Wake did, and I think it brought him relief.

'Don't think I was ever your rival. I would no more have proposed to Mary than I would have married one of her aunts. She was so sure of herself, so happy in her single-heartedness that she terrified me. My type of man is not meant for marriage, for women must be in the centre of life, and we must always be standing aside and looking on. It is a damnable thing to be left-handed.'

'The trouble about you, my dear chap,' I said, 'is that you're too hard to please.'

'That's one way of putting it. I should put it more harshly. I hate more than I love. All we humanitarians and pacifists have hatred as our mainspring. Odd, isn't it, for people who preach brotherly love? But it's the truth. We're full of hate towards everything that doesn't square in with our ideas, everything that jars on our lady-like nerves. Fellows like you are so in love with their cause that they've no time or inclination to detest what thwarts them. We've no cause—only negatives, and that means hatred, and self-torture, and a beastly jaundice of soul.'

Then I knew that Wake's fault was not spiritual pride, as I had diagnosed it at Biggleswick. The man was abased with humility.

'I see more than other people see,' he went on, 'and I feel more. That's the curse on me. You're a happy man and you get things done, because you only see one side of a case, one thing at a time. How would you like it if a thousand strings were always tugging at you, if you saw that every course meant the sacrifice of lovely and desirable things, or even the shattering of what you know to be unreplaceable? I'm the kind of stuff poets are made of, but I haven't the poet's gift, so I stagger about the world left-handed and game-legged ... Take the war. For me to fight would be worse than for another man to run away. From the bottom of my heart I believe that it needn't have happened, and that all war is a blistering iniquity. And yet belief has got very little to do with virtue. I'm not as good a man as you, Hannay, who have never thought out anything in your life. My time in the Labour battalion taught me something. I knew that with all my fine aspirations I wasn't as true a man as fellows whose talk was silly oaths and who didn't care a tinker's curse about their soul.'

I remember that I looked at him with a sudden understanding. 'I think I know you. You're the sort of chap who won't fight for his country because he can't be sure that she's altogether in the right. But he'd cheerfully die for her, right or wrong.'

His face relaxed in a slow smile. 'Queer that you should say that. I think it's pretty near the truth. Men like me aren't afraid to die, but they haven't quite the courage to live. Every man should be happy in a service like you, when he obeys orders. I couldn't get on in any service. I lack the bump of veneration. I can't swallow things merely because I'm told to. My sort are always talking about "service", but we haven't the temperament to serve. I'd give all I have to be an ordinary cog in the wheel, instead of a confounded outsider who finds fault with the machinery ... Take a great violent high-handed fellow like you. You can sink yourself till you become only a name and a number. I couldn't if I tried. I'm not sure if I want to either. I cling to the odds and ends that are my own.'

'I wish I had had you in my battalion a year ago,' I said.

'No, you don't. I'd only have been a nuisance. I've been a Fabian since Oxford, but you're a better socialist than me. I'm a rancid individualist.'

'But you must be feeling better about the war?' I asked.

'Not a bit of it. I'm still lusting for the heads of the politicians that made it and continue it. But I want to help my country. Honestly, Hannay, I love the old place. More, I think, than I love myself, and that's saying a devilish lot. Short of fighting—which would be the sin against the Holy Spirit for me—I'll do my damnedest. But you'll remember I'm not used to team work. If I'm a jealous player, beat me over the head.'

His voice was almost wistful, and I liked him enormously.

'Blenkiron will see to that,' I said. 'We're going to break you to harness, Wake, and then you'll be a happy man. You keep your mind on the game and forget about yourself. That's the cure for jibbers.'

As I journeyed to St Anton I thought a lot about that talk. He was quite right about Mary, who would never have married him. A man with such an angular soul couldn't fit into another's. And then I thought that the chief thing about Mary was just her serene certainty. Her eyes had that settled happy look that I remembered to have seen only in one other human face, and that was Peter's ... But I wondered if Peter's eyes were still the same.

I found the cottage, a little wooden thing which had been left perched on its knoll when the big hotels grew around it. It had a fence in front, but behind it was open to the hillside. At the gate stood a bent old woman with a face like a pippin. My make-up must have been good, for she accepted me before I introduced myself.

'God be thanked you are come,' she cried. 'The poor lieutenant needed a man to keep him company. He sleeps now, as he does always in the afternoon, for his leg wearies him in the night ... But he is brave, like a soldier ... Come, I will show you the house, for you two will be alone now.'

Stepping softly she led me indoors, pointing with a warning finger to the little bedroom where Peter slept. I found a kitchen with a big stove and a rough floor of planking, on which lay some badly cured skins. Off it was a sort of pantry with a bed for me. She showed me the pots and pans for cooking and the stores she had laid in, and where to find water and fuel. 'I will do the marketing daily,' she said, 'and if you need me, my dwelling is half a mile up the road beyond the new church. God be with you, young man, and be kind to that wounded one.'

When the Widow Summermatter had departed I sat down in Peter's arm-chair and took stock of the place. It was quiet and simple and homely, and through the window came the gleam of snow on the diamond hills. On the table beside the stove were Peter's cherished belongings—his buck-skin pouch and the pipe which Jannie Grobelaar had carved for him in St Helena, an aluminium field match-box I had given him, a cheap large-print Bible such as padres present to well-disposed privates, and an old battered *Pilgrim's Progress* with gaudy pictures. The illustration at which I opened showed Faithful going up to Heaven from the fire of Vanity Fair like a woodcock that has just been flushed. Everything in the room was exquisitely neat, and I knew that that was Peter and not the Widow Summermatter. On a peg behind the door hung his much-mended coat, and sticking out of a pocket I recognized a sheaf of my own letters. In one corner stood something which I had forgotten about—an invalid chair.

The sight of Peter's plain little oddments made me feel solemn. I wondered if his eyes would be like Mary's now, for I could not conceive what life would be for him as a cripple. Very silently I opened the bedroom door and slipped inside.

He was lying on a camp bedstead with one of those striped Swiss blankets pulled up round his ears, and he was asleep. It was the old Peter beyond doubt. He had the hunter's gift of breathing evenly through his nose, and the white scar on the deep brown of his forehead was what I had always remembered. The only change since I last saw him was that he had let his beard grow again, and it was grey.

As I looked at him the remembrance of all we had been through together flooded back upon me, and I could have cried with joy at being beside him. Women, bless their hearts! can never know what long comradeship means to men; it is something not in their lives—something that belongs only to that wild, undomesticated world which we forswear when we find our mates. Even Mary understood only a bit of it. I had just won her love, which was the greatest thing that ever came my way, but if she had entered at that moment I would scarcely have turned my head. I was back again in the old life and was not thinking of the new.

Suddenly I saw that Peter was awake and was looking at me.

'Dick,' he said in a whisper, 'Dick, my old friend.'

The blanket was tossed off, and his long, lean arms were stretched out to me. I gripped his hands, and for a little we did not speak. Then I saw how woefully he had changed. His left leg had shrunk, and from the knee down was like a pipe stem. His face, when awake, showed the lines of hard suffering and he seemed shorter by half a foot. But his eyes were still like Mary's. Indeed they seemed to be more patient and peaceful than in the days when he sat beside me on the buck-waggon and peered over the hunting-veld.

I picked him up—he was no heavier than Mary—and carried him to his chair beside the stove. Then I boiled water and made tea, as we had so often done together.

'Peter, old man,' I said, 'we're on trek again, and this is a very snug little *rondavel.* We've had many good yarns, but this is going to be the best. First of all, how about your health?'

'Good, I'm a strong man again, but slow like a hippo cow. I have been lonely sometimes, but that is all by now. Tell me of the big battles.'

But I was hungry for news of him and kept him to his own case. He had no complaint of his treatment except that he did not like Germans. The doctors at the hospital had been clever, he said, and had done their best for him, but nerves and sinews and small bones had been so wrecked that they could not mend his leg, and Peter had all the Boer's dislike of amputation. One doctor had been in Damaraland and talked to him of those baked sunny places and made him homesick. But he returned always to his dislike of Germans. He had seen them herding our soldiers like brute beasts, and the commandant had a face like Stumm and a chin that stuck out and wanted hitting. He made an exception for the great airman Lensch, who had downed him.

'He is a white man, that one,' he said. 'He came to see me in hospital and told me a lot of things. I think he made them treat me well. He is a big man, Dick, who would make two of me, and he has a round, merry face and pale eyes like Frickie Celliers who could put a bullet through a pauw's head at two hundred yards. He said he was sorry I was lame, for he hoped to have more fights with me. Some woman that tells fortunes had said that I would be the end of him, but he reckoned she had got the thing the wrong way on. I hope he will come through this war, for he is a good man, though a German ... But the others! They are like the fool in the Bible, fat and ugly in good fortune and proud and vicious when their luck goes. They are not a people to be happy with.'

Then he told me that to keep up his spirits he had amused himself with playing a game. He had prided himself on being a Boer, and spoken coldly of the British. He had also, I gathered, imparted many things calculated to deceive. So he left Germany with good marks, and in Switzerland had held himself aloof from the other British wounded, on the advice of Blenkiron, who had met him as soon as he crossed the frontier. I gathered it was Blenkiron who had had him sent to St Anton, and in his time there, as a disgruntled Boer, he had mixed a good deal with Germans. They had pumped him about our air service, and Peter had told them many ingenious lies and heard curious things in return.

'They are working hard, Dick,' he said. 'Never forget that. The German is a stout enemy, and when we beat him with a machine he sweats till he has invented a new one. They have great pilots, but never so many good ones as we, and I do not think in ordinary fighting they can ever beat us. But you must watch Lensch, for I fear him. He has a new machine, I hear, with great engines and a short wingspread, but the wings so cambered that he can climb fast. That will be a surprise to spring upon us. You will say that we'll soon better it. So we shall, but if it was used at a time when we were pushing hard it might make the little difference that loses battles.'

'You mean,' I said, 'that if we had a great attack ready and had driven all the Boche planes back from our front, Lensch and his circus might get over in spite of us and blow the gaff?'

'Yes,' he said solemnly. 'Or if we were attacked, and had a weak spot, Lensch might show the Germans where to get through. I do not think we are going to attack for a long time; but I am pretty sure that Germany is going to fling every man against us. That is the talk of my friends, and it is not bluff.'

That night I cooked our modest dinner, and we smoked our pipes with the stove door open and the good smell of woodsmoke in our nostrils. I told him of all my doings and of the Wild Birds and Ivery and the job we were engaged on. Blenkiron's instructions were that we two should live humbly and keep our eyes and ears open, for we were outside suspicion—the cantankerous lame Boer and his loutish servant from Arosa. Somewhere in the place was a rendezvous of our enemies, and thither came Chelius on his dark errands.

Peter nodded his head sagely, 'I think I have guessed the place. The daughter of the old woman used to pull my chair sometimes down to the village, and I have sat in cheap inns and talked to servants. There is a fresh-water pan there, it is all covered with snow now, and beside it there is a big house that they call the Pink Chalet. I do not know much about it, except that rich folk live in it, for I know the other houses and they are harmless. Also the big hotels, which are too cold and public for strangers to meet in.'

I put Peter to bed, and it was a joy to me to look after him, to give him his tonic and prepare the hot water bottle that comforted his neuralgia. His behaviour was like a docile child's, and he never lapsed from his sunny temper, though I could see how his leg gave him hell. They had tried massage for it and given it up, and there was nothing for him but to endure till nature and his tough constitution deadened the tortured nerves again. I shifted my bed out of the pantry and slept in the room with him, and when I woke in the night, as one does the first time in a strange place, I could tell by his breathing that he was wakeful and suffering.

Next day a bath chair containing a grizzled cripple and pushed by a limping peasant might have been seen descending the long hill to the village. It was clear frosty weather which makes the cheeks tingle, and I felt so full of beans that it was hard to remember my game leg. The valley was shut in on the east by a great mass of rocks and glaciers, belonging to a mountain whose top could not be seen. But on the south, above the snowy fir-woods, there was a most delicate lace-like peak with a point like a needle. I looked at it with interest, for beyond it lay the valley which led to the Staub pass, and beyond that was Italy—and Mary.

The old village of St Anton had one long, narrow street which bent at right angles to a bridge which spanned the river flowing from the lake. Thence the road climbed steeply, but at the other end of the street it ran on the level by the water's edge, lined with gimcrack boarding-houses, now shuttered to the world, and a few villas in patches of garden. At the far end, just before it plunged into a pine-wood, a promontory jutted into the lake, leaving a broad space between the road and the water. Here were the grounds of a more considerable dwelling—snow-covered laurels and rhododendrons with one or two bigger trees—and just on the water-edge stood the house itself, called the Pink Chalet.

I wheeled Peter past the entrance on the crackling snow of the highway. Seen through the gaps of the trees the front looked new, but the back part seemed to be of some age, for I could see high walls, broken by few windows, hanging over the water. The place was no more a chalet than a donjon, but I suppose the name was given in honour of a wooden gallery above the front door. The whole thing was washed in an ugly pink. There were outhouses—garage or stables among the trees—and at the entrance there were fairly recent tracks of an automobile.

On our way back we had some very bad beer in a cafe and made friends with the woman who kept it. Peter had to tell her his story, and I trotted out my aunt in Zurich, and in the end we heard her grievances. She was a true Swiss, angry at all the belligerents who had spoiled her livelihood, hating Germany most but also fearing her most. Coffee, tea, fuel, bread, even milk and cheese were hard to get and cost a ransom. It would take the land years to recover, and there would be no more tourists, for there was little money left in the world. I dropped a question about the Pink Chalet, and was told that it belonged to one Schweigler, a professor of Berne, an old man who came sometimes for a few days in the summer. It was often let, but not now. Asked if it was occupied, she remarked that some friends of the Schweiglers—rich people from Basle—had been there for the winter. 'They come and go in great cars,' she said bitterly, 'and they bring their food from the cities. They spend no money in this poor place.'

Presently Peter and I fell into a routine of life, as if we had always kept house together. In the morning he went abroad in his chair, in the afternoon I would hobble about on my own errands. We sank into the background and took its colour, and a less conspicuous pair never faced the eye of suspicion. Once a week a young Swiss officer, whose business it was to look after British wounded, paid us a hurried visit. I used to get letters from my aunt in Zurich, Sometimes with the postmark of Arosa, and now and then these letters would contain curiously worded advice or instructions from him whom my aunt called 'the kind patron'. Generally I was told to be patient. Sometimes I had word about the health of 'my little cousin across the mountains'. Once I was bidden expect a friend of the patron's, the wise doctor of whom he had often spoken, but though after that I shadowed the Pink Chalet for two days no doctor appeared.

My investigations were a barren business. I used to go down to the village in the afternoon and sit in an out-of-the-way cafe, talking slow German with peasants and hotel porters, but there was little to learn. I knew all there was to hear about the Pink Chalet, and that was nothing. A young man who ski-ed stayed for three nights and spent his days on the alps above the fir-woods. A party of four, including two women, was reported to have been there for a night—all ramifications of the rich family of Basle. I studied the house from the lake, which should have been nicely swept into ice-rinks, but from lack of visitors was a heap of blown snow. The high old walls of the back part were built straight from the water's edge. I remember I tried a short cut through the grounds to the high-road and was given 'Good afternoon' by a smiling German manservant. One way and another I gathered there were a good many serving-men about the place—too many for the infrequent guests. But beyond this I discovered nothing.

Not that I was bored, for I had always Peter to turn to. He was thinking a lot about South Africa, and the thing he liked best was to go over with me every detail of our old expeditions. They belonged to a life which he could think about without pain, whereas the war was too near and bitter for him. He liked to hobble out-of-doors after the darkness came and look at his old friends, the stars. He called them by the words they use on the veld, and the first star of morning he called the *voorlooper*—the little boy who inspans the oxen—a name I had not heard for twenty years. Many a great yarn we spun in the long evenings, but I always went to bed with a sore heart. The longing in his eyes was too urgent, longing not for old days or far countries, but for the health and strength which had once been his pride.

One night I told him about Mary.

'She will be a happy *mysie*,' he said, 'but you will need to be very clever with her, for women are queer cattle and you and I don't know their ways. They tell me

English women do not cook and make clothes like our vrouws, so what will she find to do? I doubt an idle woman will be like a mealie-fed horse.'

It was no good explaining to him the kind of girl Mary was, for that was a world entirely beyond his ken. But I could see that he felt lonelier than ever at my news. So I told him of the house I meant to have in England when the war was over—an old house in a green hilly country, with fields that would carry four head of cattle to the Morgan and furrows of clear water, and orchards of plums and apples. 'And you will stay with us all the time,' I said. 'You will have your own rooms and your own boy to look after you, and you will help me to farm, and we will catch fish together, and shoot the wild ducks when they come up from the pans in the evening. I have found a better countryside than the Houtbosch, where you and I planned to have a farm. It is a blessed and happy place, England.'

He shook his head. 'You are a kind man, Dick, but your pretty *mysie* won't want an ugly old fellow like me hobbling about her house ... I do not think I will go back to Africa, for I should be sad there in the sun. I will find a little place in England, and some day I will visit you, old friend.'

That night his stoicism seemed for the first time to fail him. He was silent for a long time and went early to bed, where I can vouch for it he did not sleep. But he must have thought a lot in the night time, for in the morning he had got himself in hand and was as cheerful as a sandboy.

I watched his philosophy with amazement. It was far beyond anything I could have compassed myself. He was so frail and so poor, for he had never had anything in the world but his bodily fitness, and he had lost that now. And remember, he had lost it after some months of glittering happiness, for in the air he had found the element for which he had been born. Sometimes he dropped a hint of those days when he lived in the clouds and invented a new kind of battle, and his voice always grew hoarse. I could see that he ached with longing for their return. And yet he never had a word of complaint. That was the ritual he had set himself, his point of honour, and he faced the future with the same kind of courage as that with which he had tackled a wild beast or Lensch himself. Only it needed a far bigger brand of fortitude.

Another thing was that he had found religion. I doubt if that is the right way to put it, for he had always had it. Men who live in the wilds know they are in the hands of God. But his old kind had been a tattered thing, more like heathen superstition, though it had always kept him humble. But now he had taken to reading the Bible and to thinking in his lonely nights, and he had got a creed of his own. I dare say it was crude enough, I am sure it was unorthodox; but if the proof of religion is that it gives a man a prop in bad days, then Peter's was the real thing. He used to ferret about in the

Bible and the *Pilgrim's Progress*—they were both equally inspired in his eyes—and find texts which he interpreted in his own way to meet his case. He took everything quite literally. What happened three thousand years ago in Palestine might, for all he minded, have been going on next door. I used to chaff him and tell him that he was like the Kaiser, very good at fitting the Bible to his purpose, but his sincerity was so complete that he only smiled. I remember one night, when he had been thinking about his flying days, he found a passage in Thessalonians about the dead rising to meet their Lord in the air, and that cheered him a lot. Peter, I could see, had the notion that his time here wouldn't be very long, and he liked to think that when he got his release he would find once more the old rapture.

Once, when I said something about his patience, he said he had got to try to live up to Mr Standfast. He had fixed on that character to follow, though he would have preferred Mr Valiant-for-Truth if he had thought himself good enough. He used to talk about Mr Standfast in his queer way as if he were a friend of us both, like Blenkiron ... I tell you I was humbled out of all my pride by the sight of Peter, so uncomplaining and gentle and wise. The Almighty Himself couldn't have made a prig out of him, and he never would have thought of preaching. Only once did he give me advice. I had always a liking for short cuts, and I was getting a bit restive under the long inaction. One day when I expressed my feelings on the matter, Peter upped and read from the *Pilgrim's Progress*: 'Some also have wished that the next way to their Father's house were here, that they might be troubled no more with either hills or mountains to go over, but the Way is the Way, and there is an end.'

All the same when we got into March and nothing happened I grew pretty anxious. Blenkiron had said we were fighting against time, and here were the weeks slipping away. His letters came occasionally, always in the shape of communications from my aunt. One told me that I would soon be out of a job, for Peter's repatriation was just about through, and he might get his movement order any day. Another spoke of my little cousin over the hills, and said that she hoped soon to be going to a place called Santa Chiara in the Val Saluzzana. I got out the map in a hurry and measured the distance from there to St Anton and pored over the two roads thither—the short one by the Staub Pass and the long one by the Marjolana. These letters made me think that things were nearing a climax, but still no instructions came. I had nothing to report in my own messages, I had discovered nothing in the Pink Chalet but idle servants, I was not even sure if the Pink Chalet were not a harmless villa, and I hadn't come within a thousand miles of finding Chelius. All my desire to imitate Peter's stoicism didn't prevent me from getting occasionally rattled and despondent.

The one thing I could do was to keep fit, for I had a notion I might soon want all my bodily strength. I had to keep up my pretence of lameness in the daytime, so I used to take my exercise at night. I would sleep in the afternoon, when Peter had his siesta, and then about ten in the evening, after putting him to bed, I would slip out-of-doors and go for a four or five hours' tramp. Wonderful were those midnight wanderings. I pushed up through the snow-laden pines to the ridges where the snow lay in great wreaths and scallops, till I stood on a crest with a frozen world at my feet and above me a host of glittering stars. Once on a night of full moon I reached the glacier at the valley head, scrambled up the moraine to where the ice began, and peered fearfully into the spectral crevasses. At such hours I had the earth to myself, for there was not a sound except the slipping of a burden of snow from the trees or the crack and rustle which reminded me that a glacier was a moving river. The war seemed very far away, and I felt the littleness of our human struggles, till I thought of Peter turning from side to side to find ease in the cottage far below me. Then I realized that the spirit of man was the greatest thing in this spacious world ... I would get back about three or four, have a bath in the water which had been warming in my absence, and creep into bed, almost ashamed of having two sound legs, when a better man a yard away had but one.

Oddly enough at these hours there seemed more life in the Pink Chalet than by day. Once, tramping across the lake long after midnight, I saw lights in the lake-front in windows which for ordinary were blank and shuttered. Several times I cut across the grounds, when the moon was dark. On one such occasion a great car with no lights swept up the drive, and I heard low voices at the door.

Another time a man ran hastily past me, and entered the house by a little door on the eastern side, which I had not before noticed ... Slowly the conviction began to grow on me that we were not wrong in marking down this place, that things went on within it which it deeply concerned us to discover. But I was puzzled to think of a way. I might butt inside, but for all I knew it would be upsetting Blenkiron's plans, for he had given me no instructions about housebreaking. All this unsettled me worse than ever. I began to lie awake planning some means of entrance ... I would be a peasant from the next valley who had twisted his ankle ... I would go seeking an imaginary cousin among the servants ... I would start a fire in the place and have the doors flung open to zealous neighbours...

And then suddenly I got instructions in a letter from Blenkiron.

It came inside a parcel of warm socks that arrived from my kind aunt. But the letter for me was not from her. It was in Blenkiron's large sprawling hand and the style of it was all his own. He told me that he had about finished his job. He had got his line on Chelius, who was the bird he expected, and that bird would soon wing its way southward across the mountains for the reason I knew of.

'We've got an almighty move on,' he wrote, 'and please God you're going to hustle some in the next week. It's going better than I ever hoped.' But something was still to be done. He had struck a countryman, one Clarence Donne, a journalist of Kansas City, whom he had taken into the business. Him he described as a 'crackerjack' and commended to my esteem. He was coming to St Anton, for there was a game afoot at the Pink Chalet, which he would give me news of. I was to meet him next evening at nine-fifteen at the little door in the east end of the house. 'For the love of Mike, Dick,' he concluded, 'be on time and do everything Clarence tells you as if he was me. It's a mighty complex affair, but you and he have sand enough to pull through. Don't worry about your little cousin. She's safe and out of the job now.'

My first feeling was one of immense relief, especially at the last words. I read the letter a dozen times to make sure I had its meaning. A flash of suspicion crossed my mind that it might be a fake, principally because there was no mention of Peter, who had figured large in the other missives. But why should Peter be mentioned when he wasn't on in this piece? The signature convinced me. Ordinarily Blenkiron signed himself in full with a fine commercial flourish. But when I was at the Front he had got into the habit of making a kind of hieroglyphic of his surname to me and sticking J.S. after it in a bracket. That was how this letter was signed, and it was sure proof it was all right.

I spent that day and the next in wild spirits. Peter spotted what was on, though I did not tell him for fear of making him envious. I had to be extra kind to him, for I could see that he ached to have a hand in the business. Indeed he asked shyly if I couldn't fit him in, and I had to lie about it and say it was only another of my aimless circumnavigations of the Pink Chalet.

'Try and find something where I can help,' he pleaded. 'I'm pretty strong still, though I'm lame, and I can shoot a bit.'

I declared that he would be used in time, that Blenkiron had promised he would be used, but for the life of me I couldn't see how.

At nine o'clock on the evening appointed I was on the lake opposite the house, close in under the shore, making my way to the rendezvous. It was a coal-black night, for though the air was clear the stars were shining with little light, and the moon had not yet risen. With a premonition that I might be long away from food, I had brought some slabs of chocolate, and my pistol and torch were in my pocket. It was bitter cold, but I had ceased to mind weather, and I wore my one suit and no overcoat.

The house was like a tomb for silence. There was no crack of light anywhere, and none of those smells of smoke and food which proclaim habitation. It was an eerie job scrambling up the steep bank east of the place, to where the flat of the garden started, in a darkness so great that I had to grope my way like a blind man.

I found the little door by feeling along the edge of the building. Then I stepped into an adjacent clump of laurels to wait on my companion. He was there before me.

'Say,' I heard a rich Middle West voice whisper, 'are you Joseph Zimmer? I'm not shouting any names, but I guess you are the guy I was told to meet here.'

'Mr Donne?' I whispered back.

'The same,' he replied. 'Shake.'

I gripped a gloved and mittened hand which drew me towards the door.

CHAPTER SIXTEEN

I Lie on a Hard Bed

The journalist from Kansas City was a man of action. He wasted no words in introducing himself or unfolding his plan of campaign. 'You've got to follow me, mister, and not deviate one inch from my tracks. The explaining part will come later. There's big business in this shack tonight.' He unlocked the little door with scarcely a sound, slid the crust of snow from his boots, and preceded me into a passage as black as a cellar. The door swung smoothly behind us, and after the sharp out-of-doors the air smelt stuffy as the inside of a safe.

A hand reached back to make sure that I followed. We appeared to be in a flagged passage under the main level of the house. My hobnailed boots slipped on the floor, and I steadied myself on the wall, which seemed to be of undressed stone. Mr Donne moved softly and assuredly, for he was better shod for the job than me, and his guiding hand came back constantly to make sure of my whereabouts.

I remember that I felt just as I had felt when on that August night I had explored the crevice of the Coolin—the same sense that something queer was going to happen, the same recklessness and contentment. Moving a foot at a time with immense care, we came to a right-hand turning. Two shallow steps led us to another passage, and then my groping hands struck a blind wall.

The American was beside me, and his mouth was close to my ear.

'Got to crawl now,' he whispered. 'You lead, mister, while I shed this coat of mine. Eight feet on your stomach and then upright.'

I wriggled through a low tunnel, broad enough to take three men abreast, but not two feet high. Half-way through I felt suffocated, for I never liked holes, and I had a momentary anxiety as to what we were after in this cellar pilgrimage. Presently I smelt free air and got on to my knees.

'Right, mister?' came a whisper from behind. My companion seemed to be waiting till I was through before he followed.

'Right,' I answered, and very carefully rose to my feet.

Then something happened behind me. There was a jar and a bump as if the roof of the tunnel had subsided. I turned sharply and groped at the mouth. I stuck my leg down and found a block.

'Donne,' I said, as loud as I dared, 'are you hurt? Where are you?'

But no answer came.

Even then I thought only of an accident. Something had miscarried, and I was cut off in the cellars of an unfriendly house away from the man who knew the road and had a plan in his head. I was not so much frightened as exasperated. I turned from the tunnel-mouth and groped into the darkness before me. I might as well prospect the kind of prison into which I had blundered.

I took three steps—no more. My feet seemed suddenly to go from me and fly upward. So sudden was it that I fell heavy and dead like a log, and my head struck the floor with a crash that for a moment knocked me senseless. I was conscious of something falling on me and of an intolerable pressure on my chest. I struggled for breath, and found my arms and legs pinned and my whole body in a kind of wooden vice. I was sick with concussion, and could do nothing but gasp and choke down my nausea. The cut in the back of my head was bleeding freely and that helped to clear my wits, but I lay for a minute or two incapable of thought. I shut my eyes tight, as a man does when he is fighting with a swoon.

When I opened them there was light. It came from the left side of the room, the broad glare of a strong electric torch. I watched it stupidly, but it gave me the fillip needed to pick up the threads. I remembered the tunnel now and the Kansas journalist. Then behind the light I saw a face which pulled my flickering senses out of the mire.

I saw the heavy ulster and the cap, which I had realized, though I had not seen, outside in the dark laurels. They belonged to the journalist, Clarence Donne, the trusted emissary of Blenkiron. But I saw his face now, and it was that face which I had boasted to Bullivant I could never mistake again upon earth. I did not mistake it now, and I remember I had a faint satisfaction that I had made good my word. I had not mistaken it, for I had not had the chance to look at it till this moment. I saw with acid clearness the common denominator of all its disguises—the young man who lisped in the seaside villa, the stout philanthropist of Biggleswick, the pulpy panic-stricken creature of the Tube station, the trim French staff officer of the Picardy chateau ... I saw more, for I saw it beyond the need of disguise. I was looking at von Schwabing, the exile, who had done more for Germany than any army commander ... Mary's words came back to me—'the most dangerous man in the world' ... I was not afraid, or broken-hearted at failure, or angry—not yet, for I was too dazed and awestruck. I looked at him as one might look at some cataclysm of nature which had destroyed a continent.

The face was smiling.

'I am happy to offer you hospitality at last,' it said.

I pulled my wits farther out of the mud to attend to him. The cross-bar on my chest pressed less hard and I breathed better. But when I tried to speak, the words would not come.

'We are old friends,' he went on. 'We have known each other quite intimately for four years, which is a long time in war. I have been interested in you, for you have a kind of crude intelligence, and you have compelled me to take you seriously. If you were cleverer you would appreciate the compliment. But you were fool enough to think you could beat me, and for that you must be punished. Oh no, don't flatter yourself you were ever dangerous. You were only troublesome and presumptuous like a mosquito one flicks off one's sleeve.'

He was leaning against the side of a heavy closed door. He lit a cigar from a little gold tinder box and regarded me with amused eyes.

'You will have time for reflection, so I propose to enlighten you a little. You are an observer of little things. So? Did you ever see a cat with a mouse? The mouse runs about and hides and manoeuvres and thinks it is playing its own game. But at any moment the cat can stretch out its paw and put an end to it. You are the mouse, my poor General—for I believe you are one of those funny amateurs that the English call Generals. At any moment during the last nine months I could have put an end to you with a nod.'

My nausea had stopped and I could understand what he said, though I had still no power to reply.

'Let me explain,' he went on. 'I watched with amusement your gambols at Biggleswick. My eyes followed you when you went to the Clyde and in your stupid twistings in Scotland. I gave you rope, because you were futile, and I had graver things to attend to. I allowed you to amuse yourself at your British Front with childish investigations and to play the fool in Paris. I have followed every step of your course in Switzerland, and I have helped your idiotic Yankee friend to plot against myself. While you thought you were drawing your net around me, I was drawing mine around you. I assure you, it has been a charming relaxation from serious business.'

I knew the man was lying. Some part was true, for he had clearly fooled Blenkiron; but I remembered the hurried flight from Biggleswick and Eaucourt Sainte-Anne when the game was certainly against him. He had me at his mercy, and was wreaking his vanity on me. That made him smaller in my eyes, and my first awe began to pass.

'I never cherish rancour, you know,' he said. 'In my business it is silly to be angry, for it wastes energy. But I do not tolerate insolence, my dear General. And my country has the habit of doing justice on her enemies. It may interest you to know that the end is not far off. Germany has faced a jealous world in arms and she is about to be justified of her great courage. She has broken up bit by bit the clumsy organization of her opponents. Where is Russia today, the steam-roller that was to crush us? Where is the poor dupe Rumania? Where is the strength of Italy, who was once to do wonders for what she called Liberty? Broken, all of them. I have played my part in that work and now the need is past. My country with free hands is about to turn upon your armed rabble in the West and drive it into the Atlantic. Then we shall deal with the ragged remains of France and the handful of noisy Americans. By midsummer there will be peace dictated by triumphant Germany.'

'By God, there won't!' I had found my voice at last.

'By God, there will,' he said pleasantly. 'It is what you call a mathematical certainty. You will no doubt die bravely, like the savage tribes that your Empire used to conquer. But we have the greater discipline and the stronger spirit and the bigger brain. Stupidity is always punished in the end, and you are a stupid race. Do not think that your kinsmen across the Atlantic will save you. They are a commercial people and by no means sure of themselves. When they have blustered a little they will see reason and find some means of saving their faces. Their comic President will make a speech or two and write us a solemn note, and we will reply with the serious rhetoric which he loves, and then we shall kiss and be friends. You know in your heart that it will be so.'

A great apathy seemed to settle on me. This bragging did not make me angry, and I had no longer any wish to contradict him. It may have been the result of the fall, but my mind had stopped working. I heard his voice as one listens casually to the ticking of a clock.

'I will tell you more,' he was saying. 'This is the evening of the 18th day of March. Your generals in France expect an attack, but they are not sure where it will come. Some think it may be in Champagne or on the Aisne, some at Ypres, some at St Quentin. Well, my dear General, you alone will I take into our confidence. On the morning of the 21st, three days from now, we attack the right wing of the British Army. In two days we shall be in Amiens. On the third we shall have driven a wedge as far as the sea. Then in a week or so we shall have rolled up your army from the right, and presently we shall be in Boulogne and Calais. After that Paris falls, and then Peace.'

I made no answer. The word 'Amiens' recalled Mary, and I was trying to remember the day in January when she and I had motored south from that pleasant city.

'Why do I tell you these things? Your intelligence, for you are not altogether foolish, will have supplied the answer. It is because your life is over. As your Shakespeare says, the rest is silence ... No, I am not going to kill you. That would be crude, and I hate crudities. I am going now on a little journey, and when I return in twenty-four hours' time you will be my companion. You are going to visit Germany, my dear General.'

That woke me to attention, and he noticed it, for he went on with gusto.

'You have heard of the *Untergrundbahn*? No? And you boast of an Intelligence service! Yet your ignorance is shared by the whole of your General Staff. It is a little organization of my own. By it we can take unwilling and dangerous people inside our frontier to be dealt with as we please. Some have gone from England and many from France. Officially I believe they are recorded as "missing", but they did not go astray on any battle-field. They have been gathered from their homes or from hotels or offices or even the busy streets. I will not conceal from you that the service of our Underground Railway is a little irregular from England and France. But from Switzerland it is smooth as a trunk line. There are unwatched spots on the frontier, and we have our agents among the frontier guards, and we have no difficulty about passes. It is a pretty device, and you will soon be privileged to observe its working ... In Germany I cannot promise you comfort, but I do not think your life will be dull.'

As he spoke these words, his urbane smile changed to a grin of impish malevolence. Even through my torpor I felt the venom and I shivered.

'When I return I shall have another companion.' His voice was honeyed again. 'There is a certain pretty lady who was to be the bait to entice me into Italy. It was so? Well, I have fallen to the bait. I have arranged that she shall meet me this very night at a mountain inn on the Italian side. I have arranged, too, that she shall be alone. She is an innocent child, and I do not think that she has been more than a tool in the clumsy hands of your friends. She will come with me when I ask her, and we shall be a merry party in the Underground Express.'

My apathy vanished, and every nerve in me was alive at the words.

'You cur!' I cried. 'She loathes the sight of you. She wouldn't touch you with the end of a barge-pole.'

He flicked the ash from his cigar. 'I think you are mistaken. I am very persuasive, and I do not like to use compulsion with a woman. But, willing or not, she will come with me. I have worked hard and I am entitled to my pleasure, and I have set my heart on that little lady.'

There was something in his tone, gross, leering, assured, half contemptuous, that made my blood boil. He had fairly got me on the raw, and the hammer beat violently in my forehead. I could have wept with sheer rage, and it took all my fortitude to keep my mouth shut. But I was determined not to add to his triumph.

He looked at his watch. 'Time passes,' he said. 'I must depart to my charming assignation. I will give your remembrances to the lady. Forgive me for making no arrangements for your comfort till I return. Your constitution is so sound that it will not suffer from a day's fasting. To set your mind at rest I may tell you that escape is impossible. This mechanism has been proved too often, and if you did break loose from it my servants would deal with you. But I must speak a word of caution. If you tamper with it or struggle too much it will act in a curious way. The floor beneath you covers a shaft which runs to the lake below. Set a certain spring at work and you may find yourself shot down into the water far below the ice, where your body will rot till the spring ... That, of course, is an alternative open to you, if you do not care to wait for my return.'

He lit a fresh cigar, waved his hand, and vanished through the doorway. As it shut behind him, the sound of his footsteps instantly died away. The walls must have been as thick as a prison's.

I suppose I was what people in books call 'stunned'. The illumination during the past few minutes had been so dazzling that my brain could not master it. I remember very clearly that I did not think about the ghastly failure of our scheme, or the German plans which had been insolently unfolded to me as to one dead to the world. I saw a single picture—an inn in a snowy valley (I saw it as a small place like Peter's cottage), a solitary girl, that smiling devil who had left me, and then the unknown terror of the Underground Railway. I think my courage went for a bit, and I cried with feebleness and rage. The hammer in my forehead had stopped for it only beat when I was angry in action. Now that I lay trapped, the manhood had slipped out of my joints, and if Ivery had still been in the doorway, I think I would have whined for mercy. I would have offered him all the knowledge I had in the world if he had promised to leave Mary alone.

Happily he wasn't there, and there was no witness of my cowardice. Happily, too, it is just as difficult to be a coward for long as to be a hero. It was Blenkiron's phrase about Mary that pulled me together—'She can't scare and she can't soil'. No, by heavens, she couldn't. I could trust my lady far better than I could trust myself. I was still sick with anxiety, but I was getting a pull on myself. I was done in, but Ivery would get no triumph out of me. Either I would go under the ice, or I would find a chance of putting a bullet through my head before I crossed the frontier. If I could do nothing else I could perish decently ... And then I laughed, and I knew I was past the worst. What made me laugh was the thought of Peter. I had been pitying him an hour ago for having only one leg, but now he was abroad in the living, breathing world with years before him, and I lay in the depths, limbless and lifeless, with my number up.

I began to muse on the cold water under the ice where I could go if I wanted. I did not think that I would take that road, for a man's chances are not gone till he is stone dead, but I was glad the way existed ... And then I looked at the wall in front of me, and, very far up, I saw a small square window.

The stars had been clouded when I entered that accursed house, but the mist must have cleared. I saw my old friend Orion, the hunter's star, looking through the bars. And that suddenly made me think.

Peter and I had watched them by night, and I knew the place of all the chief constellations in relation to the St Anton valley. I believed that I was in a room on the lake side of the Pink Chalet: I must be, if Ivery had spoken the truth. But if so, I could not conceivably see Orion from its window ... There was no other possible conclusion, I must be in a room on the east side of the house, and Ivery had been lying. He had already lied in his boasting of how he had outwitted me in England and at the Front. He might be lying about Mary ... No, I dismissed that hope. Those words of his had rung true enough.

I thought for a minute and concluded that he had lied to terrorize me and keep me quiet; therefore this infernal contraption had probably its weak point. I reflected, too, that I was pretty strong, far stronger probably than Ivery imagined, for he had never seen me stripped. Since the place was pitch dark I could not guess how the thing worked, but I could feel the cross-bars rigid on my chest and legs and the side-bars which pinned my arms to my sides ... I drew a long breath and tried to force my elbows apart. Nothing moved, nor could I raise the bars on my legs the smallest fraction.

Again I tried, and again. The side-bar on my right seemed to be less rigid than the others. I managed to get my right hand raised above the level of my thigh, and then with a struggle I got a grip with it on the cross-bar, which gave me a small leverage. With a mighty effort I drove my right elbow and shoulder against the side-bar. It seemed to give slightly ... I summoned all my strength and tried again. There was a crack and then a splintering, the massive bar shuffled limply back, and my right arm was free to move laterally, though the cross-bar prevented me from raising it.

With some difficulty I got at my coat pocket where reposed my electric torch and my pistol. With immense labour and no little pain I pulled the former out and switched it on by drawing the catch against the cross-bar. Then I saw my prison house.

It was a little square chamber, very high, with on my left the massive door by which Ivery had departed. The dark baulks of my rack were plain, and I could roughly make out how the thing had been managed. Some spring had tilted up the flooring, and dropped the framework from its place in the right-hand wall. It was clamped, I observed, by an arrangement in the floor just in front of the door. If I could get rid of that catch it would be easy to free myself, for to a man of my strength the weight would not be impossibly heavy.

My fortitude had come back to me, and I was living only in the moment, choking down any hope of escape. My first job was to destroy the catch that clamped down the rack, and for that my only weapon was my pistol. I managed to get the little electric torch jammed in the corner of the cross-bar, where it lit up the floor towards the door. Then it was hell's own business extricating the pistol from my pocket. Wrist and fingers were always cramping, and I was in terror that I might drop it where I could not retrieve it.

I forced myself to think out calmly the question of the clamp, for a pistol bullet is a small thing, and I could not afford to miss. I reasoned it out from my knowledge of mechanics, and came to the conclusion that the centre of gravity was a certain bright spot of metal which I could just see under the cross-bars. It was bright and so must have been recently repaired, and that was another reason for thinking it important. The question was how to hit it, for I could not get the pistol in line with my eye. Let anyone try that kind of shooting, with a bent arm over a bar, when you are lying flat and looking at the mark from under the bar, and he will understand its difficulties. I had six shots in my revolver, and I must fire two or three ranging shots in any case. I must not exhaust all my cartridges, for I must have a bullet left for any servant who came to pry, and I wanted one in reserve for myself. But I did not think shots would be heard outside the room; the walls were too thick.

I held my wrist rigid above the cross-bar and fired. The bullet was an inch to the right of the piece of bright steel. Moving a fraction I fired again. I had grazed it on the left. With aching eyes glued on the mark, I tried a third time. I saw something leap apart, and suddenly the whole framework under which I lay fell loose and mobile

... I was very cool and restored the pistol to my pocket and took the torch in my hand before I moved ... Fortune had been kind, for I was free. I turned on my face, humped my back, and without much trouble crawled out from under the contraption.

I did not allow myself to think of ultimate escape, for that would only flurry me, and one step at a time was enough. I remember that I dusted my clothes, and found that the cut in the back of my head had stopped bleeding. I retrieved my hat, which had rolled into a corner when I fell ... Then I turned my attention to the next step.

The tunnel was impossible, and the only way was the door. If I had stopped to think I would have known that the chances against getting out of such a house were a thousand to one. The pistol shots had been muffled by the cavernous walls, but the place, as I knew, was full of servants and, even if I passed the immediate door, I would be collared in some passage. But I had myself so well in hand that I tackled the door as if I had been prospecting to sink a new shaft in Rhodesia.

It had no handle nor, so far as I could see, a keyhole ... But I noticed, as I turned my torch on the ground, that from the clamp which I had shattered a brass rod sunk in the floor led to one of the door-posts. Obviously the thing worked by a spring and was connected with the mechanism of the rack.

A wild thought entered my mind and brought me to my feet. I pushed the door and it swung slowly open. The bullet which freed me had released the spring which controlled it.

Then for the first time, against all my maxims of discretion, I began to hope. I took off my hat and felt my forehead burning, so that I rested it for a moment on the cool wall ... Perhaps my luck still held. With a rush came thoughts of Mary and Blenkiron and Peter and everything we had laboured for, and I was mad to win.

I had no notion of the interior of the house or where lay the main door to the outer world. My torch showed me a long passage with something like a door at the far end, but I clicked it off, for I did not dare to use it now. The place was deadly quiet. As I listened I seemed to hear a door open far away, and then silence fell again.

I groped my way down the passage till I had my hands on the far door. I hoped it might open on the hall, where I could escape by a window or a balcony, for I judged the outer door would be locked. I listened, and there came no sound from within. It was no use lingering, so very stealthily I turned the handle and opened it a crack.

It creaked and I waited with beating heart on discovery, for inside I saw the glow of light. But there was no movement, so it must be empty. I poked my head in and then followed with my body.

It was a large room, with logs burning in a stove, and the floor thick with rugs. It was lined with books, and on a table in the centre a reading-lamp was burning. Several dispatch-boxes stood on the table, and there was a little pile of papers. A man had been here a minute before, for a half-smoked cigar was burning on the edge of the inkstand.

At that moment I recovered complete use of my wits and all my self-possession. More, there returned to me some of the old devil-may-careness which before had served me well. Ivery had gone, but this was his sanctum. Just as on the roofs of Erzerum I had burned to get at Stumm's papers, so now it was borne in on me that at all costs I must look at that pile.

I advanced to the table and picked up the topmost paper. It was a little typewritten blue slip with the lettering in italics, and in a corner a curious, involved stamp in red ink. On it I read:

'*Die Wildvoegel muessen heimkehren.*'

At the same moment I heard steps and the door opened on the far side, I stepped back towards the stove, and fingered the pistol in my pocket.

A man entered, a man with a scholar's stoop, an unkempt beard, and large sleepy dark eyes. At the sight of me he pulled up and his whole body grew taut. It was the Portuguese Jew, whose back I had last seen at the smithy door in Skye, and who by the mercy of God had never seen my face.

I stopped fingering my pistol, for I had an inspiration. Before he could utter a word I got in first.

'*Die Voegelein schweigen im Walde,*' I said.

His face broke into a pleasant smile, and he replied:

'*Warte nur, balde rubest du auch.*'

'Ach,' he said in German, holding out his hand, 'you have come this way, when we thought you would go by Modane. I welcome you, for I know your exploits. You are Conradi, who did so nobly in Italy?'

I bowed. 'Yes, I am Conradi,' I said.

CHAPTER SEVENTEEN

The Col of the Swallows

He pointed to the slip on the table.

'You have seen the orders?'

I nodded.

'The long day's work is over. You must rejoice, for your part has been the hardest, I think. Some day you will tell me about it?'

The man's face was honest and kindly, rather like that of the engineer Gaudian, whom two years before I had met in Germany. But his eyes fascinated me, for they were the eyes of the dreamer and fanatic, who would not desist from his quest while life lasted. I thought that Ivery had chosen well in his colleague.

'My task is not done yet,' I said. 'I came here to see Chelius.'

'He will be back tomorrow evening.'

'Too late. I must see him at once. He has gone to Italy, and I must overtake him.'

'You know your duty best,' he said gravely.

'But you must help me. I must catch him at Santa Chiara, for it is a business of life and death. Is there a car to be had?'

'There is mine. But there is no chauffeur. Chelius took him.'

'I can drive myself and I know the road. But I have no pass to cross the frontier.'

'That is easily supplied,' he said, smiling.

In one bookcase there was a shelf of dummy books. He unlocked this and revealed a small cupboard, whence he took a tin dispatch-box. From some papers he selected one, which seemed to be already signed.

'Name?' he asked.

'Call me Hans Gruber of Brieg,' I said. 'I travel to pick up my master, who is in the timber trade.'

'And your return?'

'I will come back by my old road,' I said mysteriously; and if he knew what I meant it was more than I did myself.

He completed the paper and handed it to me. 'This will take you through the frontier posts. And now for the car. The servants will be in bed, for they have been preparing for a long journey, but I will myself show it you. There is enough petrol on board to take you to Rome.'

He led me through the hall, unlocked the front door, and we crossed the snowy lawn to the garage. The place was empty but for a great car, which bore the marks of having come from the muddy lowlands. To my joy I saw that it was a Daimler, a type with which I was familiar. I lit the lamps, started the engine, and ran it out on to the road.

'You will want an overcoat,' he said.

'I never wear them.'

'Food?'

'I have some chocolate. I will breakfast at Santa Chiara.'

'Well, God go with you!'

A minute later I was tearing along the lake-side towards St Anton village.

I stopped at the cottage on the hill. Peter was not yet in bed. I found him sitting by the fire, trying to read, but

I saw by his face that he had been waiting anxiously on my coming.

'We're in the soup, old man,' I said as I shut the door. In a dozen sentences I told him of the night's doings, of Ivery's plan and my desperate errand.

'You wanted a share,' I cried. 'Well, everything depends on you now. I'm off after Ivery, and God knows what will happen. Meantime, you have got to get on to Blenkiron, and tell him what I've told you. He must get the news through to G.H.Q. somehow. He must trap the Wild Birds before they go. I don't know how, but he must. Tell him it's all up to him and you, for I'm out of it. I must save Mary, and if God's willing I'll settle with Ivery. But the big job is for Blenkiron—and you. Somehow he has made a bad break, and the enemy has got ahead of him. He must sweat blood to make up. My God, Peter, it's the solemnest moment of our lives. I don't see any light, but we mustn't miss any chances. I'm leaving it all to you.'

I spoke like a man in a fever, for after what I had been through I wasn't quite sane. My coolness in the Pink Chalet had given place to a crazy restlessness. I can see Peter yet, standing in the ring of lamplight, supporting himself by a chair back, wrinkling his brows and, as he always did in moments of excitement, scratching gently the tip of his left ear. His face was happy.

'Never fear, Dick,' he said. 'It will all come right. *Ons sal 'n plan maak.*'

And then, still possessed with a demon of disquiet, I was on the road again, heading for the pass that led to Italy.

The mist had gone from the sky, and the stars were shining brightly. The moon, now at the end of its first quarter, was setting in a gap of the mountains, as I climbed the low col from the St Anton valley to the greater Staubthal. There was frost and the hard snow crackled under my wheels, but there was also that feel in the air which preludes storm. I wondered if I should run into snow in the high hills. The whole land was deep in peace. There was not a light in the hamlets I passed through, not a soul on the highway.

In the Staubthal I joined the main road and swung to the left up the narrowing bed of the valley. The road was in noble condition, and the car was running finely, as I mounted through forests of snowy Pines to a land where the mountains crept close together, and the highway coiled round the angles of great crags or skirted perilously some profound gorge, with only a line of wooden posts to defend it from the void. In places the snow stood in walls on either side, where the road was kept open by man's labour. In other parts it lay thin, and in the dim light one might have fancied that one was running through open meadowlands.

Slowly my head was getting clearer, and I was able to look round my problem. I banished from my mind the situation I had left behind me. Blenkiron must cope with that as best he could. It lay with him to deal with the Wild Birds, my job was with Ivery alone. Sometime in the early morning he would reach Santa Chiara, and there he would find Mary. Beyond that my imagination could forecast nothing. She would be alone—I could trust his cleverness for that; he would try to force her to come with him, or he might persuade her with some lying story. Well, please God, I should come in for the tail end of the interview, and at the thought I cursed the steep gradients I was climbing, and longed for some magic to lift the Daimler beyond the summit and set it racing down the slope towards Italy.

I think it was about half-past three when I saw the lights of the frontier post. The air seemed milder than in the valleys, and there was a soft scurry of snow on my right cheek. A couple of sleepy Swiss sentries with their rifles in their hands stumbled out as I drew up.

They took my pass into the hut and gave me an anxious quarter of an hour while they examined it. The performance was repeated fifty yards on at the Italian post, where to my alarm the sentries were inclined to conversation. I played the part of the sulky servant, answering in monosyllables and pretending to immense stupidity.

'You are only just in time, friend,' said one in German. 'The weather grows bad and soon the pass will close. Ugh, it is as cold as last winter on the Tonale. You remember, Giuseppe?'

But in the end they let me move on. For a little I felt my way gingerly, for on the summit the road had many twists and the snow was confusing to the eyes. Presently came a sharp drop and I let the Daimler go. It grew colder, and I shivered a little; the snow became a wet white fog around the glowing arc of the headlights; and always the road fell, now in long curves, now in steep short dips, till I was aware of a glen opening towards the south. From long living in the wilds I have a kind of sense for landscape without the testimony of the eyes, and I knew where the ravine narrowed or widened though it was black darkness.

In spite of my restlessness I had to go slowly, for after the first rush downhill I realized that, unless I was careful, I might wreck the car and spoil everything. The surface of the road on the southern slope of the mountains was a thousand per cent worse than that on the other. I skidded and side-slipped, and once grazed the edge of the gorge. It was far more maddening than the climb up, for then it had been a straight-forward grind with the Daimler doing its utmost, whereas now I had to hold her back because of my own lack of skill. I reckon that time crawling down from the summit of the Staub as some of the weariest hours I ever spent.

Quite suddenly I ran out of the ill weather into a different climate. The sky was clear above me, and I saw that dawn was very near. The first pinewoods were beginning, and at last came a straight slope where I could let the car out. I began to recover my spirits, which had been very dashed, and to reckon the distance I had still to travel ... And then, without warning, a new world sprang up around me. Out of the blue dusk white shapes rose like ghosts, peaks and needles and domes of ice, their bases fading mistily into shadow, but the tops kindling till they glowed like jewels. I had never seen such a sight, and the wonder of it for a moment drove anxiety from my heart. More, it gave me an earnest of victory. I was in clear air once more, and surely in this diamond ether the foul things which loved the dark must be worsted ...

And then I saw, a mile ahead, the little square red-roofed building which I knew to be the inn of Santa Chiara.

It was here that misfortune met me. I had grown careless now, and looked rather at the house than the road. At one point the hillside had slipped down—it must have been recent, for the road was well kept—and I did not notice the landslide till I was on it. I slewed to the right, took too wide a curve, and before I knew the car was over the far edge. I slapped on the brakes, but to avoid turning turtle I had to leave the road altogether. I slithered down a steep bank into a meadow, where for my sins I ran into a fallen tree trunk with a jar that shook me out of my seat and nearly broke my arm. Before I examined the car I knew what had happened. The front axle was bent, and the off front wheel badly buckled.

I had not time to curse my stupidity. I clambered back to the road and set off running down it at my best speed. I was mortally stiff, for Ivery's rack was not good for the joints, but I realized it only as a drag on my pace, not as an affliction in itself. My whole mind was set on the house before me and what might be happening there.

There was a man at the door of the inn, who, when he caught sight of my figure, began to move to meet me. I saw that it was Launcelot Wake, and the sight gave me hope.

But his face frightened me. It was drawn and haggard like one who never sleeps, and his eyes were hot coals.

'Hannay,' he cried, 'for God's sake what does it mean?'

'Where is Mary?' I gasped, and I remember I clutched at a lapel of his coat.

He pulled me to the low stone wall by the roadside.

'I don't know,' he said hoarsely. 'We got your orders to come here this morning. We were at Chiavagno, where Blenkiron told us to wait. But last night Mary disappeared ... I found she had hired a carriage and come on ahead. I followed at once, and reached here an hour ago to find her gone ... The woman who keeps the place is away and there are only two old servants left. They tell me that Mary came here late, and that very early in the morning a closed car came over the Staub with a man in it. They say he asked to see the young lady, and that they talked together for some time, and that then she went off with him in the car down the valley ... I must have passed it on my way up ... There's been some black devilment that I can't follow. Who was the man? Who was the man?'

He looked as if he wanted to throttle me.

'I can tell you that,' I said. 'It was Ivery.'

He stared for a second as if he didn't understand. Then he leaped to his feet and cursed like a trooper. 'You've botched it, as I knew you would. I knew no good would come of your infernal subtleties.' And he consigned me and Blenkiron and the British army and Ivery and everybody else to the devil.

I was past being angry. 'Sit down, man,' I said, 'and listen to me.' I told him of what had happened at the Pink Chalet. He heard me out with his head in his hands. The thing was too bad for cursing.

'The Underground Railway!' he groaned. 'The thought of it drives me mad. Why are you so calm,

Hannay? She's in the hands of the cleverest devil in the world, and you take it quietly. You should be a raving lunatic.'

'I would be if it were any use, but I did all my raving last night in that den of Ivery's. We've got to pull ourselves together, Wake. First of all, I trust Mary to the other side of eternity. She went with him of her own free will. I don't know why, but she must have had a reason, and be sure it was a good one, for she's far cleverer than you or me ... We've got to follow her somehow. Ivery's bound for Germany, but his route is by the Pink Chalet, for he hopes to pick me up there. He went down the valley; therefore he is going to Switzerland by the Marjolana. That is a long circuit and will take him most of the day. Why he chose that way I don't know, but there it is. We've got to get back by the Staub.'

'How did you come?' he asked.

'That's our damnable luck. I came in a first-class six-cylinder Daimler, which is now lying a wreck in a meadow a mile up the road. We've got to foot it.'

'We can't do it. It would take too long. Besides, there's the frontier to pass.'

I remembered ruefully that I might have got a return passport from the Portuguese Jew, if I had thought of anything at the time beyond getting to Santa Chiara.

'Then we must make a circuit by the hillside and dodge the guards. It's no use making difficulties, Wake. We're fairly up against it, but we've got to go on trying till we drop. Otherwise I'll take your advice and go mad.'

'And supposing you get back to St Anton, you'll find the house shut up and the travellers gone hours before by the Underground Railway.'

'Very likely. But, man, there's always the glimmering of a chance. It's no good chucking in your hand till the game's out.'

'Drop your proverbial philosophy, Mr Martin Tupper, and look up there.'

He had one foot on the wall and was staring at a cleft in the snow-line across the valley. The shoulder of a high peak dropped sharply to a kind of nick and rose again in a long graceful curve of snow. All below the nick was still in deep shadow, but from the configuration of the slopes I judged that a tributary glacier ran from it to the main glacier at the river head.

'That's the Colle delle Rondini,' he said, 'the Col of the Swallows. It leads straight to the Staubthal near Grunewald. On a good day I have done it in seven hours, but it's not a pass for winter-time. It has been done of course, but not often.... Yet, if the weather held, it might go even now, and that would bring us to St Anton by the evening. I wonder'—and he looked me over with an appraising eye—'I wonder if you're up to it.'

My stiffness had gone and I burned to set my restlessness to physical toil.

'If you can do it, I can,' I said.

'No. There you're wrong. You're a hefty fellow, but you're no mountaineer, and the ice of the Colle delle Rondini needs knowledge. It would be insane to risk it with a novice, if there were any other way. But I'm damned if I see any, and I'm going to chance it. We can get a rope and axes in the inn. Are you game?'

'Right you are. Seven hours, you say. We've got to do it in six.'

'You will be humbler when you get on the ice,' he said grimly. 'We'd better breakfast, for the Lord knows when we shall see food again.'

We left the inn at five minutes to nine, with the sky cloudless and a stiff wind from the north-west, which we felt even in the deep-cut valley. Wake walked with a long, slow stride that tried my patience. I wanted to hustle, but he bade me keep in step. 'You take your orders from me, for I've been at this job before. Discipline in the ranks, remember.'

We crossed the river gorge by a plank bridge, and worked our way up the right bank, past the moraine, to the snout of the glacier. It was bad going, for the snow concealed the boulders, and I often floundered in holes. Wake never relaxed his stride, but now and then he stopped to sniff the air.

I observed that the weather looked good, and he differed. 'It's too clear. There'll be a full-blown gale on the Col and most likely snow in the afternoon.' He pointed to a fat yellow cloud that was beginning to bulge over the nearest peak. After that I thought he lengthened his stride.

'Lucky I had these boots resoled and nailed at Chiavagno,' was the only other remark he made till we had passed the seracs of the main glacier and turned up the lesser ice-stream from the Colle delle Rondini.

By half-past ten we were near its head, and I could see clearly the ribbon of pure ice between black crags too steep for snow to lie on, which was the means of ascent to the Col. The sky had clouded over, and ugly streamers floated on the high slopes. We tied on the rope at the foot of the bergschrund, which was easy to pass because of the winter's snow. Wake led, of course, and presently we came on to the icefall.

In my time I had done a lot of scrambling on rocks and used to promise myself a season in the Alps to test myself on the big peaks. If I ever go it will be to climb the honest rock towers around Chamonix, for I won't have anything to do with snow mountains. That day on the Colle delle Rondini fairly sickened me of ice. I daresay I might have liked it if I had done it in a holiday mood, at leisure and in good spirits. But to crawl up that couloir with a sick heart and a desperate impulse to hurry was the worst sort of nightmare. The place was as steep as a wall of smooth black ice that seemed hard as granite. Wake did the step-cutting, and I admired him enormously. He did not seem to use much force, but every step was hewn cleanly the right size, and they were spaced the right distance. In this job he was the true professional. I was thankful Blenkiron was not with us, for the thing would have given a squirrel vertigo. The chips of ice slithered between my legs and I could watch them till they brought up just above the bergschrund.

The ice was in shadow and it was bitterly cold. As we crawled up I had not the exercise of using the axe to warm me, and I got very numb standing on one leg waiting for the next step. Worse still, my legs began to cramp. I was in good condition, but that time under Ivery's rack had played the mischief with my limbs. Muscles got out of place in my calves and stood in aching lumps, till I almost squealed with the pain of it. I was mortally afraid I should slip, and every time I moved I called out to Wake to warn him. He saw what was happening and got the pick of his axe fixed in the ice before I was allowed to stir. He spoke often to cheer me up, and his voice had none of its harshness. He was like some ill-tempered generals I have known, very gentle in a battle.

At the end the snow began to fall, a soft powder like the overspill of a storm raging beyond the crest. It was just after that that Wake cried out that in five minutes we would be at the summit. He consulted his wrist-watch. 'Jolly good time, too. Only twenty-five minutes behind my best. It's not one o'clock.'

The next I knew I was lying flat on a pad of snow easing my cramped legs, while Wake shouted in my ear that we were in for something bad. I was aware of a driving blizzard, but I had no thought of anything but the blessed relief from pain. I lay for some minutes on my back with my legs stiff in the air and the toes turned inwards, while my muscles fell into their proper place.

It was certainly no spot to linger in. We looked down into a trough of driving mist, which sometimes swirled aside and showed a knuckle of black rock far below. We ate some chocolate, while Wake shouted in my ear that now we had less step-cutting. He did his best to cheer me, but he could not hide his anxiety. Our faces were frosted over like a wedding-cake and the sting of the wind was like a whiplash on our eyelids.

The first part was easy, down a slope of firm snow where steps were not needed. Then came ice again, and we had to cut into it below the fresh surface snow. This was so laborious that Wake took to the rocks on the right side of the couloir, where there was some shelter from the main force of the blast. I found it easier, for I knew something about rocks, but it was difficult enough with every handhold and foothold glazed. Presently we were driven back again to the ice, and painfully cut our way through a throat of the ravine where the sides narrowed. There the wind was terrible, for the narrows made a kind of funnel, and we descended, plastered against the wall, and scarcely able to breathe, while the tornado plucked at our bodies as if it would whisk us like wisps of grass into the abyss.

After that the gorge widened and we had an easier slope, till suddenly we found ourselves perched on a great tongue of rock round which the snow blew like the froth in a whirlpool. As we stopped for breath, Wake shouted in my ear that this was the Black Stone.

'The what?' I yelled.

'The Schwarzstein. The Swiss call the pass the Schwarzsteinthor. You can see it from Grunewald.'

I suppose every man has a tinge of superstition in him. To hear that name in that ferocious place gave me a sudden access of confidence. I seemed to see all my doings as part of a great predestined plan. Surely it was not for nothing that the word which had been the key of my first adventure in the long tussle should appear in this last phase. I felt new strength in my legs and more vigour in my lungs. 'A good omen,' I shouted. 'Wake, old man, we're going to win out.'

'The worst is still to come,' he said.

He was right. To get down that tongue of rock to the lower snows of the couloir was a job that fairly brought us to the end of our tether. I can feel yet the sour, bleak smell of wet rock and ice and the hard nerve pain that racked my forehead. The Kaffirs used to say that there were devils in the high berg, and this place was assuredly given over to the powers of the air who had no thought of human life. I seemed to be in the world which had endured from the eternity before man was dreamed of. There was no mercy in it, and the elements were pitting their immortal strength against two pigmies who had profaned their sanctuary. I yearned for warmth, for the glow of a fire, for a tree or blade of grass or anything which meant the sheltered homeliness of mortality. I knew then what the Greeks meant by panic, for I was scared by the apathy of nature. But the terror gave me a kind of comfort, too. Ivery and his doings seemed less formidable. Let me but get out of this cold hell and I could meet him with a new confidence.

Wake led, for he knew the road and the road wanted knowing. Otherwise he should have been last on the rope, for that is the place of the better man in a descent. I had some horrible moments following on when the rope grew taut, for I had no help from it. We zigzagged down the rock, sometimes driven to the ice of the adjacent couloirs, sometimes on the outer ridge of the Black Stone, sometimes wriggling down little cracks and over evil boiler-plates. The snow did not lie on it, but the rock crackled with thin ice or oozed ice water. Often it was only by the grace of God that I did not fall headlong, and pull Wake out of his hold to the bergschrund far below. I slipped more than once, but always by a miracle recovered myself. To make things worse, Wake was tiring. I could feel him drag on the rope, and his movements had not the precision they had had in the morning. He was the mountaineer, and I the novice. If he gave out, we should never reach the valley.

The fellow was clear grit all through. When we reached the foot of the tooth and sat huddled up with our faces away from the wind, I saw that he was on the edge of fainting. What that effort must have cost him in the way of resolution you may guess, but he did not fail till the worst was past. His lips were colourless, and he was choking with the nausea of fatigue. I found a flask of brandy in his pocket, and a mouthful revived him.

'I'm all out,' he said. 'The road's easier now, and I can direct YOU about the rest ... You'd better leave me. I'll only be a drag. I'll come on when I feel better.'

'No, you don't, you old fool. You've got me over that infernal iceberg, and I'm going to see you home.'

I rubbed his arms and legs and made him swallow some chocolate. But when he got on his feet he was as doddery as an old man. Happily we had an easy course down a snow gradient, which we glissaded in very unorthodox style. The swift motion freshened him up a little, and he was able to put on the brake with his axe to prevent us cascading into the bergschrund. We crossed it by a snow bridge, and started out on the seracs of the Schwarzstein glacier.

I am no mountaineer—not of the snow and ice kind, anyway—but I have a big share of physical strength and I wanted it all now. For those seracs were an invention of the devil. To traverse that labyrinth in a blinding snowstorm, with a fainting companion who was too weak to jump the narrowest crevasse, and who hung on the rope like lead when there was occasion to use it, was more than I could manage. Besides, every step that brought us nearer to the valley now increased my eagerness to hurry, and wandering in that maze of clotted ice was like the nightmare when you stand on the rails with the express coming and are too weak to climb on the platform. As soon as possible I left the glacier for the hillside, and though that was laborious enough in all conscience, yet it enabled me to steer a straight course. Wake never spoke a word. When I looked at him his face was ashen under a gale which should have made his cheeks glow, and he kept his eyes half closed. He was staggering on at the very limits of his endurance ...

By and by we were on the moraine, and after splashing through a dozen little glacier streams came on a track which led up the hillside. Wake nodded feebly when I asked if this was right. Then to my joy I saw a gnarled pine.

I untied the rope and Wake dropped like a log on the ground. 'Leave me,' he groaned. 'I'm fairly done. I'll come on later.' And he shut his eyes.

My watch told me that it was after five o'clock.

'Get on my back,' I said. 'I won't part from you till I've found a cottage. You're a hero. You've brought me over those damned mountains in a blizzard, and that's what no other man in England would have done. Get up.'

He obeyed, for he was too far gone to argue. I tied his wrists together with a handkerchief below my chin, for I wanted my arms to hold up his legs. The rope and axes I left in a cache beneath the pine-tree. Then I started trotting down the track for the nearest dwelling.

My strength felt inexhaustible and the quicksilver in my bones drove me forward. The snow was still falling, but the wind was dying down, and after the inferno of the pass it was like summer. The road wound over the shale of the hillside and then into what in spring must have been upland meadows. Then it ran among trees, and far below me on the right I could hear the glacier river churning in its gorge. Soon little empty huts appeared, and rough enclosed paddocks, and presently I came out on a shelf above the stream and smelt the wood-smoke of a human habitation.

I found a middle-aged peasant in the cottage, a guide by profession in summer and a woodcutter in winter.

'I have brought my Herr from Santa Chiara,' I said, 'over the Schwarzsteinthor. He is very weary and must sleep.'

I decanted Wake into a chair, and his head nodded on his chest. But his colour was better.

'You and your Herr are fools,' said the man gruffly, but not unkindly. 'He must sleep or he will have a fever. The Schwarzsteinthor in this devil's weather! Is he English?'

'Yes,' I said, 'like all madmen. But he's a good Herr, and a brave mountaineer.'

We stripped Wake of his Red Cross uniform, now a collection of sopping rags, and got him between blankets with a huge earthenware bottle of hot water at his feet. The woodcutter's wife boiled milk, and this, with a little brandy added, we made him drink. I was quite easy in my mind about him, for I had seen this condition before. In the morning he would be as stiff as a poker, but recovered.

'Now I'm off for St Anton,' I said. 'I must get there tonight.'

'You are the hardy one,' the man laughed. 'I will show you the quick road to Grunewald, where is the railway. With good fortune you may get the last train.'

I gave him fifty francs on my Herr's behalf, learned his directions for the road, and set off after a draught of goat's milk, munching my last slab of chocolate. I was still strung up to a mechanical activity, and I ran every inch of the three miles to the Staubthal without consciousness of fatigue. I was twenty minutes too soon for the train, and, as I sat on a bench on the platform, my energy suddenly ebbed away. That is what happens after a great exertion. I longed to sleep, and when the train arrived I crawled into a carriage like a man with a stroke. There seemed to be no force left in my limbs. I realized that I was leg-weary, which is a thing you see sometimes with horses, but not often with men.

All the journey I lay like a log in a kind of coma, and it was with difficulty that I recognized my destination, and stumbled out of the train. But I had no sooner emerged from the station of St Anton than I got my second wind. Much snow had fallen since yesterday, but it had stopped now, the sky was clear, and the moon was riding. The sight of the familiar place brought back all my anxieties. The day on the Col of the Swallows was wiped out of my memory, and I saw only the inn at Santa Chiara, and heard Wake's hoarse voice speaking of

Mary. The lights were twinkling from the village below, and on the right I saw the clump of trees which held the Pink Chalet.

I took a short cut across the fields, avoiding the little town. I ran hard, stumbling often, for though I had got my mental energy back my legs were still precarious. The station clock had told me that it was nearly half-past nine.

Soon I was on the high-road, and then at the Chalet gates. I heard as in a dream what seemed to be three shrill blasts on a whistle. Then a big car passed me, making for St Anton. For a second I would have hailed it, but it was past me and away. But I had a conviction that my business lay in the house, for I thought Ivery was there, and Ivery was what mattered.

I marched up the drive with no sort of plan in my head, only a blind rushing on fate. I remembered dimly that I had still three cartridges in my revolver.

The front door stood open and I entered and tiptoed down the passage to the room where I had found the Portuguese Jew. No one hindered me, but it was not for lack of servants. I had the impression that there were people near me in the darkness, and I thought I heard German softly spoken. There was someone ahead of me, perhaps the speaker, for I could hear careful footsteps. It was very dark, but a ray of light came from below the door of the room. Then behind me I heard the hall door clang, and the noise of a key turned in its lock. I had walked straight into a trap and all retreat was cut off.

My mind was beginning to work more clearly, though my purpose was still vague. I wanted to get at Ivery and I believed that he was somewhere in front of me. And then I thought of the door which led from the chamber where I had been imprisoned. If I could enter that way I would have the advantage of surprise.

I groped on the right-hand side of the passage and found a handle. It opened upon what seemed to be a dining-room, for there was a faint smell of food. Again I had the impression of people near, who for some unknown reason did not molest me. At the far end I found another door, which led to a second room, which I guessed to be adjacent to the library. Beyond it again must lie the passage from the chamber with the rack. The whole place was as quiet as a shell.

I had guessed right. I was standing in the passage where I had stood the night before. In front of me was the library, and there was the same chink of light showing. Very softly I turned the handle and opened it a crack ...

The first thing that caught my eye was the profile of Ivery. He was looking towards the writing-table, where someone was sitting.

CHAPTER EIGHTEEN

The Underground Railway

This is the story which I heard later from Mary ...

She was at Milan with the new Anglo-American hospital when she got Blenkiron's letter. Santa Chiara had always been the place agreed upon, and this message mentioned specifically Santa Chiara, and fixed a date for her presence there. She was a little puzzled by it, for she had not yet had a word from Ivery, to whom she had written twice by the roundabout address in France which Bommaerts had given her. She did not believe that he would come to Italy in the ordinary course of things, and she wondered at Blenkiron's certainty about the date.

The following morning came a letter from Ivery in which he ardently pressed for a meeting. It was the first of several, full of strange talk about some approaching crisis, in which the forebodings of the prophet were mingled with the solicitude of a lover.

'The storm is about to break,' he wrote, 'and I cannot think only of my own fate. I have something to tell you which vitally concerns yourself. You say you are in Lombardy. The Chiavagno valley is within easy reach, and at its head is the inn of Santa Chiara, to which I come on the morning of March 19th. Meet me there even if only for half an hour, I implore you. We have already shared hopes and confidences, and I would now share with you a knowledge which I alone in Europe possess. You have the heart of a lion, my lady, worthy of what I can bring you.'

Wake was summoned from the *Croce Rossa* unit with which he was working at Vicenza, and the plan arranged by Blenkiron was faithfully carried out. Four officers of the Alpini, in the rough dress of peasants of the hills, met them in Chiavagno on the morning of the 18th. It was arranged that the hostess of Santa Chiara should go on a visit to her sister's son, leaving the inn, now in the shuttered quiet of wintertime, under the charge of two ancient servants. The hour of Ivery's coming on the 19th had been fixed by him for noon, and that morning Mary would drive up the valley, while Wake and the Alpini went inconspicuously by other routes so as to be in station around the place before midday.

But on the evening of the 18th at the Hotel of the Four Kings in Chiavagno Mary received another message. It was from me and told her that I was crossing the Staub at midnight and would be at the inn before dawn. It begged her to meet me there, to meet me alone without the others, because I had that to say to her which must be said before Ivery's coming. I have seen the letter. It was written in a hand which I could not have distinguished from my own scrawl. It was not exactly what I would myself have written, but there were phrases in it which to Mary's mind could have come only from me. Oh, I admit it was cunningly done, especially the love-making, which was just the kind of stammering thing which I would have achieved if I had tried to put my feelings on paper. Anyhow, Mary had no doubt of its genuineness. She slipped off after dinner, hired a carriage with two broken-winded screws and set off up the valley. She left a line for Wake telling him to follow according to the plan—a line which he never got, for his anxiety when he found she had gone drove him to immediate pursuit.

At about two in the morning of the 19th after a slow and icy journey she arrived at the inn, knocked up the aged servants, made herself a cup of chocolate out of her tea-basket and sat down to wait on my coming.

She has described to me that time of waiting. A home-made candle in a tall earthenware candlestick lit up the little *salle-a-manger*, which was the one room in use. The world was very quiet, the snow muffled the roads, and it was cold with the penetrating chill of the small hours of a March night. Always, she has told me, will the taste of chocolate and the smell of burning tallow bring back to her that strange place and the flutter of the heart with which she waited. For she was on the eve of the crisis of all our labours, she was very young, and youth has a quick fancy which will not be checked. Moreover, it was I who was coming, and save for the scrawl of the night before, we had had no communication for many weeks ... She tried to distract her mind by repeating poetry, and the thing that came into her head was Keats's 'Nightingale', an odd poem for the time and place.

There was a long wicker chair among the furnishings of the room, and she lay down on it with her fur cloak muffled around her. There were sounds of movement in the inn. The old woman who had let her in, with the scent of intrigue of her kind, had brightened when she heard that another guest was coming. Beautiful women do not travel at midnight for nothing. She also was awake and expectant.

Then quite suddenly came the sound of a car slowing down outside. She sprang to her feet in a tremor of excitement. It was like the Picardy chateau again—the dim room and a friend coming out of the night. She heard the front door open and a step in the little hall ...

She was looking at Ivery.... He slipped his driving-coat off as he entered, and bowed gravely. He was wearing a green hunting suit which in the dusk seemed like khaki, and, as he was about my own height, for a second she was misled. Then she saw his face and her heart stopped.

'You!' she cried. She had sunk back again on the wicker chair.

'I have come as I promised,' he said, 'but a little earlier. You will forgive me my eagerness to be with you.'

She did not heed his words, for her mind was feverishly busy. My letter had been a fraud and this man had discovered our plans. She was alone with him, for it would be hours before her friends came from Chiavagno. He had the game in his hands, and of all our confederacy she alone remained to confront him. Mary's courage was pretty near perfect, and for the moment she did not think of herself or her own fate. That came later. She was possessed with poignant disappointment at our failure. All our efforts had gone to the winds, and the enemy had won with contemptuous ease. Her nervousness disappeared before the intense regret, and her brain set coolly and busily to work.

It was a new Ivery who confronted her, a man with vigour and purpose in every line of him and the quiet confidence of power. He spoke with a serious courtesy.

'The time for make-believe is past,' he was saying. 'We have fenced with each other. I have told you only half the truth, and you have always kept me at arm's length. But you knew in your heart, my dearest lady, that there must be the full truth between us some day, and that day has come. I have often told you that I love you. I do not come now to repeat that declaration. I come to ask you to entrust yourself to me, to join your fate to mine, for I can promise you the happiness which you deserve.'

He pulled up a chair and sat beside her. I cannot put down all that he said, for Mary, once she grasped the drift of it, was busy with her own thoughts and did not listen. But I gather from her that he was very candid and seemed to grow as he spoke in mental and moral stature.

He told her who he was and what his work had been. He claimed the same purpose as hers, a hatred of war and a passion to rebuild the world into decency. But now he drew a different moral. He was a German: it was through Germany alone that peace and regeneration could come. His country was purged from her faults, and the marvellous German discipline was about to prove itself in the eye of gods and men. He told her what he had told me in the room at the Pink Chalet, but with another colouring. Germany was not vengeful or vainglorious, only patient and merciful. God was about to give her the power to decide the world's fate, and it was for him and his kind to see that the decision was beneficent. The greater task of his people was only now beginning.

That was the gist of his talk. She appeared to listen, but her mind was far away. She must delay him for two hours, three hours, four hours. If not, she must keep beside him. She was the only one of our company left in touch with the enemy ...

'I go to Germany now,' he was saying. 'I want you to come with me—to be my wife.'

He waited for an answer, and got it in the form of a startled question.

'To Germany? How?'

'It is easy,' he said, smiling. 'The car which is waiting outside is the first stage of a system of travel which we have perfected.' Then he told her about the Underground Railway—not as he had told it to me, to scare, but as a proof of power and forethought.

His manner was perfect. He was respectful, devoted, thoughtful of all things. He was the suppliant, not the master. He offered her power and pride, a dazzling career, for he had deserved well of his country, the devotion of the faithful lover. He would take her to his mother's house, where she would be welcomed like a princess. I have no doubt he was sincere, for he had many moods, and the libertine whom he had revealed to me at the Pink Chalet had given place to the honourable gentleman. He could play all parts well because he could believe in himself in them all.

Then he spoke of danger, not so as to slight her courage, but to emphasize his own thoughtfulness. The world in which she had lived was crumbling, and he alone could offer a refuge. She felt the steel gauntlet through the texture of the velvet glove.

All the while she had been furiously thinking, with her chin in her hand in the old way ... She might refuse to go. He could compel her, no doubt, for there was no help to be got from the old servants. But it might be difficult to carry an unwilling woman over the first stages of the Underground Railway. There might be chances ... Supposing he accepted her refusal and left her. Then indeed he would be gone for ever and our game would have closed with a fiasco. The great antagonist of

England would go home rejoicing, taking his sheaves with him.

At this time she had no personal fear of him. So curious a thing is the human heart that her main preoccupation was with our mission, not with her own fate. To fail utterly seemed too bitter. Supposing she went with him. They had still to get out of Italy and cross Switzerland. If she were with him she would be an emissary of the Allies in the enemy's camp. She asked herself what could she do, and told herself 'Nothing.' She felt like a small bird in a very large trap, and her chief sensation was that of her own powerlessness. But she had learned Blenkiron's gospel and knew that Heaven sends amazing chances to the bold. And, even as she made her decision, she was aware of a dark shadow lurking at the back of her mind, the shadow of the fear which she knew was awaiting her. For she was going into the unknown with a man whom she hated, a man who claimed to be her lover.

It was the bravest thing I have ever heard of, and I have lived my life among brave men.

'I will come with you,' she said. 'But you mustn't speak to me, please. I am tired and troubled and I want peace to think.'

As she rose weakness came over her and she swayed till his arm caught her. 'I wish I could let you rest for a little,' he said tenderly, 'but time presses. The car runs smoothly and you can sleep there.'

He summoned one of the servants to whom he handed Mary. 'We leave in ten minutes,' he said, and he went out to see to the car.

Mary's first act in the bedroom to which she was taken was to bathe her eyes and brush her hair. She felt dimly that she must keep her head clear. Her second was to scribble a note to Wake, telling him what had happened, and to give it to the servant with a tip.

'The gentleman will come in the morning,' she said. 'You must give it him at once, for it concerns the fate of your country.' The woman grinned and promised. It was not the first time she had done errands for pretty ladies.

Ivery settled her in the great closed car with much solicitude, and made her comfortable with rugs. Then he went back to the inn for a second, and she saw a light move in the *salle-a-manger*. He returned and spoke to the driver in German, taking his seat beside him.

But first he handed Mary her note to Wake. 'I think you left this behind you,' he said. He had not opened it.

Alone in the car Mary slept. She saw the figures of Ivery and the chauffeur in the front seat dark against the headlights, and then they dislimned into dreams. She had undergone a greater strain than she knew, and was sunk in the heavy sleep of weary nerves.

When she woke it was daylight. They were still in Italy, as her first glance told her, so they could not have taken the Staub route. They seemed to be among the foothills, for there was little snow, but now and then up tributary valleys she had glimpses of the high peaks. She tried hard to think what it could mean, and then remembered the Marjolana. Wake had laboured to instruct her in the topography of the Alps, and she had grasped the fact of the two open passes. But the Marjolana meant a big circuit, and they would not be in Switzerland till the evening. They would arrive in the dark, and pass out of it in the dark, and there would be no chance of succour. She felt very lonely and very weak.

Throughout the morning her fear grew. The more hopeless her chance of defeating Ivery became the more insistently the dark shadow crept over her mind. She tried to steady herself by watching the show from the windows. The car swung through little villages, past vineyards and pine-woods and the blue of lakes, and over the gorges of mountain streams. There seemed to be no trouble about passports. The sentries at the controls waved a reassuring hand when they were shown some card which the chauffeur held between his teeth. In one place there was a longish halt, and she could hear Ivery talking Italian with two officers of Bersaglieri, to whom he gave cigars. They were fresh-faced, upstanding boys, and for a second she had an idea of flinging open the door and appealing to them to save her. But that would have been futile, for Ivery was clearly amply certificated. She wondered what part he was now playing.

The Marjolana route had been chosen for a purpose. In one town Ivery met and talked to a civilian official, and more than once the car slowed down and someone appeared from the wayside to speak a word and vanish. She was assisting at the last gathering up of the threads of a great plan, before the Wild Birds returned to their nest. Mostly these conferences seemed to be in Italian, but once or twice she gathered from the movement of the lips that German was spoken and that this rough peasant or that black-hatted bourgeois was not of Italian blood.

Early in the morning, soon after she awoke, Ivery had stopped the car and offered her a well-provided luncheon basket. She could eat nothing, and watched him breakfast off sandwiches beside the driver. In the afternoon he asked her permission to sit with her. The car drew up in a lonely place, and a tea-basket was produced by the chauffeur. Ivery made tea, for she seemed too listless to move, and she drank a cup with him. After that he remained beside her.

'In half an hour we shall be out of Italy,' he said. The car was running up a long valley to the curious hollow between snowy saddles which is the crest of the Marjolana. He showed her the place on a road map. As the altitude increased and the air grew colder he wrapped the rugs closer around her and apologized for the absence of a foot-warmer. 'In a little,' he said, 'we shall be in the land where your slightest wish will be law.'

She dozed again and so missed the frontier post. When she woke the car was slipping down the long curves of the Weiss valley, before it narrows to the gorge through which it debouches on Grunewald.

'We are in Switzerland now,' she heard his voice say. It may have been fancy, but it seemed to her that there was a new note in it. He spoke to her with the assurance of possession. They were outside the country of the Allies, and in a land where his web was thickly spread.

'Where do we stop tonight?' she asked timidly.

'I fear we cannot stop. Tonight also you must put up with the car. I have a little errand to do on the way, which will delay us a few minutes, and then we press on. Tomorrow, my fairest one, fatigue will be ended.'

There was no mistake now about the note of possession in his voice. Mary's heart began to beat fast and wild. The trap had closed down on her and she saw the folly of her courage. It had delivered her bound and gagged into the hands of one whom she loathed more deeply every moment, whose proximity was less welcome than a snake's. She had to bite hard on her lip to keep from screaming.

The weather had changed and it was snowing hard, the same storm that had greeted us on the Col of the Swallows. The pace was slower now, and Ivery grew restless. He looked frequently at his watch, and snatched the speaking-tube to talk to the driver. Mary caught the word 'St Anton'.

'Do we go by St Anton?' she found voice to ask.

'Yes,' he said shortly.

The word gave her the faintest glimmering of hope, for she knew that Peter and I had lived at St Anton. She tried to look out of the blurred window, but could see nothing except that the twilight was falling. She begged for the road-map, and saw that so far as she could make out they were still in the broad Grunewald valley and that to reach St Anton they had to cross the low pass from the Staubthal. The snow was still drifting thick and the car crawled.

Then she felt the rise as they mounted to the pass. Here the going was bad, very different from the dry frost in which I had covered the same road the night before. Moreover, there seemed to be curious obstacles. Some careless wood-cart had dropped logs on the highway, and more than once both Ivery and the chauffeur had to get out to shift them. In one place there had been a small landslide which left little room to pass, and Mary had to descend and cross on foot while the driver took the car over alone. Ivery's temper seemed to be souring. To the girl's relief he resumed the outside seat, where he was engaged in constant argument with the chauffeur.

At the head of the pass stands an inn, the comfortable hostelry of Herr Kronig, well known to all who clamber among the lesser peaks of the Staubthal. There in the middle of the way stood a man with a lantern.

'The road is blocked by a snowfall,' he cried. 'They are clearing it now. It will be ready in half an hour's time.'

Ivery sprang from his seat and darted into the hotel. His business was to speed up the clearing party, and Herr Kronig himself accompanied him to the scene of the catastrophe. Mary sat still, for she had suddenly become possessed of an idea. She drove it from her as foolishness, but it kept returning. Why had those tree-trunks been spilt on the road? Why had an easy pass after a moderate snowfall been suddenly closed?

A man came out of the inn-yard and spoke to the chauffeur. It seemed to be an offer of refreshment, for the latter left his seat and disappeared inside. He was away for some time and returned shivering and grumbling at the weather, with the collar of his greatcoat turned up around his ears. A lantern had been hung in the porch and as he passed Mary saw the man. She had been watching the back of his head idly during the long drive, and had observed that it was of the round bullet type, with no nape to the neck, which is common in the Fatherland. Now she could not see his neck for the coat collar, but she could have sworn that the head was a different shape. The man seemed to suffer acutely from the cold, for he buttoned the collar round his chin and pulled his cap far over his brows.

Ivery came back, followed by a dragging line of men with spades and lanterns. He flung himself into the front seat and nodded to the driver to start. The man had his engine going already so as to lose no time. He bumped over the rough debris of the snowfall and then fairly let the car hum. Ivery was anxious for speed, but he did not want his neck broken and he yelled out to take care. The driver nodded and slowed down, but presently he had got up speed again.

If Ivery was restless, Mary was worse. She seemed suddenly to have come on the traces of her friends. In the St Anton valley the snow had stopped and she let down the window for air, for she was choking with suspense. The car rushed past the station, down the hill by Peter's cottage, through the village, and along the lake shore to the Pink Chalet.

Ivery halted it at the gate. 'See that you fill up with petrol,' he told the man. 'Bid Gustav get the Daimler and be ready to follow in half in hour.'

He spoke to Mary through the open window.

'I will keep you only a very little time. I think you had better wait in the car, for it will be more comfortable than a dismantled house. A servant will bring you food and more rugs for the night journey.'

Then he vanished up the dark avenue.

Mary's first thought was to slip out and get back to the village and there to find someone who knew me or could take her where Peter lived. But the driver would prevent her, for he had been left behind on guard. She looked anxiously at his back, for he alone stood between her and liberty.

That gentleman seemed to be intent on his own business. As soon as Ivery's footsteps had grown faint, he had backed the car into the entrance, and turned it so that it faced towards St Anton. Then very slowly it began to move.

At the same moment a whistle was blown shrilly three times. The door on the right had opened and someone who had been waiting in the shadows climbed painfully in. Mary saw that it was a little man and that he was a cripple. She reached a hand to help him, and he fell on to the cushions beside her. The car was gathering speed.

Before she realized what was happening the newcomer had taken her hand and was patting it.

About two minutes later I was entering the gate of the Pink Chalet.

CHAPTER NINETEEN

The Cage of the Wild Birds

'Why, Mr Ivery, come right in,' said the voice at the table. There was a screen before me, stretching from the fireplace to keep off the draught from the door by which I had entered. It stood higher than my head but there were cracks in it through which I could watch the room. I found a little table on which I could lean my back, for I was dropping with fatigue.

Blenkiron sat at the writing-table and in front of him were little rows of Patience cards. Wood ashes still smouldered in the stove, and a lamp stood at his right elbow which lit up the two figures. The bookshelves and the cabinets were in twilight.

'I've been hoping to see you for quite a time.' Blenkiron was busy arranging the little heaps of cards, and his face was wreathed in hospitable smiles. I remember wondering why he should play the host to the true master of the house.

Ivery stood erect before him. He was rather a splendid figure now that he had sloughed all disguises and was on the threshold of his triumph. Even through the fog in which my brain worked it was forced upon me that here was a man born to play a big part. He had a jowl like a Roman king on a coin, and scornful eyes that were used to mastery. He was younger than me, confound him, and now he looked it.

He kept his eyes on the speaker, while a smile played round his mouth, a very ugly smile.

'So,' he said. 'We have caught the old crow too. I had scarcely hoped for such good fortune, and, to speak the truth, I had not concerned myself much about you. But now we shall add you to the bag. And what a bag of vermin to lay out on the lawn!' He flung back his head and laughed.

'Mr Ivery—' Blenkiron began, but was cut short.

'Drop that name. All that is past, thank God! I am the Graf von Schwabing, an officer of the Imperial Guard. I am not the least of the weapons that Germany has used to break her enemies.'

'You don't say,' drawled Blenkiron, still fiddling with his Patience cards.

The man's moment had come, and he was minded not to miss a jot of his triumph. His figure seemed to expand, his eye kindled, his voice rang with pride. It was melodrama of the best kind and he fairly rolled it round his tongue. I don't think I grudged it him, for I was fingering something in my pocket. He had won all right, but he wouldn't enjoy his victory long, for soon I would shoot him. I had my eye on the very spot above his right ear where I meant to put my bullet ... For I was very clear that to kill him was the only way to protect Mary. I feared the whole seventy millions of Germany less than this man. That was the single idea that remained firm against the immense fatigue that pressed down on me.

'I have little time to waste on you,' said he who had been called Ivery. 'But I will spare a moment to tell you a few truths. Your childish game never had a chance. I played with you in England and I have played with you ever since. You have never made a move but I have quietly countered it. Why, man, you gave me your confidence. The American Mr Donne ...'

'What about Clarence?' asked Blenkiron. His face seemed a study in pure bewilderment.

'I was that interesting journalist.'

'Now to think of that!' said Blenkiron in a sad, gentle voice. 'I thought I was safe with Clarence. Why, he brought me a letter from old Joe Hooper and he knew all the boys down Emporia way.'

Ivery laughed. 'You have never done me justice, I fear; but I think you will do it now. Your gang is helpless in my hands. General Hannay ...' And I wish I could give you a notion of the scorn with which he pronounced the word 'General'.

'Yes—Dick?' said Blenkiron intently.

'He has been my prisoner for twenty-four hours. And the pretty Miss Mary, too. You are all going with me in a little to my own country. You will not guess how. We call it the Underground Railway, and you will have the privilege of studying its working.... I had not troubled much about you, for I had no special dislike of you. You are only a blundering fool, what you call in your country easy fruit.'

'I thank you, Graf,' Blenkiron said solemnly.

'But since you are here you will join the others ... One last word. To beat inepts such as you is nothing. There is a far greater thing. My country has conquered. You and your friends will be dragged at the chariot wheels of a triumph such as Rome never saw. Does that penetrate your thick skull? Germany has won, and in two days the whole round earth will be stricken dumb by her greatness.'

As I watched Blenkiron a grey shadow of hopelessness seemed to settle on his face. His big body drooped in his chair, his eyes fell, and his left hand shuffled limply among his Patience cards. I could not get my mind to work, but I puzzled miserably over his amazing blunders. He had walked blindly into the pit his enemies had dug for him. Peter must have failed to get my message to him, and he knew nothing of last night's work or my mad journey to Italy. We had all bungled, the whole wretched bunch of us, Peter and Blenkiron and myself ... I had a feeling at the back of my head that there was something in it all that I couldn't understand, that the catastrophe could not be quite as simple as it seemed. But I had no power to think, with the insolent figure of Ivery dominating the room ... Thank God I had a bullet waiting for him. That was the one fixed point in the chaos of my mind. For the first time in my life I was resolute on killing one particular man, and the purpose gave me a horrid comfort.

Suddenly Ivery's voice rang out sharp. 'Take your hand out of your pocket. You fool, you are covered from three points in the walls. A movement and my men will make a sieve of you. Others before you have sat in that chair, and I am used to take precautions. Quick. Both hands on the table.'

There was no mistake about Blenkiron's defeat. He was done and out, and I was left with the only card. He leaned wearily on his arms with the palms of his hands spread out.

'I reckon you've gotten a strong hand, Graf,' he said, and his voice was flat with despair.

'I hold a royal flush,' was the answer.

And then suddenly came a change. Blenkiron raised his head, and his sleepy, ruminating eyes looked straight at Ivery.

'I call you,' he said.

I didn't believe my ears. Nor did Ivery.

'The hour for bluff is past,' he said.

'Nevertheless I call you.'

At that moment I felt someone squeeze through the door behind me and take his place at my side. The light was so dim that I saw only a short, square figure, but a familiar voice whispered in my ear. 'It's me—Andra Amos. Man, this is a great ploy. I'm here to see the end o't.'

No prisoner waiting on the finding of the jury, no commander expecting news of a great battle, ever hung in more desperate suspense than I did during the next seconds. I had forgotten my fatigue; my back no longer needed support. I kept my eyes glued to the crack in the screen and my ears drank in greedily every syllable.

Blenkiron was now sitting bolt upright with his chin in his hands. There was no shadow of melancholy in his lean face.

'I say I call you, Herr Graf von Schwabing. I'm going to put you wise about some little things. You don't carry arms, so I needn't warn you against monkeying with a gun. You're right in saying that there are three places in these walls from which you can shoot. Well, for your information I may tell you that there's guns in all three, but they're covering *you* at this moment. So you'd better be good.'

Ivery sprang to attention like a ramrod. 'Karl,' he cried. 'Gustav!'

As if by magic figures stood on either side of him, like warders by a criminal. They were not the sleek German footmen whom I had seen at the Chalet. One I did not recognize. The other was my servant, Geordie Hamilton.

He gave them one glance, looked round like a hunted animal, and then steadied himself. The man had his own kind of courage.

'I've gotten something to say to you,' Blenkiron drawled. 'It's been a tough fight, but I reckon the hot end of the poker is with you. I compliment you on Clarence Donne. You fooled me fine over that business, and it was only by the mercy of God you didn't win out. You see, there was just the one of us who was liable to recognize you whatever way you twisted your face, and that was Dick Hannay. I give you good marks for Clarence ... For the rest, I had you beaten flat.'

He looked steadily at him. 'You don't believe it. Well, I'll give you proof. I've been watching your Underground Railway for quite a time. I've had my men on the job, and I reckon most of the lines are now closed for repairs. All but the trunk line into France. That I'm keeping open, for soon there's going to be some traffic on it.'

At that I saw Ivery's eyelids quiver. For all his self-command he was breaking.

'I admit we cut it mighty fine, along of your fooling me about Clarence. But you struck a bad snag in General Hannay, Graf. Your heart-to-heart talk with him was poor business. You reckoned you had him safe, but that was too big a risk to take with a man like Dick, unless you saw him cold before you left him ... He got away from this place, and early this morning I knew all he knew. After that it was easy. I got the telegram you had sent this morning in the name of Clarence Donne and it made me laugh. Before midday I had this whole outfit under my hand. Your servants have gone by the Underground Railway—to France. Ehrlich—well, I'm sorry about Ehrlich.'

I knew now the name of the Portuguese Jew.

'He wasn't a bad sort of man,' Blenkiron said regretfully, 'and he was plumb honest. I couldn't get him to listen to reason, and he would play with firearms. So I had to shoot.'

'Dead?' asked Ivery sharply.

'Ye-es. I don't miss, and it was him or me. He's under the ice now—where you wanted to send Dick

Hannay. He wasn't your kind, Graf, and I guess he has some chance of getting into Heaven. If I weren't a hard-shell Presbyterian I'd say a prayer for his soul.'

I looked only at Ivery. His face had gone very pale, and his eyes were wandering. I am certain his brain was working at lightning speed, but he was a rat in a steel trap and the springs held him. If ever I saw a man going through hell it was now. His pasteboard castle had crumbled about his ears and he was giddy with the fall of it. The man was made of pride, and every proud nerve of him was caught on the raw.

'So much for ordinary business,' said Blenkiron. 'There's the matter of a certain lady. You haven't behaved over-nice about her, Graf, but I'm not going to blame you. You maybe heard a whistle blow when you were coming in here? No! Why, it sounded like Gabriel's trump. Peter must have put some lung power into it. Well, that was the signal that Miss Mary was safe in your car ... but in our charge. D'you comprehend?'

He did. The ghost of a flush appeared in his cheeks.

'You ask about General Hannay? I'm not just exactly sure where Dick is at the moment, but I opine he's in Italy.'

I kicked aside the screen, thereby causing Amos almost to fall on his face.

'I'm back,' I said, and pulled up an arm-chair, and dropped into it.

I think the sight of me was the last straw for Ivery. I was a wild enough figure, grey with weariness, soaked, dirty, with the clothes of the porter Joseph Zimmer in rags from the sharp rocks of the Schwarzsteinthor. As his eyes caught mine they wavered, and I saw terror in them. He knew he was in the presence of a mortal enemy.

'Why, Dick,' said Blenkiron with a beaming face, 'this is mighty opportune. How in creation did you get here?'

'I walked,' I said. I did not want to have to speak, for I was too tired. I wanted to watch Ivery's face.

Blenkiron gathered up his Patience cards, slipped them into a little leather case and put it in his pocket.

'I've one thing more to tell you. The Wild Birds have been summoned home, but they won't ever make it. We've gathered them in—Pavia, and Hofgaard, and Conradi. Ehrlich is dead. And you are going to join the rest in our cage.'

As I looked at my friend, his figure seemed to gain in presence. He sat square in his chair with a face like a hanging judge, and his eyes, sleepy no more, held Ivery as in a vice. He had dropped, too, his drawl and the idioms of his ordinary speech, and his voice came out hard and massive like the clash of granite blocks.

'You're at the bar now, Graf von Schwabing. For years you've done your best against the decencies of life. You have deserved well of your country, I don't doubt it. But what has your country deserved of the world? One day soon Germany has to do some heavy paying, and you are the first instalment.'

'I appeal to the Swiss law. I stand on Swiss soil, and I demand that I be surrendered to the Swiss authorities.' Ivery spoke with dry lips and the sweat was on his brow.

'Oh, no, no,' said Blenkiron soothingly. 'The Swiss are a nice people, and I would hate to add to the worries of a poor little neutral state ... All along both sides have been outside the law in this game, and that's going to continue. We've abode by the rules and so must you ... For years you've murdered and kidnapped and seduced the weak and ignorant, but we're not going to judge your morals. We leave that to the Almighty when you get across Jordan. We're going to wash our hands of you as soon as we can. You'll travel to France by the Underground Railway and there be handed over to the French Government. From what I know they've enough against you to shoot you every hour of the day for a twelvemonth.'

I think he had expected to be condemned by us there and then and sent to join Ehrlich beneath the ice.

Anyhow, there came a flicker of hope into his eyes. I daresay he saw some way to dodge the French authorities if he once got a chance to use his miraculous wits. Anyhow, he bowed with something very like self-possession, and asked permission to smoke. As I have said, the man had his own courage.

'Blenkiron,' I cried, 'we're going to do nothing of the kind.'

He inclined his head gravely towards me. 'What's your notion, Dick?'

'We've got to make the punishment fit the crime,' I said. I was so tired that I had to form my sentences laboriously, as if I were speaking a half-understood foreign tongue.

'Meaning?'

'I mean that if you hand him over to the French he'll either twist out of their hands somehow or get decently shot, which is far too good for him. This man and his kind have sent millions of honest folk to their graves. He has sat spinning his web like a great spider and for every thread there has been an ocean of blood spilled. It's his sort that made the war, not the brave, stupid, fighting Boche. It's his sort that's responsible for all the clotted beastliness ... And he's never been in sight of a shell. I'm for putting him in the front line. No, I don't mean any Uriah the Hittite business. I want him to have a sporting chance, just what other men have. But, by God, he's going to learn what is the upshot of the strings he's been pulling so merrily ... He told me in two days' time Germany would smash our armies to hell. He boasted that he would be mostly responsible for it. Well, let him be there to see the smashing.'

'I reckon that's just,' said Blenkiron.

Ivery's eyes were on me now, fascinated and terrified like those of a bird before a rattlesnake. I saw again the shapeless features of the man in the Tube station, the residuum of shrinking mortality behind his disguises. He seemed to be slipping something from his pocket towards his mouth, but Geordie Hamilton caught his wrist.

'Wad ye offer?' said the scandalized voice of my servant. 'Sirr, the prisoner would appear to be trying to puishon hisself. Wull I search him?'

After that he stood with each arm in the grip of a warder.

'Mr Ivery,' I said, 'last night, when I was in your power, you indulged your vanity by gloating over me. I expected it, for your class does not breed gentlemen. We treat our prisoners differently, but it is fair that you should know your fate. You are going into France, and I will see that you are taken to the British front. There with my old division you will learn something of the meaning of war. Understand that by no conceivable chance can you escape. Men will be detailed to watch you day and night and to see that you undergo the full rigour of the battlefield. You will have the same experience as other people, no more, no less. I believe in a righteous God and I know that sooner or later you will find death—death at the hands of your own people—an honourable death which is far beyond your deserts. But before it comes you will have understood the hell to which you have condemned honest men.'

In moments of great fatigue, as in moments of great crisis, the mind takes charge and may run on a track independent of the will. It was not myself that spoke, but an impersonal voice which I did not know, a voice in whose tones rang a strange authority. Ivery recognized the icy finality of it, and his body seemed to wilt, and droop. Only the hold of the warders kept him from falling.

I, too, was about at the end of my endurance. I felt dimly that the room had emptied except for Blenkiron and Amos, and that the former was trying to make me drink brandy from the cup of a flask. I struggled to my feet with the intention of going to Mary, but my legs would not carry me ... I heard as in a dream Amos giving thanks to an Omnipotence in whom he officially disbelieved. 'What's that the auld man in the Bible said? Now let thou thy servant depart in peace. That's the way I'm feelin' mysel'.' And then slumber came on me like an armed man, and in the chair by the dying wood-ash I slept off the ache of my limbs, the tension of my nerves, and the confusion of my brain.

CHAPTER TWENTY

The Storm Breaks in the West

The following evening—it was the 20th day of March—I started for France after the dark fell. I drove Ivery's big closed car, and within sat its owner, bound and gagged, as others had sat before him on the same errand. Geordie Hamilton and Amos were his companions. From what Blenkiron had himself discovered and from the papers seized in the Pink Chalet I had full details of the road and its mysterious stages. It was like the journey of a mad dream. In a back street of a little town I would exchange passwords with a nameless figure and be given instructions. At a wayside inn at an appointed hour a voice speaking a thick German would advise that this bridge or that railway crossing had been cleared. At a hamlet among pine woods an unknown man would clamber up beside me and take me past a sentry-post. Smooth as clockwork was the machine, till in the dawn of a spring morning I found myself dropping into a broad valley through little orchards just beginning to blossom, and I knew that I was in France. After that, Blenkiron's own arrangements began, and soon I was drinking coffee with a young lieutenant of Chasseurs, and had taken the gag from Ivery's mouth. The bluecoats looked curiously at the man in the green ulster whose face was the colour of clay and who lit cigarette from cigarette with a shaky hand.

The lieutenant rang up a General of Division who knew all about us. At his headquarters I explained my purpose, and he telegraphed to an Army Headquarters for a permission which was granted. It was not for nothing that in January I had seen certain great personages in Paris, and that Blenkiron had wired ahead of me to prepare the way. Here I handed over Ivery and his guard, for I wanted them to proceed to Amiens under French supervision, well knowing that the men of that great army are not used to let slip what they once hold.

It was a morning of clear spring sunlight when we breakfasted in that little red-roofed town among vineyards with a shining river looping at our feet. The General of Division was an Algerian veteran with a brush of grizzled hair, whose eye kept wandering to a map on the wall where pins and stretched thread made a spider's web.

'Any news from the north?' I asked.

'Not yet,' he said. 'But the attack comes soon. It will be against our army in Champagne.' With a lean finger he pointed out the enemy dispositions.

'Why not against the British?' I asked. With a knife and fork I made a right angle and put a salt dish in the centre. 'That is the German concentration. They can so mass that we do not know which side of the angle they will strike till the blow falls.'

'It is true,' he replied. 'But consider. For the enemy to attack towards the Somme would be to fight over many miles of an old battle-ground where all is still desert and every yard of which you British know. In Champagne at a bound he might enter unbroken country. It is a long and difficult road to Amiens, but not so long to Chilons. Such is the view of Petain. Does it convince you?'

'The reasoning is good. Nevertheless he will strike at Amiens, and I think he will begin today.'

He laughed and shrugged his shoulders. '*Nous verrons*. You are obstinate, my general, like all your excellent countrymen.'

But as I left his headquarters an aide-de-camp handed him a message on a pink slip. He read it, and turned to me with a grave face.

'You have a flair, my friend. I am glad we did not wager. This morning at dawn there is great fighting around St Quentin. Be comforted, for they will not pass. Your *Marechal* will hold them.'

That was the first news I had of the battle.

At Dijon according to plan I met the others. I only just caught the Paris train, and Blenkiron's great wrists lugged me into the carriage when it was well in motion. There sat Peter, a docile figure in a carefully patched old

R.F.C. uniform. Wake was reading a pile of French papers, and in a corner Mary, with her feet up on the seat, was sound asleep.

We did not talk much, for the life of the past days had been so hectic that we had no wish to recall it. Blenkiron's face wore an air of satisfaction, and as he looked out at the sunny spring landscape he hummed his only tune. Even Wake had lost his restlessness. He had on a pair of big tortoiseshell reading glasses, and when he looked up from his newspaper and caught my eye he smiled. Mary slept like a child, delicately flushed, her breath scarcely stirring the collar of the greatcoat which was folded across her throat. I remember looking with a kind of awe at the curve of her young face and the long lashes that lay so softly on her cheek, and wondering how I had borne the anxiety of the last months. Wake raised his head from his reading, glanced at Mary and then at me, and his eyes were kind, almost affectionate. He seemed to have won peace of mind among the hills.

Only Peter was out of the picture. He was a strange, disconsolate figure, as he shifted about to ease his leg, or gazed incuriously from the window. He had shaved his beard again, but it did not make him younger, for his face was too lined and his eyes too old to change. When I spoke to him he looked towards Mary and held up a warning finger.

'I go back to England,' he whispered. 'Your little *mysie* is going to take care of me till I am settled. We spoke of it yesterday at my cottage. I will find a lodging and be patient till the war is over. And you, Dick?'

'Oh, I rejoin my division. Thank God, this job is over. I have an easy *trund* now and can turn my attention to straight-forward soldiering. I don't mind telling you that I'll be glad to think that you and Mary and Blenkiron are safe at home. What about you, Wake?'

'I go back to my Labour battalion,' he said cheerfully. 'Like you, I have an easier mind.'

I shook my head. 'We'll see about that. I don't like such sinful waste. We've had a bit of campaigning together and I know your quality.'

'The battalion's quite good enough for me,' and he relapsed into a day-old *Temps*.

Mary had suddenly woke, and was sitting upright with her fists in her eyes like a small child. Her hand flew to her hair, and her eyes ran over us as if to see that we were all there. As she counted the four of us she seemed relieved.

'I reckon you feel refreshed, Miss Mary,' said Blenkiron. 'It's good to think that now we can sleep in peace, all of us. Pretty soon you'll be in England and spring will be beginning, and please God it'll be the start of a better world. Our work's over, anyhow.'

'I wonder,' said the girl gravely. 'I don't think there's any discharge in this war. Dick, have you news of the battle? This was the day.'

'It's begun,' I said, and told them the little I had learned from the French General. 'I've made a reputation as a prophet, for he thought the attack was coming in Champagne. It's St Quentin right enough, but I don't know what has happened. We'll hear in Paris.'

Mary had woke with a startled air as if she remembered her old instinct that our work would not be finished without a sacrifice, and that sacrifice the best of us. The notion kept recurring to me with an uneasy insistence. But soon she appeared to forget her anxiety. That afternoon as we journeyed through the pleasant land of France she was in holiday mood, and she forced all our spirits up to her level. It was calm, bright weather, the long curves of ploughland were beginning to quicken into green, the catkins made a blue mist on the willows by the watercourses, and in the orchards by the red-roofed hamlets the blossom was breaking. In such a scene it was hard to keep the mind sober and grey, and the pall of war slid from us. Mary cosseted and fussed over Peter like an elder sister over a delicate little boy. She made him stretch his bad leg full length on the seat, and when she made tea for the party of us it was a protesting Peter who had the last sugar biscuit. Indeed, we were almost a merry company, for Blenkiron told stories of old hunting and engineering days in the West, and Peter and I were driven to cap them, and Mary asked provocative questions, and Wake listened with amused interest. It was well that we had the carriage to ourselves, for no queerer rigs were ever assembled. Mary, as always, was neat and workmanlike in her dress; Blenkiron was magnificent in a suit of russet tweed with a pale-blue shirt and collar, and well-polished brown shoes; but Peter and Wake were in uniforms which had seen far better days, and I wore still the boots and the shapeless and ragged clothes of Joseph Zimmer, the porter from Arosa.

We appeared to forget the war, but we didn't, for it was in the background of all our minds. Somewhere in the north there was raging a desperate fight, and its issue was the true test of our success or failure. Mary showed it by bidding me ask for news at every stopping-place. I asked gendarmes and *Permissionnaires*, but I learned nothing. Nobody had ever heard of the battle. The upshot was that for the last hour we all fell silent, and when we reached Paris about seven o'clock my first errand was to the bookstall.

I bought a batch of evening papers, which we tried to read in the taxis that carried us to our hotel. Sure enough there was the announcement in big headlines. The enemy had attacked in great strength from south of Arras to the Oise; but everywhere he had been repulsed and held in our battle-zone. The leading articles were confident, the notes by the various military critics were almost braggart. At last the German had been driven to an offensive, and the Allies would have the opportunity they had longed for of proving their superior fighting strength. It was, said one and all, the opening of the last phase of the war.

I confess that as I read my heart sank. If the civilians were so over-confident, might not the generals have fallen into the same trap? Blenkiron alone was unperturbed. Mary said nothing, but she sat with her chin in her hands, which with her was a sure sign of deep preoccupation.

Next morning the papers could tell us little more. The main attack had been on both sides of St Quentin, and though the British had given ground it was only the outposts line that had gone. The mist had favoured the enemy, and his bombardment had been terrific, especially the gas shells. Every journal added the old old comment—that he had paid heavily for his temerity, with losses far exceeding those of the defence.

Wake appeared at breakfast in his private's uniform. He wanted to get his railway warrant and be off at once, but when I heard that Amiens was his destination I ordered him to stay and travel with me in the afternoon. I was in uniform myself now and had taken charge of the outfit. I arranged that Blenkiron, Mary, and Peter should go on to Boulogne and sleep the night there, while Wake and I would be dropped at Amiens to await instructions.

I spent a busy morning. Once again I visited with Blenkiron the little cabinet in the Boulevard St Germain, and told in every detail our work of the past two months.

Once again I sat in the low building beside the Invalides and talked to staff officers. But some of the men I had seen on the first visit were not there. The chiefs of the French Army had gone north.

We arranged for the handling of the Wild Birds, now safely in France, and sanction was given to the course I had proposed to adopt with Ivery. He and his guard were on their way to Amiens, and I would meet them there on the morrow. The great men were very complimentary to us, so complimentary that my knowledge of grammatical French ebbed away and I could only stutter in reply. That telegram sent by Blenkiron on the night of the 18th, from the information given me in the Pink Chalet, had done wonders in clearing up the situation.

But when I asked them about the battle they could tell me little. It was a very serious attack in tremendous force, but the British line was strong and the reserves were believed to be sufficient. Petain and Foch had gone north to consult with Haig. The situation in Champagne was still obscure, but some French reserves were already moving thence to the Somme sector. One thing they did show me, the British dispositions. As I looked at the plan I saw that my old division was in the thick of the fighting.

'Where do you go now?' I was asked.

'To Amiens, and then, please God, to the battle front,' I said.

'Good fortune to you. You do not give body or mind much rest, my general.'

After that I went to the *Mission Anglaise*, but they had nothing beyond Haig's communique and a telephone message from G.H.Q. that the critical sector was likely to be that between St Quentin and the Oise. The northern pillar of our defence, south of Arras, which they had been nervous about, had stood like a rock. That pleased me, for my old battalion of the Lennox Highlanders was there.

Crossing the Place de la Concorde, we fell in with a British staff officer of my acquaintance, who was just starting to motor back to G.H.Q. from Paris leave. He had a longer face than the people at the Invalides.

'I don't like it, I tell you,' he said. 'It's this mist that worries me. I went down the whole line from Arras to the Oise ten days ago. It was beautifully sited, the cleverest thing you ever saw. The outpost line was mostly a chain of blobs—redoubts, you know, with machine-guns—so arranged as to bring flanking fire to bear on the advancing enemy. But mist would play the devil with that scheme, for the enemy would be past the place for flanking fire before we knew it... Oh, I know we had good warning, and had the battle-zone manned in time, but the outpost line was meant to hold out long enough to get everything behind in apple-pie order, and I can't see but how big chunks of it must have gone in the first rush.... Mind you, we've banked everything on that battle-zone. It's damned good, but if it's gone—'He flung up his hands.

'Have we good reserves?' I asked.

He shrugged his shoulders.

'Have we positions prepared behind the battle-zone?'

'I didn't notice any,' he said dryly, and was off before I could get more out of him.

'You look rattled, Dick,' said Blenkiron as we walked to the hotel.

'I seem to have got the needle. It's silly, but I feel worse about this show than I've ever felt since the war started. Look at this city here. The papers take it easily, and the people are walking about as if nothing was happening. Even the soldiers aren't worried. You may call me a fool to take it so hard, but I've a sense in my bones that we're in for the bloodiest and darkest fight of our lives, and that soon Paris will be hearing the Boche guns as she did in 1914.'

'You're a cheerful old Jeremiah. Well, I'm glad Miss Mary's going to be in England soon. Seems to me she's right and that this game of ours isn't quite played out yet. I'm envying you some, for there's a place waiting for you in the fighting line.'

'You've got to get home and keep people's heads straight there. That's the weak link in our chain and there's a mighty lot of work before you.'

'Maybe,' he said abstractedly, with his eye on the top of the Vendome column.

The train that afternoon was packed with officers recalled from leave, and it took all the combined purchase of Blenkiron and myself to get a carriage reserved for our little party. At the last moment I opened the door to admit a warm and agitated captain of the R.F.C. in whom I recognized my friend and benefactor, Archie Roylance.

'Just when I was gettin' nice and clean and comfy a wire comes tellin' me to bundle back, all along of a new battle. It's a cruel war, Sir.' The afflicted young man mopped his forehead, grinned cheerfully at Blenkiron, glanced critically at Peter, then caught sight of Mary and grew at once acutely conscious of his appearance. He smoothed his hair, adjusted his tie and became desperately sedate.

I introduced him to Peter and he promptly forgot Mary's existence. If Peter had had any vanity in him it would have been flattered by the frank interest and admiration in the boy's eyes. 'I'm tremendously glad to see you safe back, sir. I've always hoped I might have a chance of meeting you. We want you badly now on the front. Lensch is gettin' a bit uppish.'

Then his eye fell on Peter's withered leg and he saw that he had blundered. He blushed scarlet and looked his apologies. But they weren't needed, for it cheered Peter to meet someone who talked of the possibility of his fighting again. Soon the two were deep in technicalities, the appalling technicalities of the airman. It was no good listening to their talk, for you could make nothing of it, but it was bracing up Peter like wine. Archie gave him a minute description of Lensch's latest doings and his new methods. He, too, had heard the rumour that Peter had mentioned to me at St Anton, of a new Boche plane, with mighty engines and stumpy wings cunningly cambered, which was a devil to climb; but no specimens had yet appeared over the line. They talked of Bali, and Rhys Davids, and Bishop, and McCudden, and all the heroes who had won their spurs since the Somme, and of the new British makes, most of which Peter had never seen and had to have explained to him.

Outside a haze had drawn over the meadows with the twilight. I pointed it out to Blenkiron.

'There's the fog that's doing us. This March weather is just like October, mist morning and evening. I wish to Heaven we could have some good old drenching spring rain.'

Archie was discoursing of the Shark-Gladas machine.

'I've always stuck to it, for it's a marvel in its way, but it has my heart fairly broke. The General here knows its little tricks. Don't you, sir? Whenever things get really excitin', the engine's apt to quit work and take a rest.'

'The whole make should be publicly burned,' I said, with gloomy recollections.

'I wouldn't go so far, sir. The old Gladas has surprisin' merits. On her day there's nothing like her for pace and climbing-power, and she steers as sweet as a racin' cutter. The trouble about her is she's too complicated. She's like some breeds of car—you want to be a mechanical genius to understand her ... If they'd only get her a little simpler and safer, there wouldn't be her match in the field. I'm about the only man that has patience with her and knows her merits, but she's often been nearly the death of me. All the same, if I were in for a big fight against some fellow like Lensch, where it was neck or nothing, I'm hanged if I wouldn't pick the Gladas.'

Archie laughed apologetically. 'The subject is banned for me in our mess. I'm the old thing's only champion, and she's like a mare I used to hunt that loved me so much she was always tryin' to chew the arm off me. But I wish I could get her a fair trial from one of the big pilots. I'm only in the second class myself after all.'

We were running north of St Just when above the rattle of the train rose a curious dull sound. It came from the east, and was like the low growl of a veld thunderstorm, or a steady roll of muffled drums.

'Hark to the guns!' cried Archie. 'My aunt, there's a tidy bombardment goin' on somewhere.'

I had been listening on and off to guns for three years. I had been present at the big preparations before Loos and the Somme and Arras, and I had come to accept the racket of artillery as something natural and inevitable like rain or sunshine. But this sound chilled me with its eeriness, I don't know why. Perhaps it was its unexpectedness, for I was sure that the guns had not been heard in this area since before the Marne. The noise must be travelling down the Oise valley, and I judged there was big fighting somewhere about Chauny or La Fere. That meant that the enemy was pressing hard on a huge front, for here was clearly a great effort on his extreme left wing. Unless it was our counter-attack. But somehow I didn't think so.

I let down the window and stuck my head into the night. The fog had crept to the edge of the track, a gossamer mist through which houses and trees and cattle could be seen dim in the moonlight. The noise continued—not a mutter, but a steady rumbling flow as solid as the blare of a trumpet. Presently, as we drew nearer Amiens, we left it behind us, for in all the Somme valley there is some curious configuration which blankets sound. The countryfolk call it the 'Silent Land', and during the first phase of the Somme battle a man in Amiens could not hear the guns twenty miles off at Albert.

As I sat down again I found that the company had fallen silent, even the garrulous Archie. Mary's eyes met mine, and in the indifferent light of the French railway-carriage I could see excitement in them—I knew it was excitement, not fear. She had never heard the noise of a great barrage before. Blenkiron was restless, and Peter was sunk in his own thoughts. I was growing very depressed, for in a little I would have to part from my best friends and the girl I loved. But with the depression was mixed an odd expectation, which was almost pleasant. The guns had brought back my profession to me, I was moving towards their thunder, and God only knew the end of it. The happy dream I had dreamed of the Cotswolds and a home with Mary beside me seemed suddenly to have fallen away to an infinite distance. I felt once again that I was on the razor-edge of life.

The last part of the journey I was casting back to rake up my knowledge of the countryside. I saw again the stricken belt from Serre to Combles where we had fought in the summer of '17. I had not been present in the advance of the following spring, but I had been at Cambrai and I knew all the down country from Lagnicourt to St Quentin. I shut my eyes and tried to picture it, and to see the roads running up to the line, and wondered just at what points the big pressure had come. They had told me in Paris that the British were as far south as the Oise, so the bombardment we had heard must be directed to our address. With Passchendaele and Cambrai in my mind, and some notion of the difficulties we had always had in getting drafts, I was puzzled to think where we could have found the troops to man the new front. We must be unholily thin on that long line. And against that awesome bombardment! And the masses and the new tactics that Ivery had bragged of!

When we ran into the dingy cavern which is Amiens station I seemed to note a new excitement. I felt it in the air rather than deduced it from any special incident, except that the platform was very crowded with civilians, most of them with an extra amount of baggage. I wondered if the place had been bombed the night before.

'We won't say goodbye yet,' I told the others. 'The train doesn't leave for half an hour. I'm off to try and get news.'

Accompanied by Archie, I hunted out an R.T.O. of my acquaintance. To my questions he responded cheerfully.

'Oh, we're doing famously, sir. I heard this afternoon from a man in Operations that G.H.Q. was perfectly satisfied. We've killed a lot of Huns and only lost a few kilometres of ground ... You're going to your division? Well, it's up Peronne way, or was last night. Cheyne and Dunthorpe came back from leave and tried to steal a car to get up to it ... Oh, I'm having the deuce of a time. These blighted civilians have got the wind up, and a lot are trying to clear out. The idiots say the Huns will be in Amiens in a week. What's the phrase? "*Pourvu que les civils tiennent.*" 'Fraid I must push on, Sir.'

I sent Archie back with these scraps of news and was about to make a rush for the house of one of the Press officers, who would, I thought, be in the way of knowing things, when at the station entrance I ran across Laidlaw. He had been B.G.G.S. in the corps to which my old brigade belonged, and was now on the staff of some army. He was striding towards a car when I grabbed his arm, and he turned on me a very sick face.

'Good Lord, Hannay! Where did you spring from? The news, you say?' He sank his voice, and drew me into a quiet corner. 'The news is hellish.'

'They told me we were holding,' I observed.

'Holding be damned! The Boche is clean through on a broad front. He broke us today at Maissemy and Essigny. Yes, the battle-zone. He's flinging in division after division like the blows of a hammer. What else could you expect?' And he clutched my arm fiercely. 'How in God's name could eleven divisions hold a front of forty miles? And against four to one in numbers? It isn't war, it's naked lunacy.'

I knew the worst now, and it didn't shock me, for I had known it was coming. Laidlaw's nerves were pretty bad, for his face was pale and his eyes bright like a man with a fever.

'Reserves!' and he laughed bitterly. 'We have three infantry divisions and two cavalry. They're into the mill long ago. The French are coming up on our right, but they've the devil of a way to go. That's what I'm down here about. And we're getting help from Horne and Plumer. But all that takes days, and meantime we're walking back like we did at Mons. And at this time of day, too ... Oh, yes, the whole line's retreating. Parts of it were pretty comfortable, but they had to get back or be put in the bag. I wish to Heaven I knew where our right divisions have got to. For all I know they're at Compiegne by now. The Boche was over the canal this morning, and by this time most likely he's across the Somme.'

At that I exclaimed. 'D'you mean to tell me we're going to lose Peronne?'

'Peronne!' he cried. 'We'll be lucky not to lose Amiens! ... And on the top of it all I've got some kind of blasted fever. I'll be raving in an hour.'

He was rushing off, but I held him.

'What about my old lot?' I asked.

'Oh, damned good, but they're shot all to bits. Every division did well. It's a marvel they weren't all scuppered, and it'll be a flaming miracle if they find a line they can stand on. Westwater's got a leg smashed. He was brought down this evening, and you'll find him in the hospital. Fraser's killed and Lefroy's a prisoner—at least, that was my last news. I don't know who's got the brigades, but

Masterton's carrying on with the division ... You'd better get up the line as fast as you can and take over from him. See the Army Commander. He'll be in Amiens tomorrow morning for a pow-wow.'

Laidlaw lay wearily back in his car and disappeared into the night, while I hurried to the train.

The others had descended to the platform and were grouped round Archie, who was discoursing optimistic nonsense. I got them into the carriage and shut the door.

'It's pretty bad,' I said. 'The front's pierced in several places and we're back to the Upper Somme. I'm afraid it isn't going to stop there. I'm off up the line as soon as I can get my orders. Wake, you'll come with me, for every man will be wanted. Blenkiron, you'll see Mary and Peter safe to England. We're just in time, for tomorrow it mightn't be easy to get out of Amiens.'

I can see yet the anxious faces in that ill-lit compartment. We said goodbye after the British style without much to-do. I remember that old Peter gripped my hand as if he would never release it, and that Mary's face had grown very pale. If I delayed another second I should have howled, for Mary's lips were trembling and Peter had eyes like a wounded stag. 'God bless you,' I said hoarsely, and as I went off I heard Peter's voice, a little cracked, saying 'God bless you, my old friend.'

I spent some weary hours looking for Westwater. He was not in the big clearing station, but I ran him to earth at last in the new hospital which had just been got going in the Ursuline convent. He was the most sterling little man, in ordinary life rather dry and dogmatic, with a trick of taking you up sharply which didn't make him popular. Now he was lying very stiff and quiet in the hospital bed, and his blue eyes were solemn and pathetic like a sick dog's.

'There's nothing much wrong with me,' he said, in reply to my question. 'A shell dropped beside me and damaged my foot. They say they'll have to cut it off ... I've an easier mind now you're here, Hannay. Of course you'll take over from Masterton. He's a good man but not quite up to his job. Poor Fraser—you've heard about Fraser. He was done in at the very start. Yes, a shell. And Lefroy. If he's alive and not too badly smashed the Hun has got a troublesome prisoner.'

He was too sick to talk, but he wouldn't let me go.

'The division was all right. Don't you believe anyone who says we didn't fight like heroes. Our outpost line held up the Hun for six hours, and only about a dozen men came back. We could have stuck it out in the battle-zone if both flanks hadn't been turned. They got through Crabbe's left and came down the Verey ravine, and a big wave rushed Shropshire Wood ... We fought it out yard by yard and didn't budge till we saw the Plessis dump blazing in our rear. Then it was about time to go ... We haven't many battalion commanders left. Watson, Endicot, Crawshay ...' He stammered out a list of gallant fellows who had gone.

'Get back double quick, Hannay. They want you. I'm not happy about Masterton. He's too young for the job.' And then a nurse drove me out, and I left him speaking in the strange forced voice of great weakness.

At the foot of the staircase stood Mary.

'I saw you go in,' she said, 'so I waited for you.'

'Oh, my dear,' I cried, 'you should have been in Boulogne by now. What madness brought you here?'

'They know me here and they've taken me on. You couldn't expect me to stay behind. You said yourself everybody was wanted, and I'm in a Service like you. Please don't be angry, Dick.'

I wasn't angry, I wasn't even extra anxious. The whole thing seemed to have been planned by fate since the creation of the world. The game we had been engaged in wasn't finished and it was right that we should play it out together. With that feeling came a conviction, too, of ultimate victory. Somehow or sometime we should get to the end of our pilgrimage. But I remembered Mary's forebodings about the sacrifice required. The best of us. That ruled me out, but what about her?

I caught her to my arms. 'Goodbye, my very dearest. Don't worry about me, for mine's a soft job and I can look after my skin. But oh! take care of yourself, for you are all the world to me.'

She kissed me gravely like a wise child.

'I am not afraid for you,' she said. 'You are going to stand in the breach, and I know—I know you will win. Remember that there is someone here whose heart is so full of pride of her man that it hasn't room for fear.'

As I went out of the convent door I felt that once again I had been given my orders.

It did not surprise me that, when I sought out my room on an upper floor of the Hotel de France, I found Blenkiron in the corridor. He was in the best of spirits.

'You can't keep me out of the show, Dick,' he said, 'so you needn't start arguing. Why, this is the one original chance of a lifetime for John S. Blenkiron. Our little fight at Erzerum was only a side-show, but this is a real high-class Armageddon. I guess I'll find a way to make myself useful.'

I had no doubt he would, and I was glad he had stayed behind. But I felt it was hard on Peter to have the job of returning to England alone at such a time, like useless flotsam washed up by a flood.

'You needn't worry,' said Blenkiron. 'Peter's not making England this trip. To the best of my knowledge he has beat it out of this township by the eastern postern. He had some talk with Sir Archibald Roylance, and presently other gentlemen of the Royal Flying Corps appeared, and the upshot was that Sir Archibald hitched on to Peter's grip and departed without saying farewell. My notion is that he's gone to have a few words with his old friends at some flying station. Or he might have the idea of going back to England by aeroplane, and so having one last flutter before he folds his wings. Anyhow, Peter looked a mighty happy man. The last I saw he was smoking his pipe with a batch of young lads in a Flying Corps waggon and heading straight for Germany.'

CHAPTER TWENTY-ONE

How an Exile Returned to His Own People

Next morning I found the Army Commander on his way to Doullens.

'Take over the division?' he said. 'Certainly. I'm afraid there isn't much left of it. I'll tell Carr to get through to the Corps Headquarters, when he can find them. You'll have to nurse the remnants, for they can't be pulled out yet—not for a day or two. Bless me, Hannay, there are parts of our line which we're holding with a man and a boy. You've got to stick it out till the French take over. We're not hanging on by our eyelids—it's our eyelashes now.'

'What about positions to fall back on, sir?' I asked.

'We're doing our best, but we haven't enough men to prepare them.' He plucked open a map. 'There we're digging a line—and there. If we can hold that bit for two days we shall have a fair line resting on the river. But we mayn't have time.'

Then I told him about Blenkiron, whom of course he had heard of. 'He was one of the biggest engineers in the States, and he's got a nailing fine eye for country. He'll make good somehow if you let him help in the job.'

'The very fellow,' he said, and he wrote an order. 'Take this to Jacks and he'll fix up a temporary commission. Your man can find a uniform somewhere in Amiens.'

After that I went to the detail camp and found that Ivery had duly arrived.

'The prisoner has given no trouble, sirr,' Hamilton reported. 'But he's a wee thing peevish. They're saying that the Gairmans is gettin' on fine, and I was tellin' him that he should be proud of his ain folk. But he wasn't verra weel pleased.'

Three days had wrought a transformation in Ivery. That face, once so cool and capable, was now sharpened like a hunted beast's. His imagination was preying on him and I could picture its torture. He, who had been always at the top directing the machine, was now only a cog in it. He had never in his life been anything but powerful; now he was impotent. He was in a hard, unfamiliar world, in the grip of something which he feared and didn't understand, in the charge of men who were in no way amenable to his persuasiveness. It was like a proud and bullying manager suddenly forced to labour in a squad of navvies, and worse, for there was the gnawing physical fear of what was coming.

He made an appeal to me.

'Do the English torture their prisoners?' he asked. 'You have beaten me. I own it, and I plead for mercy. I will go on my knees if you like. I am not afraid of death—in my own way.'

'Few people are afraid of death—in their own way.'

'Why do you degrade me? I am a gentleman.'

'Not as we define the thing,' I said.

His jaw dropped. 'What are you going to do with me?' he quavered.

'You have been a soldier,' I said. 'You are going to see a little fighting—from the ranks. There will be no brutality, you will be armed if you want to defend yourself, you will have the same chance of survival as the men around you. You may have heard that your countrymen are doing well. It is even possible that they may win the battle. What was your forecast to me? Amiens in two days, Abbeville in three. Well, you are a little behind scheduled time, but still you are prospering. You told me that you were the chief architect of all this, and you are going to be given the chance of seeing it, perhaps of sharing in it—from the other side. Does it not appeal to your sense of justice?'

He groaned and turned away. I had no more pity for him than I would have had for a black mamba that had killed my friend and was now caught to a cleft tree. Nor, oddly enough, had Wake. If we had shot Ivery outright at St Anton, I am certain that Wake would have called us murderers. Now he was in complete agreement. His passionate hatred of war made him rejoice that a chief contriver of war should be made to share in its terrors.

'He tried to talk me over this morning,' he told me. 'Claimed he was on my side and said the kind of thing I used to say last year. It made me rather ashamed of some of my past performances to hear that scoundrel imitating them ... By the way, Hannay, what are you going to do with me?'

'You're coming on my staff. You're a stout fellow and I can't do without you.'

'Remember I won't fight.'

'You won't be asked to. We're trying to stem the tide which wants to roll to the sea. You know how the Boche behaves in occupied country, and Mary's in Amiens.'

At that news he shut his lips.

'Still—' he began.

'Still,' I said. 'I don't ask you to forfeit one of your blessed principles. You needn't fire a shot. But I want a man to carry orders for me, for we haven't a line any more, only a lot of blobs like quicksilver. I want a clever man for the job and a brave one, and I know that you're not afraid.'

'No,' he said. 'I don't think I am—much. Well. I'm content!'

I started Blenkiron off in a car for Corps Headquarters, and in the afternoon took the road myself. I knew every inch of the country—the lift of the hill east of Amiens, the Roman highway that ran straight as an arrow to St Quentin, the marshy lagoons of the Somme, and that broad strip of land wasted by battle between Dompierre and Peronne. I had come to Amiens through it in January, for I had been up to the line before I left for Paris, and then it had been a peaceful place, with peasants tilling their fields, and new buildings going up on the old battle-field, and carpenters busy at cottage roofs, and scarcely a transport waggon on the road to remind one of war. Now the main route was choked like the Albert road when the Somme battle first began—troops going up and troops coming down, the latter in the last stage of weariness; a ceaseless traffic of ambulances one way and ammunition waggons the other; busy staff cars trying to worm a way through the mass; strings of gun horses, oddments of cavalry, and here and there blue French uniforms. All that I had seen before; but one thing was new to me. Little country carts with sad-faced women and mystified children in them and piles of household plenishing were creeping westward, or stood waiting at village doors. Beside these tramped old men and boys, mostly in their Sunday best as if they were going to church. I had never seen the sight before, for I had never seen the British Army falling back. The dam which held up the waters had broken and the dwellers in the valley were trying to save their pitiful little treasures. And over everything, horse and man, cart and wheelbarrow, road and tillage, lay the white March dust, the sky was blue as June, small birds were busy in the copses, and in the corners of abandoned gardens I had a glimpse of the first violets.

Presently as we topped a rise we came within full noise of the guns. That, too, was new to me, for it was no ordinary bombardment. There was a special quality in the sound, something ragged, straggling, intermittent, which I had never heard before. It was the sign of open warfare and a moving battle.

At Peronne, from which the newly returned inhabitants had a second time fled, the battle seemed to be at the doors. There I had news of my division. It was farther south towards St Christ. We groped our way among bad roads to where its headquarters were believed to be, while the voice of the guns grew louder. They turned out to be those of another division, which was busy getting ready to cross the river. Then the dark fell, and while airplanes flew west into the sunset there was a redder sunset in the east, where the unceasing flashes of gunfire were pale against the angry glow of burning dumps. The sight of the bonnet-badge of a Scots Fusilier made me halt, and the man turned out to belong to my division. Half an hour later I was taking over from the much-relieved Masterton in the ruins of what had once been a sugar-beet factory.

There to my surprise I found Lefroy. The Boche had held him prisoner for precisely eight hours. During that time he had been so interested in watching the way the enemy handled an attack that he had forgotten the miseries of his position. He described with blasphemous admiration the endless wheel by which supplies and reserve troops move up, the silence, the smoothness, the perfect discipline. Then he had realized that he was a captive and unwounded, and had gone mad. Being a heavy-weight boxer of note, he had sent his two guards spinning into a ditch, dodged the ensuing shots, and found shelter in the lee of a blazing ammunition dump where his pursuers hesitated to follow. Then he had spent an anxious hour trying to get through an outpost line, which he thought was Boche. Only by overhearing an exchange of oaths in the accents of Dundee did he realize that it was our own ... It was a comfort to have Lefroy back, for he was both stout-hearted and resourceful. But I found that I had a division only on paper. It was about the strength of a brigade, the brigades battalions, and the battalions companies.

This is not the place to write the story of the week that followed. I could not write it even if I wanted to, for I don't know it. There was a plan somewhere, which you will find in the history books, but with me it was blank chaos. Orders came, but long before they arrived the situation had changed, and I could no more obey them than fly to the moon. Often I had lost touch with the divisions on both flanks. Intelligence arrived erratically out of the void, and for the most part we worried along without it. I heard we were under the French—first it was said to be Foch, and then Fayolle, whom I had met in Paris. But the higher command seemed a million miles away, and we were left to use our mother wits. My problem was to give ground as slowly as possible and at the same time not to delay too long, for retreat we must, with the Boche sending in brand-new divisions each morning. It was a kind of war worlds distant from the old trench battles, and since I had been taught no other I had to invent rules as I went along. Looking back, it seems a miracle that any of us came out of it. Only the grace of God and the uncommon toughness of the British soldier bluffed the Hun and prevented him pouring through the breach to Abbeville and the sea. We were no better than a mosquito curtain stuck in a doorway to stop the advance of an angry bull.

The Army Commander was right; we were hanging on with our eyelashes. We must have been easily the weakest part of the whole front, for we were holding a line which was never less than two miles and was often, as I judged, nearer five, and there was nothing in reserve to us except some oddments of cavalry who chased about the whole battle-field under vague orders. Mercifully for us the Boche blundered. Perhaps he did not know our condition, for our airmen were magnificent and you never saw a Boche plane over our line by day, though they bombed us merrily by night. If he had called our bluff we should have been done, but he put his main strength to the north and the south of us. North he pressed hard on the Third Army, but he got well hammered by the Guards north of Bapaume and he could make no headway at Arras. South he drove at the Paris railway and down the Oise valley, but there Petain's reserves had arrived, and the French made a noble stand.

Not that he didn't fight hard in the centre where we were, but he hadn't his best troops, and after we got west of the bend of the Somme he was outrunning his heavy guns. Still, it was a desperate enough business, for our flanks were all the time falling back, and we had to conform to movements we could only guess at. After all, we were on the direct route to Amiens, and it was up to us to yield slowly so as to give Haig and Petain time to get up supports. I was a miser about every yard of ground, for every yard and every minute were precious. We alone stood between the enemy and the city, and in the city was Mary.

If you ask me about our plans I can't tell you. I had a new one every hour. I got instructions from the Corps, but, as I have said, they were usually out of date before they arrived, and most of my tactics I had to invent myself. I had a plain task, and to fulfil it I had to use what methods the Almighty allowed me. I hardly slept, I ate little, I was on the move day and night, but I never felt so strong in my life. It seemed as if I couldn't tire, and, oddly enough, I was happy. If a man's whole being is focused on one aim, he has no time to worry ... I remember we were all very gentle and soft-spoken those days. Lefroy, whose tongue was famous for its edge, now cooed like a dove. The troops were on their uppers, but as steady as rocks. We were against the end of the world, and that stiffens a man ...

Day after day saw the same performance. I held my wavering front with an outpost line which delayed each new attack till I could take its bearings. I had special companies for counter-attack at selected points, when I wanted time to retire the rest of the division. I think we must have fought more than a dozen of such little battles. We lost men all the time, but the enemy made no big scoop, though he was always on the edge of one. Looking back, it seems like a succession of miracles. Often I was in one end of a village when the Boche was in the other. Our batteries were always on the move, and the work of the gunners was past praising. Sometimes we faced east, sometimes north, and once at a most critical moment due south, for our front waved and blew like a flag at a masthead ... Thank God, the enemy was getting away from his big engine, and his ordinary troops were fagged and poor in quality. It was when his fresh shock battalions came on that I held my breath ... He had a heathenish amount of machine-guns and he used them beautifully. Oh, I take my hat off to the Boche performance. He was doing what we had tried to do at the Somme and the Aisne and Arras and Ypres, and he was more or less succeeding. And the reason was that he was going bald-headed for victory.

The men, as I have said, were wonderfully steady and patient under the fiercest trial that soldiers can endure. I had all kinds in the division—old army, new army, Territorials—and you couldn't pick and choose between them. They fought like Trojans, and, dirty, weary, and hungry, found still some salt of humour in their sufferings. It was a proof of the rock-bottom sanity of human nature. But we had one man with us who was hardly sane....

In the hustle of those days I now and then caught sight of Ivery. I had to be everywhere at all hours, and often visited that remnant of Scots Fusiliers into which the subtlest brain in Europe had been drafted. He and his keepers were never on outpost duty or in any counter-attack. They were part of the mass whose only business was to retire discreetly. This was child's play to Hamilton, who had been out since Mons; and Amos, after taking a day to get used to it, wrapped himself in his grim philosophy and rather enjoyed it. You couldn't surprise Amos any more than a Turk. But the man with them, whom they never left—that was another matter.

'For the first wee bit,' Hamilton reported, 'we thocht he was gaun daft. Every shell that came near he jumped like a young horse. And the gas! We had to tie on his mask for him, for his hands were fushionless. There was whiles when he wadna be hindered from standin' up and talkin' to hisself, though the bullets was spittin'. He was what ye call demoralized ... Syne he got as though he didna hear or see onything. He did what we tell't him, and when we let him be he sat down and grat. He's aye greetin' ... Queer thing, sirr, but the Gairmans canna hit him. I'm aye shakin' bullets out o' my claes, and I've got a hole in my shoulder, and Andra took a bash on his tin that wad hae felled onybody that hadna a heid like a stot. But, sirr, the prisoner taks no scaith. Our boys are feared of him. There was an Irishman says to me that he had the evil eye, and ye can see for yerself that he's no canny.'

I saw that his skin had become like parchment and that his eyes were glassy. I don't think he recognized me.

'Does he take his meals?' I asked.

'He doesna eat muckle. But he has an unco thirst. Ye canna keep him off the men's water-bottles.'

He was learning very fast the meaning of that war he had so confidently played with. I believe I am a merciful man, but as I looked at him I felt no vestige of pity. He was dreeing the weird he had prepared for others. I thought of Scudder, of the thousand friends I had lost, of the great seas of blood and the mountains of sorrow this man and his like had made for the world. Out of the corner of my eye I could see the long ridges above Combles and Longueval which the salt of the earth had fallen to win, and which were again under the hoof of the Boche. I thought of the distracted city behind us and what it meant to me, and the weak, the pitifully weak screen which was all its defence. I thought of the foul deeds which had made the German name to stink by land and sea, foulness of which he was the arch-begetter. And then I was amazed at our forbearance. He would go mad, and madness for him was more decent than sanity.

I had another man who wasn't what you might call normal, and that was Wake. He was the opposite of shell-shocked, if you understand me. He had never been properly under fire before, but he didn't give a straw for it. I had known the same thing with other men, and they generally ended by crumpling up, for it isn't natural that five or six feet of human flesh shouldn't be afraid of what can torture and destroy it. The natural thing is to be always a little scared, like me, but by an effort of the will and attention to work to contrive to forget it. But Wake apparently never gave it a thought. He wasn't foolhardy, only indifferent. He used to go about with a smile on his face, a smile of contentment. Even the horrors—and we had plenty of them—didn't affect him. His eyes, which used to be hot, had now a curious open innocence like Peter's. I would have been happier if he had been a little rattled.

One night, after we had had a bad day of anxiety, I talked to him as we smoked in what had once been a French dug-out. He was an extra right arm to me, and I told him so. 'This must be a queer experience for you,' I said.

'Yes,' he replied, 'it is very wonderful. I did not think a man could go through it and keep his reason. But I know many things I did not know before. I know that the soul can be reborn without leaving the body.'

I stared at him, and he went on without looking at me.

'You're not a classical scholar, Hannay? There was a strange cult in the ancient world, the worship of Magna Mater—the Great Mother. To enter into her mysteries the votary passed through a bath of blood——I think I am passing through that bath. I think that like the initiate I shall be *renatus in aeternum*—reborn into the eternal.'

I advised him to have a drink, for that talk frightened me. It looked as if he were becoming what the Scots call 'fey'. Lefroy noticed the same thing and was always speaking about it. He was as brave as a bull himself, and with very much the same kind of courage; but Wake's gallantry perturbed him. 'I can't make the chap out,' he told me. 'He behaves as if his mind was too full of better things to give a damn for Boche guns. He doesn't take foolish risks—I don't mean that, but he behaves as if risks didn't signify. It's positively eerie to see him making notes with a steady hand when shells are dropping like hailstones and we're all thinking every minute's our last. You've got to be careful with him, sir. He's a long sight too valuable for us to spare.'

Lefroy was right about that, for I don't know what I should have done without him. The worst part of our job was to keep touch with our flanks, and that was what I used Wake for. He covered country like a moss-trooper, sometimes on a rusty bicycle, oftener on foot, and you couldn't tire him. I wonder what other divisions thought of the grimy private who was our chief means of communication. He knew nothing of military affairs before, but he got the hang of this rough-and-tumble fighting as if he had been born for it. He never fired a shot; he carried no arms; the only weapons he used were his brains. And they were the best conceivable. I never met a staff officer who was so quick at getting a point or at sizing up a situation. He had put his back into the business, and first-class talent is not common anywhere. One day a G. S. O. from a neighbouring division came to see me.

'Where on earth did you pick up that man Wake?' he asked.

'He's a conscientious objector and a non-combatant,' I said.

'Then I wish to Heaven we had a few more conscientious objectors in this show. He's the only fellow who seems to know anything about this blessed battle. My general's sending you a chit about him.'

'No need,' I said, laughing. 'I know his value. He's an old friend of mine.'

I used Wake as my link with Corps Headquarters, and especially with Blenkiron. For about the sixth day of the show I was beginning to get rather desperate. This kind of thing couldn't go on for ever. We were miles back now, behind the old line of '17, and, as we rested one flank on the river, the immediate situation was a little easier. But I had lost a lot of men, and those that were left were blind with fatigue. The big bulges of the enemy to north and south had added to the length of the total front, and I found I had to fan out my thin ranks. The Boche was still pressing on, though his impetus was slacker. If he knew how little there was to stop him in my section he might make a push which would carry him to Amiens. Only the magnificent work of our airmen had prevented him getting that knowledge, but we couldn't keep the secrecy up for ever. Some day an enemy plane would get over, and it only needed the drive of a fresh storm-battalion or two to scatter us. I wanted a good prepared position, with sound trenches and decent wiring. Above all I wanted reserves—reserves. The word was on my lips all day and it haunted my dreams. I was told that the French were to relieve us, but when—when? My reports to Corps Headquarters were one long wail for more troops. I knew there was a position prepared behind us, but I needed men to hold it.

Wake brought in a message from Blenkiron. 'We're waiting for you, Dick,' he wrote, 'and we've gotten quite a nice little home ready for you. This old man hasn't hustled so hard since he struck copper in Montana in '92. We've dug three lines of trenches and made a heap of pretty redoubts, and I guess they're well laid out, for the Army staff has supervised them and they're no slouches at this brand of engineering. You would have laughed to see the labour we employed. We had all breeds of Dago and Chinaman, and some of your own South African blacks, and they got so busy on the job they forgot about bedtime. I used to be reckoned a bit of a slave driver, but my special talents weren't needed with this push. I'm going to put a lot of money into foreign missions henceforward.'

I wrote back: 'Your trenches are no good without men. For God's sake get something that can hold a rifle. My lot are done to the world.'

Then I left Lefroy with the division and went down on the back of an ambulance to see for myself. I found Blenkiron, some of the Army engineers, and a staff officer from Corps Headquarters, and I found Archie Roylance.

They had dug a mighty good line and wired it nobly. It ran from the river to the wood of La Bruyere on the little hill above the Ablain stream. It was desperately long, but I saw at once it couldn't well be shorter, for the division on the south of us had its hands full with the fringe of the big thrust against the French.

'It's no good blinking the facts,' I told them. 'I haven't a thousand men, and what I have are at the end of their tether. If you put 'em in these trenches they'll go to sleep on their feet. When can the French take over?'

I was told that it had been arranged for next morning, but that it had now been put off twenty-four hours. It was only a temporary measure, pending the arrival of British divisions from the north.

Archie looked grave. 'The Boche is pushin' up new troops in this sector. We got the news before I left squadron headquarters. It looks as if it would be a near thing, sir.'

'It won't be a near thing. It's an absolute black certainty. My fellows can't carry on as they are another day. Great God, they've had a fortnight in hell! Find me more men or we buckle up at the next push.' My temper was coming very near its limits.

'We've raked the country with a small-tooth comb, sir,' said one of the staff officers. 'And we've raised a scratch pack. Best part of two thousand. Good men, but most of them know nothing about infantry fighting. We've put them into platoons, and done our best to give them some kind of training. There's one thing may cheer you. We've plenty of machine-guns. There's a machine-gun school near by and we got all the men who were taking the course and all the plant.'

I don't suppose there was ever such a force put into the field before. It was a wilder medley than Moussy's camp-followers at First Ypres. There was every kind of detail in the shape of men returning from leave, representing most of the regiments in the army. There were the men from the machine-gun school. There were Corps troops—sappers and A.S.C., and a handful of Corps cavalry. Above all, there was a batch of American engineers, fathered by Blenkiron. I inspected them where they were drilling and liked the look of them. 'Forty-eight hours,' I said to myself. 'With luck we may just pull it off.'

Then I borrowed a bicycle and went back to the division. But before I left I had a word with Archie. 'This is one big game of bluff, and it's you fellows alone that enable us to play it. Tell your people that everything depends on them. They mustn't stint the planes in this sector, for if the Boche once suspicions how little he's got before him the game's up. He's not a fool and he knows that this is the short road to Amiens, but he imagines we're holding it in strength. If we keep up the fiction for another two days the thing's done. You say he's pushing up troops?'

'Yes, and he's sendin' forward his tanks.'

'Well, that'll take time. He's slower now than a week ago and he's got a deuce of a country to march over. There's still an outside chance we may win through. You go home and tell the R.F.C. what I've told you.'

He nodded. 'By the way, sir, Pienaar's with the squadron. He would like to come up and see you.'

'Archie,' I said solemnly, 'be a good chap and do me a favour. If I think Peter's anywhere near the line I'll go off my head with worry. This is no place for a man with a bad leg. He should have been in England days ago. Can't you get him off—to Amiens, anyhow?'

'We scarcely like to. You see, we're all desperately sorry for him, his fun gone and his career over and all that. He likes bein' with us and listenin' to our yarns. He has been up once or twice too. The Shark-Gladas. He swears it's a great make, and certainly he knows how to handle the little devil.'

'Then for Heaven's sake don't let him do it again. I look to you, Archie, remember. Promise.'

'Funny thing, but he's always worryin' about you. He has a map on which he marks every day the changes in the position, and he'd hobble a mile to pump any of our fellows who have been up your way.'

That night under cover of darkness I drew back the division to the newly prepared lines. We got away easily, for the enemy was busy with his own affairs. I suspected a relief by fresh troops.

There was no time to lose, and I can tell you I toiled to get things straight before dawn. I would have liked to send my own fellows back to rest, but I couldn't spare them yet. I wanted them to stiffen the fresh lot, for they were veterans. The new position was arranged on the same principles as the old front which had been broken on March 21st. There was our forward zone, consisting of an outpost line and redoubts, very cleverly sited, and a line of resistance. Well behind it were the trenches which formed the battle-zone. Both zones were heavily wired, and we had plenty of machine-guns; I wish I could say we had plenty of men who knew how to use them. The outposts were merely to give the alarm and fall back to the line of resistance which was to hold out to the last. In the forward zone I put the freshest of my own men, the units being brought up to something like strength by the details returning from leave that the Corps had commandeered. With them I put the American engineers, partly in the redoubts and partly in companies for counter-attack. Blenkiron had reported that they could shoot like Dan'l Boone, and were simply spoiling for a fight. The rest of the force was in the battle-zone, which was our last hope. If that went the Boche had a clear walk to Amiens. Some additional field batteries had been brought up to support our very weak divisional artillery. The front was so long that I had to put all three of my emaciated brigades in the line, so I had nothing to speak of in reserve. It was a most almighty gamble.

We had found shelter just in time. At 6.30 next day—for a change it was a clear morning with clouds beginning to bank up from the west—the Boche let us know he was alive. He gave us a good drenching with gas shells which didn't do much harm, and then messed up our forward zone with his trench mortars. At 7.20 his men began to come on, first little bunches with machine-guns and then the infantry in waves. It was clear they were fresh troops, and we learned afterwards from prisoners that they were Bavarians—6th or 7th, I forget which, but the division that hung us up at Monchy. At the same time there was the sound of a tremendous bombardment across the river. It looked as if the main battle had swung from Albert and Montdidier to a direct push for Amiens. I have often tried to write down the events of that day. I tried it in my report to the Corps; I tried it in my own diary; I tried it because Mary wanted it; but I have never been able to make any story that hung together. Perhaps I was too tired for my mind to retain clear impressions, though at the time I was not conscious of special fatigue. More likely it is because the fight itself was so confused, for nothing happened according to the books and the orderly soul of the Boche must have been scarified ... At first it went as I expected. The outpost line was pushed in, but the fire from the redoubts broke up the advance, and enabled the line of resistance in the forward zone to give a good account of itself. There was a check, and then another big wave, assisted by a barrage from field-guns brought far forward. This time the line of resistance gave at several points, and Lefroy flung in the Americans in a counter-attack. That was a mighty performance. The engineers, yelling like dervishes, went at it with the bayonet, and those that preferred swung their rifles as clubs. It was terribly costly fighting and all wrong, but it succeeded. They cleared the Boche out of a ruined farm he had rushed, and a little wood, and re-established our front. Blenkiron, who saw it all, for he went with them and got the tip of an ear picked off by a machine-gun bullet, hadn't any words wherewith to speak of it. 'And I once said those boys looked puffy,' he moaned.

The next phase, which came about midday, was the tanks. I had never seen the German variety, but had heard that it was speedier and heavier than ours, but unwieldy. We did not see much of their speed, but we found out all about their clumsiness. Had the things been properly handled they should have gone through us like rotten wood. But the whole outfit was bungled. It looked good enough country for the use of them, but the men who made our position had had an eye to this possibility. The great monsters, mounting a field-gun besides other contrivances, wanted something like a highroad to be happy in. They were useless over anything like difficult ground. The ones that came down the main road got on well enough at the start, but Blenkiron very sensibly had mined the highway, and we blew a hole like a diamond pit. One lay helpless at the foot of it, and we took the crew prisoner; another stuck its nose over and remained there till our field-guns got the range and knocked it silly. As for the rest—there is a marshy lagoon called the Patte d'Oie beside the farm of Gavrelle, which runs all the way north to the river, though in most places it only seems like a soft patch in the meadows. This the tanks had to cross to reach our line, and they never made it. Most got bogged, and made pretty targets for our gunners; one or two returned; and one the Americans, creeping forward under cover of a little stream, blew up with a time fuse.

By the middle of the afternoon I was feeling happier. I knew the big attack was still to come, but I had my forward zone intact and I hoped for the best. I remember I was talking to Wake, who had been going between the two zones, when I got the first warning of a new and unexpected peril. A dud shell plumped down a few yards from me.

'Those fools across the river are firing short and badly off the straight,' I said.

Wake examined the shell. 'No, it's a German one,' he said.

Then came others, and there could be no mistake about the direction—followed by a burst of machine-gun fire from the same quarter. We ran in cover to a point from which we could see the north bank of the river, and I got my glass on it. There was a lift of land from behind which the fire was coming. We looked at each other, and the same conviction stood in both faces. The Boche had pushed down the northern bank, and we were no longer in line with our neighbours. The enemy was in a situation to catch us with his fire on our flank and left rear. We couldn't retire to conform, for to retire meant giving up our prepared position.

It was the last straw to all our anxieties, and for a moment I was at the end of my wits. I turned to Wake, and his calm eyes pulled me together.

'If they can't retake that ground, we're fairly carted,' I said.

'We are. Therefore they must retake it.'

'I must get on to Mitchinson.' But as I spoke I realized the futility of a telephone message to a man who was pretty hard up against it himself. Only an urgent appeal could effect anything ... I must go myself ... No, that was impossible. I must send Lefroy ... But he couldn't be spared. And all my staff officers were up to their necks in the battle. Besides, none of them knew the position as I knew it ... And how to get there? It was a long way round by the bridge at Loisy.

Suddenly I was aware of Wake's voice. 'You had better send me,' he was saying. 'There's only one way—to swim the river a little lower down.'

'That's too damnably dangerous. I won't send any man to certain death.'

'But I volunteer,' he said. 'That, I believe, is always allowed in war.'

'But you'll be killed before you can cross.'

'Send a man with me to watch. If I get over, you may be sure I'll get to General Mitchinson. If not, send somebody else by Loisy. There's desperate need for hurry, and you see yourself it's the only way.'

The time was past for argument. I scribbled a line to Mitchinson as his credentials. No more was needed, for Wake knew the position as well as I did. I sent an orderly to accompany him to his starting-place on the bank.

'Goodbye,' he said, as we shook hands. 'You'll see, I'll come back all right.' His face, I remember, looked singularly happy. Five minutes later the Boche guns opened for the final attack.

I believe I kept a cool head; at least so Lefroy and the others reported. They said I went about all afternoon grinning as if I liked it, and that I never raised my voice once. (It's rather a fault of mine that I bellow in a scrap.) But I know I was feeling anything but calm, for the problem was ghastly. It all depended on Wake and Mitchinson. The flanking fire was so bad that I had to give up the left of the forward zone, which caught it fairly, and retire the men there to the battle-zone. The latter was better protected, for between it and the river was a small wood and the bank rose into a bluff which sloped inwards towards us. This withdrawal meant a switch, and a switch isn't a pretty thing when it has to be improvised in the middle of a battle.

The Boche had counted on that flanking fire. His plan was to break our two wings—the old Boche plan which crops up in every fight. He left our centre at first pretty well alone, and thrust along the river bank and to the wood of La Bruyere, where we linked up with the division on our right. Lefroy was in the first area, and Masterton in the second, and for three hours it was as desperate a business as I have ever faced ... The improvised switch went, and more and more of the forward zone disappeared. It was a hot, clear spring afternoon, and in the open fighting the enemy came on like troops at manoeuvres. On the left they got into the battle-zone, and I can see yet Lefroy's great figure leading a counter-attack in person, his face all puddled with blood from a scalp wound ...

I would have given my soul to be in two places at once, but I had to risk our left and keep close to Masterton, who needed me most. The wood of La Bruyere was the maddest sight. Again and again the Boche was almost through it. You never knew where he was, and most of the fighting there was duels between machine-gun parties. Some of the enemy got round behind us, and only a fine performance of a company of Cheshires saved a complete breakthrough.

As for Lefroy, I don't know how he stuck it out, and he doesn't know himself, for he was galled all the time by that accursed flanking fire. I got a note about half past four saying that Wake had crossed the river, but it was some weary hours after that before the fire slackened. I tore back and forward between my wings, and every time I went north I expected to find that Lefroy had broken. But by some miracle he held. The Boches were in his battle-zone time and again, but he always flung them out. I have a recollection of Blenkiron, stark mad, encouraging his Americans with strange tongues. Once as I passed him I saw that he had his left arm tied up. His blackened face grinned at me. 'This bit of landscape's mighty unsafe for democracy,' he croaked. 'For the love of Mike get your guns on to those devils across the river. They're plaguing my boys too bad.'

It was about seven o'clock, I think, when the flanking fire slacked off, but it was not because of our divisional guns. There was a short and very furious burst of artillery fire on the north bank, and I knew it was British. Then things began to happen. One of our planes—they had been marvels all day, swinging down like hawks for machine-gun bouts with the Boche infantry—reported that Mitchinson was attacking hard and getting on well. That eased my mind, and I started off for Masterton, who was in greater straits than ever, for the enemy seemed to be weakening on the river bank and putting his main strength in against our right ... But my G.S.O.2 stopped me on the road. 'Wake,' he said. 'He wants to see you.'

'Not now,' I cried.

'He can't live many minutes.'

I turned and followed him to the ruinous cowshed which was my divisional headquarters. Wake, as I heard later, had swum the river opposite to Mitchinson's right, and reached the other shore safely, though the current was whipped with bullets. But he had scarcely landed before he was badly hit by shrapnel in the groin. Walking at first with support and then carried on a stretcher, he managed to struggle on to the divisional headquarters, where he gave my message and explained the situation. He would not let his wound be looked to till his job was done. Mitchinson told me afterwards that with a face grey from pain he drew for him a sketch of our position and told him exactly how near we were to our end ... After that he asked to be sent back to me, and they got him down to Loisy in a crowded ambulance, and then up to us in a returning empty. The M.O. who looked at his wound saw that the thing was hopeless, and did not expect him to live beyond Loisy. He was bleeding internally and no surgeon on earth could have saved him.

When he reached us he was almost pulseless, but he recovered for a moment and asked for me.

I found him, with blue lips and a face drained of blood, lying on my camp bed. His voice was very small and far away.

'How goes it?' he asked.

'Please God, we'll pull through ... thanks to you, old man.'

'Good,' he said and his eyes shut.

He opened them once again.

'Funny thing life. A year ago I was preaching peace ... I'm still preaching it ... I'm not sorry.'

I held his hand till two minutes later he died.

In the press of a fight one scarcely realizes death, even the death of a friend. It was up to me to make good my assurance to Wake, and presently I was off to Masterton. There in that shambles of La Bruyere, while the light faded, there was a desperate and most bloody struggle. It was the last lap of the contest. Twelve hours now, I kept telling myself, and the French will be here and we'll have done our task. Alas! how many of us would go back to rest? ... Hardly able to totter, our counter-attacking companies went in again. They had gone far beyond the limits of mortal endurance, but the human spirit can defy all natural laws. The balance trembled, hung, and then dropped the right way. The enemy impetus weakened, stopped, and the ebb began.

I wanted to complete the job. Our artillery put up a sharp barrage, and the little I had left comparatively fresh I sent in for a counter-stroke. Most of the men were untrained, but there was that in our ranks which dispensed with training, and we had caught the enemy at the moment of lowest vitality. We pushed him out of La Bruyere, we pushed him back to our old forward zone, we pushed him out of that zone to the position from which he had begun the day.

But there was no rest for the weary. We had lost at least a third of our strength, and we had to man the same long line. We consolidated it as best we could, started to replace the wiring that had been destroyed, found touch with the division on our right, and established outposts. Then, after a conference with my brigadiers, I went back to my headquarters, too tired to feel either satisfaction or anxiety. In eight hours the French would be here. The words made a kind of litany in my ears.

In the cowshed where Wake had lain, two figures awaited me. The talc-enclosed candle revealed Hamilton and Amos, dirty beyond words, smoke-blackened, blood-stained, and intricately bandaged. They stood stiffly to attention.

'Sirr, the prisoner,' said Hamilton. 'I have to report that the prisoner is deid.'

I stared at them, for I had forgotten Ivery. He seemed a creature of a world that had passed away.

'Sirr, it was like this. Ever sin' this mornin', the prisoner seemed to wake up. Ye'll mind that he was in a kind of dream all week. But he got some new notion in his heid, and when the battle began he exheebited signs of restlessness. Whiles he wad lie doun in the trench, and whiles he was wantin' back to the dug-out. Accordin' to instructions I provided him wi' a rifle, but he didna seem to ken how to handle it. It was your orders, sirr, that he was to have means to defend hisself if the enemy cam on, so Amos gie'd him a trench knife. But verra soon he looked as if he was ettlin' to cut his throat, so I deprived him of it.'

Hamilton stopped for breath. He spoke as if he were reciting a lesson, with no stops between the sentences.

'I jaloused, sirr, that he wadna last oot the day, and Amos here was of the same opinion. The end came at twenty minutes past three—I ken the time, for I had just compared my watch with Amos. Ye'll mind that the Gairmans were beginning a big attack. We were in the front trench of what they ca' the battle-zone, and Amos and me was keepin' oor eyes on the enemy, who could be obsairved dribblin' ower the open. Just then the prisoner catches sight of the enemy and jumps up on the top. Amos tried to hold him, but he kicked him in the face. The next we kenned he was runnin' verra fast towards the enemy, holdin' his hands ower his heid and crying out loud in a foreign langwidge.'

'It was German,' said the scholarly Amos through his broken teeth.

'It was Gairman,' continued Hamilton. 'It seemed as if he was appealin' to the enemy to help him. But they paid no attention, and he cam under the fire of their machine-guns. We watched him spin round like a teetotum and kenned that he was bye with it.'

'You are sure he was killed?' I asked.

'Yes, sirr. When we counter-attacked we fund his body.'

There is a grave close by the farm of Gavrelle, and a wooden cross at its head bears the name of the Graf von Schwabing and the date of his death. The Germans took Gavrelle a little later. I am glad to think that they read that inscription.

CHAPTER TWENTY-TWO

The Summons Comes for Mr Standfast

I slept for one and three-quarter hours that night, and when I awoke I seemed to emerge from deeps of slumber which had lasted for days. That happens sometimes after heavy fatigue and great mental strain. Even a short sleep sets up a barrier between past and present which has to be elaborately broken down before you can link on with what has happened before. As my wits groped at the job some drops of rain splashed on my face through the broken roof. That hurried me out-of-doors. It was just after dawn and the sky was piled with thick clouds, while a wet wind blew up from the southwest. The long-prayed-for break in the weather seemed to have come at last. A deluge of rain was what I wanted, something to soak the earth and turn the roads into water-courses and clog the enemy transport, something above all to blind the enemy's eyes ... For I remembered what a preposterous bluff it all had been, and what a piteous broken handful stood between the Germans and their goal. If they knew, if they only knew, they would brush us aside like flies.

As I shaved I looked back on the events of yesterday as on something that had happened long ago. I seemed to judge them impersonally, and I concluded that it had been a pretty good fight. A scratch force, half of it dog-tired and half of it untrained, had held up at least a couple of fresh divisions ... But we couldn't do it again, and there were still some hours before us of desperate peril. When had the Corps said that the French would arrive? ... I was on the point of shouting for Hamilton to get Wake to ring up Corps Headquarters, when I remembered that Wake was dead. I had liked him and greatly admired him, but the recollection gave me scarcely a pang. We were all dying, and he had only gone on a stage ahead.

There was no morning strafe, such as had been our usual fortune in the past week. I went out-of-doors and found a noiseless world under the lowering sky. The rain had stopped falling, the wind of dawn had lessened, and I feared that the storm would be delayed. I wanted it at once to help us through the next hours of tension. Was it in six hours that the French were coming? No, it must be four. It couldn't be more than four, unless somebody had made an infernal muddle. I wondered why everything was so quiet. It would be breakfast time on both sides, but there seemed no stir of man's presence in that ugly strip half a mile off. Only far back in the German hinterland I seemed to hear the rumour of traffic.

An unslept and unshaven figure stood beside me which revealed itself as Archie Roylance.

'Been up all night,' he said cheerfully, lighting a cigarette. 'No, I haven't had breakfast. The skipper thought we'd better get another anti-aircraft battery up this way, and I was superintendin' the job. He's afraid of the Hun gettin' over your lines and spying out the nakedness of the land. For, you know, we're uncommon naked, sir. Also,' and Archie's face became grave, 'the Hun's pourin' divisions down on this sector. As I judge, he's blowin' up for a thunderin' big drive on both sides of the river. Our lads yesterday said all the country back of Peronne was lousy with new troops. And he's gettin' his big guns forward, too. You haven't been troubled with them yet, but he has got the roads mended and the devil of a lot of new light railways, and any moment we'll have the five-point-nines sayin' Good-mornin' ... Pray Heaven you get relieved in time, sir. I take it there's not much risk of another push this mornin'?'

'I don't think so. The Boche took a nasty knock yesterday, and he must fancy we're pretty strong after that counter-attack. I don't think he'll strike till he can work both sides of the river, and that'll take time to prepare. That's what his fresh divisions are for ... But remember, he can attack now, if he likes. If he knew how weak we were he's strong enough to send us all to glory in the next three hours. It's just that knowledge that you fellows have got to prevent his getting. If a single Hun plane crosses our lines and returns, we're wholly and utterly done. You've given us splendid help since the show began, Archie. For God's sake keep it up to the finish and put every machine you can spare in this sector.'

'We're doin' our best,' he said. 'We got some more fightin' scouts down from the north, and we're keepin' our eyes skinned. But you know as well as I do, sir, that it's never an ab-so-lute certainty. If the Hun sent over a squadron we might beat 'em all down but one, and that one might do the trick. It's a matter of luck. The Hun's got the wind up all right in the air just now and I don't blame the poor devil. I'm inclined to think we haven't had the pick of his push here. Jennings says he's doin' good work in Flanders, and they reckon there's the deuce of a thrust comin' there pretty soon. I think we can manage the kind of footler he's been sendin' over here lately, but if Lensch or some lad like that were to choose to turn up I wouldn't say what might happen. The air's a big lottery,' and Archie turned a dirty face skyward where two of our planes were moving very high towards the east.

The mention of Lensch brought Peter to mind, and I asked if he had gone back.

'He won't go,' said Archie, 'and we haven't the heart to make him. He's very happy, and plays about with the Gladas single-seater. He's always speakin' about you, sir, and it'd break his heart if we shifted him.'

I asked about his health, and was told that he didn't seem to have much pain.

'But he's a bit queer,' and Archie shook a sage head. 'One of the reasons why he won't budge is because he says God has some work for him to do. He's quite serious about it, and ever since he got the notion he has perked up amazin'. He's always askin' about Lensch, too—not vindictive like, you understand, but quite friendly. Seems to take a sort of proprietary interest in him. I told him Lensch had had a far longer spell of first-class fightin' than anybody else and was bound by the law of averages to be downed soon, and he was quite sad about it.'

I had no time to worry about Peter. Archie and I swallowed breakfast and I had a pow-wow with my brigadiers. By this time I had got through to Corps H.Q. and got news of the French. It was worse than I expected. General Peguy would arrive about ten o'clock, but his men couldn't take over till well after midday. The Corps gave me their whereabouts and I found it on the map. They had a long way to cover yet, and then there would be the slow business of relieving. I looked at my watch. There were still six hours before us when the Boche might knock us to blazes, six hours of maddening anxiety ... Lefroy announced that all was quiet on the front, and that the new wiring at the Bois de la Bruyere had been completed. Patrols had reported that during the night a fresh German division seemed to have relieved that which we had punished so stoutly yesterday. I asked him if he could stick it out against another attack. 'No,' he said without hesitation. 'We're too few and too shaky on our pins to stand any more. I've only a man to every three yards.' That impressed me, for Lefroy was usually the most devil-may-care optimist.

'Curse it, there's the sun,' I heard Archie cry. It was true, for the clouds were rolling back and the centre of the heavens was a patch of blue. The storm was coming—I could smell it in the air—but probably it wouldn't break till the evening. Where, I wondered, would we be by that time?

It was now nine o'clock, and I was keeping tight hold on myself, for I saw that I was going to have hell for the next hours. I am a pretty stolid fellow in some ways, but I have always found patience and standing still the most difficult job to tackle, and my nerves were all tattered from the long strain of the retreat. I went up to the line and saw the battalion commanders. Everything was unwholesomely quiet there. Then I came back to my headquarters to study the reports that were coming in from the air patrols. They all said the same thing—abnormal activity in the German back areas. Things seemed shaping for a new 21st of March, and, if our luck were out, my poor little remnant would have to take the shock. I telephoned to the Corps and found them as nervous as me. I gave them the details of my strength and heard an agonized whistle at the other end of the line. I was rather glad I had companions in the same purgatory.

I found I couldn't sit still. If there had been any work to do I would have buried myself in it, but there was none. Only this fearsome job of waiting. I hardly ever feel cold, but now my blood seemed to be getting thin, and I astonished my staff by putting on a British warm and buttoning up the collar. Round that derelict farm I ranged like a hungry wolf, cold at the feet, queasy in the stomach, and mortally edgy in the mind.

Then suddenly the cloud lifted from me, and the blood seemed to run naturally in my veins. I experienced the change of mood which a man feels sometimes when his whole being is fined down and clarified by long endurance. The fight of yesterday revealed itself as something rather splendid. What risks we had run and how gallantly we had met them! My heart warmed as I thought of that old division of mine, those ragged veterans that were never beaten as long as breath was left them. And the Americans and the boys from the machine-gun school and all the oddments we had commandeered! And old Blenkiron raging like a good-tempered lion! It was against reason that such fortitude shouldn't win out. We had snarled round and bitten the Boche so badly that he wanted no more for a little. He would come again, but presently we should be relieved and the gallant blue-coats, fresh as paint and burning for revenge, would be there to worry him.

I had no new facts on which to base my optimism, only a changed point of view. And with it came a recollection of other things. Wake's death had left me numb before, but now the thought of it gave me a sharp pang. He was the first of our little confederacy to go. But what an ending he had made, and how happy he had been in that mad time when he had come down from his pedestal and become one of the crowd! He had found himself at the last, and who could grudge him such happiness? If the best were to be taken, he would be chosen first, for he was a big man, before whom I uncovered my head. The thought of him made me very humble. I had never had his troubles to face, but he had come clean through them, and reached a courage which was for ever beyond me. He was the Faithful among us pilgrims, who had finished his journey before the rest. Mary had foreseen it. 'There is a price to be paid,' she had said—'the best of us.'

And at the thought of Mary a flight of warm and happy hopes seemed to settle on my mind. I was looking again beyond the war to that peace which she and I would some day inherit. I had a vision of a green English landscape, with its far-flung scents of wood and meadow and garden ... And that face of all my dreams, with the eyes so childlike and brave and honest, as if they, too, saw beyond the dark to a radiant country. A line of an old song, which had been a favourite of my father's, sang itself in my ears:

There's an eye that ever weeps and a fair face will be fain
When I ride through Annan Water wi' my bonny bands again!

We were standing by the crumbling rails of what had once been the farm sheepfold. I looked at Archie and he smiled back at me, for he saw that my face had changed. Then he turned his eyes to the billowing clouds.

I felt my arm clutched.

'Look there!' said a fierce voice, and his glasses were turned upward.

I looked, and far up in the sky saw a thing like a wedge of wild geese flying towards us from the enemy's country. I made out the small dots which composed it, and my glass told me they were planes. But only Archie's practised eye knew that they were enemy.

'Boche?' I asked.

'Boche,' he said. 'My God, we're for it now.'

My heart had sunk like a stone, but I was fairly cool. I looked at my watch and saw that it was ten minutes to eleven.

'How many?'

'Five,' said Archie. 'Or there may be six—not more.'

'Listen!' I said. 'Get on to your headquarters. Tell them that it's all up with us if a single plane gets back. Let them get well over the line, the deeper in the better, and tell them to send up every machine they possess and down them all. Tell them it's life or death. Not one single plane goes back. Quick!'

Archie disappeared, and as he went our anti-aircraft guns broke out. The formation above opened and zigzagged, but they were too high to be in much danger.

But they were not too high to see that which we must keep hidden or perish.

The roar of our batteries died down as the invaders passed westward. As I watched their progress they seemed to be dropping lower. Then they rose again and a bank of cloud concealed them.

I had a horrid certainty that they must beat us, that some at any rate would get back. They had seen thin lines and the roads behind us empty of supports. They would see, as they advanced, the blue columns of the French coming up from the south-west, and they would return and tell the enemy that a blow now would open the road to Amiens and the sea. He had plenty of strength for it, and presently he would have overwhelming strength. It only needed a spear-point to burst the jerry-built dam and let the flood through ... They would return in twenty minutes, and by noon we would be broken. Unless—unless the miracle of miracles happened, and they never returned.

Archie reported that his skipper would do his damnedest and that our machines were now going up. 'We've a chance, sir,' he said, 'a good sportin' chance.' It was a new Archie, with a hard voice, a lean face, and very old eyes.

Behind the jagged walls of the farm buildings was a knoll which had once formed part of the high-road. I went up there alone, for I didn't want anybody near me.

I wanted a viewpoint, and I wanted quiet, for I had a grim time before me. From that knoll I had a big prospect of country. I looked east to our lines on which an occasional shell was falling, and where I could hear the chatter of machine-guns. West there was peace for the woods closed down on the landscape. Up to the north, I remember, there was a big glare as from a burning dump, and heavy guns seemed to be at work in the Ancre valley. Down in the south there was the dull murmur of a great battle. But just around me, in the gap, the deadliest place of all, there was an odd quiet. I could pick out clearly the different sounds. Somebody down at the farm had made a joke and there was a short burst of laughter. I envied the humorist his composure. There was a clatter and jingle from a battery changing position. On the road a tractor was jolting along—I could hear its driver shout and the screech of its unoiled axle.

My eyes were glued to my glasses, but they shook in my hands so that I could scarcely see. I bit my lip to steady myself, but they still wavered. From time to time I glanced at my watch. Eight minutes gone—ten—seventeen. If only the planes would come into sight! Even the certainty of failure would be better than this harrowing doubt. They should be back by now unless they had swung north across the salient, or unless the miracle of miracles—

Then came the distant yapping of an anti-aircraft gun, caught up the next second by others, while smoke patches studded the distant blue sky. The clouds were banking in mid-heaven, but to the west there was a big clear space now woolly with shrapnel bursts. I counted them mechanically—one—three—five—nine—with despair beginning to take the place of my anxiety. My hands were steady now, and through the glasses I saw the enemy.

Five attenuated shapes rode high above the bombardment, now sharp against the blue, now lost in a film of vapour. They were coming back, serenely, contemptuously, having seen all they wanted.

The quiet was gone now and the din was monstrous. Anti-aircraft guns, singly and in groups, were firing from every side. As I watched it seemed a futile waste of ammunition. The enemy didn't give a tinker's curse for it ... But surely there was one down. I could only count four now. No, there was the fifth coming out of a cloud. In ten minutes they would be all over the line. I fairly stamped in my vexation. Those guns were no more use than a sick headache. Oh, where in God's name were our own planes?

At that moment they came, streaking down into sight, four fighting-scouts with the sun glinting on their wings and burnishing their metal cowls. I saw clearly the rings of red, white, and blue. Before their downward drive the enemy instantly spread out.

I was watching with bare eyes now, and I wanted companionship, for the time of waiting was over.

Automatically I must have run down the knoll, for the next I knew I was staring at the heavens with Archie by my side. The combatants seemed to couple instinctively. Diving, wheeling, climbing, a pair would drop out of the melee or disappear behind a cloud. Even at that height I could hear the methodical rat-tat-tat of the machine-guns. Then there was a sudden flare and wisp of smoke. A plane sank, turning and twisting, to earth.

'Hun!' said Archie, who had his glasses on it.

Almost immediately another followed. This time the pilot recovered himself, while still a thousand feet from the ground, and started gliding for the enemy lines. Then he wavered, plunged sickeningly, and fell headlong into the wood behind La Bruyere.

Farther east, almost over the front trenches, a two-seater Albatross and a British pilot were having a desperate tussle. The bombardment had stopped, and from where we stood every movement could be followed. First one, then another, climbed uppermost and dived back, swooped out and wheeled in again, so that the two planes seemed to clear each other only by inches. Then it looked as if they closed and interlocked. I expected to see both go crashing, when suddenly the wings of one seemed to shrivel up, and the machine dropped like a stone.

'Hun,' said Archie. 'That makes three. Oh, good lads! Good lads!'

Then I saw something which took away my breath. Sloping down in wide circles came a German machine, and, following, a little behind and a little above, a British. It was the first surrender in mid-air I had seen. In my amazement I watched the couple right down to the ground, till the enemy landed in a big meadow across the high-road and our own man in a field nearer the river.

When I looked back into the sky, it was bare. North, south, east, and west, there was not a sign of aircraft, British or German.

A violent trembling took me. Archie was sweeping the heavens with his glasses and muttering to himself. Where was the fifth man? He must have fought his way through, and it was too late.

But was it? From the toe of a great rolling cloud-bank a flame shot earthwards, followed by a V-shaped trail of smoke. British or Boche? British or Boche? I didn't wait long for an answer. For, riding over the far end of the cloud, came two of our fighting scouts.

I tried to be cool, and snapped my glasses into their case, though the reaction made me want to shout. Archie turned to me with a nervous smile and a quivering mouth. 'I think we have won on the post,' he said.

He reached out a hand for mine, his eyes still on the sky, and I was grasping it when it was torn away. He was staring upwards with a white face.

We were looking at the sixth enemy plane.

It had been behind the others and much lower, and was making straight at a great speed for the east. The glasses showed me a different type of machine—a big machine with short wings, which looked menacing as a hawk in a covey of grouse. It was under the cloud-bank, and above, satisfied, easing down after their fight, and unwitting of this enemy, rode the two British craft.

A neighbouring anti-aircraft gun broke out into a sudden burst, and I thanked Heaven for its inspiration. Curious as to this new development, the two British turned, caught sight of the Boche, and dived for him.

What happened in the next minutes I cannot tell. The three seemed to be mixed up in a dog fight, so that I could not distinguish friend from foe. My hands no longer trembled; I was too desperate. The patter of machine-guns came down to us, and then one of the three broke clear and began to climb. The others strained to follow, but in a second he had risen beyond their fire, for he had easily the pace of them. Was it the Hun?

Archie's dry lips were talking.

'It's Lensch,' he said.

'How d'you know?' I gasped angrily.

'Can't mistake him. Look at the way he slipped out as he banked. That's his patent trick.'

In that agonizing moment hope died in me. I was perfectly calm now, for the time for anxiety had gone. Farther and farther drifted the British pilots behind, while Lensch in the completeness of his triumph looped more than once as if to cry an insulting farewell. In less than three minutes he would be safe inside his own lines, and he carried the knowledge which for us was death.

Someone was bawling in my ear, and pointing upward. It was Archie and his face was wild. I looked and gasped—seized my glasses and looked again.

A second before Lensch had been alone; now there were two machines.

I heard Archie's voice. 'My God, it's the Gladas—the little Gladas.' His fingers were digging into my arm and his face was against my shoulder. And then his excitement sobered into an awe which choked his speech, as he stammered—'It's old—'

But I did not need him to tell me the name, for I had divined it when I first saw the new plane drop from the clouds. I had that queer sense that comes sometimes to a man that a friend is present when he cannot see him.

Somewhere up in the void two heroes were fighting their last battle—and one of them had a crippled leg.

I had never any doubt about the result, though Archie told me later that he went crazy with suspense. Lensch was not aware of his opponent till he was almost upon him, and I wonder if by any freak of instinct he recognized his greatest antagonist. He never fired a shot, nor did Peter ... I saw the German twist and side-slip as if to baffle the fate descending upon him. I saw Peter veer over vertically and I knew that the end had come. He was there to make certain of victory and he took the only way. The machines closed, there was a crash which I felt though I could not hear it, and next second both were hurtling down, over and over, to the earth.

They fell in the river just short of the enemy lines, but I did not see them, for my eyes were blinded and I was on my knees.

After that it was all a dream. I found myself being embraced by a French General of Division, and saw the first companies of the cheerful bluecoats whom I had longed for. With them came the rain, and it was under a weeping April sky that early in the night I marched what was left of my division away from the battle-field. The enemy guns were starting to speak behind us, but I did not heed them. I knew that now there were warders at the gate, and I believed that by the grace of God that gate was barred for ever.

They took Peter from the wreckage with scarcely a scar except his twisted leg. Death had smoothed out some of the age in him, and left his face much as I remembered it long ago in the Mashonaland hills. In his pocket was his old battered *Pilgrim's Progress*. It lies before me as I write, and beside it—for I was his only legatee—the little case which came to him weeks later, containing the highest honour that can be bestowed upon a soldier of Britain.

It was from the *Pilgrim's Progress* that I read next morning, when in the lee of an apple-orchard Mary and Blenkiron and I stood in the soft spring rain beside his grave. And what I read was the tale in the end not of Mr Standfast, whom he had singled out for his counterpart, but of Mr Valiant-for-Truth whom he had not hoped to emulate. I set down the words as a salute and a farewell:

Then said he, 'I am going to my Father's; and though with great difficulty I am got hither, yet now I do not repent me of all the trouble I have been at to arrive where I am. My sword I give to him that shall succeed me in my pilgrimage, and my courage and skill to him that can get it. My marks and scars I carry with me, to be a witness for me that I have fought His battles who now will be my rewarder.'

So he passed over, and all the trumpets sounded for him on the other side.

www.ingramcontent.com/pod-product-compliance
Lightning Source LLC
Chambersburg PA
CBHW071726110726
47908CB00006B/1518

* 9 7 8 1 4 7 3 3 1 7 7 2 7 *